AMERICAN
REVOLUTIONS

AMERICAN REVOLUTIONS

A Continental History,
1750–1804

ALAN TAYLOR

W. W. NORTON & COMPANY

Independent Publishers Since 1923

New York   London

Copyright © 2016 by Alan Taylor

All rights reserved
Printed in the United States of America
First Edition

For information about permission to reproduce selections from this book, write to Permissions, W. W. Norton & Company, Inc., 500 Fifth Avenue, New York, NY 10110

For information about special discounts for bulk purchases, please contact W. W. Norton Special Sales at specialsales@wwnorton.com or 800-233-4830

Manufacturing by Quad Graphics Fairfield
Book design by Helene Bevinsky
Production manager: Anna Oler

ISBN 978-0-393-08281-4

W. W. Norton & Company, Inc.
500 Fifth Avenue, New York, N.Y. 10110
www.wwnorton.com

W. W. Norton & Company Ltd.
Castle House, 75/76 Wells Street, London W1T 3QT

1 2 3 4 5 6 7 8 9 0

For the Kelmans: Ari, Lesley, Jacob, Ben,
and especially
WYATT

And in memory of Caroline Cox

By what means, this great and important Alteration in the religious, Moral, political and Social Character of the People of thirteen Colonies, all distinct, unconnected and independent of each other, was begun, pursued and accomplished is surely interesting to Humanity to investigate, and perpetuate to Posterity.

—JOHN ADAMS, 1818

CONTENTS

CONTENTS

LIST OF MAPS

LIST OF ILLUSTRATIONS

AMERICAN
REVOLUTIONS

Introduction

May not a man have several voices, Robin,
as well as two complexions?
—Nathaniel Hawthorne,
from "My Kinsman, Major Molineux"

On a summer evening, a rustic "youth of barely eighteen years" arrived in a seaport capital, "the little metropolis of a New England colony." Although dressed in homespun and having little money, Robin was handsome, alert, and ambitious. The clever son of a country clergyman, he came to seek his celebrated kinsman, Major Molineux, a wealthy gentleman in royal favor. With the major's patronage, Robin expected to rise quickly in society. Passing through "a succession of crooked and narrow streets," he became confused and angry when no one would direct him to his kinsman's mansion. Instead, people mocked Robin. At last, a stranger replied, "Watch here an hour, and Major Molineux will pass by." Robin noticed the stranger's face painted half black and half red "as if two individual devils, a fiend of fire and a fiend of darkness, had united themselves to form this infernal visage."

The young man waited by a moonlit church, where he encountered "a gentleman in his prime, of open, intelligent, cheerful, and altogether

---

"The Procession," engraving by Elkanah Tisdale, 1795. Accompanied by musicians, a Patriot mob hauls a tarred-and-feathered Tory in a cart. Courtesy of the Library of Congress (LC-USZ62-7709).

prepossessing countenance." Learning of Robin's mission, the gentleman lingered from "a singular curiosity to witness your meeting." In the distance, they heard the advancing roar of a crowd. "There were at least a thousand voices went up to make that one shout," Robin noted. "May not a man have several voices, Robin, as well as two complexions?" the gentleman replied.

The painted stranger reappeared at the head of a torch-lit parade of "wild figures in the Indian dress" attended by raucous musicians and "applauding spectators," including women. The cavalcade accompanied an open cart holding "an elderly man, of large and majestic person" covered with tar and feathers. Robin recognized the victim as his kinsman suffering from "overwhelming humiliation." His face was "pale as death . . . his eyes were red and wild, and the foam hung white upon his quivering lip." The rioters halted and fell silent, looking to Robin for reaction, and the major recognized his kinsman. "They stared at each other in silence, and Robin's knees shook, and his hair bristled, with a mixture of pity and terror." Suddenly, Robin felt "a bewildering excitement" as he erupted into a loud and long laugh shared with the mob at the major's expense. The rioters marched on "like fiends that throng in mockery around some dead potentate, mighty no more, but majestic still in his agony."

As the street reclaimed silence, the watching gentleman asked, "Well, Robin, are you dreaming?" Having lost all hope of patronage from his disgraced kinsman, Robin prepared to leave town, but the gentleman advised Robin to stay "as you are a shrewd youth, you may rise in the world without the help of your kinsman, Major Molineux."[1]

A story published by Nathaniel Hawthorne in 1832, "My Kinsman, Major Molineux" specifies neither dates nor places and names no historical characters, operating instead as a dreamy metaphor rich in symbol and suggestion. But nothing done since by historian or novelist so concisely conveys the internal essence of the revolution. Hawthorne recognized that the struggle was our first civil war, rife with divisions, violence and destruction. The fiends of fire and darkness were busy during the revolution.

Hawthorne understood the power of stylized violence to compel the wavering to endorse revolution. Patriots built popular support, and intimidated opponents, through rituals that invited public participation to shame others. Robin's sudden laugh represents the decisions made by thousands when they helped to disgrace Loyalists as enemies to American liberty.

Historians and politicians often miscast the American Revolution as the polar opposite of even bloodier revolutions elsewhere. They recall the American version as good, orderly, restrained, and successful when contrasted against the excesses of the French and Russian revolutions. Polarities, however, mislead by insisting on perfect opposites. Only by the especially destructive standards of other revolutions was the American more restrained. During the Revolutionary War, Americans killed one another over politics and massacred Indians, who returned the bloody favors. Patriots also kept one-fifth of Americans enslaved, and thousands of those slaves escaped to help the British oppose the revolution. After the war, 60,000 dispossessed Loyalists became refugees. The dislocated proportion of the American population exceeded that of the French in their revolution. The American revolutionary turmoil also inflicted an economic decline that lasted for fifteen years in a crisis unmatched until the Great Depression of the 1930s. During the revolution, Americans suffered more upheaval than any other American generation, save that which experienced the Civil War of 1861 to 1865.

The conflict embroiled everyone, including women and children, rather than just soldiers in set-piece battles. A plundered farm was a more common experience than a glorious and victorious charge. Some historians treat the notorious wartime violence in the South as exceptional in an otherwise restrained war. This bracketing neglects the brutal war zones around British enclaves in New York and Philadelphia; the devastation of frontier settlements and native villages from New York to Georgia; and the Patriot repression of disaffection in much of New Jersey, Delaware, and the eastern shore of Maryland and Virginia. The true exceptions were the few pockets bypassed by war's brutality, primarily towns in New England. If the American Revolution was less devastating than some conflicts elsewhere, it still featured much cruelty, violence, and destruction.[2]

In popular history books and films, a united and heroic American people rise up against unnatural foreign domination by Britons, cast as snooty villains. That story of irrepressible nationalism inverts cause and effect in the revolution. The colonists were reluctant nationalists, and the revolution began, rather than culminated, a long, slow, and incomplete process of creating an American identity and nation. During the mid-eighteenth century, British America was developing closer cultural, economic, and political ties to Britain. In 1775, Benjamin Franklin recalled, "I never had heard in any Conversation from any Person drunk or sober, the least Expression of a Wish for a Separation, or Hint that such a Thing would be advantageous to America." Rather than an inevitable ripening of difference, the revolution violently wrenched reluctant colonists into a new and uncertain future as an independent country.[3]

By writing of the American Revolution as pitting "Americans" against the British, historians prematurely find a cohesive, national identity. If we equate Patriots with Americans, we recycle the canard that anyone who opposed the revolution was an alien at heart. We also read American nationalism backwards, obscuring the divisions and uncertainties of the revolutionary era. This book refers to the supporters of independence as Patriots and to the opponents as Loyalists, but many more people wavered in the middle, and all were Americans.[4]

But that upheaval also generated political and cultural creativity. Indeed, the accomplishments of independence, union, and republican government seem all the more remarkable given the grim civil war at the heart of the revolution. The founders had formidable enemies, internal divisions, and their own doubts, fears, and contentions to overcome. If they fell short in producing equality and liberty for all, they established ideals worth striving for.

To sustain support among war-weary people, Patriot leaders had to make political concessions that promised greater respect and political power for common men. In "My Kinsman, Major Molineux," Hawthorne defines the internal social meaning of revolution, when the Patriot gentleman assures Robin that he can get ahead without the colonial patronage of his kinsman. As an alternative to British-led hierarchy, the gentleman promises a new meritocracy that will reward shrewd young men for their abilities rather than their birth. To win their civil war, genteel Patriots had to build a cross-class coalition that appealed to thousands of common men and women—as Hawthorne noted. Without mass participation, Patriots could not sustain riots and boycotts against British taxes or the later war against British and Loyalist troops. Hawthorne conveys the appeal of the republican society promoted by the Patriots. It might not achieve more equal results, in the distribution of wealth and power, but it promised fairer competition. Whether we have fulfilled or defaulted on that promise is the essential question of American politics.[5]

The harsh experiences of war shaped the legacies of the revolution. More than byproducts of war, civilian sufferings helped to define the new republican government. During the 1780s, nationalists pushed for a stronger federal government by appealing to people who remembered the bloody anarchy of the war. Dorothea Gamsby, a wartime refugee, remembered, "Dismay and terror, wailing and distraction impressed their picture on my memory, never to be effaced."[6]

Turmoil persisted after the formal peace treaty. During the 1780s, the United States remained roiled by internal conflicts, meddling by other empires, and resistance by native peoples. Few Americans felt confident that their union could hang together given the interplay of their internal divisions with external threats. Most citizens favored their home state and feared political power exercised by a distant, central government. Their suspicion undermined the initial confederacy of the states, generating a crisis that led to adoption of the Federal Constitution of 1787. Rather than reflecting confidence in American unity, the new constitutional order was a "peace pact" meant to manage dangerous distrust and potential conflicts between the states. Instead of resolving the union's problems, the Federal Constitution postponed the day of reckoning until 1861, when the union plunged into a bigger civil war that nearly destroyed the nation. That later civil war erupted over western expansion: whether territorial growth would commit the nation to free labor or, instead, extend slave society and its political power.[7]

The importance of the West to making America's future emerged during the revolutionary generation, when that vast region began just beyond the Appalachian Mountains. Between 1754 and 1763, the British and their colonists conquered French Canada and claimed the West as far as the Mississippi River. Colonists expected to share in the imperial fruits of victory. Instead, the British government treated them as second-class subjects by imposing new taxes and trying to protect Indian lands from settler expansion. The British also made unexpected concessions to their new Francophone and Catholic subjects in Canada. British rulers treated their coastal colonists as just another subordinate group within a composite empire of diverse peoples managed from London. This new treatment dismayed colonists who had counted on their British culture and white skins to justify superior privileges. If denied dominion over natives and Francophones, the colonists worried that they would become dependents ruled by Britain. They called this anticipated fate "slavery," an anxiety fueled by the growing population of the enslaved among them.[8]

In the trans-Appalachian West, the British Empire displayed a fatal combination: threatening pretensions without sufficient power to enforce them. Defying British troops, settlers continued to flow west to take Indian lands. The British failure in the West discredited imperial rulers at the same time that they tried to impose new taxes on coastal colonists. Most interpretations of the revolution's causes subordinate western issues, treating them as minor irritants less significant than the clash over taxes. *American Revolutions* balances the scales by linking western conflict with resistance to parliamentary taxes as equal halves of a constitutional crisis that disrupted the British Empire in North America.[9]

Essential to understanding the causes of the revolution, the West

proved even more important to its consequences. After the war, th
sands of settlers moved across the mountains to make more farms
and towns. That growth would define, for better or worse, the new
nation's prospects. During the 1780s and early 1790s, the exodus compounded the fissures within American society and threatened to dissolve the weak confederation of the states. Newcomers settled along
vast river systems that drew their trade either north to British Canada
or south to Spanish-held Louisiana. American leaders needed to overcome that geography to win western allegiance. If they could succeed,
the growing settler population would become the nation's greatest
asset rather than its chief liability. Westerners might form a national
constituency stronger that anything in the East, where state loyalties
dominated.

To prevail in the West, Patriots had to learn lessons from the British failure there. Thomas Jefferson noted that frontier folk "will settle
the lands in spite of every body," including any government, American or British. Unable to restrain settlers, American leaders needed to
help them. By leading, rather than slowing, the process of Indian dispossession, the federal government could gain influence in the West.
Jefferson promised equal rights for common white men and promoted
their prosperity through westward expansion. After much trial and
error, and close calls with collapse, an American union would succeed where the British had failed by sustaining an "empire of liberty"
beyond the Appalachians. But that new empire came at the expense of
Indians who lost their homelands.[10]

By emphasizing the broader North America, including the West,
this book breaks with an older view of colonial America as limited
to the Atlantic coast and almost entirely British in culture. By adopting "Atlantic" or "Continental" approaches, recent historians have
broadened the geographic stage and diversified the human cast of colonial America. New scholarship pays more attention to rival Spanish,
French, Dutch, and even Russian colonizers. We also now understand
that relations with native peoples were pivotal in shaping every colonial region and in framing the competition of rival empires. Enslaved

Africans also now appear as central, rather than peripheral, to building colonies that overtly celebrated liberty.[11]

Most books on the revolution and early republic, however, still focus on the national story of the United States, particularly the political development of republican institutions. That approach demotes neighboring empires and native peoples to bit players and minor obstacles to inevitable American expansion. Canada, Spanish America, and the West Indies virtually vanish when American historians turn to the period after 1783.[12]

American Revolutions offers a sequel to my earlier book, *American Colonies*, which presented a continental history of colonial experiences. Drawing attention to multiple, competing empires, that book avoided a singular focus on British America. *American Revolutions* similarly emphasizes the multiple and clashing visions of revolution pursued by the diverse American peoples of the continent. It differs from books which suggest a singular purpose and vision to the conflict and its legacy. The revolutionary upheavals spawned new tensions and contradictions rather than neat resolutions.

American Revolutions situates the creation of the United States in the continental and global dynamics of the rival Spanish, British, and French empires and the many natives who still held most of North America. Although shorn of thirteen colonies by the revolution, the British Empire retained Canada and parts of the West Indies and gained ground in India. In Canada, Britons redesigned their colonies to avoid an American-style revolution. In Latin America, the war initially seemed to revitalize the Spanish Empire but ultimately increased tensions between colonial elites and imperial authorities. In the next generation, those tensions would create republican revolutions throughout Spanish America. Beyond the Appalachian Mountains, native nations created confederations to halt expansion by American settlers. Further west, on the Great Plains, some Indian peoples gained power over others by deploying guns and horses to control immense herds of bison.[13]

The founders of the American union understood that they were enmeshed in global networks of trade, culture, diplomacy, and war. As they expected, their actions affected, and were affected by, the rest of the world. In 1818, John Adams noted, "The American Revolution was not a common event. Its Effects and Consequences have already been Awful over a great Part of the globe. And when and Where are they to cease?" Indeed, those consequences have not yet ceased.[14]

The politics of the early republic remained entangled with those of the broader world. By helping the Patriots win independence, the French reaped national debts and republican ideas that led to their own revolution in 1789. During the 1790s, the American political parties polarized as Republicans embraced the new revolution, while Federalists denounced its radical turn. In 1791, the French Revolution inspired a massive slave revolt in the French Caribbean colony of Saint-Domingue, which led to the creation of a new nation, Haiti. When black people became revolutionaries, white Americans recoiled. They set new, racial limits to the spread of republicanism, retreating from the implicitly universal promises of their revolution. But the American Revolution generated many conflicting meanings, and some Americans kept alive an alternative, broader vision of revolution that might lead to a "new birth of freedom" in a later generation.[15]

1
COLONIES

*It is truly a miserable thing that we no sooner
leave fighting our neighbors, the French, but we
must fall to quarrelling among ourselves.*

—REVEREND SAMUEL JOHNSON of Connecticut, 1763[1]

I n 1760 in Boston, colonists gathered to hear the proclamation of a
new king, George III. They vowed "all Faith and constant Obedience, with all hearty and humble Affection" and hoped that the
monarch would have many "happy Years to Reign over us." The proclamation concluded with a resounding, "God save the King!" The
crowd erupted in huzzahs, militiamen fired three volleys in the air,
and the harbor fort discharged cannon. In the evening, bonfires blazed,
fireworks lit up the skies, and candles illuminated the windows of the
town. A Bostonian noted, "I have been here about sixteen years and I
don't know of one single man but would risque his life and property
to serve King George the Third." Colonists rejoiced in the British constitution, which provided a benevolent monarchy to promote prosperity, defend their liberties, and protect the Protestant faith. They had
not always been so lucky.[2]

---

*"A Representation of the Sugar-Cane and the Art of Making Sugar," by John Hinton,
from the* Universal Magazine of Knowledge and Pleasure *(London, 1749). West
Indian slaves work a donkey mill on the right to crush the cane, creating a flow of
juice to the boil works on the left. Palm trees and cane plants decorate the landscape.
Courtesy of the Library of Congress (LC-USZ62-7841).*

During the early 1680s, England's king, James II, had embraced Catholicism and sought to concentrate power at the expense of Parliament and the colonies. In the so-called "Glorious Revolution" of 1688, most of the English aristocracy supported a military coup that cast out James II, and substituted his Protestant daughter, Mary, and her Dutch husband, William of Orange. Jointly reigning for the rest of the century, the new monarchs accepted limits to their powers, which enhanced cooperation with Parliament.[3]

The Glorious Revolution plunged Britain into prolonged warfare with the French Empire, which sought to restore James II to power. To compete with mighty France, the English built a larger military managed by an expanded bureaucracy and funded by heavy new taxes. Prior to 1688, Parliament had held taxes down to keep the Crown weak. After casting its lot with William and Mary, however, Parliament had to fund their military survival. In return, Parliament won control over expenditures, which provided new leverage over foreign and military policy, previously Crown prerogatives.[4]

Unable to rule without the other, Parliament and the Crown formed a new, composite sovereign known as "King-in-Parliament." In that bicameral legislature, great aristocrats inherited seats in the House of Lords while gentry and merchants dominated an elected House of Commons. The government's cabinet ministers came from the aristocracy, but they needed majority support in the Commons. Those ministers conducted the Privy Council, through which the king exercised executive power. At mid-century, King George II complained, "Ministers are Kings in this country," for he could not govern without them. His lament was the boast of his subjects, who claimed greater freedom than their European counterparts governed by more powerful rulers.[5]

As the imperial wars became global, the "King-in-Parliament" needed cooperation from colonial governments. In a key compromise, the Crown accepted assemblies elected by property-holders as responsible for setting taxes and appropriations within each colony. Most colonies received royal governors and tolerated trade regulations and military coordination. The Crown could also veto any colonial law that contradicted a statute of Parliament.[6]

During the early eighteenth century, the colonies and Britain became more closely intertwined in a shared empire in which political, economic, cultural, and military initiatives came from the great metropolis of London. Imperial success in war and restraint in politics led colonial leaders to glory in the identity of transplanted Englishmen endowed with the same liberties enjoyed by their peers in the mother country. Rather than thinking of themselves as a distinct new people in America, colonists proudly claimed the status of Britons who lived west of the Atlantic.[7]

During the eighteenth century, the king became a revered symbol of the empire's prosperity, power, liberties, and Protestant faith. George III declared, "The pride, the glory of Britain, and the direct end of its constitution is political liberty." As the protector of his subjects and their rights, this king warranted allegiance. Colonists idealized the king as their champion against their Catholic enemies, the French and Spanish, for politics and religion were entangled in colonial culture. By comparison, colonists felt little fondness for Parliament, where they had no representatives. Proud of their British liberty, the colonists looked south and north to see their supposed inferiors in the more authoritarian Spanish and French empires.[8] *sense of superiority*

Americas

During the sixteenth century, the Spanish developed the first, most populous, and richest European empire in the Americas. They began in the West Indies, an arc of islands stretching north and then west from the South American coast to embrace the Caribbean Sea. The Spanish settled the larger islands, Cuba, Hispaniola, and Puerto Rico, which served as bases for raiding the mainland to enslave Indians and plunder their villages and cities. Those raids led to the conquest of Mexico, which became the great center of the Spanish Empire, where Hispanic colonists prospered by exploiting native labor to cultivate crops, raise livestock, and mine silver.[9]

Taking Indian wives and concubines, male colonists produced mixed offspring known as "mestizos," who became especially numer-

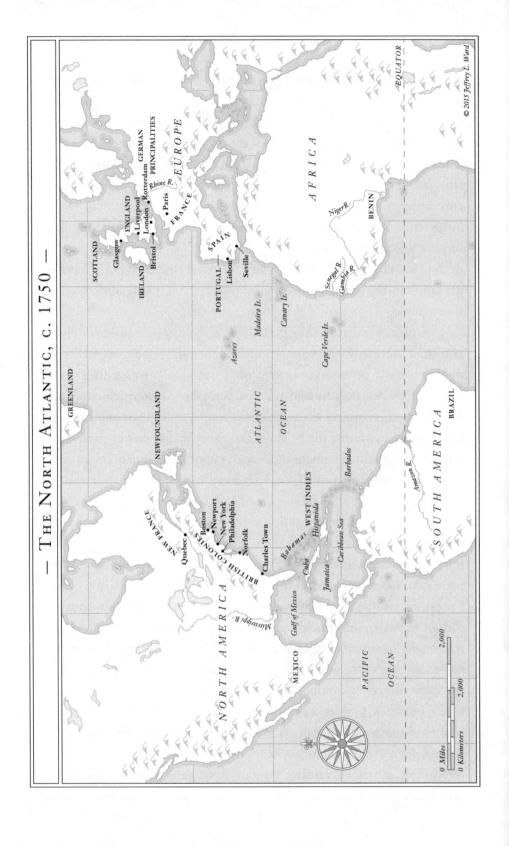

THE NORTH ATLANTIC, c. 1750

© 2015 Jeffrey L. Ward

GREENLAND

NORTH AMERICA

NEWFOUNDLAND

NEW FRANCE

Quebec

BRITISH COLONIES

Boston
Newport
New York
Philadelphia
Norfolk

Charles Town

MEXICO

Mississippi R.

Gulf of Mexico

Bahamas
WEST INDIES
Cuba
Hispaniola
Jamaica
Caribbean Sea

Barbados

PACIFIC
OCEAN

SOUTH AMERICA

BRAZIL

Amazon R.

ATLANTIC
OCEAN

Azores

Madeira Is.

Canary Is.

Cape Verde Is.

SCOTLAND
Glasgow
IRELAND
ENGLAND
Liverpool
London
Bristol

GERMAN
PRINCIPALITIES
Rotterdam
Rhine R.
Paris
FRANCE

EUROPE

SPAIN
PORTUGAL
Lisbon
Seville

AFRICA

Niger R.
BENIN
Senegal R.
Gambia R.

EQUATOR

0 Miles   2,000
0 Kilometers   2,000

ous in the cities and towns. By 1700, mestizos outnumbered Indians in central Mexico, while imported African slaves peopled the tropical coasts. Hispanic authorities developed a complex racial hierarchy known as the *castas*, which rose from Africans and Indians at the bottom through mixed-race peoples in the middle to the lighter-skinned Spaniard imagined at the pinnacle. The higher *castas* enjoyed superior status and greater legal privileges at the expense of the lower. Spanish colonies created many market towns featuring spacious grids of streets around a central plaza with a town hall and church or cathedral. The whitest and wealthiest families dwelled near the central plaza, while the lower-caste people with darker complexions lived on the outskirts.[10]

To the north, the Spanish established marginal colonies in Arizona, Florida, New Mexico, and Texas. Lacking the mineral riches of Mexico, the colonies attracted few colonists, so Indians remained the majority. Spanish authorities tried to compensate by transforming Indians into Hispanics through missions run by Franciscan friars. To support the missions, the Spanish built fortified *presidios* garrisoned by soldiers. Although these outposts operated at a financial loss, the Crown valued the frontier colonies as a broad buffer zone meant to keep rival empires at a safe distance from precious Mexico.[11]

Near the missions, most Indians made peace with the powerful newcomers by incorporating Christian beliefs and Spanish practices into their native cultures. The missionized natives allied with the Spanish against the surrounding and more mobile natives who violently resisted conversion and domination. In Arizona and New Mexico, Pimas, Papagos, and Pueblo peoples converted and joined the Spanish in wars against the Apaches, Comanches, Navajos, and Utes of the surrounding deserts and mountains. In Texas, similar enemies pushed the beleaguered Coahuiltecan peoples into the missions. In Florida, the Apalachees, Guales, and Timucuans accepted missions and fought against Yamasee and Creek peoples to the north.[12]

During the early eighteenth century, Spain's frontier colonies suffered from increased raiding by native enemies who obtained guns from French or British traders. Seeking livestock and slaves, raiders destroyed Florida's missions and damaged those in New Mexico and Texas. Resourceful and adaptive, <u>natives became essential to the imperial competition in North America.</u> <u>Rival empires measured their strength by the range and number of their Indian allies.</u> During the eighteenth century, trade trumped missions in sustaining an imperial alliance with native peoples. And the British and the French produced better trade goods at a lower cost than did the Spanish. A Creek chief explained, "Indians will attach themselves to & Serve them best who Supply their Necessities."[13]

During the seventeenth century, the French created colonies on the West Indian islands: principally Martinique, Guadeloupe, and Saint-Domingue on the west coast of Hispaniola. The French West Indians developed thriving plantations devoted to sugar, coffee, and indigo cultivation by <u>slaves</u> imported from Africa.[14]

Far to the north, the French also founded mainland colonies known as Acadia and Canada. At first, they came to fish for cod, hunt whales and seals, and trade with native peoples for furs. But fishermen, hunters, and traders needed food, so French officials also sent peasants, known as *habitants*, to develop farms beside the Bay of Fundy in Acadia and along the St. Lawrence River in Canada, which featured the great fortified seaport and capital town of Quebec. <u>To convert Indians to the Catholic faith, the French supported Jesuit missionaries,</u> who established churches in native villages. Initially, the Crown subcontracted colonization to trading companies with royal charters. During the 1660s and 1670s, the Crown revoked the charters and consolidated imperial control through appointed governors, intendants, and councils of leading colonists.[15]

The St. Lawrence reached westward deep into the continent, drawing waters from the Great Lakes, where the French erected trading posts to procure furs from the natives. French traders adapted to native culture with help from Indian wives, who provided kinship ties and produced mixed-race offspring, known as *métis*. In that "upper country," the French, *métis*, and natives developed an alliance based upon mutual accommodations. <u>Lacking the power to dominate the other, the French and Indians had to treat one another with wary respect.</u> In return for generous presents of trade goods, natives protected trading posts and supported the French in wars against the English colonists to the east. Entangled with native allies, who sought to preserve their independence and maximize their presents, the French could not fulfill their fantasies of dominating Indians.[16]

In the late seventeenth century, the French established the colony of Louisiana along the lower Mississippi River, where New Orleans became the capital and main seaport. The Louisiana colonists raised tobacco and provisions or traded with Indians for deerskins to export. Distant from the European market and rife with deadly subtropical diseases, the colony languished, attracting even fewer colonists than did Canada. Costing more to administer than they yielded in revenue, Canada and Louisiana lagged far behind the West Indies in economic importance to the empire. The French subsidized their continental colonies in the faint hope of future profits and from an immediate need for native allies to hold the continental interior and contain the English colonies along the Atlantic Seaboard. (Those English colonies became "British" after the 1707 union of England and Scotland).[17]

During the early seventeenth century, the English created their own plantation colonies in the West Indies: principally Antigua, Barbados, and Jamaica, where planters exploited thousands of enslaved Africans who cultivated sugarcane. In great and growing demand in Europe, sugar generated the immense profits that enabled plantation owners annually to buy thousands of slaves to replace those worked to death or killed by tropical fevers. Despite the diseases, the West Indian colonies were also the richest and most cherished by the empire, for their exports exceeded in value those from every other region. The West Indies also became the primary market for Britain's lucrative slave trade. In 1740, a writer praised Jamaica as "a Constant Mine, whence Britain draws prodigious riches." A few hundred slaves did escape and defended their autonomy as "maroons" in the rugged hills and mountains of Jamaica's undeveloped interior. Unable to suppress them, the colonial government sought to contain the maroons by paying them bounties for returning more recently escaped slaves.[18]

To the north on the Atlantic coast of the continent, South Carolina (founded in 1670), North Carolina (1712), and Georgia (1733) also produced commodities for export. Too far north for sugarcane cultivation, the mainland planters instead forced slaves to grow rice and indigo in the low country near the coast. In 1737, a visitor remarked that "Carolina looks more like a negro country than like a country settled by white people." Further inland, farmers raised cattle and grains to help feed the coastal slaves and those in the West Indies. Carolinians also profited by trading guns and ammunition to hinterland Indians, who paid with deerskins and enslaved captives taken from less well-armed native peoples, often those from Florida's Spanish missions. In 1701, feeling cheated by the Carolina traders, some Santee natives tried to take their deerskins directly to England by crossing the Atlantic in dugout canoes. Of course, they underestimated the distance and powerful ocean swells, which swamped their open canoes. They were rescued by passing sailors but then promptly sold into slavery: it did not pay to cross Carolinians, whom, a pious visitor insisted, "walk[ed] the straight path to hell."[19]

North of the Carolinas lay the Chesapeake colonies of Virginia and Maryland, founded in 1607 and 1634. Their colonists cultivated tobacco for the English market and corn for themselves. The profits of tobacco attracted thousands of immigrants who dispossessed and killed natives and then cleared the forests to make hundreds of new farms and plantations. In the late seventeenth and early eighteenth centuries, the Chesapeake colonists imported thousands of enslaved Africans, who comprised 40 percent of the region's population by 1750.[20]

Continuing north, the Atlantic Seaboard's middle colonies consisted of New York (begun in 1614 as New Netherland), Delaware (1638 as New Sweden), New Jersey (1664), and Pennsylvania (1680). The colder climate and shorter growing season encouraged farmers to raise more wheat and less tobacco. Because family-run farms prevailed, slaves comprised less than a tenth of the population. The middle colo-

slave dependent economy [handwritten marginal note]

nies also featured greater ethnic and cultural diversity than elsewhere in British America. The original Dutch and Swedish colonies had recruited a mix of Dutch, Finns, Jews, Norwegians, Swedes, and Walloons. After the English conquest in 1664, the region attracted a new wave of immigrants from Scotland, Ireland, and the German principalities. Most were Protestants, but they divided into many denominations.[21]

Greater cultural homogeneity prevailed farther north in New England: the colonies of New Hampshire, Massachusetts, Rhode Island, and Connecticut. Most New Englanders descended from English migrants who arrived during the 1630s and subscribed to a demanding form of Protestantism known as "Puritanism." In this relatively cold and infertile region, colonists raised cattle, sheep, and grain on thousands of small, rocky farms. After supplying family needs, they shipped modest surpluses to the West Indies to feed planters and their slaves. New England merchant ships returned with molasses, rum, and sugar or carried those cargoes to Britain to exchange for manufactured goods. New Englanders prospered by becoming shipbuilders, fishermen, and long-distance traders active throughout the growing empire. The populous New England colonies expanded rapidly, displacing natives, who fled northward to become French allies in Canada.[22]

In 1713, the British took Acadia from the French and renamed the colony Nova Scotia. In alliance with Micmac Indians, Acadians ignored British officials, who had little authority beyond their small garrison at Annapolis Royal. In the mid eighteenth century, Britons established a stronger presence on the colony's eastern shore by subsidizing immigrants and founding a seaport and naval base at Halifax.[23]

At the start of the seventeenth century, the English had developed seasonal fishing camps along the shores of Newfoundland, a large island near the mouth of the St. Lawrence River. The fishermen caught codfish, which they dried in the sun on the shores and packed into barrels for shipment to Britain, the West Indies, or southern Europe. Dried codfish ranked as the third-most-valuable export from British America, exceeded only by West Indian sugar and Chesapeake tobacco.[24]

Further north and west, English merchants formed the Hudson's

Bay Company in 1670 and founded fur-trading posts at the mouths of rivers along the arctic shores of Rupert's Land. The frigid conditions forbade agriculture and limited navigation to the summer months. There were no true settlers, merely four hundred corporate employees recruited for a few years' work and primarily drawn from the Orkney Islands of Scotland. In contrast to the empire's settler colonies, the Hudson's Bay posts avoided war with the region's natives, Crees and Chipewyans, who supplied furs in exchange for British manufactures and alcohol. In their restraint, the company's employees resembled the French traders of Canada more than the aggressive farmers of New England, the Chesapeake, and Carolinas.[25]

In the colonies along the Atlantic Seaboard, prospering farms attracted immigrants and promoted a higher birth rate and longer life expectancy than in the sickly West Indies to the south, or the colder, northern outposts of the British Empire. As a result, in 1750 four-fifths of British Americans lived in the thirteen colonies of the temperate latitudes on the continent. Those colonies had 1.5 million people compared to a mere 60,000 in French Canada and 10,000 in Louisiana. Still fewer Spaniards lived in Arizona, Florida, Texas, and New Mexico. The rapid growth of the British mainland colonies alarmed their imperial and native neighbors, who feared being overwhelmed by British expansion.[26]

After 1700, British America imported 1,500,000 slaves: more than four times the number of white immigrants. The massive escalation of the slave trade produced an unprecedented, transatlantic displacement of people. A brutal business, the slave trade killed a tenth of the enslaved, primarily from disease, during transit across the Atlantic from West Africa. The survivors then suffered the shock of enslavement in a strange and distant land. Separated from friends and kin, they were ordered about in a new language and brutally punished if they balked, resisted, or tried to escape. New masters put the enslaved to work on colonial farms and plantations raising crops for export. Arriving with many distinct languages and ethnic identities, they gradually created new cultures as African Americans.[27]

Three-quarters of the newly enslaved landed in the West Indies, where the sugar plantations were especially profitable but lethal. Masters could afford to work slaves to death and then replace them. Although the West Indies imported more slaves, by 1775 the British mainland colonies had more living slaves, because of their healthier conditions. In continental British America, a fifth of the people were enslaved, with the largest numbers in the Carolina and Chesapeake colonies. Slavery proved less profitable in New England and the middle colonies, where farmers could not raise the more lucrative southern crops: rice, tobacco, indigo, and sugar. The enslaved comprised only 2 percent of the population in New England and 8 percent in the middle colonies, but slavery was legal in every colony, and only Quakers questioned the enslavement of Africans.[28]

To lower their costs, masters provided the enslaved with minimal food, crude shelter, and ragged clothes. Most slaves had to work at least twelve hours a day and six days a week under the close supervision and cutting whip of a white overseer. A Jamaican governor reported that planters thought that "Negroes are not of the same Species with us, but that being of a different Mold and Nature, as well as Colour, they were made intirely for our Use, . . . having as great a Propensity to Subjection, as we have to command, and loving Slavery as naturally as we do Liberty." Masters and overseers compelled enough labor and obedience to profit from slavery, but they did so with great difficulty and in lurking fear of a slave revolt. To punish resisting slaves and terrify the rest, planters relied on torture, mutilation, and executions.[29]

Compared to the Spanish or French, British Americans imposed harsher conditions on slaves and discouraged freeing any of them. The marriages of slaves lacked legal standing, allowing masters to rupture families by selling husbands apart from wives and children from their parents. Because British colonists balked at freeing any slaves, a mere 1 percent of African Americans enjoyed freedom and only under harsh restrictions. In Virginia, an Anglican minister concluded, "These two words Negro and Slave" had, "by custom, grown Homogeneous and Convertible."[30]

*another
direction
for hate
displace*

During the early eighteenth century, as slaves increased and indentured servitude declined, a racial divide developed between freedom and slavery, which tended to soften class divisions among white men. United by dread of slave revolt, British Americans asserted legal equality within their race and a shared supremacy over blacks. In public life and rights, a white racial solidarity trumped the considerable variation in wealth among the colonists. Freedom seemed all the more precious because colonists daily saw the humiliation and exploitation of the enslaved.[31]

In Spanish America, class and race worked in a less binary, indeed in a more kaleidoscopic, fashion thanks to the prevalence of Roman law, the Catholic Church, and complex combinations of racial mixing, which included many more people of Indian descent. By 1775, Spanish America had more free than enslaved blacks because the Catholic Church promoted manumission in wills, and imperial policy allowed slaves to purchase freedom by hiring out for wages. Always keen for more revenue, the Crown sold certificates of Spanish status to mestizos and free mulattoes. After 1760, Spanish authorities armed and organized free blacks in militias to defend their colonies and hunt down runaway slaves. Hispanic colonies also offered greater social mobility than did the British. Spanish-American towns hosted many successful craftsmen with dark skins but richer possessions than many poor whites of supposedly pure blood. Spanish elites distrusted poor whites as little if any better than people of Indian or African descent. In the Spanish Empire, whites without wealth enjoyed less legal privilege and fewer political rights than in British America.[32]

Comparing themselves to Spanish and French colonists, British Americans took great pride in their superior liberty, especially their right to elect assembly representatives. But race limited freedom, for British America was simultaneously and inseparably a land of black slavery and white opportunity. In Georgia, early settlers bristled when their paternalistic colonial government initially banned slavery as a security threat. The dissidents prevailed under the revealing slogan of "Liberty and Property without restrictions," for they insisted that white men became fully free by owning blacks. The British offered just one of several formulas for freedom and race in the Americas.[33]

Commerce

During the eighteenth century, British America became more closely tied to the economy of Great Britain. The mother country provided a protected market for the produce of American farms and plantations, while British manufacturers increasingly relied on sales to colonial consumers. More than 90 percent of the mainland colonists lived in the countryside as farmers and planters, and just a few seaports qualified as cities. In 1760, only Philadelphia, Boston, and New York exceeded 16,000 inhabitants. Nothing in the colonies could compare to the teeming metropolis of London, the largest city in Europe and home to 750,000 people.[34]

Lacking industries, save for shipbuilding, colonial seaports specialized in exporting farm produce and importing British manufactures on credit extended by British firms. Colonial merchants repaid these loans with produce shipped after the harvest to Europe or the West Indies. As rural domains of farmers, the colonies complemented the more urbanized and industrializing mother country.[35]

Beginning in 1651, Parliament promoted that economic synergy with a series of "Navigation Acts," which closed colonial ports to foreign rivals including the Dutch, French, and Spanish. Colonial ships qualified as English and so could trade throughout the empire. The acts also mandated that a few especially valuable "enumerated commodities" produced in the colonies (principally sugar and tobacco) had to be shipped only to the mother country. But the colonists could export other produce, such as Pennsylvania wheat or New England fish anywhere they could find a profitable market. Finally, the acts stipulated that all European goods bound for British America had to pass through an English port and pay customs duty. In sum, the Navigation Acts sought to enhance Crown revenue, bolster the colonial market for British manufactures, and maximize the sailors and

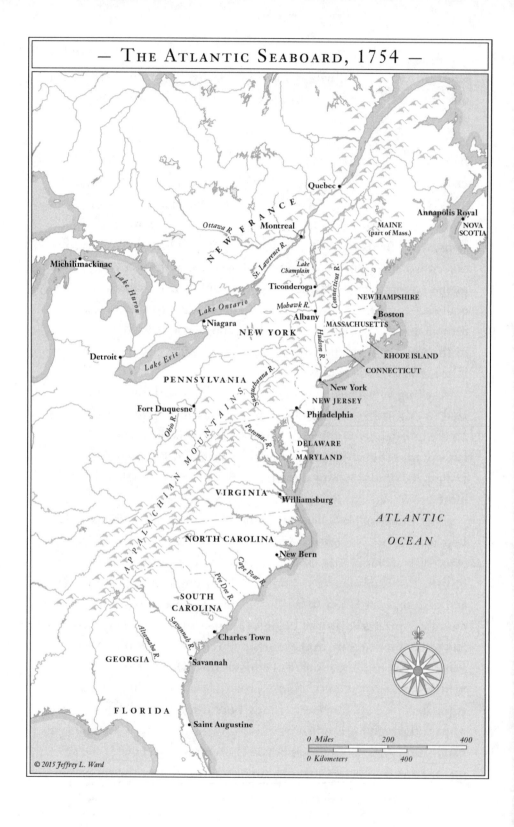

— THE ATLANTIC SEABOARD, 1754 —

Quebec

NEW FRANCE

Ottawa R. Montreal

Annapolis Royal

MAINE
(part of Mass.)

NOVA
SCOTIA

Michilimackinac

Lake Huron

St. Lawrence R.

Lake Champlain

Ticonderoga

NEW HAMPSHIRE

Lake Ontario

Mohawk R.

Connecticut R.

Niagara

Albany

Boston

NEW YORK

MASSACHUSETTS

Detroit

Lake Erie

Hudson R.

RHODE ISLAND

CONNECTICUT

PENNSYLVANIA

Susquehanna R.

New York

NEW JERSEY

Fort Duquesne

Philadelphia

Ohio R.

Potomac R.

DELAWARE

MARYLAND

APPALACHIAN MOUNTAINS

VIRGINIA

Williamsburg

ATLANTIC

OCEAN

NORTH CAROLINA

New Bern

Cape Fear R.

Pee Dee R.

SOUTH
CAROLINA

Alatamaha R.

Savannah R.

Charles Town

GEORGIA

Savannah

FLORIDA

Saint Augustine

0 Miles   200   400

0 Kilometers   400

© 2015 Jeffrey L. Ward

ships of the empire. In 1708, a writer explained that Britain had no other way to become "considerable in the World, but by our Fleets; and of supporting them, but by our Trade, which breeds Seamen; and brings in Wealth to maintain them." Overseas trade sustained the naval supremacy that enabled the relatively small realm of Britain to exercise global power.[36]

Far from dividing the colonists from the mother country, the Atlantic Ocean drew them together during the eighteenth century. As transatlantic shipping tripled, colonists became better supplied with British consumer goods and better informed about events in, and ideas from, the mother country. Thanks to the swelling volume of trade, the colonial economy grew faster than did Britain's. From just 4 percent of England's gross domestic product in 1700, the colonial economy blossomed to 40 percent by 1770, assuming greater importance to the empire. A romantic myth miscasts the common colonists as self-sufficient "yeomen farmers," who allegedly raised all that they needed or wanted. In fact, colonial farms produced crops *both* for household needs *and* for the external market. By raising a surplus for export, colonists could buy imported consumer goods. Between 1720 and 1770 per capita colonial imports from Britain increased by 50 percent.[37]

The growing transatlantic commerce generated a "consumer revolution," as British workshops produced more diverse goods in greater abundance and at lower cost. Colonial prosperity enabled consumers to buy more manufactured goods, more sugar and rum from the West Indies, and more spices and tea from Asia. Only the poorest and most rustic people wore homespun; everyone else donned clothing made from imported textiles. Wealthy colonists imported fine furniture from England, and their grand mansions emulated British models. Women welcomed and promoted the consumer revolution, for the imports reduced their long and hard labor to spin thread and weave cloth. By acquiring fashionable clothing, women obtained a new means for self-expression. Sharing goods and ideas with the mother country, the colonists became more British than ever before.[38]

Among free people, the primary social distinction contrasted the genteel few, who possessed wealth and some leisure, from the many common folk who toiled as laborers, farmers, and artisans. Common people worked with their hands in the dirt; gentlemen did not. In Virginia, a young gentleman declared that "it would derogate greatly" from his character "to learn a trade; or to put his hand to any servile employment." In the mainland colonies, the genteel comprised about one in every twenty free people; the rest were common. The genteel enjoyed social esteem and powerful advantages in education, business, law, politics, and marriage. A traveler noted that gentlemen and ladies had to "distinguish themselves from the common sort of people, by a good garb, genteel air, or good education, wealth or learning." They ate with silver knives and forks, wore silk stockings and frilled shirts, and rode in carriages. Expensive and tasteful possessions and precise words and manners marked the genteel few as possessing the honor, sensibility, and refinement deemed beyond the dull abilities of common people driven by brute impulses and hungers. Colonel Landon Carter of Virginia dismissed most common folk as "but Idiots." Yet gentlemen needed common folk as an audience expected to show deference in public encounters with the privileged few.[39]

Although powerful, the line between genteel and common was also porous. Despite the worship of stability and hierarchy, colonial society had plenty of social mobility, both up and down. Some sons of common farmers and artisans prospered as merchants and lawyers, while the wealthy could lose inherited fortunes to the volatile twists of fate and trade. Emulation drove conspicuous consumption as commoners bought clothes, furniture, tea sets, and houses above their original "sort" and beyond their means. A traveler marveled at American society as "one continued Race in which everyone is endeavoring to distance all behind him, and to overtake or pass by, all before him: every one flying from his Inferiors in Pursuit of his Superiors, who fly from him with equal Alacrity." But social ascent was only respectable when the ambitious could master and display genteel learning and manners. Gentlemen and ladies closely watched and fiercely criticized anyone who flaunted wealth without cultivating a genteel style.[40]

Coverture

Per the law of coverture, a British colonial woman passed by marriage from legal dependence on her father to reliance on a husband, losing her last name and gaining no civil rights. The influential jurist William Blackstone explained, "By marriage, the husband and wife are one person in law: that is, the very being or legal existence of the woman is suspended during the marriage, or . . . consolidated into that of the husband." Almost all women married, dreading as contemptible the poor life of a "spinster" or "old maid." Because men headed and represented their families in public life, women could not vote, hold political office, or serve on juries. Only widows could own property and bring lawsuits to protect it. Women were supposed to obey, and men were obliged to protect. Newspapers ridiculed any suggestion that women could participate in public life or deserved greater legal rights.[41]

The culture taught women to define their lives by motherhood and domesticity. A young wife wrote, "For my part, I own that we are made but for little things and our employments ought to extend at the furthest to the interior economy and policy of the family, and the care of our Children when they are little." Some women, however, privately resented their subordination. In Philadelphia, Grace Growden balked at marriage, writing in her private journal:

> Never get Tyed to a Man
> For once you are yoked
> Tis all a Mere Joke
> Of seeing your freedom again

But she did marry—and lived to regret it as Joseph Galloway's wife. She later described herself as a "wretched Wife Whose doom'd with him to spend her Life."[42]

Hard work in and around the home also restricted the lives of common women. Wives and mothers had to prepare hefty meals for large families, tend a garden, milk a cow or two, sew, mend, and wash clothing, make soap and candles, help butcher the livestock, and somehow keep the house clean. Mary Holyoke, the wife of a country doctor, recorded one workweek:

> Washed. Ironed, Scoured pewter. Scoured rooms. Scoured furniture Brasses and put up the chintz bed and hung pictures. Sowed Sweet marjoram. Sowed pease. Sowed cauliflower. Sowed 6 week beans. Pulled radishes. Set out turnips. Cut 36 asparagus. Killed the pig, [which] weighed 164 pounds. Made bread. Put beef in pickle. Salted Pork, put bacon in pickle. Made the Dr. 6 cravats marked H. Quilted two petticoats since yesterday. Made 5 shirts of the doctor.

In their twenties and thirties, women also had to tend several children, for most wives were pregnant every other year, for want of birth control save for abstinence. A colonial woman usually married in her late teens or early twenties and bore seven to ten children. Although she performed work essential to her household, her husband or father owned the fruits of that labor. And when urban women worked for hire as seamstresses, laundresses, and domestics, they received half the wages paid to men.[43]

Faiths

Most colonial leaders believed that social morality, political harmony, and community order demanded public conformity in religion. In most provinces, colonists had to pay taxes for one established church even if they belonged to a dissenting congregation. The establishment varied by colony, depending on the faith of the founders: Congregational in New England (except Rhode Island) and Anglican in most other colonies. Save for New York, the middle colonies had no establishment because ethnic diversity promoted an array of denominations: Anglicans, Baptists, Lutherans, Presbyterians, Quakers, Dutch and German Reformed, Mennonites, and Amish. In that region, no single church could dominate the others, so all had to compete for adherents and rely on voluntary contributions.[44]

In the established churches, ministers preached the sacredness of social stability and deference to a hierarchy of authority. Reverend Jonathan Edwards insisted that everyone had an "appointed office, place, and station, according to their several capacities and talents, and everyone keeps his place, and continues in his proper business." Colonial churches assigned pews on the basis of family status, with the most prestigious people sitting closest to the minister. That insistence on ranking and order derived from a pervasive anxiety over status competition and social mobility in British America.[45]

During the mid eighteenth century, religious revivals promoted a more emotional and popular style of worship. Revivals were local bursts of religious fervor as many people embraced a passionate new birth of their faith. During the late 1730s, those revivals became more frequent, widespread, and similar in New Jersey and New England, a synchronicity that pious folk interpreted as a sign of God's intervening power. The revivals accelerated from 1739 to 1741, when a celebrated English evangelist, George Whitefield, took his show on the road to the colonies. A masterful promoter, Whitefield exploited the latest marketing techniques, employing advance men, handbills, and newspaper notices to build his celebrity and audiences. In the colonies, he had a masterful promoter: Benjamin Franklin, then a printer and publisher in Philadelphia. Although a religious skeptic, Franklin admired Whitefield's talents and saw a precious opportunity to sell his books and improve the morality of colonists.[46]

Touring from New England to Georgia, Whitefield drew huge crowds and reached even more colonists through his publications. This impact revealed the transatlantic integration of the British Empire as a common market of shared goods and ideas. After Whitefield returned to England, his American supporters sustained the momentum by leading many local revivals, which became collectively known as the Great Awakening. During the 1760s and early 1770s, a second round of revivals spread in Virginia, where evangelical Presbyterians and Baptists challenged the Anglican establishment.[47]

Itinerant preachers stirred controversy by blaming old-fashioned ministers for neglecting their duty to seek, experience, and preach evangelical conversion. In every denomination, such rebukes divided ministers, as some adopted the spontaneous, impassioned, evangelical style while others hardened in opposition. Evangelicals became known as "New Lights," because they believed in sudden, new dispensations of divine grace, while their foes were "Old Lights," who defended venerable institutions and scriptural traditions. Preferring a dispassionate style of worship, Old Lights distrusted evangelical outbursts: weeping, crying out, twitching, and falling down during worship. An Old Light complained that revivalists "screw up the people to the greatest heights of religious phrenzy and then leave them in that wild state, for perhaps ten or twelve months, till another enthusiast comes among them, to repeat the same thing over again." In many colonies, Old Light ministers and magistrates tried to outlaw and punish evangelical itinerants, but their stubborn persistence foiled that persecution.[48]

The revivals became even more controversial when they inspired common people of little education and low status to become preachers who censored prestigious ministers as godless frauds. This was more than the well-educated Whitefield had ever bargained on. By emphasizing the overwhelming, miraculous, and fundamental power of God acting directly and indiscriminately upon souls, evangelicals weakened the social conventions of their hierarchical society. By insisting that everyone had the right to choose his or her own minister, evangelicals championed individualism, a concept then considered divisive and anarchic. Free choice had radical implications for an unequal society in which husbands commanded wives, fathers dictated to sons, masters owned servants and slaves, and gentlemen claimed deference from common people. Evangelicals argued that no worldly authority should obstruct religious choice, and they charged that great wealth and power rendered men too proud to humble themselves before God: the prerequisite for salvation by a new birth.[49]

Rejecting the traditional conviction that society should unite under one church, evangelicals promoted a more pluralistic, egalitarian, and voluntary social order. Their itinerant preachers and converts sought freely to cross community and denominational lines. The evangelical style influenced the younger ministers in established churches, for they had to compete to retain parishioners, who liked to sample a range of preachers. Evangelical values prepared many colonists to seek a new society premised on individualism and voluntary association.[50]

Constitution *British system doesn't work in America*

During the early seventeenth century, the English Crown had lacked revenue, so kings chartered private interests, known as proprietors, to found and manage colonies. These proprietors obtained both title to sell colonial lands and the power to govern colonists. Proprietors appointed a governor, who had to share power with an assembly elected by propertied colonists. The latter cherished legislative control over taxation as their most fundamental liberty.[51]

During the seventeenth century, many proprietors became bankrupt or alienated their colonists (or did both). In such cases, the Crown took over a colony and appointed the governor while retaining the elected assembly. The eighteenth-century British Empire had a ramshackle structure of diverse constitutional arrangements, for older proprietary models survived beside the more numerous royal colonies. The Calvert and Penn families kept Maryland and Pennsylvania as proprietary possessions, while the Hudson's Bay Company clung to Rupert's Land. Connecticut and Rhode Island preserved charters that allowed the propertied colonists to elect governors as well as legislators. These petty republics poorly fit the imperial structure headed by a king and his Parliament, but neither had the energy or resources to rationalize this empire. British imperial officials were too few and too busy to supervise the colonies closely. Their colonial information was spotty, their attention divided, and their communication with distant governors slow.[52]

The British also lacked the military manpower to coerce colonists. *weak rulers* Possessing only a third of France's population, the British struggled to raise a considerable army and devoted most of their troops to defending the mother country or its German partner, the principality of

Hanover. Prior to 1755, Britain rarely sent troops across the Atlantic except to defend the West Indies. On the North American mainland, the British relied on colonial militiamen and volunteers. Unable to deploy intimidating force, imperial officials had to negotiate with leading colonists, seeking compromises and making concessions. Colonial lobbyists in Britain had clout as experts who could secure some cooperation with imperial initiatives: usually military expeditions against French and Spanish colonies. Those lobbyists got support from influential British merchants and manufacturers who relied on the colonies as an export market.[53]

On both sides of the Atlantic, Britons insisted that their constitution preserved the liberties of subjects better than in any other realm on earth. Unlike the later American Federal Constitution, the British constitution was not a written document but, instead, a consensus understanding of political institutions and legal precedents. In 1763, James Otis, a lawyer in Boston, extolled that constitution as a font of "liberty and knowledge, civil and religious. . . . No other constitution of civil government has yet appeared in the world, so admirably adapted to these great purposes." Britons overlooked the contradictions that the empire also enslaved thousands of Africans and dominated the conquered Irish. British Americans claimed the liberty that their supposed inferiors—Africans, Catholics, and Indians—allegedly did not deserve.[54]

Conventional thinking insisted that Britain enjoyed a "mixed constitution," which balanced the three elements of any civilized society: the one (a monarch), the few (aristocrats), and the many (common people). The monarch led the executive branch, while a House of Lords assembled the few, and an elected House of Commons represented the many, albeit only those who met the property requirement to vote. Britons celebrated their mixed constitution as better than tyranny (the rule of one), oligarchy (domination by a few), or democracy (government by the many). A tyrant or oligarchs would exploit common people by ruling with an iron fist, while democracy would empower unscrupulous politicians known as "demagogues" to encourage the poor to plun-

der the rich. In theory, only a mixed constitution provided the checks
and balances on each social order needed to sustain liberty and social
stability. John Adams credited the idealized combination of "monarchical splendor, the aristocratical independency, and the democratical
freedoms" in Britain with "the preservation of the subject's liberty."[55]

Colonial governments were supposed to operate as subordinate
versions of the British constitution. A Bostonian explained, "By the
governor, representing the King, the colonies are monarchical; by the
Council, they are aristocratical; by a house of representatives . . . from
the people, they are democratical." He concluded, "The concurrence
of these three forms of government seems to be the highest perfection
that human civil government can attain."[56]

In fact, colonial governments fell short of the British model in
three ways: they had weaker governors, unstable councils, and powerful assemblies responsive to a broader electorate. Imperial officials
regarded colonial governments as out of balance, as too democratic
because assemblies dominated governors and councils. Without the
life tenure of a monarch, royal governors were appointed by imperial bureaucrats and served at their pleasure, which proved fickle and
fleeting. On average, a colonial governor lasted for merely five years:
far less than most councillors or assemblymen. Governors also lacked
local connections, for only a fifth of them grew up in the colonies. Most
were British gentlemen with great debts and a powerful patron in Britain. Seeking to recoup impaired fortunes, governors tried to maximize
their salary and the official fees earned by granting licenses and lands.
Those goals compelled them to curry favor with colonial councillors
and assemblymen.[57]

The assemblies were more responsive to a broader electorate than in
Britain. The same property requirement prevailed on both sides of the
Atlantic: in order to vote, a man had to own enough property to support himself and his family, which meant at least a small farm or shop.
Only a quarter of English men owned enough to vote, while two-thirds
of free colonial men qualified for political rights. The unintended difference derived from the broader distribution of farms in the mainland

colonies, which grew rapidly by taking land from the Indians. Currying favor with voters, assemblymen <u>sought to limit taxes</u> by curtailing the authority of councils and governors—to the dismay of imperial officials.[58]

The colonies also lacked the true aristocrats needed to render a council an equivalent to the British House of Lords. British America had no lords, dukes, earls, and marquises to inherit titles and large, landed estates worked by tenants. The colonies did have rich and influential men, but they were lawyers, merchants, and planters who relied on buying and selling property to make money. In the mainland colonies, the richest men were not in the same league with the great merchants and landlords of England (or the grandees of the West Indies). For example, a Philadelphia merchant commonly had a capital worth £400 compared to £3,000 for a London merchant. Still on the make, most assemblymen and councillors were commercial men who sought to limit the royal governor.[59]

In theory, a colonial governor held formidable powers: to summon or dissolve the assembly and to veto laws without any override by a supermajority. The governor's royal instructions also demanded his jealous protection of the Crown's share of colonial power, known as "the prerogative," from aggressive assemblies. In addition, the governor had some patronage to build "an interest" with the leading men in the assembly and on the council. He could nominate a few to serve in the lucrative posts of attorney general, colonial secretary, surveyor general, and treasurer. With the council's approval, the governor also appointed county sheriffs and clerks, justices of the peace, and militia officers. Colonists coveted those offices as sources of honor, influence, and some income. If the council cooperated, a governor could reward his friends with large grants of frontier land and could withhold that largesse from his foes.[60] *really value any power they have*

But no governor possessed enough offices and lands to satisfy all of the ambitious and competitive colonial politicians. And both the governor's superiors in London and his opponents in the assembly tended over time to reduce his patronage. In most colonies by the 1750s, assertive assemblymen had gained control of appointing county justices, clerks, and sheriffs. And imperial bureaucrats in London began to fill many of the best colonial posts, including chief justice, attorney general, and clerk of the assembly. Deprived of sufficient patronage, a governor could rarely manage his restive assembly. Instead of following the governor's lead, assemblymen usually heeded constituents who wanted their taxes kept low and their governors kept weak.[61]

By controlling appropriations, assemblymen held the trump card in colonial politics: the governor's precious salary. A governor who strictly adhered to his royal instructions got nowhere fast and had to live without his pay. After much initial wrangling, most governors eventually learned to get along and go along with the leaders in their assemblies. Of course, a governor who neglected his instructions risked recall by his imperial superiors. In sum, he was doomed to fail either for colluding, or for clashing, with the colonial elite. That inexorable trap compounded the pressure on a governor to make as much money as soon as possible before his inevitable recall.[62]

Colonial politics lacked formal parties, but there was an unstable polarity pitting a faction that supported the governor against his more numerous opponents, who resented exclusion from his patronage. Posing as "Patriots," the opponents claimed to defend colonial liberty and property against the greed of a grasping governor and his corrupt minions. In Pennsylvania, a governor lamented that "the people" were "always fondest of those that opposed the Gov't." Another governor noted the conviction of Virginians "that he is the best Patriot that most violently opposes all Overtures for raising money."[63]

The arrival of a new governor often rearranged the sides, as the old governor's critics became the new governor's cronies, obliging former supporters to become Patriots. New York's Philip Livingston candidly explained, "We change Sides as Serves our Interest best." Because one year's "court men" could become the next year's Patriots, the popular leaders were just as genteel, wealthy, and well educated as those who stuck with the governor. No leader on either side sought a more democratic society of greater equality. Both factions agreed that Indians should be dispossessed and that women, servants, and slaves should remain dependent.[64]

The political wrangling did not imply any alienation from king and empire. Indeed, colonial Patriots opposed governors in the name of the king, who allegedly wanted nothing but the best for his subjects. In 1733, during an election in New York, an assembly candidate held a parade beneath "a Banner; on one Side of which was affixed in gold Capitals, KING GEORGE, and on the Other, in like golden Capitals LIBERTY & LAW." The same voters who distrusted governors also worshiped the king, for an idealized monarchy lay at the heart of the political culture.[65]

Beyond the petty republics of Connecticut and Rhode Island, voters chose only members for the assembly: a mere third of the provincial government. In most colonies every county, no matter how populous or small, could elect two representatives. Although chosen by voters, the assembly was no democratic institution, for gender, poverty, or race disqualified most adults from voting. Women, children, slaves, indentured servants, free blacks, or white men without property were deemed dependent on others. Even widows with land lacked the vote because the culture denigrated all females as unstable and untrustworthy.[66]

Elections served as a political carnival: a brief reversal of social roles that ultimately reaffirmed the unequal social order. Genteel candidates had to flatter and treat common voters, who ordinarily had to defer to their betters. At the poll, each voter briefly held center stage, while genteel candidates looked on in suspense. An election was a safety valve, giving common men a brief taste of power.[67]

Turnout, however, rarely topped a quarter of the qualified voters. The roads were bad, the weather often stormy, and the polling places few and far between: usually only one per county. Most voters had more pressing business to attend to on their farms, and many elections went uncontested. In Virginia between 1728 and 1775, two-thirds of the elections lacked any competition. Colonial America was a poor place to look for democracy.[68]

A few elite families dominated most counties, and most assemblies were relatively small conclaves of like-minded men. Massachusetts alone had an assembly with more than a hundred members. More typical was New Jersey with twenty and New York with twenty-eight members. In most colonies, representation favored the older counties at the expense of newer, frontier districts. In 1769 in New York, landlords and merchants held twenty-one seats compared to only seven members from the colony's farmer majority. A royal governor reported that New York's assembly "consists of the Owners of these Extravagent [land] grants, the Merchants of New York, the principal of them strongly connected with the Owners of these great Tracts by family Interest, and of Common Farmers, which last are Men easily deluded and led away with popular Arguments of Liberty and Privilege." But common colonists could express their politics by rioting rather than voting.[69]

Boston had an especially vibrant popular culture that could erupt into mass protest. Every November 5, the working people celebrated "Pope's Day," the Boston version of Guy Fawkes Day, which honored the suppression of a Catholic plot to blow up Parliament and the king in 1605. Making a great show of rowdy Protestantism, men in the rival neighborhoods of the South End and North End made garish effigies of the pope, devil, and Guy Fawkes. To raise funds, they called on gentlemen for contributions and woe to the windows of anyone who refused. On Pope's Day, the rival gangs mounted their effigies on carts, which they hauled in raucous procession to the town's central common, where they battled with fists and clubs to capture the other side's trophies. In 1764, the South Enders triumphed at the cost of one boy's life and many bloodied noses and broken bones. The victors then hauled both carts to the public gallows at the southern edge of town for a massive bonfire of the effigies. Pope's Day allowed common laborers and artisans to rule the streets and extort contributions from gentlemen for one day in the year, a venting of energy that enabled social and political order to prevail during the rest of the year.[70]

Ordinarily deferential to authority, common people claimed the right to act violently when their supposed betters committed some glaring abuse or neglect. In 1747, hundreds of common Bostonians took to the streets to protest the forcible impressments of local sailors by a Royal Navy squadron commanded by Commodore Charles Knowles. The violence escalated after a press gang killed two resisting sailors. Governor William Shirley described the rioters as "working artificers, seafaring men, and low sorts of people." Behind the scenes, however, they had support from "Persons of Influence in the Town": merchants who disliked losing sailors to the Royal Navy. Armed with stones, clubs, and cutlasses, rioters smashed the statehouse windows, seized and burned a barge thought to belong to the commodore, and drove the frightened governor to take refuge in the harbor fort. Local militiamen ignored his call to turn out and suppress the riot. Rather than seeking a revolution in government, the rioters wanted a limited but immediate response: the return of impressed men to their families. Understanding the rules of the game, Shirley persuaded Knowles to release the sailors. Triumphant rioters then returned to their work and homes, while the governor demanded and received an apology from the Boston town meeting, thereby restoring the normative deference of the political culture.[71]

When powerful and wealthy men abused their power, common people sought to nullify the local operation of the law. In New Jersey, eastern New York, Maine, northern Maryland, and North Carolina, powerful land speculators demanded payments from common people, who insisted that they already had bought title to their farms. They feared reduction to tenancy or wage labor by wealthy landlords. When farmers refused to pay, landlords sued and threatened eviction and jail. In response, farmers assembled with clubs and crowbars to break open jails and liberate their friends. Rural rioters also wrecked the houses of wayward neighbors who submitted to speculators and their courts. Although adept at destroying property and roughing up opponents, the rioters almost never killed anyone. They sought immediate redress for a particular grievance rather than to overthrow the government and social structure. Common rioters called themselves "regulators," for they sought to regulate the law rather than destroy it.[72]

not revolutionary

Enemies

Britons and British Americans shared an identity defined against the Catholic French and Spanish, cast as economically backward, religiously superstitious, culturally decadent, and submissive to despotic rule. By contrast, Britons felt especially blessed and enlightened by commerce, civil liberties, the common law, and their Protestant faith. As evidence, they cited the superior prosperity and naval power of the British Empire. In wartime, the Royal Navy defended the empire's trade and ravaged the commerce of rival empires to the double benefit of colonial producers and shippers. In 1700, a New Englander preached, "It is no little Blessing of God that we are part of the English nation." During the eighteenth century, the many imperial wars against France and Spain promoted the colonists' identification with Britain. Making much of their supposed racial purity, British Americans accused the French and Spanish of indiscriminately mixing with natives and Africans. In Virginia, a leading minister prayed for "the reduction of that mongrel race of *French* and *Indian* savages, who . . . have been the eternal enemies of humanity, peace, religion and *Britons.*"[73]

Blessed with a more temperate climate and better seaport access to the Atlantic, British America sustained the denser settlement of farmers, while most of New France remained hunting territory possessed by Indians. Pinned east of the Appalachian Mountains (approximately 200 miles from the coast), British colonists occupied less land but did so more intensively than did the French, who were dispersed in a broad arc from Louisbourg, at the mouth of the St. Lawrence in the northeast, up that river to the Great Lakes and down the Mississippi River to New Orleans.[74]

The larger British-American population should have generated an army big enough to overwhelm the fewer and more dispersed French colonists. But the many, distinct British colonies lost that advantage by bickering over who should bear the costs of war. The growing British colonial population also alarmed native peoples, who felt less pressure from the smaller French numbers. Rendered arrogant by their larger population, British colonists mistreated their Indian neighbors, and colonial juries would rarely convict settlers for murdering natives.[75]

In sum, Indians faced a greater threat from the many British Americans than from the fewer French. To cultivate native support and trade, the French built many small forts along the Great Lakes and the Ohio and Mississippi rivers. Lightly built and garrisoned, the posts depended upon Indians for protection. Rather than intimidate natives, the forts served them by providing trade, presents, and rallying points for war parties to attack British settlements.[76]

Although diminished by disease, the natives of the interior remained formidable guerilla fighters who dominated the vast forests between the rival empires. Advancing stealthily along paths through the woods, they struck suddenly before slipping away and eluding pursuit. Haudenosaunee (Iroquois) chiefs warned Virginia's governor, "Our Young Warriors are like the Wolves of the Forrest." To counter native raids, colonial officials had to build and garrison many frontier forts at great expense in men and money. To attack another empire's colonies by land through dense forests, each side needed Indian scouts and warriors to avoid falling into a deadly ambush.[77]

The balance of power in North America hinged upon the French ability to maintain, or the British capacity to subvert, an alliance with native peoples. In 1755, a Carolinian noted:

> The importance of the Indians is now generally known and understood. A Doubt remains not, that the prosperity of our Colonies on the Continent will stand or fall with our Interest and favour among them. While they are our Friends, they are the Cheapest and Strongest Barrier for the Protection of our Settlements; when Enemies, they are capable of ravaging in their method of War, in spite of all we can do, to render those Possessions almost useless.

In the competition for native allies, the British had one great advantage. They offered better-quality trade goods at lower prices than could the French.[78]

Some imperialists had dangerous illusions of controlling Indians, who, in fact, fought in their own way for their own interests. The fissuring of authority in native communities also worked against imperial command and control. Divided into many tribes and subdivided into hundreds of autonomous villages, Indians were further riven by competing factions led by rival chiefs. Colonial officials complained that presents purchased only the limited and unpredictable support of one faction. Where imperial commanders wanted prolonged, disciplined campaigns of endurance, natives preferred quick raids and a prompt return home to celebrate and recover. They were volatile allies prone to switch sides if their colonial partners faltered in war or failed to supply trade goods, especially guns and ammunition. None would take orders from outsiders. A French officer reported, "They are unwilling to recognize any foreigner as their master, just as they have none among themselves."[79]

Natives exploited the competition between rival empires to procure presents from both. Favored chiefs bolstered their influence by distributing these gifts among their warriors. Then they could parlay that enhanced influence in their village to seek still more presents from imperial patrons. Recognizing the advantages of their middle position, savvy chiefs hoped to keep one empire from conquering the colonies of the other. In New York, a colonial official acknowledged, "To preserve the Ballance between us & the French is the great ruling Principle of Modern Indian Politics."[80]

Wars

Between 1689 and 1763, the British and French waged four massive wars throughout the world's oceans and in far-flung colonies as well as in Europe. The first war (1689–1697) ended in a stalemate, but the second (1702–1713) featured impressive British victories. In the peace treaty of 1713, Britons secured Nova Scotia, Newfoundland, Hudson's Bay, and the West Indian island of St. Kitts. The third war (1743–1748) proved inconsequential, for the British again concentrated their forces in Europe, entrusting most of the fighting in America to colonists. Massachusetts and New Hampshire bore the brunt of the fighting, suffering raids by the French and their Indian allies. The other British colonies provided little help, save for South Carolina and Georgia, which tangled with the Spanish of Florida.[81]

Beginning in 1754, the fourth war became known in Europe as the <u>Seven Years War</u> and in the British colonies as the French and Indian War. Mutual dread drove both sides to fight, casting the other as the aggressor. Britons insisted that the French had a great plot to seek "universal monarchy" by dominating Europe and all colonies. Meanwhile, the French feared suffocation by the growing naval and commercial power of the British Empire. The two colonial flash points were the Ohio Valley and the northwestern margins of Nova Scotia. To defend their claims in both areas, the French built forts and armed nearby native allies, measures which the British regarded as provocations.[82]

The fertile Ohio Valley lay just west of the Appalachian Mountains, which had long hemmed in the British colonists to the east. To block British expansion westward, the French built Fort Duquesne at the strategic forks of the Ohio River (present-day Pittsburgh). In 1754, the royal governor of Virginia sent George Washington with a regiment of colonial troops to oust the French garrison. Inexperienced and rash, Washington bungled the expedition by making a premature and unprovoked attack on a French patrol. "Nothing could be more shameful, so base or so black as the train of thought of this Washington," declared the governor-general of New France. Counterattacking in overwhelming force, the French and their native allies surrounded the Virginians, who huddled in a crude fort poorly located in swampy low ground. Washington surrendered on July 4, unaware that the date would later assume a happier meaning for him. Fortunately for Washington, the French wanted to prevent a full-scale war, so they disarmed the Virginians and sent them home.[83]

Angered by Washington's defeat, the British blamed French aggression. Denouncing the "insults and encroachments of the French," the Duke of Newcastle warned, "All North America will be lost if these practices are tolerated." Noting the growing importance of colonial commerce to the empire, Britain's rulers wanted a vigorous military response. Another imperial official explained that British wealth had become "so linked in with, and dependent upon, the American revenues and remittances, that if they are ruined and stopt, the whole system of public credit in this country will receive a fatal shock."[84]

Most colonial legislatures again sought to evade the costs of war by shunting them onto their neighbors. Pennsylvania, for example, saw little reason to help Virginians seize western lands that Pennsylvanians also claimed. Appalled by the bickering, the Earl of Halifax denounced "the absurd and false oeconomy, the ill-tim'd deficiency of spirit and the lethargic insensibility of the colonies."[85]

During the summer of 1754, delegates from seven colonies met at Albany to try to improve their military coordination by proposing a daring plan for colonial union. Drafted by Benjamin Franklin, the "Albany Plan" called for a "Grand Council" chosen by colonists and a Crown-appointed "President General" to serve as the executive. The new union would control colonial defense and Indian affairs and have the power to levy taxes. The individual colonies would retain responsibility for their internal affairs, and the new union would remain subordinate to the King-in-Parliament. But both the colonial legislatures and imperial government jealously rejected the plan as an intrusion on their prerogatives. Franklin despaired of unifying colonies with such "different forms of government, different laws, different interests, and some of them different religious persuasions and different manners." British colonists entered a dangerous new war as divided as ever.[86]

Colonial dithering led the British to take charge of the war effort in America. In 1755, General Edward Braddock crossed the Atlantic with redcoats and orders to push the French back along the frontier. Braddock sent one force of British regulars and New England volunteers to overwhelm the French posts at the head of the Bay of Fundy in Nova Scotia. The victors deported most of the 6,000 Acadian French and confiscated their farms and livestock for appropriation by land speculators and settlers from New England.[87]

Braddock led 2,200 regular and colonial troops in an overland march against Fort Duquesne. Brave but arrogant, Braddock neglected to cultivate native allies and scouts. Within seven miles of the fort, his troops plunged into a devastating Indian ambush that killed Braddock and hundreds of his men. The debacle had one silver lining: after the senior British officers died, Washington took command and redeemed his military reputation by leading a retreat that saved two-thirds of the troops. His skill at retreating would prove invaluable in his next war, when his outnumbered and outgunned army often needed to escape from defeat to fight another day.[88]

After Braddock's defeat, French-allied warriors ravaged the settlements of Virginia, Maryland, and Pennsylvania. Highly mobile warriors could pin down greater numbers of colonial troops. A French officer boasted that British Americans were defenseless: "What can they do against these invisible enemies who strike then flee with the speed of lightning[?] They are the exterminating angel[s]." Thanks to these raids, initiative in the frontier war passed to the French during 1756 and 1757. Under the able leadership of Governor-General Pierre de Rigaud de Vaudreuil and General Louis-Joseph de Montcalm, French forces captured British forts on Lake Ontario and Lake George. Meanwhile, in Europe, the British suffered an even more humiliating loss when the French captured Minorca, a prime naval base in the Mediterranean.[89]

In Britain, the embarrassing defeats brought to power a more competent administration headed by William Pitt as Secretary of State for the Southern Department. Bombastic, egotistical, energetic, and ambitious, Pitt reorganized his empire's military resources to conquer the French colonies in North America: a great escalation in British war aims. In 1758 in British America, Pitt deployed 45,000 troops, about half British regulars and half colonial volunteers, and five times the number of French troops in Canada. The British also sent forces to fight in India, Germany, and Portugal and to raid the coast of France. In all theaters, the British employed 167,000 soldiers and sailors at an annual expense of £18 million. Never before had any empire spent so much money to wage war on a transoceanic scale.[90]

Instead of ordering colonial cooperation, Pitt bought it by reimbursing two-fifths of the military expenditures made by colonial legislatures. The new policy increased their contributions of men and supplies, particularly from New England. Although politically expedient, Pitt's policies were financially reckless. By compounding the public debt, Pitt saddled colonists and Britons with a burden that later would disrupt the empire.[91]

In 1758, the Royal Navy won control of the Atlantic and devastated French shipping, reducing the reinforcements and supplies that reached New France. As trade goods became scarce at French forts, many Indians ran short of the guns, gunpowder, and shot needed for hunting and war. When a new British force advanced on Fort Duquesne, the local natives deserted the French to reopen trade with Pennsylvanians. Abandoned by their allies, the French blew up that fort and fled northward to Canada. Without native warriors, the French could not defend their frontier posts.[92]

The British overwhelmed New France with sheer numbers of soldiers and sailors, warships, and cannon. In 1758, a massive British fleet and 13,000 regulars captured the great fortress at Louisburg on Cape Breton Island near the mouth of the St. Lawrence River. A year later, the invaders swept up the river to attack and capture Quebec. In 1760, British forces from Quebec and New York converged on Montreal, compelling Vaudreuil to surrender all of Canada, including the forts around the Great Lakes to the west. The French Crown had failed to reinforce Canada, instead giving priority to fighting in Europe.[93]

In 1762, the Spanish belatedly entered the war as French allies. Instead of turning the military tide, Spain promptly shared in the defeats inflicted by British forces, who captured the great Spanish colonial port of Havana, Cuba. In the Pacific another British fleet seized Manila, the capital of the Philippines. For the Manila attack, the British relied on troops raised in India, which attested to the increasingly global and multiracial nature of the British Empire. The British also made gains in

"General Wolfe Killed at the Siege of Quebec, September 14, 1759," engraving by W. & J. Stratford, 1792. While British troops surge to victory in the background, a messenger brings news to the dying commander, General James Wolfe, in the center foreground. Courtesy of the Library of Congress (LC-USZ62-53).

India and West Africa by routing the French and their local allies. In the West Indies, Britons conquered the French islands of Guadeloupe, Martinique, St. Lucia, Grenada, and St. Vincent.[94]

But the British also had to weather a slave revolt in Jamaica, the biggest uprising ever in the largest and richest colony of the British West Indies. Disrupting imports of food, the war put slaves on short rations. In April 1760 on the north shore, about 5,000 of the enslaved rose up to plunder and burn their plantations before retreating with stolen weapons into the forested hills to defend themselves as defiant maroons. British regulars and colonial militiamen counterattacked, killing Tackey, the charismatic rebel leader. Resistance crumbled, and the victors tortured and executed more than 100 rebels, decorating crossroads with impaled heads as intimidating examples to other slaves. Given a terrible scare, Jamaican planters clung more closely to the empire, petitioning for more redcoats to garrison the colony.[95]

white fear

Britain won the Seven Years War because advanced financial institutions and abundant investment capital enabled the government to raise more money than could the French and Spanish. By 1763, however, mounting taxes and national debt had become alarming. Britons grew especially sullen after 1760, when Parliament levied higher taxes on beer. That year, a new king, George III, ascended to the throne and, in late 1761, sacked Pitt and, a year later, opened peace negotiations with the French and Spanish.[96]

Reforms

In February 1763, the European belligerents made peace in the Treaty of Paris. The French conceded Canada and all of their claims east of the Mississippi (including the Ohio Valley) to the British. The victors also retained Senegal, a valuable West African base for the slave trade, and the lesser of their West Indian conquests: Dominica, Grenada, St. Vincent, and Tobago. To mollify the French, the British returned the Caribbean islands of Guadeloupe, Martinique, and St. Lucia. The French also recovered their fishing stations at Saint Pierre and Miquelon, near the rich cod-fishery of the Grand Banks off Newfoundland. The French readily sacrificed Canada, which had run a great annual deficit, preferring to regain profitable sugar islands and access to the northern fisheries.[97]

To appease their Spanish allies, the French gave them New Orleans and most of Louisiana (west of the Mississippi River). Although Louisiana was a money-loser, the Spanish hoped to enhance the security of Mexico by deepening the frontier buffer zone meant to keep the British far away. To regain Havana and Manila, the Spanish ceded Florida to the British. The Mississippi became the new boundary between the British and the Spanish empires. After the Treaty of Paris, British America stretched from the Arctic to the Caribbean.[98]

Britons gloated over their global triumphs, but the French exited the war with a leaner and more effective empire, while Britain took on vast debts and expensive new responsibilities. The leading French negotiator, the Duc de Choiseul, boasted that he had burdened the British with future woes. Indeed, the great conquests created new tensions between colonists and the empire, while inspiring the French and Spanish to adopt reforms that bolstered their colonial and military resources. In the next war, the French would have a modernized army and a bigger navy of better-designed warships.[99]

During the 1760s and 1770s, the Spanish adopted new colonial policies meant to enhance their empire's revenues and defenses. Named for Spain's ruling dynasty, the "Bourbon reforms" promoted economic development and strengthened fortifications and garrisons. Increasing the power of Spanish-born officials, the centralizing reforms came at the expense of colonial aristocrats, whom imperialists derided as selfish and backward obstacles to economic growth. Thanks to new and increased taxes, Crown revenues from Mexico soared from 12 million to 50 million pesos annually. While freeing most trade within the Spanish Empire, the Crown toughened enforcement of bans on colonial trade with other empires.[100]

In 1766, the new Spanish governor of Louisiana, Antonio de Ulloa, alienated New Orleans merchants by enforcing stricter customs regulations. Hoping to entice France to reclaim Louisiana, the merchants stirred up the common people to revolt, driving Ulloa away to Cuba in October 1768. A year later, General Alejandro O'Reilly, an Irish-born officer, arrived with 2,000 Spanish soldiers to restore order. O'Reilly tried, convicted, and executed five leading rebels at New Orleans.[101]

After this show of force, the Spanish governed Louisiana with judicious restraint, loosening the commercial restrictions that had provoked the revolt. O'Reilly and his successors as governor relied on French magistrates for local government and on French traders to manage native diplomacy. Aside from a few Spanish officials at the top (and 2,000 immigrants from the Canary Islands), most Louisianans remained French. Eager to procure settlers, the Spanish regime welcomed French *habitants* and traders who moved across the Mississippi when the British occupied the Illinois country. The Spanish also enticed nearly 3,000 dislocated Acadians, who became Cajuns in Louisiana. Anticipating a future conflict with the British, O'Reilly wanted to settle the colony "with people who are irreconcilable enemies of England on account of the contempt and persecution they have suffered." More Francophones came to Louisiana under Spanish rule than in the previous French administration of the colony. Britons naïvely regarded Spain as a decrepit power inferior to France. In fact, Spanish rule revitalized the long-neglected colony.[102]

Spanish officials also pushed their colonial frontier northwestward from Mexico into California in response to alarming rumors of Russian advances eastward from Siberia via Alaska. Other reports suggested that British fur traders were approaching the Pacific Coast via Hudson's Bay. Vague in their knowledge of the vast Pacific Northwest region, the Spanish prematurely concluded that Russians and Britons were closing in on California and would soon outflank New Mexico to attack Mexico. In fact, the imperial rivals were fewer and farther away than the Spanish imagined. In distant and subarctic Alaska, a few dozen Russian traders were busy harvesting sea otter pelts, while the Hudson's Bay Company had not yet breached the Rocky Mountains to find the Pacific. Among imperial officials, however, fearful misunderstanding was more motivating than reassuring truth. Beginning in 1768, the Spanish occupied the California coast with a string of missions and small *presidios*, which stretched northward to Monterey by 1774. Lacking colonists, Spanish officials attempted to turn natives into Hispanics at the new missions.[103]

A more substantial threat to Spain came from the Pacific voyages of exploration led by Captain James Cook of the Royal Navy. By documenting and mapping the islands, shores, currents, and peoples of the Pacific, Cook sought new trade routes and potential colonies in a quarter of the globe that especially imperiled Spanish interests. From Peru and Mexico, the Spanish shipped silver across that ocean to the Philippines and China, a lucrative commerce at risk if the Royal Navy could dominate the Pacific. Britain threatened to complete its global superiority by breaking into the Pacific.[104]

To guard the southeastern approach to the Pacific, the Spanish asserted their claim to the Falkland Islands in the South Atlantic. Although unpopulated, cold, and relatively barren, the Falklands offered coveted harbors for sailing ships. In 1766, British marines constructed a fort on West Falkland Island, which provoked the Spanish governor of Buenos Aires in 1770 to oust the intruders with military force. While the Royal Navy mobilized for war, Spain looked to France for support. But France's financial and naval recovery from the last war remained painfully incomplete. Denied French support, the Spanish had to back down, grudgingly conceding the Falklands to Britain. That new lesson in British aggression compounded the French and Spanish zeal to narrow the naval gap and prepare for another war.[105]

Within a dozen years of the peace of 1763, a global conflict would erupt from a surprising source: a rebellion by thirteen British colonies along the Atlantic Seaboard of North America. A Briton later recognized that his empire's triumph in the Seven Years War had borne bitter fruit: "What did Britain gain by the most glorious and successful war on which she ever engaged? A height of Glory which excited the Envy of the surrounding nations and . . . an extent of empire we were equally unable to maintain, defend or govern." *Because* of that triumph, the empire would reap a revolution in British America.[106]

Divisions

The great British victories in the Seven Years War had thrilled the colonists, who danced around bonfires, fired volleys of cannon, rang church bells, lit up the sky with fireworks, and toasted Pitt, King George III, the Royal Navy, British army, and colonial volunteers. Far from seeking independence, colonists cherished the liberties, military security, and profitable trade provided by a triumphant empire. Addressing Boston's town meeting in 1763, James Otis praised the war for strengthening colonial ties to the empire: "We in America have certainly abundant reason to rejoice. . . . The true interests of Great Britain and her plantations are mutual, and what God in his providence has united, let no man dare attempt to pull asunder." A year later he added, "We love, esteem and reverence our mother country and adore our king."[107]

By conquering French Canada, however, Britons and colonists unwittingly created a crisis within their shared empire. ~~After their victories, Britons felt emboldened to rearrange the empire, and colonial leaders felt freer to defy those changes.~~ In 1775 a London newspaper blamed the conquests for spoiling the colonists: "the moment their fears . . . were removed by the cession of all Canada to Great Britain, that moment the dutiful colonies began to change their tone; ~~America was no longer *ours*, but *theirs*.~~"[108] CHANGE

[margin annotation: privilege of skin color + British culture]

Victory had not come cheap, for the conflict nearly doubled the British national debt from a prewar £74 million to a postwar £133 million. During the mid-1760s, servicing that debt consumed £5 million of the empire's annual budget of £8 million. The government also needed £360,000 annually to sustain 10,000 troops to garrison the conquests in North America. Already paying higher taxes than the French and Spanish, Britons demanded that Parliament find new sources of revenue in the colonies.[109]

After making such a major investment of men and money to fight in North America, Britain's rulers were not about to revert to their prewar policy of neglecting the colonies. During the war, British officers and officials had discovered just how prosperous the colonists had become. Yet on a per capita basis, the colonists paid only 1 shilling in tax directly to the empire compared to 26 shillings per capita paid in England. Britons insisted that colonists should pay new and higher taxes as the chief beneficiaries of an expensive war.[110]

Imperial officials also complained that the colonists had performed poorly and selfishly during the war. Sticklers for discipline, British officers derided colonial troops as laxly trained, insubordinate, and ineffective in combat. General James Wolfe denounced them as "the dirtiest, most contemptible, cowardly dogs that you can conceive." Britons also denounced colonial merchants who had profiteered by trading with the enemy in the West Indies. Pitt declared that American smuggling had "principally, if not alone, enabled [France] to sustain, and protract, this long and expensive war."[111]

Frustrated with colonial legislators, troops, and merchants, British officials decided to tighten their control over the colonies. Public opinion in Britain agreed. In 1763 in England, William Smith struggled to raise money for a colonial college thanks to "a strong prejudice that we stand in need of no help, have got all the benefits of a war that has plunged the mother country so deep in debt." Britons told Smith that colonists "were able enough to build our colleges ourselves; that we had got all the advantages of the war, had born little of the burden, and were impudent beggars that would do nothing for ourselves."[112]

Fed up with negotiating and compromising with colonial elites, imperial reformers wanted to compel greater obedience and raise more revenue. Rejecting colonial pretensions to a privileged place in the empire, imperial officials wanted to govern colonists as subordinates and tax them to fund the enhanced garrisons needed for an enlarged empire. Colonists, however, resented the new garrisons as an unnecessary expense and a potential threat to their liberty. Britons took colonial opposition lightly because they credited victory in the recent war almost entirely to the regular army and Royal Navy, which allegedly had rescued inept, conniving, and bickering colonists from French and Indian aggression. British leaders doubted that colonists could defy the empire.[113]

British hubris was on a collision course with inflated American expectations of a partnership in the empire. Colonists considered themselves "free-born Englishmen" of tried and true loyalty to their king. As British subjects in America, colonial leaders expected the same rights as their counterparts in the mother country. They balked at the label "American" as implying cultural degradation by association with Indians and enslaved Africans.

After the war, British officials and writers increasingly derided colonists as distant and wayward inferiors who deserved restraint for the greater good of the empire. In London as a colonial lobbyist, Benjamin Franklin bristled at hearing colonists described as "a mixed rabble of Scotch, Irish and foreign vagabonds, [the] descendants of convicts, ungrateful rebels, &c." British writers and readers cast colonists as the "lowest of Mankind, and almost a different Species from the English" and "fit only to be snubb'd, curb'd, shackled and plundered." Franklin worried that Britons would treat colonists as the "subjects of subjects," rather than as partners in the empire. If denied equality with Britons, colonists feared that they sat on the slippery slope to dependence, dispossession, and even (they claimed) enslavement. A Member of Parliament dismissed Franklin as "a most complete American, a perfect anti-Briton." In fact, he clung to an inclusive vision of empire imperiled by the new demands of British officials.[115]

After the triumphant war, colonists expected a privileged position as Britons in America. Instead, to their horror, imperial reformers sought a more centralized empire. Thomas Jefferson later rebuked Britons for an imperial partnership lost: "We might have been a free and a great people together." But that imagined empire of freedom depended on a shared superiority over natives and the enslaved.[116]

2

LAND

I see plainly how it is now throughout the Continent.
People expect to do now as they please.
—SIR WILLIAM JOHNSON, 1768[1]

During the eighteenth century, the population grew faster in British America than in the mother country. Thanks to abundant land, early marriages, and healthy conditions, the number of colonists doubled every twenty-five years. In 1751, Benjamin Franklin calculated that, within a century, "the greatest number of Englishmen will be on this side of the Water." Rather than anticipate American independence, Franklin praised that growth as an "accession of Power to the British Empire by Sea as well as Land!" But he also expected power to shift westward with the flow of population, increasing colonial clout and diminishing that of the mother country.[2]

Colonial expansion westward accelerated after the triumphant conquest of Canada, which opened to settlement the vast domain beyond the Appalachian Mountains. Blessed with fertile soil and navigable rivers, the West enticed settlers to make new farms at the expense of native peoples. Those new settlements promised to draw more immi-

[handwritten margin note: population growth]

"A View of a Saw Mill and Block House upon Fort Anne Creek," by W. Lane, 1789. The sawmill and the blockhouse exemplify the environmental transformation wrought by settlement. Courtesy of the Library of Congress (LC-USZ62-1799).

grants to the colonies, hastening the shift of people and power across the Atlantic.[3]

As America expanded, worried British leaders feared losing control of their empire. Some regarded the colonies as hostile rivals bent on creating their own empire at British expense. Britons began to think of the colonists as aliens—as Americans—far sooner than did colonists like Franklin who dreamed of a shared empire of equals. A British newspaper anticipated two centuries in the future when visitors "from the empire of America" came to tour the ruins of a depopulated London where Parliament had become a hollow, forsaken shell. In the story, a Londoner explained that most Britons had "settled in Imperial America," which "was the original cause of our poverty and of your power and grandeur."[4]

Pushed by rising rents, stagnant wages, and poor grain harvests in Britain, migrants also felt pulled by the abundant, fertile, and cheap lands of the colonies. Between 1760 and 1775, 30,000 English, 40,000 Scots, and 55,000 northern Irish (a total of 125,000) moved to British America. During the same period, 12,000 Germans and 85,000 enslaved Africans joined them, raising the total to 222,000. On average, 15,000 immigrants arrived annually, a tripling of the prewar rate. An Irish observer worried that "if the numbers of inhabitants constitute the riches of a state, Heaven knows, Ireland will soon be the poorest country under the canopy of Heaven." And America would become the richest.[5]

The worriers included the Earl of Hillsborough, who, as president of the Board of Trade and later as Secretary of State, played a leading role in colonial policy. The owner of nearly 100,000 acres of Irish land, Hillsborough benefited from high rents and cheap labor, so he was loath to see any of his 20,000 tenants and laborers leave for the colonies. He insisted that the emigrants departed "for no other reason but because they hope to live better, or to earn more money in those countries than they can do at home." Insisting that they suffered instead of prospering in America, Hillsborough argued that "it would be doing them a service" and "for the public good to lay a restraint upon poor people leaving the place of their birth without leave from the magistrates of the place."[6]

But what could the British government do? For all its imperial pretensions, the Crown lacked the means to police its many seaports to regulate departures. Proposed restrictions also ran afoul of British pride in their cherished liberty to move freely within the empire.

Unable to control Britons, the empire tried instead to restrain colonists by vetoing subsidies offered by some colonies to attract immigrants from Britain and by restricting western settlement. In addition to preserving Britain's hegemony, the restrictive policy sought to avoid expensive wars with Indians. Burdened by a great national debt, the empire could ill afford to spend more money policing the West.[7]

Fear

The British conquest of New France alarmed native peoples, who lost the leverage of playing off one empire against another. Indians also resented the British claim to territories that the French had held by native sufferance. Rejecting the transfer made by the Treaty of Paris, a Creek chief, Yahatatastonake, warned British officials that natives were "surprized how People can give away Land that does not belong to them." An Ojibwa chief assured the British, "Although you have conquered the French, you have not yet conquered us. We are not your slaves." Natives protested as colonial hunters and settlers invaded Indian country, sweeping natives aside to remake their homelands into farms and towns. "People is mad to be Settelling upon the Indians Land," a barely literate colonist warned, "it is bringing the hole Contrey in to troblle." Reckless traders also cheated the natives after plying them with alcohol. Meanwhile, the British army commander, Sir Jeffrey Amherst, built new forts without native permission and cut costs by curtailing the customary delivery of diplomatic presents to chiefs.[8]

Disgust spread among the natives around the Great Lakes and in the Ohio Valley. A British Indian agent, George Croghan, warned his superiors that Indians had "the highest notions of Liberty of any

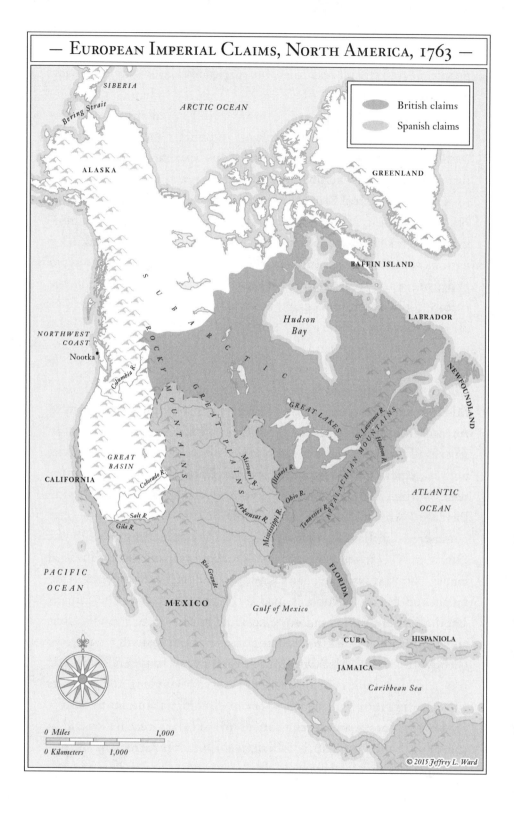

— European Imperial Claims, North America, 1763 —

British claims
Spanish claims

SIBERIA

ARCTIC OCEAN

Bering Strait

ALASKA

GREENLAND

BAFFIN ISLAND

NORTHWEST COAST

Nootka

Columbia R.

S U B A R C T I C

ROCKY MOUNTAINS

GREAT PLAINS

Hudson Bay

LABRADOR

NEWFOUNDLAND

GREAT LAKES

St. Lawrence R.

Hudson R.

APPALACHIAN MOUNTAINS

GREAT BASIN

CALIFORNIA

Colorado R.

Missouri R.

Illinois R.

Ohio R.

Tennessee R.

ATLANTIC OCEAN

Salt R.

Gila R.

Arkansas R.

Mississippi R.

PACIFIC OCEAN

Rio Grande

FLORIDA

MEXICO

Gulf of Mexico

CUBA

HISPANIOLA

JAMAICA

Caribbean Sea

0 Miles   1,000
0 Kilometers   1,000

© 2015 Jeffrey L. Ward

people on Earth" and had "become exceeding jealous of our growing power in that Country." The superintendent for Indian affairs in the northern colonies, Sir William Johnson, agreed: "They are greatly disgusted at the great Thirst which we all seem to shew for their Lands."[9]

Alienated natives felt inspired by religious prophets, who promised that the Master of Life would destroy the greedy intruders if Indians revitalized their traditional ways and ceremonies. A leading prophet, Neolin, insisted that natives could create on earth a "Heaven where there was no White people but all Indians." Seeking to unite native nations, prophets urged Indians to forsake their traditional divisions and enmities. By rising up against the British garrisons of the interior, chiefs hoped to induce the French to come back and reclaim their proper place in a middle ground of presents, respect, and restraint.[10]

During the spring and summer of 1763, far-flung native peoples surprised and captured most of the British forts around the Great Lakes and in the Ohio Valley, killing or capturing the soldiers. At Michilimackinac, warriors fooled the garrison by playing a game of lacrosse in front of the fort. In pursuit of a ball, they rushed through an open gate and grabbed guns from native women, who had entered with weapons hidden beneath their robes. But the natives failed to capture the three largest and strongest western forts: Detroit, Niagara, and Pitt (the former Fort Duquesne and the future Pittsburgh).[11]

Britons called this uprising "Pontiac's Rebellion" after a chief of the Ottawas. Although talented and influential, Pontiac could not command the many diverse peoples who dwelled in dozens of scattered villages. For shared reasons but under their own chiefs, many natives attacked British posts and colonial settlements. Calling them rebels also misses their point, for Indians were free peoples who had never become British subjects. One chief assured a British officer: "This land is ours, and not yours."[12]

The brutal war hardened animosities along racial lines. Raiders ravaged the settlements of western Pennsylvania, Maryland, and Virginia, killing or capturing 2,000 colonists. Outraged by the atrocities of frontier war, many settlers treated all Indians, regardless of allegiance, as violent brutes best exterminated. In Pennsylvania in December 1763, vigilantes, known as the "Paxton Boys," massacred the peaceful Indians of Conestoga, who had sought colonial protection. The Paxton Boys tomahawked men, women, and children as they prayed.[13]

Outraged by the murders, Franklin considered the Conestogas guilty only of having "had a reddish brown Skin, and black Hair." He concluded: "If it be right to kill Men for such a Reason, then should any Man with a freckled Face and red Hair, kill a Wife or Child of mine, it would be right for me to revenge it, by killing all the freckled red-haired Men, Women, and Children, I could afterwards anywhere meet with." Most colonists rejected his logic, preferring their racism. None of the Paxton killers ever faced trial for their crimes.[14]

In February 1764, 500 armed Paxton Boys marched on Philadelphia to intimidate the leaders of Pennsylvania into adopting harsher measures against Indians. On the outskirts of the city, the vigilantes agreed to return home when promised a redress of their grievances. The colony allocated more money for frontier defense and offered bounties for Indian scalps: $134 for a man, $130 for a woman, and $50 for a child. The bounties promoted indiscriminate Indian hunting, for the scalp of a peaceable native told no tales, paid as well, and cost fewer pains to take.[15]

In 1764, the imperial government sought to end the expensive and frustrating frontier war. Blaming Amherst for the crisis, British leaders replaced him with a more pragmatic commander, General Thomas Gage. The new commander heeded the advice of Sir William Johnson, who denounced the folly of treating Indians with contempt "without considering that it is in their power at pleasure to lay waste and destroy the Frontiers." Johnson recognized that presents and respect for Indians were far cheaper than military expeditions. From 1764 to 1766, chiefs made peace with Johnson, who lavishly distributed presents. In return, Indians allowed the British to rebuild and reoccupy their forts. Although the uprising failed to return the French to North America, Indians had shocked Britons into adopting the conciliatory policies associated with the French.[16]

British officers concluded that settlers, rather than Indians, posed the greatest threat to imperial peace and order on the frontier. Determined to avoid another expensive war, British officials sought to protect natives from settlers. While colonists drew a harder racial line against Indians, Britons felt a new sympathy for them. In 1767, Gage noted, "I find everywhere that the Soldiers agree perfectly well with the Indians, and they seem to look upon them at present, as People who are to protect them from Injurys." But colonists longed to crush and dispossess native peoples, if only the British would get out of the way.[17]

Proclamation

In an age when bulky goods moved best by water rather than over land, the Appalachian Mountains posed an obstacle for transporting produce from the new settlements to the seaports of the Atlantic Seaboard. Instead, the West's navigable rivers, including the Ohio and Mississippi, flowed south to New Orleans, near the Gulf of Mexico. Because that seaport belonged to Spain, British officials worried that an imperial rival would benefit from the produce of the new settlements. Imperial officials also expected that political allegiance would follow economic interest, alienating settlers from the British Empire as they traded with the Spanish.[18]

In October 1763, a Royal Proclamation ordered settlers to stay east of the Appalachians and barred colonial governors from granting western lands to speculators. The proclamation shocked colonists, who, after helping to conquer Canada, had expected the British to help them dispossess the Indians in the West.[19]

Providing no civil government for the vast interior, the Proclamation left administration to the military and two Indian superintendents: Colonel John Stuart in the southern colonies and Sir William Johnson in the north. Born in Scotland, Stuart had migrated to South Carolina, where he became adept at Indian trade and diplomacy after marrying a Cherokee woman, who bore him several children. By restraining traders and settlers, Stuart won the trust of most southeastern nations.[20]

Johnson was an Irish immigrant of great charm, cunning, ambition, and powerful connections through his uncle, an admiral in the Royal Navy. During the late 1730s, Johnson settled in the Mohawk Valley of New York, where he shrewdly cultivated good relations with the Mohawk Indians. Learning their language and ways, he prospered in the fur trade and obtained a landed estate, which he settled with tenants from Germany and Scotland. As the common-law husband of Molly Brant, a prestigious Mohawk, he won influence in the broader Haudenosaunee confederation of New York, rallying them against the French during the Seven Years War.[21]

Banning western settlement, the Royal Proclamation instead invited settlers into three new southern, coastal colonies: East Florida, West Florida, and the Ceded Islands in the West Indies. Fearful of inland development as anarchic, British officials expected to exercise closer oversight in coastal colonies with military garrisons supported by the Royal Navy. Coastal settlement also favored economic integration into the transatlantic trade of the empire. In the new provinces, imperial officials promoted a more compact pattern of settlements better suited for defense against the French, Spanish, and Indians. Imperial officials also hoped to cultivate more deferential societies than those of the empire's older settler colonies, which had such assertive, elected assemblies.[22]

Located in the West Indies, the Ceded Islands consisted of Dominica, Grenada, St. Vincent, and Tobago, which the British had taken from France during the war. Although totaling only 700 square miles, the fertile Ceded Islands were promising for sugarcane and coffee plantations. To draw planters from the other British West Indies, imperial officials promised the standard colonial government: appointed governors and councils with an elected assembly. The British also sent troops to destroy maroon communities of escaped slaves but faced especially fierce resistance on St. Vincent from "Black Caribs": the mixed-race descendants of natives and former slaves. In 1773, the British made a peace that reserved the northern quarter of St. Vincent for the Black Caribs.[23]

British officials sought to modify the standard Caribbean development, which featured large plantations with many slaves and few whites. Lacking enough white men for the militia, West Indian colonies were doubly vulnerable: to slave revolt from within and French invasion from without. To attract more common whites and fewer great planters to the Ceded Islands, the Board of Trade capped land grants at 500 acres. The grantees faced stiff fines if they failed promptly to develop plantations and to settle at least one white man on every 100 acres. The land policy also reserved small lots of ten to thirty acres to accommodate the poorest settlers. To further discourage speculative hoarding of wild lands, the Crown required an annual "quit-rent" of 6 pence per acre, which a productive plantation could better afford than could idle lands.[24]

The land policy sought to generate a broad class of small-scale planters grateful to the government. Governor Valentine Morris of St. Vincent championed the "small and middling white Settlers" as "by far the most useful" colonists because they gave "the greatest strength to infant colonies." By contrast, the "opulent planter, who solicits for a large tract" sought to make a great fortune while living safely in England. Of course, the land policy offended great planters as an obstacle to their expansion. But the policy promoted rapid development, particularly on Grenada, where the value of sugar exports to Britain surged from £62,915 in 1763 to £859,981 a decade later.[25]

In the Treaty of Paris, the British also obtained Florida, which had never prospered under Spanish rule. The few Hispanic colonists lived around the towns of St. Augustine on the Atlantic coast and Pensacola on the Gulf coast. The rest of Florida remained native country largely settled by Seminoles: Creek Indians who had moved south and developed a new identity during the preceding generation. Unwilling to accept British rule, nearly all of Spain's 3,700 subjects withdrew from Florida in 1763.[26]

To promote British settlement, imperial officials divided Florida into two new provinces: East Florida along the Atlantic coast and West Florida on the Gulf coast and east bank of the Mississippi. The empire provided a governor and appointed councils for both colonies, but deferred an assembly until the population grew. East Florida never qualified for an assembly, but West Florida obtained one in November 1766—although it had a mere dozen representatives. The British kept garrisons of 300 men in each colony, but yellow fever, malaria, dysentery, typhus, and alcoholism took a steady toll on the troops.[27]

The royal Privy Council in London controlled land grants in East Florida, a policy that favored British rather than American speculators. The warm climate, long growing season, and supposed fertility allured well-connected Britons, including the colony's governor, General James Grant, and Lord Adam Gordon, who noted that promotional literature had "sett us all Florida mad." During the 1760s, the Privy Council issued 227 grants for 2,800,000 acres.[28]

fear of retribution

Fearing a large enslaved population as a security risk, imperial officials hoped to attract poor white Britons imported as indentured servants. Imperialists forgot the failure of a similar social experiment in neighboring Georgia during the preceding generation. In the tropics and subtropics, colonists longed to become planters with slaves to perform the hard, dirty labor of clearing the forest and cultivating crops. And East Florida was an especially wretched place for a settler colony. Swampy, thickly vegetated, and crawling with snakes, the land was difficult to clear with hand tools, particularly where mangroves and palmettos filled the soil with tough, thick roots. While suffering from heat and humidity, laborers attracted clouds of mosquitoes, which carried debilitating diseases, including malaria. The newcomers also dreaded the immense, bellowing, carnivorous alligators. Once cleared, East Florida's sandy soil produced scantier crops than expected.[29]

New Smyrna was the most spectacular of East Florida's many failed settlements that relied on indentured servants and pipe dreams. Most servants from Britain quickly ran away, so speculators sought southern European peasants, deemed ideal settlers for Florida: hardworking, used to heat, and rendered desperate by poverty. An agent for the developers recruited 1,400 migrants, a mix of Corsicans, Italians, Greeks, and Minorcans, imposing indentures that obliged them to work as unpaid servants for fourteen years before obtaining their own farms. In 1768, he settled them seventy-five miles south of St. Augustine at a place ominously known as Mosquito Inlet. Changing the name to New Smyrna failed to fool the millions of biting insects who bled the newcomers. Shocked by harsh conditions and brutal overseers, the servants rebelled and fled, but Governor Grant's troops captured and returned them. Grant sentenced three to die but pardoned one who agreed to execute the other two. Within seven years of arrival, three-quarters of the immigrants died from a combination of disease, heat prostration, and brutal treatment. After Grant left the colony, a more sympathetic governor allowed the survivors to move to St. Augustine.[30]

Grant noted that servants quickly figured out that they had to evade menial labor to be considered white: "Upon their landing they are immediately seized with the pride which every man is possessed of who wears a white face in America, and they say they won't be slaves and so they make their escape." Wealthier planters imported enslaved Africans, who became half of the population by 1776. Embracing the convenient fiction that Africans were well suited to brutal treatment and hard labor, Grant concluded, "Africans are the only people to go to work in warm climates."[31]

West Florida developed more rapidly thanks to better land, fewer absentee speculators, and more experienced settlers, who favored the fertile Natchez District on the east bank of the Mississippi, where they could trade with neighbors in Spanish Louisiana on the west bank. Rather than draw servants from Europe, West Florida attracted American settlers used to frontier hardships. Most came from North Carolina, Virginia, and Pennsylvania and crossed the mountains to descend the Ohio and Mississippi rivers in flatboats. The newcomers raised pigs, corn, and vegetables for subsistence as well as rice, indigo, tobacco, and cotton for export. By 1775, West Florida had 5,000 colonists (a quarter of them slaves) compared to 3,000 (half of them slaves) in East Florida. The colony did suffer from an especially fractious government in which leaders shot each other in duels and one depressed governor hanged himself in his study.[32]

Independence

In the mainland colonies, most free men owned farms by "freehold title," which promised a cherished independence from a landlord, employer, or master. Franklin explained, "No man who can have a piece of land of his own, sufficient by his labour to subsist his family in plenty, is poor enough to be a manufacturer and work for a master." The allure of independence also drew immigrants across the Atlantic. "The hopes of having land of their own & becoming independent of Landlords is what chiefly induces people into America," noted a New York official.[33] *no authority, no meddling*

But the cost of land in older colonial counties soared beyond the reach of many young people as the population doubled between 1750 and 1770. Colonial families often had eight to a dozen children, but only one could inherit the whole farm. The other sons could rent land from wealthy landlords who had monopolized immense tracts, particularly in New York, Maryland, eastern Pennsylvania, and northern Virginia.[34]

expansion problem solving To escape tenancy and secure independence, poorer families moved west to make new farms. New York's governor noted that, when the terms of indentured servants expired, "They immediately quit their masters and get a small tract of land, in settling which for the first three or four years they lead miserable lives, and in the most abject poverty. But all this is patiently borne and submitted to with the greatest cheerfulness [because] the satisfaction of being land holders smooths every difficulty."[35]

After the conquest of Canada, settlers surged into the backcountry from New England to Georgia. Between 1760 and 1776, the New England colonies created 283 new towns: an average of 18 new towns per year, which represented a tripling of the pre-1760 rate. "They are crowding up to this Country as if all New England was set on fire," a Vermont settler observed in 1771. In a single decade, New York's population more than doubled, from 80,000 in 1761 to 168,000 in 1771. Most of that growth occurred in new settlements in the Mohawk and upper

Hudson valleys. Pennsylvanians pushed west through the Appalachians into the Ohio Valley. Other settlers flowed southwestward from Pennsylvania along a rocky, rutted, and stumpy road via the "Great Valley" into the backcountry of Virginia, the Carolinas, and Georgia. North Carolina's population increased sixfold between 1750 and 1775, while Georgia's grew by a factor of fourteen.[36]

Living far from stores, mills, and decent roads, settlers initially struggled against immense trees, dense brush, howling wolves, and passing Indians. While carving new farms out of the forest, the settlers often went hungry and could rarely afford to buy imported consumer goods. Rough men and women with crude manners and morals bore the shock of early settlement. An Anglican missionary, Charles Woodmason, described Carolina settlers as "Banditti, profligates, Reprobates, and the vilest Scum of Mankind." They dwelled "like Hogs" in cramped and drafty cabins with "little or no Bedding" and wore few clothes while "swopping their Wives as Cattel, and living in a state of Nature, more irregularly and unchastely than the Indians." Bored with Woodmason's preaching, many got drunk, set their dogs to barking, and began "firing, hooping, and hallowing like Indians." The missionary sighed, "How hard the Lot of any Gentleman in this Part of the World."[37]

Common settlers sought freehold farms, but frontier land was not free, for speculators demanded payments for title to the terrain. Wealthy men with political connections procured thousands of acres from friendly governors and their councils. Paying only modest fees, speculators profited by retailing smaller parcels to the families whose labor made farms in the forest. In granting land, governors and councillors favored one another and leading assemblymen who cooperated in politics. Once procured, these large land grants enjoyed legal protection from judges and lawyers, who were related to, or worked for, the great landed families.[38]

After 1753, royal instructions limited American land grants to no more than 1,000 acres per individual, but colonial officials and speculators colluded to evade the limit. In 1772, New York's Governor William Tryon justified such evasions to a superior in England: "I conceive it, My Lord, good policy to lodge large Tracts of Land in the hands of Gentlemen of weight and consideration. They will naturally farm out their lands to Tenants: a method which will ever create subordination and counterpoise, in some measure, the general leveling spirit, that so much prevails in some of His Majesty's Governments." Tryon referred to the New England colonies, where freehold title prevailed and the colonists resisted British taxes. He later added that no New York governor could "keep his ground or preserve his Government in peace" unless he satisfied the wealthy land speculators who dominated the legislature.[39]

The colonial land system favored speculators and governors at the expense of Indians, who lost the land, and settlers, who had to rent or buy their new farms. In New York's counties along the border with New England, however, settlers allied with the local Indians to resist wealthy landlords, who held fraudulent seventeenth-century deeds from supposed chiefs. During the 1760s, 225 Wappinger Indians clung to 205,000 acres in New York's Dutchess County along the Connecticut line. Adapting to colonial culture, the Wappingers became Christians and assisted the British invasion of French Canada. At war's end, however, they returned home to find their villages taken over by speculating landlords.[40]

To retrieve some value for their lands, the Wappingers made a shrewd alliance with settlers from nearby Connecticut, granting them large farms at slight rents for 999-year terms. In return, the settlers agreed to resist the landlords while mounting a legal challenge to their title, providing the money that natives lacked. Daniel Nimham, a Wappinger chief, and Samuel Monroe, a farmer, led the alliance. Because so much colonial land depended upon suspect Indian deeds, an alliance of intruding Yankees with defiant natives was a double nightmare for New York's leaders. In 1763, landlords persuaded the courts and governor to have Monroe arrested on a charge of treason. Settlers concluded that they could not obtain justice "in a Course of Law because they were poor and . . . poor men were always oppressed by the rich."[41]

Armed with clubs, they acted as regulators to block the land-lords' agents from collecting rents and ejecting settlers. When sheriffs arrested a defiant settler, his friends broke open the county jail to liberate him. To enforce local solidarity, they also ousted anyone who paid rent to the landlords. In June 1766, Governor Sir Henry Moore sent redcoats to suppress the resistance. After several sharp skirmishes wounded a few soldiers, they arrested sixty settlers and burned many farms. Tried and convicted of riot, most suffered heavy fines and short jail terms, but the court sentenced one leader, William Prendergast, to death for committing high treason. To calm further resistance, however, Moore secured the king's pardon for Prendergast.[42]

The Wappingers and their settler allies sent Chief Nimham to London to appeal to the king for justice. Suspicious of colonial predation on native lands, imperial officials welcomed an opportunity to patronize Indian appellants. In August 1766, the Board of Trade concluded that New York's government had behaved with "unreasonable Severity, [and] the Colour of great Prejudice & Partiality . . . to intimidate these Indians from prosecuting their claims." The Privy Council then ordered Governor Moore to reconsider the Wappinger case.[43]

Sir William Johnson warned the imperial lords that the Wappingers could expect no justice from a colonial government led by land speculators. Indeed, in March 1767, the New York council and governor dismissed the Wappinger appeal as "vexatious and unjust." Defeated in courtroom, council, and battlefield, the Wappingers and their settler allies either had to pay rent to the landlords or move away.[44]

Although victorious, colonial leaders resented that the imperial government had tried to help the Wappingers. With other eastern natives pressing similar appeals to London, colonial gentlemen worried that the Crown would show greater resolve in the future. Indeed, some imperialists claimed that natives were sovereign allies of the Crown rather than dependent subjects of particular colonies. If eastern Indians obtained Crown protection for their enclaves, the colonial elite would lose the coveted power to control their dispossession. At the Wappinger hearing, a lawyer for the landlords insisted that challenging their title threatened to "open a Door to the greatest Mischiefs, inasmuch as a great part of the Lands in this Province . . . lie under much the Same Scituation." Colonial leaders regarded the imperial intervention to protect eastern Indians, and Parliament's new taxes, as related threats to private property and local rule in America.[45]

Regulators

In the North Carolina backcountry, settlers faced similar demands for payments from speculators who claimed millions of acres. If settlers balked, they faced expensive lawsuits, which they almost always lost because the county sheriffs and justices were appointed by a royal governor in cahoots with the speculators. The county cliques also enriched themselves by levying heavy fees and regressive poll taxes on the farmers. Lacking cash, settlers lost livestock and farms to foreclosure if they failed to pay their fees and taxes.[46]

Settlers found an inspirational spokesman in Herman Husband. Although born into a wealthy, slaveholding family in Maryland, Husband had been transformed by his religious conversion during the Great Awakening. Rejecting slavery and privilege, he moved with his family to North Carolina in search of "a new government of liberty." Instead, he found land speculators with shaky titles and corrupt county officials who fleeced the farmers. Husband lamented "the unequal chances the poor and the weak have in contentions with the rich and powerful." To justify armed resistance, he invoked the higher authority of God, who favored justice for the humble over further enrichment of the powerful.[47] *american way*

Taking up clubs and firearms, backcountry regulators drove away sheriffs who tried to satisfy court orders by dispossessing farmers. When sheriffs arrested Husband, 700 armed men assembled to liberate him in May 1768. In September 1770, regulators disrupted the Hillsborough Court, driving away Judge Richard Henderson and beating up three lawyers. The rioters also broke into the village stores, smashing windows and taking goods. Then they destroyed the buildings and furniture of Colonel Edmund Fanning, the county's leading lawyer and sheriff. Two months later, arsonists torched Henderson's property.[48]

In response, Governor Tryon rallied the militia in eastern North Carolina and marched west to suppress the regulators. At Alamance on May 16, 1771, Tryon led 1,100 militiamen into battle against 2,500 regulators, who were poorly armed and lacked artillery to counter Tryon's two cannon. After two hours of fighting, the regulators broke and fled. Tryon hanged one captive and had many more whipped. The victors also looted and burned the homes of regulators, including that of Herman Husband. A month later, the authorities hanged six more regulators, including Husband's brother-in-law James Pugh. Condemned to hang, Pugh loudly denounced official corruption until silenced by the noose when Fanning kicked out the barrel that Pugh stood on. Husband fled north to Pennsylvania, where he adopted the fitting alias of "Tuscape Death."[49]

Later in 1771, the imperial government promoted Tryon to govern New York, where he found an even more formidable regulation in that colony's northeastern counties, the future Vermont. During the early 1760s, the greedy governor of New Hampshire, Benning Wentworth, had reaped fees by granting lands west of the Connecticut River to aspiring land speculators. During the late 1760s, the equally reckless governor of New York, Sir Henry Moore, made even more money by granting the same lands in larger quantities to his friends.[50]

To win the race to settle the region, the New Hampshire grantees sold lands at rock-bottom prices, which allured laborers and tenants eager to own farms. To defend their bargains, the settlers organized town governments and a militia known as the Green Mountain Boys, who burned out and drove away any settlers foolish enough to prefer New York's government and land title. Compared to the vast land claims of leading New Yorkers, the New Hampshire grantees were small-scale speculators, dealing in single townships and selling farms at lower prices. That combination made them plausible populists who could rally regulators against the New York grandees.[51]

Tall, strong, bold, and profane, Ethan Allen led the Green Mountain Boys. Allen denounced the "great state and magnificence" of New York's "junto of land thieves," who sought to exploit hardworking settlers by demanding premium prices for frontier land. He insisted that justice favored possession "sealed and confirmed with the Sweat and Toil of the Farmer." Confronting "Yorkers," Allen declared "that his name was Ethan Allen, Captain of that Mob, and his authority was his arms, pointing to his gun, that he and his companions were a Lawless Mob, their Law being Mob Law." After burning a Yorker's farm, Allen told him: "God Damn your Governour, Laws, King, Council, and Assembly." Try as he might, Tryon could never catch and hang the Green Mountain Boys, as he had done to the North Carolina regulators. Allen would outlast the governor and lead Vermont to independence during the coming revolution.[52]

Lines

Dozens of native nations held the land west of the Appalachians, north of the Gulf of Mexico, south of the Canadian subarctic, and east of the Great Plains. The approximately 150,000 natives greatly outnumbered the settlers and soldiers, who occupied small outposts in the vast West. Natives reserved most of their domains for hunting game and gathering roots, herbs, and berries. Men hunted, fished, and built cabins, while women tended crops of corn, beans, and squash planted near their villages. Lacking courts, jails, bureaucracies, and professional armies, the Indian nations were communities of extended kin. Native nations subdivided into many scattered villages, each with several, competing chiefs who led rival clans. Natives preferred dispersed, weak, and competitive leadership as the best guarantor of their cherished freedom. A Cherokee explained that bullying chiefs would "lose their Authority in the nation, as they hold it on no other foundation than the Love of the People." Britons considered Indians blessed with perfect freedom or cursed with virtual anarchy.[53]

Indians often adopted outsiders, including Africans and Europeans, as kin provided they accepted native ways and identities. After capturing and beating Simon Kenton, Shawnees announced, "You [are] no more a white man but an Indian and a brother." Kenton later recalled, "They say when a man comes among a parcel of people that are harsh to him, and they moderate towards him, he will be more attached to them, and I believe it." Unlike most settlers, who insisted on hard and harsh boundaries between the races, Indians believed that they could convert white captives because natives regarded identities as cultural and fluid rather than biological and fixed.[54]

During the late 1760s and early 1770s, the settler influx threatened the 1,800 Shawnees, 3,500 Delawares, and 600 Mingoes of the upper Ohio Valley. Far from unchanging primitives clinging to some ancient life of subsistence, these Indians drank alcohol, wore manufactured cloth, wielded iron hoes and steel axes, and used guns for hunting and war. Enmeshed in the transatlantic market, they procured manufactured goods in exchange for furs and pelts. Native dwellings resembled the log cabins of their settler rivals. Some even had stone chimneys and glass windows. But Indians clustered their cabins in villages, while settlers usually scattered their homes to claim larger farms as private property. Natives also acquired horses, pigs, cows, and poultry, which roamed about their villages. In addition to their native languages, the valley's Indians spoke a smattering of English and French, often adopted colonial names, and exchanged spiritual ideas with Christian missionaries. While selectively borrowing from the intruding culture, natives clung to their distinctive identities and homelands, for they despised assimilation into colonial society lest they become laboring inferiors. Despite the partial convergence of frontier cultures, most settlers preferred to exaggerate differences to justify dispossessing Indians as supposed savages.[55]

The British lacked the manpower to enforce the Royal Proclamation against the defiant settlers who poured over the Appalachian Mountains into Indian country. In 1773, the *Virginia Gazette* insisted, "Not even a second Chinese wall, unless guarded by a million soldiers, could prevent the settlement of the Lands on the Ohio." In fact, General Gage had only 7,000 soldiers scattered through North America. His troops did burn a few cabins in western Pennsylvania, but the settlers quickly returned and rebuilt. Gage wearily reported that they were "too Numerous, [and] too Lawless and Licentious ever to be restrained." He regarded "driving the Settlers off the Lands, and destroying a parcel of vile Hutts, to be of little use, for they meet with no Punishment and return again in greater Numbers."[56]

Indeed, the British struggled to protect their own troops against settlers who resented the warming relationship between redcoats and Indians. In western Pennsylvania's Cumberland County, armed vigilantes called themselves "Black Boys" because they disguised their faces with soot. In March 1765, Black Boys ambushed redcoats guarding a train of eighty-one packhorses bearing British presents meant for Indians in the Ohio Valley. The attackers scared away teamsters and soldiers, killed four horses, and burned Indian goods worth £25,000. The Black Boys continued to harass British garrisons in central Pennsylvania. In May 1766, Gage reported, "This Spring they surrounded Fort Loudoun for the space of a day and a night, firing some thousands of Shot at it." Regulators rather than revolutionaries, the Black Boys sought to frustrate a particular measure—supplying Indians—rather than to overthrow the government.[57]

Some settlers murdered peaceful Indians who ventured into the settlements. In August 1766, Sir William Johnson counted 20 victims during the preceding six months in Pennsylvania, New Jersey, and New York. In February 1768, Frederick Stump and a servant slaughtered ten Indians, including a woman and her three children, and burned their bodies or stuffed them under the ice of a frozen river. The killers claimed revenge for Indian atrocities committed during the recent war, but often the murders were a grim sport or meant to cover the theft of natives' guns, horses, and furs.[58]

The authorities could arrest few suspects. When they did, frontier mobs broke open a jail to liberate the imprisoned, as they did for Stump and his accomplice, or jurors refused to convict. According to Johnson, settlers insisted that "killing an Indian . . . was the same thing as killing a wild beast!" New Jersey did execute two drifters who had raped and murdered a pair of native women. In a gallows speech to the crowd, one murderer boasted that it was "a meritorious act to kill Heathens whenever they were found." Johnson reported that "this seems to be the opinion of all the common people." In 1768, an Oneida chief, Conoghquieson, embarrassed Johnson by declaring, "You often tell us we don't restrain our people and that you do so with yours, but Brother your words differ more from your Actions than ours do."[59]

Unable to restrain settlers, British officers hoped that Indians would take bloody revenge on intruders and murderers. In 1765, John Stuart assured Creeks, "We will set up Marks and if any white People settle beyond them we shall never enquire how they came to be Killed." In 1768, Gage reported, "At present there is a total Dissolution of Law and Justice on this head, amongst the People of the Western Frontier; and the Indians can get no Satisfaction but in their own way, by retaliating on those who unhappily fall into their hands." By wishing for Indian vengeance, Gage confessed to British impotence on the American frontier.[60]

Imperial officers also could not control the speculators who defied the Proclamation Line to stake illicit claims to vast tracts. The speculators feared that common squatters were taking the best lands while the Proclamation deprived gentlemen of the legal standing to prosecute and evict intruders. In 1767, George Washington directed his land agent "to secure some of the most valuable Lands in the King's part . . . notwithstanding the Proclamation that restrains it at present & prohibits the Settling of them at all, for I can never look upon that Proclamation in any other light (but this I may say between ourselves) than as a temporary expedient to quiet the Minds of the Indians & must fall of course in a few years." His agent dutifully marked and claimed 25,000 acres. Washington urged him "to keep this whole matter a profound Secret" and "leave the rest to time & my own Assiduity to Accomplish." He wanted to avoid the publicity that might call imperial attention to his land grab or invite rival speculators to seek the same, prime lands. Perhaps Washington never told a lie, but he did not always tell the whole truth.[61]

Cessions

With colonial protests blocking new taxes, British leaders felt compelled to cut their frontier expenditures to the bone. In March 1768, they slashed the superintendents' budgets for Indian presents and revoked their authority to regulate traders. Lord Hillsborough ordered British troops to abandon most of the forts in Indian country because, he explained, the empire could not afford "the enormous expence attending Indian affairs upon the former plan." Imperial officials let the colonies assume responsibility for regulating the tricky interactions of traders, speculators, settlers, and natives. Johnson protested that the empire had entrusted the chicken coop to foxes.[62]

The new policy also authorized Johnson and Stuart to negotiate an extension westward of the boundary line established by the Royal Proclamation. Imperial officials hoped to head off trouble by buying the upper Ohio Valley, an area already compromised by the intrusions of speculators and squatters. Unable to stop settlement, the empire could at least purchase some grudging consent from the affected Indian nations. In October 1768 at Hard Labor, South Carolina, Stuart concluded a land cession treaty with southern chiefs, setting a new boundary compatible with his imperial instructions.[63]

Johnson, however, pursued his self-interest instead of his instructions. Hillsborough had ordered both superintendents to purchase no lands farther westward than the Great Kanawha River (which flowed into the Ohio River). Stuart complied, but Johnson pushed the line westward as far as the Tennessee River in October 1768, when he secured a massive land cession in the Treaty of Fort Stanwix. While Haudenosaunee chiefs collected the payment—trade goods worth £10,604—most of the ceded lands belonged to Cherokees, Delawares, Mingoes, and Shawnees, who got nothing. Johnson earmarked vast tracks for his land-speculating friends, including Benjamin and William Franklin, who gave Johnson thousands of acres as a kickback. Johnson acted selfishly and cynically because he resented the imperial government for weakening his authority over westward expansion and the Indian trade.[64]

Outraged by the theft of their lands, the Ohio Valley Indian nations threatened to unite and push settlers back across the Appalachians. The renewed threat of frontier conflict infuriated Hillsborough, who rebuked Johnson for violating his instructions. "Every day discovers more and more the fatal policy of departing from the line prescribed by the Proclamation of 1763," complained Hillsborough, who expected to reap "a general Indian War, the Expence whereof will fall upon this Kingdom."[65]

To avert war, Hillsborough directed Virginia's governor to void all surveys and reject all applications for land in the contested zone. Hillsborough also compelled Johnson to reconvene the Haudenosaunee during the summer of 1770 to renounce the cession west of the Great Kanawha, thereby depriving Virginian speculators of 10 million acres in what is now Kentucky. The frustrated Virginians included Patrick Henry, Thomas Jefferson, and George Washington, who resented the empire's restrictions on their western ambitions. Their anger grew as squatters began to occupy lands denied to speculators. They also feared competition from an immense rival speculation launched in England by Benjamin Franklin.[66]

Vandals

In a bid to reduce the imperial tensions, Franklin worked to reconcile colonial and British elites by uniting them in one big land-speculating company. As the "Grand Ohio Company," the partners sought a royal grant of 20 million acres along the Ohio River as a new colony named Vandalia in honor of the queen, who claimed descent from ancient Germans known as the Vandals. In London, Franklin recruited wealthy aristocrats and bankers with political clout by promising them fabulous profits from selling fertile lands to settlers. The British partners included Thomas and Richard Walpole, the wealthy and powerful nephews of a late prime minister. The American investors included Franklin's son, William, who was the royal governor of New Jersey, Sir William Johnson and his leading deputy, George Croghan, and the wealthy Philadelphia merchants Samuel and Thomas Wharton. Because Benjamin Franklin irritated Hillsborough, Samuel Wharton became the company's front man. A British investor declared that Wharton had drawn into the scheme "better *Connections* . . . than any American I know of ever did." Many investors also had a political agenda: to discredit Hillsborough and oust him as Secretary of State.[67]

The Vandalia scheme appalled Hillsborough as a corrupt threat to his power and a violation of his cherished policy of restricting western expansion. Gage and Stuart also opposed the proposed colony as a dangerous provocation to the Indians. In 1772, Hillsborough persuaded the Board of Trade to reject the scheme, but the speculators appealed to the Privy Council, which accepted their offer of a mere £10,604 for the vast domain. Embarrassed by defeat, Hillsborough resigned and was replaced by the Earl of Dartmouth.[68]

But the empire's leaders were a diverse lot often working at cross purposes, and many remained hostile to Vandalia and the speculators, particularly the devious Franklin. The Crown's Law Officers tied up the proposed colony in a thicket of legal technicalities over boundaries, quit-rents, and a charter. Franklin explained that they considered him "unworthy of the Favours of the Crown." To deceive them into completing the grant, Franklin wrote a phony letter resigning from the company, but he secretly kept his shares.[69]

Frontier turmoil also imperiled Franklin's grand land speculation, for Indians threatened to attack the new colony, and rival colonial speculators also claimed the region. A leading Virginian warned that settlers would resist Vandalia and produce "such convulsions and insurrections as happened in the colony of New York . . . between the great landholders and their tenants." By creating one big land-speculating company, Franklin had sought to reconcile leaders in Britain and America. Instead, his scheme widened the gap between elites on opposite shores of the Atlantic, hastening the empire's rupture.[70]

In 1772, British troops completed their evacuation of twenty-two frontier forts, including Fort Pitt, the gateway to the Ohio Valley. The empire retained only a few posts on the Great Lakes at Michilimackinac, Detroit, and Niagara and at Vincennes on the Wabash River. General Gage declared, "I wish most sincerely that there was neither Settler nor Soldier in any part of the Indian country." Instead, the military withdrawal accelerated settlement. By 1774, 50,000 settlers lived beyond the old Proclamation Line, but Gage washed his British hands of the bloodshed that they would provoke: "Let them feel the Consequences, [for] we shall be out of the Scrape." The military withdrawal increased frontier chaos, which further discredited the empire as impotent.[71]

Imperial officials had expected the colonies to assume responsibility for regulating Indian trade, punishing frontier murders, and ousting squatters on native lands. But colonial assemblies balked at any financial burden. Consequently, the British withdrawal created a power vacuum that attracted a rush of competing settlers and speculators. In 1773, a missionary reported that gangs had formed to "rove through the country in search of land, either to settle on or for speculation." Rival speculators and squatter gangs competed to secure the best locations: fertile valleys blessed with springs. While the poor man had to seek his own spots, the wealthy could employ agents and surveyors. By marking trees, making maps, and perhaps locating a loyal settler or two in crude cabins, a speculator hoped to preempt prime locations from the competition. But overlapping claims soon rendered the Ohio Valley a lawyer's paradise and a farmer's lament.[72]

Defying their royal instructions, colonial governors helped speculators grab western lands. To manage his colony's legislature, a governor "made interest" with leading colonists by granting to them large tracts on the frontier. Virginia's new governor, the Earl of Dunmore, quickly mastered the game. A friend described Dunmore as a "very good natured, Jolly Fellow & loves his Bottle." To frustrate Vandalia, Dunmore claimed the entire Ohio Valley, including western Pennsylvania, for Virginia's land speculators.[73]

In January 1774, Dunmore sent an agent, Dr. John Connolly, to seize Fort Pitt, which British troops had abandoned. Connolly installed a garrison of pro-Virginia militia and renamed the post Fort Dunmore.

Intruding Virginians clashed with Pennsylvania's settlers. By toppling fences and burning cabins, rival gangs tried to drive each other from the contested region. The partisans also arrested and jailed the other side's leaders, but mobs broke open rough-hewn frontier jails to liberate them. A British general worried that the upper Ohio Valley had become "the asylum of the lawless."[74]

AGAIN?

During the spring of 1774, Virginia partisans began attacking native encampments to butcher men, women, and children. The murders provoked Shawnee revenge raids on the hated settlements, which played the settlers into Connolly's hands, as they sought his protection under Virginia's authority. To consolidate that support, Virginia's leaders cynically protected the murderers from prosecution. A Virginia partisan noted that "it would be easier to find 100 men to screen" an Indian killer "from the Law than ten to bring him to Justice." Indeed, leading Virginians welcomed the war as a golden opportunity to drive Shawnees from the Ohio Valley. A speculator explained, "The Oppertun[i]ty we hav[e] So long wished for, is now before us."[75]

To resist Virginia's expansion, Shawnees tried to restore Pontiac's pan-Indian alliance, but Sir William Johnson sowed bribes and distrust among the other native nations. On July 11, 1774, Johnson assembled Haudenosaunee chiefs at his house in the Mohawk Valley to consult about the crisis, but he suffered a fatal heart attack. Colonists and Indians worried that Johnson's death would complete the empire's collapse and intensify anarchy along the frontier.[76]

Without seeking Crown approval, Dunmore invaded Shawnee country with hundreds of volunteers recruited with promises of plunder and land. At Point Pleasant on the Ohio River, an advance force repelled a Shawnee attack on October 10. Then Dunmore arrived to take command, crossing the Ohio River with 2,000 men to menace native villages. To save their homes, the outnumbered Shawnees ceded their lands south of the Ohio River, including Kentucky. Dunmore assured his superiors in Britain that, although the war "undoubtedly was attended with circumstances of Shocking inhumanity," the victory "may be the means of producing happy effects" by impressing "an Idea of the power of the White People upon the minds of the Indians."[77]

By murdering Indians, Virginia partisans had ignited a war that enabled Dunmore and his speculator friends to secure millions of acres of western lands. Common settlers did the fighting, but wealthy speculators scooped up the spoils. By organizing a settler militia to defeat Shawnees, Dunmore pressured the imperial government to accept Virginia's expansive claims, which reached westward to the Mississippi. Dunmore's triumph doomed the proposed Vandalia Colony, for the settlers had become subject to Virginia law and magistrates, so the royal attorney general killed the Vandalia grant.[78]

Although victorious over Shawnees and Vandalia, Virginians faced a new challenge from North Carolina land speculators, who formed the Transylvania Company in August 1774. They were led by Richard Henderson, a backcountry judge notorious for greed. Offended by his treatment of squatters and debtors, regulators had burned his house, barn, and stables in 1770. One former debtor, Daniel Boone, proved more forgiving, entering a partnership with Henderson in 1774. A veteran hunter, Boone knew the best routes over the mountains to the finest lands in Kentucky. Folklore casts Boone as a nature-loving refugee from settled civilization; in fact, he helped land speculators fill the forest with farmers.[79]

With Virginians poised to seize Kentucky, a few Cherokees made the best of their bad situation by selling their claim for a heap of trade goods offered by Henderson in a hasty gathering at Sycamore Shoals in March 1775. Getting something seemed better than the nothing offered by Virginia, which claimed the contested region by conquest. By offering just £10,000 (and ultimately paying much less), Henderson and Boone acquired a shaky Cherokee title to 20 million acres in Kentucky. Most Cherokees and Shawnees disavowed the sale by a few rogue chiefs as illegitimate. A Cherokee chief, Dragging Canoe, warned Henderson that his people would pay dearly in lives because the region was "bloody ground and would be dark and difficult to settle."[80]

To wrest Kentucky away from Virginia and the Indians, Hender-

son initially offered settlers a good deal: 100 acres for just 20 shillings. He followed the Vermont model of selling cut-rate land titles to
attract many supporters willing to defend their bargains. A Virginian
complained, "When they get possession, it may be almost impossible
to remove or reduce them to obedience." During the spring of 1775,
Boone led emigrants through the Cumberland Gap in the mountains
to found settlements along the Kentucky River in the fertile "Blue-
grass Country." Most of the settlers were young men of little property
and less reputation. Henderson described them as "a set of scoundrels
who scarcely believe in God or fear a devil." Anticipating trouble with
the Indians, Boone and Henderson urged them to build a substantial
fort. Instead, they pursued self-interest by scattering to claim large
farms. Henderson despaired of getting the fort built "unless the Indians should do us the favor of . . . regularly scalping a man every week
until it is performed." Henderson had learned Dunmore's lesson: that
war against the natives could compel western settlers to accept the
restraining authority of government. Only fear could trump greed on
the frontier.[81]

By 1775, the British Empire had lost all credibility and influence
in the Ohio Valley. Imperial authority shrank into a few, small forts
scattered along the Great Lakes to the north. When apprised of Henderson's land grab, Stuart lamented that "in our present state of anarchy and confusion there can be no remedy for this Evil." Henderson
had defied British policy, which forbade any purchase of Indian lands
without supervision by a Crown superintendent for Indian affairs:
Johnson or Stuart. Henderson even tried to collect quit-rents, a Crown
prerogative. Although Dunmore was a royal governor, he had gone
rogue to wage war without imperial permission. In December 1774,
Haudenosaunee chiefs urged imperial authorities to restrain the Virginians, "who are white Men, and supposed to be under [your] command." But Indians, settlers, speculators, and even royal governors all
ignored imperial policy to do as they pleased. In November, an Ohio
Valley settler boasted: "When without a king, [one] doeth according
to the freedom of his own will." The king had become irrelevant on

the frontier. In desperation, his ministers decided to extend Quebec's jurisdiction into the troubled West.[82]

Quebec

In 1763, about 70,000 French Canadians reluctantly became British subjects. The top military officers, civil officials, and wholesale merchants left for France, but most of the landlords (*seigneurs*) and common French Canadians (*habitants*) stayed on their lands. To reconcile them to their new empire, the British promised to protect their lives, property, and Catholic faith, but imperial officials faced bitter protests from Anglophone newcomers.[83]

Britons cherished their laws and government as the freest in the world but insisted that only English-speaking Protestants could govern themselves. In the Royal Proclamation, the Crown substituted English for French law and provided Quebec with a royal governor and an appointed council. The proclamation vaguely promised an assembly to entice British immigrants into the colony, but few came, so imperial officials kept postponing that assembly. The Anglophone newcomers were merchants, shopkeepers, artisans, and demobilized soldiers. Clustering in Montreal and Quebec, the newcomers remained a small minority among many Francophone Catholics. Despite their paltry numbers, the Anglophones clamored for an assembly, which they expected to dominate by excluding Francophone Catholics from political rights.[84]

The newcomers irritated Quebec's governor, James Murray, a veteran military officer who spoke fluent French. Fond of hierarchy and order, he preferred Francophones as more deferential subjects, deeming them "the most faithful & useful Set of Men in this American Empire." He derided the colony's Anglophones as "disbanded soldiers of little Property and mean capacity" or "Licentious Fanaticks Trading here," who sought "to Lord it over the Vanquished." Bending his instructions, Murray permitted Catholics to serve on juries and as lawyers. If the imperial government overruled his concessions, he asked for permission to return home "as I cannot be [a] witness to the Misery of a people I love and admire." Rather than force French Canadians into a British mold, Murray favored adapting the empire to their culture.[85]

Appalled by Murray's compromises, the newcomers derided the governor as a traitor to British traditions: as, in their words, "Vexatious, Oppressive, unconstitutional, [and] injurious to civil Liberty and the Protestant Cause." They also resented his vigorous suppression of smuggling and collection of taxes without authorization by an elected assembly in the colony. The critics even accused Murray of encouraging disguised soldiers to break into the house of a critic, Thomas Walker, to beat him and slice off an ear.[86]

In 1766 the imperial government recalled Murray but retained his legal concessions to the French Canadians. Viscount Barrington explained, "The two great points in respect to Canada was to make the Colony affectionate to us and to make the people happy." The new governor was another military paternalist, Sir Guy Carleton, who agreed that Francophone Catholics could neither be converted to Protestantism and British culture nor replaced with British immigrants. Because of the "severe Climate" Carlton believed that "this Country must, to the end of Time, be peopled by the Canadian Race." Unwilling to impose an assembly that would exclude Francophone Catholics, Carleton concluded, "The Province is in no degree ripe for that Form of Government which generally prevails throughout Your Majesty's other Colonies upon the Continent."[87]

To bolster Canadian "zeal for the king's government," Carleton favored restoring French civil law and supporting the Catholic Church. In June 1774, Parliament endorsed Carleton's proposals by passing the Quebec Act, which broke with the British constitutional tradition that had excluded Catholics from government. Unlike the Irish, Canadian Catholics could own land and serve on the governing council. The Catholic Church also retained control over its parishes with the power to collect tithes. Troubled by defiance in other colonies, Parliament sought to secure Canada by mollifying French Canadians.[88]

The Quebec Act also enlarged Quebec by shifting its bounds south to the Ohio River and west to the Mississippi. The British hoped that Quebec's authoritarian government might succeed where the more restive colonies of the seaboard had failed: at restraining the invasion of colonial settlers and speculators into Indian country. Murderous settlers would be tried in Canada by stern British judges without any indulgent frontier jurors. The Quebec government also would favor Montreal-based fur merchants, who wanted to preserve native hunting grounds by keeping settlers out of the Ohio Valley. The act's primary author, Alexander Wedderburn, assured Parliament that the act sent a clear message to American settlers: "This is the border, beyond which, for the advantage of the whole empire, you shall not extend yourselves."[89]

But colonial gentlemen resented any restriction for the greater good of an empire based in distant London. The *New York Journal* claimed that the West should belong to colonial Protestants: "The finger of God points out a mighty empire to your sons: the Savages of the wilderness were never expelled to make room in this, the best part of the Continent, for idolators and slaves." By slaves, the writer meant French Canadians supposedly enslaved to Catholic superstition and idolatry, for many colonial speculators aspired to fill the West with their own enslaved Africans.[90]

British colonists to the south interpreted the act as meant to constrain and intimidate them. Massachusetts colonists regarded French Catholics as "fit instruments in the hands of power, to reduce the ancient free Protestant Colonies to the same state of slavery with themselves." The act allegedly debased the proper superiority of Protestant Britons by favoring French Catholics. A Bostonian insisted that "a superstitious, bigoted Canadian Papist, though ever so profligate, is now esteemed a better subject to our Gracious Sovereign George the Third, than a liberal, enlightened New England Dissenter, though ever so virtuous." Having long celebrated their king as the Protestant champion against Catholicism and absolute monarchy, the colonists felt betrayed when George III endorsed the Quebec Act. In 1775 an English visitor heard colonists declare, "*it is a pity the King of England was turned Papist.*"[91]

Patriots dreaded the precedent set by establishing a colonial government without an elected assembly. In July 1774, Virginians denounced the Quebec Act as part of "a premeditated Design and System, formed and pursued by the British Ministry, to introduce an arbitrary Government into his Majesty's American Dominions." In October 1774, Richard Henry Lee of Virginia insisted that the Quebec Act was "the worst grievance" suffered by the colonists. Lee understood that the imperial crisis pivoted on issues of western land as well as eastern taxes.[92]

Patriots also feared a new imperial land policy announced in February 1774. The new policy enhanced imperial power over land-granting at the expense of colonial speculators and royal governors. The Crown required the prior survey and public sale in relatively small lots (100 to 1,000 acres) of frontier land in every colony. The reform promised to help smaller-scale buyers obtain farms while generating revenue for the Crown (rather than simply for the governors as personal income). In addition to selling title to land, the Crown expected thereafter annually to collect quit-rents attached to the premises.[93]

The policy antagonized the most powerful and influential men in the colonies: the speculators who dominated colonial assemblies and councils. In Virginia, Edmund Pendleton denounced "the Ministry for degrading Royaltie into the Pedlar hawking lands for sale." While Pendleton affected to defend royal dignity, Thomas Jefferson sought to undermine it by insisting that the king had "no right to grant lands of himself." The colonial gentry felt aggrieved because the reformed system would block their speculation in vast tracts of land acquired for paltry fees. The land reform threatened efforts by colonial elites to increase their fortunes and extend their power westward into Indian country.[94]

Royal Populism

Imperial officials blamed unregulated expansion and land speculation for provoking expensive Indian wars and clashes between landlords and settlers. Imperialists also distrusted colonial leaders who benefited from speculation and expansion. Lacking aristocratic origins, leading colonists were relative upstarts and strivers apparently driven by greed and ambition to defy any restraints sought by the empire.

Imperial officials dreamed of slowing expansion by compelling more compact settlement under new rules imposed by the empire. During the 1760s, they had tested a reformed land policy in the new Crown colonies of East and West Florida and the Ceded Islands. Imperial leaders also considered protecting Wappingers and other enclave Indians in the older colonies from dispossession by grasping colonists. In addition, the empire tried to limit western expansion beyond the Appalachians. After the Proclamation Line of 1763 collapsed under settler and speculator pressure, imperial officials entrusted much of the West to the more pliant colony of Quebec. In 1774, imperial lords also announced a sweeping reform of land grants in all colonies, restricting large-scale land speculation in favor of public sales of smaller tracts. While encouraging common buyers, the new policy also promised greater revenue for the Crown: a doubly damning prospect for colonial gentlemen who speculated in lands and sought to keep the empire weak within the colonies.

But royal governors often worked at cross-purposes with the Crown on landed issues. Imperial rulers had grown suspicious of leading colonists, but most royal governors coveted their political cooperation. Without their support, a governor would reap opposition instead of a salary and lose his own chance to get rich through speculation. As a consequence, governors favored landlords against settlers. In 1766, Sir Henry Moore sent redcoats to suppress the restive tenants in Dutchess County, New York. Five years later, Governor Tryon led the militia that crushed North Carolina's Regulators. In 1774, Lord Dunmore helped Virginia's speculators preempt the Ohio Valley from squatters by attacking Shawnees. Acting on their own, Moore, Tryon, and Dunmore exceeded their instructions from London.

While royal governors played the old land game in the colonies, imperial rulers sought to impose new rules. In 1773 and 1774, Tryon pressed the British army commanders to send redcoats to suppress resistance in Vermont. This time, generals Gage and Haldimand refused, for they no longer believed that helping land speculators would improve colonial cooperation with the empire. Why, commanders asked, antagonize settlers to assist wealthy men who exploited the taxation issue to make so much trouble for the empire? Perhaps the empire should instead help aggrieved settlers and exploited Indians at the expense of the speculating elite.[95]

In 1772, one new royal governor concluded that his predecessor had taken the wrong side in the colonial land disputes. Replacing Tryon as North Carolina's governor, Josiah Martin initially agreed that the regulators had gotten their just desserts, but a tour of the backcountry changed his mind. Writing to Hillsborough, Martin explained, "My progress through this Country, My Lord, hath opened my eyes exceedingly." He concluded that the farmers had "been provoked by insolence and cruel advantages taken of the people's ignorance by mercenary tricking Attorneys, Clerks and other little Officers." When "the wretched people," turned to regulation, crafty speculators and county officials used "artful misrepresentations" to deploy the government against common folk.[96]

Turning the tables, Martin sought to build popular support for the empire by mollifying backcountry farmers. In effect, he played the populist card against the leading men who had supported Tryon. Martin pardoned regulators, sacked extortionate officials, and demanded restitution from embezzling sheriffs. A delighted regulator concluded that, because Martin had "given us every satisfaction," the county cabals "hate [him] as bad as we hated Tryon." Throughout British America, regulators wishfully believed that a just king favored them against local elites. Martin gave substance to that legend of the protecting king. During the coming revolution, most North Carolina regulators would either support the empire or at least avoid helping the Patriots. On the other hand, North Carolina's leading Patriots had supported Tryon's suppression of the regulation.[97]

Imperial measures seemed to threaten the landed interests and ambitions of leading colonists, but the Crown lacked the means to enforce its reforms. By withdrawing troops from the backcountry while escalating its pretensions to control settlers and speculators, the

British created a credibility gap. Imperial measures combined potential threat with real impotence. That combination rendered the empire irritating yet contemptible to colonists who wanted to profit from westward expansion.

Everything the British touched seemed to generate disorder. While seaport mobs raged against Parliament's taxes, frontier settlers and speculators frustrated imperial policy in the West. Johnson denounced "the riotous Conduct of Persons worse than Savages" for preventing "us from ever again possessing the friendship of the Indians, or from enjoying a peace." Croghan tied western defiance to the seaport riots; given the "repeated Insults" to imperial officials in the east, how could they expect respect from "those unruly Settlers at this distance"? But Croghan helped to discredit imperial authorities by defying them to speculate in thousands of frontier acres. The empire could not even control its own officials.[98]

Colonial leaders decided that they could do better without imperial meddling. Troubled by backcountry turmoil, they wanted to impose their own order, as Virginia's speculators did by waging Dunmore's War. But constructing an alliance of settlers and speculators would prove tricky given their clashing interests. In April 1766, hundreds of regulators marched on New York City, seeking to free their jailed leader, Samuel Monroe. They turned back when blocked by the city's militia commanded by merchants and lawyers who also had led the seaport protests against British taxes. A British officer wryly noted that "Sons of Liberty" were "great opposers to these rioters. They are of opinion that no one is entitled to riot but themselves."[99]

Patriots struggled against the double challenge of British taxes *and* popular discontent. They dreaded losing power over the common colonists to an empire that seized control over revenue *and* access to frontier land. Worse still, a triumphant empire might deploy Indian allies as frontier enforcers. Although the empire was, in fact, losing that control, its robust pretensions sufficed to scare Patriots into uniting to complete the collapse of imperial authority in the West, where farms, fortunes, and futures were made.

3

SLAVES

*For shame, let us either cease to enslave our fellow-men, or
else let us cease to complain of those that would enslave us.*

—REVEREND NATHANIEL NILES, 1774[1]

Eighteenth-century Britons celebrated their mixed constitution
as the surest foundation for liberty in history and on earth.
They also insisted that Parliament was supreme throughout the
empire, trumping every colonial legislature. In 1765, a colonial lobbyist reported that "the power of Parliament was asserted and so universally agreed to, that no petition disputing it will be received." Although
Parliament had regulated colonial commerce through customs duties,
it had never tried to levy direct taxes within the colonies for revenue.
By imposing new taxes on the colonists, imperial reformers asserted
Britain's ultimate sovereignty.[2]

Colonial gentlemen countered that their legislatures were coequal
with, rather than subordinate to, Parliament. In 1770, the Massachusetts assembly declared, "This house has the same inherent rights in
this province, as the house of commons in Great Britain." Cherishing
the king rather than Parliament, colonial leaders imagined the empire
as a federated body of legislatures united only by a shared monarch. A

---

*"Portrait of Phyllis Wheatley," engraving after Scipio Moorhead, 1773. Courtesy of
the Library of Congress (LC-USZ62-56850).*

royal governor noted that colonists claimed to live in "perfect States, not otherwise dependent upon Great Britain than by having the same King." They even petitioned the king to reclaim the power to veto Parliament's laws: a power that had lapsed during the preceding half century.[3]

Appalled Britons accused the colonists of reviving the reactionary doctrine of royal supremacy, which Parliament had defeated in a prolonged struggle during the seventeenth century. Lord Hillsborough warned a colonist, "It is essential to the constitution to preserve the supremacy of Parliament inviolate; and tell your friends in America . . . that it is as much their interest to support the constitution and preserve the supremacy of Parliament as it is ours." Britons insisted that they defended liberty by upholding Parliament's supremacy throughout the empire. They added that the empire could not survive and prosper without a supreme legislature. In 1773, a royal governor warned his assembly that it was playing with constitutional fire: "I know of no Line that can be drawn between the supreme Authority of Parliament and the total independence of the Colonies. It is impossible there should be two independent Legislatures in one and the same State."[4]

To justify resistance, colonists cited political writings by British critics of Parliament. During the 1720s, John Trenchard and Thomas Gordon published eloquent essays, known as *Cato's Letters*, in a London newspaper. Suspicious of all power as selfish and malevolent, Trenchard and Gordon insisted that government officials chronically imperiled liberty: "Power is like fire; it warms, scorches, or destroys according as it is watched, provoked, or increased." By accumulating power, corrupt officials became rich by impoverishing people with heavy taxes. To preserve property and the liberty that it sustained, people needed closely to watch and strictly to limit power. Rather than blame the king, the critics accused his ministers of distorting the will of a benevolent monarch, who sustained the world's freest constitution. Trenchard and Gordon declared, "We have a constitution that abhors absolute power; we have a king that does not desire it; and we are a people that will never suffer it."[5]

Defiantly old-fashioned, the critics distrusted the growing British financial-military complex of the eighteenth century. They despised the rising importance of banks, stock markets, and large trading companies that rewarded financial manipulators with great wealth. Preferring the tangible productivity of farming, critics longed to restore an allegedly simpler time of sterner morality sustained by agriculture. They insisted that farmers made the best citizens because they sustained "virtue," which meant the sacrifice of private interests to benefit the community. Such virtue abounded where people were relatively equal in owning productive farmland (or artisans' shops). The ideal society maximized the number of modest property holders but denied political rights to anyone without independence: women, children, servants, slaves, and wage laborers. Virtue's corrosive opposite was corruption, the use of money and luxury to render people dependent on others.[6]

Trenchard and Gordon and other critics had little clout within Britain, where the empire's growing prosperity and military prowess vindicated the government. Political criticism flourished in the press but swayed only a few backbenchers in Parliament. Most Britons believed that they enjoyed a unique liberty well defended by Parliament in a mixed and balanced constitution that was the envy of the world.[7]

British colonists, however, embraced the critics, often reprinting and quoting *Cato's Letters* and other opposition works. Charges of ministerial corruption resonated with colonists who distrusted royal governors and customs officials as greedy outsiders. Colonial Patriots insisted that they defended the idealized society described by Trenchard and Gordon—a rural society that apparently had decayed in Britain. Less urbanized than the mother country, the mainland colonies had the broad class of the farmers deemed especially capable of virtue and devoted to liberty. Patriots warned that Parliament's taxes would deplete the property that sustained colonists' independence as landowners. Rendered dependent on officials and landlords, the exploited colonists would lose virtue and with it their liberty. This critique of corrupting power helped colonists justify resisting taxes as a moral imperative in defense of liberty. But like the opposition in Britain, the colonists exempted the king from the blame heaped on his ministers and their allegedly corrupt management of Parliament.[8]

After 1763, a constitutional crisis roiled the empire as parliamentary supremacy confronted colonists who insisted on the virtual autonomy of their own legislatures. As both sides dug in on their constitutional positions, they distrusted their foils as reckless conspirators against liberty. Patriots detected a malevolent plot by British leaders to "enslave" the colonists by imposing new taxes and regulations. Boston's town meeting insisted that "a deep-laid and desperate plan of imperial despotism has been laid, and partly executed, for the extinction of all civil liberty." That rhetoric struck Britons as so irrational that it must cover a colonial conspiracy by reckless demagogues out to destroy the empire by seeking American independence. Neither plot existed save in the powerful imaginations of political opponents who distrusted one another. A rare moderate on imperial issues, Benjamin Franklin, lamented, "To be apprehensive of chimerical dangers, to be alarmed at trifles, to suspect plots and deep designs where none exist, to regard as mortal enemies those who are really our nearest and best friends, and to be very abusive, are all symptoms of this distemper."[9]

Taxes

In 1763, George Grenville was the prime minister for a British administration deeply indebted and saddled with the costs of running a bigger empire. In North America, the empire had tripled its territory, which required a standing army of 10,000 men to defend. As the most heavily taxed people in Europe, Britons wondered why the colonists paid so little for imperial protection. A popular English ballad, "America Triumphant; or Old England's Downfall," insisted that the uneven tax burdens of empire impoverished the English and encouraged migration to the colonies:

Who'd stay in musty England,
And work himself to death,
Where choaked with debts and taxes,
No man can fetch his breath
Then to America we'll go,
Where we will merry be;
Since there no taxes need be paid,
As wise men all agree.

Surely, Britons concluded, colonists could afford to pay 2 shillings per person annually to fund the £225,000 needed for garrisons in the colonies. As precedent, Members of Parliament pointed to Ireland, which they taxed to support the redcoats posted there.[10]

To enhance revenue, the British tightened enforcement of the customs laws, so long evaded by colonists. Indeed, during the early 1760s, colonial customs yielded only £200,000 annually: a mere quarter of the empire's administrative costs in British America. In 1763, imperial officials reorganized the colonial customs service, increasing the officers and demanding closer attention to their duties. The Royal Navy added patrols along the North American coast to search merchant ships for smuggled goods. Entitled to a share of what they confiscated, naval officers were highly motivated to seize suspected ships. In 1764, the empire also transferred smuggling cases from colonial courts, where jurors favored the accused, to new vice-admiralty courts, where Crown judges presided without juries.[11]

But even if the empire fully suppressed smuggling and collected all of the customs duties, revenues would fall short of the funds needed for the army in America. In March 1764, Parliament passed the Sugar Act: the first attempt to tax the colonists for revenue. The act barred any importation of rum from outside the empire and raised the duty on sugar imports from 5 shillings to 19 shillings per hundred pounds. The Sugar Act benefited British West Indian planters, who needed the protected market provided by the empire, for they could not compete with the French West Indies, which produced sugar at a lower cost and sold it for a cheaper price. Superior wealth and family connections also gave the West Indian lobby greater clout in London than the main-landers enjoyed. While West Indians cheered the new duties levied on their French competitors, mainland colonists seethed over their higher price for sugar.[12]

In 1764, Parliament also passed the Currency Act, which barred the colonies from issuing paper money as legal tender. Lacking specie (gold and silver coins), many colonies issued paper money as an economic necessity. British merchants, however, despised the stuff as inflation-ary, which undercut the value of debts owed by the colonial importers of British manufactures. By banning paper money, Parliament favored a powerful British interest at the colonists' expense, reducing their means to pay the elevated duties on imported sugar. In combination, the Sugar and Currency acts showed that the mainland colonists lacked the clout in Parliament enjoyed by British merchants and West Indian planters.[13]

Colonists disliked the Sugar and Currency acts but reluctantly complied with them, limiting their protests to a few formal com-plaints by their assemblies. That muted colonial response encouraged Grenville to propose a bolder measure: a stamp tax levied within the colonies on legal documents, newspapers, and even playing cards. Brushing aside protests from colonial lobbyists in London, Grenville ruled out the old alternative of requesting that each colony raise, in its own way, a certain sum to contribute to imperial defense, for he distrusted colonial assemblies.[14]

Grenville also wanted to prove a point: that Parliament could exer-cise its sovereign power to tax the colonists. Members of Parliament agreed, passing the Stamp Act by a five-to-one margin in February 1765. One member noted, "If America looks to Great Britain for pro-tection, she must enable [us] to protect her. If she expects our fleets, she must assist our revenue." Defending Parliament's right to tax the colonists, Edmund Burke concluded, "If Great Britain were stripped of this right, every principle of unity and subordination in the empire was gone for ever." The tax would take effect on November 1.[15]

To minimize pushback from the colonists, Grenville set their stamp tax at a relatively low level: only two-thirds of what Britons paid. He also stipulated that the money would remain in the colonies to fund the military, and he appointed leading colonists to the lucrative positions selling stamps. Surely, he reasoned, colonists would pay the new tax with no more than the grumbling that had met the Sugar Act.[16]

Instead, the stamp tax horrified the colonists, who were suffering from a postwar depression in trade. At war's end, the empire's military expenditures dried up in the mainland colonies as the British removed troops, sailors, and their subsidies. Meanwhile, demobilized soldiers and sailors poured into the seaports, depressing wages paid for labor. Facing ruin for want of customers, merchants sued their many debtor-customers, who stood to lose their shops and farms for want of specie. Hard-pressed colonists bristled at paying another new imperial tax, no matter how small.[17]

Without savings to fall back on, artisans and laborers suffered most from the depression. Poor families also bore the heaviest burdens of the recent war, as their men performed military services in larger numbers and under the most dangerous conditions. More poor men died or suffered dismemberment, and they left more widows and orphans in hungry, shivering poverty. Unprecedented numbers sought relief by entering the grim poorhouses of colonial seaports.[18]

Patriot politicians sought to focus the anger of common people on the stamp tax, British officials, and their colonial supporters. Boston's Patriots targeted Thomas Hutchinson, the Massachusetts-born lieutenant governor who had also become the colony's chief justice in 1760. Adept at patronage politics and nepotism, Hutchinson helped his relatives secure well-paying and powerful posts as judges or executive officials.[19]

Hutchinson and his conservative friends made easy marks for populist outrage. As chief justice, Hutchinson supported blanket search warrants to help customs officers suppress smuggling. Disdaining the town meeting that governed Boston, Hutchinson wanted to substitute an English-style city corporation run by an oligarchy of wealthy merchants. He and his allies also favored the hard-money policy cherished by British merchants but despised by most colonists. Defeated in town and assembly elections, Hutchinson and friends lost their little faith in common voters and looked to imperial leaders for political support. By doing so, they compounded their unpopularity in Boston.[20]

Hutchinson opposed the stamp tax but conceded that Parliament had the sovereign right to pass it. Cautious, hesitant, and temperate, Hutchinson lacked the Patriots' passion for confrontation. He feared that they would blow up an empire, which he cherished as essential to the security and prosperity of the colonies: "The rights of parts and individuals must be given up when the safety of the whole shall depend on it . . . in return for the protection received against foreign enemies." Patriots, however, refused to sacrifice any rights for the benefit of the whole empire.[21]

Hutchinson's greatest foe was Samuel Adams, the son of a Boston brewer. Unlike the wealthy and restrained Hutchinson, Adams possessed only moderate means but a fierce focus on his political goals. In contrast to his dapper and slender rival, Adams was stocky and shabbily dressed. "I glory in being what the world calls a poor Man," Adams wrote. Secretive, patient, and cautious, he cultivated popularity as the basis for power. Instead of putting on airs, Adams carefully learned the names and views of shipwrights and other artisans. A leader in Boston's town meeting, Adams secured appointment as a local tax collector, where he became more popular by neglecting to collect from his neediest supporters. A political rival characterized Adams as "by no means remarkable for brilliant abilities" but "equal to most men in popular intrigue, and the management of a faction. He eats little, drinks little, sleeps little, thinks much, and is most decisive and indefatigable in pursuit of his objects." Adams aptly described his political strategy as to "keep the attention of his fellow citizens awake to their grievances; and not suffer them to be at rest, till the causes of their just complaints are removed."[22]

The Patriot cause also appealed to ambitious young lawyers who felt blocked by Hutchinson's powerful cabal. "Is not this amazing ascendancy of one Family [a] Foundation sufficient on which to erect a Tyranny?" demanded John Adams, the younger cousin of Samuel Adams. A farmer's son, John Adams graduated from Harvard in 1754 with an enormous chip on his round shoulders. Fiercely ambitious and easily insulted, he suspected that men of inherited wealth and prestige mocked and blocked him. "I have a dread of Contempt, a quick sense of Neglect, a strong Desire of Distinction," he confessed to his diary. Hutchinson also infuriated the fiery young lawyer James Otis, who insisted that his father should have become chief justice. Otis vowed to "set the whole province in a flame, though he perished in the attempt."[23]

During the mid-1760s, competing elites divided Boston and other seaports. By winning royal favor, some prestigious families had secured the most lucrative and powerful offices. Gentlemen with less clout posed as Patriots to champion the rights of common people. They sought to channel anger over growing poverty in a depressed economy. Rather than denounce all of the rich as a predatory class, Patriots encouraged laboring people to focus their animus more narrowly on a few gentlemen who seemed especially menacing because of their imperial connections. Those connections became a liability as people blamed their economic woes on Parliament's new taxes.[24]

To mobilize a broad following, Patriots subsidized newspapers and pamphlets and staged political theater in the streets by holding mock funerals around a black coffin representing liberty. These performances attracted large crowds of working people, many of them without the property required to vote. To spread word into the countryside and beyond to other colonies, Patriots organized committees of correspondence, which shared information, provocative essays for the press, strategies for resistance, and talking points. A conservative critic paid a backhanded compliment to the Patriot impresarios of protest: "They were intimately acquainted with the feelings of man and knew all the avenues of the human heart."[25]

Patriots insisted that the stamp tax threatened the liberties cherished by colonists. A writer asserted that the tax would "deprive us of all our invaluable charter rights and privileges, drain us suddenly of our cash, occasion an entire stagnation of trade, discourage every kind of industry, and involve us in the most abject slavery." Colonists bristled because stamp tax evaders could be prosecuted in the vice-admiralty courts, which lacked juries. They felt discriminated against as inferiors, for such courts could not try revenue cases in England. Patriots also opposed funding the British garrisons as potential threats to colonial liberty.[26]

Far from seeking seats in the distant Parliament, colonists simply argued that only their own assemblies could tax them. Pennsylvania's assemblymen asserted that colonists were "entitled to all the Liberties, Rights and Privileges of his Majesty's Subjects in *Great-Britain*," and it was "the inherent Birth-right . . . of every *British* Subject, to be taxed only by his own Consent, or that of his legal Representatives." In Virginia, a fiery young assemblyman, Patrick Henry, declared "that the General Assembly of this Colony have the *only and sole exclusive* Right and Power to lay Taxes and Impositions upon the Inhabitants of this Colony."[27]

Loyal to the king, colonists wanted him to intervene and overrule Parliament. A New Yorker assured George III that "the pretence of your parliament of Great-Britain to tax your American subjects, is an absolute insult upon your Majesty's understanding, and a robbery of your sole right to govern them." In Boston, a mob paraded behind a banner with the slogan "King, Pitt and Liberty." Samuel Adams assured a British friend that colonists were "so sensible . . . of their happiness and safety, in their union with, and dependence upon, the mother country, that they would by no means be inclined to accept of an independency, if offered to them." Instead, they wanted to revert to the good old days of protection and prosperity without paying taxes directly to Parliament.[28]

Sons

To intimidate Hutchinson and other conservatives, Boston's Patriot gentlemen turned to Ebenezer Mackintosh, a twenty-eight-year-old shoemaker and a veteran of colonial wars and Pope's Day rumbles.

Mackintosh brokered a peace between rival North and South End gangs to create a united mob in support of the Patriots. By forcing Hutchinson's brother-in-law, Andrew Oliver, to resign as collector, they meant to prevent anyone from paying the stamp tax in Boston. On the evening of August 14, 1765, three thousand men tore apart Oliver's wharfside office and then marched to his home to trash it. The next day, a shaken Oliver resigned, but Hutchinson remained defiant. On August 26, the mob attacked and destroyed his mansion, while the chief justice and his family fled for their lives.[29]

Similar riots erupted in other colonies. On August 28 in Newport, Rhode Island, a mob plundered the tax collector and sacked the houses of two wealthy men who had urged submission to the Stamp Act. The terrified customs officers fled for safety aboard a British warship in the harbor. On September 2 in Annapolis, Maryland, a mob demolished the warehouse of the stamp distributor, who fled to New York, where another mob captured him and extorted his resignation. In Connecticut on September 18, five hundred armed men captured a tax collector and compelled him to resign and then to lead their cheers for "liberty and property." In one colony after another, tax collectors resigned to save their homes.[30]

Siding with the mob, local militiamen refused to protect tax collectors, and the seaports lacked regular troops for the job. New York did have a garrison of 180 redcoats, which inspired the cranky acting governor, Cadwallader Colden, to land and store stamps in the harborside fort. On November 1, an enraged mob of 2,000 drove the governor into the fort while they burned his effigy, two carriages, and two sleighs before destroying the elegant home of the garrison's commander. Fearing that the mob would storm the fort, Colden surrendered the stamps on November 5.[31]

Without collectors to sell stamps, the ports could not legally function after November 1, when the law took effect. But shutting the ports threatened the jobs of thousands. In Boston, New York, and Philadelphia, Patriots compelled merchants, lawyers, and judges to conduct business without the required stamp on their documents. In Wilming-

ton, North Carolina, a thousand men gathered to seize customs officers, holding them hostage until they allowed ships freely to come and
go without stamps on their documents. Throughout the mainland colonies, ships sailed with cargoes but without the stamped documents
required by law.[32]

Only about half the British colonies—all on the continental
mainland—resisted the Stamp Act. In Bermuda, the Bahamas, Quebec,
Nova Scotia, East and West Florida, Jamaica, and Barbados, colonists
grudgingly accepted the tax as a small price to pay for doing business
within a great empire. Smaller, weaker, and newer provinces were too
dependent on the British military to make trouble over a modest tax.
Indeed, most benefited from military expenditures funded by a tax primarily paid by Atlantic Seaboard colonists. The absence of an assembly in Quebec and East Florida also promoted political calm.[33]

In the West Indies, violent resistance was limited to the islands of
St. Kitts and Nevis, where mobs did burn stamps, effigies of stamp-tax
collectors, and the houses of those who refused to resign. Especially
dependent on imported food and lumber from the mainland colonies,
the colonists of St. Kitts and Nevis felt greater solidarity with the Patriots. But the leaders of the larger islands of Antigua, Barbados, and
Jamaica accepted the tax after much grumbling, for they raised more
of their own food and relied on trade with Britain. The Barbadian and
Jamaican newspapers paid the tax and printed almost nothing against
it. Mainland Patriots denounced the West Indians as too corrupt to
defend liberty.[34]

British leaders had expected little resistance from the diverse mainland colonies with their deep suspicions of one another. But the Stamp
Act touched a raw nerve, their aversion to taxes imposed by Parliament, so the crisis generated unprecedented intercolonial communication and cooperation. In 1765, colonial newspapers reprinted Franklin's
cartoon, depicting a snake cut in pieces, each labeled as a colony, above
the motto "Join or Die." Christopher Gadsden of South Carolina
declared, "There ought to be no New England men, no New Yorker,
&c., known on the Continent, but all of us Americans" sharing "essential and common rights as Englishmen."[35]

As Americans, however, they meant to defend their British heritage of rights within the empire. In October 1765 in New York, delegates from nine mainland colonies met as the "Stamp Act Congress" to coordinate an appeal to Parliament. The twenty-seven delegates were gentlemen experienced in colonial assemblies. They deemed it "unreasonable and inconsistent with the Principles and Spirit of the *British* Constitution, for the People of *Great-Britain*, to grant to his Majesty the Property of the Colonists."[36]

In support of the Stamp Act Congress, two hundred merchants gathered at a New York tavern in late October to organize a boycott of British goods. Newspapers spread this news, inspiring similar associations in other seaports. By inflicting economic pain on British manufacturers and their workers, Patriots pressured Parliament to repeal the hated stamp tax. Writing anonymously in the *Boston Gazette*, John Adams hoped that unemployed "weavers should pull down all the houses in old England, and knock the brains out of all the wicked great men there."[37]

Pressure from British manufacturers and merchants did sway Parliament. The colonists also benefited from a change in the imperial government. In July 1765, the king sacked George Grenville as prime minister from a personal dislike for a tiresome bore who failed to show enough respect for the royal family. Lord Rockingham led the new cabinet, which saw no need to defend Grenville's measures, including the Stamp Act. Parliament also balked at the high cost of sending a large army to suppress colonial riots and enforce a tax that would raise little revenue at best.[38]

In March 1766, Parliament repealed the Stamp Act but unanimously passed a Declaratory Act, which asserted the sovereign power of Parliament "to bind the colonies and people of America in all cases whatsoever." The Declaratory Act emulated a 1720 act that rendered Parliament supreme over Ireland. While repealing one tax, Parliament clung to its sovereign right to pass other taxes on the colonies in the future.[39]

Despite the Declaratory Act, colonists exulted in news of the repeal and felt renewed pride in an empire apparently ruled by a benevolent king. Church bells rang and festive colonists gathered for banquets and bonfires to celebrate the passing of a constitutional crisis and the anticipated revival of prosperity. The North Carolina legislature praised the "Justice of Parliament" and conveyed to the king their "gratitude for the paternal goodness which has so graciously relieved them." Britons, however, faced higher excise and land taxes after Parliament failed to tax Americans. In London in March 1767, a colonial lobbyist heard British complaints "that they are to pay infinite taxes and we none; they are to be burdened that we may be eased; and, in a word, that the interests of Britain are to be sacrificed to those of America."[40]

The Stamp Act Crisis taught the colonists how to frustrate British measures by combining protest resolutions by elite writers with violent intimidation by common mobs and economic boycotts by everyone. The three forms of resistance worked together. Boycotts required a common front, which intimidation and ostracism helped to produce. In turn, published arguments by leading Patriots vindicated the boycotters and bully boys as defending colonial liberty against a plot by British tyrants.[41]

By seizing the initiative, rallying popular support, and wielding intimidating power, Patriots discredited conservatives, including Hutchinson and Oliver. John Adams exulted, "So universal has been the Resentment of the People, that every Man who has dared to speak in favour of the Stamps, ... how great soever his Abilities and Virtues had been esteemed before, or whatever his fortune, Connections and Influence had been, has been seen to sink into universal Contempt and Ignominy."[42]

But Boston's leading Patriots did not want to wrest power from Hutchinson only to lose it to Ebenezer Mackintosh, who had attacked wealthy men with an alarming glee. Samuel and John Adams sought to marginalize Parliament's supporters and nullify the stamp tax without unleashing class warfare. Rich Patriots needed reassurance that the resistance did not threaten them. Working behind the scenes in ways that remain obscure, Patriot leaders discredited Mackintosh, who lost his clout with the mob. By 1770 he was languishing in jail for debt, which none of his former, genteel friends would help him pay.[43]

To supplant Mackintosh's leadership, Boston's leading Patriots organized a club known as "the Sons of Liberty." By early 1766, similar groups had appeared as far south as Georgia. The leaders were respectable tradesmen and merchants, but most had achieved wealth rather than inherited it, and they often worked beside common journeymen and apprentices in their shops or on their wharves.[44]

Familiarity with common men helped to mobilize hundreds of laborers and sailors for mass meetings, parades, and protests. Sons of Liberty proudly declared that their meetings drew "all ranks and condition," which was a radical development in a political culture where genteel leaders had long excluded the "rabble" from gatherings by the "respectable." Many more common people took a greater interest in seaport politics. John Adams marveled at the change: "The People, even to the lowest Ranks, have become more attentive to their Liberties, more inquisitive about them, and more determined to defend them, than they were ever before known or had occasion to be." Common households became sites of political mobilization as husbands and wives, parents and children, discussed public issues. Adams concluded, "Was not every Fireside, indeed, a Theatre of Politicks?" The Sons invited broader political participation but also sought to manage it.[45]

Class tensions persisted within the Patriot coalition, however, as laboring folk sometimes clashed with genteel leaders. In 1766 in New York, the Sons of Liberty agreed to accept in private the apology of a respectable merchant, Charles Williams, who had bought some stamps. Angered by genteel favor for an insider, 5,000 common people gathered to humiliate Williams and burn the offending stamps. A witness reported, "The Merchant who had used them was order'd himself to kindle the Fire" while the throng cheered. That evening, the witness added, "tho' the Sons of Liberty exerted themselves to the utmost, they could not prevent the gathering of the Multitude, who went to Mr. Williams's house, broke open the Door and destroyed some of the Furniture, but thro' the Influence of the Sons of Liberty and on his most earnest Entreaty and promise in the most public manner to ask pardon next day," the rioters dispersed. In the morning, Williams humbly apologized from the public gallows before a vast throng. The Sons of Liberty often had to work out similar compromises with common supporters, who had their own ideas about a proper resistance.[46]

Endorsing the authority of local magistrates, courts of law, and assemblies, the Sons did not mean to promote a revolution. We "are not attempting any change of Government," the New York Sons wrote, "only a preservation of the [British] Constitution." They promised to attack no one "farther than as he was a Promoter or Abettor of the *Stamp Act*." They professed loyalty to the king and "a strong Sense of the Superior Excellence of the English Constitution to that of any other Form of Government upon Earth." They acted as regulators of that constitution when allegedly perverted by corrupt ministers, like Grenville, who had betrayed the good king. But their actions tended to discredit the colonial regime as impotent to keep order. The Sons of Liberty increasingly had to fill a vacuum of authority that they helped to create. In Massachusetts, Governor Francis Bernard lamented that he had become a "meer nominal governor" and "a prisoner at large . . . wholly in the Power of the People."[47]

Bernard insisted that imperial leaders had made a strategic mistake by prematurely pushing for taxes without first making essential structural reforms in colonial governments. He asserted that colonial politics lacked proper balance because the elected assemblies had become too powerful at the expense of governors and councils appointed by the Crown. To bolster the councils, Bernard proposed creating a colonial nobility to "give strength and stability to the *American* governments, as effectually as an hereditary *Nobility* does to that of *Great Britain*." He also argued that colonial officials— governor, lieutenant governor, attorney general, solicitor general, and judges of the superior courts—were weakened by dependence on salaries controlled by the assemblies. Bernard wanted the empire's officials to receive fixed salaries derived from revenues raised in the colonies by Parliamentary fiat, as the British had mandated in the newer colonies of Georgia, Nova Scotia, East and West Florida, and the Ceded Islands.[48]

To fund such a "civil list," the new British chancellor of the exchequer, Charles Townshend, urged Parliament to enhance the customs duties paid by colonists. Townshend relied on a distinction between "internal" and "external" taxes made by Franklin in testimony before the House of Commons in 1766. He had attested that, while the colonists rejected the stamp tax as internal, they would accept "external" taxes such as the duties levied by the Sugar Act. A year later, Parliament imposed higher colonial taxes on imported tea, glass, paper, and paints. Although these duties would bring in only £40,000 annually, Townshend hoped that establishing this modest precedent would enable Parliament later to increase the duties.[49]

Unfortunately for Townshend, Franklin had misspoken. Long resident in London and out of touch with his colonial constituents, he did not realize how emboldened they had become by success in defying the Stamp Act. A new consensus denied that colonists should pay any tax, external as well as internal, if levied by Parliament. They also had grown too suspicious of British motives to support any tax to augment the financial independence of Crown officials from elected assemblies. In *Letters from a Farmer in Pennsylvania*, John Dickinson, a wealthy lawyer, denounced the Townshend Duties as just as unconstitutional as the hated stamp tax. In early 1768, Sons of Liberty organized a new boycott of imports until Parliament rescinded the enhanced duties.[50]

The boycott challenged colonists' love for consumer goods and merchants' pursuit of profits. George Mason, a Virginia planter, urged George Washington to sacrifice for the Patriot cause: "Our All is at Stake, & the little Conveniencys & Comforts of Life, when set in Competition with our Liberty, ought to be rejected not with Reluctance but with Pleasure." But sacrifice was easier said than done in a competitive society, where people measured status by their ability to wear the latest fashions from London. Washington noted that many a gentleman feared that "an alteration in the System of my living, will create suspicions of a decay in my fortune, & such a thought the world must not harbour." Merchants also fretted that competitors might covertly import and sell the proscribed goods.[51]

The Sons of Liberty sought to shame, isolate, and ruin as "enemies to their country" anyone who violated the boycott. Mass meetings adopted solemn resolutions and pressured all residents to pledge support for the boycott. Common people became enforcers of restraint imposed often on wealthier merchants who had previously enjoyed deference from the public. As a means to other ends, the Sons of Liberty promoted a more participatory political culture.[52]

Newspapers and broadsides posted on tavern and courthouse doors listed the names of those who refused to sign a nonimportation agreement or who violated it. To avoid shame, ostracism, and economic ruin, a suspect had to appear in public, often at the gallows, to confess, apologize, and promise to reform. The adamant risked punishment by "tarring and feathering," where the victim was seized, stripped, drenched in hot tar, and sprinkled with feathers. In addition to the pain, a victim suffered humiliation as he was carted through town while his neighbors hooted and hollered. Rioters carted some victims to the edge of town and dumped them, with a warning never to return. Others had their houses smeared with excrement, popularly known as "Hillsborough paint" in mock tribute to the despised Secretary of State.[53]

British officials marveled at the power of extra-legal committees and mobs to compel colonists to forsake their beloved consumer goods. General Thomas Gage considered it "a matter of Astonishment, to hear that British Manufactures were prohibited in British Provinces, by an illegal Combination of people . . . without the least Show of Opposition." He could not believe that common people got away with punishing reputable merchants for engaging in legal trade. Gage regarded the Sons of Liberty as hypocrites who deprived thousands of their British rights to buy and sell and speak their minds.[54]

In the name of liberty, Patriots suppressed free speech, broke into private mail, and terrorized their critics. In Boston in October 1769, a defiant conservative printer, John Mein, revealed that some Sons of Liberty, including John Hancock, covertly imported goods while exploiting the boycott to drive smaller competitors out of business. Mein's revelations threatened to discredit the boycott, so a mob of a thousand men chased him through the streets, yelling, "Kill him; kill him." Mein escaped and sailed away for England. In his absence, Hancock bought up debts owed by Mein and used them to seize control of, and shut down, his offending newspaper. Patriots believed only in the liberty of their press.[55]

In June 1768, a British warship sailed into Boston Harbor to help customs officers seize a sloop for smuggling. Unfortunately, the sloop was named the *Liberty* and belonged to Hancock, the wealthiest merchant in Boston. As a major employer and creditor, Hancock could rally lots of rowdy support. A large and angry mob roughed up customs officers, smashed the windows and some of the furniture of their homes, and burned one of their boats. They and their families took refuge on a British warship or in the harbor's fort, Castle William. When the colony's council rejected Governor Bernard's request to call out the militia, he mourned that "a trained mob" controlled Boston.[56]

In October 1768, the British government sent Gage and two regiments of redcoats to Boston to "protect and support the civil magistrates, and the officers of the Crown, in the execution of their duty." To frustrate that mission, Patriots insulted and harassed the troops. Boys and men pelted patrolling soldiers with snowballs, mud, stones, and spittle or persuaded them to desert. The *Boston Gazette* agitated readers with horrifying reports of abusive troops. One fabricated story insisted that a soldier had raped a woman so brutally that she died beneath the town's Liberty Tree. The harassment and agitation neutralized the troops, for neither Bernard nor Hutchinson, his successor as governor, dared to deploy them against civilians. Boston mobs continued to menace redcoats, bully importers of British goods, and tar and feather customs informers.[57]

On the night of March 5, 1770, about fifty men and boys gathered to harass seven soldiers guarding the custom house on Boston's main street by hurling snowballs, chunks of ice, sticks, and rocks while yelling "Kill them." The captain in charge tried to restrain his men, but they feared for their lives. One fired and the rest followed suit, hitting eleven colonists, five of whom died. Flocking to the scene, hundreds of angry colonists threatened to kill the captain and his men, so Hutchinson ordered them away to Castle William.[58]

Patriot propagandists turned the tragedy into "the Boston Massacre." Three-quarters of the town's inhabitants attended the mass funeral of the victims. Newspaper writers described the massacre as the work "of wicked and designing men to bring us into a state of bondage and ruin." In a widely reprinted engraving, Paul Revere, a Boston silversmith, depicted demonic redcoats killing well-dressed and unarmed gentlemen. For Patriots, March 5 became an annual and somber occasion publicly to mourn the victims as martyrs for liberty.[59]

In New York City in January 1770, similar tensions between soldiers and Sons of Liberty also erupted into violence. Fed up with public insults, off-duty soldiers smashed up a tavern on Golden Hill favored by the Sons of Liberty. The troops also pulled down a nearby "liberty pole": a tall post erected as a rallying point for Patriots. When the Sons gathered to counterattack, a massive brawl erupted. Getting the worst of it, soldiers retreated to their fort. While singing "God Save the King," the Sons of Liberty erected a massive new pole: eighty feet tall, cased in protective iron bands, and topped by a weather-vane inscribed with the word "Liberty."[60]

Daughters

Tradition excluded colonial women from even talking about politics, but the boycotts needed their support. Sons of Liberty invited women as well as men to sign the boycott associations. While forsaking imported consumer goods that made their lives easier and more appealing, women also had to spin and weave more homespun cloth to substitute for imports. Thirteen-year-old Anna Green Winslow wrote in her diary, "As I am (as we say) a Daughter of liberty, I chuse to w[e]ar as much of our own manufactory as pocible." Previously denied political significance, their decisions as consumers and producers became essen-

a form of power

tial to the Patriot cause. Christopher Gadsden conceded that without the assistance of "our wives, 'tis impossible to succeed."[61]

Women's participation gave depth to Patriot claims to speak for the entire community. Women joined the street protests, including the ritual shaming of boycott-breakers and Loyalists. A Boston conservative complained that "Ladys of Fashion" threw pillows out their windows to passing mobs to provide the feathers to complete a hot coat of tar. In New England towns, women stiffened the patriotism of their men. A conservative lamented, "A certain epidemical phrenzy runs through our fair country women which outdoes all the pretended patriotic virtue of the more robustic males." He complained that women were "little mischief making devils" who pressured men to act as Patriots or face a ban from parties and balls.[62]

In performances of political theater (as well as religious commitment), dozens of women gathered at a local minister's house in many New England towns to spin thread and weave homespun cloth. These spinning and weaving bees attracted throngs of supporters, and newspapers celebrated women as key actors in the Patriot cause. The publications invited other communities to stage such bees and compete in gathering the largest numbers and producing the most cloth. For the first time, the press praised women for exercising political judgment, and many women felt duty-bound to support a political cause. The *South Carolina Gazette* assured them, "[You] have it in your power more that all your committees and Congresses, to strike the stroke, and make the hills and plains of America clap their hands."[63]

In another new development, women defended their political activity in print. One rejected criticism by conservatives: "What should induce you to think, gentlemen, that those of us who are daily witnesses to the difficulty of . . . providing for a large family, should be incapable of feeling for our country, for our husbands, for our offspring, amidst the impending distress universally apprehended." The sister of one prominent Patriot (James Otis) and wife of another (James Warren), Mercy Otis Warren, insisted that political engagement was compatible with women's traditional roles: "But as every domestic enjoyment depends on the decision of the mighty contest, who can be an unconcerned and silent spectator?"[64]

Patriot women felt pride in their enhanced political awareness. In 1774, Charity Clarke, a young New Yorker, boasted, "These limbs are armed with strength, the Soul is fortified by Virtue, and the Love of Liberty is cherished within this bosom." Annis Boudinot Stockton concluded, "Tho' a female, I was born a patriot and can't help it If I would." Eliza Wilkinson of South Carolina recalled, "None were greater politicians than the several knots of ladies, who met together. All trifling discourse of fashions, and such low chat was thrown by, and we commenced perfect statesmen."[65]

Coercion

Once again, turnover in British politics benefited the colonists. In 1770, a new ministry led by Lord North took office. He preferred to blame the recently deceased Townshend rather than defend policies that had provoked so much trouble in the colonies. Thanks to the boycott, British exports to the colonies dwindled from £2.5 million in 1768 to £1.6 million in 1769. Angered by their losses, British manufacturers denounced the Townshend duties as taxes on British *exports* rather than on colonial *imports*. Balking at the expense of sending more troops to coerce the colonists, in April 1770, Parliament repealed the Townshend Duties, save for a duty on tea meant to maintain Parliament's right to tax colonists. The Sons of Liberty wanted to prolong the boycott of all imports until Parliament withdrew the tea tax, but most colonists preferred to declare victory, so they could resume buying British goods. During the early 1770s, imports from Britain doubled, and political calm returned to the colonies.[66]

The tax on tea yielded scant revenue because most colonists consumed cheaper tea smuggled in from the Dutch East Indies (now Indonesia). To undercut that smuggling and benefit the East India Company, a politically powerful corporation, Parliament in May 1773 *reduced* the tax on tea shipped by that company to the American colonies. Thereafter, the East India Company could undersell smugglers in the colonial market. Seeking a bargain, consumers might accept taxed tea, establishing the precedent coveted by Parliament. Lord North doubted "that the Americans would resist at being able to drink their tea at ninepence in the pound cheaper."[67]

But the Tea Act angered colonial merchants, who stood to lose their profitable business in smuggled tea. They denounced the act as a plot to seduce Americans to sell their liberty for the tea of a British monopoly. This line of attack revived opposition to any tea tax, no matter how small. The *Boston Gazette* ominously warned that importers of taxed tea would "be considered and treated as Wretches unworthy to live, and [will] be made the first Victims of our just Resentment."[68]

Into this firestorm of protest, the East India Company sent seven ships laden with taxed tea bound for four colonial ports: Boston, New York, Philadelphia, and Charles Town. In Philadelphia, a Patriot newspaper denounced the chests of tea as "filled with poverty, oppression, slavery, and every other hated disease." Patriots threatened to turn any colonial collaborators over to "The Committee for Tarring and Feathering," which persuaded most merchants to reject the company's tea. In Boston, however, the consignees were the sons of Thomas Hutchinson, and they would not be intimidated. As governor, Hutchinson also refused to permit the ships to return to Britain without unloading their cargoes. To prevent them from landing the tea in December 1773, fifty Patriots thinly disguised as Indians stormed aboard the three company ships in Boston harbor. Smashing open 340 chests with hatchets, they dumped 90,000 pounds of tea into the dirty water.[69]

The "Boston Tea Party" infuriated Members of Parliament, who concluded that they had compromised too long, reaping an insulting defiance. Reversing Patriot rhetoric, Lord Buckinghamshire argued that the issue had become whether the British "were to be free, or slaves to our colonies." One hotheaded Member asserted: "The town of Boston ought to be knocked about their ears and destroyed" because "you will never meet with that proper obedience to the laws of this country until you have destroyed that nest of locusts." General Gage declared "that the crisis is come, when the provinces must be either British colonies, or independent and separate states."[70]

In the spring, Parliament adopted four "Coercive Acts" by overwhelming margins: the Boston Port Act, Massachusetts Government Act, Impartial Administration of Justice Act, and Quartering Act. The first closed the port of Boston, save for shipments of food and fuel, until the town paid the East India Company in full for the destroyed tea. The second act reformed the charter government of Massachusetts, which Britons considered turbulent because dominated by an assembly. The act made the council dependent for appointment and retention solely on the governor—rather than on governor and assembly as in the past. The act also strictly regulated town meetings and allowed sheriffs to appoint jurors. To protect Crown officials and soldiers from harassing prosecutions, the third act transferred their trials to Britain or another colony. The fourth act enabled a military commander to claim housing for troops posted in a colonial town or city. The Crown appointed Gage to perform double duty as both governor of Massachusetts and commander of British troops in North America. He brought along four regiments to enforce the Coercive Acts in Massachusetts.[71]

By crushing resistance in Boston, British leaders sought to save their empire. If deprived of its American colonies, the empire would, they feared, collapse, exposing Britain to domination by the French and Spanish. In June 1774, Lord Dartmouth assured Gage:

> The constitutional authority of this kingdom over its colonies must be vindicated, and its laws obeyed throughout the whole empire. It is not only its dignity and its reputation but its power, nay its very existence depends upon the present moment; for should those ideas of independence . . . once take root, that relation between the kingdom and its colonies which is the bond of peace and power will soon cease to exist and destruction must follow disunion.

Patriots regarded the British as powerful aggressors imposing their domination, but leading Britons acted from a fear for the security of their vulnerable empire. The competing colonial and British fears became intertwined in an escalating crisis.[72]

Somerset

Colonists worried that submission to Parliament's taxes would impose a dependency that they called "slavery." In May 1764, Boston's assemblymen insisted, "If Taxes are laid upon us in any shape without ever having a Legal Representation where they are laid, are we not reduced from the Character of Free Subjects to the miserable state of Tributary Slaves?" They regarded secure private property as freedom's foundation. Two of their favorite political writers concluded, "Happiness is the Effect of Independency and Independency [is] the effect of Property." If compelled to accept Parliament's taxes, colonists would become, they believed, a subject people without the property rights that defined Britons as uniquely free.[73]

The fear assumed a special salience because so many colonists owned enslaved people of African origins or descent. Washington insisted that the British meant to "make us as tame & abject Slaves as the Blacks we Rule over with such arbitrary Sway." In 1765, John Adams denounced the British and declared: "We won't be their negroes." Living among growing numbers of slaves, masters could see the dreadful consequences of losing freedom. Patriots feared having the tables turned upon them by some combination of external taxation and internal slave revolt.[74]

While colonists faced new parliamentary taxes, real slavery became more conspicuous among them. During the 1760s, the colonists imported 365,000 slaves: more than in any preceding ten-year period. Indeed, between 1760 and 1776 more people arrived in the colonies (including the West Indies) as slaves than as free people. Most of the enslaved lived in the southern, plantation colonies, accounting for 90 percent of the population in the West Indies, 60 percent in South Carolina, and 40 percent in Virginia. But slavery was legal throughout the colonies, including the northern seaports. In Boston in 1761, 1,000 of the city's 15,000 people were enslaved and only 18 black residents were free. In the mainland colonies as a whole, the enslaved comprised a fifth of the population.[75]

Carolinians and West Indians continued to import slaves, but the leaders of Virginia and Maryland worried that they had more than enough for their economy and too many for security from revolt. To discourage slave imports, their legislators levied heavy provincial duties, but the Crown vetoed them at the behest of British slave traders. In a deep irony, the Chesapeake colonists then resented the British for sparing them from their own tax. Claiming the moral high ground, Virginians implausibly blamed the persistence of slavery on the British.[76]

Patriots sought to protect both liberty and property, which they understood as interdependent, but that property included thousands of enslaved people. In 1765 in Charles Town, South Carolina, white protesters denounced the stamp tax while chanting "Liberty!" When watching slaves took up the chant, alarmed whites called out militiamen to patrol the streets and enforce a curfew. In a particularly obtuse performance, Richard Henry Lee, a wealthy Patriot in Virginia, had his slaves parade around a county courthouse, carrying banners which denounced Parliament's taxes as "chains of slavery."[77]

British critics cast Americans as canting hypocrites who preached liberty while practicing slavery. The English writer Samuel Johnson was appalled that colonists likened Parliament's small new taxes to slavery: "How is it that we hear the loudest yelps for liberty among the drivers of negroes?" Ambrose Serle, a British official, declaimed: "Such men are no Enemies to absolute Rule: they only hate it in others, but ardently pursue it for themselves." By keeping and abusing slaves, colonists allegedly disqualified themselves as true Britons and needed restraint by a paternalistic empire.[78]

An enslaved Bostonian, Phillis Wheatley, won celebrity in Britain for her pious poetry. A slave ship had carried her from West Africa to

Boston in 1761, when she was seven years old and half dead with sickness. Purchased by a tailor, Wheatley recovered, learned to read, and published poetry that extolled liberty and evangelical Christianity. Impressed by her talent, an English critic rebuked those who kept her enslaved: "The people of Boston boast themselves chiefly on their principles of liberty. One such act as the purchase of her freedom would, in our opinion, have done more honour than hanging a thousand [liberty] trees with ribbons and emblems." Apparently shamed by the criticism, her master freed Wheatley in 1773: an example of how professions of liberty could invite British charges of hypocrisy that slaves might exploit to seek freedom.[79]

By claiming the language of liberty, northern slaves pressured their masters to free them. Defying efforts to exclude them, blacks joined seaport mobs that attacked officials in the name of liberty. An escaped slave of mixed African and Indian ancestry, Crispus Attucks, died in "the Boston Massacre." Other black people petitioned legislatures to abolish slavery. In 1773 in Boston, slaves declared: "We expect great things from men who have made such a noble stand against the designs of their *fellow men* to enslave them." Although the petitions failed, Patriots no longer could deny that their slaves longed for freedom.[80] no more deniability

The ridicule by Britons and pressure of colonial slaves obliged some Patriots to confront the contradiction between their professions and practices. Patrick Henry agreed that slavery was "as repugnant to humanity as it is inconsistent with the Bible and destructive to liberty." A Philadelphia doctor and Patriot, Benjamin Rush, warned that it was "useless for us to denounce the servitude to which the Parliament of Great Britain wishes to reduce us, while we continue to keep our fellow creatures in slavery just because their color is different from ours."[81]

Most Patriots, however, clung to slavery as essential to their profits and security, for they distrusted free blacks. Despite his antislavery eloquence, Henry did not liberate his slaves, citing "the general inconvenience of living without them." In 1771, the Massachusetts legislature prepared a bill to emancipate the enslaved, but leading Patriots killed it because, James Warren explained, it would "have a bad effect on the union of the colonies." Making common cause with southern colonists trumped acting against literal slavery.[82]

Denied freedom by Patriots, most of the enslaved looked to the British as potential liberators. Black preachers insisted that the king "was about to alter the World and set the Negroes Free," but warned that selfish colonial masters had blocked a royal decree for emancipation. This wishful conviction implied that, if slaves revolted, they would enjoy powerful support from the benevolent king. A Carolinian reported that the enslaved "entertained ideas that the present contest [with Britain] was for obliging us to give them liberty."[83]

The legend of a liberating king reflected news of a recent antislavery ruling by England's highest court in the celebrated case of *Somerset v. Stewart*. A former customs officer in Boston, Charles Stewart, had brought a slave, James Somerset, to England in 1769. When Stewart subsequently tried to send Somerset away to Jamaica, the slave sued for his freedom with the support of an abolitionist attorney who argued that the enslaved became free when brought to England. In 1772, the chief justice, Lord Mansfield, ruled that slavery had no just basis in "natural law" or in English common law, so it required "positive law," a statute passed by Parliament, to legitimate the system in England: "It's so odious, that nothing can be suffered to support it, but positive law." For want of such a statute, Mansfield ruled that Stewart could not force Somerset to leave the mother country for renewed slavery in a colony. Although technically narrow, Mansfield's ruling became broadly interpreted as upholding the legal maxim that any slave became free upon setting foot in England, deemed the great land of liberty.[84]

Widely reported in the American press, Mansfield's *Somerset* ruling caused a sensation in the colonies. Although the ruling did not apply there, colonial masters felt shocked by the suggestion that their property system defied English traditions of liberty. The *Somerset* decision implied that colonial slaveholders were backward people who warranted imperial control. Americans preferred to think of themselves as champions of liberty against British tyranny, so they hated being cast instead as barbaric for keeping slaves. By challenging the constitutional parity claimed by colonists, the *Somerset* ruling seemed to bolster Parliament's claim to hold legislative supremacy over the entire empire. And if Parliament could tax colonists, it could also interfere with slavery in America.[85]

Learning of the ruling, some slaves sought to exploit the new loophole in the slave system. In 1773, a master advertised in the *Virginia Gazette* for the recapture of two runaway slaves, man and wife. The master predicted that they would seek a ship for England, "where they imagine they will be free (a Notion now prevalent among the Negroes greatly to the vexation and prejudice of their Masters)." As the enslaved became more restive, prone to run away and perhaps rebel, masters *retribution* worried about their property and lives if ruled by an empire so apparently indifferent to their interests.[86] *fear for safety*

The *Somerset* ruling coincided with an imperial veto of Virginia's latest attempt to discourage further slave imports. As a result of that combination, Virginians feared being trapped with a growing population of slaves longing for freedom. The empire seemed implicitly to stir up slave discontent while preventing colonies from restricting the threatening growth of their numbers. The traditional history of the American Revolution emphasizes the role of Massachusetts in resisting British taxes, but Virginia proved equally important to the Patriot coalition. And Virginia's leaders interpreted the imperial taxes through the ominous prism of the *Somerset* ruling and the imperial vetoes. To preserve their freedom, colonial masters believed that they had to keep blacks securely enslaved.[87]

(reluctant revolutionaries)

Alarms

In 1774, most colonists still hoped to stay in the empire while compelling Parliament to rescind the Coercive Acts. In September, Washington organized a Patriot volunteer unit whose members vowed "to defend to the utmost of our Power, the legal prerogatives of our Sovereign King George the third, and the just Rights & Privileges of our Country, our Posterity & ourselves upon the Principles of the British Constitution." Patriots wanted to remain Britons in America rather than become Americans freed from Britain.[88]

The empire's leaders promised to lift the Coercive Acts provided Bostonians paid for the destroyed tea and acknowledged Parliament's sovereignty. But Boston's town meeting, Sons of Liberty, and newspapers remained defiant, insisting that submission would sacrifice their liberties forever. To sustain that resistance, Boston's Patriots needed political support from the countryside. Would the farmers of New England stand by the Bostonians or blame them as reckless for destroying the tea?[89]

Rural New Englanders felt pinched by a decaying standard of living, as a growing population tried to cultivate the thin and rocky soil of old farms. Southern New England was thickly settled with many modest farms of 50 to 100 acres and worked by free families rather than enslaved labor. By the 1770s, crop yields were declining from the effects of ploughing and erosion over several generations. The price of land soared and the size of farms shrank as fathers divided homesteads among several sons. Rural vagrancy increased, and lawsuits to collect debts soared. Most farmers remained solvent, but they worried that social and economic trends would threaten conditions for their children.[90]

Farmers feared losing their precious independence as freeholders. Patriots gave those anxieties a focus by warning that the revised Massachusetts government would favor corrupt elites and impose heavy provincial taxes. Groaning under these burdens, common farmers would have to sell their homesteads to parasitical landlords like the aristocrats of England. Boston's Patriots warned, "If the breath of a British house of commons can originate an act for taking away all our money, our lands will go next or be subject to rack rents from haughty and relentless landlords who will ride at ease, while we are trodden in the dirt." Rural Patriots saw their own grim potential future in the British exploitation of Irish peasants, who lacked political rights, suffered from heavy taxes, and paid rising rents to absentee landlords.[91]

In Massachusetts, most country folk agreed that the Coercive Acts threatened their liberties and freeholds. Their town meetings adopted firm resolutions, which filled the columns of Patriot newspaper in the seaports. Rural towns voted contributions to relieve the Boston poor, who were suffering from the port's closure. They also set up committees to erect liberty poles and coordinate enforcement of a renewed boycott of British manufactures. Clergymen preached fiery sermons to justify armed resistance, if necessary, to defy the Coercive Acts. Reverend Jonathan Parsons of Newburyport insisted that "the spirit of Christian benevolence would animate us to fill our streets with blood, rather than suffer others to rob us of our rights."[92]

Rural Patriots rejected the authority of any provincial officials who accepted commissions under the arbitrary new charter mandated by the Massachusetts Government Act. In August and September 1774, thousands of common men gathered at the shire town in each county. Armed with clubs and accompanied by drummers and fifers, they confronted the judges to demand their suspension of legal proceedings under the new charter. Popular anger focused on the thirty-six gentlemen appointed to the new council. Prestigious men of old families, substantial wealth, and elite educations no longer could count on deference from their common neighbors. Gathering outside the mansion of a counsellor, hundreds demanded his immediate, public resignation lest he face "the consequences of refusing the demands of an enraged People." Some mobs forced a humbled counsellor to doff his hat and walk through their ranks in a ceremony that asserted the ultimate sovereignty of the people. Many terrified council members fled from the countryside to take refuge with the redcoats in Boston.[93]

In defense of their old charter, Patriots nullified the Massachusetts Government Act, depriving Gage of any authority beyond the reach of his troops occupying Boston. The country people also stopped paying taxes into the provincial treasury. Refusing commissions issued by Gage as governor, rural militia officers answered to local committees and prepared for armed resistance by stockpiling munitions and drilling their young men as "minutemen," who could rally at a moment's notice. "In truth, the People here have taken the Government into their own hands," a Worcester conservative reported. In Hampshire County, another noted, "Everybody submitted to our Sovereign Lord the Mob."[94]

Gage feared an armed uprising, which he nearly provoked on September 1 by sending 250 troops at dawn to Charlestown and Cambridge to seize gunpowder and cannons from militia arsenals. The British got away with the munitions without killing anyone, but wild rumors spread far and wide that they were massacring civilians while warships bombarded Boston. From as far away as New Hampshire, Rhode Island, and Connecticut, 20,000 militiamen took up arms and rushed to Cambridge. A witness recalled seeing "armed Men rushing forward, some on foot, some on horseback, at every house Women & Children making Cartridges" while "animating their Husbands & Sons to fight for their liberties." He concluded that the women "surpassed the Men for Eagerness & Spirit in the Defense of Liberty by Arms."[95]

Although the redcoats returned to Boston, and the militiamen then went home, the rapid and widespread militia mobilization provided a dress rehearsal for revolution, which thrilled Patriots but depressed conservatives. A government supporter warned, "I really fear, should the General send his troops out of Boston [again], he will lose them. . . . How to resist such an inraged multitude is not for me to say, or even pretend to guess."[96]

In an echo chamber of dread, Patriot defiance alarmed Gage into a reaction that provoked still deeper opposition. Fearing attack from the countryside, Gage fortified the approaches to Boston, which angered Patriots as an escalation. Meeting in Suffolk County on September 9, they adopted radical resolves, declaring the Coercive Acts null and void because imposed by "a wicked administration to enslave America." The Suffolk Resolves justified colonial preparations for war. In October 1774, Patriots organized the Provincial Congress, with delegates from every town, to govern the colony and coordinate local committees. Their resistance was evolving into a revolution. Stunned by the breadth and intensity of Patriot opposition, Gage despaired in reports to his superiors in London, "The Disease was believed to have been confined to the town of Boston. . . . But now it's so universal there is no knowing where to apply a Remedy."[97]

But how would colonists beyond New England react to the armed resistance in Massachusetts? Samuel Adams wondered whether "the people of America" would consider the Coercive Acts "as an attack on the Constitution of an individual Province, in which the rest are not interested, or will they view the model of Government prepared for us as a system for the whole Continent[?]" Given the widespread prejudices against New Englanders as sharp traders, their colonial neighbors might dismiss them as reckless troublemakers who had reaped what they had sowed. Instead, newspapers and public meetings in other colonies applauded resistance in New England and urged colonial unity in defiance of Parliament. Gage warned his superiors that the colonists were "strangely violent in support of Boston."[98]

Association

Patriot gentlemen feared losing control over the popular and increasingly violent resistance. To maintain their authority, leading Patriots held provincial meetings to choose delegates to assemble in Philadelphia in September 1774 as the "First Continental Congress." So assembled, they could coordinate a firm but restrained response to the empire. As an end run around the colonial governments, the Congress was unconstitutional, but the delegates hoped to preserve some imperial tie. Henry Laurens of South Carolina assured a British friend, "Independence is not the view of America, not a Sober Sensible Man wishes for it." But Patriots had hardened their stance against Parliament. In addition to the old insistence that Parliament could not tax colonists, they added that Parliament had no power to legislate for the colonies in any way, not even to regulate trade. Regarding the king as their sole link to the empire, the Patriots would still accept royal governors but would heed no British legislature as superior to any of their own.[99]

The fifty-six delegates to the Congress represented twelve diverse colonies (none came from Georgia) with long traditions of deep distrust. Few knew one another save for those of their own colony. John Adams, reported that they were "Strangers" unfamiliar "with Each others' Language, Ideas, Views, Design. They are therefore jealous, of each other—fearfull, timid, skittish." Endowed with robust egos, most wanted to show off rather than defer in this conclave of talents. Adams confided: "The Deliberations of the Congress are spun out to an immeasurable Length. There is so much Wit, Sense, Learning, Acuteness, Subtlity, Eloquence, &c. among fifty Gentlemen, each of whom has been habituated to lead and guide in his own Province, that an immensity of Time is spent unnecessarily."[100]

When Congress got down to business, New Englanders had firm support from the Virginians, especially the orators Patrick Henry and Richard Henry Lee. Although more taciturn, George Washington carried great weight with his dignified stature and military exploits during the last war. The delegates from the middle colonies were more cautious and led by John Dickinson and Joseph Galloway of Pennsylvania and James Duane and John Jay of New York.[101]

The delegates debated how to compel Parliament to abandon its legislative power over the colonies. Galloway hoped to resolve the crisis with constitutional reform and avoid "all the horrors of a civil war" and the "inevitable ruin of America." He offered a new "Plan of Union" modeled on the Albany Plan proposed by his friend Franklin in 1754. Galloway wanted to institutionalize and perpetuate Congress as an American parliament, with members chosen by colonial legislatures. A president-general appointed by the Crown would head an executive branch and possess a veto power. Both the American and British parliaments would have to approve any legislation affecting all the colonies, while local matters would remain to the jurisdiction of individual colonial legislatures.[102]

Moderates supported Galloway's plan, but most delegates had

"Joseph Galloway," etching by Max Rosenthal.
Courtesy of Library of Congress (LC-USZ62-47131).

become too soured on British rule to consider any constitutional partnership. Henry warned, "We shall liberate our Constituents from a
corrupt House of Commons, but thro[w] them into the Arms of an
American Legislature that may be bribed" by the British. Henry distrusted any powerful legislature beyond the bounds of his own colony.
Most Patriots regarded Congress as an emergency, short-term expedient rather than a true legislature for a united America. For true governance, they wanted only a shared king and their colonial legislatures.
Voting as blocs by colony, the delegates tabled the Galloway Plan by
a vote of six to five (Rhode Island did not vote because its delegates
divided evenly).[103]

But Congress also rejected the most radical proposals to attack and
drive British troops from Boston. Most delegates feared that war would

divide and ruin the colonists. Washington insisted "that it is the ardent wish of the warmest advocates for liberty that peace and tranquility, upon Constitutional grounds, may be restored & the horrors of Civil Discord prevented." Writing to a friend, John Adams explained, "They Shudder at the Prospect of Blood."[104]

Most delegates hoped that economic warfare would again suffice to induce Parliament to back down. Congress recommended a comprehensive trade boycott, known as the "Continental Association." Barring colonial exports as well as British imports, the new boycott demanded far more sacrifice by Americans, who could not prosper if their crops remained locked in colonial warehouses. To soften that blow, and give Parliament time to reconsider, Congress forbade all imports effective December 1, 1774, but postponed the ban on exports until September 10, 1775. Adjourning in late October, the delegates planned to reconvene on May 10, 1775, to assess the British response.[105]

To enforce the Continental Association, Congress urged "every county, city, and town" to elect a committee of inspection. These committees were to publish the names of violators so "that all such foes to the rights of British America may be publicly known, and universally contemned as the enemies of American liberty; and thenceforth we respectively will break off all dealings with him or her." Such ostracism could ruin a person socially and economically. By sponsoring committees answerable to Congress rather than the empire, the Continental Association accelerated the collapse of colonial governments. Begun in New England during the preceding summer and fall, that shift spread to the middle and southern colonies during the winter and spring of 1774–1775. Linked to provincial congresses in each colony and ultimately to Congress, the committees provided new political structures, which initiated a revolution beyond what the delegates had anticipated.[106]

The committees created hundreds of new positions, broadening the opportunities for common men of modest means to exercise public authority. A Patriot explained that a committeeman "acquired a degree of importance, which was new to him; and by this means, whole com-

munities and societies were cemented together." Some committees
grew to more than 100 members as Patriots sought active support from
every corner of a big county. In 1775, at least 7,000 colonists served as
Patriot committeemen. But the democratization had limits, for only
property holders could elect committee members, which excluded the
landless poor as well as women and the enslaved. The committees
proved remarkably effective, for the value of British imports plum-
meted from about £3,000,000 in 1774 to just £220,000 during the first
six months of 1775.[107]

Becoming de facto local governments, the committees took over
collecting taxes and managing the militia. Many committees even
enforced price controls, inspected merchants' books, and shunned violators until they publicly confessed and mended their ways. Under the
traditional social order, men of wealth and prestige had exercised public
authority and commanded deference from their neighbors. That pattern became more complicated under the association, where support
for the Patriots trumped traditional prestige. A gentleman still received
deference if he endorsed the Continental Association, but opponents
reaped disrespect and violence. The new weight given to ideology challenged a traditional culture that had conceived of social and political
hierarchies as interlocked.[108]

Going door-to-door, committeemen urged every man and woman
to sign the association or suffer the consequences. Inviting everyone to
spy on their neighbors, the committees ferreted out, seized, and burned
stashes of tea and conservative books while a crowd gathered at the
county courthouse to hoot at the culprits. After confessing, the suspects had to ignite the condemned items in festive bonfires that rallied
public support for the new committees and intimidated the wavering.[109]

Shaming and shunning usually sufficed in the intimate communities of colonial America, so only the most persistent and vocal conservatives suffered violence. In Connecticut, Dr. Abner Beebe continued
to deride Congress, so a mob seized him. According to a friend, Beebe
was "stripped naked, & hot Pitch was poured upon him, which blis-
tered his Skin. He was then carried to a Hog Sty & rubbed over with

Hog's Dung. They threw the Hog's Dung in his Face, & rammed some of it down his Throat. . . . His House was attacked, his Windows broke."[110]

Acting in the name of liberty, the committees suppressed speech by their critics. The Philadelphia Committee insisted that "no person has the right to the protection of a community or society he wishes to destroy . . . by speeches and writings" which "aid and assist our enemies." Patriots broke open mail to read letters from suspected critics of Congress. A merchant begged his correspondents to censor their words because "the temper of the people is such that misconstructions are put on the most innocent expressions" by "those who call themselves the Assertors of American Freedom."[111]

Conservatives denounced the Continental Association as more tyrannical, intrusive, and dangerous than anything attempted by Parliament. Insisting that liberty could not survive without law and order, conservatives bristled at the assumed power of local committees and their mobs. In Maryland, a conservative asked a friend, "What think you of this land of liberty, where a man's property is at the mercy of anyone that will lead the mob!" Critics feared that the social upheaval would culminate in a violent anarchy destructive to all property and social order. In New York, Reverend Samuel Seabury concluded, "If we must be enslaved, let it be by a KING at least, and not by a parcel of upstart, lawless committee-men. If I must be devoured, let me be devoured by the jaws of a lion and not gnawed to death by rats and vermin." Conservatives preferred to accept Parliament's sovereignty rather than risk a revolution and war led by reckless upstarts against mighty Britain.[112]

HIS EXCEL: G. WASHINGTON ESQ: LL.D. LATE COMMANDER IN CHIEF OF THE ARMIES OF THE U.S. OF AMERICA & PRESIDENT OF THE CONVENTION OF 1787

Painted & Engrav'd by C.W. Peale. 1787.

4

REBELS

*Which is better—to be ruled by one tyrant three thousand
miles away or by three thousand tyrants not a mile away?*

—MATHER BYLES, a Loyalist, 1774[1]

During the spring of 1774, after news of the Coercive Acts reached
Massachusetts, two lawyers and old friends took a break from
a court session for a walk together. Each felt dismayed with the
other over politics, for Jonathan Sewall defended the empire while John
Adams championed the Patriots. Sewall warned Adams to beware:
"Great Britain is determined on her system; her power was irresistible and would certainly be destructive to . . . all those who should
persevere in opposition to her designs." Adams replied that he "knew
Great Britain was determined on her system, and that very determination determined me on mine. . . . I had passed the Rubicon; swim
or sink, live or die, survive or perish with my country—was my unal-
terable determination." Adams spoke with a conviction still rare even
among Patriots, that America was a distinct country that could defy
the empire.[2]

Britons doubted that colonists could sustain their Continental
Association; soon enough, their parochial bickering and competition

---

*"His Excellency George Washington, Esq.," engraving by Charles Willson Peale,
1787. Courtesy of the Library of Congress (LC-DIG-ppmsca-17515).*

131

for profits would rupture their tenuous cooperation. The British also believed that Americans could not resist the empire in a war. Lord North declared, "They can hurt nobody but themselves." Lord Sandwich, the first Lord of the Admiralty, added, "They are raw, undisciplined, cowardly men." Britons also believed that a great but silenced majority in the colonies remained loyal to the empire. Convinced that ill-trained colonial militiamen could never stand up to regular troops, British leaders insisted that resistance would collapse if confronted by a determined show of force.[3]

Imperial leaders took a hard line with the colonists but balked at paying the true cost of that policy. Cooped up in Boston by Patriot control of the countryside, General Gage requested 20,000 troops to impose order in New England. Averse to that expense, the imperial lords advised Gage to make do with his smaller force and send troops into the hinterland to arrest leading Patriots and seize their arsenals. A dutiful general, Gage dispatched Lieutenant Colonel Francis Smith with 700 soldiers to march westward to Concord, where Patriots had stockpiled arms and ammunition.[4]

The troops left before dawn on April 19, 1775, but alert Patriots in Boston dispatched riders to warn their friends in the country. About 70 militiamen tried to block the British advance at Lexington at daybreak. Gunfire erupted on both sides before the outnumbered militiamen broke and fled, leaving behind eight dead or dying. Pressing ahead to Concord, the British burned the town's liberty pole and seized and destroyed some munitions, but Patriots had removed most of their supplies across the Concord River. Militiamen repelled a British attempt to cross the river, so Smith ordered his men to withdraw toward Boston.[5]

To harass that retreat, thousands of militiamen arrived from throughout eastern and central Massachusetts. Firing from houses and behind trees and stone walls, they inflicted heavy casualties on the increasingly outnumbered redcoats. To rescue them, Gage sent out a relief force of 1,400 men under Lord Percy, who escorted the retreating troops back to safety in fortified Boston at dusk. The British had lost at least 73 dead and 174 wounded: about twice the Patriot losses.[6]

Rather than return home, militiamen camped in the hills around Boston, besieging the British garrison. Their decision to stay, and of more to join them, escalated the day's battle into the start of a long war. Led primarily by Dr. Joseph Warren, the Massachusetts Provisional Congress took charge of the new army, while hoping that Congress would adopt it.[7]

On May 26, Gage received reinforcements, including three subordinate generals: William Howe, Henry Clinton, and John Burgoyne. Accomplished veterans of the Seven Years War, the new generals were supposed to stiffen Gage's resolve to crush the rebellion. But Gage still had only 6,000 men to counter the 16,000 rebel militia, who also could draw on even larger reserves of manpower in an emergency.[8]

On the night of June 16–17, 3,200 Patriots occupied and began to fortify two hills, Bunker and Breed's, on the Charlestown peninsula. Overlooking Boston from the north, the new position threatened the British garrison. In response, the British commanders rejected the simplest solution: to exploit their naval superiority to seize the narrow neck of the peninsula to trap the reckless militiamen. Instead, Gage endorsed Burgoyne's and Howe's plan to land 2,500 troops in front of the entrenched militiamen for a direct assault on their new strongholds. Burgoyne explained, "I believe in most states of the world as well as in our own, the respect, and control, and subordination of government . . . depends in a great measure upon the idea that trained troops are invincible against any numbers or any position of undisciplined rabble; and this idea was a little in suspense since the 19th of April." Ignoring the sobering lesson of the bloody retreat from Concord, British commanders sought to score a political point by demonstrating that, even if fortified, no American militiamen could resist British regulars.[9]

Meant to discredit the Patriots, the battle instead embarrassed the British. Intense fire repelled Howe's first two attacks, inflicting heavy casualties. Leading a third charge, Howe belatedly had his men shed their heavy packs. With the Patriots running out of ammunition, their fire faltered, and the British swept over the parapet on Breed's Hill. At last, the regulars could wield their bayonets to slaughter dozens

"Sir William Howe, Knight of the Bath," engraving by R.
Faulder, 1780. Courtesy of the Library of Congress (LC-
USZ62-45247)

of defenders, including Joseph Warren. But most of the militiamen
escaped across the neck to safety. The British had bought two hills
at the appalling cost of 228 dead and 826 wounded, more than two-
fifths of the attacking force and twice the Patriot losses. Gage ruefully
reported, "These People Shew a Spirit and Conduct against us, they
never shewed against the French, and every body had Judged of them

from their former Appearance, and behavior . . . which has led many into great mistakes." Concluding that Gage had made the greatest mistakes, the imperial government replaced him with Howe as commander in North America. At least Howe learned from his error, for thereafter he avoided frontal assaults on fortified Patriots.[10]

Divisions

While Howe hunkered down in Boston, keeping his army inert, Patriots grabbed control in the rest of the mainland colonies. On April 29 in New York City, a lawyer, William Smith, Jr., reported:

> It is impossible fully to describe the agitated State of the Town since last Sunday, when the News first arrived of the Skirmish between Concord and Boston. At all corners People [are] inquisitive for News. . . . Tales of all kinds invented, believed, denied, discredited. . . . Little business done in the day—few Jurors and Witnesses attend the Courts. Armed Parties summon the Town publicly to come and take Arms and learn the Manual exercise . . . and armed Individuals shew themselves at all hours in the street, consternation in the Face of the Principal Inhabitants.

After seizing the city's munitions, Patriots hauled local Loyalists to the liberty pole, where, one victim reported, they were "insulted and beaten in a Cruel manner, if they refused to kneel down and Curse the King and his Government." On May 6, Governor William Franklin of New Jersey reported, "All legal authority and government seems to be drawing to an end here, and that of congresses, conventions and committees establishing in their places." Fearing arrest or even assassination, several royal governors fled to British warships during June and July.[11]

The newly aggressive politics of common men troubled many gentlemen. Gouverneur Morris of New York worried, "The mob begins to think and to reason. . . . I see it with fear and trembling, that if the disputes with Britain continue, we shall be under the domination of

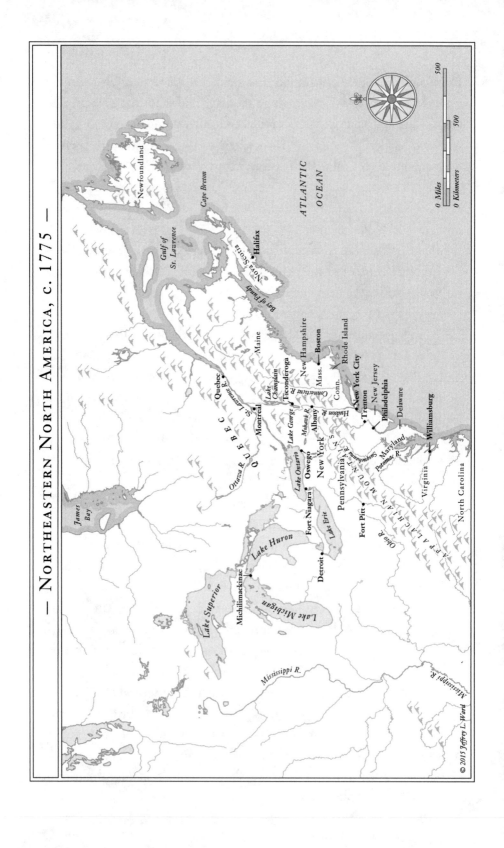

— Northeastern North America, c. 1775 —

Newfoundland

Cape Breton

Gulf of
St. Lawrence

ATLANTIC
OCEAN

Halifax

Nova Scotia

Bay of Fundy

Maine

New Hampshire

Boston

Rhode Island

Mass.

Conn.

Lake Champlain

Ticonderoga

St. Lawrence R.

Quebec

Montreal

Lake George

Connecticut R.

New York City

New Jersey

Trenton

Delaware

Philadelphia

Ottawa R.

QUEBEC

Albany

Mohawk R.

Hudson R.

Oswego

New York

Pennsylvania

Maryland

Williamsburg

Lake Ontario

Fort Niagara

Susquehanna R.

Potomac R.

Virginia

APPALACHIAN MOUNTAINS

James
Bay

Lake Huron

Lake Erie

Detroit

Fort Pitt

Ohio R.

North Carolina

Lake Superior

Michilimackinac

Lake Michigan

Mississippi R.

Mississippi R.

0 Miles   500
0 Kilometers   500

© 2015 Jeffrey L. Ward

a riotous mob." He concluded that the "mobility grow dangerous to the gentry, and how to keep them down is the question." The revolution divided gentlemen, with the most conservative becoming Loyalists who defended British rule as essential to social stability. But Patriot gentlemen felt more confident that they could manage the common people. James Duane advised, "Let [the people] be rather followed than driven." Cadwallader Colden noted that "gentlemen of property" took charge of Patriot committees lest "the most dangerous men among us would take the lead." While Loyalist leaders dreaded the politicized common people, genteel Patriots hoped to control them.[12]

Both Patriots and Loyalists were cross-class coalitions led by rival gentlemen who rallied common supporters. In the northern colonies the wealthy divided, but the richest southerners overwhelmingly became Patriots (or "Whigs"). "There were in no part of America more determined Whigs than the opulent slaveholders in Virginia, the Carolinas, and Georgia," recalled David Ramsay of South Carolina. Where the gentlemen of a county united, for one side or the other, they drew almost all of their neighbors with them. But in many counties, gentlemen divided into rival camps and competed for popular support.[13]

To defeat the British, Patriot gentlemen needed to maximize their popular support, so they promised enhanced respect and opportunities for common men. The Patriot movement created many new leadership roles as committeemen, provincial legislators, and militia officers, which common men often filled.[14]

Attacking the colonial order as artificial and corrupt, Patriots promised an equal and open competition for property and office. Merit rather than connections would reap wealth and leadership. But like the paternalism favored by Loyalists, Patriots described an elusive ideal that they often compromised in practice. Interests and connections persisted in the new order, as in the old empire, but in a more egalitarian guise. Those contradictions disgusted some common people, who preferred the elitism of leading Loyalists as more honest and transparent. Common men could despise those who suddenly waxed powerful as committeemen or grew rich as contractors by so busily embracing the revolt.[15]

Loyalists favored imperial rule because it demanded less of them than did the pushy new committees and mobs of the Patriots. Where Patriotism attracted especially ambitious colonists, Loyalism appealed to traditionalists who cherished stability. A New Yorker explained, "The height of my Ambition was and is to live and die a British subject." Uneasy with political passion, Loyalists denounced the anger and violence of the Patriots as mass insanity. In Massachusetts, a Loyalist declared, "To such a pitch of madness have the people arrived that we are now forbidden not only to speak but to think." Relatively passive, Loyalists proved slow to challenge Patriots, who were more passionate, resolute, and better organized.[16]

Loyalists claimed to defend true American liberty, for they regarded Patriot committees and mobs as greater threats to freedom than the small taxes levied by Parliament. Loyalists also denounced Patriots for rupturing an empire that had long provided protection and prosperity. A New York Loyalists explained, "It is the Cause of Truth against Falsehood, of Loyalty against Rebellion, of legal Government against Usurpation, of Constitutional Freedom against Tyranny—in short— it is the Cause of human happiness, the happiness of Millions against Outrage and Oppression."[17]

Loyalists despised Patriot leaders as cunning and reckless demagogues deluding the people with specious grievances and false hopes. Allegedly driven by greed and a lust for power, Patriots threatened the traditional foundations of social order, initiating a violent collapse into anarchy. Dreading a tyranny of the majority, Loyalists regarded British oversight as essential to preserve law and order in America. Given "how thin the partition is, between excess of liberty and absolute tyranny," a Rhode Islander felt grateful that "in the last resort his liberty and property were subject to the care of Britain."[18]

Elite Loyalists resented the social mobility promoted by Patriots. In 1775, a Loyalist complained of the proliferating "Committees, new raised militia, petty officers, and other persons officially busy, in hopes

of being distinguished." Urging every man to "keep his own rank, and
. . . do his own duty, in his own station," a South Carolinian lamented
that "every silly Clown and illiterate Mechanic will take upon him[self]
to censure the conduct of his Prince or Governor." A satirical Loyalist composed a recipe to make a supposed Patriot: "Take of conspiracy
and the root of pride three handfuls, two of ambition and vain glory.
Pound them in the mortar of faction and discord. Boil it in 3 quarts of
dissembling tears and a little New England rum over the fire of sedition until you find the scum of falsehood to rise to the top."[19]

Loyalists opposed armed resistance to Britain as futile and ruinous. Joseph Galloway warned that the colonists "may as well attempt
to scale the moon, and wrench her from her orbit as withstand the
powers of Britain." Impressed by British might and colonial weakness,
Loyalists worried that America would reap a bloody, destructive retribution. William Franklin warned New Jersey's legislators, "You have
now pointed out to you, Gentlemen, two Roads—one evidently leading to Peace, Happiness, and a Restoration of the Public Tranquility—
the other inevitably conducting you to Anarchy, Misery, and all the
Horrors of a Civil War."[20]

Congress

On May 10, 1775, the Continental Congress reassembled in Philadelphia and sought to take charge of the armed resistance to Britain.
Fifty of the sixty-five delegates had attended the previous, fall session of Congress, providing a continuity that boosted confidence in
their authority. Samuel and John Adams, John Dickinson, George
Washington, Patrick Henry, and Richard Henry Lee all returned.
The newcomers included some especially talented politicians: Benjamin Franklin (recently returned from London), James Wilson, John
Hancock, George Clinton, Robert R. Livingston, and Thomas Jefferson. And there was a notable subtraction, for Galloway stayed away
in disgust.[21]

Divisions among the colonists compounded the difficulties facing

Congress. In addition to the split between Loyalists and Patriots, the latter subdivided into radicals and moderates. Radicals wanted to declare independence and create state republics that would dispense with the king as well as his Parliament. But they dared not quickly sever imperial ties for fear of alienating moderates, who would fight Britain in the short term, while hoping ultimately to reconcile with the empire. If the British troops withdrew and Parliament renounced its colonial taxes and Coercive Acts, moderate Patriots would restore royal governors and accept imperial regulation of overseas trade. Like the Loyalists, moderates respected British power, valued imperial trade, and feared mob violence. Unlike the Loyalists, however, moderate Patriots hoped to tame the popular fervor by guiding it toward reunion.[22]

Dickinson was the leading moderate in Congress. Born to landed wealth and educated as a lawyer in England, Dickinson admired the empire and had much to lose from its rupture. He feared that an independent America would suffer a catastrophic series of civil wars: "A multitude of Commonwealths, Crimes & Calamities, Centuries of mutual Jealousies, Hatreds, Wars of Devastation; till at last the exhausted Provinces shall sink into Slavery under the yoke of some fortunate Conqueror." To mollify the moderates, Congress adopted in July an "Olive Branch Petition" addressed to the king. Written by Dickinson, the petition sought reconciliation in deferential language. Congress faced the contradiction of fighting the empire while praying for reunion.[23]

Radicals neither wanted nor expected reconciliation, but they regarded unity in Congress as essential to rally the public behind the war, so they could not press ahead without the moderates. Adams explained, "America is . . . like a large fleet sailing under convoy. The fleetest sailors must wait for the dullest and slowest."[24]

Local radicals continued to push Congress toward more decisive action. Congressmen had urged colonists outside of New England to stay on the defensive. On May 17, however, congressmen learned that Ethan Allen and the Green Mountain Boys had seized Ticonderoga, a British fort on Lake Champlain in northern New York. Although in a ruinous state, Ticonderoga had a large and precious stock of the cannon and gunpowder that Patriots so desperately needed. The fort also controlled the strategic waterway that led south to Albany or north to Montreal. In Patriot hands, the fort opened the way to invading Canada and barred that route to a British invasion of New York. Unable to resist the great prize, Congress agreed on May 31 to retain and reinforce Ticonderoga. As his reward, Allen collected a colonel's commission from Congress.[25]

Without declaring independence, congressmen began to act as the leaders of a sovereign nation. Lacking precedents, they faced a dizzying array of complex issues. "Such a vast Multitude of Objects, civil, political, commercial and military, press and crowd upon Us so fast, that We know not what to do first," Adams reported. Congress also began with no revenue, no bureaucracy, no national bank, no army, and no navy to challenge the world's most powerful empire. For money, they relied on a printing press, which produced paper dollars that diminished daily in value. The British population of 11 million greatly outnumbered the 2.5 million mainland colonists, and a fifth of the latter were slaves more apt to support the British than help the Patriots. The free colonists were also bitterly divided, for a fifth remained loyal to the empire. Unlike industrializing Britain, the colonies lacked factories to produce uniforms, weapons, and munitions, all of which had to be imported. The Patriots' great advantage was also a liability, for the vast, sprawling, and heavily wooded terrain poorly linked by bad roads would frustrate American logistics as well as British conquest.[26]

In early June, Congress resolved to recruit troops in Pennsylvania, Virginia, and Maryland to reinforce the New Englanders around Boston, transforming a regional force into the Continental Army. By seeking a commander from Virginia, John and Samuel Adams hoped to consolidate southern support for the siege of Boston. As the largest, most populous, and most powerful colony, Virginia was critical to the Patriot coalition.[27]

By wearing his military uniform to Congress, Washington advertised his experience and availability. Tall, strong, and erect, he looked the masculine part of a commander. Reserved and dignified, he was popular with the other delegates, who preferred to hear the sound of their own voices. "He possessed the Gift of Silence," recalled John Adams, who did not. On June 14, Adams nominated Washington as "a Gentleman whose Skill and Experience as an Officer, whose independent fortune, great Talents and excellent universal Character, would . . . unite the cordial Exertions of all the Colonies better than any other Person in the Union." Another delegate endorsed Washington: "He seems discreet and virtuous, no harum-scarum, ranting, swearing fellow, but sober, steady, and calm." Few Congressmen sensed the fierce inner emotions that Washington suppressed by exerting his powerful will. But they did recognize that he was too devoted to civilian authority to seize power as a military dictator. On June 15, Congress unanimously chose Washington to command the Continental Army.[28]

Departing Philadelphia on June 23, Washington rode north with an entourage that included two of his slaves. His arrival at New York City caused a crisis for the city's moderate leaders because the royal governor, William Tryon, was returning from England on the same day. An official delegation arranged for Washington to enter the city in the afternoon, welcomed by a military band, nine companies of militia, and a cheering throng. As soon as they had whisked him through town, the delegation rushed to the docks to welcome Tryon, landing from a British warship in the harbor. "What a farce! What cursed hypocrisy!" remarked a watching Loyalist. In the uncertainties of June 1775, moderates had to prepare for all possibilities as they fought a war that they hoped would lead to reconciliation.[29]

Washington and Congress opted to build a conventional army along European lines, rather than rely entirely on ill-trained militiamen and irregulars like the Green Mountain Boys. "Our armies must be disciplined and learn to fight," Adams declared. That meant fighting in close ranks in open fields, firing synchronized volleys before charging forward to slash with the bayonet. British regulars could stand the punishment while getting off more volleys per minute—usually three or four—than could untrained militiamen. Because rifles were slower to load and quicker to jam, most soldiers, American as well as British, fought as infantry with smoothbore muskets. Only by firing in massed volleys could troops compensate for the relative inaccuracy of their muskets. To achieve group cohesion and a rapid pace of fire required months of drilling, which did not sit well with Americans. With support from Congress, Washington enforced a hierarchy of command based on stark social distinctions between genteel officers and common troops. While fighting for liberty for civilians, Congress enforced inequality on its troops.[30]

On July 2, 1775, two weeks after the Battle of Bunker Hill, Washington rode into Cambridge, Massachusetts, to take command of his new army. He was dismayed by the filthy hodgepodge of crude huts and tents behind some poorly built earthworks. Almost no one had a proper uniform, and gunpowder was in short supply. "I found," he reported, "a mixed multitude of People here, under very little discipline, order or Government." He privately denounced common New Englanders as "an exceeding[ly] dirty and nasty people" with "an unaccountable kind of stupidity." Regarding his undisciplined men as unprepared to face British regulars in open-field battle, Washington doubted that he could train them before their enlistments expired at the end of the year.[31]

Men of local popularity, few New England officers were ready to whip their neighbors for any dereliction in duty. Washington felt disgusted when he spotted some captains shaving their soldiers or repairing their shoes. Washington assured his troops "that an Army without Order, Regularity & Discipline, is no better than a Commission[e]d mob." He faced a great contradiction: in the name of liberty, he had to compel men to forsake their freedom and individuality to become regimented cogs in a military machine.[32]

Washington discharged the worst officers, drilled his soldiers, and had the defiant whipped. A visitor reported, "The strictest government is taking place, and great distinction is made between officers and soldiers. Everyone is made to know his place and keep in it." But the progress was far slower than Washington liked, and his limited stock of cannon and gunpowder ruled out an attack on fortified Boston. Then, in January, he had to rebuild the army with raw recruits because most of his men had gone home as their enlistments expired.[33]

Empire

Although Patriots denied seeking independence, imperial leaders considered them liars out to destroy and replace the British Empire. Gage concluded, "The Stroke is leveled at the British Nation, on whose Ruins they hope to build their so much Vaunted American Empire, and to rise like a Phoenix out of the Ashes of the Mother Country." On August 23, the king issued a Proclamation to denounce the resisting colonists as rebels. George III also refused to receive Dickinson's Olive Branch Petition sent by Congress to seek a cease-fire and reconciliation. Lord North explained, "I am afraid that declaring a cessation of arms at this time would establish that independence which the leaders of the faction in America have always intended."[34]

To coordinate the war effort, in November 1775 the king appointed Lord George Germain as Secretary of State for the colonies. Tall and vigorous, Germain possessed a sharp mind, stirring eloquence, and great administrative skills. He also felt driven to overcome the great disgrace of his life: a court-martial conviction for apparent cowardice as a general during the Seven Years War in Europe. While Lord North managed the government's finances and majority in Parliament, Germain conducted the war effort. By organizing massive fleets and armies, he hoped to crush the rebellion before the French and Spanish could enter the fray.[35]

Britain retained the loyalty of half of their empire in America, for fourteen colonies rejected the rebellion embraced by thirteen. While the Patriot cause prospered in the thickly settled mainland colonies, it withered along the northern and southern margins, where Anglophones were few and needed British military aid. East and West Florida, for example, were sparsely settled, depended on British subsidies, and relied on redcoats for protection against Indians and the Spanish in nearby Louisiana. Both colonies also lacked newspapers and active legislatures (West Florida's assembly did not meet for six years after 1772) to agitate the public. Florida's colonists had little reason to revolt and scant hope of success if they tried.[36]

Far to the north, Nova Scotia was also thinly settled by newcomers. To replace deported Acadians, the British recruited settlers from New England, but the colony still had only 14,000 colonists in 1770. As a long, rocky peninsula with wretched roads and many harbors, Nova Scotia relied on water transportation, so it was poorly positioned to defy the Royal Navy. Indeed, the colonists regarded that navy as an economic asset that sustained the port of Halifax.[37]

Nova Scotia's constitution also favored imperial rather than local rule. In contrast to New England, Nova Scotia's local governance relied on counties run by Crown-appointed magistrates. Nova Scotia's county establishments made far less trouble than did the town meetings of New England. Accepting Parliament's taxes, Nova Scotia's assembly declined to send delegates to the Continental Congress.[38]

Most Nova Scotians sought to stay neutral or profit from the war by supplying the Royal Navy and operating pro-British privateers to prey on Patriot shipping. In 1776, on the colony's western fringe, a few settlers tried to seize Fort Cumberland, a small British post. Failing, they fled and had their homes burned by the victors. When Patriot privateers raided the colony's shores to loot homes and shops, Nova Scotians rallied as loyal militia to defend their property. Under the pressures of war, they broke with their relatives in revolutionary New England.[39]

Most of the loyal colonies were Caribbean islands, including Barbados and Jamaica. Like their mainland counterparts, British West Indians disliked taxation by Parliament, and their assemblies wrangled with royal governors over political supremacy. But the West Indians ultimately depended on Britain for investment, credit, and a protected market. They shipped 90 percent of their sugar to the mother country, where the people consumed more rum and sugar per capita than anyone else on the planet—and had the bad teeth and diseased livers to prove it. Between 1763 and 1777, surging sugar production and rising sugar prices combined to enrich planters as never before. While Patriots were denouncing some small new taxes, West Indians counted their profits as favored members of the empire.[40]

The West Indians also relied on Britain for military security. The powerful Royal Navy protected them against French and Spanish attacks, convoyed their cargoes to Britain, and secured imported shipments of new slaves. The 50,000 white West Indians also counted on redcoats to suppress uprisings by their 275,000 slaves. West Indian legislatures generously appropriated funds to build outposts, barracks, and military hospitals and even to supplement the soldiers' pay. The empire could pressure West Indian assemblies by threatening to *withdraw* troops, while it had to send redcoats to cow the mainland colonists. A Briton concluded that so long as they relied "on Planting by Negroes" the West Indies "can never become independent of these kingdoms."[41]

Secrets

Southern mainland planters also sustained slavery, but they felt more threatened than protected by the British Empire. They also felt more secure in resisting the naval power of the empire because of the vast hinterland of their continental setting. Where whites were less than a tenth of the West Indian population, they accounted for 60 percent of the people in the southern mainland colonies. North American planters could rally thousands of common whites as militiamen to watch slaves and resist British rule. West Indians, however, could neither resist the redcoats (and Royal Navy) nor do without their protection.

In the southern mainland colonies, Patriots fought to preserve slavery for blacks as well as the liberty of whites. Indeed, they regarded slave labor as an essential economic foundation for sustaining the freedom of white men. The enslaved, however, longed for their own liberty, and looked to the British as potential liberators. A Lutheran minister reported that the enslaved "secretly wished that the British army might win, for then all Negro slaves will gain their freedom."

In 1775 in Dorchester County, Maryland, the Patriot committee reported, "The insolence of the Negroes in this county is come to such a height, that we are under a necessity of disarming them. . . . We took about eighty guns, some bayonets, swords, etc. The malicious and imprudent speeches of some among the lower classes of whites have induced them to believe that their freedom depended on the success of the King's troops."[42]

Noting agitation among the enslaved, southerners feared a bloody uprising. James Madison warned of British efforts to foment a slave revolt in Virginia: "To say the truth, that is the only part in which this Colony is vulnerable & if we should be subdued, we shall fall like Achilles by the hand of one that knows that secret." Lord Dunmore knew that secret of the internal enemy. An aggressive, ambitious governor, Dunmore had helped Virginians and himself by dispossessing Indians along the Ohio River in Dunmore's War of 1774. Thereafter, he felt betrayed by ingrates when Virginians supported New England's resistance to the empire. One night in April 1775, Dunmore sent soldiers to remove the public munitions from Williamsburg, Virginia's capital, to a British warship. Without that gunpowder, Virginians feared that they lacked enough firepower to suppress a slave revolt, which rumors insisted was imminent. When local leaders protested, Dunmore threatened to "declare freedom to the slaves and reduce the City of W[illia]msburg to ashes." Patrick Henry led armed volunteers from the countryside to confront the governor, who escaped their wrath by fleeing to a British warship in June.[43]

Dunmore's threat to free and arm the enslaved began as a bluff, meant to spook Virginians into passivity, for he did not wish to ruin the plantation economy of a colony that the British hoped to recover. But the Patriot coup in Williamsburg called that bluff, forcing Dunmore to convert his bluster into black soldiers. He also recognized the military potential of the many runaway slaves who sought haven on his warships during the summer and fall. In November 1775, Dunmore issued a proclamation, offering freedom to black slaves and white servants who would help him suppress the rebellion.[44]

Carefully targeted, the proclamation promised freedom only to young men who could and would bear arms, but Dunmore learned that, to entice black men to become soldiers, he had to provide haven and freedom for their families. By January 1776, about 800 black men, and an equal number of women and children, had flocked to Dunmore, who organized the men in a special unit, known as the "Ethiopian Regiment," commanded by white officers. News of Dunmore's proclamation spread far and wide. In Pennsylvania, a master advertised for the return of a runaway: "As Negroes in general think that Lord Dunmore is contending for their liberty it is not improbable that said Negroe is on his march to join his Lordship's own black regiment." Jefferson complained that Dunmore had "raised our country into [a] perfect phrensy."[45]

Most of the runaways came from the Tidewater counties closest to Dunmore's ships and bases in the lower reaches of Chesapeake Bay. They escaped from riverside farms and plantations in canoes and boats stolen from their masters. The few who ran the longer, overland gauntlet from the hinterland included several from Washington's Mount Vernon. His farm manager warned, "There is not a man of them, but woud leave us, if they believ'd they coud make their Escape. . . . Liberty is sweet." Washington denounced Dunmore as an "Arch Traitor to the Rights of Humanity" and warned that if "that Man is not crushed before Spring, he will become the most formidable Enemy America has—his strength will Increase as a Snow Ball by Rolling." Washington hoped that a bullet soon would kill Dunmore, for then "the World would be happily rid of a Monster."[46]

Rather than recognize that runaways indicted the slave system, Virginians concocted their own wishful legend: that Britons lured away slaves to resell them in the West Indies, where they would suffer far more than in Virginia. If the British were frauds instead of liberators, the enslaved should cling to their masters as protectors rather than flee from them as exploiters. Masters assembled their slaves to warn of their West Indian peril and invite their renewed commitment to servitude in Virginia. According to Robert Carter, his slaves dutifully answered, "We all fully intend to serve you our master and we do now promise to use our whole might & force to execute your Commands." But at least thirty of Carter's slaves promptly ran away.[47]

Dunmore's mistakes as a commander soon undermined his credibility as a liberator. In early December 1775, just a month after issuing his proclamation, he rushed his raw recruits into a premature battle that culminated in their crushing defeat at Great Bridge, south of Norfolk. In a panic, Dunmore fled to his ships, evacuating Norfolk. He burned a few waterfront buildings, but Patriot militiamen torched the rest of the town and then blamed it on Dunmore.[48]

He set up a new base on Gwynn Island, where most of his black refugees succumbed to an epidemic of smallpox, for Dunmore had neglected to inoculate them. A Patriot militiaman found a nearby shore "full of Dead Bodies, chiefly negroes. We are poisoned with the stench." In August 1776, Dunmore abandoned his campaign and sailed to New York, taking away about 500 blacks, but left behind another 1,000 who were dying. Their fate provided fodder for Patriot propaganda that cast the British as duplicitous seducers of foolish slaves. But many blacks survived capture at Gwynn Island only to die gruesomely when vindictive Patriots set fire to their flimsy brush huts, ostensibly to stop the spread of their smallpox.[49]

Imperial officials lost their gamble when they threatened to free and arm slaves in 1775–1776. Meant to intimidate southern planters into submission, the threats instead pushed most to become Patriots. Richard Henry Lee declared that "Lord Dunmore's unparalleled conduct in Virginia has, a few Scotch excepted, united every man in that large Colony." In South Carolina, Edward Rutledge predicted that Dunmore's appeal to blacks would "more effectively . . . work an eternal separation between Great Britain and the Colonies, - than any other expedient, which could possibly be thought of."[50]

On May 3, 1775, a merchant ship arrived in Charles Town, South Carolina carrying the alarming (and premature) report from England that the imperial government planned "to grant freedom to such Slaves as would desert their Masters and join the King's troops." Overhearing the agitated talk of masters, the enslaved concluded the redcoats were coming to free them. A slave assured his fellows that "God would send Deliverance to the Negroes, from the power of their Masters, as He freed the Children of Israel from Egyptian Bondage." Some masters overheard the slaves and hastily concluded that, rather than await the British invasion, they would free themselves in a bloody revolt. Henry Laurens noted that Charles Town's "Inhabitants are as suddenly blown up by apprehensions as Gun powder is by Fire."[51]

In mid-June, the Charles Town magistrates arrested Thomas Jeremiah on charges of preparing a slave revolt to support the British. As a free black fisherman and harbor pilot, Jeremiah had prospered and acquired a few slaves, but that prosperity irritated his white neighbors. Laurens denounced Jeremiah as "puffed up by prosperity, ruined by Luxury and debauchery and grown to an amazing pitch of vanity and ambition." Coming from the wealthy and pompous Laurens, the accusation of vanity and ambition was misplaced, but a white skin covered most sins, including pride, in Charles Town.[52]

Despite brutal treatment in jail, Jeremiah refused to confess, clinging to his innocence. On August 11, a jury convicted and the judges sentenced him to die. Recognizing the trial as a travesty, the royal governor, William Campbell, prepared to pardon Jeremiah, provoking a firestorm of master anger: "They openly and loudly declared [that] if I granted the man a pardon they would hang him at my door." Intimidated, Campbell desisted. On August 18, from the town gallows, Jeremiah warned "his implacable and ungrateful persecutors [that] God's judgment would one day overtake them for shedding his innocent blood." After hanging Jeremiah to the verge of death, the executioner cut him down and tied him to a post atop a heap of firewood so that flames could complete his destruction. Laurens exulted, "Justice is satisfied!" But Campbell mourned the death of a "murdered" man, who "asserted his innocence to the last, [and] behaved with the greatest intrepidity as well as decency."[53]

A month later, Campbell fled from Charles Town to the security of a British warship. During the fall, scores of slaves followed his example by stealing canoes to escape to British warships in the outer harbor or to refugee camps on Sullivan's and Tybee islands. In December 1775 and March 1776, Patriot rangers attacked and burned the refugee camps, butchering or reenslaving the runaways. Colonel Stephen Bull explained to Laurens that they had to put "fugitive & Rebellious Slaves to death" to "deter other Negroes from deserting." The Charles Town City Council agreed that the massacres would "serve to humble our Negroes in general."[54]

Patriots defended freedom for white men while asserting their domination over enslaved blacks. Patriots understood that dominion in defensive terms, as meant to secure their liberty and property from slaves allegedly manipulated by the British. In the South, the enslaved sought a greater revolution, for they meant to "Alter the World" and regarded Britons, rather than Patriots, as the better champions of true liberty. Although the British performance as liberators lagged far behind the wishful hopes of the enslaved, they could find no better ally.

Evacuations

By invading Canada, Congress hoped to secure their northern flank, preventing the British from rallying Indians to raid the colonial frontier—as the French had done in previous wars. Defended by only 700 redcoats led by Sir Guy Carleton, Canada seemed ripe for invasion. To facilitate that conquest, Congress appealed to the Catholic French Canadians for support. The appeal rang hollow because the Protestant Anglophones of the rebelling colonies had for so long insulted and attacked Canadians. After denouncing the Quebec Act in 1774 for coddling Catholics, Congress had little credibility in suddenly befriending them a year later. Meanwhile, the Quebec Act had won the British some credit with the *habitants.* Most French Canadians tried to remain neutral, keeping to their farms while selling provisions to both sides.[55]

Heading north, Patriot invaders descended Lake Champlain and the Richelieu River during the summer and fall of 1775. Commanded by General Richard Montgomery, a dashing and energetic Irish veteran of the British army, the Patriots captured a British garrison at St. John on November 2 and seized Montreal ten days later. Carleton escaped downriver to Quebec, the great fortified citadel and seaport of Canada, where he confronted a second Patriot force.[56]

In September, Washington had sent Benedict Arnold with 1,000 men from the Boston siege army north via the Kennebec and Dead rivers through Maine and across a mountainous watershed to the Chaudière River, which flowed into the St. Lawrence near Quebec. After a long, hard, hungry, cold, and soggy journey through rapids and bogs, the 600 ragged, weary survivors reached Quebec in early November. Montgomery left most of his men behind to garrison St. John and Montreal, but he led 400 troops down the St. Lawrence to join Arnold outside the walls of Quebec in early December, raising the Patriot force to 1,000. Despite their ordeal, Arnold's troops impressed Montgomery, who exclaimed, "I must say he has brought with him many pretty young men."[57]

Although uglier, Carleton's men were more numerous at 1,300 (most of them sailors and Canadian militia), and they had the safety of the heavy, stone walls of Quebec, which the Patriots could not breach for want of heavy artillery. Time was also on Carleton's side, for the enlistment of Arnold's troops would expire on December 31. Desperate to strike before the year ended, Montgomery and Arnold exploited the cover of a blizzard on the night of December 30. Their troops broke into the weakest part of the city, the Lower Town below the heavy fortifications on the heights. But everything quickly went wrong in the dark, swirling with snow. The defenders shot Montgomery dead and severely wounded Arnold in the leg. In the confusion, Patriots suffered 100 casualties, and 426 men surrendered. Carleton arranged an honorable burial for his former friend, Montgomery, lamenting the political "infatuation" of "a genteel man and an agreeable companion." Defections, however, worked both ways in a civil war. To avoid the miseries of captivity, a quarter of the captured Patriots switched sides to enlist with the British.[58]

In the spring of 1776, Congress sent General John Thomas north with thousands of new recruits to bolster the invasion force in Canada. But the siege of Quebec collapsed with the arrival on May 7 of a Royal Navy squadron bearing 7,000 troops commanded by General Burgoyne. As the Patriots fled upstream, hundreds, including Thomas, succumbed to a smallpox epidemic. Losing faith in Congress, the *habitants* stopped selling their produce to hungry Patriots, who resorted to looting farms, which further alienated French Canadians from their supposed liberators.[59]

Continuing their chaotic retreat to Lake Champlain, the Patriots abandoned Montreal and St. John. The new Patriot commander, General John Sullivan, reported, "I found myself at the head of a dispirited Army, filled with horror at the thought of seeing their enemy. . . . Smallpox, famine and disorder had rendered them almost lifeless." Half of his 7,000 men were too sick or wounded for duty. "Lice and Maggots . . . were creeping in Millions over the Victims," one soldier noted. Only Carleton's painfully slow pursuit allowed the Patriots to escape. In early July, the wreckage of the northern army staggered into Ticonderoga. John Adams described the fleeing soldiers as "disgraced, defeated, discontented, diseased, naked, undisciplined, [and] eaten up with vermin." The catastrophe in Canada had cost 5,000 Patriot soldiers, either dead or captured. A British officer mocked the Patriots for offering "a resistance . . . as flimsy & absurd as were their Motives for taking up Arms against their Sovereign."[60]

The Patriots enjoyed greater success in their siege of Boston. In late 1775, Washington had sent his artillery commander, Henry Knox, to retrieve cannon and gunpowder from Ticonderoga. Teamsters and oxen hauled sledges bearing 59 cannon across the frozen countryside of New England, reaching Washington's army in February 1776. On the night of March 4, Washington sent troops with the new cannon to fortify Dorchester Heights, which overlooked Boston from the south. The next morning, the British were stunned to see fortifications, which a British officer marveled, had been "raised with an expedition equal to the Genii belonging to Aladdin's Wonderful Lamp." Unless dislodged, the Patriots could bombard Boston and its British garrison. Daunted by his casualties at Bunker Hill the year before, General Howe declined to risk a frontal assault on a fortified position. Instead, he withdrew 10,000 troops and 1,100 Loyalists from the city, completing the evacuation on March 17. Washington let them sail away peacefully in return for Howe's pledge not to burn Boston. Crowded into dirty transports and forsaking most of their property, Loyalists suffered rather than stay behind to face vindictive Patriots.[61]

Boston's liberation thrilled Patriots throughout the colonies, but Washington knew that Howe would regroup and resupply in Nova Scotia to strike again at more vulnerable Patriot targets to the south: Charles Town and New York. In the southern and middle colonies, British leaders expected to find more Loyalist support than in New England.[62]

In late 1775, the imperial government had prepared an expedition to reclaim the Carolinas with the help of southern Loyalists. Sir Peter Parker commanded the fleet and General Henry Clinton led the redcoats. Winter storms battered and delayed the fleet, depriving the Loyalist uprising and the British arrival of essential coordination. Rising too soon, 1,500 armed Loyalists began their march from the backcountry to the North Carolina coast in February 1776. At Moore's Creek Bridge, seventeen miles from Wilmington, 1,100 Patriots intercepted and crushed the Loyalists. Parker's fleet belatedly arrived in late April, too late to seize Wilmington, so Parker and Clinton sailed south along the coast to attack Charles Town.[63]

On June 28, Parker's warships bombarded Fort Sullivan, the key fortification barring entrance to Charles Town's harbor. The ships suffered heavy damage from Patriot fire, while the British cannon made little impression on the spongy palmetto logs of the fort. Three warships ran aground and one had to be burned. That evening, Parker called off his futile attack. Three weeks later, he sailed away with Clinton's troops to join General Howe's assault on New York. The surprising victory demoralized Loyalists, enabling the Patriots to consolidate their control in the Carolinas.[64]

Common Sense

Despite waging war and taking over colonial governments, Congress
held back from declaring independence through 1775 and into 1776.
Many moderate Patriots as well as Loyalists still revered the mixed
constitution of Britain and cherished the commercial benefits of the
empire. In April 1776, Franklin observed, "The Novelty of the Thing
deters some, the Doubt of Success others, [and] the vain Hope of Reconciliation, many." But he also noted "a rapid Increase of the formerly
small Party who were for an independent Government."[65]

That shift in opinion owed much to an unlikely man, Thomas
Paine. Hard-drinking, self-educated, cranky, and restless, Paine had
accomplished little during the previous thirty-seven years of his check-
ered life. The son of a poor artisan, Paine had lost his job as an excise
tax collector in England in 1774, the same year that his marriage crumbled and creditors auctioned his paltry household goods to pay his
debts. At rock bottom, Paine sought a new start by migrating to the
colonies. Arriving in Philadelphia in November 1774, he embraced
the Patriot cause and became the chief writer and editor of the *Pennsylvania Magazine*. His forceful prose impressed Dr. Benjamin Rush,
a leading Patriot who recruited Paine to publish a political pamphlet
against reconciliation.[66]

On January 10, 1776 in Philadelphia, Paine published *Common
Sense*, which became the most powerful pamphlet in American history.
The first edition of 1,000 copies sold out within two weeks. By June,
reprints raised the total to 150,000 copies: a phenomenal impact for a
public of only 2.5 million people, a fifth of them slaves. Many more colonists read excerpts from *Common Sense* in their local newspapers or
heard it read aloud in taverns and streets. Except for the Bible, no written
work had ever been so widely read and discussed in British America.[67]

Unlike previous political pamphleteers who wrote in a learned and
legalistic style, Paine addressed common people in direct and forceful
prose. Jefferson marveled, "No writer has exceeded Paine in ease and
familiarity of style; in perspicuity of expression; happiness of elucida-

"*Mr. Thomas Paine, Author of the Rights of Man,*" *engraving by George Romney. Courtesy of the Library of Congress (LC-DIG-ppmsca-31802).*

tion, and in simple and unassuming language." Avoiding the arcane works of political philosophers, Paine quoted only the Bible: the primary text known and revered by his intended readers. For Paine, style was also substance, for he sought to constitute a new readership: a broad and engaged public for a republican revolution. He insisted that common people should no longer defer to gentlemen in politics. Aptly titled, *Common Sense* spoke to and for common people.[68]

Paine pushed for immediate independence, a union of thirteen states, and republican governments for those states. All three goals broke dramatically with past experience and received wisdom. No colonies in the Americas had yet revolted from their mother empire; past bickering by the colonies augured poorly for a union; and almost all former republics in Europe had been small, contentious, and short-lived. In a daring stroke, Paine argued that Americans could triumph by *combining* all three gambles: on independence, union, and republic. Seeking one alone would certainly fail, but the *combination* would prove invincible. If united in a righteous cause, he insisted, Americans could crush the corrupt mercenaries of a royal tyrant.[69]

To justify revolution, Paine needed to destroy Americans' reverence for the mixed constitution and reigning king. Blaming Parliament for the taxes, Patriots had long looked to the monarch as a potential ally. To free Americans from that tradition, Paine exposed king and aristocrats as vicious frauds who duped and exploited common people. By dispensing with such parasites, common folk could, at last, live free and prosper. Paine concluded, "Of more worth is one honest man to society, and in the sight of God, than all the Crowned ruffians that ever lived." He denounced George III as "the Royal Brute" with "blood on his soul" for sending troops to kill Americans. By discrediting the monarch, Paine made independence and republican government desirable, indeed inevitable. He relocated sovereignty away from a royal family to the collective people of a new nation.[70]

He elevated the Patriot struggle in utopian and universal terms. By winning republican self-government, Americans could create an ideal society of peace, prosperity, and equal rights. That conspicuous success would, in turn, inspire common people throughout the world to seek freedom either through revolution at home or by migrating to America, "an asylum for mankind." Paine concluded, "The cause of America is in a great measure the cause of all mankind. . . . The birth-day of a new world is at hand."[71]

Americans now take this soaring rhetoric for granted, but it was new and radical for colonists who had long felt self-conscious about their parochial and provincial status. Paine relocated them from the colonial margins of a sophisticated empire to the center of a new and coming world of utopian potential. He invested the Patriot cause with a global purpose that could motivate people to make the sacrifices needed to win a revolutionary war against a mighty empire. "The sun never shined on a cause of greater worth," Paine concluded.[72]

Common Sense outraged Loyalists, who dreaded its allure for common people. Nicholas Cresswell wrote: "A pamphlet called 'Commonsense' makes a great noise. One of the vilest things that ever was published to the world. Full of false representations, lies, calumny and treason whose principles are to subvert all Kingly Governments and erect an Independent Republic." In New York, Charles Inglis, worried that Paine's reckless words would plunge "our once happy land" deeper into a "Ruthless war. . . . Torrents of blood will be spilt, and thousands reduced to beggary and wretchedness." Loyalists retorted in their own pamphlets, principally James Chalmers's *Plain Truth*, which defended the mixed constitution as "the pride and envy of mankind." But Loyalist writers struggled to reach readers because Patriots seized and burned most of the opposition's pamphlets.[73]

Common Sense's fiery tone and popularity alarmed some genteel Patriots, who feared that it threatened deference for them. Elias Boudinot denounced Paine as a "Crack Brain Zealot for Democracy." Gouverneur Morris disdained Paine as "a mere adventurer . . . without fortune, without family or connexions, ignorant even of grammar." Thirty years later, John Adams bristled when a friend referred to the American Revolution as the triumph of an "Age of Reason." Adams replied, "I know not whether any Man in the World has had more influence on its inhabitants or affairs for the last thirty years than Tom Paine. . . . Never before in any Age of the World was [anyone] suffered by the Poltroonery of mankind to run through Such a Career of mischief. Call it then the Age of Paine."[74]

But Paine enabled many more Patriots to overcome their fears of republican independence. In Massachusetts, Joseph Hawley remarked, "Every sentiment has sunk into my well-prepared heart." General Charles Lee asked Washington: "Have you seen the pamphlet *Common Sense*? I never saw such a masterly irresistible performance." Washington endorsed "the sound Doctrine and unanswerable reasoning contained (in the pamphlet) *Common Sense*." His Virginia correspondents reported that "*Common Sense* is working a powerful change there in the minds of many men." In the mainland colonies of 1776, Paine found the ideal conjunction of place, time, and readers for his radical words and ideas.[75]

The push for independence also fed on outrage at recent British coercive measures. In late February, colonists learned that Parliament had passed the Prohibitory Act, which exposed all American merchant ships to seizure as the property "of open enemies." The bill soured moderates, who had longed for reconciliation. John Hancock slyly remarked that "making all our Vessells lawful Prize don't look like a Reconciliation." In the spring, Patriots also discovered that the Crown had hired dreaded Hessian mercenaries from the German principalities to fight in America. Adams insisted that British policy made independence inevitable: "It throws thirteen Colonies out of the Royal Protection . . . and makes us independent in Spight of all our supplications and Entreaties."[76]

By May 1776, Patriots noted a swing in public opinion in favor of independence. Previously moderate and reluctant, New Jersey Patriots sacked the last remaining royal governor in the rebelling colonies: William Franklin, who had broken with his father, Benjamin, to remain loyal to the empire. On June 10, 1776, the New Jersey Provincial Congress denounced the governor as "an enemy to the liberties of this country." They had him arrested and hauled away to prison in Connecticut. Declaring the imperial tie dissolved, the Provincial Congress prepared a new state constitution. During the spring of 1776, many other provincial congresses pressed their delegations in Congress to declare independence.[77]

Independence would help Congress secure the foreign assistance needed to fight the British. French agents assured congressmen that France could provide little aid until the Patriots broke with Britain and formed a union strong enough to provide a stable diplomatic partner. In Congress on June 7, Richard Henry Lee of Virginia introduced a resolution to declare independence. "It is not choice then but necessity that calls for Independence, as the only means by which foreign Alliances can be obtained; and a proper Confederation by which internal peace and union can be secured," Lee explained.[78]

On July 2, twelve delegations voted for independence, with only New York abstaining (a week later the New Yorkers changed their vote to create unanimity). Adams exulted, "The Hopes of Reconciliation, which were fondly entertained by Multitudes of honest and well meaning tho weak and mistaken People, have been gradually and at last totally extinguished." Although correct about the Patriots, he ignored the Loyalists who still clung to the empire.[79]

To justify the decision to their countrymen and the world, Congress adopted a Declaration of Independence drafted by Jefferson with help from Franklin and Adams. Following the lead of *Common Sense*, the Declaration blamed the king as a tyrant who provoked a just rebellion. The philosophic preamble celebrated human equality as a natural right divinely ordained: "We hold these truths to be self-evident, that all men are created equal, that they are endowed by their Creator with certain unalienable Rights, that among these are Life, Liberty and the Pursuit of Happiness." The Declaration then indicted the king for denying life, liberty, and the pursuit of happiness to his colonial subjects. Dwelling on recent events generated by the war, that indictment slighted the issue that had started the whole conflict: Parliament's attempt to tax and restrict the colonists. As the symbol of British sovereignty, the king had to become the great villain, denounced for impressing sailors, recruiting mercenaries, burning towns, promoting slave revolts, and inciting raids by "merciless Indian savages." In a pivotal transmutation, the formerly beloved king became a despised tyrant.[80]

Adopted and published on July 4, the Declaration had a poetic quality that played to emotions as well as reason. Adams delighted in the "high tone and the flights of Oratory with which [the Declaration] abounded." He later added, "The Declaration of Independence I always considered as a Theatrical Show." Congress forwarded printed copies to state officials with directions to proclaim and circulate. At 1,337 words, it fit on one long, printed page—a broadside—which proved convenient for posting on the doors of public buildings and the walls of taverns. Newspapers reprinted the Declaration, magistrates proclaimed it at county courthouses, and clergymen announced it from their pulpits. Washington had his officers read the Declaration to their assembled troops. Crowds celebrated by ringing church bells, firing volleys, illuminating homes with candles, and lighting bonfires on the hills—all accompanied with lavish toasts of alcohol. The boisterous celebrations helped to draw many wavering people over to the Patriot cause.[81]

Patriots attacked the symbols of monarchy, tearing down and burning royal portraits and coat-of-arms posted on public buildings, churches, and tavern signs. Patriot mobs also assaulted Anglican ministers who persisted in publicly praying for the king, as was their traditional duty. Stubborn clergymen had their clothes ripped, their homes and churches ransacked, and their windows smashed. In New York City on July 9, Patriots toppled the great equestrian statue of George III and melted its lead to make 40,000 bullets to shoot at redcoats. In that blow for liberty, the Patriots employed slaves to tear down the statue.[82]

By declaring independence, Congress gave the conflict greater clarity and raised its stakes. No longer were Patriots absurdly fighting in the king's name against his Parliament. Instead, they defended an American union of republican states. A Delaware man observed, "I could hardly own the King and fight against him at the same time, but now these matters are cleared up. Heart and hand shall move together."[83]

That new clarity alienated some moderate Patriots who dreaded independence and republicanism as leading to anarchy. Congress's chaplain, Rev. Jacob Duché, resigned in disgust upon discovering "that

independency was the idol, which they had long wished to set up, &
rather than sacrifice this idol, they would deluge their Country in
Blood." James Allen belonged to a prominent and wealthy Philadelphia family. In July 1775, he had praised resistance to British taxes as "a
great & glorious cause." In March 1776, however, he anxiously wrote:
"The plot thickens; peace is scarcely thought of—Independency pre-
dominant. Thinking people uneasy, irresolute & inactive. The Mobility triumphant." He concluded, "The madness of the multitude is but
one degree better than submission to the Tea-Act."[84]

Allen denounced independence for empowering common people
to abuse and plunder their betters. Dropping out of the militia, he
retired to the countryside, where he tried to lay low and keep quiet. But
Patriots would not leave him alone, for they demanded that everyone
embrace and assist their cause. A committee hounded Allen, and militiamen slashed his carriage with bayonets. He complained, "To oppress
one's countrymen is a love of Liberty . . . & the most insignificant [men]
now lord it with impunity & without discretion over the most respectable characters." He concluded, "This convulsion has indeed brought
all the dregs to the Top." Once a firm Patriot, Allen felt alienated by
independence and its social consequences.[85]

Retreat

In late June and early July 1776, while Congress debated independence,
a massive British fleet bearing thousands of soldiers approached New
York City. On July 2, General Howe's army landed without opposition and camped on Staten Island. During the next month, more ships
and troops arrived from England and the failed Carolina foray by Clinton and Parker. The New York expedition ultimately involved half the
Royal Navy, most of the British merchant marine, two-thirds of the
British army, and 8,000 Hessians. Never before had such a huge fleet
and immense army gathered for war in North America. Lord Germain's logistical preparations had paid off, displaying the financial
and organizational might of the empire. By deploying massive force,

the British hoped to intimidate the Patriots and win the war in a single decisive campaign.[86]

Declaring independence suddenly seemed far more reckless, for Howe's 32,000 troops outnumbered Washington's 19,000, and the Britons and Hessians were well-trained, disciplined, and experienced regulars, while the Patriots were raw recruits supplemented by even rawer militia. A British general, James Grant, exulted, "If a good bleeding can bring those Bible-faced Yankees to their senses—the fever of Independence should soon abate."[87]

New York enticed the British as the second-largest city and best harbor on the Atlantic Seaboard. Occupying a square mile at the southern tip of Manhattan Island, New York was the gateway to the Hudson, a navigable river reaching deep into the interior. Adams considered it "the Nexus of the Northern and Southern Colonies, [and] a kind of Key to the whole Continent." By capturing New York and ascending the Hudson, Howe could sever New England, the hotbed of rebellion, from the middle colonies.[88]

New York also had many Loyalists, who could rally to help the British. While royal troops assembled on Staten Island, Patriot mobs terrorized Loyalists in the city. One reported, "On Monday night, some men called Tories were carried and hauled about through the streets with candles forced to be held by them or pushed in their faces, and their heads burned; but on Wed[nesday], in the open day, the scene was by far worse; several, and among them gentlemen, were carried on rails; some stripped naked and dreadfully abused." A Patriot celebrated the "grand Toory rides" for scaring the city's other Loyalists into hiding.[89]

Prudence urged Washington to abandon New York as indefensible against a superior naval force. "Whoever commands the Sea must command the Town," General Lee warned. New York also offered dangerous temptations. The city's many prostitutes conveyed venereal disease through the Continental ranks. An officer from Massachusetts lamented, "Every brutal gratification can be so easily indulged in this place that the army will be debauched here in a month more

than in twelve at Cambridge." But Congress felt a political imperative to hold the key city, which was home to "many worthy Citizens
& their Families."[90]

On August 22, 1776, Howe landed 20,000 troops on the western
end of Long Island and marched toward Washington's entrenched position on high ground. On August 27, Howe feinted a frontal assault
while sending thousands of troops nine miles around Washington's
flank through a pass revealed by Loyalists. The flank attack surprised
and routed the Patriots, who suffered 1,500 casualties, most of them
prisoners.[91]

Despite losing only 400 men in the fight, Howe failed to complete
his triumph for fear of further casualties. By holding his troops back
from a final assault, Howe gave Washington time to rally his shattered army behind earthworks on Brooklyn Heights near the East
River. Two nights later, Washington's troops escaped from Howe's
trap, crossing the river to Manhattan under the cover of darkness and
fog. Howe had lost a precious chance to cripple the Patriot cause.[92]

Howe hoped that his victory on Long Island would suffice to
bring the Patriots to terms. Obliged to hear the British offer, Congress sent Adams, Franklin, and John Rutledge to meet the general
and his brother, Admiral Richard Howe, on Staten Island on September 11. But they found no common ground. The Howes offered only
a vague future deal on taxes and pardons for Patriots who surrendered, while the three congressmen insisted that Britain had to recognize American independence. Lord Howe's secretary concluded,
"They met, they talked, they parted. And now nothing remains but
to fight it out."[93]

Washington's outnumbered troops were dispirited by defeat and
weakened by disease and desertion. Ignoring orders, they shot off their
weapons in camp for sport. Washington reported that "seldom a day
passes but some persons are shot by their friends." He warned Congress, "Our situation is truly distressing" because his soldiers' minds
were filled "with apprehension and despair." Three-quarters of the
militiamen had run away, and others kept busy looting nearby homes

and shops. "With the deepest concern I am obliged to confess my want of confidence in the generality of the Troops," he concluded.[94]

On the morning of September 15, British warships blasted the flimsy Patriot earthworks of lower Manhattan while barges carried thousands of troops to land at Kip's Bay just north of the city. Threatened with envelopment, Patriot soldiers broke and fled northward as most threw away their packs and guns to run faster. Officers cursed them as cowards, while the men damned their officers as fools. In a fury, Washington beat fleeing men with his cane. Rather than join their flight, he rode toward the advancing redcoats. His watching friend Nathanael Greene worried that Washington was "so vexed at the infamous conduct of his troops that he sought death rather than life." Forced back by his officers, Washington reluctantly joined the chaotic retreat northward to new entrenchments on Harlem Heights.[95]

Meanwhile, in the city, crowds of Loyalists came out to wave the Union Jack and cheer the redcoats as liberators. Howe's secretary reported that the New Yorkers "behaved in all respects, women as well as men, like overjoyed Bedlamites." More than 700 people signed a "declaration of dependence" affirming their loyalty to the empire. In a proclamation, Howe promised to restore the "free enjoyment of their Liberty and Properties upon the true Principles of the Constitution."[96]

On the windy night of September 20, a suspicious fire raced through New York, consuming more than 500 houses and several churches: a quarter of the city. By depriving many Loyalists of homes and Britons of barracks, the fire helped the Patriot cause, so Washington celebrated the blaze as the work of "Providence." Loyalists thought it was the work of Washington. Claiming to find evidence of arson and sabotage, a Loyalist mob hanged a suspect without a trial.[97]

In October, Howe made another end run around Washington, landing troops northeast of Manhattan. Forced to withdraw northward into Westchester County, Washington foolishly left behind two large garrisons in forts beside the Hudson. At White Plains on October 28–29, Howe battered Washington's main army, which retreated into

New Jersey. Then the British turned south to trap the two exposed garrisons. On November 16, Hessians stormed Fort Washington, taking 2,800 prisoners and a massive store of munitions: men and supplies that the Patriots could ill afford to lose. Only an abrupt evacuation saved Fort Lee's garrison from the same fate, but the fleeing Patriots lost more precious cannon and ammunition.[98]

Reeling from his defeats, Washington withdrew southwestward across New Jersey while desertion reduced his demoralized army to just 5,400 men. Another 2,000 men lingered to the north along the Hudson River under General Lee, who ignored Washington's order to rejoin the main army. A tall, thin, homely, and acerbic man with dirty clothes and crude manners, Lee had served ably as an officer in the British Army during the Seven Years War. When passed over for promotion after the war, he quit the service in a huff and moved to the colonies, where he embraced independence and republicanism. In 1775, he won a commission as a major general after dazzling Congress with his odd combination of professional expertise and confidence in raw American troops. He posed a stark contrast with Washington, who felt like an awkward amateur but longed to discipline his soldiers. Impressed by Lee's record, Washington praised him as "the first Officer in Military knowledge and experience we have in the whole Army."[99]

During the fall of 1776, however, Washington's defeats emboldened Lee to intrigue to replace his commander. He wrote to other officers: "*Entre nous*, a certain great man is damnably deficient." On November 21, Joseph Reed, a member of Washington's staff, privately replied to Lee: "I do think that it is entirely owing to you that this Army & the Liberties of America . . . are not totally cut off. You have Decision, a Quality often wanting in Minds otherwise valuable."[100]

Lee's decisive qualities proved less real than his vanity. On the evening of December 12–13, Lee rode three miles beyond his army's camp to cavort with a mistress at an inn in northern New Jersey. Tipped off by Loyalists, British cavalrymen surrounded the inn and hauled Lee away into the winter in his slippers and nightshirt.

"Charles Lee, Esqr.—Major General of the Continental Army in America," engraving by C. Shepherd, 1775. Courtesy of the Library of Congress (LC-USZ62-3617).

The British exulted in this triumph, but it bore ironic consequences. With Lee removed from competition for command, Washington could unite his men and officers for a last, desperate bid to save their cause. John Sullivan led Lee's former troops southwest to, at last, join Washington's army.[101]

Washington withdrew his troops across the broad Delaware River to the relative safety of Pennsylvania. Hungry and ragged, the men lacked tents as the weather turned nasty. Hundreds more deserted, and half of the rest would leave when their enlistments expired at the end of December. Reed described Washington's force as "the wretched remains of a broken army." In a confidential letter, Washington despaired, "Our affairs are in a very bad way. . . . I think the game is pretty near up." He warned Congress that year's end would bring "an end to the existence of our Army." And who would enlist in a new army for an apparently lost cause?[102]

In New Jersey, most people abandoned the Patriot cause. Washington reported, "From disaffection, and want of spirit & fortitude, the Inhabitants instead of resistance, are offering Submission, & taking protections from Genl. Howe in Jersey." At least 5,000 men accepted British pardons. The defectors included Richard Stockton, a signer of the Declaration of Independence. Washington grimly understood that the people "will cease to depend upon or support a force, from which no protection is given to them."[103]

Patriot despair spread to Philadelphia, where few people thought that Washington could stop the British and save the city. Packing their furniture into wagons, thousands sought refuge in the countryside. Congress fled south to Baltimore, leaving behind only a three-member executive committee, which included Robert Morris, who suspected that the Patriot cause was doomed:

> Our people knew not the hardships & Calamities of War when they so boldly dared Brittain to arms. Every man was then a bold Patriot, felt himself equal to the Contest, . . . but now when we are fairly engaged, when Death & Ruin stare us in the face and when nothing but the most intrepid Courage can rescue us from Contempt & disgrace, sorry I am to Say it, many of those who were foremost in Noise, [now] Shrink coward like from the Danger and are begging pardon without striking a Blow.

Many gentlemen, including John Dickinson, stopped accepting the paper money issued by Congress, deeming it worthless. Several leading Philadelphians defected, bolting across the Delaware to offer their services as Loyalists to the victorious Britons. They included Joseph

Galloway and three brothers of James Allen: a committeeman, a lieutenant colonel of the militia, and a member of Congress.[104]

British commanders regarded the war as nearly won. Lord Rawdon boasted that the Continental Army "is broken all to pieces, and the spirit of their leaders . . . is also broken. It is well nigh over with them." On December 14, however, Howe called off his pokey pursuit of Washington. Rather than cross the Delaware and strike for Philadelphia, Howe withdrew most of his men to winter quarters in and around New York City. He even divided his army to send General Clinton with 6,000 men to seize Newport, Rhode Island, as a base for raids to harass southern New England. To hold western New Jersey, Howe posted a Hessian garrison at Trenton on the east side of the Delaware River.[105]

A brilliant organizer and tactician, Howe had won dazzling victories, but he lacked a sense of strategic urgency. After winning a battle, he failed to press home attacks on the staggered enemy. Loyalists bitterly complained that Howe lacked the killer instinct needed to crush the Patriots. Instead, they charged, Howe preferred to linger in his luxurious quarters, gambling, drinking, and whoring. Leaving his wife behind in England, Howe took a mistress in America. Elizabeth Lloyd Loring was the wife of a Loyalist, Joshua Loring, Jr., whom Howe bought off by appointing him to the lucrative post of commissary of prisoners. One Loyalist ditty blamed Howe's sloth on his lust:

> *Sir William, he, snug as a flea,*
> *Lay all this time a-snoring;*
> *Nor dreamed of harm, as he lay warm*
> *In bed with Mrs. Loring.*

The arrangement proved less happy for imprisoned Patriots who suffered from Mr. Loring's corruption and incompetence. Denied decent shelter, clothing, food, and water, the prisoners died by droves on prison ships, especially the *Jersey*, which became notorious as a squalid deathtrap that few survived.[106]

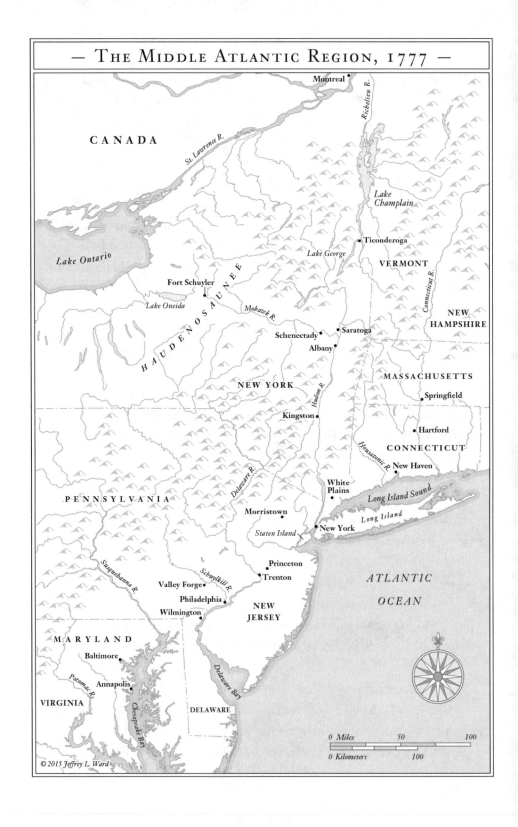

— THE MIDDLE ATLANTIC REGION, 1777 —

CANADA

St. Lawrence R.

Montreal

Richelieu R.

Lake Ontario

Lake Champlain

Ticonderoga

Lake George

VERMONT

Fort Schuyler

Lake Oneida

Mohawk R.

H A U D E N O S A U N E E

Connecticut R.

NEW HAMPSHIRE

Schenectady

Saratoga

Albany

NEW YORK

Hudson R.

MASSACHUSETTS

Springfield

Kingston

Hartford

Housatonic R.

CONNECTICUT

New Haven

Delaware R.

White Plains

Long Island Sound

PENNSYLVANIA

Long Island

Morristown

Staten Island

New York

Susquehanna R.

Schuylkill R.

Princeton

Trenton

ATLANTIC

Valley Forge

OCEAN

Philadelphia

Wilmington

NEW JERSEY

MARYLAND

Baltimore

Potomac R.

Annapolis

Delaware Bay

VIRGINIA

Chesapeake Bay

DELAWARE

© 2015 Jeffrey L. Ward

| 0 Miles | | 50 | 100 |
| 0 Kilometers | | 100 | |

Recovery

His back against the wall, Washington rallied, for he refused to accept the dishonor of surrender without one last fight. Despite the misery and doubts around him (and in his own letters), he maintained a public serenity that bolstered morale in the army. One of his lieutenants later recalled, "A deportment so firm, so dignified, but yet so modest and composed, I have never seen in any other person." Few Americans still had confidence in Washington, but those who did would fight for him.[107]

On December 25, Washington had 6,000 men, but their number would shrink to 1,400 with the expiration of most enlistments at the end of the week. He had one last chance to win the victory needed to reverse the downward spiral in Patriot morale. Washington saw an opportunity in the exposed Hessian garrison of 1,500 men posted across the Delaware at Trenton. But crossing the icy, twisting river was risky, and the Hessians were tough, veteran troops. Washington said that only "necessity, dire necessity, will, nay must, justify" an attack, for he had to "raise the spirits of the People, which are quite sunk by our misfortunes."[108]

As they crossed the Delaware River in boats, the troops endured a fierce storm that mixed hail, rain, and snow. An officer reported, "The wind is northeast and beats in the faces of the men. It will be a terrible night for the soldiers who have no shoes. Some of them have tied old rags around their feet, but I have not heard a man complain." At least the storm kept the Hessians snug in their warm quarters in Trenton.[109]

Expecting no attack, the Hessian commander, Colonel Johann Rall, had neglected to fortify Trenton, which remained an open town. Before dawn on December 26, Washington's men landed unopposed about nine miles upriver and then marched south to Trenton, surprising the waking Hessians, who were surrounded, riddled by cannon fire, and compelled to surrender. The Patriots suffered no dead and only three wounded to take 948 prisoners in Washington's first significant battlefield victory of the war. Rall died of his wounds two days later. The victorious soldiers got drunk on captured rum until

Washington ordered the hogsheads smashed to drain the liquor onto the frozen ground.[110]

On January 2 at Trenton, Washington braced for a counterattack by 5,500 British troops sent west from New York under the command of Lord Cornwallis, who thought that he had the Continentals trapped against the Delaware River. Overnight, however, Washington's men slipped away, marching around the British to the south. Instead of heading back across the Delaware, Washington turned east, passing behind the unwary Cornwallis. On the morning of January 3 at Princeton, Washington routed three British regiments posted there as a rear guard. Then Washington headed north, eluding Cornwallis's pursuit to find refuge in the hills around Morristown, New Jersey. There he again had to rebuild his army as new recruits replaced the veterans whose terms had expired.[111]

Although modest in scale, the victories at Trenton and Princeton transformed the political situation in New Jersey. Most of the inhabitants had soured on their occupiers, who had committed "every species of Rapine and plunder," according to the British adjutant general. Another general conceded that such atrocities tended to "lose you friends and gain you enemies." Many Patriot militiamen rallied to harass the British retreat, while Loyalists fled to New York or hid in the forests to live as bandits, while dodging deadly pursuit by "tory-hunters." Forsaking most of the state, Howe withdrew his troops to the outskirts of New York, where he remained inert until the spring. A British officer developed a new appreciation for the Patriots, "Though it was once the fashion of this army to treat them in the most contemptible light, they are now become a formidable enemy."[112]

After Trenton and Princeton, Washington became the great hero as Patriot morale rebounded. In Virginia, a disgusted Loyalist, Nicholas Cresswell, reported: "The minds of the people are much altered. A few days ago they had given up the cause for lost. Their late successes have turned the scale and now they are all liberty mad again.... They have recovered [from] their panic and it will not be an easy matter to throw them into that confusion again."[113]

By waging a <u>war of attrition</u>, Washington sought to wear down a better-equipped and better-trained foe, for the British could ill afford to bring more men and supplies across the Atlantic to replace their losses. A Briton worried, "Our army will be destroyed by damned driblets." Cresswell marveled that Washington, "a Negro-driver, should, with a ragged Banditti of undisciplined people, the scum and refuse of all nations on earth, so long keep a British General at bay." But Washington understood better than Howe that victory hinged on who could endure a long, hard, and bitter struggle. Cresswell conceded that Washington was a "great and wonderful man."[114]

5

ALLIES

"I can tell you S[i]r, it is trublesum[e] times for us all,
but wors[e] for the Sold[i]ers."
—SERGEANT ICHABOD WARD, 1777[1]

To win independence, the United States had to cultivate inter-dependence with European allies. Lacking industries, Patriots needed imported arms, ammunition, and uniforms to sustain their forces. For want of hard currency, they sought credit from European governments and bankers to purchase the imported supplies. Congress also coveted military advisors with expertise in artillery and engineering. Ultimately, the Patriots wanted French and Spanish naval power to fight the Royal Navy and protect merchant ships carrying the European supplies needed to sustain the war effort.[2]

But many congressman worried that any foreign alliance would lead to a new dependence. As British colonists, Patriots had long despised the absolutist regimes and Catholic faith of France and Spain. Many in Congress also cherished independence as a precious chance to escape from the imperial wars driven by European contentions. By weaning

---

A sketch of four Continental army soldiers by Baron Ludwig von Closen, a German-born officer in the French expeditionary force commanded by Rochambeau. Note the black infantryman on the far left and the artilleryman, with a burning match, on the far right. Courtesy of the Anne S. K. Brown Military Collection, Brown University Library.

Americans from the "corruption" associated with monarchical rule and imperial warfare, Patriots hoped to sustain virtue in their countrymen. They also expected their new nation to prosper by freely trading with all nations rather than accepting economic domination by another European power.[3]

Patriots also wanted a free hand to build their own empire in North America. In September 1776, Congress approved a "Model Treaty of Amity and Commerce" to propose to France and Spain. Drafted by John Adams, the document showed the Patriots' imperial ambitions and wariness of European allies. The proposed treaty required allies to recognize the United States as entitled to all of British America, including Canada, Nova Scotia, Newfoundland, and the Floridas. While claiming all potential conquests in North America, Congress expected France and Spain to fight the British without binding Americans in any way. Congressmen liked to believe that American trade alone was so enticing that European nations would assist them. In late 1776, however, after Patriot forces suffered defeats, congressmen decided that beggars could not be choosers. Desperate for French and Spanish help, Congress agreed to accept their dominance in the Caribbean.[4]

French and Spanish leaders were wary of helping an American revolt by republican states lest they set a bad example for their own colonies. Spanish leaders especially worried that the rapidly growing and westward-expanding Americans threatened the thinly settled Spanish frontier colony of Louisiana. But, the French and Spanish also felt tempted by the chance to smite and weaken their British foes.[5]

The French foreign minister, the Comte de Vergennes, was diligent, resourceful, experienced, and patient in his drive to restore France's military might and diplomatic clout. To enrich France and impoverish Britain, Vergennes sought to wrest away the profits of North American trade, but he had to proceed carefully in assessing whether the Patriot revolt provided the right moment to challenge the mighty British Empire. Betting on a lost cause would expose the French to dangerous risks and enormous costs. The finance minister, Anne-Robert Jacques Turgot, astutely warned that a new war would ruin the French Crown.[6]

In the spring of 1776, Vergennes decided covertly to help the Patriots, but he balked at alliance and open war as premature. Deeming the French fleet not yet prepared to take on the Royal Navy, he feared that war would expose French colonies in the West Indies and French fishermen off Newfoundland to devastating British attacks. Vergennes also wanted to line up the Spanish as allies, which would take persuasion and time. Meanwhile, Vergennes set up a front company to sell military supplies to Congress on credit with eventual repayment in Virginia tobacco. To head the company, Vergennes appointed Pierre-Augustin Caron de Beaumarchais, an accomplished playwright and secret agent. In December 1776, the Spanish Crown followed suit by directing their officials in Havana and Louisiana secretly to ship munitions to the Patriots. Many French and Spanish shipments slipped through the inefficient and porous British blockade of the long American coast. Unwilling to add to their open enemies in 1776, the British could only protest and seethe about the covert aid, which the French and Spanish officially denied providing. Britons hoped to crush the rebellion before it could tempt the French and Spanish to enter the war fully. Although the campaign of 1776 fell short, the British had renewed confidence that they could finish off the Patriots in 1777, when General Sir John Burgoyne would invade New York from the north.[7]

Burgoyne

During the spring and summer of 1776, Sir Guy Carleton drove the reeling Patriot troops from Canada. Preparing to attack Ticonderoga in northern New York, he first had to build a flotilla to wrest control of Lake Champlain from Patriot gunboats commanded by Benedict Arnold. On October 11 off Valcour Island, the British flotilla crushed Arnold's. The demoralized Patriot garrison at Ticonderoga promised little resistance, but Carleton decided that the season was too late, so he pulled back and put his men into winter quarters in Canada. Disgusted by Carleton's poor show, Lord Germain turned

"General Sir John Burgoyne," engraving by Robert Pollard, 1778.
Courtesy of the Library of Congress (LC-USZ62-58746).

command of the northern invasion over to a far more aggressive general, Burgoyne.[8]

Charming and gregarious, Burgoyne made a fine drinking companion and regimental commander. During the Seven Years War, he had displayed courage and flair as a cavalry officer in European campaigns, but his avid self-promotion and aristocratic connections won him promotion to major general—well beyond his abilities. The British writer Horace Walpole described Burgoyne as a "vain, very ambitious man with a half-understanding which was worse than none." But he treated common soldiers with unusual respect, and his aggressive energy promised to succeed where Carleton's slow caution had faltered. Abundantly self-assured, Burgoyne posted a bet in London that he would return "home victorious from America by Christmas Day, 1777."[9]

Burgoyne proposed, and Germain accepted, a complex strategic plan for a three-pronged attack during the campaign of 1777. First, Burgoyne would lead the Canadian army south via Lake Champlain to take Ticonderoga and Albany. Second, Colonel Barry St. Leger would command a smaller force to advance via Lake Ontario on the west to rally Indian support and descend the Mohawk River to join Burgoyne at Albany. Third, Sir William Howe would ascend the Hudson River from New York to complete the juncture of the three armies, thereby recovering New York and isolating New England to the east. But Howe preferred his own plan to attack Philadelphia. When Germain also approved that alternative, Burgoyne remained confident that he could take Albany without Howe's help.[10]

In June, Burgoyne advanced southward with 6,700 regulars, half of them Hessians, about 700 Canadians, and 500 native warriors. Issuing a bombastic proclamation, he promised to liberate "the suffering thousands" of Loyalists from the Patriots "system of Tyranny," but few Americans would welcome Hessians and Indians as liberators. In early July, Burgoyne captured Ticonderoga by posting cannon on an unguarded mountain overlooking the fort, which compelled the defenders to flee.[11]

The retreating Patriots were commanded by General Philip Schuyler, a haughty New York landlord unpopular with common New Englanders, who balked at reinforcing him. In early August 1777, the New England delegates persuaded Congress to make Schuyler the scapegoat for losing Ticonderoga. Congress replaced him with General Horatio Gates, a former British officer popular with New Englanders because of his surprisingly common manners.[12]

Gates benefited from Schuyler's efforts to clog the road south from Ticonderoga with felled trees. Burgoyne's advance slowed to a crawl as his troops took twenty-four days to cover a mere twenty-three miles. Meanwhile, Patriots scored a great propaganda coup by highlighting an atrocity committed by two of Burgoyne's Indians. In a drunken quarrel, they tomahawked Jane McCrea, the fiancée of a Loyalist officer. Gates and the Patriot press spread a lurid account and urged American men to defend their women by repelling Burgoyne's approaching army. Many wavering people, who balked at fighting for independence, would take up arms to fight Indians, whom they feared and hated. Gates's appointment and McCrea's death promoted a surge by New England militiamen into the Patriot camps on the upper Hudson.[13]

After reaching the Hudson north of Albany, Burgoyne sent Hessians east toward Bennington, Vermont, to rally Loyalists and round up horses and forage. Instead, on August 16, they were surrounded by 2,000 Patriot militiamen commanded by John Stark. After two fierce firefights, 900 of the invaders surrendered, further reducing Burgoyne's manpower. He lamented that New England "abounds in the most active and most rebellious race of the continent and hangs like a gathering storm on my left."[14]

Burgoyne suffered another loss on his western flank in the upper Mohawk Valley, where St. Leger besieged the Patriot garrison at Fort Schuyler (formerly Fort Stanwix). In August, his Haudenosaunee allies and Loyalists ambushed a relief force of Patriot militiamen and Oneida warriors commanded by General Nicholas Herkimer, who had a Loyalist brother serving with St. Leger. After a bloody, day-long battle in brutal heat, dense gunpowder smoke, and a brief but violent thunderstorm, the Oneidas and Patriots retreated after suffering 200 casualties, including a dying General Herkimer. The Loyalists and their native allies lost only 50 dead—but more than enough to erode Haudenosaunee morale. Many warriors abandoned St. Leger, returning to their distant villages to conduct condolence ceremonies for the dead. More natives deserted when they learned of the approach by another Patriot relief force. Disheartened by those desertions, St. Leger retreated in disarray to Canada in late August.[15]

Despite the ominous defeats on both flanks, Burgoyne refused to withdraw but instead pushed south toward Albany. "Britons never retreat," he told his men. Trapped by vanity, Burgoyne meant to prove that he was no Carleton. Burgoyne expected General Henry Clinton to lead a relief force from New York City to his rescue. But Clinton's force was too small to make more than a diversion by attacking Patriot forts in the highlands north of the city. After reaching Kingston, Clinton turned back, leaving Burgoyne to his fate. Meanwhile, militia reinforcements swelled Gates's army to 20,000 men, triple Burgoyne's troops.[16]

In mid-September, Burgoyne sought to dislodge General Gates, who had entrenched his army on Bemis Heights beside the Hudson south of the village of Saratoga. Although a cautious commander, Gates had aggressive and able subordinates in Daniel Morgan and Benedict Arnold. On September 19, in the forests around Freeman's Farm, Burgoyne's men suffered heavy casualties in a failed attempt to push Gates's army back. On October 7, Burgoyne again attacked at Freeman's Farm but suffered a second bloody defeat. Pulling back to Saratoga, he was surrounded by Gates's superior numbers. A British sergeant recalled that the Patriots "swarmed around the little adverse army like birds of prey." Dreading capture by vengeful Patriots, Indian warriors slipped away homeward through the forest, while Burgoyne negotiated surrender terms with Gates.[17]

Concluded on October 17, "the Convention of Saratoga" permitted Burgoyne's troops to return to Britain on condition that they never again serve in North America. Considering the terms too generous, Congress reneged on Gates's deal and instead sent the prisoners away to camps in Virginia. Burgoyne lost his bet to return triumphant to London for Christmas, and the British lost a sixth of their troops in North America. The defeat proved the folly of any British invasion of the northern countryside, far beyond naval support. Albany lay too close to New England, the great hive of Patriot numbers, for the British to win.[18]

Loyalists paid dearly for the British defeats at Bennington, Fort Schuyler, and Saratoga. Victorious and vindictive Patriots plundered and horsewhipped Loyalists suspected of favoring the invaders. In late 1777 and early 1778, hundreds of refugees fled northward to Canada or westward to Niagara. Bolstering the Loyalist battalions in British service, the refugee men joined Indian allies in raiding the Patriot settlements along the Mohawk and Susquehanna rivers. In June 1778, Niagara's British commander reported, "Scalps & Prisoners are coming in every day, which is all the News [that] this Place affords."[19]

Philadelphia

Instead of supporting Burgoyne's campaign, General Howe went west to attack Philadelphia, the largest city on the seaboard and the capital for Congress. Although his troops greatly outnumbered Washington's, Howe rejected taking the direct route overland across New Jersey. Instead, he squandered nearly two precious months by embarking 13,000 men in 260 ships for a circuitous voyage via Chesapeake Bay to the mouth of the Susquehanna in northern Maryland. He left Clinton and 9,000 troops behind to defend New York City. The long voyage removed the main British army from combat during the peak of the summer campaign, to the dismay of Howe's officers. His folly enabled Washington to send reinforcements north to help Gates destroy Burgoyne's army. Not until August 25 did Howe's army land in northern Maryland, fifty-seven miles from Philadelphia, to resume the fight against Washington. He had taken forty-seven days to shorten his approach to Philadelphia by a mere forty-three miles. Although a superb battlefield commander, Howe was a paltry strategist, obtuse to the bigger picture both military and political.[20]

Heading south from New Jersey to confront Howe, Washington paraded his troops through Philadelphia in a bid to sway "the minds of the disaffected." At Brandywine Creek on September 11, Washington arrayed 11,000 men to block Howe's advance. As in the battle of Long Island, Howe menaced the front of Washington's line but sent a strike force on a wide sweep around the Continentals to surprise their vulnerable flank. After suffering heavy casualties, Washington withdrew his battered army to safety.[21]

Abandoning Philadelphia, Congress fled to Lancaster, Pennsylvania. The Pennsylvania militia followed their lead at the first sight of British regulars. A disgusted Elias Boudinot lamented that "as soon as a Gun was fired within ¼ of a Mile of them [they] would throw down their arms & run away worse than a Company of [New] Jersey Women." On September 26, Howe's advance force entered Philadelphia unopposed. Three-quarters of the inhabitants stayed put and loudly celebrated the British as liberators, "tho' by all accounts," a Briton remarked, "many of them were publickly on the other side before our arrival." Adams denounced Philadelphia as "that Mass of Cowardice and Toryism." The former chaplain to Congress, Reverend Jacob Duche, urged Washington to disavow independence and negotiate reconciliation with British rule.[22]

But Washington remained resolute. On October 4, his troops staggered the British with a counterattack on their outer lines at Germantown, a western suburb of Philadelphia. In the morning fog and heavy smoke of gunfire, however, the Continentals became confused and began firing on one another. It did not help that one of their generals, Adam Stephen, drank himself into a stupor during the battle. Howe brought up reinforcements and counterattacked, driving back the Continentals, but the fierce battle deflated British hopes that Washington's army was spent, that losing Philadelphia had sapped the Patriot will to fight.[23]

Despite capturing the rebel capital, the British were no closer to winning the war. Beyond the city, Howe found many farmers eager to sell produce but few willing to enlist as Loyalist soldiers. While Howe won the showy battles, Washington was winning a war of attrition as the British lost men whom they could ill afford to replace. His friend General Nathanael Greene, noted: "We cannot conquer the British force at once, but they cannot conquer us at all. The limits of the British government in America are their out-sentinels," for they lacked enough committed Loyalists to hold the ground that Howe passed over. And Washington's dogged ability to preserve his army impressed French leaders almost as much as Gate's victory at Saratoga.[24]

But some congressmen and a few officers nurtured the fantasy that

Washington should have crushed Howe at Brandywine or Germantown. Impatient with a slow, inglorious war of attrition, Washington's
critics longed for a decisive military genius, who could quickly end the
war by smashing the British. In mid-October, news of Gates's great
victory at Saratoga emboldened the critics, including John Adams, who
had soured on Washington just two years after pushing for his elevation to command.[25]

This malicious chatter irritated Washington and angered his inner
circle of generals and staff officers, who admired his dignified character
and relied on his patronage. Led by Nathanael Greene, Henry Knox,
and Alexander Hamilton, Washington's "military family" interpreted
the criticism as an insidious conspiracy or "cabal" to sack Washington
in favor of Gates. They especially blamed General Thomas Conway,
an Irish-born officer formerly in the French service. Although able,
Conway was also acerbic, angering American-born officers who felt
slighted when he won promotions at their expense. They felt furious
upon discovering that Conway had denigrated Washington in an indis-
crete letter written to flatter Gates.[26]

The winter of criticism ultimately strengthened Washington's
hold over the army. By responding forcefully, Washington's partisans
put his critics on the defensive. Within the army, Conway and other
critics became shunned and marginalized, their prospects ruined.
After resigning his commission, Conway sailed back to France, nurs-
ing a wound suffered in a duel with a Washington supporter. Most
congressmen recognized that only Washington could hold the army
together and command popular support. Knox assured Washington: "The people of America look up to you as their Father." Adams
sarcastically recalled, "Northern, Middle and Southern Statesmen,
and northern, Middle and Southern Officers of The Army, expressly
agreed to blow the Trumpets of Panegyrick in concert" to render
Washington "popular and fashionable, with all Parties in all places
and with all Persons, as a Centre of Union, as the Central Stone in
the Geometrical Arch. There you have the Revelation of the whole
Mystery." An adept political infighter, Washington built a powerful

"interest" among officers and in Congress. Underestimating Washington was a fool's errand.[27]

In late December, Washington had his ragged, shivering men build log huts for the winter. Up to a dozen men crowded into a hut, each a mere fourteen by sixteen feet and without windows or wooden floor. He located the main camp at Valley Forge, in the Pennsylvania hills eighteen miles northwest of Philadelphia: close enough to watch the British but sufficiently far for some security from attack. But the nearby farms could not support 11,000 hungry soldiers, and many farmers preferred to sell food for British coin rather than the depreciating paper money issued by Congress. Soldiers also suffered because of corruption and inefficiency in the army's commissary department. In February 1778, Washington described his troops as "starving." An army surgeon reported:

> Poor food—hard lodging—Cold Weather—fatigue—Nasty Cloathes—nasty Cookery—Vomit half my time.... There comes a soldier, his bare feet are seen thro' his worn-out Shoes, his legs nearly naked from the tatter'd remains of an only pair of stockings, his Breeches not sufficient to cover his nakedness, his Shirt hanging in Strings, his hair dishevel'd, his face meager, his whole appearance pictures a person forsaken & discouraged.

Two thousand men, nearly a fifth of the army, perished that winter from a debilitating combination of filth, exposure, malnutrition, and disease.[28]

While Washington grew closer to his suffering soldiers, he felt more distant from the civilians whom they defended. He rebuked Pennsylvania's legislators for criticizing, rather than supplying, his army: "I can assure those gentlemen that it is a much easier and less distressing thing to draw remonstrances in a comfortable room by a good fireside than to occupy a cold bleak hill and sleep under frost and snow without clothes or blanket." He blamed the army's plight on prosperous and selfish citizens who pursued profits instead of sacrificing for the cause: "Is the paltry consideration of a little dirty pelf to individuals to be placed in competition with the essential rights and liberties of the present generation, and of Millions yet unborn? . . . And shall we at last become the victims of our own abominable lust of gain?" As a planter and land speculator, Washington had chased profits, but at Valley Forge, he saw more clearly the human costs of profiteering.[29]

Washington had his troops whip and even shoot civilians caught conveying provisions to Philadelphia. He left their bodies beside the road as a warning to others. His troops also destroyed the flour mills within twenty miles of the city and seized all the grain and livestock in that no-man's-land for the Continental Army. General Greene reported, "The Inhabitants cry out and beset me from all quarters—but like Pharo[a]h, I harden my heart" and "forage the Country very bare." Greene's troops converted once prosperous farms into a barren landscape of "poverty and distress."[30]

In late winter, as their food supply improved, the soldiers also got their first systematic training in battlefield maneuvers and the manual of arms. In previous battles, their movements and firing had been ragged and uncoordinated: a poor match for disciplined British regulars. A Patriot officer declared that the typical Continental Army soldier had never learned how to wield the bayonet "but to roast his beefsteak"—and beefsteaks were rare in a starving army. To supervise the new drill instruction, Washington relied on a mercenary officer who called himself Baron von Steuben and claimed to have served as a general in the fabled Prussian army of Frederick the Great. Like most of the mercenaries who offered their services to Congress, Steuben greatly inflated his qualifications. Neither a general nor a baron, he had served as a mere captain in Prussia, but Steuben had real talents and adapted resourcefully to new circumstances. Admiring Washington's persistent soldiers, Steuben marveled that no European army would have held together under such suffering.[31]

Steuben's powerful build, profane passion, and blundering English amused and intimidated his soldiers, who learned to fire more rapidly in synchronized volleys and to wield bayonets. Their morale improved as they took pride in their conspicuous progress in performing Steuben's drills. Thrilled by the results, Washington longed to have another go at the British in a European-style battle in an open field. That opportunity would come in the summer thanks to an alliance with France.[32]

Alliance

The Patriot diplomats in Paris included Benjamin Franklin, a famed scientist and talented writer, who made the most of his international celebrity. During the early 1770s in London, Franklin had taken pains to appear wealthy and genteel, but in Paris he shrewdly cultivated a new persona as the plain and honest American of simple but digni-*clever* fied clothes and manners. He deftly appealed to the French fashion for romanticizing America as a land of purer simpletons, early versions of Jerry Lewis. Taken with Franklin, the French mass-produced his image on engravings, medallions, busts, and statuettes.[33]

But the Patriot diplomats were mismatched men, who bickered chronically and openly. Rigid, ideological, jealous, and suspicious, Arthur Lee clashed with the pragmatic and indulgent Franklin and the corrupt Silas Deane, an inveterate wheeler-dealer. Franklin and Deane worked more easily together, which infuriated Lee, who wrote long diatribes to Congress charging his colleagues with embezzlement and treason. Delighting in flatterers, Franklin was an easy mark for spies, including his secretary, Edward Bancroft. A charming doctor and amateur scientist, Bancroft won Franklin's friendship and trust, which he betrayed by selling secrets to a British spymaster. Once a week, Bancroft strolled through the Tuileries gardens of Paris to leave documents in the hollow of a tree for his British handler to pick up. Deane and Lee proved equally oblivious to their own secretaries, who also sold information to the British. Recognizing that the American delegation was a sieve for information, French officials avoided entrusting it with secrets.[34]

In early 1778, Vergennes concluded that the French navy was ready for war. News arrived then of Gates's triumph at Saratoga and of Washington's dogged persistence in fighting Howe. The Patriot pluck reassured Vergennes and his king, Louis XVI, that a French-American alliance could beat the British. On February 6, 1778, French and American commissioners signed treaties for trade and alliance. Both parties agreed to make no separate peace and accept no British terms short of American independence. France renounced retaking Canada but could seize British colonies in the West Indies. Retreating from the naïve principles of the Model Treaty of 1776, Congress accepted an entangling alliance in 1778.[35]

The Patriots and French hoped to draw the Spanish into their alliance, but the latter balked at encouraging an expansive, republican empire peopled by Protestants. The cautious Spanish foreign minister, Conde de Floridablanca, preferred to seek territorial concessions from Britain to buy Spain's neutrality. Floridablanca wanted everything that Britain had taken from Spain after 1700: Florida, Minorca, and Gibraltar. Rebuffed by Britain, in April 1779 Spain allied with France, which agreed to sustain the war until the British surrendered Gibraltar. Spanish leaders still refused to ally with the United States, ignored its ambassador to Madrid, John Jay, and advanced only modest loans and arms shipments. But the Patriots benefited from the combined naval might of France and Spain deployed around the globe against British forces and interests.[36]

The British failed to find any allies in Europe to counterbalance the French and Spanish. Far too successful in the Seven Years War, the British had upset the balance of power, arousing fear and jealousy in other European capitals. The Russians organized the League of Armed Neutrality with Denmark, Austria, Sweden, and Prussia to defy British efforts to blockade their trade with France and Spain. In late 1780, the British even added the Dutch Republic to their enemies by attempting to suppress its profitable neutral trade with the French and Americans.[37]

Shocked by France's alliance with the Patriots, Lord North sought reconciliation with the Patriots in early 1778. Responding to North's urgent lobbying, Parliament reluctantly rescinded the Coercive Acts of 1774 and promised to exempt colonists from parliamentary taxation forever (save for duties to regulate trade). In return, Patriots would have to demobilize their army, abandon the French alliance, and restore colonial governments with royal governors. To negotiate with Congress, Parliament appointed a commission headed by the Earl of Carlisle. The Carlisle Commissioners proposed something like Joseph Galloway's plan of 1774 by accepting Congress as an enduring body albeit subordinate to the Crown. They also agreed to guarantee colonial charters in perpetuity against alteration; to post no British regulars in the colonies in peacetime; reserve all colonial offices to Americans; and offer them some seats in the imperial Parliament. Britain would even help finance the massive debt that Congress had incurred fighting British forces. Upon arriving in Philadelphia in June, the commissioners wrote to Congress, offering to "reestablish on the Basis of equal Freedom and mutual Safety the tranquility of this once happy Empire."[38]

These humbling concessions disgusted many Members of Parliament, but they supported Lord North for want of an alternative prime minister acceptable to the king. A London newspaper denounced offering "terms of humiliating reconciliation" to a "race of unnatural and ungrateful bastards." A despairing Loyalist in London committed suicide after learning of the new policy, which also disgusted many British troops. One of Howe's aides noted, "The common English soldiers are so angry about the Act of Parliament on non-taxation, etc. which is posted here that they tear down these proclamations during the night."[39]

If offered in 1774, the concessions would have resolved the American crisis short of war. By 1778, however, Patriots would accept no dependence, however limited, on the empire. Clinging to independence and the French alliance, Congress refused to meet with the Carlisle commissioners. With all hope for reconciliation dashed, British officers urged a harder war meant to punish civilians and shatter the American economy. Increasingly distrustful and contemptuous of all Americans, hardline officers longed to take bloody, burning revenge for their own losses. Colonel Banastre Tarleton insisted that "nothing will serve these people but fire and sword." Hardened by years of indecisive war, British and Loyalist officers preferred to ravage rather than reconcile with the Patriots.[40]

In response, Gouverneur Morris wrote a pamphlet to warn the British that, in retaliation, Congress could hire terrorists in England to "wrap their metropolis in flames." Morris even threatened to send hit squads of frontiersmen across the Atlantic: "and the dreaded scalping-knife itself may, in the hands of our riflemen, spread horror through their island."[41]

Morris's threats seemed credible thanks to a real terrorist, a young Scot named James Aitken but commonly known as "John the Painter" because John was his alias and he worked as a house painter. Aitken had spent two years in British America, initially as an indentured servant in Virginia, but he had returned to England in the spring of 1775 just as the war began. Short, slim, hard-drinking, and prickly, he wanted revenge against the many English who mocked his poverty and stutter. He hoped to return to a hero's welcome in America after burning Royal Navy dockyards in Britain. In 1776, he visited Paris to pitch his plan to Silas Deane, who provided some encouragement and money. In late 1776 and early 1777, Aitkin set fires that damaged the Portsmouth dockyard and the city of Bristol, which spread public terror via the newspapers through England. Arrested in January, he was tried, convicted, and executed in March at the age of twenty-four. Hoisted in an iron gibbet, his rotting body hung for years as a warning to others at the entrance to Portsmouth Harbor on the Channel coast.[42]

Clinton

The entry of the French and Spanish (and later the Dutch) escalated the conflict into a world war. Facing attacks on colonies and shipping around the globe, the British no longer could concentrate troops and warships in North America to suppress the rebellion. Instead, they had to divert military resources to defend Gibraltar and Minorca, the

West Indian sugar colonies, the slaving entrepot at Senegal, and the East India Company's holdings in India. Dreading a French and Spanish invasion across the English Channel, Britain kept half of the Royal Navy in home waters. In America, the British had to deploy their reduced military resources more cautiously and efficiently. The crushing defeat at Saratoga highlighted the high costs and low rewards of trying to conquer the northern countryside, where Patriots outnumbered Loyalists. Germain assured General Sir Henry Clinton that "the War must be prosecuted upon a different Plan from That upon which it has hitherto been carried on."[43]

Clinton replaced Howe as the British commander in North America, and Germain ordered the diversion of 10,000 troops to defend the Floridas, West Indies, and Canada. Clinton regarded his new command as thankless and probably hopeless. While his army shrank to about two-thirds of the size previously entrusted to Howe, Clinton noted that "the rebels were every day growing stronger in number, confidence and discipline." He understood that battlefield victories were necessary but insufficient to win a war that ultimately demanded that Britons "gain the hearts and subdue the minds of America." Although able, insightful, well educated, and experienced, Clinton was also hypersensitive, grumpy, and quarrelsome. "I am hated—nay, detested—in this army," Clinton sadly concluded a year after taking command.[44]

To consolidate the remaining British forces in the northern colonies, Germain directed Clinton to evacuate Philadelphia and retreat to New York. The evacuation dismayed Loyalists, led by Joseph Galloway, whom Howe had appointed to supervise the city as "Superintendent General of the Police." Galloway complained that he was "exposed to the Rage of his bitter Enemies, deprived of a Fortune of about £70,000 and now left to wander like Cain upon the Earth, without Home & without Property." A British official agreed that the evacuation would wither Loyalist support in the northern colonies: "No man can be expected to declare for us when he cannot be assured a fortnight's protection."[45]

In June 1778, Clinton withdrew from Philadelphia to New York.

By marching his 10,000 men with 1,500 wagons across New Jersey, Clinton freed up his transports to carry away heavy stores and 5,000 Loyalists from Philadelphia by sea. Washington pursued and sought to force a fight to test the improved discipline of his army. But he entrusted command of the advance force to General Charles Lee, who recently had returned from his British captivity in an exchange of prisoners. Doubting the wisdom of risking a major battle, Lee preferred merely to harass the retreating British. On the morning of June 28 at Monmouth Courthouse, Clinton counterattacked and routed Lee's men, who became confused and disorganized in the searing heat and smoke of a summer battle on rough terrain. "It was almost impossible to breathe," recalled one soldier. Disgusted by the chaotic retreat, Washington rushed to the front and publicly ripped into Lee with profane rage. A listening colonel later recalled, "Never have I enjoyed such swearing before or since." Taking command, Washington renewed the attack and sustained a tough fight through the afternoon, but he could not defeat Clinton, who disengaged his men that night to resume their retreat.[46]

A court-martial suspended Lee and then Congress dismissed him from the army in January 1780. Lee's downfall completed the triumph of Washington's military family in the army. After suffering a nearly fatal wound in a duel with John Laurens, one of Washington's aides, Lee retired to a ruinous house in Virginia. He died in obscurity in 1782, still looking for "a Country where power was in righteous hands."[47]

Newport

In April 1778, Congress unanimously ratified the treaty with France. "I believe no event was ever received with a more heart felt joy," Washington exulted. "America is at last saved by almost a Miracle," declared another Patriot. American Protestants had to shed their colonial prejudices against the French as the devious minions of a Catholic king. A congressman, Elbridge Gerry, marveled:

What a miraculous change in the political world! ... The government of France an advocate of liberty, espousing the cause of protestants and risking a war to secure their independence. The king of England considered by every whig in the nation as a tyrant and the king of France applauded by every whig in America as the protector of the rights of man! ... These, my friend, are astonishing changes.

To celebrate the alliance, Washington staged a pageant where his republican troops chanted "Long Live the King of France." After three years of hard struggle against long odds, Patriots expected to reap easier victories with French help.[48]

By rushing a fleet to American waters, the French government sought to demonstrate the benefits of alliance. After flirting with an attack on New York, the Comte d'Estaing led his fleet northeast to besiege the smaller, outlying British garrison at Newport, Rhode Island. To assist the French, Washington sent Continental troops and New England militia commanded by John Sullivan. The allied force of 14,000 outnumbered the 3,000 defenders, but the allies bungled their cooperation. Deeming Sullivan inept, d'Estaing sailed away to Boston to repair his ships damaged by a gale. Despite the lack of French support, Sullivan attacked Newport and suffered a bloody defeat, so he retreated.[49]

Sullivan publicly blasted d'Estaing and denigrated the French as unreliable allies. Further trouble erupted in Boston, where French and American sailors staged a bloody brawl that killed a French officer. John Laurens noted, "I saw very plainly when I was at Boston, that our a[nc]ient, hereditary prejudices" against the French "were very far from being eradicated." A French officer insisted that Americans disdained their new allies as "dwarfs, pale, ugly specimens who lived exclusively on frogs and snails." To placate the French, Massachusetts officials funded a statue in honor of the dead officer; Congress passed a resolution vindicating French courage and wisdom; and Washington wrote fawning letters to soothe the wounded feelings of d'Estaing. In November, the admiral sailed away for the West Indies, per his orders from France, restoring British naval supremacy along the Atlantic seaboard.[50]

Aside from pushing the British to evacuate Philadelphia, the allies had little to show for their first campaign together. Coordinating their interests and forces proved more difficult than either had expected during the euphoria of spring. Giving priority to the West Indies, the French could spare their fleet for North American operations only during the late summer and early fall, when hurricanes menaced ships in the Caribbean.[51]

In the northern states, the war became a dreary struggle that both sides seemed to be losing. The British idled 25,000 men in and around New York. Occasionally, Clinton sent out some troops to burn and plunder vulnerable towns in eastern New Jersey, southern New York, and coastal Connecticut. After one raid, a sarcastic British captain declared, "A very pretty expedition; six thousand men having penetrated 12 miles into the country—burnt a village and returned." Washington's counterattacks captured British outposts at Stony Point, on the Hudson, in July 1779 and at Paulus Hook, New Jersey, a month later. Those setbacks led the British to further consolidate their forces in New York by evacuating Newport in October 1779. But Washington could not attack the main British garrison for want of men and money.[52]

Mutiny

Washington's army shrank as fewer men would join a service notorious for hunger, exposure, hard marching, scant pay, harsh discipline, and brutal combat. Fond of their liberty, most free Americans balked at prolonged military service as, in the words of one officer, "temporary slavery." Indeed, Henry Laurens considered Continental service "infinitely worse than slavery" because of the greater risk of mutilation and death.[53]

During the great initial enthusiasm of 1775–1776 the sons of substantial farmers and artisans had served as Continentals, but they enlisted for only one-year terms, which compelled Washington to rebuild his army every winter. In 1777, Congress increased the term of service to at least three years or the duration of the war. Washington welcomed the change, but the longer terms daunted anyone who had much choice in the matter. Adams noted that the army could no longer recruit "Men who could get at home [a] better living, more comfortable Lodgings, more than double the Wages, in Safety, not exposed to the Sickness of the Camp." Therefore, the army could only enlist "the meanest, idlest, most intemperate and worthless" men.[54]

For want of sufficient volunteers, in 1777 the states began draft-ing men from the militia. Most served for just three or six months and remained militiamen under local officers. A more dreaded draft con-signed men to the Continental Army for three or more years. Draft-ees received a notice: "This is to inform you [that you] are this evening drafted as one of the Continental men to go to General Washington's headquarters, and you must go or find an able bodied man in your Room, or pay a fine of twenty pounds in law[ful] money in twenty-four hours." A prosperous conscript paid the fine or hired a substitute, but poor men had no choice but to serve or run away. The savvy poor man made the best of his bad situation by selling his services as the substitute for a drafted man of means. Joseph Plumb Martin recalled, "I thought, as I must go, I might as well endeavor to get as much for my skin as I could." A French officer noted that Continental regiments "were composed entirely of vagabonds and paupers; no enticement or trick could force solid citizens to enlist as regulars."[55]

Apprentices, transients, beggars, drunks, slaves, and indentured immigrants abounded among the new recruits, as communities thrust military duty on marginal men. A Continental officer described most of his recruits as "only *Food for* Worms . . . hungry, lean faced Vil-lains." In Maryland, a gentleman helped two officers recruit a tavern haunter "who would do to stop a bullet as well as a better man, and as he was a truly worthless dog, he held, that the neighbourhood would be much indebted to us for taking him away." To save the costs of jailing and hanging Loyalists or criminals, judges reprieved those who would serve as Continentals for at least three years. Many captured Loyalists, Britons, and Hessians also got out of American prison camps by enlisting in Patriot forces.[56]

As poor men filled the ranks, politicians became more indifferent to supplying the army with pay, clothing, and food. Congress also mismanaged the commissary and quartermaster departments, which were supposed to supply the troops. Confusion, corruption, and incompetence brought rancid meat, spoiled flour, or nothing at all to the encampments. For want of proper uniforms, soldiers often looked like ragged beggars. "Poor fellows, my heart bleeds for them, while I Damn my country as void of gratitude," declared Lieutenant Colonel Ebenezer Huntington of Connecticut.[57]

The primary problem was that Congress lacked the power to tax and relied on quotas assessed on the individual states, which often failed to pay in full or on schedule. For want of gold and silver, Congress and the states printed millions of paper dollars, which rapidly depreciated toward worthlessness. A pound of beef cost 4 cents in 1777 but $1.69 three years later. In April 1779, Washington complained that "a waggon load of money will scarcely purchase a waggon load of provision." A year later, a Connecticut congressman deemed the Continental currency fit "for little Else but to Make the Tail of a Paper Kite."[58]

Soldiers seethed as they suffered while so many civilians prospered at home. The troops also felt neglected by many officers preoccupied with their own honor, perks, and comfort as gentlemen. After a day's march, when a regiment camped for the night, officers claimed beds in houses, leaving soldiers to sleep in stables or out in the cold, rain, and snow without tents. Martin recalled "venting our spleen at our country and government, then at our officers, and then at ourselves for our imbecility in staying there and starving in detail for an ungrateful people who did not care what became of us, so they could enjoy themselves while we were keeping a cruel enemy from them." Another barely literate soldier complained, "we are yoused wors than

Beests or hogs at home." He and his fellow men "Cu[r]se[d] the day thay [en]Listed."[59]

Troops felt betrayed by recruiting officers, local committees, and state governments which had promised them decent food and clothing and regular pay. In December 1778, Huntington lamented,

> Not a Day Passes . . . but some Soldier with Tears in his Eyes, hands me a letter from his Wife Painting forth the Distresses of his family in such strains as these, "I am without bread, and Cannot get any, the Committee will not Supply me, my Children will Starve, or if they do not, they must freeze, we have no wood, neither Can we get any. *Pray Come Home.*"

Another officer asked his state's governor, "If any of them desert, how can I punish them when they plead in their justification that on your part the Contract is broken? That you promised and engaged to . . . make them comfortable here, and the situation of their families tolerable at home, this they say they had an undoubted right to expect."[60]

Many soldiers slipped away from their camps at night to steal food from orchards, barns, gardens, and chicken coops. Fearful of alienating civilians, Washington demanded, "How disgraceful to the army is it, that the peaceable inhabitants, our countrymen and fellow citizens, dread our halting among them, even for a night and are happy when they get rid of us?" He whipped and sometimes executed culprits, but he dared not punish too many, for his army was so shorthanded.[61]

Fed up with hunger, exposure, and no pay, a fifth of the Continentals deserted. Some joined the British, but most fled homeward to pass as civilians. If going home seemed too risky, they bolted to a frontier settlement in Kentucky or Vermont. The army could sentence deserters to death but rarely did so, preferring whipping, for soldiers were too scarce to kill except on the battlefield.[62]

Soldiers also could band together to go on strike, which officers called "mutiny." During mutinies, enlisted men refused to do duty until satisfied for their grievances, or they could march away as regiments bound for home. Rare in the early, active years of the northern war, mutinies became more common between 1779 and 1781. Soldiers usually mutinied during the winter or spring: the hungriest seasons of their service. Rather than embroiling the entire army, mutinies were sporadic and involved regiments from the same state. Not yet thinking of themselves as Americans, soldiers lacked bonds and trust across state lines. Officers relied on the animosities and prejudices between states to suppress mutinies. During the spring of 1780, when Connecticut regiments went on strike, Pennsylvania troops forced them to submit.[63]

On January 1, 1781, however, those Pennsylvanians mutinied. They claimed that their three-year enlistments had expired at the end of December, while officers insisted that the troops could not leave before the war ended. The troops killed an officer and wounded two others, who tried to suppress the mutiny. Led by their sergeants, the mutineers marched under arms from their camp at Morristown, New Jersey, toward Philadelphia to intimidate Congress into releasing them from service and providing their overdue pay. General Clinton sent two agents to entice the mutineers to join his army at New York. But they considered themselves true Patriots, so they seized the agents and turned them over for trial and execution as spies. Congress and the Pennsylvania legislature then gave way, discharging 1,250 Pennsylvania soldiers, paying their arrears, and promising legal immunity for the mutiny. In return for generous bonus payments, many reenlisted.[64]

The deal appalled Washington, who thought it set a reckless precedent: "Unless this dangerous spirit can be suppressed by force, there is an end to all subordination in the Army, and indeed to the Army itself." He took a hard line later in January, when 200 New Jersey Continentals mutinied and demanded releases, back pay, and rum. Their small numbers enabled Washington to crush them with troops from New England. Then he made a few grim examples to deter other soldiers from considering mutiny. Officers compelled twelve convicted mutineers to serve as a firing squad to execute two of their companions. A witness reported that the "wretched victims, overwhelmed by the terrors of death, had neither time nor power to implore the mercy and forgiveness of their God."[65]

Ann Glover was the widow of a sergeant executed as a mutineer in 1779 after he and his fellow North Carolina soldiers had endured fifteen months without pay. In a protest to her state legislature, she asked, "What must the Feeling of the Man be who fought at Brandywine, at Germantown, and at Stony Point and did his duty, and when on another March in defence of his Country, with Poverty staring him full in the face, he was denied his Pay?" A veteran concluded, "As affairs are now going on, the common soldiers have nothing to expect, but that if America maintain her independency, they must become slaves to the rich."[66]

The post-1776 Continental Army belied the myth of heroic citizen-soldiers putting down the plow to pick up their muskets and win the war. In fact, a small regular army of poor men sustained the Patriot cause by enduring years of hard duty and public neglect. Although often initially conscripted, soldiers developed a commitment to the cause greater than their more fortunate neighbors who stayed home. Washington declared that "the unparalleled perseverance" of the soldiers "through almost every possible suffering and discouragement, for the space of eight long years, was little short of a standing Miracle." A Pennsylvania officer deemed the common soldiers "the best in the world Else they would Mutiny and Desert in Bodys. I think they have more virtue than half the Country." By enduring what civilians would not bear, Continental troops won the war so that others might enjoy the fruits of victory.[67]

All Her Mite

The Patriot war effort needed support from women. Because men especially sought to impress women, female patriotism could goad them into enlisting. When war broke out, a Philadelphia woman reported, "I will tell you what I have done. . . . My only brother I have sent to the American camp with my prayers and blessings. I hope he will not disgrace me." Rejecting domestic passivity, she considered herself a political influence in her household, and her brother had to match her commitment or disgrace the family.[68]

With so many men away fighting, wives and daughters had to run family farms and shops, or the economy would collapse. Women helped harvest and process the food and clothing that sustained Patriot forces. Rachel Wells noted, "If She did not fight She threw in all her mite which bought the Sogers food & Clothing & Let them have Blankets." Women even collected urine in chamber pots to help produce saltpeter, an essential but scarce component for making gunpowder. Many letters showed a growing confidence by women who had referred to the farm or shop as "his" but later began to call it "ours" or even "my farm" in letters to distant husbands.[69]

As women grew more self-assured, absent husbands did well to acknowledge a shifting balance in their relationships. One astute soldier ceased providing detailed instructions, "but must Leave all to your good Management," he assured his wife. Another man conceded, "This war which has so often & long separated us, has taught me how to value you." General Henry Knox proved a slower study, writing some hectoring letters that provoked his wife, Lucy Flucker Knox. Considering herself "quite a woman of business," she encouraged him to bring a new attitude when he returned home: "I hope you will not consider yourself as commander in chief of your own house—but be convinced . . . that there is such a thing as equal command."[70]

In 1780 in Philadelphia, genteel Patriot women led by Esther DeBerdt Reed and Sarah Franklin Bache raised funds for Washington's suffering troops. After organizing a committee of correspondence, they published an address, urging women in every county to organize a chapter, select a "treasuress," and solicit collections for forwarding to the wife of the governor in each state. Reaching out from Pennsylvania to New Jersey, Maryland, and Virginia, they created the first interstate women's organization. To collect money, they drew on both tradition and a new assertiveness. A Loyalist female critic complained that the Patriot activists "reminded" a reluctant man "of the extreme rudeness of refusing anything to the fair sex," and "at length they left him, after threatening to hand his name down to posterity with infamy." Benjamin Rush reported that his formerly apolitical wife had "distinguished herself by her zeal and address in this business, and is now so thoroughly enlisted in the cause of her country that she reproaches me with lukewarmness."[71]

Women raised about $340,000, which they submitted to Martha Washington for delivery to her husband, General Washington. The organizers wanted the troops to receive cash payments, but the general overruled them for fear that his men would spend it to get drunk. Instead, at his request, the women bought cloth and made 2,200 shirts. Each shirt bore the embroidered name of she who made it. Washington's intervention narrowed their initiative to a more traditional, domestic role.[72]

A few hundred women accompanied the Continental Army and drew rations and small pay as camp followers. Some were prostitutes, but most were soldiers' wives, often with young children. Poverty drove them to follow the army rather than starve at home. Washington complained that they slowed his army's march but conceded that some were "absolutely necessary," for they nursed the sick and wounded, prepared meals, cleaned hospitals, and did laundry. One regiment's women went on strike and obtained better pay for their work. Subject to court-martial, they could be whipped and ousted from camp for crimes.[73]

Genteel observers and officers despised camp women as dirty and disorderly. After the army passed through Philadelphia, a snooty gentleman complained, "These camp followers poured after their soldiers again, their hair flying, their brows beady with the heat, their belongings slung over one shoulder, chattering and yelling in sluttish shrills as they went and spitting in the gutters." But the army needed their help, and their presence kept husbands from deserting. When a sergeant's wife marched ahead of General Benedict Arnold on one especially brutal journey, he marveled, "Now Mrs. Grier had got before me. My mind was humbled, yet astonished, at the exertions of this good woman."[74]

During battle, camp women brought up food, water, and ammunition to refresh and resupply the troops. They also rushed forward to plunder enemy corpses of cash, watches, and clothing. Some joined the fighting by helping to load and fire cannon. In 1779. Congress granted a military pension to a woman who suffered a crippling wound and British capture in battle. Another received a pension from Virginia for her war service. On the frontier, many women took up arms to defend their homes against Indian attacks.[75]

A few women dressed and passed as men to enlist as full-time soldiers. Deborah Sampson of Massachusetts served as Robert Shurtleff for nearly two years, suffering a wound and winning a commendation. A nearly fatal fever subjected her to care by a doctor, who discovered her secret, which led to her discharge from the army. After the war, Sampson married, bore children, published her story, and won a veteran's pension (paid to her husband). She also became a public performer, reenacting her service in uniform for paying audiences.[76]

Other Patriot women served as spies. When British and Loyalist forces occupied their villages and farms, these women listened and watched carefully before slipping away to inform Patriot commanders of enemy numbers, positions, and plans. Mistaking women as uninformed and apolitical, British commanders spoke indiscreetly in their presence and let them pass on the roads. The officers should have known better, for they employed Loyalist women in the same role. One captured Patriot spy refused to give up any information, not even her name, so she died aboard a British prison ship known to her captors only as prisoner 355.[77]

In a brutal war that raged across the countryside, women endured the plundering and torching of their homes and many became impoverished refugees along with their children. Even if far from combat, women suffered from the absence of husbands and from an economy disrupted by shortages and hyperinflation. Military camps and marching troops also spread deadly epidemics. No previous war in British

America had brought so much misery to so many families. Suffering bred hatred. A Patriot girl assured a captured Hessian that she longed to tear out George III's heart to "fry it over these coals, and eat it."[78]

Traitor

Most American officers were the sons of merchants, lawyers, and land-speculators rather than true aristocrats, so they felt insecure about their honor and gentility. Prickly about any slight or insult, they avidly competed over pay, praise, and promotions. In Congress, Adams felt "wearied to Death with the Wrangles between military officers . . . Scrambling for Rank and Pay like Apes for Nuts." A French diplomat regarded the contention for rank as "an epidemic sickness among the Americans."[79]

Paid in increasingly worthless paper money, officers resented that so many speculators and contractors made fortunes at home. "I despise my Countrymen," insisted one officer. Another bluntly told Congress that, in a war fought "for Empire and Liberty" by "a people whose object is Property," the "army expects some of that property which the citizen seeks, and which the army protects for him." Continental officers envied their British counterparts assured of lifetime pensions at half pay after their service. Similar postwar pensions would, officers argued, partially compensate them for the inflation that consumed their paper salaries. Most congressmen, however, disdained pensions as corrupt marks of aristocratic privilege at odds with republican equality and selfless virtue. One complained that officers had "forgotten that this *was* in its beginnings a patriotic war." Washington warned Congress that many able but impatient officers would resign if denied pensions. In May 1778, Congress relented by approving pensions but for no more than seven years after the war.[80]

The promised pension was too little, too late for Captain Moore Fauntleroy, who despaired of Patriot victory as the economy verged on collapse. In 1779, he concluded, "Our affairs are as dark as they can be; & I really believe the game is up." He explained, "The whole continent

"Benedict Arnold," by a British engraver, 1781.
Courtesy of the Library of Congress (LC-USZ62-45217).

is starving. . . . The Continental money is not worth a curse, . . . everybody is tired; & those red-hot Virginians who were so violent [for revolution] are all crying out for Peace." Anticipating defeat, he sought to help it along by becoming a British spy.[81]

Benedict Arnold also was discontented, for his ambition never rested. Although a short man, Arnold was powerfully built and striking for his black hair, dark complexion, and light blue eyes. Born in Connecticut as the son of an alcoholic merchant of decaying fortune, Arnold longed to acquire wealth, prove his gentility, and assert superiority over others. Although an early Patriot, his hot temper, impa-

another American dream

tience, and self-assertion irritated his many rivals for promotion in the Continental Army. He raged when Congress instead advanced officers of less seniority and courage. Belatedly promoted to major general, Arnold won fame as an inspirational leader during the Saratoga campaign, but he quarreled bitterly with his theater commander, Gates, and suffered a crippling wound in his left leg.[82]

Slow to recuperate, Arnold could no longer serve in the field, so Washington gave him command of Philadelphia after the British evacuation in June 1778. Arnold courted an eighteen-year-old beauty, Margaret "Peggy" Shippen, the vivacious daughter of a wealthy judge with Loyalist leanings. The couple married in April 1779. Needing money to live grandly, Arnold engaged in shady business deals that exploited government wagons to move private goods. Irritated with his protégé, Washington reprimanded Arnold's conduct as "Imprudent and improper." Thin-skinned, Arnold brooded over every slight, which he regarded as rank injustice given his serious wounds suffered in the Patriot cause.[83]

He began to question the pursuit of independence. In starving soldiers, decaying currency, bankrupt treasuries, rampant profiteering, and public weariness, he discerned pervasive corruption. With so many of his countrymen cutting corners to make money, Arnold felt scapegoated for misusing a few wagons. Blaming the French alliance as the moral poison that had ruined the Patriot cause, he mourned Congress's rejection of the Carlisle Commission as a great, lost opportunity for reconciliation. Arnold concluded that "the Reunion of the British Empire, was the best and only means to dry up the streams of misery that have deluged this country."[84]

Feeding Arnold's resentments, Peggy urged him to seek greater justice and rewards with the British. She helped him open a covert correspondence with Major John André, who had been her friend during the British occupation of Philadelphia and later became General Clinton's spymaster. Through intermediaries, Arnold, André, and Clinton reached a deal in August 1780, when Arnold obtained a new command: of West Point, the pivotal fortification in the Patriot defenses on the

Hudson River north of New York City. In return for betraying the garrison and embracing Loyalism, Arnold would receive a whopping £20,000 payment, a lifetime pension of £500 annually, and a commission and command as a major general in the British service. Clinton hoped that such a high-profile defection would discredit Congress and initiate a cascading series of conversions that would doom the revolution. With Arnold's help, Clinton predicted that "the Rebellion would end suddenly in a Crash."[85]

In September 1780, a disguised André visited Arnold at West Point to make the final arrangements. On André's return journey, he was stopped and searched by Patriot scouts, who found incriminating documents written by Arnold. Learning of the capture, Arnold slipped away down the Hudson in a barge to reach a British warship. Delivering himself but not his post, Arnold received a cut-rate price from the British: £6,000 instead of £20,000. Still, he made more money from his service than did any other American general during the war.[86]

"Arnold has betrayed us! Whom can we trust now?" Washington demanded in confusion and rage. Unable to get his hands on the traitor, Washington settled for convicting and hanging André as a spy. Left behind by her fleeing husband, Peggy gave a masterful, wailing performance of utter shock and raving depression, which fooled Washington and his gallant officers, who pronounced her innocent of everything but great beauty. She left West Point for her father's home in Philadelphia but later slipped away to join her husband in New York.[87]

Arnold's shocking defection tormented Continental officers. "I cannot get Arnold out of my head," one confessed. If a great hero could betray the Patriot cause, who would be next? How extensive was the moral rot? To limit such demoralizing questions, Patriot leaders depicted Arnold as a uniquely desperate villain driven by a distinctive greed. Nathanael Greene declared, "How black, how despised, loved by none, and hated by all. Once his Country's Idol, now her horror." The Patriot press cast Arnold as an aberration, a satanic monster and perverse exception who proved a rule: that other Americans remained virtuous and true. By cursing Arnold and burning his effigy, Patri-

"The Unfortunate Death of Major André," engraving by John Goldar, 1783. This represents the execution on October 2, 1780, of Major John André as a spy by order of a Continental Army court-martial. Courtesy of the Library of Congress (LC-USZ62-52)

ots found reassurance that *they* would never betray their cause. Phil-adelphians staged the largest demonstration and most elaborate float, where a devil tempted and tormented a two-faced Arnold before all ended in a bonfire. Thousands turned out to hoot and holler, form-ing the largest gathering ever seen in the city. Clinton had hoped that Arnold's betrayal would discredit the Patriot cause and promote mass defections. Instead, the Patriots spun Arnold's betrayal as the consum-mate, but selfish and isolated, act of treason.[88]

In another transformation, the three capturing scouts, who were accomplished looters, became celebrated as, in Washington's words, "men of great virtue" because they resisted André's proffer of a bribe. In fact, they had calculated wisely, for they won silver medals and life-time pensions from Congress, which sought new heroes to replace the fallen general. Arnold's betrayal also benefited his fellow officers. In October 1780, Congress bolstered their allegiance by extending the promised pensions beyond seven years to become lifetime awards.[89]

While Arnold emerged as a Patriot monster, André became a British martyr, killed for serving his king and empire. An elegant and hand-some young man with talents as a poet, artist, and actor, André had been beloved by his fellow officers. In death, they exalted him as the finest gentleman in the world, a paragon who died with a brave and stoic dignity. Even common soldiers reviled the Patriots for killing the noblest of men. A British sergeant reported, "No language can describe the mingled sensations of horror, grief, sympathy, and revenge that agi-tated the whole garrison." George III awarded André's mother a pen-sion and knighted his brother. The Patriot degradation of Arnold and the British elevation of André worked together to sharpen national dis-tinctions, American versus British.[90] *distinct national identities*

Embers

In 1776, Adams had opposed a French military alliance for fear that Patriots would relax their own efforts and let their allies do the heavy lifting. That fear proved apt after 1778, as the war shifted south and the northern public grew weary of the financial and bloody burdens of the struggle. As their initial enthusiasm waned, many citizens tried to shunt the hazards and costs of war onto someone else. Meanwhile, Congress lost credibility as it failed to supply the soldiers or control rampant inflation. In early 1781, Congress lacked the funds even to publish its own proceedings.[91]

Starved for money and men, Washington's ragged little army usually remained on the defensive, playing the long game of attrition by necessity. Growing impatient, Vergennes sought more decisive measures to win the war quickly before French finances collapsed under the strain. In October 1780, a French officer serving as a Patriot general, the Marquis de Lafayette, warned Washington that the "French Court have often complained to me of the inactivity of that American Army, who before the alliance had distinguished themselves by their spirit of enterprise." French officials suspected that Patriots expected their partners to fight their battles for them. "I confess," Vergennes wrote to a friend, "I have only a feeble confidence in the energy of the United States."[92]

The American union seemed on the verge of collapse, which threatened to expose France to British retaliation. This compelled Vergennes to offer additional loans to Congress and send 5,000 troops under Comte de Rochambeau to bolster Washington. In July 1780, Clinton rued the French reinforcement: "Its arrival gave additional animation to the spirit of rebellion whose almost expiring embers began to blaze up fresh on its appearance." But Rochambeau cautioned Vergennes to expect little from the Americans: "Don't count on these people here."[93]

A View of the GUARD-HOUSE and SIMSBURY-MINES now called Newgate, A Prison for the Confinement of Loyalists in Connecticut

6

LOYALTIES

When once the Dogs of Civil War are let loose
it is no easy matter to Call them back.
—PIERCE BUTLER[1]

At the close of the war, we fought the enemy
with British soldiers; and they fought
us with those of America.
—NATHANAEL GREENE[2]

A popular myth casts the revolution as waged by a united American people against British rule. That myth derives from Patriot claims to speak for all true Americans, dismissing Loyalists as a deluded few corrupted by the British. A Patriot declared, "A Tory is a thing whose head is in England and its body in America, and its neck ought to be stretched" by hanging. After the revolution triumphed, nationalist historians endorsed the Patriot view, marginalizing or ignoring Loyalists to concoct a unifying American identity. In fact, the revolution divided families and neighborhoods. Benjamin

"A View of the Guard-House and Simsbury-Mines, Now Called Newgate—a Prison for the Confinement of Loyalists in Connecticut," engraving by J. Bew, 1781. This Loyalist print depicts the guardhouse aboveground with a shaft leading below, described as "opening the descent to Hell," which contains the dank and dark prison and mine. Courtesy of the Library of Congress (LC-USZ62-50390).

Franklin hated his son William for clinging to loyalty. In New York, Gouverneur Morris was a leading Patriot, but his brother served in the British army. Horatio Gates commanded an American army while his brother-in-law was a British officer. Pennsylvania's chief justice conceded that America "was not a nation at war with another nation, but a country in a state of *civil war.*"[3]

Revolutions breed civil wars: triangular struggles in which two sides compete for civilian support. British leaders wishfully believed that most colonists were Loyalists temporarily cowed by a minority of brazen and bullying rebels. "I may safely assert," General Howe reported, "that the insurgents are very few, in comparison with the whole of the people." Although committed Patriots were a minority outside of New England in 1775, Howe confused the colonial majority, which preferred to remain neutral, with committed Loyalists, who, in fact, were a minority even smaller than the Patriots.[4]

John Adams famously calculated that, at the start of the revolution, "We were about one third Tories, one third timid and one third true Blue." Adams overestimated the Loyalist proportion, which probably peaked early at a fifth of the population or about half the proportion of Patriots. He also undercounted the wavering, who comprised about two-fifths of the people.[5]

The wavering tried to stay out of the fight as the best means to protect their lives and property. Nathanael Greene noted that Carolina farmers were, "notwithstanding their danger, very intent upon their own private affairs." Mocking the wavering, Thomas Paine insisted, "Your conduct is an invitation to the enemy, yet not one in a thousand of you has heart enough to join them. Howe is as much deceived by you as the American cause is injured by you." In December 1776, Washington confessed that he did not "apprehend half so much danger from Howe's Army, as from the disaffection of the three States of New York, Jersey & Pensylvania."[6]

Patriots called them Tories, but alienated neutrals were better described as "disaffected." They wanted neither to pay taxes to Parliament nor submit to Patriot boycotts, new oaths, militia service, impressed livestock, and depreciating money. A New York farmer and writer, John Hector St. John de Crèvecoeur, satirically observed: "We have so many more masters than we used to have. There is the high and mighty Congress, and there is our Governor, and our Senators, and our Assemblymen, and there is our captain of Light Horse . . . and there are the honorable committee[men]. And there are, let me see, one, two, three, four, five commissaries who want nothing but our horses, grain, hay, etc." Crèvecoeur denounced the Patriots as "malevolent men who have set the world to gaze at the majestic Tree of Liberty, which they pretend to have planted, whilst they are cultivating . . . the most poisonous weeds." Patriots demanded far more from common people than Parliament ever had.[7]

Longing to be left alone, the disaffected resented both sides but clashed more often with the Patriots, who demanded more of them. Crèvecoeur regarded the conflict as a bloody tragedy provoked by greedy leaders: "The innocent class are always the victims of the few. . . . It is for the sake of the great leaders on both sides that so much blood must be spilt; that of the people is counted as nothing. Great events are not achieved for us, though it is by us that they are principally accomplished, by the arms, the sweat, [and] the lives of the people."[8]

For refusing to take a Patriot oath, Crèvecoeur suffered jail and fines. In February 1779, he fled to British-occupied New York City and found work as a surveyor, but other Loyalists suspected Crèvecoeur of spying for the Patriots, so he landed in a rat-infested jail for three months, until cleared. In one of Crèvecoeur's stories, a disaffected man laments that "we should be thus suspended between poverty, neglect, and contempt if we go to New York, and fines, imprisonment, and exile if we stay!"[9]

Choices

By sorting Americans into Loyalists and Patriots, we suggest that individuals made quick and definitive decisions based on political principles. Some did, but many more committed slowly, reluctantly, and provisionally. In one North Carolina county, the vaguely divided militiamen decided to cast their united lot based on the result of a fistfight between a Loyalist and a Patriot. Choosing sides in a civil war was painful and confusing for rural folk, who rarely read a pamphlet or saw a newspaper. People balked at the risks of clear allegiance: exposing their farms to looters, suffering the hardships of a military camp or political prison, or killing others and risking death in combat.[10]

Although remembered as just a few elitists, Loyalists included a broad array of common people from diverse backgrounds and with varying motives. Most people chose sides based on relationships with neighbors and kin, bonding with those of similar faith and ethnicity and against those who differed. Loyalism or disaffection was especially strong in regions with the greatest ethnic and cultural diversity and contention: New Jersey, New York, Pennsylvania, and the backcountry of the Carolinas. A writer noted that New Jersey had "almost every religious persuasion under heaven. . . . They were like so many jarring elements pent up together." Add competing armies moving through and you have a formula for the bitter divisions of civil war.[11]

In the most common pattern, Loyalists belonged to local minorities who feared living in a republican society where a distrusted majority could dominate them. Unpopular and harassed by their neighbors, the Scots in North Carolina and Virginia rallied to the king as their protector. Anglicans and Quakers dreaded falling under the sway of their more numerous Congregationalist and Presbyterian rivals, who were early and staunch Patriots. A New Jersey Loyalist explained, "The Presbyterians were Striving to Get the Rule into their own hands And that he Never Wold be Subject to a Presbyterian Government." Held prisoner in a Patriot camp, a South Carolina Loyalist had to listen to "a Presbyterian sermon truly adapted to the rebels' principles and the times; or, rather, stuffed as full of Republicanism as their camp is of horse thieves."[12]

Political choices were often unstable and temporary. The ebb and flow of victory and defeat in a long war flipped many people from one side to another and sometimes back again with sojourns along the way in the broad ranks of the wavering. Many profited by selling their produce or services to the likely victors: a probability which changed as one force surged at the expense of the other. More often, people acted defensively, switching sides to save farms and lives from the power of the ascendant party. Paine complained of the many Pennsylvanians "who are changing to whig and tory with the circumstances of every day."[13]

Patriots appeared loud and numerous until a British army swept into a county; when Loyalism suddenly surfaced and surged. A Loyalist explained: "We are at present all Whigs until the arrival of the King's troops." Formerly "a good Liberty Man," Robert Weir defected when the British invaded his neighborhood, reasoning that "he'd be with the Strongest party." But Loyalists also lapsed. The Earl of Carlisle noted that thousands welcomed victorious British troops to a particular region, "but no sooner our situation was the least altered for the worse, but these friends were the first to fire upon us." A British captain warned a superior, "They swallow the Oaths of Allegiance to the King and Congress Alternately with as much ease as your Lordship does poached Eggs."[14]

Many common soldiers deserted from one side to join the other especially if captured and facing the alternative of prison. Struck by the rampant two-way desertions, General Nathanael Greene noted, "At the close of the war, we fought the enemy with British soldiers; and they fought us with those of America." Greene experienced a war very different from the popular history version of a united and resolute American people committed through thick and thin to the revolution.[15]

Outnumbering the Loyalists, the disaffected included Methodists, Quakers, or German pietists (Amish, Dunkers, and Mennonites) with religious commitments to pacifism. Giving priority to godly matters, they insisted that Christians should avoid political strife, and they saw no good or just reason for revolution. In January 1776, Philadelphia's leading Quakers declared "that the setting up, and putting down [of] kings and governments, is God's peculiar prerogative; . . . and that it is not our business, to have any hand or contrivance therein; nor to be busy bodies above our station, much less to plot and contrive the ruin, or overturn of any of them, but to pray for the king, and safety of our nation, and good of all men." When pressed to say what side he supported, one man answered, "I am for peace."[16]

Patriot militiamen resented religious pacifists for avoiding military hardships, and Patriot leaders worried that draft dodgers would claim faith as their loophole. So Patriots treated pacifists as crypto-Loyalists subject to heavy fines, imprisonment, and impressment of their livestock, blankets, and wagons. Rocks or clubs smashed their windows if they failed to put candles in them to celebrate Patriot victories.[17]

Others became disaffected from a populist resentment of leading Patriots as greedy exploiters. In Maryland, Robert Gassaway argued that "it was better for the poor people to lay down their arms and pay the duties and taxes laid upon them by King and Parliament than to be brought into slavery and to be commanded and ordered about as they were." In North Carolina, a defiant and folksy Baptist preacher declared, "Shew him a great man with [a] half moon in his hatt and Liberty Rote on it and . . . he would Shew you a devil and the poor men was bowing and Sc[r]aping to them . . . that he did not value the Congress nor Commitye no more than a passel of Rackoon Dogs."[18]

Repression

During the period 1774 to 1776, Patriots seized control of almost all the printing presses and militia units. As in other revolutions, a committed and organized minority led the way, demanded that others follow, and punished those who balked. In a hard fight against a powerful empire, Patriots refused to tolerate doubters and critics in their midst. "Those who are not for us are against us," they insisted. Toasting the king or singing "God Save the King" at a tavern sufficed to attract prosecution and persecution. In Massachusetts, a man got in trouble for calling committeemen "a set of idiots and lunaticks." "Join or die!" militiamen told the wavering. "I would have hanged my own brother had he taken part with our enemy in the contest," declared John Adams. To win the civil war, Patriots needed to silence Loyalists and compel at least grudging support from the disaffected.[19]

Dissidents faced intense pressure from committees and mobs to take Patriot oaths and serve in their militias. Patriots shunned dissidents. "I never knew how painful it is to be secluded from the free conversation of one's friends," a Pennsylvanian lamented. In South Carolina, a Loyalist complained that he and his friends faced ruin because they were "not allowed the Liberty to pass over any Ferry, nor deal in any Store, nor have their Corn ground at any Mill: they are not allowed to purchase Salt to eat with their Provisions, [and] their Estates are threat[e]ned to be taken from them."[20]

When social pressure failed, Patriots resorted to violence. At night, they fired into the homes of dissidents, toppled fences, and smashed windows. Sometimes, they broke in to drag out a man for tarring and feathering before forcing him to ride atop a sharp rail as a fifer and drummer played the rogue's march for his parade through a mocking community. In Virginia in 1775, a teacher noted, "'Tar and Feathers with their necessary Appendages, *Scoff and Shame*, are *popular* Terrors, and of great Influence." In Georgia, Thomas Brown refused to sign the Continental Association. Patriots knocked him unconscious with the butt end of a musket, tied him to a tree, tarred his legs, and set them on fire, which cost him two toes. After partially scalping Brown, they carted him through the streets for public ridicule. By abusing and shaming Loyalists as despised outsiders, rituals of intimidation helped draw wavering neighbors into the Patriot ranks.[21]

Thanks to superior communication and coordination across counties and colonies, Patriots could bring overwhelming force to bear on pockets of disaffection. In November 1775, the people of Queens County on Long Island voted against supporting New York's Provincial Congress. Deeming them "incapable of resolving to live and die [as] freemen," the Provincial Congress sent Continental troops to disarm them and arrest their leaders.[22]

Where Patriots controlled the courts, sheriffs, and jails, they treated

Loyalists as criminals, and an eighteenth-century jail was a grim place to languish. Disease or insanity frequently claimed shivering and starving inmates. Connecticut cast accused dissidents into the Simsbury copper mines, "the Catacomb of Loyalism," where they had to live and work in dank darkness forty yards below ground. Meanwhile, farms and families suffered from the incarceration of a father or son. When released, a Loyalist often returned home to find it looted and burned and his family scattered. Some courts had Loyalists branded on the face or cut off their ears so that Patriots could recognize enemies in their midst. "Your law is treason and your government is treason," declared a defiant Loyalist.[23]

State laws heavily fined and denied political rights to those who refused to take Patriot oaths, serve in a Patriot militia, or accept payment in paper money. States banned suspected Loyalists and the disaffected from practicing law, preaching, printing, and teaching. Some laws ruined Loyalists by barring them from collecting on debts owed by Patriots. States confiscated the properties of Loyalists who ran away to join the British. Declared outlaws, the refugees faced the death penalty if they came home to try to save their estates. Jonathan Sewell lamented, "My pew in the church is converted into a pork tub; my house into a den of rebels, thieves & lice; my farm in possession of the very worst of all God's creation; my few debts all gone to the devil with my debtors." Losing her coach to a Patriot, Grace Galloway had to walk through the streets of Philadelphia "like a common Woman." She fantasized that somehow and someday "all will be right yet & I shall ride when these Harpies walk as they Use[d] to do." Usually sold at rock-bottom prices, confiscated properties helped the Patriots to "interest" buyers in the success of the revolution, for its defeat would cost them their bargains.[24]

Persecution drove some waverers into an overt and active Loyalism. Where they were the local majority, the disaffected formed armed bands, toasted the king, toppled liberty poles, refused militia service, and harassed their foes. Organized disaffection prevailed on the Eastern Shore of Maryland and in adjoining southern Delaware. A Patriot sheriff declared that "two thirds of the people are Tories in spirit if not in action." Another Patriot (or "Whig") reported that on an election day, "As soon as they had collected, they began in their usual strain of drinking prosperity to King George and damning the whigs and swearing there was not rebel[s] enough in town to take them up." A committeeman felt disgusted that such poor men would defy their Patriots betters: "With a poor wretched hut crowded with children, naked, hungry and miserable without bread or a penny of money to buy any. . . . Yet, these are the wretches, who set up to be the arbiters of government; to knock down independence and restore the authority of the British King in Parliament."[25]

More often, the disaffected laid low and pretended to support Congress. Nicholas Cresswell confessed, "I am obliged to act the hypocrite and extol these proceedings [of Congress] as the wisest productions of any assembly on Earth, but in my heart I despise them." Another Loyalist lamented the Patriots' skill at swaying the wavering majority: "The Congress use every art in the world to bring over the disaffected to espouse their cause. They hang the turbulent, imprison the dangerous, fine the wealthy. They allure the ambitious with the hopes of preferment and distribute [confiscated] estates to [them]."[26]

Only the highly principled or utterly foolish openly defied Patriots where they were powerful. In Richmond, Virginia, a shoemaker confronted Continental troops marching through town in 1777. Bolting out of his shop, he shouted "Hurrah for King George!" General Francis Nash had his troops seize the malcontent and dunk him in the James River, but a witness reported, "every time he got his head above water he would cry for King George." An exasperated Nash ordered the shoemaker tarred and feathered while his wife and daughters were "crying and beseeching their father to hold his tongue . . . but still [he] would hurrah for King George." At last, he ran away when the general threatened to have him shot.[27]

"British Heroism," engraving by Elkanah Tisdale, 1795. *A Patriot artist mocks British troops for plundering American farms. Courtesy of the Library of Congress (LC USZ62-51679).*

Zones

Popular history books dwell on the big battles between formal armies and treat the conflict as relatively restrained. That approach neglects the broader and more vicious war conducted by many small raiding parties, composed of a mix of regulars and irregulars, militia and bandits. They ravaged farms and towns to take forage, livestock, clothing, and silver, and they kidnapped or killed the partisans of the other side. Swirling around the army camps, this array of "nasty little raids, ambushes, and encounters" ruined thousands of civilians.[28]

Hungry and cold soldiers cut down orchards and toppled fences for firewood; stole poultry and killed livestock for food; and looted and burned houses and barns. Some troops had the cover of official orders to strip a region of livestock and extra blankets to deny them to the enemy. Patriot and Loyalist officers gave certificates promising eventual payment, but farmers could rarely collect, so they saw no difference between impressment and looting. A Patriot officer confessed, "Any Army, even a friendly one, if any can be called so, are a dreadful Scourge to any People—you cannot conceive what Devastation and Distress mark their Steps." General Greene considered it "impossible to carry on a war without oppressing the inhabitants."[29]

The greatest sufferers lived in contested "neutral zones" around British strongholds, particularly within fifty miles of New York City in eastern New Jersey, southern New York, and southeastern Connecticut. In those lawless zones, raiders from both sides and freelancing bandits looted the farmers. Reverend Timothy Dwight, a Patriot chaplain, pitied the civilians of Westchester County, New York:

> Their furniture was extensively plundered or broken to pieces. The walls, floors, and windows were injured both by violence and decay, and were not repaired because they had not the means of repairing them, and because they were exposed to the repetition of the same injures. Their cattle were gone. Their [fences] were burnt where they were capable of becoming fuel, and in many cases

thrown down where they were not. Their fields were covered with a rank growth of weeds and wild grass.

Robbers completed their ruin by torturing farmers to reveal hidden caches of money. The people of Westchester experienced the revolution as a disaster.[30]

hate both sides

Many farmers wished a pox on both sides. Dwight reported that the Westchester folk "feared everybody who they saw and loved nobody. . . . To every question they gave such an answer as would please the inquirer; or, if they despaired of pleasing, such a one as would not provoke him. Fear apparently was the only passion by which they were animated." In harm's way, the people in contested zones learned to have no politics or to keep them better hidden than their money.[31]

Although both armies committed atrocities, British and Hessian misdeeds did more damage to their cause. Sniped at by militiamen who emerged from the civilian population, British soldiers soon despised and distrusted every American as, in the words of one officer, "crafty, skulking, [and] assassinating." Seeking revenge, Britons looted and burned the homes of potential friends as well as certain foes. And Patriots were masterful at turning enemy brutalities into vivid stories to demonize the British. Possessing less skilled polemicists and fewer printing presses, Loyalists faltered in the competition to convert atrocities into compelling propaganda.[32]

The savvier British officers recognized that they had to win a civil war. General James Robertson explained, "I never had an idea of subduing the Americans; I meant to assist the good Americans subdue the bad." But many Britons struggled to tell the good from the bad Americans, preferring to distrust and plunder them all. British commanders treated even leading Loyalists as fickle subordinates rather than as reliable partners. When military expeditions failed, British commanders made Loyalists into scapegoats, blamed for failing to rally in sufficient numbers to help the redcoats. In turn, Loyalists felt misused and slighted by obtuse Britons, who disappointed expectations as liberators and protectors.[33]

Loyalists urged commanders quickly to restore civil law and government in liberated regions so that the empire could prove that it
better protected lives and property than did Patriot committees and
mobs. Lord Germain favored restoring civil administration in pacified
zones, but he deferred to British commanders, who clung to martial
law. They feared that civil courts and an elected assembly would complicate military operations and the policing of occupied towns. Commanders wanted no magistrates to interfere with officers impressing
horses, wagons, and supplies or imprisoning suspected spies. In sum,
British generals gave priority to winning the war over restoring civil
government and law in the colonies. In vain Loyalists protested that
martial law would lose the war by alienating Americans who cherished
rule by civil law.[34]

Loyalists had rallied to the empire as a font of constitutional law
and order only to discover that British generals would not compromise their martial power. Driven from their homes by Patriot mobs
and committees, Loyalists had to make the best of their bad bargain
in occupied New York City. Severely damaged by the fire of September 1776, much of the city became a crowded, filthy, and sickly shan-
tytown for thousands of refugees fleeing from Patriot persecution in
the countryside. British officers and officials claimed the best remaining homes, often at the expense of loyal owners, while rents rose to
four times their prewar levels, compounding the poverty and irrita-
tion of the refugees.[35]

For want of civil justice, civilians suffered abuse, theft, and rape by
the worst redcoats. A disgusted Loyalist concluded, "This robbing was
done by people sent to America to protect loyalists against the persecution and depredations of Rebels." General Howe conceded "that it
was not in the power of a few officers to keep the men under proper
restraint." Generals often issued new orders against abuses but rarely
could catch (or would punish) culprits, whom they needed to fight the
war. Some commanders found the abuses more amusing than criminal. On British-occupied Staten Island, Lord Rawdon reported, "A girl
cannot step into the bushes to pluck a rose without running the most

imminent risk of being ravished, and they are so little accustomed to these vigorous methods that they don't bear them with proper resignation, and of consequence we have the most entertaining courtsmartial every day."[36]

Many British officers also expressed contempt for Loyalists. General Howe's secretary complained, "Alas, they all prate & profess much; but when you call upon them they will do nothing." Britons wanted to manipulate rather than empower leading Loyalists like William Franklin and Joseph Galloway. British commanders were also slow to enlist Loyalist troops, disdaining colonists as military amateurs averse to discipline and cowardly in combat. "Provincials, if not sustained by regular troops are not to be trusted," General Clinton explained. During the early campaigns of 1775 to 1777, British commanders relied on redcoats and Hessians, authorizing only a handful of Loyalist units.[37]

In 1778, when Lord Germain withdrew thousands of regulars from New York for service elsewhere, the shorthanded Clinton had to recruit more Loyalist troops. In New York City, enlistment appealed to refugees, who could find no other work and welcomed the pay, steady rations, and decent clothing of British military service. Recruiters also promised them at least 50 acres (later raised to 200) of land in some colony after the war. By 1781, the British employed at least 10,000 Loyalists: comparable to the numbers then in George Washington's Continental Army besieging New York.[38]

Although Loyalists usually fought well, British generals often employed them as laborers and teamsters rather than rely upon them in battle. Disgusted by British restraint and slights, many Loyalists joined irregular bands that operated independently to raid and burn Patriot farms and villages. Unpaid, these raiders profited by selling their loot, especially horses and cattle. They included a former New Jersey slave named Titus who escaped to join the British in New York City. Adopting the name "Colonel Tye," he rallied a mixed-race gang, which stole horses and attacked Patriot militiamen until 1780, when he died in a raid on his home county.[39]

Rather than treat Loyalists as prisoners of war who could be exchanged, Patriots often prosecuted and executed them as horse thieves, spies, traitors, murderers, and burglars. In Virginia, Patriots whipped Loyalists until they shouted "Liberty Forever" and pledged allegiance to the new order. Suspects also could be hoisted by their thumbs or hung by the neck until near death or past it. In 1778, on Easter Sunday in Gloucester County, New Jersey, Patriot militiamen disturbed religious services by whipping to death a captured Loyalist. In Monmouth County, New Jersey, the farm of a Patriot militia general became known as "the Hanging Place," after he executed a dozen of his enemies. For hanging Loyalists after quick, mock trials, Colonel Charles Lynch of Virginia turned his name into a verb.[40]

Loyalists wanted to retaliate against captured Patriots, but British commanders refused lest the Patriots execute imprisoned redcoats. In exchanging prisoners, the generals also preferred to retrieve Britons rather than Loyalists, who resented the double standard that treated them as inferior to redcoats. Captain Richard Lippincott protested, "If I took a Rebel Prisoner, he was subject to be exchanged, according to the Laws of war and of Nations. If I should happen to have fallen into the hands of Rebels, my life was subject to be taken, as a Rebel to a Rebel state." Champions of traditional law and order, Loyalists bristled at their treatment as rebels by the real rebels.[41]

Deposed as New Jersey's royal governor and arrested in June 1776, William Franklin was embittered by harsh imprisonment—and by the death of his wife during his absence. Exchanged in 1778, he chafed under General Clinton's restraints on the Loyalists in New York City. In the fall of 1779, Franklin organized a militant association that sought command of Loyalist troops and the prisoners they took. The Associated Loyalists wanted to control captured Patriots as leverage to protect their own people held by the enemy. More Loyalists would survive captivity if Patriots feared retribution.[42]

Late in the war, members of the Associated Loyalists captured a Patriot militia captain, Joshua Huddy, who had plundered and executed Loyalists in New Jersey. Rather than turn Huddy over to the

British, Franklin ordered him executed by Captain Lippincott. On the New Jersey shore, Lippincott left the dangling corpse with a placard for Patriots to read:

> We the Reffugees having with Greif Long beheld the Cruel Murders of our Brethren and finding Nothing [done] . . . We therefore Determine not to Suffer without takeing Vengeance for numerous Cruelties and thus begin and have made use of Capt. Huddy as the first Object to present to your Views, and Further *Determine* to Hang Man for Man as Long as a Reffugee is Left Existing.

Washington demanded that Clinton surrender Lippincott for trial by the Patriots. Clinton was tempted, for he regarded the execution as an affront to his authority, but he instead had the captain tried by a British court-martial. Acquitted, Lippincott fled to Canada. Washington nearly executed a British officer in retaliation for Huddy's death but ultimately held back, perhaps because the British disbanded the Associated Loyalists and sent Franklin off to exile in England.[43]

South

In 1778, Lord Germain retrenched British military operations in the northern colonies and ordered a partial shift southward by the army. In Georgia and South Carolina, Germain hoped to find and recruit many more Loyalists. With British regulars in short and shrinking supply, the empire relied more heavily on American support where it still could be found. "[The] Assistance of the Loyal Inhabitants is essential to the Success of all Operations," Germain explained. In the South, Britons also expected to cultivate more native allies, particularly Cherokees, Chickasaws, and Choctaws. In addition, the enslaved could become a liability for the Patriots and an asset for the British. While the invaders drew upon runaways for recruits, Patriots would have to reserve men to guard their slaves, reducing the troops available to resist invasion. With the threat of blacks and Indians, the British

— THE SOUTHERN STATES, 1780 —

Chesapeake Bay

Richmond

VIRGINIA

Yorktown

Roanoke R.

Albemarle Sound

Guilford
Courthouse

NORTH CAROLINA

CHEROKEE

Neuse R.

New Bern

APPALACHIAN MOUNTAINS

Hannah's Cowpens

King's Mountain

Cape Fear R.

CATAWBA

Ninety-Six

Camden

Pee Dee R.

Wilmington

SOUTH CAROLINA

Santee R.

Augusta

Eutaw Springs

Savannah R.

Charles Town

UPPER
CREEK

Ocmulgee R.

Oconee R.

GEORGIA

Savannah

ATLANTIC
OCEAN

Chattahoochee R.

LOWER
CREEK

Flint R.

St. Marys R.

Apalachicola R.

Saint Augustine

FLORIDA

St. Johns R.

Gulf of
Mexico

0 Miles   100   200

0 Kilometers   200

© 2015 Jeffrey L. Ward

hoped to intimidate southern Patriot leaders into quick submission. John Stuart, the British Indian agent, had noted, "Nothing can be more alarming" to southern whites "than the Idea of an Attack from Indians and Negroes."[44] *b/c it wld be revenge + therefore no mercy consequence*

But British commanders underestimated the incompatibility of the racial elements in their southern coalition, for white Loyalists distrusted Indians and wanted to keep blacks enslaved. Loyalists and Indians preferred to take slaves as plunder rather than liberate them as brethren. Out to suppress a rebellion, the British balked at making their own revolution to emancipate all of the enslaved or to protect native lands.[45]

Slavery in revolution The British treated some blacks as allies but most as property. In their contradictory southern strategy, Britons wanted to undermine slavery where it benefited Patriots but to bolster it in Loyalist districts. While enticing slaves away from Patriot owners, the British forced runaways to return to Loyalist masters. British officers even sent troops to suppress slave strikes on Loyalist-owned plantations by whipping the leaders. Some officers also sold blacks taken as plunder from Patriot plantations. Rather than destroy plantation slavery, the British sought to capture it. Germain targeted the Deep South for recovery because Georgia and South Carolina were so valuable for their profitable export crops of indigo and rice. If only some mainland colonies could be saved from revolution, let them be Georgia and South Carolina. Primarily seeking support from whites, the British were ambivalent and limited liberators of blacks.[46]

Most slaves stayed put on their farms and plantations because they feared execution if captured by Patriots, dreaded revenge taken on their families left behind, or worried about losing precious ties to their kin. A plantation mistress, Eliza Lucas Pinckney, noted that the enslaved were "attached to their homes and the little they have." Many also wondered how they would fare with the British in dirty and sickly military encampments, where hundreds died of smallpox, dysentery, and typhus. Boston King, a Carolina runaway, recalled that he felt "much grieved at first, to be obliged to leave my friends, and reside among strangers." Only slowly did he begin to "feel the happiness of liberty"—of the limited sort allowed to blacks by the British.[47]

By exploiting the turmoil of war, many slaves did claim greater autonomy on their plantations. Pinckney complained that her slaves became "insolent and quite their own masters." Rather than raise market crops, such as rice, for masters, many slaves tended their own gardens to ensure survival in troubled times. But persistent slaves also risked falling prey to roaming partisans and bandits who stole human beings for resale.[48]

Despite the dangers and uncertainty, thousands of enslaved people did flee to the invaders. Banastre Tarleton concluded, "Upon the approach of any detachment of the King's troops, all negroes, men, women, and children . . . thought themselves absolved from all respect to their American masters, and . . . they quitted the plantations and followed the army." Other slaves ran away, seized guns, and formed gangs of bandits to plunder their former plantations. A British officer exulted that the "Negroes who flock to the conquerors . . . do ten thousand times more Mischief than the whole Army put together."[49]

But they could have done far more damage to the Patriots if the British had deployed them more aggressively as soldiers. In the Deep South, British commanders proved less daring than Lord Dunmore had been in 1775. While he had recruited black soldiers, his successors in Georgia and the Carolinas usually deployed runaways as laborers or as foraging irregulars. In return for wages, runaways built earthworks, drove wagons, washed clothes, and served as orderlies and nurses in hospitals. By failing to train more black troops for combat, the British lost their best chance to win the war in the South. Indeed, half measures proved worse than none at all, for the few blacks armed by the British sufficed to outrage southern whites. General Thomas Sumter insisted that armed blacks aroused "the resentment and detestation of every American."[50]

Patriots rallied popular support by associating the British with slaves, bandits, and Indians. With characteristics hyperbole, Thomas Lynch damned the British for calling "in Savages to ravage our frontiers—to

massacre our defenceless women—and children—offers every incite-
ment to our Slaves to rebel—and murder their masters." Henry Laurens agreed, "While Men of War & Troops are to attack us in front, the
Indians are to make inroads on our backs—Tories & Negro Slaves to
rise in our Bowels." Although insufficient to intimidate Patriots, the
limited British outreach to Indians and blacks was more than enough
to outrage most southern whites.[51]

In late 1778, General Clinton began the southern invasion by sending 3,000 troops in ships from New York to Georgia. The weakest
and most vulnerable of Patriot states, Georgia had a long frontier with
native peoples, and the small free population of about 18,000 feared their
15,000 slaves. Reinforced by 2,000 British and Loyalist troops from East
Florida, the expedition seized Savannah, the capitol and major seaport
of Georgia. A runaway slave had revealed a path through the swamps,
enabling the British to surprise and rout the 1,800 defenders.[52]

During the next year, the British consolidated their hold on Georgia. In January 1779, Lieutenant Colonel Archibald Campbell advanced
up the Savannah River to Augusta, finding little resistance and attracting many armed supporters. Campbell boasted, "I have got the Country in arms against the Congress" and "ripped one star and one stripe
from the rebel flag of America." In October 1779, the British and Loyalists also repelled an attack on Savannah by Continentals, led by General Benjamin Lincoln, supported by French troops and a fleet led
by the Comte d'Estaing. After suffering heavy casualties, the French
sailed back to the West Indies while Lincoln retreated to Charles Town.
The victory gave British General Charles Grey new hope that the war
could be won in America: "It is the first time I have seen day light in
this business." At last, it seemed, the British had found the soft under-
belly of the Patriot rebellion.[53]

Black Troops

The British conquest of Georgia inspired some Patriots to promote
a desperate countermeasure: arming some slaves with the promise of

freedom upon completing their service. With so few white men volunteering for Continental service, it seemed foolish to turn away black people eager to fight for their freedom. In 1775, the New England states enlisted 200 blacks, but Washington forbade recruiting any more. He subscribed to the prevailing, although contradictory, conviction that black people were too cowardly to fight and, yet, that training them as soldiers menaced white domination. A Pennsylvania captain declared that black soldiers "had a disagreeable, degrading effect" on the army. General Philip Schuyler of New York, a slave owner, asked whether it was "consistent with the Sons of Freedom to trust their all to be defended by slaves."[54]

In January 1778, to bolster his undermanned army, Washington belatedly endorsed plans by the New England states to recruit the enslaved, promise them eventual freedom, and compensate their masters. Taking the lead, Rhode Island raised a regiment with a black majority but white officers. Describing the black soldiers as "merry, confident, and sturdy," a French officer praised the Rhode Island regiment as "the most neatly dressed, the best under arms, and the most precise in its maneuvers." By the end of the war, blacks comprised a tenth of the Continental Army, serving at a rate double that of their proportion in the northern population. The strain of a long war compelled Patriots to adopt bolder measures than they had intended when the conflict began, and northern blacks seized the chance to seek freedom through military service.[55]

The courage of black troops impressed John Laurens, a Continental officer who saw them repulse veteran Hessian troops in Rhode Island in August 1778. Laurens seemed an unlikely proponent of black freedom, for his father, Henry Laurens, had bought and sold more than 10,000 slaves in his sordid career. But John was young, idealistic, educated in Europe, and open to new ideas. He concluded, "I think we Americans, at least in the Southern Colonies, cannot contend with a *good grace*, for Liberty, until we have enfranchised our Slaves." He hated hearing "the Groans of despairing multitudes toiling for the Luxuries of Merciless Tyrants."[56]

Handsome, brave, and dashing, Laurens impressed Washington, who brought him onto his staff. In February 1779, Laurens proposed enlisting of slaves in the South: "It will be my duty and my pride to transform the timid Slave into a firm defender of Liberty and render him worthy to enjoy it himself." Laurens blamed the degradation of slaves on their treatment rather than their race. If provided with equal opportunity, he reasoned, they could improve their character and condition. He also sought to redeem white Americans by providing "the glory of triumphing over deep rooted national prejudices."[57]

The British victory at Savannah and threat to Charles Town persuaded Henry Laurens to support his son's plan as essential to save the Patriot cause in the South. He assured Washington that "had we Arms for 3000 such black men as I could select in Carolina I should have no doubt of success in driving the British out of Georgia & subduing East Florida before the end of July." While promising support to John Laurens, Washington privately expressed qualms to Henry Laurens: that freeing and arming some slaves would breed dangerous resentments among the rest, inviting bloody revolts. Although Washington had come around to enlisting northern blacks, he feared recruiting them in the South as too risky.[58]

In May 1779, Congress endorsed the Laurens plan and recommended that South Carolina and Georgia arm 3,000 slaves, who would receive no wartime pay, only their freedom and $50 if they survived the conflict. Congress promised to compensate owners for the value of their slaves who enlisted. General Lincoln endorsed the plan because it promised to relieve hundreds of common white militiamen from having to serve.[59]

South Carolina legislators, however, overwhelmingly rejected the proposal as a threat to their way of life. Christopher Gadsden declared, "We are much disgusted here at Congress recommending [to] us to arm our Slaves; it was received with great resentment, as a very dangerous and impolitic Step." Fearing their own blacks more than the redcoats, masters insisted that training and freeing some slaves would inspire the rest to kill their masters. And few common whites wished to serve

beside blacks as their military equals. As a stark alternative, legislators sought to enlist more white men by promising each a bounty that
included a slave paid for by the state. If they had to lose any slaves, Carolinians wanted them to become the property of other white men.[60]

Writing to his son, Henry Laurens noted, "I learn your black Air
Castle is blown up with contemptuous huzzas." He consoled John that
it was "certainly a great task effectually to persuade Rich Men to part
willingly with the very source of their wealth." Despite his private
qualms about the plan, Washington similarly assured John, "I must
confess that I am not at all astonished at the failure of your Plans. That
Spirit of Freedom, which at the commencement of this contest would
have gladly sacrificed everything to the attainment of its object, has
long since subsided and every selfish Passion has taken its place." The
long, hard war had amplified Americans' vices at the expense of their
virtue.[61]

Home to more than half the slaves in the new nation and menaced by British raids, Virginia considered raising black troops in late
1780. As in South Carolina, however, Virginia's legislators preferred
to bolster the slave system by offering each white recruit a slave along
with 100 acres of land. The offer appalled James Madison, who asked:
"Would it not be as well to liberate and make soldiers at once of the
blacks themselves as to make them instruments for enlisting white
Soldiers? It w[oul]d certainly be more consonant to the principles of
liberty which ought never to be lost sight of in a contest for liberty."
But few Virginians shared Madison's premise that all men were created equal. Instead, the state legislators promoted white solidarity in
racial supremacy as the antidote to class tensions between poor and
rich whites.[62]

Despite the new inducements, few whites enlisted to fill Virginia's
quota in the Continental Army. Farmers and their sons preferred to
stay home to tend their crops. When drafted to serve, some sent slaves
as substitutes, promising freedom to those who survived the war. Desperate for soldiers, Virginia's leaders reluctantly accepted about 500
enslaved substitutes.[63]

Carolinas

In early 1780, General Clinton assembled 12,500 troops, drawn from New York and Savannah, to attack Charles Town. To defend the city, General Lincoln had only 5,100 men, half Continentals and half militia (and no armed African Americans). On May 12, after suffering British artillery bombardment, Lincoln surrendered the city and his starving men in the greatest disaster suffered by Patriot forces during the war. An amused British officer described the surrender ceremony: "Lincoln limp'd out at the Head of the most ragged Rabble I ever beheld."[64]

Patriot support in South Carolina virtually collapsed. In Charles Town, two hundred gentlemen welcomed the British for liberating them from "a rank democracy" that had exercised a "tyrannic domination, only to be found among the uncivilized part of mankind." In the backcountry, a militia regiment seized their officers and marched into Charles Town to surrender them to the British. The hundreds who took a British oath of allegiance included Henry Middleton, who had presided over the Continental Congress, and General Andrew Williamson, who commanded a backcountry district. Facing almost no resistance, British troops occupied the South Carolina Piedmont in early June. A British officer exulted, "This Country is intirely conquered; the People crowd in from all quarters to deliver up their arms." A disgusted Patriot officer declared, "With a few exceptions, the Men are all Tories & the Women all Whores."[65]

But Clinton overplayed his hand by declining to restore civil government. Ruling through martial law, he left civilians without recourse when abused by soldiers. The absence of civil law also crippled the Loyalist insistence that the British championed true liberty, order, and property. Patriots could argue that they alone provided a legitimate government and so could cast the Loyalists as criminals and traitors. Worse still, on June 3, Clinton issued a proclamation that required submitting men to serve in a Loyalist militia. By ruling out neutrality, the most popular option in the Carolinas, Clinton drove many wavering men to join Patriot partisans hiding out in the swamps. A Loyalist noted that men had submitted to "enjoy a respite from the Calamities of war" rather than to help the British win that war.[66]

In the Piedmont, Patriots and Loyalists coalesced around local leaders—millers, storekeepers, and large landowners—whose political commitments drew in their many clients, debtors, and relatives. When Colonel Thomas Fletchall defected to the Loyalists, a Patriot regretted the local impact because "Col. Fletchall has all those people at his beck, and reigns amongst them like a little King." But the Patriots had plenty of local kingpins to rally their neighbors for war. A Loyalist described the Carolina Piedmont as "a piece of patch work, the inhabitants of every settlement, when united in sentiment, being in arms for the side they liked best, and making continual inroads into one another's settlements." Because ethnic and denominational groups tended to settle in clusters, their affinities reinforced the powerful localism of political allegiances.[67]

To pacify the countryside, the British needed to reconcile Loyalists and Patriots. But the Loyalists wanted revenge for past sufferings while Patriots could not abide submitting to their local enemies. A Loyalist explained, "There is such a fund of Hatred and Animosity in the Hearts of the People, as Time only can extinguish." In vain, Britons struggled to control their Loyalist partisans, whose indiscriminate plundering and killing kept Patriots from surrendering and antagonized wavering people.[68]

Sailing back to New York in June 1780, Clinton left 8,000 troops and the southern campaign to the command of Lord Cornwallis. Although an élegant aristocrat, Cornwallis was also brave, sensible, contemptuous of pretense, and attentive to his troops. A veteran of the Seven Years War in Germany, he disliked waging civil war in America, but felt duty-bound and ambition-driven to serve the empire. But Clinton denied him enough men to win the war in the South. Taking care of himself, Clinton kept 72 percent of the redcoats idle in and around New York, allowing only 28 percent for active duty with Cornwallis.[69]

Cornwallis relied on a daring and ruthless subordinate, Lieutenant Colonel Banastre Tarleton, who led a fast-moving Loyalist legion

"Lord Cornwallis," engraving by John Fielding, 1786.
Courtesy of the Library of Congress (LC-UCZ62-45340).

of cavalry and light infantry. Tarleton intimidated the enemy through terror, burning farms and slaughtering prisoners. After the fall of Charles Town, Colonel Abraham Buford commanded the sole remaining regiment of Continentals in South Carolina. They retreated north toward North Carolina, but Tarleton overtook them at Waxhaws on May 29. He attacked and massacred half of them, ignoring Buford's offer to surrender. Instead of cowing Patriots, the atrocity outraged and motivated them to fight back with their own brutality. "Remember Buford!" bellowed Patriots when they butchered captured Loyalists.[70]

After posting a string of garrisons to hold the South Carolina backcountry, Cornwallis led his army north toward North Carolina. To counter that advance, Congress sent General Horatio Gates, the victor of Saratoga, south with some Continentals to rally the North Carolina militia. His men were hungry and unnerved by the summer heat, leading Gates to lament, "Our Army is like a dead whale upon the Sea Shore—a monstrous Carcass without Life or Motion." Gates got them moving but felt compelled to fight a hasty battle before the militiamen lost heart and went home. With 4,100 men, two-thirds of them militia, Gates attacked Cornwallis's smaller but veteran force at Camden on August 16. British discipline triumphed as the militiamen broke and ran, often without firing a shot. While some Continentals fought on until surrounded, Gates panicked and fled on his fast horse, not stopping until he reached Charlotte, sixty miles from the battlefield. Patriots lost 250 dead and 800 wounded or captured.[71]

Longing to fight a regular war, Cornwallis felt disgusted with the guerilla conflict and murderous banditry that raged in the Carolina backcountry. Rather than try to restore order, he moved on to seek a conventional battle with the wreckage of Gates's force. To protect his western flank, Cornwallis relied on Major Patrick Ferguson, a talented and ambitious Scot who commanded a Loyalist regiment, the American Volunteers. But 1,400 frontier militiamen surrounded his 1,000 Loyalists, who sought refuge on King's Mountain in North Carolina. On October 7, 1780, the Patriots stormed the mountain, killing Ferguson and 150 Loyalists.[72]

Ferguson's surviving men tried to surrender, but enraged victors shot or hanged many and left the wounded to die without medical help. The executed included Lieutenant Colonel Ambrose Mills. A prisoner reported, "Mrs. Mills with a young child in her arms sat out all night in the rain with her husband's corps[e]." When Cornwallis protested, the governor of South Carolina, John Rutledge, retorted that Loyalists had "hanged many more of our People" and "his Lordship has mistaken the Side on which the Cruelty lies." Cornwallis threatened to retaliate against his prisoners, but Patriots called his bluff. In turn, the Loyalists felt deflated by the British failure to stand up for their prisoners in Patriot hands. Where British atrocities stiffened Patriots' resistance, their cruelties spooked the Loyalists, a difference which predicted who would ultimately win the partisan war in the backcountry.

A Patriot exulted, "The tories, who after the defeat of Genl. Gates had a full range, are chased from their homes, hunted thro' the woods and shot with as much indifference as you would a buck."[73]

Greene

Despite the setback on his western flank, Cornwallis pressed deep into North Carolina in pursuit of the Continentals under a new commander: Nathanael Greene. A self-educated and genial former blacksmith from Rhode Island, Greene had a surprising self-confidence that impressed his men and superiors, especially Washington, who became his great patron. No general in the war, not even Washington, could do more with less than Greene, a talent which served the Patriots very well indeed in the embattled South.[74]

Thirty-eight years old in December 1780, Greene took command of the shattered southern army: 1,500 ragged, hungry, and demoralized men, about half Continentals and half North Carolina militia. They were, Greene reported, "so addicted to plundering that they were a terror to the inhabitants." He described his prospects as "dismal," for, in contrast to New England, "where most of the people are warm friends, here the greater part are inveterate enemies." While restoring the discipline of his troops, Greene also had to make do with scanty accommodations. One night he took shelter from a cold rain in a crude hovel, sharing a mound of straw with Governor Rutledge. During the night both awoke and accused the other of kicking, only to discover that a hog had slipped in to share their crude bed. Greene did his best to round up supplies and hound state governors to send him more militia—but with scant success.[75]

Greene dodged Cornwallis's superior army of veteran troops despite their forced marches to catch him. Greene wryly noted, "There are few generals that have run oftener . . . than I have done. But I have taken care not to run too far, and commonly have run as fast forward as backward, to convince the Enemy that we were like a Crab, that could run either way." To distract Cornwallis, Greene gambled by

"General N[athanael] Greene," engraving after a portrait by Charles Willson Peale. Courtesy of the Library of Congress (LC-USZ62-121991).

dividing his already-too-small army, sending Brigadier General Daniel Morgan with 1,000 men to harass the Loyalists to Cornwallis's west. Forced to react, Cornwallis sent Tarleton with 1,100 troops, a mix of Britons and Loyalists, in pursuit of Morgan. A brawny former teamster during the Seven Years War, Morgan had suffered a brutal flogging by the British after brawling with an officer. Fueled by that pain and humiliation, he became an especially active and resourceful Patriot during the next war.[76]

Overtaken by Tarleton at Hannah's Cowpens, Morgan drew up his little force to confront the attack on January 17, 1781. Able to charm tough men, Morgan persuaded his militia to hold their ground for at least two volleys. Their surprisingly deadly fire disordered Tarleton's line, which Morgan compounded by sending his Continentals forward with a bayonet charge. Morgan's cavalry cut off the fleeing enemy, who lost 110 dead and 702 captured. Riding away fast, Tarleton was one of 250 to escape. After the victory, Morgan led his men and captives on a hard-driving retreat to elude Cornwallis's pursuit and reunite with Greene's army.[77]

Morgan's victory emboldened more North Carolina and Virginia militia to join Greene's force, which grew to 4,200 men. Although Cornwallis had only 2,000 troops, he welcomed the chance to attack Greene at Guilford Court House, North Carolina. On March 15, 1781, after a bloody, seesaw, two-hour fight, Greene retreated rather than risk his army's survival on further combat. Like Washington, Greene understood that preserving his army was more important than risking all in a go-for-broke attack. "The [Continental] Army is all that the States have to depend upon for their political existence," he explained.[78]

Cornwallis had won the battlefield at a prohibitive cost, for a quarter of his already small force became casualties: twice the losses suffered by the Patriots. Cornwallis withdrew 175 miles to the seaport of Wilmington to rest and resupply his battered army. The sight of Cornwallis's shrunken force and many wounded dispirited even the most committed Loyalists. Cornwallis complained that "many of the inhabitants rode into the [British] camp, shook me by the hand, said they were glad to see us, and to hear we had beat Greene, and then rode home again." In their rags and hunger, the redcoats looked nearly as bad as the Continentals.[79]

As his little army recovered at Wilmington, Cornwallis learned that Greene had broken away, marching southwestward bound for the South Carolina Piedmont to menace the garrisons commanded by Lord Rawdon. Rather than follow Greene, on April 25 Cornwallis turned north to invade Virginia. Weary of the brutal and inconclusive warfare in the Carolinas, he no longer wanted to chase the elusive Greene for hundreds of miles across many broad rivers. By instead ravaging Virginia, a heartland of Patriot resources and home for many leaders, Cornwallis hoped to make his enemy stand and fight on his terms.[80]

Reaching Virginia in mid-May, Cornwallis joined a British expeditionary force active along the James River since December 1780. Commanded by Benedict Arnold and his British guardian, General William Phillips, the force raided plantations, liberating hundreds of slaves. In January, Arnold marched into Richmond, the new state capital, brushing aside militia resistance. Governor Jefferson and other state leaders fled westward while Arnold looted and burned most of the town. Poorly armed, Virginia militiamen felt spooked by the British regulars, especially Tarleton's cavalry, "whom the militia fear as they would so many wild beasts," a Patriot officer complained. Shocked by the easy British victories, the state's former lieutenant governor, John Page, declared that the impotent resistance had "disgraced our Country."[81]

In early June, Tarleton led 250 mounted men westward to Charlottesville, where Jefferson and the Virginia legislature had sought refuge. The raiders captured munitions and seven state legislators, including Daniel Boone, who represented Virginia's county in Kentucky. Jefferson escaped on a fast horse: the culminating humiliation of his unhappy tenure as governor. The raiders drank his wine and took away twenty-three slaves, who would try their luck in freedom with the British.[82]

In Virginia during 1781, the British attracted 4,000 runaways, including sixteen from George Washington's Mount Vernon. As his refugee following grew, Cornwallis's army strained the countryside's resources. A Hessian officer reported, "Any place this horde approached was eaten clean, like an acre invaded by a swarm of locusts."[83]

British raids exposed Virginia's military weakness and internal divisions. Common farmers and artisans resented wartime taxes, military impressments of livestock, and drafts for militia service. With crops to cultivate, they wanted to stay home rather than march off to fight and perhaps die. Their families might starve without a good harvest, for, as some militiamen explained, "One day's Labour is necessary for the Next day's Support." Plain folk bristled when wealthy planters exempted themselves, their sons, and overseers from militia duty so that they could stay home to guard the enslaved. A common farmer complained, "The Rich wanted the Poor to fight for them, to defend their property, whilst they refused to fight for themselves."[84]

Appropriating revolutionary rhetoric, disaffected Virginians insisted that staying home was the best way to defend their cherished liberty and property. One militiaman "swore by God if the enemy came upon the spott, he would not take up arms in defence of his country, but would stay by his property and would make the best terms he could." A leading Patriot concluded, "The same Principles which attach them to the American Cause will incline them to resist [the] Injustice or Oppression" of taxes, drafts, and impressments.[85]

The British invasion increased militia drafts and popular resistance to them. A Patriot colonel complained that some desperate draftees "cut off their fingers after the draft" to win discharges. Many militia officers resigned their commissions to avoid having to enforce the drafts. Others fulfilled the letter but not the spirit of the law by selecting old, infirm, and underage draftees certain to be sent home by disgusted Continental officers. One commander complained that many Virginia counties provided only "little dwarfs and children." Many able-bodied draftees quickly deserted. Others flocked to the British to surrender and receive paroles as prisoners, which let them return home exempted from further military service. Insisting that he was no Loyalist, a deserter declared that "he never would fight against his Country." A Patriot retorted "That was not enough; that he ought to fight for it."[86]

During the spring and summer of 1781 in at least six counties, militiamen "armed with Clubs, swords, guns, and pistols" rioted to block drafts of men, the collection of taxes, and impressment of farmers' livestock and produce. An officer noted, "The People are tired of the War & come to the Field most reluctantly." Despite the military crisis, Virginia produced only a quarter of the men needed to fill its quota for the Continental Army. Unable to collect supplies from the people, a state contractor sadly concluded, "The Citizen will do nothing without being compelled by Military Force." A board of frustrated tax collectors concluded, "Anarchy, confusion and disorder reigns triumphant amongst us." But the popular discontent did not translate into any enthusiasm for the British.[87]

In Virginia, as in the Carolinas, Cornwallis won every battle, burned many buildings, and looted widely but got no closer to winning the war. British officers grew frustrated with their inability to turn battlefield success into strategic triumph. General Charles O'Hara despaired of conquering a country "where repeated successes cannot ensure permanent advantages." General Clinton blamed Cornwallis for pursuing an "unmeaning and unprofitable ramble through Virginia." Clinton, however, sent vague and contradictory orders, while doing precious little with his own army at New York. The main British hope was that the staggering Patriot cause would collapse from war-weariness, rampant inflation, and internal divisions. With neither side winning, each had to hope for the foe to lose. The belligerents resembled two battered boxers waiting for the other to stumble and fall.[88]

Anarchy

Cornwallis had entrusted command in South Carolina to Lord Rawdon, an able officer. His 8,000 troops, a mix of Loyalists and redcoats, outnumbered Greene's men by more than two to one, but Rawdon diffused them to garrison ten posts, and Greene gained strength by rallying Patriot partisans in the backcountry. On April 25, Rawdon attacked Greene at Hobkirk's Hill, a sandy ridge covered with pines. Once again, Greene withdrew at the peak of combat, leaving the battlefield to Rawdon, but it was littered with more Loyalist than Patriot bodies. "We fight, get beat, rise, and fight again," Greene explained.[89]

By preoccupying Rawdon, Greene enabled Patriot partisans led by Thomas Sumter and Francis Marion to capture the outlying British posts one by one. Veteran Indian-fighters and successful planters, Marion and Sumter proved elusive and cunning at guerilla warfare. By June 6, the British retained only three garrisons in Georgia and South Carolina: Charles Town and Savannah on the coast and Ninety-Six, the last Loyalist oasis in the Piedmont. In late May, Greene besieged 550 Loyalists at Ninety-Six, but they repelled his attacks. Despite that victory, Rawdon evacuated the post, abandoning the region to the

Patriots. A dismayed British major grudgingly praised Greene, "The more he is beaten, the further he advances in the end."[90]

In early September, Greene attacked the retreating British and Loyalists at Eutaw Springs, on the Santee River forty miles from Charles Town. A fierce Patriot charge captured the enemy camp, but that success undid the hungry and thirsty victors, who broke ranks to get drunk on captured rum. When the British counterattacked, Greene withdrew his disordered men to avert disaster. He had lost another battle while inflicting heavier casualties on the British, who bought a field for two-fifths of their men (while Greene lost a quarter of his force). Once again a tactical setback yielded a strategic windfall for the Patriots as Rawdon withdrew to Charles Town, where the Royal Navy could protect and supply his men. By October, the Patriots had reclaimed the rest of the Carolinas, while the garrisons at Charles Town and Savannah became as useless to the British war effort as the inert force in occupied New York. Hundreds of ruined Loyalists and black runaways fled from the interior to seek safety near Charles Town in a shanty community known as "Rawdontown."[91]

In mid-1780, Patriot prospects had appeared bleak after crushing defeats at Savannah, Charles Town, and Camden. During the next year, however, the British cause collapsed into a few coastal refuges. Ultimately, British regulars were too few to control the vast hinterland, and Loyalist militias proved too weak to suppress Patriot partisans. Rather than pacifying the backcountry, British victories spread a vicious and shocking anarchy. Greene worried, "The whole country is in danger of being laid waste by the Whigs and Torrys, who pursue each other with as much relentless fury as beasts of prey." A British officer lamented, "The violence and passions of these people are beyond every curb of religion and humanity."[92]

Desperate for fodder and food, both armies stole from civilians, ruining hundreds of farms and impoverishing thousands of people. On both sides, officers reasoned that any resources left behind would only fall to the enemy. But the worst looting and killing derived from the vicious competition of irregular partisans. Rarely paid, they sought compensation in plunder, which discouraged morality and restraint. They assassinated foes, executed prisoners, and looted and burned the homes of civilians caught in the middle. A Patriot partisan recalled victory in a skirmish where "*Not one* [Loyalist was] taken prisoner— for that occurred but seldom, the rifle usually saved us that trouble." Both sides applied to whites the cruelties previously practiced in frontier war against Indians.[93]

At night, both sides attacked houses to kill helpless, sleeping foes in their beds or to haul them out for brutal floggings that could become fatal. Hundreds of desperate families became "Outlyers," abandoning their homes to live in hovels secreted in forests or swamps. A North Carolinian reported, "Fear of being called into the militia has driven many to hide in the woods, [and] as they have nothing on which to live they resort to highway robbery." Bandit gangs added to the chaos by preying upon everyone.[94]

Partisans claimed to act in just revenge for a prior atrocity committed by the other side. Patriots often recalled Tarleton's butchery of Buford's regiment at the Waxhaws, while Loyalists remembered the executions after the Battle of King's Mountain. Moses Hall, a Patriot militiaman, recalled the fate of six captured Loyalists: "I heard some of our men cry out, 'Remember Buford,' and the prisoners were immediately hewed to pieces with broadswords." Initially troubled by the massacre, Hall reconsidered after finding the corpse of a local boy bayoneted by the British. That sight, he remembered, "relieved me of my distressful feelings for the slaughter of the Tories, and I desired nothing so much as the opportunity of participating in their destruction."[95]

Men took pride and pleasure in killing their foes. A Loyalist reported the Patriot execution of a Loyalist captain: "As his murderers never took the trouble of pinioning his arms, in his struggles, while dying, he attempted several times to take hold of the limbs of the tree on which he was hanged; and it afforded them high amusement to beat down his hands with their whips and sticks." A North Carolina Loyalist hoped "to see the day that we shall ride to Our horses knees in

Liberty Men's Blood & Guts." In South Carolina, Aedanus Burke, a leading Patriot, knew a militia officer who "kept a tally of men he has killed on the barrel of his pistol, and the notches amount to twenty-five." Burke calculated that, if subject to the laws against arson, theft, and murder, "there are not one thousand men in the Country [of South Carolina] who c[oul]d escape the Gallows." He sadly concluded that "man by custom may be so brutalized as to relish human blood."[96]

The taboo against harming women broke down. In North Carolina, backcountry folk denounced the atrocities by the Patriot militia. "Numbers of persons such as Women and Children have been tortured, hung up and strangled, cut down, and hung up again, som[e]-times branded with brands or other hot irons in order to extort Confessions from them." In Georgia, Loyalists tortured a Patriot woman by using a musket lock as a thumbscrew. A French officer reported finding a pregnant Patriot murdered in her bed with a message scrawled on the bed's canopy by her Loyalist killers: "Thou shalt never give birth to a rebel."[97]

Survivors became selfish, suspicious, and vicious. In North Carolina, pious Moravians lamented that civil war "made life harder and harder, for men became more and more brutal." Reverend Archibald Simpson of South Carolina, reported, "Every person keeps close on his own plantation. . . . The people that remain have been peeled, pillaged, & plundered. Poverty, want, & hardship appear in almost every countenance. A dark, melancholy gloom appears everywhere, and the morals of the people are almost entirely extirpated."[98]

The violence and looting devastated the landscape. Tarleton noted that military foraging had "made a desert of the country." After crossing the North Carolina backcountry, a traveler reported that "most of the plantations that we passed were either abandoned or burned, now and then one was inhabited, but they had nothing." Traversing South Carolina, a Patriot general saw "no living creature" save for vultures "picking the bones of some unfortunate fellows, who had been shot or cut down, and left in the woods above ground."[99]

Initially so promising, the British bid to conquer the South withered as they alienated most of the white people, including many formerly inclined to Loyalism. The superiority of Patriot partisans also swayed the wavering majority. Cornwallis complained, "Colonel [Francis] Marion had so wrought on the minds of the people, partly by the terror of his threats and cruelty of his punishments, and partly by the promise of plunder, that there was scarcely an inhabitant between the Santee and Pedee [rivers], that was not in arms against us." Marion's mood was not improved when Loyalists captured and executed his son.[100]

The British also lost local support by encouraging bandit gangs that included runaway slaves. Interracial banditry by poor whites and blacks threatened the interests of propertied men who sought to protect their farms and slaveholdings. Patriots made special efforts to capture and execute black bandits. "Yesterday the famous Maj[o]r Gray, the infamous Spy and Notorious Horse thief, lost His Mullatto Head. It is exhibited at Cherraw Hill as a terror to Tories," a Patriot officer reported.[101]

The British also suffered from association with Indians. Although the invaders did little for their Indian allies, that limited aid sufficed to alienate backcountry whites. Cornwallis regarded Indian warriors as unreliable and expensive, more interested in extorting presents than in obeying his orders. To save money, he failed to provide them with enough munitions to defend their villages against settler attacks. In December 1780, Patriots devastated the "Overhill Cherokee Country" west of the Appalachian Mountains. A chief mourned that the attackers "dyed their hands in the Blood of many of our Women and Children, burnt 17 towns, destroyed all our provisions by which we & our families were almost destroyed by famine this Spring." The Patriot commander boasted, "The Over Hill Country were chiefly made a Field of desolation, the Families dispersed in the Mountains to starve." Patriot raiders burned fifteen more towns in March 1781. Burning out Indians proved wildly popular with southern settlers, who rallied to the Patriots and despised the British. Cherokees served the Patriot cause better as enemies than they could have as allies.[102]

The alienation of white folk also fed on the ambivalent British policy toward enslaved Africans, which produced more chaos than liberation. While the British armed only a few hundred of the thousands of black refugees, that precedent outraged most white men as a threat to their way of life. The black refugees also became alluring plunder for Patriot partisans. Thomas Sumter recruited men by offering one prime field hand for every private who served for at least ten months. Officers got more slaves, which helped to enrich Sumter and other leading partisans. This violent redistribution of the enslaved disrupted their families and communities—dividing relatives and friends forever. By flirting with Indians, bandits, and runaways, the British unwittingly alienated most white southerners, who defended private property and white supremacy by rallying to the Patriots.[103]

Cycles

Early in the war, Loyalist leaders begged for quick and powerful British interventions in every colony before their supporters ebbed away under the pressure of Patriot domination. If the British hesitated, there might be few Loyalists left to welcome and support them. William Rankin complained that in his county in Pennsylvania, the Loyalists' "unabated zeal in the Royal Cause was never called into Action and they were obliged to Submit." But invading a region might only expose and ruin Loyalists when the regulars moved on and the stronger Patriot militias came back for revenge. Although unreliable when thrust into combat with regulars, Patriot militiamen were plenty good at suppressing their Loyalist counterparts. Clinton warned that British incursions "might induce a Number of persons to declare for us, whom we might afterwards be obliged to abandon" and so "only serves to inflame men's minds, and to sacrifice those friends you abandon to the rage and fury of an incensed multitude." The Loyalists and British desperately needed one another to hold captured districts, but even together they could never control more than a shifting fraction of the vast territory and dispersed settlements of rural America.[104]

The cycles of invasion, exposure, and suppression eventually taught the Loyalists and the disaffected to keep a low profile. The longer the war dragged on, the fewer the Americans who would risk helping the British. The greatest decline in Loyalist support came in the South, where it had been strongest. Cornwallis was far too impatient in marching his army about in futile search of a climatic battle somewhere else, giving too little time for Loyalists to consolidate their control over occupied counties. Despite some showy, early victories, the British forces were big enough to spread chaos but far too small to restore peace. Civilians increasingly blamed the British invasion for the violence that rippled through the backcountry—and for the threat of Indian war and slave revolt. A disgruntled Loyalist explained, "The lower sort of People, who were in many parts, particularly in South Carolina, originally attached to the British Government, have suffered so severely, & been so frequently deceived, that Great Britain has now a hundred enemies, where it had one before." Most people concluded that a Patriot victory offered the best prospect for restoring peace and stability.[105]

7

WESTS

Since the year 1777 We have lived
in a State of Anarchey.
—WESTERN PENNSYLVANIA SETTLERS, 1782[1]

The Patriot cause merged a frontier hunger for Indian land with a dread of British power. Colonists feared confinement within a boundary patrolled by savage warriors allied to a domineering empire. In May 1775, a Patriot committee denounced "the Indians, whom we dread most" because "they are to be made use of in keeping us in awe." Patriots regarded the British alliance with native peoples as a tyrannical obstacle to the colonists' right to make private property from Indian lands. By allying with natives, Britons allegedly betrayed the racial solidarity of white men upheld by Patriots.[2]

Indians suspected that American independence would accelerate their dispossession and enslavement. Joseph Brant urged his fellow Mohawks "to defend their Lands & Liberty against the Rebels, who in a great measure begin this Rebellion to be sole Masters of this Continent." Playing on this fear, a British agent asked Haudenosaunee chiefs, "Are you willing to go with them, and suffer them to make horses and oxen of you, to put you into wheelbarrows, and to bring us all into

---

"Chief of the Little Osages," engraving by Charles Balthazar Julien Févret de Saint-Mémin, c. 1804. Courtesy of the Library of Congress (LC-DIG-pga-04426).

251

slavery?" Along the settler frontier, both sides dreaded domination by the other.[3]

In the east, where Indians lived in poverty and small enclaves enveloped by settlements, Patriots demanded their armed support. Bowing to that pressure, southern New England's Indians sent men to fight and die for the Patriot cause. Indeed, a greater proportion of enclave natives served in Patriot forces than did their white neighbors. Similarly situated in the Carolinas, Catawbas fought beside, and caught slaves for, the Patriots. By serving as allies, eastern natives sought Patriot protection for their enclaves. Instead, they suffered especially heavy casualties, which emboldened white neighbors to grab more native land.[4]

On the frontier, where natives remained numerous, autonomous, and powerful, Patriots hope to secure their neutrality in the conflict. During 1775–1776, Congress's agents assured native chiefs: "This is a family quarrel between us and Old England. You Indians are not concerned in it. . . . We desire you to remain at home, and not join on either side, but keep the hatchet buried deep."[5]

When Indians threatened to break their neutrality, Patriots took a harder line. In May 1776, an officer warned the Mohawks that, if they helped the enemy, "He would burn their upper & lower Castles on the Mohawk River, would burn all their houses, destroy their Towns & Cast the Mohawks with their Wifes & Children off of the face of the Earth."[6]

Most native chiefs initially accepted <u>neutrality</u> as their best policy. In August 1775, a Patriot noted, "It is plain to me that the Indians understand their game, which is to play into both hands." Natives needed to find and hold the tipping point in a balance of power between external rivals: formerly the British and French, now Britons and Patriots. During the volatile uncertainty of 1775 and 1776, it seemed dangerously premature to embrace either side, lest natives gamble their lives and lands on an eventual loser. Instead, most chiefs sought presents from both sides while making no commitments. A British agent reported that Indians preferred "to enjoy the advantages of a neutrality by being paid from both parties."[7]

Initially, the British also favored native neutrality as they focused on fighting Patriots on the east coast. While offering alluring words and generous presents, British leaders avoided explicit promises to preserve native lands, for they still hoped to find Loyalist support among frontier settlers. Britons also worried that Patriots would take propaganda advantage of any women or children killed by native warriors. But the British kept their options open should the war expand to the frontier.[8]

British delays cost the Cherokees dearly. About 12,000 in number including 3,000 warriors, they lived in forty-three villages in the foothills of the southern Appalachian Mountains. Dragging Canoe led a militant faction fed up with encroaching settlers and resolved "to die like men" rather "than to dwindle away by inches." He ignored the British southern Indian superintendent, John Stuart, who urged patience and restraint. In July 1776, Dragging Canoe's warriors attacked settlements in the western counties of North and South Carolina. Patriots insisted that Cherokees acted as British pawns and provided bloody proof that settlers must unite in support of the revolution. No matter how little the British did to help Indian raids, they bore the blame so skillfully cast by Patriot writers.[9] *propaganda war*

Rallying 6,000 militiamen from Virginia and both Carolinas, Patriots attacked and destroyed most Cherokee villages, neutral as well as hostile. Cherokee resistance crumbled as they ran out of ammunition for want of an adequate supply from the British. By striking during August through October, Patriots ruined ripening crops, sentencing survivors to a hungry winter and spring. A Patriot commander directed the militiamen to "cut up every Indian cornfield, and burn every Indian town" and promised "that every Indian taken shall be the slave and property of the taker; that the nation be extirpated, and the lands become the property of the public."[10]

Forced into the mountains, starving Cherokees sued for peace, save for Dragging Canoe and his warriors, who moved west to the Chickamauga Valley (in northern Georgia), at a safer distance from their enemies. In July 1777, the other chiefs paid a heavy price for peace, ceding 5 million acres to the Patriots. Exulting in their victory and British weakness, the Patriots warned other natives to note that when the Cherokees were driven "out of their Country, like a Gang of Cattle & their Corn all destroyed, that the people over the great Water cannot help them."[11]

In 1777, the third year of the war, British leaders belatedly recognized that they needed Indian help. Few settlers had rallied to the Loyalist cause, so there was little to lose and much to gain from encouraging natives to raid Patriot settlements. Daunted by the Cherokee defeats, the southern nations held back, but a surge in British presents and bellicose rhetoric drew most of the northern natives into the war.[12]

Most Indians believed that the British would probably win the war and could best supply trade goods. A Choctaw chief bluntly told a British official: "Whoever gives us the most will be the most regarded." A Delaware chief, Captain Pipe, warned a Patriot, "We are ridiculed by your Enemies for being attached to you who cannot even furnish us with a pair of Stockings or a Blanket." Patriots lacked the manufacturing capacity to produce the goods coveted by natives.[13]

In stark contrast, British allies reaped abundant presents of rum, guns, ammunition, cloth, clothing, hatchets, hoes, mirrors, and jewelry. In 1781, at the Great Lakes posts of Niagara, Detroit, and Michilimackinac, British agents delivered goods worth £100,000—up dramatically from the £500 given there in 1775.[14]

With British help, natives hoped to roll back invading settlers. Choctaw chiefs explained, "The Americans, a great deal more ambitious and numerous than the English, put us out of our lands, forming therein great settlements, extending themselves like a plague of locusts." A Creek chief reasoned, "The Virginians are now come very near my nation and I do not want them to come any nearer."[15]

Many Indians, however, regarded the British as just the lesser of two evils. Too often they were manipulative allies who cast natives in harm's way. A Delaware chief, Silver Heels, rebuked Detroit's commander: "We Indians are the only Sufferers [in] this War, as we day-by-day lose our people while you are quietly in your Fort." Native support for the British was volatile, waxing when they won battles but waning after defeats. A Spanish official reported that the shifting fortunes of war were "causing a great number of Indian tribes to go from one side to the other without knowing which side to take."[16]

Raids

Poorly garrisoned by a few hundred men, the British forts along the Great Lakes were vulnerable to Patriot attack unless screened by native allies adept at forest warfare. Because the best defense was an aggressive offense, Britons promoted native raids on the settlements of New York, Pennsylvania, western Virginia, and Kentucky. At a minimum, these attacks kept frontier Patriots pinned down and unable to send men and supplies to help the Continental Army operating along the Atlantic Seaboard. Better still, frontier raids might force Patriot leaders to divert soldiers to defend the beleaguered settlements, weakening eastern resistance to British armies operating along the coast.[17]

Natives insisted on fighting in their own manner, under their own leaders, and returned home when they wished. Stuart explained that warriors were "willing to assist us but it must be in their own way . . . by excursions in small parties upon the settlements." Such volatile allies frustrated British officers, who naïvely expected obedience. One complained, "Hiding in bushes and behind trees, waiting to take a shot at someone, and upon meeting with the slightest resistance, taking flight with amazing agility, but showing up at another place just as quickly— these are their principal military virtues." Unimpressed with those skills, he insisted that natives "cost many times more than real soldiers and do more harm than good."[18]

Patriots, however, sorely felt the Indian raids. Seeking revenge, Washington diverted part of his army to invade the Haudenosaunee country in 1779. In April, Colonel Goose Van Schaick surprised and destroyed the main Onondaga village. Because the most militant Onondagas had already withdrawn westward to Niagara, the attack victimized peaceable villagers who were easy pickings for a surprise attack. According to an Onondaga chief, the soldiers raped and killed women captured at the village, "yet these Rebels call themselves Christians."

General James Clinton rebuked Van Schaick, "Bad as the savages are, they never violate the chastity of any women, their prisoners."[19]

During the summer, General John Sullivan led 3,000 Patriot troops deep into the Haudenosaunee country of the Seneca and Cayuga nations. Sullivan had Washington's orders to effect "the total destruction and devastation of their settlements . . . that the country may not be merely *overrun* but *destroyed*." During August and September, Sullivan's soldiers methodically located, looted, and burned forty villages around Seneca and Cayuga lakes and in the Genesee Valley. Soldier marveled as they torched substantial villages of log cabins, broad fields of Indian corn, and extensive orchards of apple, peach, and cherry trees. Impressed by the fertile soil, many troops eagerly anticipated returning after the war as conquering settlers. Haudenosaunees blamed the destruction on Washington, whom they called Hanodagonyes, which meant "Town Destroyer." A Seneca chief later assured Washington, "We called you the town destroyer; and to this day, when that name is heard, our women look behind them and turn pale, and our children cling close to the necks of their mothers."[20]

Driven from their homes, 5,000 Haudenosaunees fled westward to refuge villages, which stretched for eight miles along the Niagara River. During the long, cold winter of 1779–1780, hundreds died from malnutrition, exposure, and disease. Far from breaking the Haudenosaunees, dispossession and suffering enhanced their grim determination to take revenge by raiding during the spring of 1780. One of Sullivan's officers conceded, "The nests are destroyed but the birds are still on the wing."[21]

Most Haudenosaunees assisted the British, but their Oneida kin allied with the Patriots to secure guarantees for their lands. General Schuyler had made them promises that he would not keep: "You will then partake of every Blessing we enjoy, and united with a free people, your Liberty and Property will be safe." Located at the western head of the Mohawk Valley, Oneidas provided a security buffer for Patriot settlements to the east.[22]

In 1780, Loyalists and the other Haudenosaunees expelled the

Oneidas and burned their villages. A third of them defected to join the refugees at Niagara, but two-thirds fled eastward to find haven with the Patriots at Schenectady. Because Patriot finances and logistics were a mess, the Oneida refugees suffered from ragged clothing, scant food, and cold, leaky huts. In October 1780, Schuyler warned Congress, "I fear their virtue will, at last, yield to a continuation of distress which no human being can endure and that they will renounce an alliance which has exposed them to such abuse."[23]

After eliminating the Oneida villages as a buffer, Loyalist and Indian raids could devastate the settlements in the Mohawk Valley. By the end of 1781, raiders had burned most of the towns, driving two-thirds of the inhabitants from their homes, widowing 380 women, and leaving 2,000 children without fathers.[24]

Kentucky

Renowned as fertile, Kentucky attracted hundreds of settlers in 1775–1776, just as revolution disrupted the empire. Cherokees, to the south, and Shawnees, to the north, resented the intrusion on their cherished hunting grounds. By promising to provide security, Virginia's leaders wrested the region from the rival claim of the Transylvania Company, a cartel of North Carolina land speculators led by Judge Richard Henderson. After offering cheap land on easy terms in 1775, the company alienated settlers in 1776 by abruptly doubling prices and monopolizing the best locations: salt licks, mines, and mill seats. Exploiting Henderson's unpopularity, Virginia's Patriot governor, Patrick Henry, organized Kentucky into counties, appointed magistrates and militia officers, and promised generous land grants at bargain prices.[25]

Virginia's leading man in Kentucky was George Rogers Clark, a twenty-four-year-old captain who had served in Lord Dunmore's Shawnee war. Although hard-drinking, Clark was also ambitious, brave, shrewd, and ruthless. To extend Virginia's claim north and west of Kentucky, Clark organized a military expedition to seize the Francophone settlements at Cahokia, Kaskaskia, and Vincennes in the Illinois country. In July 1778, Clark and 150 men easily captured the villages, for they lacked British garrisons, and the *habitants* did not want a fight.[26]

Detroit's commander, Major Henry Hamilton, rallied a mixed force of Britons, French Canadians, and Indians to head south to retake the Illinois country. After traveling 600 miles, Hamilton's men seized the leading village, Vincennes, while Clark was away at Kaskaskia to the west. Hastening back through cold rains and soggy swamps, Clark's Virginians besieged Hamilton's weak fort in February 1779. To terrify the defenders, Clark had three captured Indians conspicuously tomahawked. Most of Hamilton's French Canadians promptly deserted, which led Hamilton to surrender, while denouncing Clark as a madman "reeking from the human sacrifice in which he had acted as chief priest."[27]

Accusing Hamilton of having paid bounties to Indians for scalps taken from settlers and "embrued your hands in the blood of our women and children," Clark clapped him into irons and paraded him through the Kentucky settlements on a march eastward to Virginia, where he landed in a dank dungeon. In fact, Hamilton had bought no scalps and instead saved lives by ransoming captives from the Indians. Meanwhile, Patriots bought many scalps, for South Carolina and Pennsylvania offered up to $1,000 for one, regardless of the corpse's age or gender. But Patriots insisted that they scalped only in just revenge for an original sin that they ascribed to the alleged savages.[28]

Virginia's triumph in Illinois accelerated the land rush into Kentucky, boosting the population from 1,000 in 1778 to 8,000 by 1782. But the complex Virginia land laws soon revealed deep flaws. To secure official surveys and legal documents of title, settlers had to make costly trips east to the distant state capital, Richmond. The many dispersed surveyors also produced plans that overlapped multiple claims to the best properties. The tangled legal titles delighted only lawyers, as litigation clogged the county courts for decades. Lacking cash and education, many common settlers lost their claims to clever speculators with Richmond connections and expensive attorneys.[29]

Virginia's hold on Kentucky weakened as many settlers came to distrust "the officers of the State" as "a Damn'd Set of thieves and Robers only come to this Country to Rob and Pilage the Inhabitants." Active, brave, and resolute when on campaign, Clark proved lax, inept, and often drunk as an administrator in Kentucky. With leaders acting selfishly, common settlers feared becoming, they explained, "Slaves to those Engrossers of Lands and to the Court of Virginia." Many settlers defied official surveyors and speculators to claim lands as squatters, defending them with their rifles. A frustrated speculator complained, "With what a Jealous Eye we view one another, every Man looking upon his neighbor as his Enemy."[30]

Virginia's control of Illinois proved even weaker. After Clark's victories, the state organized the vast region as a Virginia county, but the *habitants* preferred to be left alone. A Virginia captain deemed them "a set of ignorant asses," who "deserve[d] to be ruled with a rod of iron or droved at the Point of the bayonet." While asserting their own liberty, Virginians denounced others, who did not cooperate, as unfit for freedom. With British troops ravaging eastern Virginia in 1780 and 1781, the state could spare neither men nor money to control a distant region of restive Francophones. In 1783 an *habitant* declared that his people "are now altogether without authority."[31]

Hate

Armed by Britons and infuriated by settlers, Indian warriors raided the settlements of Kentucky, Pennsylvania, and western Virginia during the summer of 1777. Over the next six years, Shawnee, Delaware, and Mingo raiders killed or captured hundreds of settlers and destroyed their livestock, crops, and cabins. A Loyalist officer boasted that raids had "reduced the extensive frontier upon the Ohio, to a heap of ashes." A Patriot lamented, "It is truly disturbing to see how this Country is laid waste, and more so to hear the lamentations of Widows for their murdered Husbands and Children, and sometimes the Husband for his Wife and Children." A militia commander calculated that the war killed at least 860 Kentuckians.[32]

Many settlers fled eastward, while those who stayed behind "forted up" by moving into communal stockades and forming local associations for self-defense. Members agreed to assemble every morning, at the beat of a drum, to receive daily orders from three overseers. While most men worked in the fields, the rest stood guard. At day's end, they withdrew to the security of the local "station": a cluster of cabins surrounded by a protective stockade of logs.[33]

Frontier militiamen also crossed the Ohio River to attack and burn native villages and their crops. A militia general explained that warriors might flee, "but their huts and cornfields must remain, the destruction whereof greatly affects their old men, their women, and their children." But Patriots lacked the men, provisions, and money to attack Detroit, the distant British post that supplied native raiders.[34]

The war became racialized as most settlers sought to destroy all Indians, even those who tried to help them. Clark vowed that "he would never spare Man, woman, or child of them on whom he could lay his hands." He reasoned that "to excel them in barbarity was and is the only way to make war upon Indians." Hard-liners butchered the most vulnerable Indians, those who tried to keep the peace. In November 1777, vigilantes murdered and mutilated the Shawnee chief Cornstalk, who was then negotiating with Continental officers. A year later, militiamen killed a Delaware chief, White Eyes, while he was guiding a Patriot military expedition. The murders discredited peacemakers among the natives, who became more united in attacking settlements. An unusual frontier captain warned Clark, "If there is not a stop put to Killing Indian friends, we must Expect to have all foes." Rejecting coexistence with any Indians, Clark retorted, "The same world will scarcely do for them and us."[35]

Hard-liners marginalized moderates, who included Daniel Boone. While leading an armed settler party harvesting salt for their cattle, Boone surrendered without a fight to a larger force of warriors. Accepting adoption by Blackfish, a Shawnee chief, Boone encouraged his compatriots to do the same. Blackfish released and followed them to Boonesborough, where his adopted son urged the settlers to surrender.

Rejecting Boone's advice, they defended their stockade until the Shawnees withdrew. Distrusted thereafter by his neighbors, Boone moved
away, forsaking the settlement that bore his name.[36]

The racial polarization distressed Continental officials based at
Fort Pitt, for they wanted to cultivate some Indians as allies. When
the Continental Indian agent, George Morgan, protested the murders of Indian peacemakers, Virginia's supporters had him arrested
on trumped-up charges of Loyalism. In the spring of 1778, three other
agents defected from federal service, fleeing to join the Loyalists at
Detroit. Forty Continental soldiers also deserted from Fort Pitt and
fled to Detroit.[37]

Compromised by the defections, federal authority dwindled in the
West. While Fort Pitt's commander, Colonel Daniel Brodhead was
meeting with a Delaware chief, a settler came up behind and tomahawked that chief. Rather than prosecute the killer, Brodhead resigned
his command as hopeless. His successor at Fort Pitt, William Irvine,
noted "the general and common opinion of the people of this Country is that all Continental officers are too fond of Indians." Several
families of peaceful Delawares sought federal protection as refugees
on Killbuck Island in the Ohio River near Fort Pitt. In 1782, scores of
militiamen seized and disarmed the Continental troops guarding the
refugees before slaughtering and scalping the Indians, most of them
women and children.[38]

Nearly bankrupt and preoccupied with war in the East, Congress
could sustain just 200 unpaid, ragged, and hungry soldiers in the Ohio
Valley, primarily at Fort Pitt. Only desperate, impoverished, and alcoholic men would enlist for federal service in the West. In late 1781,
General Irvine complained, "I never saw troops cut so truly a deplorable, and at the same time despicable, a figure. . . . Nay! It would be
difficult to determine whether they were white men." After botching
a campaign against Detroit, another federal general, Lachlan McIntosh, convened the valley's chiefs to boast of his power to compel their
submission, "upon which declaration they Set up a General Laugh."[39]

By 1782, the western collapse of federal authority freed settlers to pursue ~~genocidal goals.~~ In March, David Williamson, an accomplished Indian killer, rallied western Pennsylvania's militiamen to cross the Ohio River to invade Indian country. Unable to track down elusive enemies, the vigilantes instead seized Gnadenhutten, a peaceful Delaware village led by Moravian missionaries. Irvine reported that they "had built a pretty Town and made good improvements and lived for some years past quite in the style of Christian white people." Irvine promised them protection, and they sent crops to feed his garrison. But the Delaware chief Buckongahelas told the villagers: "Remember that this day I have warned you to beware of such friends as these. I know the long knives; they are not to be trusted."[40]

At Gnadenhutten, Williamson's militiamen interpreted the European kettles and clothing as damning proof that the villagers had raided settlements rather than as evidence of their Christian conversion and civility. The militiamen butchered 96 captives—28 men, 29 women, and 39 children—by smashing their skulls with wooden mallets before scalping them for trophies. The natives died while singing Christian hymns. The victors burned the entire village to consume the bodies of their victims. Although appalled by news of the massacre, Irvine had to keep quiet rather than outrage settlers. He explained, "People who have had Fathers, Mothers, Brothers or Children Butchered, tortured, [and] Scalped by the savages, reason very differently on the subject of killing the Moravians."[41]

During the following spring, another genocidal raid targeted Delaware and Wyandot villages at Sandusky. Commanded by Washington's old friend William Crawford, the invaders confronted many enraged warriors seeking revenge for the massacre at Gnadenhutten. Routed after the loss of 40 dead, most of the militiamen fled homeward, but Indians butchered 5 captives and then slowly roasted Crawford to death. The final blow, a scalping, came from a Moravian convert who had escaped from the massacre of his kin at Gnadenhutten. Conveniently forgetting that massacre, frontier folklore instead dwelled on Crawford's torture as proof of a savagery that settlers had to overcome by slaughtering Indians.[42]

By 1782, British-allied Indians had gained a slight edge in the frontier war both in the Ohio Valley and the Haudenosaunee country. Although Patriot forays had destroyed many native villages, warriors devastated the settlements in Kentucky, Tennessee, central New York, and western Pennsylvania. Because neither side could impose order on the chaos, they jointly produced a broad and anarchic borderland of butchered families and smoldering cabins.

Louisiana

While Patriots reaped a bloody, burning mess along their frontier, the Spanish hoped to restore order on their own terms. After suffering defeats during the Seven Years War, they adopted the "Bourbon reforms," which increased Crown revenues and power in the Americas. In the Patriot revolution, Spanish officials saw both opportunity and peril. On the one hand, perhaps they could punish Britain by taking colonies, especially East and West Florida. On the other hand, they feared American expansion westward and worried that their republican ideas might spread into Latin America to subvert Spain's empire. While balking at an open alliance with the Patriots, the Spanish did provide financial and logistical support to facilitate their attacks on British positions.[43]

The Spanish had to proceed carefully because of their weakness in Louisiana. Sprawled along the entire western side of the Mississippi River, the colony stretched across the Great Plains to the Rocky Mountains to include about 828,000 square miles. But Spain had only 500 soldiers and 30,000 colonists: about an eighth of the native numbers within that vast expanse. Most of the colonists lived in two modest clusters on Louisiana's eastern margin in the Mississippi Valley. The main cluster occupied the lower river around the capital and seaport at New Orleans. In upper Louisiana, a secondary set of settlements emerged at the confluence of the Mississippi, Missouri, and Ohio Rivers (in the future state of Missouri) with St. Louis as the primary town. Most of the colonists were Francophones who had lingered after the colony's transfer from French to Spanish rule in 1763. Enslaved Africans comprised the second-largest group. The Spanish-speaking minority consisted primarily of newcomers from the Canary Islands, who settled along the river below New Orleans. Unable to control the vast hinterland, Spanish officials cultivated Indian allies with present of guns, ammunition, flags, and medals. Generating scant revenue from its limited trade, Louisiana was heavily subsidized by the Crown to provide a protective buffer zone for Mexico to the southwest.[44]

In 1776, Louisiana had an enterprising young (twenty-nine) governor, Bernardo de Gálvez. More open to aiding the Patriots than his superiors, Gálvez cooperated with their agent, the merchant Oliver Pollock, who lived in New Orleans. Through Pollock, Gálvez loaned money and supplies to support George Rogers Clark's expedition and the federal garrison at Fort Pitt. Pollock reciprocated with information on British plans.[45]

In 1778, James Willing strained Gálvez's support for the Patriots. Born in Philadelphia, Willing had moved to West Florida in 1772, acquiring 1,250 acres near Natchez. His mercantile business there failed because, as a neighbor noted, Willing "frequently indulged his natural propensity of getting drunk." An opportunist, he sought to recoup his fortunes by embracing the revolution. Returning to Philadelphia in 1777, he lobbied Congress for a captain's commission and authorization to seize West Florida. In early 1778, he led 100 volunteers down the Ohio and Mississippi rivers in a large, clumsy boat aptly named the *Rattletrap*. They surprised the riverside settlements of West Florida, which had become havens for wartime refugees from the southern states. Disaffected from the revolution, but passive in their Loyalism, the refugees wanted to be left alone as neutrals until Willing's raid forced them into the war.[46]

Despite initial pledges to protect the property of those who submitted, Willing's men pillaged and burned farms and plantations. A British officer noted that "the bare walls of the houses remain as a monument of the cruel depredations that have been committed by a rebel banditti."[47]

*"Bernardo de Gálvez, Conde de Gálvez, 1746–1786," by an
unknown engraver. Gálvez was the dynamic Spanish governor
of Louisiana. Courtesy of the Library of Congress (LC-
USZ62-58746).*

In April, West Florida's settlers rose up to ambush Willing's patrols
and capture his outposts. In November, he sailed away from New
Orleans in defeat, but a British cruiser intercepted his vessel and sent
him off to prison in occupied New York City. Thanks to his misguided
raid, the Patriot cause lost credibility in West Florida, and the British
sent 400 regulars to restore order in the region.[48]

During the summer of 1779, Gálvez learned that Spain had declared
war on Great Britain. To preempt a British attack on New Orleans,
Gálvez resolved to strike first. In August and September 1779, Gálvez
assembled 650 men, primarily local militiamen, to capture the Brit-

ish posts on the east bank of the Mississippi River at Manchac, Baton Rouge, and Natchez. To protect their property, the settlers submitted to Spanish rule.[49]

During the next two years, Gálvez conquered the rest of West Florida while his deputies on the upper Mississippi River bolstered the Spanish position around St. Louis. In January 1780, with reinforcements from Cuba, Gálvez sailed east to capture the British post at Mobile. At St. Louis in May 1780, Gálvez's subordinates repulsed an attack from Canada by 1,000 men, a mix of Britons and native allies. Counterattacking, the victors seized and destroyed the British post at St. Joseph, on the shore of Lake Michigan, in February 1781. A month later and far to the south, Gálvez landed 7,000 men to besiege Pensacola, the British capital of West Florida. His armed force included more than 400 free blacks, whom the Spanish more readily employed as soldiers than did either Britons or Patriots. Pensacola's defenders numbered 2,000 men, a quarter of them Choctaws. After two months of siege operations, the Spanish captured a key British redoubt, which enabled a closer and more deadly bombardment of the main fort. On May 10, the British commander surrendered his troops, while their Choctaw allies escaped into the backcountry. With the conquest of West Florida, Spain dominated the entire Gulf of Mexico.[50]

The Spanish also defeated Louisiana's maroons by deploying free black militiamen. Exploiting the turmoil of war, scores of slaves had slipped away from farms and plantations to make havens in swamps that presented a disorienting maze of waterways, tall cane, and cattails to outsiders. Maroons lived by hunting, fishing, tending small gardens, and rustling livestock from nearby plantations. In the spring of 1783, Spanish officers led black militiamen in an expedition that found and destroyed the largest maroon settlement and took more than fifty prisoners. In the public square of New Orleans, the victors tortured and executed four maroon leaders, including Jean St. Malo, who became a legendary martyr in the tales and songs of the enslaved in Louisiana.[51]

Impressed by Spanish victories and presents, Choctaws swapped their British flags and medals for Spanish equivalents. But Spain could only buy influence with, rather than control over, chiefs who would accept presents but take no orders. A Spanish official concluded, "More than anything, the wheel of their goodwill spins on the axis of gifts." The Spanish lacked enough trade goods to sway all of the hinterland's many native nations. Because British traders in Canada offered better goods at lower prices, Spanish influence dissipated farther up the Mississippi. Defiant Osages rustled horses along the Arkansas River, and Chickasaws attacked Spanish supply boats operating on the Mississippi. They often fenced their loot to traders based in St. Louis, for the Spanish also could not control their own distant subjects.[52]

Shadows

After conquering West Florida, Gálvez hoped to seize East Florida and Jamaica, the prize British colony in the West Indies. But two massive rebellions in South America staggered the Spanish Empire between 1781 and 1783, compelling imperial officials to divert troops to suppress the rebels. Like the American Revolution, both rebellions began as protests against new imperial taxes, which rose in wartime and were highly regressive, bearing hardest on the poor. During the 1770s, Spanish officials tripled their sales tax and applied it, for the first time, to coca, which Peruvian natives depended on to cope with the cold and thin air of their mountainous region.[53]

Although well educated as a Jesuit, José Gabriel Condorcanqui Noguera claimed descent from the Incan royal line and adopted the regal name of Tupac Amaru. With critical assistance from his wife, Micaela Bastidas, an influential merchant, Tupac Amaru rallied native peasants by arresting and executing Spanish tax collectors in the Andean Mountains. He promised to restore the Incan Empire by driving the Spanish from Peru, but the rebel siege of the key inland city of Cuzco failed in early 1781 thanks to reinforcements from the colonial capital, Lima, on the Pacific coast. Pursued by Spanish forces high into the snowy mountains, Tupac Amaru lost a crucial battle in April 1781. Vindictive in victory, the Spanish viceroy assembled a great crowd in

the central plaza of Cuzco to watch the execution of scores of captured rebels, including Tupac Amaru's wife and son. The grim spectacle culminated with a butchering of that rebel leader by drawing and
quartering. Resistance persisted to the south around Lake Titicaca for
another two years. By the end of the rebellion in 1783, 100,000 natives
and 10,000 Spaniards had died.[54]

Increased imperial taxes also provoked a revolt in 1781 in New
Granada: modern-day Colombia, Ecuador, and Venezuela. Led by
a prosperous farmer, Juan Francisco Berbeo, the uprising attracted
support from the mestizos and white creoles of the towns as well as
native peasants of the countryside. Calling themselves Comuneros,
the armed rebels marched on the provincial capital of Santa Fe de
Bogotá. Claiming to act on behalf of the king, they sought to overthrow corrupt provincial officials accused of betraying his justice.
Comuneros demanded tax relief and the removal of Spanish-born
officials (known as *peninsulares*). New Granada's viceroy blamed
the troubles on the corrosive example set by the American Revolution: "News of the independence of the English colonies of the north
goes from mouth to mouth among everyone in the uprising." In New
Granada, the Spanish restored order by compromising. Taxes temporarily went down, but *peninsulares* retained their offices, while the
Comuneros dispersed to their homes.[55]

A third native revolt set limits to Hispanic expansion northwestward into California. In 1774, California hosted the weakest and most
isolated of Spain's frontier colonies. Based at two presidios (San Diego
and Monterey) and five missions, 180 colonists struggled to dominate
the 60,000 natives along a 500-mile coast. The colony grew slowly
because of the high cost of living and low returns on exports, for adverse
currents and winds rendered a sea voyage from Mexico long, difficult,
and expensive. In 1774, however, an enterprising commander based in
northern Mexico, Juan Bautista de Anza, persuaded a native guide to
reveal an overland route that crossed the Colorado River to reach California. A year later, Anza more than doubled the colony's population
by delivering 242 colonists and founding a new presidio and mission at

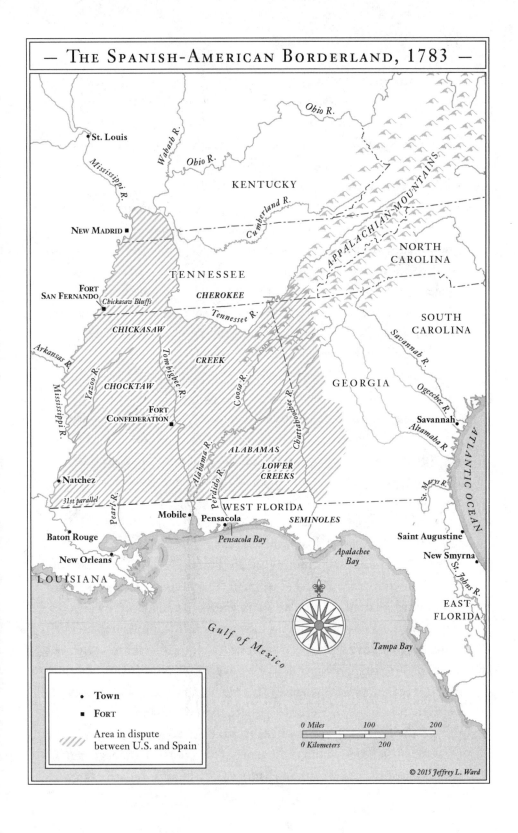

— The Spanish-American Borderland, 1783 —

Ohio R.

St. Louis

Mississippi R.

Wabash R.

Ohio R.

KENTUCKY

Cumberland R.

NEW MADRID ■

APPALACHIAN MOUNTAINS

FORT
SAN FERNANDO
Chickasaw Bluffs

TENNESSEE

CHEROKEE

Tennessee R.

NORTH
CAROLINA

CHICKASAW

SOUTH
CAROLINA

Arkansas R.

Yazoo R.

Tombigbee R.

CREEK

Coosa R.

Savannah R.

Mississippi R.

CHOCTAW

FORT
CONFEDERATION ■

Chattahoochee R.

GEORGIA

Ogeechee R.

Savannah
Altamaba R.

ATLANTIC OCEAN

Alabama R.

ALABAMAS

LOWER
CREEKS

Natchez

31st parallel

Pearl R.

Perdido R.

WEST FLORIDA

SEMINOLES

St. Marys R.

Mobile •

Pensacola

Baton Rouge

Pensacola Bay

Apalachee
Bay

Saint Augustine

New Smyrna •

New Orleans

LOUISIANA

Gulf of Mexico

St. Johns R.

EAST
FLORIDA

Tampa Bay

• **Town**

■ **Fort**

Area in dispute
between U.S. and Spain

0 Miles	100	200
0 Kilometers	200	

© 2015 Jeffrey L. Ward

San Francisco, located beside the best harbor on the west coast. Thrilled by the founding ceremony, a missionary exclaimed, "The only ones who did not enjoy this happy day were the heathens." The natives had reason to worry. The newcomers carried epidemic diseases, which spread outward from the missions, reducing the region's Indian population to a fraction within twenty years.[56]

To protect the critical Yuma crossing of the Colorado River, Anza brought the leading chief of the nearby Quechan Indians, Olleyquotequiebe, to Mexico City in the fall of 1776. Colonial officials tried to impress him with lavish hospitality and gifts. Olleyquotequiebe accepted Catholic baptism and the Christian name of Salvador Palma. Believing they had converted the chief into a pawn, the Spanish built a presidio, village, and mission at the Yuma crossing in 1780. But rapes and whippings by soldiers alienated their Quechan hosts. Led by Olleyquotequiebe, they rebelled on the morning of July 17, 1781, surprising and killing fifty-five Hispanics, including all four priests, and destroying their buildings. Stretched thin by war and rebellions elsewhere in the Americas, the Spanish could spare no soldiers to retake the Yuma crossing. This loss stifled the growth of Hispanic California, which remained thinly populated and vulnerable to a hostile takeover by another empire.[57] US

Spain's empire remained overstretched and internally volatile. Like the British, the Spanish had imposed reforms meant to rationalize and centralize control, undermining the local power long enjoyed by elite colonists. Unlike the British, the Spanish succeeded in imposing their taxes, more than doubling Crown revenues. Emboldened by success, imperial rulers issued grandiose dictates, which commanded colonial officials to impose tighter control over natives and colonists. Wearied by a spate of impossible orders, the viceroy of New Spain, Antonio María Bucareli, privately lamented, "Not everything believed possible on paper is possible in execution, especially in so vast an area." Bucareli prayed to "God to grant me strength to disentangle myself from the chaos of difficulties which enclose me in the confused management of these vast provinces. I walk in shadows."[58]

freedom from restraint

The rationality of imperial bureaucrats was madness when imposed on an American (frontier) where colonists and natives pursued their own interests. Between 1766 and 1768, the Crown's inspector general, the Marqués de Rubí, toured the long frontier from Arizona to Texas, noting "the tremendous damage His Majesty's subjects suffer daily from the barbarians." But Rubí proposed a solution that was surreal in its rigid rationality: a system of fifteen uniform, stone presidios at hundred-mile intervals, which neither the mountainous and arid landscape nor the finances of the empire could afford. Rubí's successor, José de Gálvez (Bernardo's older brother), cracked in 1769 under the strain of fighting elusive Indians on the northern frontier. One night, Gálvez burst from his tent to announce a plan to "destroy the Indians in three days simply by bringing 600 monkeys from Guatemala, dressing them like soldiers, and sending them against" the natives. He then assumed, in succession, the identities of Moctezuma, the king of Sweden, St. Joseph, and finally God. But none of them could defeat the Indians. The viceroy decided that Gálvez needed to rest and recuperate. Two years later, he sailed back to Spain and won promotion to Secretary of the Indies, the cabinet post responsible for American policy. Madness in America was no bar to power in Spain.[59]

Despite its showy victories in war, the reformed Spanish empire irritated colonial elites known as creoles (or *criollos*) because of their American birth. Prior to 1760, the Spanish Empire, like the British, had relied on negotiating compromises with, and subcontracting administration to, elites in their colonies. The most powerful colonists claimed aristocratic status as descendants of sixteenth-century conquistadores who had built the empire by destroying Indian kingdoms. During the 1760s and 1770s, however, they felt marginalized by the reforms that enhanced imperial power.[60]

At the recommendation of José de Gálvez, the Crown subordinated colonial leaders to imperial officials from Spain, known as *peninsulares*. Creoles bitterly resented pretentious newcomers who expressed the European prejudice that New World environments degraded the morals and intellect of those born there. Thanks to imperial favor in overseas trade, *peninsulares* also drove many creole merchants out of business.[61]

While restricted from above, the creoles also felt threatened from below. Claiming the pride and privilege of allegedly pure blood and pale skin, creoles denigrated as inferiors the empire's colonial majority: a medley of Indians, blacks, and mestizos. A creole denounced them as "positively ugly, with very bad color, coarse features, notorious slovenliness when they are not completely naked, no cleanliness, and even less culture and rationality. . . . They eat in the greatest squalor and filthiness, and their food is worse than their dress." Creole elites despised the imperial policy of raising revenue by selling certificates of legal whiteness (*limpieza de sangre*, or purity of blood) to mestizos and mulattoes who had prospered. Defending their position atop a racial hierarchy, creoles denounced the certificates for producing "a system of anarchy."[62]

Like their counterparts in British America, Hispanic elites reacted against imperial reforms that altered an indulgent *ancien régime* that had better served their interests. Spanish-American creoles envied the independence won by the North Americans. Some creoles covertly read republican texts, especially Thomas Paine's *Common Sense*. They were also impressed by the superior population and economic growth of the American states, which they interpreted as the fruits of republicanism, meritocracy, and free trade. "Good God, What a contrast to the Spanish System!" wrote Francisco de Miranda, an ambitious Venezuelan who regarded the American Revolution as "the infallible preliminary to our own." An officer in Bernardo de Gálvez's command, Miranda had served at the siege of Pensacola. He subsequently visited New York City, where he was befriended by Alexander Hamilton.[63]

The prospect of autonomy and free trade tempted creoles to seek independence, but they feared the risks to their wealth and power. Amounting to only a fifth of the Spanish-American population, creoles dreaded losing their domination over the impoverished and darker-colored majority. No revolutionary army could succeed without enlisting men from the lower orders, who then might throw off the slavery, tenancy, or debt-peonage that profited the creole elite. Creoles grimly remembered how Tupac Amaru's rebellion had become a race and class war, during which Indian peasants massacred white officials and landlords. Creoles eloquently spoke the Enlightenment rhetoric of freedom but did so to defend their privileged position in an unequal society.[64]

New Spain did not have the substantial middling class of white farmers that prevailed in North America. Most of those farmers felt a racial solidarity with their elites, a solidarity that trumped class tensions between them. Because white landowners predominated, Patriots felt confident that their revolt against British rule would preserve their advantages as white men. Hispanics also lacked the institutions that enabled British Americans to hone their protests and organize resistance, for New Spain had neither a free press nor any elected assembly. Despite their grievances with the empire, few creoles would seek independence until early in the next century, when the Napoleonic Wars disrupted the regime in Madrid. Only then would they make revolutions while trying to contain popular revolts from below.[65]

Plains

While the Spanish claimed the Gulf coast, and American settlers pressed westward into the Ohio Valley, a very different revolution developed on the Great Plains west of the Mississippi, as native peoples obtained horses and guns. Two thousand miles long by four hundred miles wide, the Great Plains are a wind-swept and arid grassland bounded by the Rocky Mountains on the west. The grass sustained vast herds of bison (or "buffalo"): immense, shaggy, grazing beasts that provided hundreds of pounds of meat and warm robes to successful hunters.[66]

The Missouri River flows east and south out of the Rockies and through the northern Great Plains to empty into the Mississippi near St. Louis. Along the Missouri and its major tributaries, Indians lived in earthen lodges surrounded by ditches and stockades for security against attack. Known as Pawnees, Mandans, Hidatsas, and Arikaras, the earth-lodge villagers cultivated corn, beans, and squash on fertile floodplains. During the summer, they ventured onto the plains to hunt bison: a dodgy business for men without horses. On the plains they also encountered small bands of nomads who lived by hunting and gathering.[67]

During the eighteenth century, the nomads and villagers of the Great Plains acquired horses by trading with or raiding the Hispanics of New Mexico to the southwest. The horses seemed a divine gift to people engaged in bison hunting. Mounted men could cover far more ground in much less time to find and overtake herds. Faster and nimbler than bison, mounted men armed with bows could maneuver and attack with deadly skill. By killing more bison, the Great Plains natives became better fed, clothed, and housed. Enriched by meaty protein, they raised the tallest children on the continent, taller even than the relatively well-fed people of the United States. The alluring combination of horses and bison drew more native nations to relocate onto the Great Plains. Coming from either the Rocky Mountains to the west or the Mississippi Valley to the east, the newcomers included Osages, Comanches, Cheyennes, Arapahos, Blackfeet, and the especially numerous peoples known to others as the Sioux and to themselves as Lakotas or Dakotas.[68]

By trading buffalo hides, Great Plains peoples procured guns and ammunition from Francophone traders, who ventured up the Missouri River from St. Louis, or from their British rivals to the north along the Great Lakes and Hudson's Bay. By combining guns and horses, natives became formidable in war against Indian nations that fell behind in the arms race. The strong became stronger by taking horses, women, and children and prime hunting territory from their defeated rivals. With their loot, victors could buy more firearms. Moving southeastward out of the Rocky Mountains, Comanches drove out, killed, or captured their predecessors on the southern plains, primarily peoples known to outsiders as Apaches. Determined to keep their enemies weak, Comanches blocked efforts by French gun traders to push through to deal with desperate Apaches. By 1800, Comanches had grown in number to 20,000—twice as many as all other native peoples on the southern plains and more than the Hispanics of Texas and New Mexico.[69]

Comanche expansion had a domino effect as defeated Apaches fled westward into New Mexico or southward into Texas. There they raided Hispanic ranches and missions and the allied villages of Pueblo peoples to take horses, cattle, women, and children. During the 1770s, raiders killed at least 243 Hispanics in New Mexico: an unprecedented loss for any decade in the century. In 1777, the governor reported that raiding Apaches had reduced his province "to the most deplorable state and greatest poverty." Increasingly beleaguered, Texas and New Mexico were shrinking Hispanic pockets amid increasingly powerful Indian enemies. Preoccupied with fighting the British to the east in Florida, Gálvez could spare no reinforcements for the hard-pressed Hispanic settlements to the west.[70]

In 1778, New Mexico obtained a resourceful new governor, Juan Bautista de Anza, who had discovered the Yuma Crossing route into California. In 1786, he negotiated a treaty of peace and alliance with the Comanches, who received generous annual presents and a profitable trade through Taos. In return, Comanche warriors helped Hispanics attack Apaches, capturing hundreds for sale as slaves to distant Cuba. The bloody alliance reduced Apache pressure on New Mexico, which began again to grow and prosper.[71]

During the 1770s, the American Revolution on the east coast sent out shock waves that accelerated the upheavals underway among native peoples on the Great Plains. In 1775–1776, the Patriot invasion and occupation of Canada disrupted the primary route for Indian trade goods from Europe. Nearly 2,000 miles to the west, natives on the upper Mississippi suffered when suddenly denied access to guns, gunpowder, and ammunition. Some Lakota warriors responded by traveling east to help the British reconquer Canada in 1776. Others shifted westward onto the Great Plains, where they could hunt bison and exploit new trade corridors from either the north at Hudson's Bay or to the south at St. Louis.[72]

The growing number of native nations on the Great Plains increased their violent competition over bison herds. During the mid-eighteenth century, the earth-lodge villagers had held their own because they outnumbered the nomadic newcomers. During the 1770s and 1780s, however, epidemic diseases turned the tables of war, for the traders who brought guns and horses unknowingly carried microscopic pathogens in their bodies and on their breath. Disease and trade revealed the interconnections of native and non-native peoples throughout the continent.[73]

Smallpox spread as a deadly by-product of the American Revolution, for it proliferated in crowded military and refugee camps. In 1776, smallpox ravaged the Patriot army in Canada and the black refugees who joined Lord Dunmore's British force in Virginia. Highly contagious, the disease spread as a virus through the breath of early victims to newer ones. A gruesome scourge, smallpox immobilized, depleted, disfigured, and often killed its victims, who endured intense pain from open sores, splitting headaches, abdominal distress, and raging fevers.[74]

In 1780 and 1781, travelers carried smallpox northward from the Hispanic settlements of Texas, New Mexico, and Louisiana into the native villages and camps of the Great Plains. Raiders then unwittingly spread the disease westward into the Rocky Mountains, where the epidemic afflicted distant Shoshones, who lived 2,000 miles northwest of New Orleans. Smallpox was deadlier for natives than for Euro-Americans, and people in the close quarters of an earth-lodge village suffered greater losses than did the nomads of dispersed and transient encampments. Often an epidemic affected everyone in a village, so that victims had no one to care for them. Affected villages became easy pickings for enemy warriors. One Assiniboine raid on a Hidatsa village on the upper Missouri overwhelmed feeble resistance to discover "the lodges filled with dead bodies" and the nearly dead. By scalping their diseased foes, victors unwittingly carried away the virus to afflict their own friends and kin. The epidemic probably halved the native population of the Great Plains between 1779 and 1783.[75]

The great smallpox epidemic altered the balance of power on the northern Great Plains. No longer outnumbering the nomads, the diminished Mandans, Arikaras, Hidatsas, and Pawnees suffered defeats and the destruction of many earth-lodge villages. Lakotas proved especially aggressive and victorious. "Their very name causes terror, they having so often ravaged and carried off the wives and children of the [A]ricaras," a French trader remarked. Abandoning most of their villages, the survivors crowded into fewer, larger, and heavily fortified towns. From thirty-two villages in 1770, Arikaras shrank into just two towns by 1785. While improving their security against raiders, the consolidation increased their exposure to future epidemics, which facilitated the triumph of the Lakotas on the northern plains.[76]

While Comanches controlled the southern plains and Lakotas dominated the north, Osages prevailed between them on the middle plains. Originally from the Mississippi Valley, 5,000 Osages had moved southwestward to dominate the region between the Arkansas and Missouri rivers. Better armed than their native neighbors, Osages doubled their hunting territory at mid-century, driving Caddos and Wichitas southward into Texas. The victors also stole horses, mules, women, and children from the weak Spanish posts and settlements along the Arkansas River. Ignoring Spanish threats of retribution and defying a trade embargo imposed by that empire, Osages dealt with British traders in Illinois or French traders at St. Louis to procure arms and ammunition. St. Louis merchants happily profited at the expense of their competitors along the Arkansas. A Spanish official found "no lack of persons . . . overcome by greed." Once again, Hispanic imperialists discovered the limits on their power beyond New Orleans.[77]

Thomas Jefferson recognized that nomadic nations, rather than the Spanish, dominated the Great Plains. While Americans were struggling for independence in the east, Comanches, Lakotas, and Osages were aggressively expanding in the west. Referring to Osages and Lakotas, Jefferson concluded "with these two powerful nations we must stand well, because in their quarter we are miserably weak."[78]

While waging war in the east against British rule, Patriots fought west of the Appalachians to suppress the independence of native peoples. Patriots meant to create an "empire of liberty" premised on the

freedom from restraint

ability of common whites to obtain private property by taking land from Indians. Noting that frontier folk "will settle the lands in spite of every body," Jefferson reminded Congress that all "endeavours to discourage and prevent the settling [of] our Western Country" had failed, so it was "necessary to give way to the torrent." Jefferson understood the paradoxical lesson that had eluded the British: an empire in America could only hope to *appear* strong by facilitating the wishes of its citizens, who wanted cheap and fertile land taken as quickly as possible from natives. American leaders needed to ride, rather than resist, the settler wave heading west. While the revolution had western roots, it would also bear western consequences but only after a generous peace treaty rescued the United States.[79]

8

OCEANS

*Our countrymen have all the folly of the ass and all
the passiveness of the sheep in their compositions. . . . If we
are [to be] saved, France and Spain must save us.*
—ALEXANDER HAMILTON, 1780[1]

During the eighteenth century, the great powers maintained navies of wooden vessels powered by wind caught in canvas sails. The mainstay of a fleet was the "ship-of-the-line," a massive battleship of two or three decks. Each vessel mounted at least sixty-four cannons, but seventy-four was more common, and a few behemoths had more than one hundred. A battleship required a crew of at least 500 men, who were expensive to feed and water especially on longer voyages. Organized into fleets, battleships fought in a line against those of the enemy, exchanging close-range broadsides meant to splinter vessels and decimate crews. A commanding admiral tried to coordinate his vessels by means of signal flags from his "flagship," but the signals often produced confusion during battle and recrim-

---

"The Phoenix *and the* Rose *Engaged by the Enemy's Fire Ships and Galleys on the
16 Aug. 1776," engraving by Sir James Wallace, 1778. During Lord Howe's offensive
against New York City, two British frigates forced their passage up the Hudson River
past Forts Washington and Lee despite resistance by galleys and fire ships. Courtesy of
the Library of Congress (LC-USZ62-45594).*

inations afterward. Eighteenth-century naval battles tended to be bloody but indecisive as both sides withdrew to their home ports to repair battered ships. Occasionally an unusually aggressive British admiral broke through the enemy's line to destroy and capture several battleships. French and Spanish admirals fought more cautiously rather than gamble their precious fleets.[2]

Navies also employed lighter and faster ships known as frigates, which had one or two gun decks, twenty-eight to thirty-eight cannon, and a crew of about 300 men. Avoiding combat with ships-of-the-line, frigates instead conducted long-distance scouting and convoying duties. Still smaller vessels—brigs, sloops, and schooners—provided lesser firepower but greater economy to operate.[3]

In eighteenth-century wars, the British sustained the largest fleet with the most experienced and able sailors and officers. Such a fleet was costly to maintain, so the empire discharged most of the sailors and idled or broke up most of the ships during interludes of peace. At the start of the War of the American Revolution, the Royal Navy struggled to recover from budget and manpower cuts imposed after the Seven Years War by the empire. Even as Parliament adopted the confrontational Coercive Acts in 1774, the economy-minded prime minister, Lord North, had mandated a further reduction in sailors and the shipwrights needed to repair and build warships. In 1775, the navy employed only 18,000 sailors: too few to sustain the global reach of the empire. The head of the Admiralty, the Earl of Sandwich (who gets credit for inventing the sandwich), found "the ships decaying and unfit for service, the storehouses empty, and a general despondency running through the whole naval department."[4]

In 1775 and 1776, the Royal Navy was stretched thin by its vast and conflicting duties. In addition to ferrying troops and supplies across the Atlantic, the navy tried to enforce a blockade on American ports to hurt the Patriots' economy and deprive them of imported munitions. Struggling with those assignments, the navy also failed to protect British merchant ships from Patriot privateers—fast-sailing and lightly armed warships financed by private interests. A frustrated admiral described his command in American waters as a "choice of difficulties and scarcity of means."[5]

The Royal Navy faced a small but annoying adversary in the Continental Navy created by Congress in 1775. Unable to afford ships-of-the-line, Patriots instead relied on frigates and smaller vessels. In March 1776, the little navy surprised, captured, and plundered a minor British naval base at New Providence in the Bahamas. Thereafter, the Continental vessels dispersed to prey on merchant ships.[6]

The most celebrated Patriot commander was John Paul Jones. Slight and short, he compensated with a fiery temper to intimidate the tough men who worked as sailors. Born in Scotland and initially named John Paul, he had captained British ships in the slave trade. After killing a defiant sailor, Paul fled from prosecution, enhanced his name by adding Jones, and escaped to America. He obtained a commission from Congress in 1776 and raided the Scottish port of Whitehaven in April 1778. A year-and-a-half later on the Yorkshire coast, Jones won the Continental Navy's greatest sea victory by capturing a superior British frigate after a bloody, three-hour battle that wrecked his ship and killed nearly half of his crew. Although much celebrated by Patriots, Jones's victory was a last hurrah for the Continental Navy, which shrank into insignificance through budget woes and the capture or destruction of most of its remaining ships by the enemy.[7]

While the Continental Navy faded away, the Royal Navy steadily grew under the leadership of Lord Sandwich, who by the end of 1779, more than doubled the fleet to 314 warships manned by 70,000 sailors and marines. Two years later, that complement grew to 105,000 men: an unprecedented number in that service.[8]

That expansion came in the nick of time, for the French entered the war in early 1778. British leaders feared that the enemy fleet would seize control of the English Channel and ferry across an army to invade England. Preoccupied with that threat, Sandwich concentrated the Royal Navy at the western approach to the Channel, stinting naval forces elsewhere on the world's oceans. Opposing that concentration, Lord Germain predicted, "Lord Sandwich will not risk the country upon any account, so that I apprehend we shall have some misfortunes abroad."[9]

In 1778, the French massed troops along the English Channel but did so only as a diversion, for they instead planned to exploit their naval initiative to dispatch a fleet with troops to make trouble elsewhere in the world. The Comte d'Estaing led France's Mediterranean fleet of twelve battleships and five frigates westward across the Atlantic to help the Patriots attack the British garrisons and ships at New York and Newport. But the attacks failed and d'Estaing sailed away to the West Indies, which were more important to the French.[10]

West Indies

The French and British valued their West Indian colonies more than anything on the North American continent. Sugar cane raised by slave labor enriched planters and the merchants who transported sugar and rum to Europe. Taxes on slave imports and sugar exports generated greater revenue for the rival empires than any other colonial trade. By capturing sugar-rich islands, each belligerent hoped to enhance its financial and naval strength while weakening the enemy.[11]

To guard a dozen islands scattered across 500 miles and interspersed with French possessions, the British had only 1,060 regulars fit for duty in 1778. Nor could the British West Indies rally a significant militia, for free whites comprised less than a tenth of the population and were busy guarding the enslaved majority. In the event of invasion, many planters preferred to surrender quickly, before prolonged resistance provoked the enemy to burn houses, mills, and workshops or take away slaves.[12]

Only naval supremacy could protect island colonies and capture those of the enemy. Raising more cane than food, the islanders would starve if cut off from imported provisions by an enemy with a dominant fleet. The planters also risked bankruptcy if they could not export their annual produce to satisfy creditors in Great Britain. But maintaining a fleet in the Caribbean was dangerous, difficult, and expensive, for wooden ships, canvas sails, and hemp ropes rotted more quickly in

— The West Indies, 1780 —

FLORIDA

Gulf of Mexico

BAHAMAS

Havana

CUBA

GREATER ANTILLES

JAMAICA   Port Royal

SAINT-DOMINGUE

HISPANIOLA

Santo Domingo

Caribbean Sea

Cartagena

PANAMA

SOUTH AMERICA

ATLANTIC OCEAN

PUERTO RICO   VIRGIN IS.

ST. MARTIN

SABA

ST. EUSTATIUS

ST. CHRISTOPHER

NEVIS

ANTIGUA

MONTSERRAT

GUADALOUPE

DOMINICA

MARTINIQUE

ST. LUCIA

BARBADOS

ST. VINCENT

GRENADA

TOBAGO

TRINIDAD

LESSER ANTILLES

0 Miles   500

0 Kilometers   500

© 2015 Jeffrey L. Ward

"Le vaisseau le Languedoc rematé en pleine mer ainsi que le Marseillais . . . 17 Aoust 1778," engraving by Pierre Ozanne. *After undergoing repairs, the French warships* Languedoc *and* Marseillais *rejoin the fleet of Comte d'Estaing in August 1778. Courtesy of the Library of Congress (LC-USZ62-903).*

the hot and humid conditions. And mosquito-borne tropical diseases depleted military garrisons and naval crews.[13]

With 8,000 troops already in the West Indies, the French had a great initial advantage over the 1,000 scattered redcoats in 1778. Striking first, 2,000 French troops easily captured Dominica, defended by a mere 41 redcoats. That defeat alarmed Britain's powerful West Indian lobby of merchants and planters, who demanded more troops and warships, even at the cost of weakening the Channel fleet. The king agreed, "If we lose our sugar islands, it will be impossible to raise money to continue the war."[14]

Thereafter, the British subordinated their war effort in North America to the defense of the West Indies. An imperial official declared, "The war has and ever must be determined in the West Indies." For the rest of the conflict, the empire sent more reinforcements to the Caribbean than to North America. Indeed, imperial officials drew on the New York garrison as a reserve to bolster West Indian defenses at moments of crisis. New York's commander, Sir Henry Clinton, complained "of expeditions sent out everywhere, reinforcements to every place but this. Is it because America is become no object? If so, withdraw before you are disgraced!"[15]

war was more in WI than North America

In late 1778, orders from London compelled Clinton to send 5,000 men from New York to the West Indies under the command of General James Grant. That expedition attacked St. Lucia, a French-held island with a good harbor and strategic location near the main French naval base in the Caribbean: Martinique. Grant's men repelled a powerful French counterattack by d'Estaing, who launched ill-conceived frontal assaults that killed or wounded nearly a third of his soldiers. D'Estaing withdrew to Martinique in defeat, obliging the French governor of St. Lucia to surrender. Consolidating their victory, the British constructed substantial new fortifications to render St. Lucia their premier naval station in the eastern Caribbean and a looming menace to Martinique.[16]

In April 1779, Spain entered the war, compounding Britain's problems. As the world's second- and third-largest naval powers, the French and Spanish could combine to outnumber the Royal Navy's warships by 44 percent. During the summer, the allies threatened to seize control of the English Channel and then ferry 31,000 French troops across to invade England. "Everything is now at stake," Sandwich worried. George III agreed that Britain confronted "the most serious crisis this nation ever knew." But coordinating and supplying two massive fleets from different nations delayed the allied combination until early August, when sixty-six battleships belatedly entered the Channel. They outnumbered the British warships, but the allied fleet's crews and officers were demoralized by hunger, depleted by disease, and buffeted by adverse winds. Losing their nerve, the French and Spanish commanders withdrew without a fight, canceling the invasion threat for the rest of the war.[17]

In the West Indies, during the summer of 1779, d'Estaing won his first victories by capturing the islands of St. Vincent and Grenada. The British feared that the French would next attack Jamaica, the most precious of their colonies. In September, British leaders ordered 4,000 redcoats to hasten from New York to reinforce Jamaica. Their arrival dissuaded d'Estaing from assaulting the island. Instead, he sailed north to attack the smaller British garrison at Savannah, Georgia, where he suffered another defeat. Returning to France, he left operations in the West Indies to a new French commander, the Comte de Guichen, who arrived with a fresh squadron in early 1780.[18]

French and American privateers took a toll on merchant ships trading with the British West Indies. The smaller, eastern Caribbean islands especially suffered from the interruption of their food imports. The price of scarce provisions also soared because of increased demand from thousands of sailors and soldiers sent to the West Indies in wartime. Kept at the end of the food chain, slaves suffered famine conditions. Between 1778 and 1781, at least 2,000 starved to death on the islands of Barbados, Montserrat, Nevis, and St. Kitts. Another 7,000 died on Antigua, where a severe drought and an outbreak of dysentery compounded their miseries.[19]

Planters worried that famine would provoke a bloody rebellion by the enslaved. In fact, the influx of soldiers depressed rebellions in wartime, but the turmoil did invite many slaves to run away. Some enlisted for one side or the other in the conflict. Given the desperate shortage of men for warships and regiments, some officers accepted black recruits although that angered planters and their legislators. Other runaways became maroons by stealing arms and making refuges in the mountainous recesses of some islands, principally St. Vincent, Tobago, and Jamaica.[20]

While bearing soaring costs for imported lumber and food, planters also suffered from diminished harvests and exports. Malnourished slaves lagged in cutting and processing sugarcane. When war interrupted the slave trade, planters could not replace their losses from disease, hunger, and escape. Predation by enemy warships pushed up the planters' insurance premiums on cargoes from a prewar 2 percent of value to 28 percent. Freight charges also tripled as merchant ships became harder to come by, and sailors got higher wages as naval demand increased their scarcity. Sometimes planters could not export their produce because the Royal Navy had impressed all available merchant ships for use as troop transports. In 1781, British West Indian sugar exports fell to half of their prewar level. Pinched between soaring costs and diminished production, planters' profits dwindled, as bankruptcies and foreclosures soared.[21]

Planters demanded more soldiers and sailors to repel enemy invasion and suppress maroons. But the empire struggled to sustain a large force of Britons on islands where malaria and yellow fever killed so many newcomers. The 15 percent annual loss of troops to disease in the West Indies exceeded the 6 percent of those serving in New York or the 1 percent in Canada. In Jamaica, one regiment had 1,008 men in 1778 but only 18 survivors in 1783.[22]

Convinced that black people were less vulnerable to tropical diseases, imperial officers proposed recruiting free blacks or slaves (with the promise of freedom) to bolster depleted garrisons. The proposal appalled planters, who wanted only white men as reinforcements because black military service threatened to discredit the myth of white racial superiority that justified slavery. In 1778, the governor of Jamaica organized a black regiment but had to disband it after fierce protests from the West Indian lobby, which insisted that it was "a policy . . . promising relief for the present but pregnant with future evils." Masters did tolerate conscription of their slaves to build and repair fortifications, so long as they carried no arms and remained enslaved.[23]

The French and Spanish could sustain larger forces in the Caribbean in part because they more readily enlisted and armed free blacks. *whereas the Cath. actually owned slaves* These empires also had more free blacks to recruit because the Catholic church and their laws encouraged manumissions. A quarter of the blacks in Spanish America were free, compared to less than a twentieth in the British West Indies. More pragmatic in tincturing their racism, the Spanish and French recognized that an armed and intermediary caste of free blacks tended to secure, rather than imperil, the slave system. Struggling to defend their islands, Britons paid a premium to cling to especially rigid racial prejudices.[24]

Despite the pressures and losses of war, British West Indians remained loyal to the empire unlike their North American counterparts. The Barbadian legislature regretted "the delusion of those unhappy people, who have been seduced to exchange their former unbounded happiness for ... a ruinous state of anarchy and confusion." West Indian theater performances concluded with rousing sing-alongs to the imperial anthem "Rule Britannia." West Indian legislatures voted generous subsidies for the military despite the pain of raising taxes during the economic woes of war. British planters expected their mighty empire eventually to triumph yet again. They also hated the French and despised the Spanish, so their entry into the war heightened its stakes and clarified its issues to British West Indians.[25]

Rodney

In late 1779, George III favored sending more warships and troops to the West Indies, weakening the fleet defending the English Channel. Despite the danger at home, he declared, "We must risk something, otherwise we shall only vegetate in this war. I own I wish either to get through it with spirit, or with a crash be ruined." In January 1780, the empire dispatched General Sir John Vaughan with 7,000 troops in transports for the West Indies: the largest reinforcement sent across the Atlantic since 1776.[26]

The empire awarded the West Indian naval command to Sir George Rodney, an energetic but controversial admiral. Tall and lean, he had a prominent nose and angular cheeks. Although elegant, voluble, and sociable, he was also egotistical and opinionated, dwelling with delight on his favorite subject: the feats and plans of Sir George Rodney. Victorious during the Seven Years War, Rodney had been knighted and promoted to vice admiral. Elected to Parliament, he became a hard-liner on American issues, favoring taxes and coercion. His expensive tastes in gaming, women, food, drink, and electioneering embarrassed his foolhardy creditors. The admiral's notoriety for playing fast and loose with public funds made Sandwich reluctant to give him the new command, but Rodney had a champion in Germain, who recognized that the empire needed a more aggressive naval commander in the Caribbean.[27]

Rodney's self-assurance inspired subordinates and intimidated enemy commanders. Although a stickler for naval discipline, Rodney also took pains to improve the diet and health of his sailors. Far fewer died on his watch than under previous commanders in the West Indies.[28]

In May 1780, he attacked the Comte de Guichen and the French Caribbean fleet near Martinique. For once, Rodney's luck failed as most of his captains were new to him and easily confused by faulty signals from his flagship. Both fleets suffered severe damage but neither captured any battleships. For the rest of 1780, the two evenly matched fleets (twenty-three battleships each) jockeyed for position and occasionally clashed without decisive consequences.[29]

In December 1780, the British declared war on the Dutch to stop their profitable trade in munitions and naval stores with France and the French West Indies. Reacting quickly to the news, Rodney targeted the Dutch West Indian island of St. Eustatius for attack. Only five miles long by two-and-a-half miles wide, St. Eustatius produced little sugar, but the Dutch had made it a free port, attracting merchants and ships from throughout the Caribbean and Europe. Rodney complained that the little island had done "more harm than all the arms of her most potent enemies, and alone supported the infamous American Rebellion." He longed to plunder the well-stocked warehouses and many merchant ships in the island's harbor. In early 1781, he attacked with fifteen warships and 3,000 troops. Defended by no warships and only sixty Dutch regulars, the surprised governor of St. Eustatius surrendered on February 3.[30]

Rather than sailing on to a new target, Rodney settled down for three months to ransack the island's homes, warehouses, and ships. His men even dug up graves to search for treasure. By keeping the Dutch flag flying over the port during his occupation, Rodney enticed scores of unwary trading ships into his trap. He auctioned the loot to profiteering merchants, who obtained ships and cargoes at half their value. He estimated the returns as £2 million, from which he would reap a sixteenth as his prize share. Rodney hoped to retire his massive debts, buy a London mansion, and procure "the best harpsichord money can purchase." A subordinate admiral described Rodney and his partner in plunder, General Vaughan, as "wickedly rapacious." Indeed, they sold plunder to anyone who paid well, including bidders with French and American accents, so many captured munitions reached Britain's enemies after all. Sadly for Rodney, French warships intercepted much of his own loot in transit back to England.[31]

The long, slow sack of St. Eustatius immobilized Rodney's fleet at a critical period in the war. He canceled plans to attack the Dutch colonies of Surinam and Curacao. His distraction also enabled a new French fleet of twenty-four battleships from Europe to slip into Martinique under the Comte de Grasse. Awarded naval superiority by Rodney's negligence, the French seized the island of Tobago in early June. Two days too late, Rodney showed up and then withdrew without a fight, exhibiting uncharacteristic restraint. Evidently, Rodney wanted to live long enough to enjoy his new wealth.[32]

Many of the plundered shipowners at St. Eustatius were British merchants, whom Rodney derided as smugglers and traitors who got what they deserved. Back in London, the merchants sued Rodney in the courts, and the opposition in Parliament launched an investigation of the admiral's conduct. To defend his financial and political interests, Rodney sailed back to England, departing the Caribbean on August 1 during the fateful summer of 1781. He took away part of his fleet, leaving behind only fourteen serviceable battleships under the command of Sir Samuel Hood. Rodney's abrupt departure compounded the damage wrought by his failure to intercept de Grasse, who proved unusually daring and resourceful for a French admiral.[33]

In June, de Grasse received an alarming dispatch from the Chevalier de la Luzerne, the French ambassador to the United States. Luzerne worried that the British invasion of Virginia, under Lord Cornwallis, would complete the accelerating collapse of Patriot resolve and unity. Luzerne warned de Grasse, "It is you alone who can deliver the invaded states from that crisis which is so alarming that . . . for their existence it is necessary to do all you can." The French admiral decided to sail north with his fleet to trap Cornwallis in Virginia. With hurricane season about to begin in the Caribbean, sailing north was also prudent.[34]

To procure supplies and pay his crews, de Grasse got financial assistance from Cuba's Spanish governor, Bernardo de Gálvez, and his deputy, Francisco de Saavedra. Although no Spanish warships joined de Grasse's expedition, they assumed responsibility for defending the allies' islands and shipping in his absence. This financial and naval support proved the most important aid that the Spanish gave to the Patriots during the war. Saavedra recognized that the allies "could not waste the most decisive opportunity in the whole war." In the summer of 1781, the key French and Spanish officers acted decisively to rescue the faltering United States. In early August, de Grasse's twenty-eight battle ships, supported by frigates, sailed from Cuba bound for the Chesapeake, bringing along 3,000 troops. That fleet included the largest warship in the Americas, his flagship the *Ville de Paris*, which mounted 110 guns.[35]

Yorktown

The British Admiral Hood led fourteen battleships northward in belated search of de Grasse. Unable to find him on the ocean, Hood headed to New York, where he and his ships passed under the command of the senior naval officer, Rear-Admiral Sir Thomas Graves. They sailed south with nineteen battleships to attack de Grasse's fleet guarding the mouth of Chesapeake Bay on September 5. With twenty-four battleships, 1,800 guns (to the British 1,400), and 19,000 sailors (compared to 13,000 Britons), de Grasse simply had to play defense, fending off attack. The British faltered at the more daunting task of breaking through into the bay to rescue Cornwallis. Neither side captured any ships, but the British ships suffered greater damage, so Graves drew away to New York for repairs, leaving Cornwallis to fend for himself.[36]

On August 14, George Washington had learned that de Grasse's fleet was bound for the Chesapeake. At that time, his soldiers and a

French division under the Comte de Rochambeau were probing the defenses of New York, seeking a weak point to attack Clinton's garrison. By making a feint at Staten Island, Washington and Rochambeau fooled Clinton into keeping his 20,000 men immobilized in their entrenchments, while the allied force hastened south via Philadelphia to the Chesapeake. In the best-conducted, longest, and most important march of the war, Washington and Rochambeau covered 450 miles in thirty days. French money bought supplies, while Washington arranged horses, teamsters, boats, and provisions along the way. He gambled in leaving the main British army behind, while he marched into uncertainty. Washington had no guarantee that the French fleet could fend off the Royal Navy, which might swoop in to rescue Cornwallis. In this long war, the coordination of distant forces from different nations had faltered before as the defeats at Newport and Savannah had shown. Fortunately, Washington had good reason to trust in de Grasse's ability and Clinton's inertia.[37]

Cornwallis and Clinton indulged in the petty squabbling that so often divided commanders. Shunting blame back and forth like a shuttlecock, both helped to paralyze the British force in Virginia. Regretting his foray there, Cornwallis wanted to return to South Carolina, but Clinton ordered him to stay put and fortify a riverside base. Cornwallis holed up at the village of Yorktown, on the southwestern bank of the York River. With nearly 1,000 sailors and 7,000 troops, a mix of redcoats, Hessians, and Loyalists, Cornwallis still had a strong position until de Grasse, Washington, and Rochambeau closed the trap around him on September 29. On land, Washington commanded 16,000 troops, nearly half of them French. Add the 19,000 sailors of de Grasse's fleet, and the siege involved more than twice as many French as American combatants.[38]

Conducting a classic siege in the European manner, Washington pushed his trenches ever closer to the British lines to facilitate fire by heavy artillery, most of it French. On October 14, Washington's men stormed two key British redoubts, one taken by French troops and the other by Patriots led by Alexander Hamilton. That victory enabled the allies to advance their cannon and mortars from the former 600 yards to within 350 yards of the British lines. Increasingly accurate and intense, artillery fire destroyed the village's sixty houses, inflicted heavy casualties, and demoralized the defenders. A Hessian soldier noted that Yorktown was filled with bodies "whose heads, arms, and legs had been shot off." Another reported that trapped Loyalists "fled to the waterside and hid in hastily contrived shelters on the banks, but many of them were killed by bursting bombs." While the allied commanders acted decisively, Cornwallis stayed within his lines, "passive beyond conception," Washington marveled, save for one ineffective sortie on October 16.[39]

Running short on food, Cornwallis ousted hundreds of runaway slaves who had joined his force. Many also suffered from disease. A Patriot officer saw "numbers in that condition starving and helpless, begging of us as we passed them for God's sake to kill them, as they were in great pain and misery." A Virginian reported, "An immense number of Negroes have died in the most miserable Manner in York[town]."[40]

On October 17, 1781, Cornwallis opened negotiations to surrender his army. The formal capitulation came two days later, when the British marched out of their ruined refuge and through the allied ranks to stack their arms and become prisoners. Too late, Clinton sailed from New York with a relief force of twenty-five battleships and 7,000 troops on October 19: the day of the surrender. Reaching Chesapeake Bay on October 24, Clinton learned of his fool's errand and sailed back to New York. He was right about one thing: "If Lord Cornwallis's army fails, I should have little hope of seeing British Dominion re-established in America, as our country cannot replace that Army." Cornwallis had surrendered a quarter of the redcoats in America, and the empire was too hard-pressed elsewhere to replace them.[41]

Cornwallis also crippled British prospects by accepting surrender terms that denied his Loyalist troops the protection of prisoner-of-war status. Unlike the redcoats, Loyalists taken at Yorktown risked harsh punishment, even execution, as deserters and traitors by the Patriots.

News of Cornwallis's indifference shocked and demoralized Loyalists elsewhere.[42]

Washington's victory was a remarkable turnabout, for the Patriot cause had been desperate, verging on collapse, in early 1781. Americans were sick of war and hyperinflation. Mutinies had rippled through the Continental Army, and new enlistments dwindled while desertions soared. Washington's main army shrank to just 3,500 men in the spring. Meanwhile, Congress ran out of money as the states dodged making their payments, while citizens evaded paying taxes to their states. Respect for Congress dissolved into mockery, suspicion, and contempt. "Our affairs are in a most wretched situation," a Maryland congressman noted, "Congress is at its wits End . . . and unless the French fleet and Army arrive very soon we shall in all probability be in the most deplorable situation." Hamilton concluded, "If we are [to be] saved, France and Spain must save us." Thanks to those two powers, desperate Patriots got the crucial help that saved their cause and won the war at Yorktown.[43] *depended on the French*

Shocks

Yorktown stunned Britain's leaders. Germain conveyed the bad news to the prime minister, Lord North, who received it "as he would have taken a ball in his breast," crying out "Oh God! It is all over!" The British still had 30,000 men in North America, occupying the seaports of New York, Charles Town, and Savannah. But the public will to keep fighting the Patriots (and paying taxes to do so) withered after the demoralizing news from Yorktown. Parliament no longer would support throwing good money and lives after bad in North America. As the first sacrifice to the political shift, North pushed Germain to resign as the American Secretary in January 1782. Defections by war-weary Members of Parliament cost the administration its majority in March 1782, inducing North to resign. When the king balked at accepting that resignation, North reminded his sovereign, "The torrent is too strong to be resisted. Your Majesty is well apprized that, in this country

depends largely on homefront

the Prince on the Throne cannot, with prudence, oppose the deliberate resolutions of the House of Commons. . . . Their sentiments, whether just or erroneous, must ultimately prevail."[44]

Former leaders of the opposition conducted the new administration with the Marquis of Rockingham as prime minister, and the Earl of Shelburne as American Secretary. In July, Rockingham died and Shelburne replaced him as prime minister. In April, the British had opened peace negotiations with Patriot diplomats in Paris.[45]

While support for the American war withered, Britons kept fighting the French and Spanish elsewhere in the world. The French foreign minister, the Comte de Vergennes, recognized that Yorktown was not yet decisive: "One would be wrong to believe that it means an immediate peace; it is not in the English character to give up so easily." Instead of ending the war, Yorktown redirected the conflict to the Mediterranean, India, and the West Indies.[46]

The British reaped more bad news in late 1781 and early 1782. In August 1781 in the Mediterranean, a French and Spanish force of 14,000 men besieged a British garrison of 2,000 on the island of Minorca. Suffering from scurvy, the Britons surrendered in February 1782. In the West Indies in late 1781, the French captured St. Eustatius, where the take included a treasure chest with £250,000 meant to pay the redcoats in America. In February 1782, de Grasse seized the British islands of St. Kitts, Montserrat, and Nevis. Lord John Cavendish lamented that "the great and splendid empire of Britain was nearly overturned; calamity, disgrace, and disaster were pouring on us from every quarter."[47]

To save imperiled Jamaica, the Crown turned to Rodney. Despite his notorious and untimely looting of St. Eustatius, he remained the best fighting admiral in the Royal Navy. The government promoted him and sent him back to the West Indies to deal with de Grasse. The imperial cabinet also bolstered his force by reducing the Channel fleet, affording Rodney thirty-six battleships to counter de Grasse's thirty-three. Determined to refute his critics, Rodney brought an enhanced resolve to his renewed command.[48]

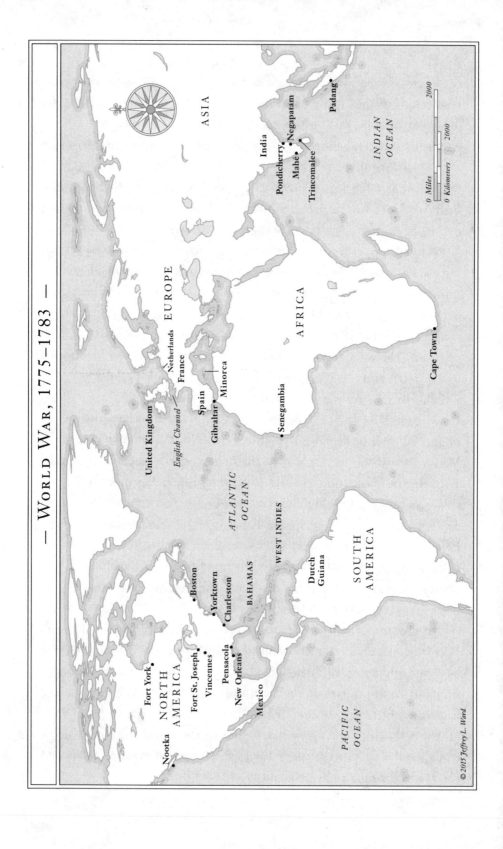

— WORLD WAR, 1775–1783 —

ASIA

Padang

Negapatam
India
Pondicherry
Mahé
Trincomalee

INDIAN
OCEAN

2000

2000

0 Miles
0 Kilometers

EUROPE

Netherlands
France

United Kingdom

English Channel

Spain
Gibraltar
Minorca

AFRICA

Senegambia

Cape Town

ATLANTIC
OCEAN

WEST INDIES

BAHAMAS

Dutch
Guiana

SOUTH
AMERICA

Boston
Yorktown
Charleston

Fort York

Fort St. Joseph
Vincennes
Pensacola
New Orleans
Mexico

NORTH
AMERICA

Nootka

PACIFIC
OCEAN

© 2015 Jeffrey L. Ward

In early April, de Grasse sailed from Martinique bound to Santo Domingo with a convoy of 150 merchant ships and transports bearing 10,000 troops. After rendezvousing with Spanish forces, de Grasse planned to attack Jamaica. But the French fleet had to pass through the Iles des Saintes between the larger islands of Dominica (to the south) and Guadeloupe (to the north). Sailing into that passage, Rodney forced de Grasse to protect his convoy by drawing up his fleet into line for battle. A gust of wind pushed some of the French vessels ahead, creating a gap. Rodney alertly pounced, sailing his flagship and several others into the gap to rake exposed French ships with broadsides, compounding the chaos in their line. After twelve hours of close, bloody conflict, five French battleships surrendered, including the mighty *Ville de Paris* along with Admiral de Grasse, who became Rodney's prisoner. Two more battleships surrendered to British pursuit a week later. The loss of seven ships, 6,000 lives, and one admiral discouraged the French, who canceled their attack on Jamaica.[49]

Giddy with relief, the British public erupted in celebration at the news, particularly the capture of de Grasse and his massive flagship, which multiplied the impression made by the victory. Jamaica's merchants, planters, and legislators funded an octagonal stone temple to house a neoclassical statue of the heroic Rodney. Medals, ballads, poems, pottery, and prints celebrated him as the greatest of British admirals. "Rodney Forever" became the hit song that summer in London. After seven years of frustration and mounting gloom, the Battle of the Saintes restored optimism in Britain. A Member of Parliament noted, "The country, exhausted and humiliated, seemed to revive in its own estimation and to resume once more its dignity among nations."[50]

Instead of the looter who helped to lose America, Rodney became the hero who saved the more important colonies in the West Indies. The Crown promoted him to the aristocracy as a baronet and awarded a lifetime, annual pension of £2,000. His former critics in Parliament joined in extolling the admiral. Lacking such acclaim, Sir Henry Clinton (rather than Rodney) bore the blame for the debacle at Yorktown because empires need scapegoats as well as heroes.[51]

"Count de Grasse, the French Admiral, Resigning His Sword to Admiral Rodney,"
British engraving by George Frederick Raymond, 1785. Courtesy of the Library of
Congress (LC-USZ62-45213).

The British faced another great test in defending Gibraltar, a naval base at the strategic entrance to the Mediterranean Sea. In July 1779, the Spanish and their French allies had launched a close siege by land and sea forces. Three years later, the allies sought to break the stalemate by building ten massive floating batteries. Thickly timbered and mounting a total of 152 cannon, they threatened to overwhelm the King's Bastion, the key seaside defense at Gibraltar. In September 1782, French and Spanish sailors rowed the batteries, supported by gunboats, toward their target, but they mishandled the clumsy vessels in high winds and rough seas. During eighteen hours of intense bombardment, the British set ablaze and destroyed the batteries, killing 2,000 allied sailors. The demoralized allies declined to fight in October, when a British relief fleet, under Lord Richard Howe, arrived with reinforcements and supplies to lift the siege.[52]

In addition to their victories at the Saintes and Gibraltar, the British improved their position in India. During the 1760s and 1770s, India grew in importance to the empire as a prime source of commerce and revenue. While native princes controlled the interior, the British held four colonies on the coast: Bombay on the west and Bihar, Bengal (including the overall capital of Calcutta), and Madras on the eastern shore. The empire entrusted their management to the East India Company, which appointed an overall governor-general. Unlike in North America, British settlers were few and redundant in distant and crowded India, so several hundred officials and soldiers relied on thousands of native collaborators to run the colonies. Based in seaports, the East India Company projected power into the interior through military alliances with some princes at the expense of others in a divide-and-conquer strategy. Claiming paternalistic motives, officials insisted that British rule in India protected the Hindu majority from brutal Muslim princes and rapacious French interlopers.[53]

In 1778–1779, the British seized French posts on the southeast coast. Most of those "British" troops were, in fact, "sepoys," Indians hired and trained by the East India Company. The British victories alarmed the Maratha Confederacy of Indian princes, who dominated

the center of the subcontinent, and Haider Ali, the powerful prince of
Mysore in south India. He derided other Indian "princes, who did not
know how to hate the English like himself." Brilliant and resourceful,
Haider Ali recruited, equipped, and trained a large army with the help
of French advisors and imported weapons. In 1780, he attacked the
British in Madras, killing or capturing an army of 4,000 men in Sep-
tember at Pollilur. A defeated officer called it "the severest blow the
English ever sustained in India." But British counterattacks defeated
Haider Ali's forces in three battles in July, August, and September
1781. The British also seized the Dutch entrepôts and garrisons at
Negapatam in November 1781 and Tricomalee in January 1782.[54]

In February 1782, a French squadron of five battleships with 1,100
troops arrived in Indian waters. Although obese and rumpled, the
commander, Admiral Pierre André de Suffren, was aggressive and
competent. The French initially had sent him to southern Africa to help
defend the Dutch colony at the Cape of Good Hope. After scaring off
a British attack there, Suffren sailed eastward across the Indian Ocean
to bolster Haider Ali. The French and British fleets fought five bloody
but inconclusive battles. Suffren's only victory was the recapture of
Trincomalee. In late 1782, the death of Haider Ali and the unraveling
of the Maratha Confederacy from internal dissension abated Indian
pressure on the British. Meanwhile, substantial military reinforcements from Europe bolstered the British force. By war's end, the British had enhanced their power in India despite the best that Haider Ali
and Admiral Suffren could throw at them.[55]

beginning of empire

Peace

During the spring of 1781, Vergennes instructed Luzerne to press Congress to commit its diplomats to follow the French lead in anticipated
peace negotiations. Vergennes distrusted the blustery John Adams,
who had come to Paris in 1780, asserting that he alone could negotiate
peace for the United States. Adams added that he would neither heed

nor even inform the French of his dealings with the British. Given France's massive investment of money, warships, and troops in the faltering United States, Vergennes sought assurances via Luzerne that their client state would not make a separate peace by cutting a secret deal with the British. Weak and dependent on French aid, Congress dutifully instructed its diplomats "to undertake nothing in the negotiations for peace or truce" without informing French leaders to secure their "concurrence, and ultimately to govern yourselves by their advice and opinion." To further restrain Adams, Congress added Benjamin Franklin, John Jay, Henry Laurens, and Thomas Jefferson to the peace commission (but Jefferson declined to go).[56]

In any peace deal, American leaders longed to gain Canada and a vast western domain beyond the Appalachian Mountains as far as the Mississippi. These grand territorial ambitions far exceeded the weak military position of the United States in 1782, when the trans-Appalachian Patriots held only a few, small, and embattled settlements in Kentucky, Tennessee, and western Virginia.[57] *illogical*

Although committed to Americans' independence, Vergennes regarded their territorial claims as "foolishness not meriting serious refutation." By keeping the British in Canada, Vergennes also hoped to perpetuate their frictions with the Americans, who would then have to cling to their alliance with France. "But you will agree, Monsieur," Vergennes assured a French diplomat, "that this way of thinking ought to be an impenetrable secret from the Americans. It would be a crime that they would never pardon." But Vergennes would soon find that Americans were his superiors at deception.[58]

The French also favored their primary ally, Spain, whose leaders sought to keep the United States restricted and weak lest it expand at the expense of Spanish America. A Spanish diplomat, Conde de Aranda, aptly predicted, "This Federal Republic was born a pigmy" and "needed the aid and strength of two powerful states like Spain and France to accomplish its independence. The day will come when it will grow up, become a giant and be greatly feared in the Americas. Then it will forget the benefits that it had received from the two powers and only think [of] its own aggrandizement." To hem in Patriot America, Spain claimed a broad buffer zone east of Louisiana as far as the new settlements in Georgia and Tennessee.[59]

Meanwhile, the British prime minister, Lord Shelburne, hoped to entice Americans back into some association with the empire on "terms of reunion and reconciliation founded in a just attention to our mutual interests." Shelburne offered legislative autonomy to the Americans if they would accept British leadership in foreign and military affairs. A political crisis in Ireland presented Shelburne with an opportunity to define a constitutional model meant to lull protests there and intrigue Americans.[60]

In theory, Ireland was an independent kingdom, but its monarch was the British king, and his ministers controlled civil, military, and judicial appointments. Thousands of occupying redcoats dominated the Irish and served as a reserve for deployment overseas in an emergency. Although Catholics comprised three-quarters of the people, they were denied political and property rights. Most were poor laborers and peasants who rented small farms and cottages from Anglican landlords. Presbyterian dissenters prevailed in Ulster (in northern Ireland), and they also resented domination by the Anglican elite based in Dublin. Anglicans owned 90 percent of the land and held almost all government offices, military commissions, and seats in the Irish Parliament, which had less autonomy than a colonial assembly.[61]

After the war began in 1775, many Irish Catholics and Presbyterians openly sympathized with the Patriots in America. The situation became tense, as British leaders had to withdraw most of their troops in Ireland for deployment in America. When the French entered the war in 1778, the British lacked enough regulars to defend Ireland from invasion. Seizing the opportunity, Irish reformers pressured the British by organizing an armed militia, known as the Volunteers, ostensibly to defend the island. Desperate for men, the British reluctantly accepted the Volunteer units, which doubled as political clubs to agitate for economic and political reforms.[62]

In 1780, Parliament made economic concessions, lifting restrictions on Ireland's exports to the rest of the empire. In early 1782, the Shelburne administration also conceded legislative autonomy to the Irish Parliament, which would no longer have to answer to the imperial Parliament in London. But Ireland remained subordinated to the Crown, which still appointed the Irish executive: a lord lieutenant and his cabinet. Legislation by the Irish Parliament also still required the king's assent, and Ireland's Catholic majority still lacked political rights.[63]

Ireland's new constitution failed to entice Americans to rejoin the empire. Such a model might have appealed in 1774 but not in 1782, after seven years of bitter, bloody war for independence. Rejecting Shelburne's scheme, Franklin concluded, "We have no safety but in our own independence." As he anticipated, Ireland's supposed legislative autonomy proved hollow as its parliament remained dominated by a reactionary Anglican oligarchy tied to Britain.[64]

In April 1782, Shelburne assigned peace negotiations in Paris to Richard Oswald, a wealthy, elderly, and erudite Scot whose philosophical liberalism coexisted with investments in the slave trade. A retired merchant, he lacked diplomatic experience but had a conciliatory manner. By July, Shelburne recognized that, to make peace, Britain had to recognize American independence. Setting aside his dream of reunion, Shelburne became "most anxious, if it is to be given up, that it should be done *decidedly*, so as to avoid all future Risque of Enmity."[65]

Tensions among the American commissioners complicated the negotiations. Absent and ill, Laurens played no part until the last two days of discussions. Bedridden by kidney stones and gout, Franklin clung to his lodgings for most of the summer, leaving the negotiations to Jay, who disliked the Spanish, distrusted the French, and suspected Franklin of working for Vergennes rather than Congress. In October, Adams returned to Paris to strengthen Jay's hand and paranoia. Adams despised Franklin as a cunning liar out to ruin Adams and subordinate the United States to France. According to Adams, Vergennes meant "to keep us down if he can—to keep his Hand under our Chin to prevent

like the colonies, they don't get along

Us from drowning, but not to lift our Heads out of [the] Water." Of course, Adams resented the restraining instructions from Congress: "Those Chains I will never wear." Wearied by Adams's insistent fears, Franklin characterized him as "always an honest Man, often a wise one, but sometimes and in some things absolutely out of his Senses."[66]

In late October, Adams and Jay decided to deal directly with the British without consulting Vergennes. To their surprise, Franklin accepted that negotiating strategy. By pursuing distinct and secret negotiations with the British, the commissioners sought the best possible deal, but they did so in defiance of their instructions from Congress.[67]

In November, the British offered generous terms if the Americans made a quick peace without waiting for the French. The United States secured expansive boundaries that stretched south to Florida, west to the Mississippi, and north to the Great Lakes. The new boundary sacrificed Britain's native allies and its major forts on the southern shores of the Great Lakes, at Oswego, Niagara, Detroit, and Michilimackinac. To Adams's relief, New England's fishermen secured access to the Newfoundland fisheries with a right to dry their catch on the shore. In his one significant contribution, Laurens got a British promise to leave behind the slaves whom they had liberated in America. On that issue, his former slave-trading partner, Oswald, was happy to oblige. But the treaty also obligated Americans to pay their prewar debts to British merchants.[68]

By indulging the United States with generous boundaries, Shelburne sought to erode its alliance with France and restore American reliance on British trade. He reasoned that, if diffused over a vast territory, Americans would remain farmers, perpetuating their dependence on British manufactured goods. Perhaps, he hoped, that trade relationship would still lead to his cherished fantasy: a reunification of the empire. Shelburne asked, "If we are to look to regain the affection of America, to reunion in any shape or even to commerce and friendship, is it not of the last degree of consequence to retain every means to gratify America?" Gratifying Americans did weaken their French alliance, but that did not reunite the British Empire.[69]

The favorable terms astonished Vergennes, who declared, "The English buy peace rather than make it. Their concessions exceed all that I should have thought possible." He chided Franklin, "I am at a loss, sir, to explain your conduct and that of your colleagues on this occasion." But Franklin had the nerve to ask for more French loan money for Congress, and Vergennes complied. He could not afford to break with his erstwhile allies before completing a French and Spanish deal with Britain.[70]

American independence disgusted George III, who considered abdicating and retiring to his German principality, Hanover, in protest. How could his ministers forsake an American war, which he had waged from a "scrupulous attachment to the Rights of Parliament" to govern and tax the entire empire? Only much later and grudgingly did the king concede good riddance to Americans. Because "knavery seems to be so much the striking feature" of their characters, he concluded "that it may not in the end be an evil that they become aliens to this kingdom."[71]

Members of Parliament felt torn about Shelburne's generous peace with an independent America. Disillusioned with the Americans as dangerous ingrates, most British leaders agreed that granting them independence was unavoidable. But that same disgust with Americans meant that they should never be rewarded with such generous borders. Many Members also rued the treaty's failure to protect Indian allies and Loyalist supporters. While peace was popular, Shelburne's treaty was not, so he paid the political price. Discredited by votes in Parliament, he resigned in April 1783.[72]

Parliament did finalize the peace treaty but refused to add the favorable commercial treaty that Shelburne sought to complete reconciliation with the Americans. He had proposed opening the empire's colonial ports to American merchant ships, restoring the prewar trade that had been so mutually beneficial to American shippers and West

Indian planters. But Shelburne's generous trade proposal appalled imperial conservatives, who upheld the protective system mandated by the Navigation Acts, which favored British merchant ships at the expense of foreign carriers. Imperialists insisted that Americans should forfeit the economic benefits of the empire as the price of their rebellion. That restriction, particularly from the West Indies, would sour Anglo-American relations deep into the next century.[73]

Regeneration

a great book

Although irritated with the Americans for making a separate peace, Vergennes saw a silver lining: their British deal pressured the Spanish to negotiate. On the verge of fiscal ruin, the French could ill afford prolonging a war that seemed increasingly futile. Vergennes assured his ambassador to Spain, "The English have to some degree regenerated their navy while ours has been used up." And after the debacle at Gibraltar in September 1782, the French regretted their commitment to stay the course until the Spanish captured that fortress.[74]

To mollify the Spanish, British negotiators accepted the loss of Minorca and West Florida. Shelburne also exchanged East Florida for the Bahamas, which the Spanish had seized in May 1782. France gave up its West Indian conquests save for the small island of Tobago, but recovered St. Lucia, which was so important to Martinique's security. France also conceded its losses in India as did the Dutch, who did, however, recover St. Eustatius in the West Indies. The British, French, Spanish, and Dutch concluded an armistice and preliminary peace agreement on January 20, 1783. The winter deal saved all parties from the prodigious costs of mounting new military expeditions in the spring. France, Spain, and Britain finalized their deal on September 3, 1783, whereupon the American treaty also became firm.[75]

Despite paying an immense price in lives and money, France and Spain won precious little from the war. Instead, their military exertions primarily benefited the United States, which got independence within generous boundaries thanks to Britain's indulgent diplomacy. While Minorca's recovery soothed Spanish pride, the Floridas proved a hollow acquisition. Once again the Spanish failed to develop the region, which instead attracted covetous attention from the nearby Americans. As for the French, the small and underdeveloped island of Tobago was a paltry return for their losses of men and money. Nor did the French succeed in weaning the Americans from their economic dependence on British trade. The poor quality and high prices of French manufactures and the stingy credit terms of French merchants could not compete with British suppliers. The war also doubled France's national debt, creating a fiscal crisis that compelled the king to summon the long-suspended Estates-General, the French parliament. In 1789, that parliament initiated a revolution that destroyed the French monarchy and sucked Europe into a massive new war, which proved especially disastrous for the Spanish.[76]

Next to the Americans, the British fared best from the peace settlement. Although they had lost in America, they had won in the rest of the world. British leaders began the war dreading that losing America would lead to the collapse of the entire empire and elevate France to global supremacy. In fact, the British Empire quickly recovered the primary benefit of America: her market for British manufactures. Meanwhile, the British did more than save the rest of their empire; they added to it, especially in India. Likening the empire to an edifice, Lord Macartney declared that without America "the building not only looks much better but is a great deal stronger." In India, Africa, and the West Indies, the British secured their chief goal: an empire subject to the sovereignty and taxes of Parliament.[77]

Aside from Canada, which received an influx of Anglophone Loyalists, the preserved empire was less British in ethnicity and culture than the lost colonies had been. The revolution subtracted most of the overseas Britons but compensated with an enlarged global empire that ruled peoples of different cultures and races. The largest British colony,

Bengal in eastern India, had 20 million people, more than twice the population of England and seven times the numbers in the lost colonies of North America. But only a few officials, merchants, and soldiers in Bengal were Britons.[78]

The revolution accelerated the process of remaking the British Empire in browner tones, a trend begun during the Seven Years War. As the empire obtained more distant and non-European subjects, Britons posed as authoritarian paternalists. Claiming the top rung in a racial and cultural hierarchy, imperialists insisted that their rule protected and improved backward peoples of darker complexions and benighted traditions. Although professing to foster an enlightened civilization, Britons primarily sought to keep cultural others in long-term subordination.[79]

imperialism in earnest

Despite their wartime loyalty, British West Indians lost influence in the postwar empire. As the Patriots had warned, Britons consolidated and centralized power in London to the detriment of colonial elites. After the war, West Indian planters protested that imperial restrictions on American shipping drove up the cost of imported provisions and threatened to starve their slaves to death or into rebellion. The formerly formidable West Indian lobby, however, had lost much of its clout in Parliament. Indeed, that lobby faced increasingly active and influential opposition from evangelical abolitionists, who sought to end the slave trade and improve treatment of the enslaved. By depriving the empire of half its slaves, American independence reduced the leverage of the slaveholders in the West Indies. In 1788, an abolitionist noted, "As long as America was ours, there was no chance that a minister would have attended to the groans of the sons and daughters of Africa." British abolitionists supported strengthening the power of the empire to restrain colonial elites.[80]

West Indian planters denounced new imperial restrictions on the slave trade and slavery as attacks on the rights of property. Many regretted that they had not joined the revolution by their fellow slaveholders in North America. But the islanders had lacked that option given their dependence on the British market for their sugar and on the Royal Navy for protection. They were stuck when the empire abolished the slave trade in 1807 and emancipated the slaves during the 1830s. West Indian planters looked on with envy as their North American counterparts dominated a republican union that protected slavery.[81]

9

SHOCKS

We are all cast off. I shall ever tho' remember
with satisfaction that it was not I [who]
deserted my King, but my King that deserted me.
—J. MULLRYNE TATTNALL, a Loyalist, 1783[1]

During the spring of 1782, the British Crown sent Sir Guy Carleton to New York to replace the disgraced Sir Henry Clinton as commander in North America. With peace negotiations underway, Britain's rulers ordered Carleton to remain on the defensive and prepare to evacuate New York, Charles Town, and Savannah. Never before had a British commander withdrawn so many troops and civilian refugees. Logistically challenging, the evacuations took over a year to complete.[2]

A low-intensity war persisted in the countryside around the three seaports as British foragers clashed with Patriot patrols. In one late skirmish, John Laurens died in a reckless charge into a Loyalist ambush outside Charles Town. The Patriot champion of black enlistment and emancipation was shot by runaway slaves in the British service.[3]

The evacuations began in July 1782, when 2,000 troops, 3,100 Loy-

"Governeer Morris Esqr., Member of Congress" [Gouverneur Morris], engraving by Pierre Eugène du Simitière, 1783. Courtesy of the Library of Congress (LC-USZ62-45482).

alists, and 3,500 slaves withdrew from Savannah. Five months later, the British removed 4,000 troops, 4,200 Loyalists, 1,500 freed blacks, and 7,000 slaves from Charles Town. Most of the Georgia and Carolina refugees initially went to East Florida only to discover, in early 1783, that British negotiators had transferred the colony back to Spain. Forced to move again, most went to the Bahamas, where their slaves struggled to raise crops in the sandy soil. A refugee lamented, "The war never occasioned half the distress which this peace has done to the unfortunate Loyalists."[4]

In Georgia and the Carolinas, the British abandoned backcountry pockets of Loyalist resistance, "outliers" who had taken refuge in southern swamps and forests. Hundreds surrendered while Patriots flushed out and butchered the holdouts. In Georgia, a Loyalist recalled, "Many of them [were] caught and killed, even when begging for life, upon their knees!" In North Carolina, a Patriot colonel reported, "We had to Kill a few Outliers, which Ansured a good End."[5]

In 1783–1784, the southern enslaved experienced a counterrevolution rather than a revolution as Patriots suppressed maroon settlements created in swamps during the chaotic war. Calling themselves the "King of England's Soldiers," armed maroons lived by raising garden crops and plundering nearby plantations. A Georgian warned, "Their leaders are the very fellows that fought and maintained their ground against the brave [French] Lancers at the siege of Savannah." Militia victories culminated in many executions, and the heads of dead maroons decorated poles erected outside county courthouses in Georgia and South Carolina.[6]

Although painful to affected planters, the wartime loss of runaway slaves proved minor to the South as a whole. Concentrated in coastal districts, the losses were much lower in the Piedmont, where natural increase continued to swell the enslaved population. At the end of the war, Virginia had 236,000 slaves, up from the 210,000 at the start. Although briefly shaken, the slave system survived the war as prosperous and important as ever. Georgians and South Carolinians imported thousands of new slaves from Africa, to replace and exceed their wartime losses. A Georgia merchant confided, "The Planter will as far as in his power sacrifice every thing to attain Negroes."[7]

By the spring of 1783, New York was the last haven for British troops and their American supporters. Rounding up 183 merchant ships and military transports, Carleton shipped 18,000 troops and 32,000 Loyalists to Halifax during the spring, summer, and fall of 1783. On November 25, Washington's troops marched into New York City, ending the long British occupation. For a week, Patriots celebrated with bonfires, feasts, fireworks, illuminations, and drinking. The boisterous celebrations of victory, however, barely masked the rapid unraveling of the American confederation.[8]

During the 1780s, the end of the war created new complications and many geopolitical possibilities. The peace treaty set in motion an array of peoples with competing visions for the continent. Thousands of former slaves sought havens within the British Empire, initially in Nova Scotia and later in West Africa. Many more white Loyalists dispersed throughout the global empire with the largest clusters in the Bahamas, Nova Scotia, New Brunswick, and Quebec. The refugees helped develop counterrevolutionary regimes committed to the mixed constitution and the union of the empire. Far from accepting defeat, Loyalists and Britons hoped to display a political alternative superior to the American states. Feeling betrayed by the peace treaty, Britain's native allies sought to construct their own confederation to resist American expansion. Their victories led western settlers to consider rejecting American rule and turning to the Spanish Empire. Instead of producing clarity, the peace treaty spawned many contingencies that seemed more menacing than promising to the American union of republican states.

Drama

Lacking revenues, the federal government failed to pay its debts and struggled to sustain an army during the last three years of the war. In Congress, frustrated nationalists rallied around Robert Morris, a wealthy

"Robert Morris," by an unknown engraver after an original painting by Charles Willson Peale. Courtesy of the Library of Congress (LC-USZ62-3596).

Philadelphia merchant who became Congress's superintendent of finance in May 1781. Ambitious, arrogant, and pushy, he exploited his political connections to transport private cargoes on government ships, minimizing his risks and maximizing his profits. During the war, Morris became the richest man in America. His political allies included the New Yorkers Gouverneur Morris and Alexander Hamilton, who shared his impatience with Congress, the states, and common people.[9]

Nationalists pressed their balky colleagues and state legislatures to empower Congress to levy its own taxes, beginning with a levy on imports known as "the impost." Such a tax would free Congress from relying on requisitions from the states, which increasingly defaulted on their payments. During the first six months of 1782, only New Jersey paid anything to Congress, and that state delivered less than 1 percent of its assessment. Congress disappointed its many impatient creditors, including Continental officers, who had not been paid for years. Without its own revenue, Congress could not pay the pensions it had promised to the officers. Many Americans considered a congressional impost and officers' pensions as corrupting their revolution. A critic accused the nationalists of self-interest: "Their professed view is to strengthen the hands of government, to make us respectable in Europe, and I believe, they might add, to divide among themselves and their friends every place of honor and of profit."[10]

Peace threatened to deprive the nationalists of their leverage. Gouverneur Morris longed for "a Continuance of the War, which will convince People of the necessity of Obedience to common Counsels for general Purposes." In early 1783, nationalists worried that disbanding the army would deepen the public indifference to funding a stronger nation.[11]

In March 1783, the nationalists played a dangerous game by sending a secret emissary to meet with angry army officers in the encampment at Newburgh, north of New York City. By refusing to demobilize and threatening to march in arms on Philadelphia, the army could pressure Congress and the states to pay soldiers and pension officers by authorizing the impost. Hamilton slyly explained that "the necessity and discontents of the army presented themselves as a powerful engine" to pressure wavering politicians. If necessary, Gouverneur Morris favored staging a military coup: "When a few Men of sense and spirit get together and declare that they are the Authority, such few as are of a different opinion may easily be convinced of their Mistake by that powerful Argument, the Halter." Taking the bait, an officer exhorted his peers to resist a "country that tramples upon your rights, disdains your cries and insults your distresses. . . . Can you then consent to be the only sufferers by this revolution, and retiring from the field, grow old in poverty, wretchedness, and contempt?"[12]

Hamilton urged Washington to lead the army's demand for the nationalist program, but the general balked, lest he "open the flood Gates of Civil discord" that would "deluge our rising Empire in Blood." Washington preferred to wait and trust the states eventually to do right by soldiers and officers. In mid-March at Newburgh, he dramatically intervened in a meeting of angry officers, persuading them to stand down. Hamilton was disappointed: "I confess could force prevail I should almost wish to see it employed. I have an indifferent opinion of the honesty of this country, and ill-forebodings as to its future system." He expected little from the states once relieved by peace.[13]

Washington recognized that few soldiers would follow their officers in staging a coup. The troops had their fill of obeying officers who cared more about getting pensions than about securing food and pay for common soldiers. Hungry and restive, the troops wanted to go home. Learning of peace in early April, many sought to hasten demobilization by staging protests, insulting their officers, and refusing to do duty. Washington warned Hamilton, "I believe, it is not in the power of Congress or their officers, to hold them much, if any longer, for we are obliged at this moment to increase our Guards to prev[en]t rioting."[14]

Congress discharged four-fifths of the troops in June, although a much larger British army remained in New York City. Still broke, Congress dismissed the soldiers with mere paper certificates vaguely promising payment sometime in the future. Joseph Plumb Martin described his fellow soldiers as left "Starved, ragged and meager, not a cent to help themselves with." Martin concluded, "When the country had drained the last drop of service it could screw out of the poor soldiers, they were turned adrift like worn-out horses." Martin sold his certificates for a pittance to buy "some decent clothing" so he would not pass for a beggar on his long road homeward. If Congress ever did make good on the certificates, most payments would benefit the speculators who bought them from desperate soldiers in 1783.[15]

In June, some disgusted soldiers passed through Philadelphia, where they surrounded the State House to denounce and threaten Congress. Refusing orders to disperse the protestors, city militiamen instead joined the throngs chanting in support of the soldiers, "Stand for your rights!" Feeling insulted and helpless, congressmen adjourned and hastened away to Princeton, New Jersey. Too fearful to return to Philadelphia, Congress moved on again to Annapolis, Maryland in November. One delegate described Congress as "hated by the public creditors, insulted by the Soldiery, and unsupported by the citizens." Benjamin Rush agreed, "The Congress is abused, laughed at and cursed in every company."[16]

At the end of November, when the British evacuated New York City, Washington dismissed the last of his troops and rode south to Annapolis to resign his commission on December 23. A mere twenty congressmen attended because only seven states sent delegations to the increasingly irrelevant Congress. Although it met in Maryland, that state's delegates rarely bothered to attend. But civilians filled the hall and gallery of the statehouse to watch Washington resign. He aptly described his performance as theatrical: "Nothing now remains, but for the actors of this mighty Scene to preserve a perfect unvarying consistency of character through the very last act; to close the *Dramma* with applause, and retire from the Military Theatre." An impressed congressman praised the "solemn and affecting spectacle." Washington projected a dignified and selfless devotion to the republican cause: a precious rarity among his squabbling countrymen. John Adams later described Washington's performance as "Shakespearean" and praised his "Excellence in Dramatic Exhibitions."[17]

By surrendering power, Washington refuted Loyalists who had predicted that he would become a military dictator like Julius Caesar and Oliver Cromwell, rebel commanders who had betrayed their republics. Thomas Jefferson declared that Washington's virtuous self-restraint had "prevented this revolution from being closed, as most others have been, by a subversion of that liberty it was intended to establish." In London, the American-born artist Benjamin West had reported Washington's retirement to a skeptical George III, who allegedly replied, "If he does that, he will be the greatest man in the world."[18]

Washington returned home to attend to his long-neglected plantation, but he also accepted an unpaid, honorific post as president of the Society of the Cincinnati. In early 1783, Continental officers formed the society to preserve their social bonds and exercise political influence. The society emerged from the Newburgh agitation as Washington's alternative to the extremists who had proposed menacing Congress and the states. Every officer could pass membership on to his eldest son, and so on through the generations, perpetuating the society. That aristocratic ethos alarmed hypersensitive republicans who disdained interest groups and hereditary influence. They accused the officers of plotting to subvert state governments in favor of a more powerful and elitist national regime. A Connecticut town meeting damned the society for trying "to dissolve our present Happy and Benevolent Constitution and to erect on the Ruins, a proper Aristocracy." The uproar embarrassed Washington, who persuaded the members, at their first convention in May 1784, to adopt a lower profile and abandon hereditary membership. As soon as the furor abated, however, the society quietly restored that feature. [19]

Freetown

Citing the peace treaty, Patriots expected the British to restore runaway slaves to their American masters. Before the British completed their evacuation, some masters pushed into Charles Town and New York to demand the surrender of their former slaves. In New York, the runaway Boston King recalled, "Many of the slaves had very cruel masters so that the thoughts of returning home with them embittered life to us." But the treaty terms appalled British commanders as betraying their wartime promises of freedom to runaways from Patriot masters. General Carleton insisted that they were no longer any man's property. When Washington sought to recover some of his former slaves in New York, Carleton replied that he would not forcibly deliver them up, some "to Execution and others to severe Punishment." To do so, "would be a dishonorable Violation of the public Faith pledged to the Negroes in the Proclamations" made by British generals.[20]

Carleton's stance outraged Washington and other Patriot leaders. James Madison denounced Carleton for advancing "a palpable & scandalous misconstruction of the Treaty." Demanding the forcible return of all runaways, Congress briefly threatened to retain British prisoners of war. But the British government supported Carleton and refused to pay compensation to masters for former slaves evacuated as free people from America.[21]

The British granted only a stinted freedom to the black refugees, denying them political rights. Most landed in Nova Scotia, where the long winters came as a shock. A black preacher, David George, recalled arriving "almost naked from the burning sands of South Carolina, to the frozen Coast of Nova Scotia, destitute of almost every necessary of life." Prejudice compounded their suffering, for white Nova Scotians disdained black people as supposed inferiors who should make do with hunger and poverty. The government granted them land grudgingly, slowly, and in small parcels of inferior soil: a mere 40 acres on average, less than half of what whites received and too little for a proper farm. Forced to become sharecroppers and menial laborers, most blacks could earn precious little given the glutted labor market of a colony swamped by poor refugees, white and black. Boston King recalled, "Some killed and ate their dogs and cats, and poverty and distress prevailed on every side." To get food, clothing, and shelter, some became indentured servants to white masters for up to six years. In the port of Shelburne, white laborers drove out black competitors by pulling down and burning their houses. A mob beat David George and took away his church, which the victors converted into a tavern. According to George, the new tavernkeeper boasted, "The old Negro wanted to make a heaven of this place, but I'll make a hell of it."[22]

Thomas Peters sought to become a Moses for his fellow black refugees by leading them to a promised land. African-born, Peters had been a North Carolina slave, Loyalist sergeant, and Nova Scotia refugee. Disgusted by broken promises, in 1790 he traveled to London to complain to imperial officials that Nova Scotia's black refugees had "no more Protection by the Laws of the Colony . . . than the mere Cattel or brute Beasts." He got support from London's abolitionists, led by Granville Sharp, who organized the Sierra Leone Company to found a West African colony as a haven for free blacks. The abolitionists funded Peters to recruit black colonists with assurances of generous land grants and political equality. The company leaders promised, "No distinction is to be made, between them & the Whites."[23]

In 1791, Peters returned to Nova Scotia to pitch an African exodus to his fellow black refugees, but the company sent along an agent, John Clarkson, to pay the bills, arrange transports, and keep an eye on Peters. Clarkson and Peters recruited 1,200 black refugees, who accepted government-paid transportation to Sierra Leone. They included Boston King, who had become a Methodist preacher, and Harry Washington, a runaway from Washington's Mount Vernon. A woman of over one hundred years demanded to go along so "that she might lay her bones in her native country."[24]

Alluringly named Freetown, the colonial capital had, by 1796, four hundred homes on a grid of nine streets. The black colonists relied upon an emotional, evangelical faith that distinguished them from their white neighbors, who were often transported criminals. A governor noted, "While the white inhabitants are roaring with strong drink at one end [of Freetown], the Nova Scotians are roaring out hymns at the other."[25]

Although the London organizers meant well, they also meant to govern through white officials, who treated black colonists as inferiors best shorted on provisions, land, and political rights. Expressing the company's patronizing paternalism, Granville Sharp referred to his "poor little ill-thriven swarthy daughter, the unfortunate colony of Sierra Leone." Sharp supplied the refugees with the poorly named *Short Sketch of Temporary Regulations,* which ran to nearly 200 pages and detailed even the prayers they were supposed to offer for each day of the week. The company also sought to profit by demanding a quit-rent from the colonists, who resented this violation of the company's pledge to provide free land. Clarkson reported that they had "imbibed strange notions from Thomas Peters as to their civil rights." In June 1792, a tropical fever killed Peters, but his defiant spirit lingered among the colonists, who complained that "Free Town" had become "a Town of Slavery."[26]

In 1800, most of the black colonists refused to pay quit-rents, rejected the company's rule, and created a rival government led by Isaac Anderson. A company official sputtered, "Their government *—wow* is pure democracy, without subordination to anyone." In October, the company brutally suppressed resistance with the help of 550 former maroons recently ousted from Jamaica and brought to Freetown as mercenaries. The victors hanged Anderson and another rebel leader and exiled twenty-five others and confiscated their farms. The evicted included a former slave who had taken "British Freedom" as his name and Harry Washington, the former Mount Vernon slave. In 1808 the Crown took over the colony from the bankrupt Sierra Leone Company. But the black colonists remained a defiant lot denounced by the new governor as "runaway slaves . . . full of every species of ignorant enthusiasm and republican frenzy." During the revolution, they had fought against American slavery rather than for the British Empire.[27]

Refugees

In the peace treaty, Patriot diplomats had pledged only to "recommend" that the thirteen states welcome back Loyalists and restore their confiscated property. Patriot negotiators would do no more for the Loyalists, whom they blamed for provoking and sustaining the war. Everyone but the British negotiators knew that this recommendation was worthless, for the states meant to retain the property by keeping out the Loyalists, and Congress lacked any power to pressure the states. Feeling betrayed, a Loyalist bitterly insisted that the peace treaty "licks the feet of Congress, and of their General [Washington]."[28]

During 1783 and 1784, Patriot mobs menaced Loyalists who tried to return home. In Albany, New York, a public meeting resolved "never to be at peace with those fiends, the Refugees, whose thefts, murders, and treasons have filled the cup of woe." The state's governor, George Clinton, vowed that he would "rather roast in hell to all eternity than . . . show mercy to a damned Tory." Returning Loyalists got beatings, coats of hot tar and cool feathers, and a parade before their hooting neighbors. In the southern backcountry, Patriots lynched eight returnees at Fishing Creek in South Carolina. A conscientious Carolina judge, Aedanus Burke, resisted pressure "to be a tool to gratify the fierce revenge of the people." He vowed to provide a "spot of neutral ground in Court, where I sat, where no distinction of Whig or Tory should be admitted." That ground proved slippery. When Burke discharged a former Loyalist and accused horse thief for lack of evidence, a furious mob rushed in, seized the suspect, and hanged him in front of the courthouse door. This postwar violence troubled some elite Patriots as a threat to social order. Nathanael Greene denounced the "intolerance to persecute men for opinions which, but twenty years before, had been the universal belief of every class of society."[29]

At least 60,000 Loyalist refugees and 15,000 of their slaves scattered through the vast British Empire. In response to their lobbying, Parliament set up a London-based commission of five men to hear and rule on Loyalist claims for compensation. Examining documents and taking sworn testimony, the commissioners sought to distinguish deserving cases from fraudulent claims. In addition to holding hearings in London, some commissioners visited New York (before the evacuation) and Quebec, Montreal, St. John, and Halifax.[30]

The commissioners favored genteel claimants, particularly those who had held high office, rather than common farmers and artisans. Women and the poor, particularly blacks, usually had to settle for a few pounds (or nothing at all). But even elite Loyalists felt bitterly disappointed. A New York merchant, Alexander Wallace, lost a fortune for his loyalty, but he got only £1,500 in compensation: "It cost me double the sum to bring myself & family to England & to support them in London to prove my losses. . . . Damn them all & your good people who passed the law to deprive us of our property." By 1788, the commissioners had accepted 4,118 claims for more than £10 million in losses, but the claimants received only about £3 million.[31]

Eight thousand refugees went to Britain, which one called "The Isle of Liberty and Peace." But most of them struggled with drenching rain, bitter poverty, a high cost of living, cultural disorientation, and British prejudices against Americans as cunning cheats. A homesick Thomas Hutchinson wrote, "I would rather die in a little country farmhouse in New England than in the best nobleman's seat in old England." The miserable included Shadrack Furman. A black Virginian, Furman had guided British troops until captured by Patriots, who whipped him nearly to death and blinded him with an ax blow to the head. Escaping to Nova Scotia and on to England, he played a fiddle for spare change in London streets.[32]

Most of the Loyalists relocated to another British colony in the Americas. Eight hundred free blacks, five thousand white Loyalists, and ten thousand slaves resettled in the West Indies and the Bahamas, a cluster of sandy islands near Florida's east coast. Prior to that influx, the poor soil and shallow harbors of the Bahamas attracted only a few poor settlers who lived by fishing, hunting turtles, scavenging shipwrecks, and collecting salt. During the mid-1780s, the newcomers doubled the white population and tripled the numbers of the enslaved in the Bahamas.[33]

Many more Loyalists moved from New York City to northern colonies, with 35,000 settling in Nova Scotia, which the British divided in 1784 to create the additional province of New Brunswick. Others moved to Quebec (2,000) and the future province of Upper Canada (6,000), which stretched up the St. Lawrence River from Montreal to and along the Great Lakes as far as Detroit. As compensation for their services and suffering, the British provided free land, seed grain, tools, and provisions during their first two years on the land. Common white families received farms of 100 to 300 acres, while officers and officials got up to 5,000 acres.[34]

In the Maritime Provinces, newcomers struggled to clear and culti-
vate their new farms, for most of the land was rocky and bleak. Upon
first seeing the shores of New Brunswick, Sarah Frost blanched at "the
roughest land I ever saw." As she watched her transport ship sail away,
Frost "sat down on the damp moss with my baby in my lap and cried."
The hard winters and short growing seasons shocked many refugees.
Polly Dibblee had nothing to offer when her "poor Children . . . cried,
Mama, why don't you help me and give me Bread?" She concluded,
"Inhuman Treatment I suffered under the Power of American Mobs
and Rebels for that Loyalty, which is now thought handsomely com-
pensated for by neglect and starvation." About a third of the Maritime
Loyalists drifted back to the United States during the late 1780s or
early 1790s, after the hatreds of the civil war had cooled.[35]

Loyalists fared better in Upper Canada, which offered better soil
and a warmer climate. Their settlements prospered along the St. Lawrence River, beside the Bay of Quinte, and on the Niagara Peninsula.
In 1785, a British visitor marveled at their rapid development of new
homesteads: "It does one's heart good to see how well they are all going
on. . . . The settling [of] the Loyalists is one of the best things [that]
George III ever did. You see abundance of the wheat, Indian corn, and
potatoes wherever you go."[36]

During the late 1780s, the promising Upper Canadian settlements
attracted a second pulse of emigrants from the United States, boosting
the colony's population to 14,000. The second wave primarily consisted
of passive Loyalists who had opposed the revolution without taking
up arms for the British. In addition to the pull of free land in Canada,
they responded to the push of political turmoil and hard times in the
United States. Lord Sydney described them as "Sufferers under the
ruinous and arbitrary Laws and Constitution of the United States." A
Loyalist insisted that "the great Influx of Inhabitants from the American Frontiers (with melancholy Complaints of Taxes, Poverty & Tyranny)" proved the good fortune of Loyalists when "compared with the
Subjects of the distressed & divided States."[37]

To show the rewards of loyalty, British officials wanted the refu-

gees to prosper. Quebec's governor, Lord Dorchester (formerly known
as Sir Guy Carleton), insisted that Americans "should on all occasions
perceive how much they are fallen, and the loyalists find, upon every
comparison, strong reasons to congratulate themselves upon having
persevered in their duty." Certain that the United States was on the
road to ruin, a New Brunswick Loyalist, Edward Winslow, predicted
that the northern colonies would, "[by] rising in proportion to the
decline of the neighbouring American states, be in a condition to over-
awe them." Britons and Loyalists hoped to embarrass the Patriots by
outperforming and discrediting their republican states.[38]

In 1788 a parasite, the Hessian fly, threatened the Loyalist settlements. The fly consumed wheat plants, leading to rampant hunger
among settlers on both sides of the northern border during the spring
and summer of 1789. On the American side, settlers had to muddle
through with little or no help from their state governments (and none
from Congress). Canadians benefited from a paternalistic British
regime, which shipped to Quebec 1,000 tons of flour, 23,000 bushels
of wheat, and 24,000 bushels of peas. Lord Grenville assured Dorchester that the aid should impress "the minds of His Majesty's Subjects
under your Lordship's Government with a just sense of His Majesty's paternal regard for the welfare of all his People." Two years later
a royal prince visited Canada and explained, "My father is not a merchant to deal in bread and ask payment for food granted for the relief
of his loyal subjects." He contrasted British paternalism with American republicanism, which allegedly promoted amoral competition at
the expense of the poor.[39]

Canada Act

The Loyalist influx increased political strife within Quebec, the vast
province extending westward from the Gulf of St. Lawrence to the
Great Lakes. Under Parliament's Quebec Act of 1774, the governor
and his council of British officials and local nobles (*seigneurs*) governed without an elected assembly. Never having had an assembly

under French rule, the common *habitants* accepted political exclusion so long as the colony did not tax them or interfere with the Catholic Church. Most officials and *seigneurs* comprised a "French Party," which opposed any political change as the slippery slope to an American-style revolution. They insisted that a largely Francophone and Catholic colony could best resist subversion by republicans.[40]

The Quebec Act offended the colony's small "British Party," composed of Anglophone tradesmen and merchants, who clustered in the towns of Montreal and Quebec. Numbering only 2,000 before the war, Quebec's Protestant Anglophone population grew during the 1780s, with the influx of 8,000 Loyalist refugees. The British partisans pushed to Anglicize the legal and political system by introducing English common law, freehold land tenures, and an elected assembly. But they wanted only Anglophone Protestants like themselves to enjoy the political rights to vote and hold office. They argued that their system would pressure French Canadians to become better British subjects by learning English and converting to Protestantism. The French partisans, however, derided their opponents as greedy merchants out to exploit the *habitants*. Quebec presented a paradox where a British minority resented that imperial officials protected the culture and law of the French majority.[41]

In 1786, the British Party got a boost from the return of Lord Dorchester as the governor. Although he had championed the Quebec Act during his previous administration (1766–1778), Dorchester had moved closer to the British Party position under the influence of his friend William Smith, Jr., who became the colony's new chief justice and a member of the council. Before the war, Smith had been a powerful lawyer and politician in New York. A moderate Patriot, he opposed Parliament's taxes but cherished Britain's mixed constitution and the union of the empire. After the Patriots declared independence and adopted republican state governments, Smith defected to join the British in occupied New York City, where he served as a magistrate, spymaster, and consultant.[42]

In 1782–1783 in New York, Dorchester and Smith developed a shared constitutional vision for reviving the empire in North America. Noting economic woes and social turmoil in the United States, Smith insisted that no republic could endure for long. He predicted: "We are on the Eve of a Revolution that will lay aside the Congress and the Republican Models. The Change will be either the setting up of the British model with a Reunion, or with a *new King*." To accelerate that counterrevolution, Dorchester and Smith wanted to unite Quebec and the Maritime provinces under one governor-general and an elected parliament—subject of course to British oversight. This new regime would mandate English law, freehold land tenure, and elected assemblies in every province including Quebec.[43]

Smith and Dorchester hoped to make Quebec more enticing to Americans. At a minimum, they wanted to induce thousands to migrate north to strengthen the colony while weakening the United States. Better still, a reformed Quebec and a Canadian union might persuade Americans to abandon their chaotic experiment in republican independence by rejoining the empire. To advance both scenarios, Dorchester and Smith embraced the British Party.[44]

Evenly matched in the governing council, the British and French parties deadlocked in acrimony. Grown indecisive and reclusive in his old age, Dorchester provided little leadership. The squabbling dismayed imperial officials in London, who preferred to impose a top-down solution. In 1789, Lord Grenville drafted the Canada Constitutional Act, which Parliament adopted in 1791. The act divided Quebec into two new provinces: Upper Canada along the Great Lakes and Lower Canada in the lower St. Lawrence Valley including Montreal and Quebec City. The division was cultural as well as geographic, for Francophones predominated in Lower Canada while Anglophone Loyalists prevailed in Upper Canada. The provinces shared a governor-general based in Quebec, but he had only nominal authority over the lieutenant governor of Upper Canada. The two colonies also retained distinct legislatures and did not answer to any parliament closer than

London. Grenville thereby rejected Smith's dream of a common parliament to unite British North America and screen it from the full sovereignty of the imperial Parliament.[45]

The Canada Constitutional Act reflected the lessons of the revolution as understood by Britons, who rejected republicanism. Grenville
examined "the constitution of our former Colonies . . . in order that we
may profit by our experience there, & avoid, if possible, in the Government of Canada, those defects which hastened the independence of
our antient possessions in America." The former colonies had become
republics because "no care was taken to preserve a due mixture of the
Monarchical & Aristocratical parts of the British Constitutions."[46]

But Grenville also made concessions to avert popular discontent.
The act mandated freehold land tenure in Upper Canada and dropped
the Crown quit-rents that had, before the war, so irritated colonists.
These concessions followed Dorchester's advice "that all seeds of discord between Great Britain and her Colonies may be prevented." In
the Canadian provinces, settlers could obtain 200 acres by taking the
oath of allegiance and paying merely nominal fees.[47]

The revolution led to virtually free land for settlers in British
Canada while rendering land more expensive in the United States.
Burdened by immense public debts incurred to wage the war, federal
and state governments sold vast tracts of frontier land to speculators,
who could immediately pay large sums in cash. For example, in 1791,
New York State sold 5,542,170 acres to land speculators for $1,030,433.
Those speculators profited by retailing the land to actual settlers, who
had to pay a premium: usually $3 per acre. For American settlers, inde-
pendence did not come cheap. Those who disliked that higher price
could move to Canada to procure cheaper land by resuming their allegiance as British subjects.[48]

In a second major concession, the Canada Constitutional Act reit-
erated Parliament's 1778 pledge never again to tax North American
colonists for revenue. Indeed, Britain heavily subsidized the provincial
governments by paying for their military garrisons and Indian diplomacy. Parliament also funded the salaries for the colony's executive

and judicial officers, which ensured the Crown's control over its servants. This arrangement reflected another British lesson drawn from the thirteen rebelling colonies: that elected assemblies had used their power over salaries to sway Crown officials. In the Canadas after the war, the British government paid those salaries to prolong colonial dependence on the empire.[49]

Thanks to this British largesse, the Canadian colonists paid lower taxes than did Americans in the republican states. In 1794, Upper Canada's landholders paid only 5 shillings in tax for every £100 in assessed property: a rate of one-quarter of one percent and a fifth of the tax rate in New York. An ironic consequence of the revolution was that the Patriot "winners" had to bear higher postwar taxes to finance their war debts. In 1800, an immigrant to Canada explained why he had left the United States: "We fought seven years to get rid of taxation, and now we are taxed more than ever!" Although deemed the war's losers, Loyalist refugees secured a lighter tax burden in the Canadian colonies than that borne by either prewar colonists or postwar citizens.[50]

In a further concession to American expectations, each colony had an assembly elected by landowners, who included most men. Grenville concluded that, if properly restricted, an assembly "would afford a juster & more effectual security against the growth of a republican or independent spirit, than any which could be derived from a Government more arbitrary in its form or principles." The British defined the assembly as a royal favor, rather than as a popular right, and as the last, not the first, step toward a more popular government. The Constitutional Act limited the size of the Canadian assemblies by stretching the bounds of their electoral districts. In Upper Canada, only sixteen members represented the nineteen counties in the first assembly of 1792.[51]

The assembly also had to share power with a "legislative council" of colonial notables, who comprised the upper house of the legislature. Nominated by the governor and appointed by the Crown, councillors served for life. Grenville hoped, in the future, to bestow titles of nobility on the most worthy councillors: "to establish in the Provinces a Body of Men having that motive of attachment to the existing form of Government, which arises from . . . hereditary distinction."[52]

Both houses of the legislature were constrained by a powerful executive branch that served at the Crown's pay and pleasure. The governor could summon, prorogue, or dissolve a legislative session. He appointed the speaker of the legislative council and could veto any speaker chosen by the assembly as well as any bill, and his veto was complete, without any provision for an override. Nor could legislators review executive measures or expenditures. To become law, an assembly initiative had to survive a formidable gauntlet of increasingly elite and distant power: assent by the legislative council, the governor, and the imperial bureaucracy in London, where the Crown had up to two years to kill a colonial law.[53]

The mode of election also reduced popular influence in the assembly. The governor appointed the county sheriffs, who supervised the voting. With only one polling place per county, turnout was sparse from the dispersed settlements of vast counties with miserable roads. Located in or near the county courthouse, the poll favored voting by those most dependent upon the government's favor: nearby lawyers, clerks, and merchants. The Canadian colonies also retained the traditional English practice of public, oral voting, which discouraged independence by debtors and tenants.[54]

Parliament designed the Canadian governments to avoid popular discontent *and* to discourage popular participation. On the one hand, the British promoted a content and inert public by minimizing taxes and the price of land. On the other hand, they also restricted electoral power to prevent demagogues from fomenting unrest. Lord Thurlow explained that the British "have given them more civil liberty, without political liberty." In sum, the British worked to deny the colonists both the civil motives and the political means for agitation.[55]

The contrast between the Canadian mixed constitutions and the American states reveals the double difference made by a republican revolution. While American politics became republican, the British constructed counterrevolutionary regimes in Canada. Under the republican constitution adopted in 1777 in New York, elections were more frequent, important, and accessible to a larger electorate. The state constitution permitted polls in every township, rather than in just a single shire town per county, and written ballots replaced oral voting. Where a colonial voter could elect representatives only to the assembly, the postwar New York voter chose his governor, lieutenant governor, and state senators as well as assembly representatives. The colonial system had allocated but two assembly seats for every county no matter how large or small. The new constitution established a more proportional system that awarded more seats to the most populous counties. New York's voters chose assemblymen every year, their governor and lieutenant governor at triennial intervals, and state senators every fourth year. Only the state senators had terms as long as Upper Canada's assemblymen. Republican logic maximized the popular sovereignty that the British mixed constitution sought to contain.[56]

The postwar empire was more hierarchical, authoritarian, and paternalistic than the prerevolutionary thirteen colonies had been. Many Loyalists initially balked at the political passivity expected of them. In every colony, clashes developed between officials and the refugees. In 1785 in St. John, New Brunswick's leading town, voters chose representatives unacceptable to the government, which rejected enough votes to install its own supporters instead. When four protestors petitioned the assembly, they landed in jail (as did sympathetic newspaper printers), charged with sedition. Thereafter, protest dissipated because the moderate majority supported law and order and dreaded accusations of disloyalty.[57]

Political turmoil also erupted in the Bahamas, where refugees were especially discontented because the British had forsaken them twice: first by evacuating Savannah and Charleston and then by sacrificing their next haven, East Florida, to the Spanish. The Bahamian governor sighed, "It will be a difficult Task, I imagine, to please so dissatisfied a People." These especially disgruntled Loyalists confronted a postwar colonial regime that had grown more authoritarian, prone to interpret any public protest as leading to a republican revolution. The newcomers, however, clung to an older, prerevolutionary political culture that justified the boisterous and jealous defense of "English liberties" against colonial officials who allegedly betrayed the true wishes of a benevolent king. In the name of superior loyalty, they deployed the repertoire of resistance associated with the Patriots—electioneering, petitions, printed protests, lawsuits, and riots—to defy their governor. Outraged by the protests, Lord Sydney found it "extraordinary that Men who profess to have suffered for their Loyalty to the Crown, and adherence to the British Constitution, should so far forget themselves, and the Duty they owe to His Majesty, as to be guilty of the most daring attempts against His Royal authority, and that Constitution." Bahamian Loyalists had to accept the authoritarian paternalism of the postrevolutionary empire or move back to the states.[58]

Confederations

By drawing a new border through the Great Lakes, the peace treaty gave up key British forts, including Detroit and Niagara, to the Americans. The treaty also consigned most of Britain's Indian allies to the American side of the boundary. Shocked by the terms, the British commander in Canada in 1783, Frederick Haldimand, confided to a friend, "My soul is completely bowed down with grief at seeing that we (with no absolute necessity) have humbled ourselves so much as to accept such humiliating boundaries."[59]

Natives felt betrayed by their British allies. A Creek chief wondered whether the British king meant "to sell his friends as slaves, or only give our lands to his and our enemies?" At Niagara in May, a British general met with Indian chiefs. He reported their insistence "that the Indian were a free People subject to no Power upon Earth, that they were faithful allies of the King of England, but not his subjects—that he had no right Whatever to grant away to the States of America, their Rights or Properties." Natives wished to live as free people between, rather than be divided by, the American union and the British or Spanish empire.[60]

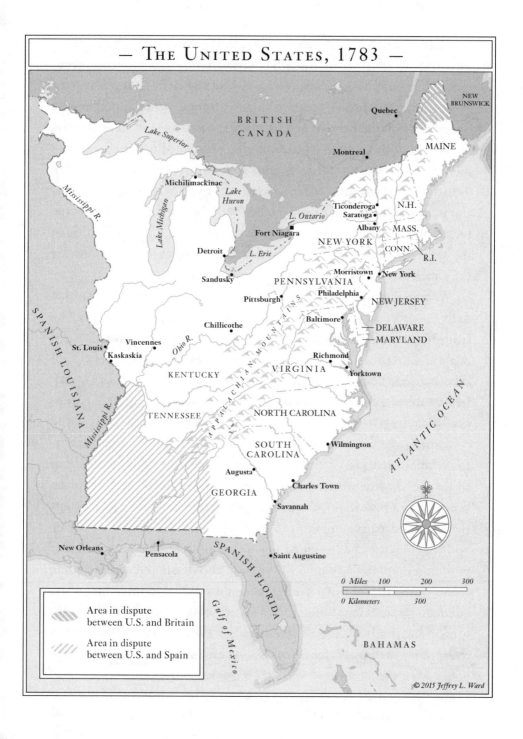

— THE UNITED STATES, 1783 —

NEW BRUNSWICK

Quebec

BRITISH CANADA

Lake Superior

MAINE

Montreal

Mississippi R.

Michilimackinac

Lake Huron

Ticonderoga

N.H.

Lake Michigan

L. Ontario

Saratoga

Albany

MASS.

Fort Niagara

NEW YORK

CONN.

Detroit

L. Erie

R.I.

Sandusky

Morristown

New York

PENNSYLVANIA

Pittsburgh

Philadelphia

NEW JERSEY

Chillicothe

Baltimore

DELAWARE

Ohio R.

MARYLAND

SPANISH LOUISIANA

Vincennes

St. Louis

Kaskaskia

Richmond

VIRGINIA

KENTUCKY

Yorktown

APPALACHIAN MOUNTAINS

Mississippi R.

TENNESSEE

NORTH CAROLINA

ATLANTIC OCEAN

SOUTH CAROLINA

Wilmington

Augusta

GEORGIA

Charles Town

Savannah

New Orleans

Pensacola

SPANISH FLORIDA

Saint Augustine

Gulf of Mexico

BAHAMAS

0 Miles 100 200 300

0 Kilometers 300

Area in dispute between U.S. and Britain

Area in dispute between U.S. and Spain

© 2015 Jeffrey L. Ward

Native peoples threatened to attack the forts rather than allow their transfer to the Americans. That Indian pressure compelled a dramatic shift in British policy, for Haldimand refused to surrender the posts to the Americans. He won support from Canada's premier economic interest, the British fur-trade firms that relied on Indian hunters around the Great Lakes. Their lobbying persuaded the home government to retain the border forts and, as justification, to cite American violations of the peace treaty. Several states had blocked British merchants from collecting prewar debts and obstructed Loyalists from reclaiming confiscated properties. By keeping the posts and cultivating Indian allies, the British also wanted to be in a strong position for the anticipated collapse of the American union.[61]

Able to compel Britain's policy shift along the American border, native peoples were more than mere pawns of imperial masters. Far from intimidating the Indians, British garrisons were hostages that enabled natives to extort concessions. Americans, however, refused to recognize Indian initiative. Instead, they reflexively blamed their frontier troubles on malicious Britons, who allegedly manipulated ignorant savages.

During the summer of 1783 at Sandusky, the chiefs from thirty-five Indian nations of the Great Lakes and the Ohio Valley met to form a confederation. They vowed to resist American expansion beyond the Ohio River, the prewar boundary between colonial settlements and native domains. Resisting American efforts to divide and conquer, the chiefs denied that any single nation could cede land without common consent. In 1788, some confederated chiefs told an American emissary "that Congress could not blame them for such a conduct, neither ought they to be jealous of them; for what had Congress done, but to unite thirteen states as one." In fact, Americans dreaded the native confederacy as a threat to the expansion deemed essential to the survival of their own union. Indeed, during the mid-1780s, the Indian confederacy grew stronger while the American union was collapsing.[62]

Articles

In 1776, Patriots found it easier to declare independence than form a confederation of their states. Diverse and fractious, the colonists lacked common bonds as Americans. Adams explained:

> The Colonies had grown up under Constitutions of Government So different, there was so great a Variety of Religions, they were composed of so many different Nations, their Customs, Manners, and Habits had So little resemblance, and their Intercourse had been so rare, and their Knowledge of each other So imperfect, that to unite them in the Same Principles in Theory and the Same System of Action, was certainly a very difficult Enterprize.

Only the pressures of war against the British superpower could force colonists to confederate.[63]

Patriots wanted a confederation just strong enough to wage the war and present a reasonably united front sufficient to persuade France to make an alliance. By keeping peace among their states, they also hoped to prevent bloody contentions for power like those that roiled Europe. During the late 1770s, congressmen felt alarmed by armed conflict between New Yorkers and New Englanders in Vermont and by rival settlers and speculators from Connecticut and Pennsylvania over the Susquehanna Valley. Only by forming a union could the member states define their boundaries and preserve their authority within those bounds. Madison explained that they "resorted to Union . . . for the common safety against powerful neighbors, and for the preservation of peace and justice among themselves." Americans needed a union to manage differences and distrust.[64]

But Patriots also meant to keep Congress too weak to interfere in the domestic policies of the member states. Having fought against Britain's centralizing power, few wanted to create a consolidated nation on this continent. While the pressures of war pushed states together, the dread of central power kept pulling them apart. The smaller states—New Jersey, Delaware, Rhode Island, and New Hampshire—especially feared domination by the larger ones that included Massachusetts, New York, and Virginia. A New Jersey delegate worried that "the smaller states will become vassals to the larger." A national, collective interest seemed elusive, as every state's leaders pushed their own agendas and threatened to secede if frustrated.[65]

Not until November 1777, more than a year after declaring independence, did Congress agree on "Articles of Confederation and perpetual union." The member states formed "a firm league of friendship with each other, for their common defense, the security of their Liberties, and their mutual and general welfare." Under the Articles, the states conceded only a few, limited powers to Congress: to wage war, conduct diplomacy, and arbitrate disputes between them. To satisfy small states, each delegation cast a single vote, so little Rhode Island's vote matched that of vast Virginia. On the major issues of war and peace, only a supermajority of nine states (out of thirteen) could commit the confederacy. The Articles required ratification by all thirteen states to become operative, and any future amendment also required unanimity, which discouraged any change.[66]

The Articles built an alliance of states rather than a cohesive nation. Adams characterized Congress as a "diplomatic assembly" of ambassadors from thirteen sovereign states. Congress was *not a national legislature that could frame laws and impose them on the states or citizens.* Able only to request, Congress relied on state legislatures to adopt and execute essential laws, such as those to recruit soldiers. Congress also lacked the powers, long exercised by the Crown over colonies, to regulate trade or veto state laws. "We have no coercive or legislative Authority," declared Thomas Burke of North Carolina: "Our Constituents are bound only in Honour to observe our Determinations." He added "that the states alone had Power to act coercively against their Citizens."[67]

Although endorsed by Congress in November 1777, the Articles remained provisional until ratified by all thirteen state legislatures.

And the smaller states first wanted to strengthen the federal govern- *expansion concern*
ment in one way: with the power to control, administer, and sell lands
west of the Appalachian Mountains. Small state leaders feared that otherwise the larger states, led by Virginia and New York, would grow
ever more powerful by monopolizing the sale of western lands. With
that revenue, the big states could pay their own debts and lower their
taxes, while small states grew poorer as their common people fled
from higher taxes to settle the West, further strengthening the land-
rich states. Small-state leaders also favored their own land speculators,
who wanted a share of the western profits.[68]

Possessing large western claims, New York and Massachusetts
compromised to mollify the small states. In March 1780, New York's
congressmen sought federal recognition of the state's claims to the
Haudenosaunee country as far west as Lake Erie. In return, New Yorkers would cede their larger but more nebulous claims to the rest of the
West as far as the Mississippi River. Following suit, Virginia's leaders
agreed to forsake their most distant land claims, to the territory north
and west of the Ohio River, in return for securing Kentucky. Facing a
British invasion, Virginians also needed federal assistance, so their leaders wanted to hasten ratification of the Articles. But Virginians insisted
that the ceded lands become "a common fund" to benefit the entire
nation (including Virginia) rather than enrich rival land speculators from
the smaller states.[69]

New York's and Virginia's partial cessions sufficed to sway the last
holdout state, Maryland, which ratified on February 2, 1781. The confederation belatedly took effect on March 1. But the federal government
remained poor and weak for want of the power to levy its own taxes.
France's minister to the United States dismissed the confederation as
"an incomplete and irregular System of government." To gain revenue
and credibility, the American confederation needed to wrest the West
away from rival empires and Indian confederations.[70]

EXPAND!

Book of Destiny

Fertile but roiled by violence, the West fed both short-term pessimism and long-term optimism for the American union. In the vast, western lands drained by navigable rivers, Americans detected a great source of wealth and power. But Indians defended those lands, and federal leaders struggled to control their own settlers. In sum, the West promised either to enrich or to unravel the fragile union. Benjamin Rush worried, "There is but one path that can lead the United States to destruction; and that is their extent of territory."[71]

The Federal domain lay north and west of the Ohio River. To the south, Virginia held Kentucky; North Carolina retained Tennessee; and Georgia claimed everything to its west as far as the Mississippi. The federal government had acquired only half of the West, and that half remained in native possession. To attract settlers to buy the land, federal officials needed to establish a territorial government with courts of law to enforce private property rights. Compelled to compete for settler allegiance, Congress could not afford to follow the unpopular British precedent of keeping a long-term set of dependent colonies in the West. Instead, Congress established temporary territories that eventually would enter the union as new states on a par with the original thirteen.[72]

Thomas Jefferson drafted the first "Northwest Ordinance," which Congress provisionally adopted in April 1784. It subdivided the federal domain into ten territories and stipulated that, once any one had 20,000 free citizens, they could convene a convention to draft a republican constitution and send a delegate to Congress. When the settler population reached the threshold of the smallest original state, Rhode Island, the territory could join the union as an equal partner in its powers and share in the national debt. While holding out future statehood, the ordinance bought time for the federal government to sell land within the territories.[73]

In 1785, Congress adopted a second Northwest Ordinance, which regulated land sales. To avoid the property disputes that had wracked

Kentucky, the ordinance mandated prior surveys of the federal domain into a grid of townships six miles on each side and subdivided into thirty-six "sections" of one square mile (640 acres). Once surveyed, the land would be sold at public auction for at least $1 per acre.[74]

By stipulating sales by sections for a dollar per acre in hard money paid immediately in full, the ordinance favored wealthy speculators rather than common settlers. In 1787 former army officers from New England formed the Ohio Company and bought nearly 2 million acres along the Ohio and Muskingum rivers at a heavily discounted price (about 10 cents per acre). A New Jersey delegate to Congress led a second cartel that procured on similar terms another million acres located around the future Cincinnati on the Ohio River. The speculators subdivided their lands for profitable retail sales to settlers, who bought on credit. Congress preferred to deal with speculators, who could pay larger sums more quickly.[75]

Eastern investors wanted a stronger and longer territorial government to protect their interests by blocking a more democratic regime dominated by the initial settlers, whom speculators distrusted as near savages. To satisfy those investors, in 1787 Congress adopted a third Northwest Ordinance, which supplanted the first ordinance and offered a more authoritarian government. The federal government would appoint a governor, secretary, and three judges who collectively would act as the legislature until a territory had 5,000 adult male inhabitants, who then could elect an assembly. But the governor retained an absolute veto on all legislation until the territory became a state. Once a territory had 60,000 free inhabitants, they could draft a constitution and apply to Congress for admission to the union. Richard Henry Lee explained that the new ordinance "seemed necessary for the security of property among uninformed and perhaps licentious people, as the greater part of those who go there are."[76]

To help the Ohio Company attract respectable settlers from New England, the new ordinance outlawed slavery in the Northwest Territory. To reconcile southern congressmen, the ordinance also mandated a fugitive slave law, requiring territorial settlers to return runaways from the slave states. The ordinance also implicitly kept open more southern territories to slavery. The combination of a partial restriction on slavery's expansion with a fugitive slave law set a precedent deemed fundamental to preserving the union.[77]

Despite the Northwest Ordinances, the federal government struggled to control the western settlements during the 1780s. Determined to pay nothing to Congress or eastern speculators, squatters pressed across the Ohio River to stake claims, build cabins, plant corn, and fight Indians. One bold squatter nailed a notice to a tree for federal soldiers to find: "I do certify that all mankind, agreeable to every constitution formed in America, have an undoubted right to pass into every vacant country, and to form their constitution." A congressman worried that the precious territory would "slip out of our hands if not speedily attended to."[78]

Federal officials worried that unruly settlers would block the development of law and order in the West. A federal surveyor denounced the squatters as a "lawless set of fellows" and "more our enemies than the most brutal savages of the country." Federal troops burned a few cabins and warned off the settlers, but the latter returned in larger numbers once the soldiers moved on. Like the British before them, the federal government would never have enough troops to restrain thousands of settlers along a broad frontier. John Jay worried that, without government control, "Shall we not fill the Wilderness with white Savages, and will they not become more formidable to us than the tawny ones who now inhabit it?"[79]

To impress and manage settlers, Congress needed to take charge of dispossessing Indians. Lacking troops, federal officials tried to compensate with bluster. Despite the weakness of the union, federal leaders promoted a provocative fiction: that they had crushed the Indians and acquired their lands by conquest during the revolution. "We are now Masters of this Island, and can dispose of the Lands as we think proper or most convenient to ourselves," General Philip Schuyler informed the Haudenosaunee. Another federal commissioner, Arthur Lee, bluntly told native chiefs, "You are subdued people." He later boasted in a private letter, "They are Animals that must be subdued and kept in awe or they will be mischievous, and fear alone will effect this submission."[80]

Acting on that theory of conquest, between 1784 and 1786 federal commissioners convened native chiefs in regional treaty councils to extort cessions of millions of acres of land. The commissioners found a few desperate (often elderly) chiefs willing to cooperate in return for extra presents, but most natives disavowed the treaties as coercive and fraudulent. Indeed, the controversial cessions increased native support for the Indian confederacy north and west of the Ohio River. The treaties were useless as long as warriors could defend their homelands.[81]

Regarding Congress as hapless and hopeless, settlers fought their own war against Indians in the Ohio Valley. In 1786, Benjamin Logan and George Rogers Clark led Kentucky militiamen in massive raids that destroyed seven Shawnee villages, although their chiefs had cooperated with federal treaty councils. One of them, Molunthy, received an American flag, which he flew over his village as a source of protection. Instead, Kentuckians seized the chief and smashed his skull with a tomahawk. After blowing his body to pieces with gunpowder, they burned his village and its crops. While smashing Shawnees, the raids also discredited the federal government that had promised to protect them.[82]

Unable to control settlers or defeat Indians, the federal government appeared impotent and irrelevant. The difficult passage over the Appalachian Mountains also threatened to alienate settlers from the eastern states. Westerners could ship their crops to market more easily either northeastward via the Great Lakes and the St. Lawrence River to British Quebec or down the Ohio and Mississippi rivers to Spanish New Orleans. A pessimistic New York congressman regarded "every emigrant to that country from the Atlantic states as forever lost to the Confederacy." Eastern leaders feared that western settlers soon would reject American rule to seek an association with the British or Spanish empire. Washington worried, "The Western settlers . . . stand as it were upon a pivot—the touch of a feather would turn them any way."[83]

Secessions also threatened to break up states. Rejecting rule by North Carolina, settlers in present-day Tennessee formed a new state called Franklin and applied for admission to the union in 1784. But only seven states, not the required nine, approved, and the Franklin experiment collapsed. Congressmen opposed admitting Franklin for fear of setting a precedent dangerous to the cohesion of every state. Anxious to retain Kentucky for Virginia, Jefferson worried that "our states will crumble to atoms by the spirit of establishing every little canton onto a separate state." A Franklin supporter concluded, "I think the affairs of America is on a tottering foundation."[84]

The growing settlements also alarmed their imperial neighbors: the British to the north in Canada and the Spanish to the southwest in Louisiana. From just 12,000 in 1783, Kentucky's population exploded to 73,000 in 1790. In 1793, the Spanish governor of Louisiana, Barón de Carondelet, warned his superiors in Spain to beware of

> the unmeasured ambition of a new people, who are vigorous, hostile to all subjection, and who have been uniting and multiplying . . . with a remarkable rapidity. . . . This vast and restless population, driving the Indian tribes continually before them and upon us, is endeavoring to gain all the vast continent occupied by the Indians between the Ohio and Misisipi Rivers, the Gulf of Mexico, and the Appalachian Mountains.

Another Spanish governor regarded the settlers as "distinguished from savages only in their color, language, and the superiority of their depraved cunning and untrustworthiness." The Spanish worried that the frontier folk would sweep across the Mississippi River into Louisiana and on across the Great Plains to take New Mexico and eventually Mexico, the silver-rich heart of the Spanish Empire.[85]

The British and Spanish frontier colonies were immense but vulnerable because so thinly populated by colonists. Sprawled along the entire western side of the Mississippi River, Louisiana stretched across the Great Plains to include about 828,000 square miles, but the vast colony had only 30,000 colonists in 1782, and Florida had only 4,000 Hispanics. By 1790, British Upper Canada had a mere 14,000 colonists in scattered settlements along the St. Lawrence River and the northern shores of the Great Lakes: a stretch of nearly 1,500 miles. In Florida, Louisiana, and Upper Canada, native peoples outnumbered colonists, who lived in a few pockets near forts.[86]

To strengthen their position, and keep American settlers away, the British and Spanish cultivated alliances with native peoples by offering generous presents, especially guns and ammunition. After the loss of the thirteen colonies, a British agent noted, "We are no longer the first landed power in North America. Therefore [we] cannot have too many Indians under our protection and countenance." By arming Indian allies, the British and Spanish sought to preserve native-held buffer zones between their colonies and the American settlements. Grateful for Spanish subsidies, a Creek chief, Alexander McGillivray, insisted, "The Crown of Spain will Gain & Secure a powerful barrier in these parts against the ambitious and encroaching Americans." The son of a Scottish trader and an elite Creek woman, McGillivray preferred "the protection of a great Monarch . . . to that of a distracted Republic." Bernardo de Gálvez exulted in the enhanced "friendship of many Indian nations who dislike the Americans, and [have] more than enough experience in forest warfare."[87]

In 1784, Spain also tried to slow American expansion by closing New Orleans to settlers' commerce via the Mississippi. Fewer settlers would move west if they could not prosper by trading their flour, hemp, corn, pork, and lumber down the great river. Playing a double game, Spanish agents also assured western leaders that they could reopen that trade by seceding from the union to accept a dependent association with the Spanish Empire. If shutting the river to trade was the stick, reopening it was the carrot. By offering a few special licenses to trade at New Orleans, the Spanish tried to buy the "interest" of western leaders to promote western secession. Noting the weakness of the United States, Louisiana's governor, Esteban Rodríguez Miró, regarded western secession as "written in the book of destiny."[88]

But the Spanish played a risky game, for armed settlers might instead reopen the trade by attacking and seizing New Orleans. The same powerful river that could carry their trade would also swiftly propel southward the boats of a military expedition, which might surprise and overwhelm New Orleans. As an early warning system, the Spanish built new forts deep within the borderland contested with the Americans, up the Tombigbee River north of Mobile and on the Chickasaw Heights, beside the Mississippi, at the future site of Memphis.[89]

To bolster those defenses, Spanish officials needed to accelerate the settlement of Florida and Louisiana. A Florida governor explained, "The best fortification would be a living wall of industrious citizens." Unable to draw enough Hispanics to their frontier colonies, Spanish officials recruited Americans by offering large grants of free land, while also providing cherished access to the New Orleans market. In return, the new subjects had to swear allegiance to the Spanish Crown and pledge to defend the colony against any invader. Governor Miró confessed that "at first glance it seems dangerous to settle foreigners in Luisiana," but he believed that land grants gave them a stake in the colony's security. Miró explained, "Once they have emigrated and sworn vassalage, anyone who takes part in a revolution will risk a great deal." But Miro conceded that "circumstances force us to take this risk."[90]

In effect, the Spanish tried to build a settler fire wall to keep away more hostile settlers from the American orbit. During the 1780s and early 1790s, about 20,000 Americans moved to Louisiana. Some newcomers, including Daniel Boone, settled near St. Louis, but most developed farms and plantations around Natchez, on the east bank of the lower Mississippi. "May God keep us Spanish," wrote one grateful settler.[91]

But the emigration policy contradicted Spain's native alliances premised on keeping settlers at a distance. McGillivray warned against gambling that Americans could become good Spanish subjects. He insisted that "filling up your country with those accursed republicans is like placing a common thief as a guard on your door and giving him the key." Indeed, Jefferson slyly noted that American immigration into

Louisiana and Florida would be "the means of delivering to us peace-ably, what may otherwise cost us a war."[92]

British officials also hoped to exploit western discontent and polit-ical instability. A British politician, Lord Sheffield, predicted: "The authority of the Congress, can never be maintained over those distant and boundless regions, and her nominal subjects will speedily imitate and multiply the examples of independence." As the union subdivided and dissolved, the British hoped to dominate the pieces. Lord Gren-ville secretly advised Lord Dorchester to encourage western secession: "It appears extremely desirable that the turn of Affairs in those Settle-ments should lead to the establishment of a Government distinct from that of the Atlantic States." Dorchester sent agents to bribe and culti-vate leaders in Vermont and Kentucky. Those leaders sought trade deals and prepared contingency plans for the apparently impending collapse of the republican union.[93]

By keeping border forts, arming Indians, and wooing settlers, Brit-ish officers sustained a cold war along the American frontier. But Brit-ish leaders hoped to avoid an escalation to another hot war with the Americans. By holding out the vague prospect that eventually they would surrender the forts, Britons strung out discussions with Amer-ican diplomats over the tangled issues of the border, Indian auton-omy, merchants' debts, and Loyalist property. Playing for time, British leaders waited for the United States to collapse, leaving the northern forts, Indians, and fur trade in the British orbit. Posted in London as a diplomat, John Adams noted, "They rely upon it, that we shall not raise an Army to take the Posts . . . and therefore they think they may play with us as long as they please." Nearly bankrupt, Congress could afford an army of only 350 men: too few to fight the empire. Consid-ering the United States too weak to survive, McGillivray predicted that the kings of Spain, Britain, and France "must settle the matter by dividing America between them."[94]

Sand

Patriot leaders had hoped that independence would bring greater prosperity through free trade with the rest of the world. Instead, they suffered from new British trade restrictions and found that the Spanish and French empires also discouraged foreign traders. In a world of mercantile empires, Americans were left on the outside looking in. In retrospect, operating within the British trade network as colonies seemed better than exclusion from it.[95]

Independence also deprived the United States of protection by the Royal Navy, which had secured colonial access to dangerous markets in the Mediterranean. Without that protection, merchant ships fell prey to Muslim pirates operating from the Barbary Coast of North Africa. Barbary's rulers offered to sell protection for tribute payments, which Congress could no more afford than it could afford a proper navy. Consequently, captured American sailors languished as slaves in Algiers, Tripoli, and Tunis. Balking at the risks of entering the Mediterranean, sea captains and merchants lost a valuable market for American fish and flour. British merchants and officials quietly delighted in the woes reaped by their American rivals, who had rejected the benefits of the empire. McGillivray also exulted, for he considered Americans and Barbary pirates as "well matched" in stealing from others.[96]

Congress could not challenge the British terms of trade, for want of money and the power to coordinate the trade policies of the states. Revenue from selling western lands withered as Indian resistance scared away potential settlers. And without that money, Congress could not raise an army to fight Indians. In 1784, Robert Morris resigned as superintendent of finance for want of any money to superintend. A year later, much of the foreign debt owed to France and Dutch investors came due, but Congress had nothing to pay. Spain's ambassador reported that the United States was "almost without Government, without a Treasury, or means of obtaining money, and torn between hope and fear of whether or not their Confederation can be consolidated." The American foreign secretary, John Jay, agreed, "Our federal Government is incompetent to its Objects."[97]

Weak and diffuse, the American union had become a diplomatic joke in Europe. "To be more exposed in the eyes of the world & more contemptible than we already are, is hardly possible," Washington lamented. He expected "the worst consequences from a half-starved, limping Government, that appears to be always moving upon crutches, & tottering at every step." Lord Sheffield declared that the United States "should not be, for a long time, either to be feared or regarded as a nation." Britons felt contempt for the weak republican union, which seemed doomed to collapse: "Their Fate seems to be—A DISUNITED PEOPLE, till the End of Time." Posted as a diplomat in Paris, Jefferson reported that Europeans "supposed everything in America was anarchy, tumult, and civil war." Without a truly national government, Americans could not secure reciprocity in foreign trade.[98]

To better fund Congress, nationalists tried to amend the Articles, but any change required unanimous approval by thirteen states. In 1782 and 1785, a single state killed proposals to allow Congress to tax imports. Giving up hope, many congressmen stayed home, often depriving Congress of a quorum. Ignoring Congress, state governments adopted their own ineffectual trade regulations and wrangled over borders. A delegate from North Carolina concluded "that the Confederated compact is no more than a rope of sand, and if a more efficient Government is not obtained, a dissolution of the Union must take place."[99]

In 1786, John Jay's negotiations with Spain threatened to hasten that dissolution. Southern leaders bristled when he offered to barter away navigation rights on the Mississippi River for commercial concessions in overseas trade. Southerners expected to benefit from economic ties with the new western settlements, which needed trade access to New Orleans. If Jay persisted, southerners threatened to secede from the union. Virginia's governor, Patrick Henry, insisted that he "would rather part with the confederation than relinquish the navigation of the

Mississippi." Westerners also threatened to secede. Jefferson warned that any "act which abandons the navigation of the Missisipi is an act of separation between the Eastern and Western country. It is a relinquishment of five parts out of eight of the territory of the United States, an abandonment of the fairest subject for the payment of our public debts, and the chaining [of] those debts on our own necks in perpetuum."[100]

Uneasy partners in an unstable union, northerners and southerners jockeyed for advantage. A Virginia congressman insisted that the "great national contest" was "whether one part of the continent shall govern the other." A Massachusetts congressman worried that a stronger union would subject New England to southern domination: "If America becomes an Empire, the seat of government will be to the southward, and the Northern States will be insignificant provinces. Empire will suit the southern gentry! They are habituated to despotism by being the sovereigns of slaves; and it is only accident and interest that has made the body of them the temporary sons of liberty."[101]

Northern and southern leaders agreed that a collapse of the union would invite bloody wars between jealous states, which would then invite manipulation, invasion, and domination by foreign empires. Hamilton denounced the states as "little, jealous, clashing, tumultuous commonwealths, the wretched nurseries of unceasing discord." Franklin agreed, "Our States are on the point of separation, only to meet hereafter for the purpose of cutting one another's throats." A South Carolina congressmen worried, "That once [the Union is] dissolved, our State establishments would be of short duration. Anarchy or internecine wars would follow till some future Caesar seized our Liberties, or we would be the sport of European policies, and perhaps parceled out as appendages to their several Governments."[102]

Nationalists longed for a stronger union that could preserve the states by binding them together in a "peace pact." Otherwise, Jay warned, the United States would split "into three or four independent and probably discordant republics or confederacies, one inclining to Britain, another to France, and a third to Spain, and perhaps played off against each other by the three" empires in perpetual, destructive wars.[103]

During the 1780s, the United States lacked any evident "Manifest Destiny" to survive and dominate the West. By blocking settler expansion, an Indian confederacy had frustrated the frontier land sales that the union desperately needed for revenue and credibility. American weakness and defeats emboldened British and Spanish leaders, who retained border forts and intrigued with Indian chiefs and leading settlers. British Canada and Spanish Louisiana offered alternative destinations and constitutional models meant to entice Americans to forsake their independence. North America was riven with competing allegiances and multiple possibilities. Would the continent ultimately belong to an expansive republic or to British and Spanish empires allied to native peoples? The empires and natives were the better bet, for the republican union was withering and internal conflict imperiled the state governments.[104]   *what changed?*

10

REPUBLICS

By the malign influence of the [moon's] eclipses, the
United States of America will be troubled with intestine jars,
and domestic quarrels, and contentions of every kind.
—SAMUEL ELLSWORTH (an astronomer), 1786.[1]

The present aera is pregnant of great & strange events.
—GEORGE WASHINGTON, 1786.[2]

Patriot leaders hoped to preserve the power derived from gen-teel manners, family connections, elite education, and supe-rior wealth. A New York grandee, Robert R. Livingston, Jr., explained that "the better sort" alone should govern because "the learned, the wise, the virtuous . . . are all aristocrats." Few gentle-men sought to empower the poor, free the enslaved, or grant rights to women. While seeking home rule, they meant still to rule at home.[3]

During the revolution, however, they faced growing pressure from common voters, who often favored ambitious men of newly gained wealth. In 1786, the French minister to the United States reported,

---

"James Madison," watercolor miniature by Charles Willson Peale, 1783. Courtesy of the Library of Congress (LC-USZC4-4097).

"Alexander Hamilton," by an unknown engraver. Courtesy of the Library of Congress (LC-USZ62-91098).

"Although there are no nobles in America, there is a class of men denominated 'gentlemen,' who by reason of their wealth, their talents, their education, their families, or the offices they hold, aspire to a preeminence which the people refuse to grant them." Gentlemen cast their new rivals as ignorant, vulgar, and greedy men aspiring to more than their due. Robert Morris complained that republican politics favored "vulgar Souls whose narrow Optics can see but the little Circle of selfish Concerns." This sounded obtuse coming from a man who had gotten rich by manipulating government contracts, subsidies, and land grants.[4]

Although gentlemen meant to govern the new states, they needed common men to fight the British, Loyalists, and Indians. Patriots also sought help from women to manage the home front and supply the armies. To secure broad, popular support, gentlemen had to persuade common folk that the revolution would improve their opportunities and status. Patriots offered a new republican order in which sovereignty derived from the people, who chose their rulers and enjoyed equal legal and civil rights. Gentlemen could continue to govern only by winning electoral consent from common voters. The revolution also appealed to religious dissenters, who longed to escape domination and taxation by the religious establishments of the colonial regime.[5]

Far from promoting an across-the-board liberation within American society, the Patriot cause appealed primarily to common white men with some property: artisans in the towns and farmers in the countryside. Patriot leaders promised to enhance their advantages in property, class, race, and gender over others. The British unwittingly aided the Patriot cause by seeking military support from Indians and the enslaved, which increased the American animus against them all.[6]

Republicanism inflated the aspirations of common men, who grumbled when wealthy gentlemen continued to grab the largest land grants, top commands, highest offices, and best contracts. Common folk also bore the greatest sacrifices and hardships of the war. As the conflict dragged on, they resented their increasing burdens from taxes and militia service. They blamed leaders for waging a rich man's war by making it a poor man's fight. The republican promise of equal opportunity invited the dissatisfied to seek more sweeping reforms meant to reduce the power and privileges of genteel leaders. During the war, petitions from common men to legislatures multiplied and dropped their deferential tone in favor of new demands for attention and action. A Maryland elitist, Charles Carroll, complained, "Every man thinks himself a judge—and an adept in the great & difficult science of Legislation." The revolution did not begin as a radical movement, but it threatened to become one during the war as many common people demanded greater changes.[7]

By disrupting traditional networks of trade and political influence, the war created opportunities for daring and ambitious men to wheel and deal their way to new wealth and greater influence. They profited from military contracts and speculation in the confiscated estates of exiled Loyalists. Ambitious men also claimed new leadership positions on Patriot committees and in the expanded militia and enlarged legislatures. During the early 1780s, three-quarters of New York's legislators had middle-class origins, unlike the wealthy gentlemen who had dominated the smaller colonial assembly.[8]

A new breed of politician appealed to the aspirations of middling farmers and artisans and to their resentments of elites who clung to the colonial emphasis on deference. The savviest of the new politicians was George Clinton, a man of common origins but fierce ambition. Although a lawyer, he played down his education to present a common, accessible style characterized by simple manners and blunt speech. A big, burly man with bushy eyebrows, he said and wrote little, preferring to build influence through deft patronage. As a militia general, he became popular for fighting Britons and suppressing Loyalists. To the shock of New York's wealthy landlord families, Clinton defeated their candidate, Philip Schuyler, to become the state's first republican governor in 1777. Schuyler complained that Clinton's "Family & Connections do not Entitle him to so distinguished a preeminence." But Clinton repeatedly won reelection, governing the state for nearly twenty years by consolidating his popularity as the farmer's champion.

Common voters appreciated that Clinton celebrated their way of life instead of displaying the traditional elitism within his grasp.[9]

Possessing limited educations and crude manners, many new leaders irritated gentlemen from older, privileged families. "When the pot boils, the scum will rise," conservatives complained. They disdained many state legislators as "the horse-jockey, the mushroom merchant, [and] the running and dishonest speculator." State legislatures allegedly belonged to "Demagogues of desperate fortunes, mere adventures in fraud." Preaching the old deference, a gentleman insisted that common folk should "be content with the station God has assigned them, and not turn politicians when their maker intended them for farmers."[10]

Genteel leaders argued that new wealth did not suffice for high political office. Instead, the proper leader also had to cultivate gentility through education and improved manners. Alexander Hamilton rose in the approved fashion to win acceptance into the New York elite. Although born poor and illegitimate in the West Indies, Hamilton secured a wealthy patron, college education, high-status wife (Schuyler's daughter), and the mores and manners of his new peers. Brilliant, short, elegant, and handsome, Hamilton wore a self-assurance that belied his origins. After serving as an officer in the army, he became a lawyer and politician who championed the interests of wealthy merchants and great landlords, obscuring his early poverty. Gentility as well as wealth jointly qualified the proper leader.[11]

Constitutions

The revolution inspired the creation of written constitutions for the new states. By the end of 1776, ten states had adopted constitutions, while two others (Connecticut and Rhode Island) clung to their old charters, which were already republican in nature. A thirteenth state, Massachusetts, wrangled over a constitution until 1780.[12]

Drawing on the written precedents of their colonial charters, Patriots wanted to avoid the ambiguity of the unwritten British constitution, which they believed had invited corruption by executive power.

lesson learned

Patriot leaders felt thrilled by their opportunity to design comprehensive republican systems. John Adams exulted, "How few of the human race have ever enjoyed an opportunity of making an election of government . . . for themselves or their children." Never before "had three millions of people full power and a fair opportunity to form and establish the wisest and happiest government that human wisdom can contrive."[13]

Most constitutions began with a bill of rights, which defined the state as committed to preserving the liberties, morality, and property of its citizens. These bills forbade the government from impairing freedom of the press, liberty of religion, the right to petition, trial by jury, access to habeas corpus, and due process under the law. Defining government in republican terms, Virginia's constitution declared that "all power is vested in and consequently derived from, the people; that magistrates are their trustees and servants, and at all times amenable to them." The constitutions rejected hereditary offices, for few Americans wanted an aristocracy.[14]

Constitution-makers reacted against the robust executive powers wielded by royal governors to prorogue legislatures, appoint local officials, and veto legislation. Thomas Hutchinson and Lord Dunmore served as negative reference points in the republican state constitutions. "The executive power," a Delaware Patriot noted, "is ever restless, ambitious, and ever grasping at increase of power." To defend liberty, Patriots dispersed power among many legislators and rendered them collectively superior to the governor. Most governors lost their powers to appoint officials and veto laws. No state constitution allowed a governor to prorogue a legislature. Virginia's legislators elected the governor annually and his decisions needed approval by a Council of State chosen by, and from, the legislators. One Virginia governor sighed that he was "no more than a reading and signing clerk to the Council."[15]

State assemblies grew by multiplying smaller districts and extending them into backcountry counties underrepresented under the colonial order. According to Adams, a republican legislature "should be in miniature an exact portrait of the people at large. It should think, feel, reason, and act like them." Where colonial elections had been held at the whim of the governor as infrequently as every seventh year, the new republican order mandated annual elections for the assembly save in South Carolina, which held biennial elections. Patriots declared, "Where annual election ends, Tyranny begins."[16]

While granting sovereignty to "the people," the state constitutions insisted that only men with property could vote or hold office. As in the colonial era, a voter had to own enough real estate to support his family, which meant having either a farm or a shop. Because small farms and workshops abounded, about two-thirds of white men qualified to vote. Patriot leaders insisted that only propertied men possessed the "independence" from a landlord or employer required to make judicious political decisions. Adams explained, "Such is the Frailty of the human Heart, that very few Men, who have no Property, have any Judgment of their own. They talk and vote as they are directed by Some Man of Property, who has attached their Minds to his Interest." Regarding states as "commonwealths" of property, constitution-makers worried that paupers and dependent laborers would sell their votes or seek laws to redistribute wealth.[17]

By modern standards, the new state governments were not all that democratic. Although two-thirds of white men could vote for the assembly, they comprised less than a third of all adults because women, black people, and the poorest whites lacked civil rights. Most states also mandated an even stricter property qualification that precluded 90 percent of men from serving as a state senator or governor. Maryland created the most elitist senate, with just fifteen members who had five-year terms and owned at least £1,000, about ten times the median property holding in the state. By design, governors and senates often blocked legislation favored by the more populist assemblies.[18]

In 1776, Pennsylvania adopted the most democratic constitution in the new union. Associations of common militiamen seized power, ousting the colony's traditional leaders, who had embraced Loyalism or Quaker pacifism. Defiantly egalitarian, the "associators" rejected traditional notions of social hierarchy and deference. When asked how many men he commanded, a militia captain replied, "Not one, but I am commanded by ninety." Some well-educated but down-on-their-luck gentlemen supported the "associators" and wrote the constitution. They included George Bryan, a bankrupt merchant; James Cannon, a college math professor; and Timothy Matlack, a brewer and gambler with deep debts. A conservative denounced them as "violent wrong-headed people of the inferior class."[19]

The new constitution broadened the electorate to include any man who had resided for at least a year in the state and had paid any tax. Where only two-thirds of men could vote under the colonial property requirement, 90 percent qualified as a result of the new taxpayer standard. Instead of a single governor, the state had a plural executive: a council of twelve elected by the people. Pennsylvania's democrats conceived of the people as having a common interest, so they mandated a legislature with just one house, dispensing with a senate. A democrat insisted, "Two or more distinct interests can never exist in society without finally destroying the liberties of the people." Legislative acts also remained provisional until another session of the assembly convened. That delay and annual elections enabled voters to select new representatives to kill any offensive law. Local voters also chose county sheriffs and justices of the peace: positions previously appointed by the colonial governor. Democrats explained, "The more simple, and the more immediately dependent the authority is upon the people, the better," for "they are the best guardians of their own liberties."[20]

The vision of a unitary society paradoxically led democrats to polarize Pennsylvania. Leading a revolution with many internal enemies, they denied the vote to anyone who would not take an oath to support the new constitution. The requirement excluded at least a third of the potential electorate, including Quakers, who refused to take any oath.[21]

Outraged conservatives denounced the Pennsylvania constitution as a threat to their liberty and property. Benjamin Rush claimed that radicals had "substituted a mob government." A conservative congressman, William Hooper, derided the state as "an execrable democracy—a Beast without a head." Hooper complained, "Taverns and dram Shops are the Councils to which the laws of the State are to be referred before they possess a binding influence."[22]

Unlike democrats, conservatives regarded society as diverse and complex. To suit that vision of society, conservatives desired a more complicated government with a separation of powers, so that two co-equal houses of the legislature, an independent judiciary, and a powerful governor could jealously watch, check, and balance each other. Where democrats concentrated electoral power to fulfill the public will, conservatives sought to limit and complicate the majority's clout. Distrusting human nature, they regarded inaction (or "gridlock" as we would put it today), as preferable to the hyperactive legislation of popular government.[23]

Conservatives favored the constitutional principles of John Adams. Admiring the British constitution as "the most stupendous fabric of human invention," Adams despised Pennsylvania's unicameral legislature because, he insisted, common people were "as unjust, tyrannical, brutal, barbarous, and cruel, as any king or senate [when] possessed of uncontrollable power." He preferred a bicameral legislature, where an upper house of fewer members from larger districts would embody prestige and wealth and could restrain the populist excesses of a lower house. According to Adams, a constitution had to manage the fundamental conflict in every civilized society, between an elite few who enjoyed superior wealth, power, and prestige and the common many, jealous of their superiors. It was folly, he insisted, to deprive the wealthy of all institutional power, for then they would subvert the government—as they were busy doing in Pennsylvania. If concentrated instead in a senate, elite power would become more conspicuous, inviting scrutiny and restraint from the lower house and common voters.[24]

To mediate between the two contentious legislative houses, Adams proposed a governor with the power to veto laws and appoint local officials. Nothing "but three different orders of men, bound by their interests to watch over each other, and stand the guardians of the laws" could preserve constitutional order. Adams concluded "that the people's rights and liberties, and the democratical mixture in a constitution, can never be preserved without a strong executive." In 1780, his ideas prevailed in the Massachusetts constitution adopted by a special convention dominated by eastern conservatives. While Pennsylvania defined the democratic end of the constitutional spectrum, Massachusetts clarified the conservative alternative. Most states adopted moderate constitutions with bicameral legislatures but without a strong governor.[25]

Charged with being aristocrats, conservatives had to learn how to mask their elitism in the language of republicanism. Posing as the people's true champions, conservatives encouraged voters to distrust their legislators as corrupt demagogues. In a stroke of political genius, conservatives packaged a separation of powers as the essence of true republicanism. In New Hampshire, a conservative insisted that the different branches of a properly complex government should, by watching one another, "become centinels in behalf of the people to guard against every possible usurpation."[26]

Muckworms

The long, hard war had devastated the American economy. Roaming armies and frontier raiders uprooted thousands of people by destroying their farms, plantations, and towns. At least 25,000 Americans died in military service, usually of disease. As a percentage of the population, the mortality exceeded every American conflict but the Civil War of the 1860s. British warships disrupted the export trade essential to prosperity. Economic historians find a 30 percent decline in national income between 1774 and 1790: a decline which they characterize as "America's greatest income slump ever," and an "economic disaster."[27]

During the spring and summer of 1783, peace brought a temporary and partial boom thanks to generous credits offered by British merchants and manufacturers eager to recapture their American market.

Americans needed that credit, for they lacked mines of gold and silver, so they were chronically short on hard money, which they could only obtain through overseas trade. Postwar British trade restrictions, however, limited American access to the West Indies. Without that market, American merchants fell deeper into debt for their imported manufactures. During the mid-1780s, Americans imported three times as much from Britain as they exported there.[28]

In 1784–1785, British merchants became nervous and tightened credit, dunning American importers, who in turn brought thousands of lawsuits against their clients. As work diminished in the seaports, urban wage levels plunged by 26 percent. As the credit constriction spread to the countryside, the demand for farm produce declined, depressing prices. Deprived of export income, farmers struggled to pay creditors in hard money and risked court-ordered foreclosures on their livestock and land. A Virginia judge, St. George Tucker, calculated that, during the mid-1780s, "barely one tidewater planter in twenty" made enough annually to pay his debts. Many old estates collapsed as lawsuits consumed the property. A merchant sighed, "We have not only had a revolution in Political government but also in many people's private circumstances."[29]

State fiscal policies worsened the economic pain borne by common farmers and artisans. During the war, states raised taxes but not enough to fund military operations, for state leaders feared alienating tax-phobic and cash-strapped voters. To bridge the gap, states and Congress resorted to printing paper money and requiring people to accept it as legal tender. With these promissory notes, governments bought supplies and paid soldiers. By 1777, however, the profusion of paper bills produced rampant inflation, which especially hurt creditors, when debtors paid with money of depreciating value. The hyperinflation also afflicted urban artisans and laborers, who struggled to earn enough to buy their daily bread.[30]

To reduce inflation, radical Patriots favored strict price controls, the confiscation and sale of Loyalist property, and tender laws that punished anyone who refused to take paper money in payment. Radicals blamed inflation on rich merchants who allegedly hoarded scarce commodities and sold them only when paid premium prices. The growing wealth of merchants like Robert Morris bred angry resentment among poor men, who blamed "greedy Muckworms."[31]

When state laws failed to curb profiteering or inflation, radicals revived local committees to set and enforce price controls, while mobs punished and shamed violators. Women often took the lead in riots, gathering to break open merchants' warehouses to seize sugar, coffee, and flour. Rioters left behind paper money at the price they deemed just. According to Abigail Adams, in July 1777 in Boston, a hundred women "assembled with a cart and trucks" to break open the warehouse of "an eminent, wealthy, stingy Merchant (who is a Batchelor)." They beat him until he gave up his keys. While they carted away his coffee, "a large concourse of Men stood [by as] amazed, silent Spectators."[32]

In 1779, Philadelphia's radicals denounced merchants as price-gougers and crypto-Loyalists bent on ruining common people. In May, an anonymous broadside appeared overnight throughout the city: "In the midst of money, we are in poverty and exposed to want in a land of plenty. You that have money, . . . down with your prices or down with yourselves." The next day, a thousand men gathered to seize a few hated merchants, parading them through the streets while drums beat out the "Rogue's March." In early October, renewed disturbances led thirty armed conservatives, including Robert Morris and James Wilson, to hole up in Wilson's mansion, which became known as "Fort Wilson." Radicals and conservatives exchanged gunfire, killing men on both sides. Just as common militiamen broke down the front door, a genteel militia unit, the City Light Horse, arrived to save the mansion and its defenders. The authorities dared not prosecute anyone on either side for the violence. The Fort Wilson riot deepened conservative hatred for the Pennsylvania constitutional regime, which apparently tolerated economic regulation by mobs.[33]

The clash over price controls revealed an emerging fault line in economic and political thought. Radicals insisted that a public good trumped private property rights; indeed property was illegitimate if derived from exploiting others. They justified local committees and mobs in intimidating wealthy men who acted selfishly. Conservatives, however, insisted that freedom was individual and required protecting private property from violent community regulation. Morris declared, "It is inconsistent with the principles of liberty to prevent a man from the free disposal of his property on such terms as he may think fit."[34]

Neither regulations nor riots could halt the spiraling inflation, as sellers refused to part with goods at below-market prices. Many artisans initially supported restricting merchants but later objected to controls on their own wages and prices. In 1780–1781, the price-control movement collapsed, and conservatives won power in most states. They introduced austerity programs meant to improve the payment of interest to state creditors and to relieve private creditors from depreciated money. Congress and most states ceased to print paper money and revoked its standing as legal tender. Citizens had to pay private debts and public taxes in hard money, which was preciously scarce. In a painful reverse, inflation gave way to deflation, afflicting especially farmers, whose incomes tanked with the plunging prices paid for their produce. The austerity programs bolstered public credit but increased tensions between the social classes.[35]

During the mid-1780s, states devoted two-thirds of their expenditures to paying interest to public creditors. To fund those payments, most states levied taxes at unprecedented rates. In 1786, for example, taxes in Massachusetts were at least four times higher than before the war. The taxes were regressive, with the poor land of common farmers paying at a higher rate than the vast tracts held by land speculators. Many states relied on poll taxes levied at the same rate on every man, poor and rich. Recalling the prewar protests over small British taxes, some rural people complained, "Our Grievances Ware Less Real and more Ideal then they are Now."[36]

Austerity policies coupled with high taxes redistributed income from common people to pay wealthy public creditors. In 1786, just sixty-seven creditors received almost all of Pennsylvania's annual interest payments. In Rhode Island, sixteen men owned half of the public debt. That debt became consolidated in fewer hands because common men rarely could afford to keep their paper certificates issued by government officials during the war. Under subsequent austerity policies, they needed specie to pay taxes and private creditors, so they sold certificates to speculators for hard pennies on the paper dollar. Then the hard-pressed former holders of the debt had to pay higher taxes to fund the full face value of the certificates to the speculators. A Massachusetts newspaper writer blamed the "great possessors" of the public debt for the "abominable system of enormous taxation, which is crushing the poor to death." When a Rhode Island speculator in military certificates rode by in a freshly painted carriage, an angry workman yelled, "Soldiers' blood makes good varnish."[37]

The postwar recession multiplied lawsuits for debts, and court judgments also demanded payment in hard money. If a debtor failed to pay, sheriffs seized his livestock and land for auctions, where property sold for a fraction of its appraised value. If a farmer hid his livestock, a creditor could cast him in jail as a hostage for the debt. A gloomy debtor insisted that New England had become "a country, which holds out nothing but poverty and prisons." Farmers dreaded losing title to their farms to become the dependent tenants of aristocratic landlords.[38]

Disgusted by austerity, many common folk questioned the revolution. A Massachusetts man asked, "Has not many been oppressed a Hundred to one more than ever they had been by Brittan Before[?]" Protestors charged that "it cost them much to maintain the *Great* Men under George the 3rd, but vastly more under the Commonwealth and Congress." They doubted that a republic could survive the growing inequality. "The security of American liberty requires a more equal distribution of property than at present," a New Yorker insisted.[39]

To reduce taxes, common people begged states to pay interest only on the depreciated value of certificates rather than on their full face value. To end deflation and ease their taxes and debts, farmers and other debtors also demanded a reversion to paper money and the suspension of lawsuits until the economy improved. Delaware farmers insisted that an inflationary policy "would afford them Immediate releaf and make them freemen instead of being slaves to a few Merciless creditors who would wish to take all they have."[40]

After the Rhode Island legislature instead increased taxes in hard money, angry voters swept in forty-five new legislators in an assembly of seventy seats. They promptly voted to inflate the economy with paper money and tender laws. Rather than accept payment in paper, Newport's merchants shuttered their stores, but mobs broke in to plunder their stocks. In other states, conservatives denounced Rhode Island as "Fool's Island" and a sinkhole of moral and financial depravity. They charged that Rhode Island's fiscal policies threatened the economies of every other state. Some shrill critics urged Connecticut or Massachusetts to annex "the little detestable corner of the Continent, called *Rhode-Island*."[41]

Reaction

Unmoved by the protests, conservatives blamed hard times on indolent spendthrifts, who allegedly preferred to shop rather than work. Newspaper moralists especially accused women of ruining their husbands by relentlessly buying imported fashions. By blaming the victims, critics denied that inequitable tax and credit policies produced their woes. Abigail Adams insisted that, if common people were "harder-prest by publick burdens than formerly, they should consider it as the price of their freedom."[42]

The leaders of Massachusetts clung to the most regressive fiscal policy in the nation. In 1785, the state's public debt of £1,600,000 was nearly triple what it could have been if Massachusetts had followed Virginia's example of funding only the depreciated value of debt certificates. No state relied more heavily on poll taxes, levied at a rate four times higher than in other states. During the mid-1780s, Massachusetts farmers paid a third of their income in state taxes, and most of that revenue went to public creditors.[43]

The state's austerity policies had strong support from eastern, coastal towns and a few commercial centers in the interior. But those policies outraged hinterland farmers who petitioned for debtor relief measures and a revision of the state constitution along more democratic lines. The legislature, however, badly represented rural interests because towns had to pay the costs of their representatives, so fifty-two poor towns economized by declining to send any. Naturally, the representatives of wealthier towns saw no reason to heed their petitions. In early 1786, most legislators rejected relief measures and constitutional reform. Instead, they *raised* taxes to help the state meet an increased requisition from Congress.[44]

Mobilizing as in the revolution, frustrated farmers organized county conventions and committees of safety and suspended the collection of taxes and debts. An eastern conservative complained, "The people have turned against their teachers the doctrines which were inculcated in order to effect the late revolution." In response, a rural writer satirized the outrage of a state legislator: "'When we had other rulers, committees and conventions of the people were lawful—they were then necessary; but since I *myself* became a ruler, they cease to be lawful—the people have no right to examine my conduct.'"[45]

In 1786, acting in the regulator tradition, militiamen in rural Massachusetts gathered to block the county courts from meeting, which prevented lawsuits from culminating in foreclosures on farms and livestock. Most of the protestors came from relatively small, poor, and hilly towns rather than from the occasional commercial town with larger populations and richer leaders. The early protests were bloodless because judges wisely withdrew when confronted by hundreds of armed and determined regulators. Rather than overthrow the government, they nullified the local operation of laws deemed oppressive until the legislature could reconsider and offer relief.[46]

But conservatives equated regulators with rebels out to destroy republican government. As lead villain, easterners cast Daniel Shays, deemed an evil mastermind who manipulated rustic dupes on behalf of shadowy "British emissaries." A conservative catechism lumped Shays with Nathan Smith and Job Shattuck as an unholy rural trinity of riot and rebellion:

> *R stands for Rebels who mobs dare to raise*
> *S stands for Satan, Smith, Shattuck, and Shays*

In fact, Shays was a reluctant local leader, a thirty-nine-year-old farmer who had served as a captain in the Continental Army. After the war, he had to sell his sword to pay his debts. As a regulator, he aspired to nothing more than helping his neighbors save their farms. But conservatives declared that they confronted "Shays's Rebellion," a misnomer that has stuck.[47]

To suppress the supposed rebellion, Governor James Bowdoin rallied 4,400 volunteers from eastern counties to march west under the command of General Benjamin Lincoln. Public creditors advanced funds to pay and supply the soldiers. In self-defense, the western and central counties formed a small army under Shays. In effect, the conservative show of force provoked regulators into becoming the rebels that elites longed to suppress. On January 25, 1787, Shays's men tried to seize badly needed firearms from the federal armory at Springfield. Botching the attack, they suffered a bloody defeat. Through a howling blizzard, the eastern force tracked the demoralized regulators to the town of Petersham, surprising and attacking them on February 4. The regulator force dissolved, while Shays and other leaders fled across state lines to New York or Vermont. Lincoln's troops rounded up lesser men for prosecution. The courts sentenced sixteen to jail terms and two to hang.[48]

Across the country, conservatives overreacted to Shays's Rebellion, which they improbably described as a leveling movement meant to abolish all debts and confiscate great property to benefit the poor. Henry Knox assured Washington, "Their creed is that the property of the United States has been protected from confiscation . . . by the joint exertion of *all*, and therefore ought to be the *common property* of all."[49]

Conservatives also felt alarmed by smaller-scale regulations in rural pockets from New Hampshire to South Carolina as farmers blocked courthouse sessions and foreclosure sales. In a few places, they burned jails and courthouses. In rural South Carolina, a debtor forced an arresting sheriff to eat his writ. In New Hampshire, regulators briefly occupied the state capitol until dispersed by armed force. James Wilson exclaimed, "The flames of internal insurrection were ready to burst out in every quarter . . . and from one end to the other of the continent; we walked in ashes concealing fire beneath our feet."[50]

Although thrilled by Shays's defeat in the winter, conservatives felt disgusted by the spring election in Massachusetts, where voters cast out Governor Bowdoin in favor of John Hancock by a margin of three-to-one. General Lincoln ran for lieutenant governor and also lost badly for want of rural support. Rejecting Bowdoin and Lincoln as callous and heavy-handed, voters preferred the vague and vapid Hancock as a conciliator. He freed most of the jailed regulators and even pardoned Shays. Having learned a lesson, more country towns paid the cost to send representatives to the legislature. The legislators suspended direct taxes for 1787 and cut them to a third of their previous level in 1788. Speculators howled as the value of state securities fell by 30 percent.[51]

Conservatives were especially upset when many other states adopted debtor relief measures as the best means to avoid armed resistance in the countryside. Seven of the thirteen states reverted to issuing paper money as legal tender. In three more states, elitist state senates rejected paper-money bills passed by assemblies. In 1787 in Virginia, Governor Edmund Randolph lamented that "paper money is hastening into popularity with great strides." Some states offered more limited measures to delay or reduce taxes or allow payments of debts or taxes in farm produce rather than in scarce cash. In South Carolina, David Ramsay noted, "Much of our quiet arises from the temporizing of the legislatures in refusing legal protection to the prosecution of the just rights of creditors."[52]

Disgusted conservatives accused states and voters of bad faith and injustice, for relief measures depreciated the value of great property. It became their turn to bemoan the consequences of the revolution. Too many common men allegedly acted "licentiously," with a selfish greed that demonstrated the folly of popular government. Ramsay complained, "This revolution has introduced so much anarchy that it will take half a century to eradicate the licentiousness of the people." John Jay concluded, "Too much has been expected from the Virtue and good Sense of the People." Washington agreed "that mankind, left to themselves are unfit for their own government."[53]

Conservatives lost confidence in state governments as too responsive to public opinion, as "too democratic." Although no state, save Pennsylvania, was particularly democratic, conservatives did not like to compromise when their property was at stake. They regarded state constitutions as pretty on paper but failures in practice, for too many alleged demagogues won legislative seats by pandering for popularity. Dr. Benjamin Rush detected a new pathology in American minds, a disease he named "Anarchia" and described as "the excess of the passion for liberty ... which could not be removed by reason, nor restrained by government." By 1787, conservatives concluded that the revolution had gone too far.[54]

Losing faith in republicanism, some gentlemen wanted to substitute a constitutional monarchy to control democracy in the states. In November 1786, the Connecticut educator Noah Webster announced in a newspaper essay, "For my own part, I confess, I was once as strong a republican as any man in America. Now a republic is among the last kinds of government I should choose. I would infinitely prefer a limited monarchy, for I would sooner be subject to the caprice of one man, than to the ignorance and passions of the multitude." Loyalists had similarly warned Patriots back in 1775. With encouragement from Nathaniel Gorham, then presiding over Congress, General von Steuben approached a Prussian prince about becoming the American king as a contingency plan "on the failure of our free institutions." The prince declined, deeming Americans too disobedient. In private letters, Hamilton, Madison, Jay, and Washington worried that great property might need a king's protection. In March 1787, Washington conceded the potential "utility" and perhaps "necessity" of a switch to monarchy but worried that such a counterrevolution would shake "the Peace of this Country to its foundation."[55]

Like Washington, most gentlemen still hoped to find, in Madison's words, a "republican remedy for the diseases most incident to republican government." They wanted to redesign republican governments to weaken the many and empower the few. Rejecting equality, Benjamin Lincoln insisted, "Men possessed of property are entitled to a greater share in political authority than those who are destitute of it." Robert Morris defined the goal as "establishing the Power of Government over a People impatient of Control." In Morris's ideal government, "the Possession of Money will acquire Influence. Influence will lead to Authority, and authority will open the Purses of the People." As he saw it, the problem was that too many people could use state governments to shut their purses to him while they reached into his pocket.[56]

Foiled at the state level, conservatives turned to an alternative: concentrating power in a national government. By ditching the weak Articles of Confederation and writing a new constitution, conservatives hoped to kill two political birds with one stone. While rescuing the federal government from impotence and irrelevance, they would also subordinate the state governments. Hamilton attributed revived nationalism to "most men of property in the several states who wish [for] a government of the union able to protect them against domestic violence and the depredations which the democratic spirit is apt to make on property." Conservative worries about the weak union merged with a growing dread of state governments as too strong and democratic. To achieve both goals, nationalists drew on the ideas of James Madison.[57]

The eldest son of the wealthiest man in a Virginia county, Madison inherited hundreds of acres, scores of slaves, and the leisure time to read widely. Attending the College of New Jersey (now Princeton), Madison studied moral philosophy and graduated in 1772. Returning to Virginia, he became active in his county's Committee of Safety and the colony's Provincial Congress. Scholarly, sickly, astute, and shy, he worked best in a library or on a committee rather than on the stump in an election. Joining Congress in 1779, he grew frustrated with regional rivalries and the weak confederacy.[58]

From a close study of state politics, Madison concluded that a popular majority could act as tyrannically as any king. During the 1770s, Patriots had sought to free the people from the tyranny of executive power. A decade later, Madison decided that in a republic "it is much more to be dreaded that the few will be unnecessarily sacrificed to the many." He insisted that a truly just republic had to "protect the minority of the opulent against the majority."[59] *tyranny of the many*

Madison saw an opportunity in the emerging consensus that the confederation was too weak and flawed. Almost everyone agreed that Congress needed new powers to levy taxes and regulate interstate and foreign commerce. But Madison sought much more: a truly national government superior to the states and able to operate directly on the American people. Such a nation would have the power to restrain state legislatures that sometimes favored debtors at the expense of creditors.[60]

Madison defied conventional thinking, which insisted that a republic could only work on a small scale, no larger than a state, so that the legislators could know their constituents and feel the local consequences of their laws. The diverse climates, landscapes, ethnicities, and classes in the vast United States seemed to defy unification in one superrepublic. Past republics had worked best on the relatively intimate scale of a city, a province, or a canton, which enjoyed relative homogeneity. Madison retorted that no American state enjoyed homogeneity and harmony, least of all the smallest one, Rhode Island.[61]

Madison insisted that the larger the territory, the better a republic could protect minorities, especially those with great property. In a big republic, he argued, "No common interest or passion will be likely to unite a majority of the whole number in an unjust pursuit." Best of all, he reasoned, "a rage for paper money, for an abolition of debts, or for any other wicked or improper project, will be less apt to pervade the whole union than a particular member of it." In one big republic, the many interest groups would have to compromise to build coalitions, which would then sustain social stability. Revolutionary republicanism had tried to manifest a common interest at the state level, as in the Pennsylvania constitution. Madison's reformed republicanism, however, sought to manage the many interests of a vast nation of diverse people.[62]

Finding a second benefit in a larger scale, Madison insisted that a national republic would filter leadership, assuring the highest quality, for voters would elect gentlemen "who possess the most attractive merit and the most diffusive and established characters." He believed that the many, small districts of a state legislature favored petty demagogues of limited education, connections, and views. By contrast, in a national republic with large congressional districts, voters would choose famous men of wider reputations and perspectives. A national republic would "extract from the mass of the Society the purest and noblest characters which it contains." On the national scale, he hoped to distill a natural aristocracy of merit.[63]

In September 1786 at Annapolis, Madison, Hamilton, and ten other nationalists held a preliminary meeting to frame an appeal to Congress for a fuller convention to meet at Philadelphia in the spring of 1787. Congress approved but limited the delegates to proposing only amendments, keeping the Articles of Confederation as the basic framework for the union. Congress also stipulated that the proposed amendments would have to win approval from "Congress and the several [state] legislatures." Given the track record of single states blocking any constitutional reform, Congress's hedging threatened to consign the convention delegates to a fool's errand. But the leading nationalists forged ahead with their own agenda: to strengthen the union *and* restrain democracy in the states. Madison later explained that the "mutability" and "injustice" of the States "contributed more to that uneasiness which produced the [Constitutional] Convention" than did "the inadequacy of the Confederation."[64]

Contrary to modern belief, the founders did not intend to create a national democracy. Instead, they designed a national republic to restrain state democracies, which they blamed for the union's woes. David Ramsay derided state governments as "elected despotisms." Elbridge Gerry claimed, "The evils we experience flow from the excess of democracy." Roger Sherman agreed that common people "wanted information and are constantly liable to be misled." Charles Carroll insisted that of all governments "Democracies" were "the worst, and will end as all other Democracies have, in despotism."[65]

By restraining democracy in the states, nationalists hoped to save republican government from a descent into anarchy or a switch to monarchy. They wanted also to preserve the union from splitting into several smaller confederacies, or many individual states, which would contest boundaries and settle differences with bloody wars. In April, Ramsay assured Jefferson, "Our eyes now are all fixed on the continental convention to be held in Philad[elphi]a in May next. Unless they make an efficient federal government I fear that the end of the matter will be an American monarch or rather three or more confederacies." At that convention, Madison assured the other delegates that they "were now digesting a plan which in its operation w[oul]d decide forever the fate of Republican Gov[ernmen]t."[66]

Plans

A dozen states sent delegations to Philadelphia, with only Rhode Island balking. Most states chose nationalists, so that they would reap blame if the convention failed. America's leading populists—Samuel Adams of Massachusetts, George Clinton of New York, and Patrick Henry of Virginia—stayed home. Henry explained that he "smelt a rat." In the New York delegation, Clinton assigned two clients to keep a close eye on the third member, Hamilton. State legislators also counted on their ultimate power to reject proposals from the convention.[67]

Madison urged Washington to come out of retirement and attend as a Virginia delegate. The most revered man in the nation, Washington could give credibility to the reform movement. Although he supported the nationalist push, he initially balked at going to Philadelphia, for he worried about tainting his reputation, which was both his greatest achievement and burden. Through self-discipline and hard service, he became known as the consummate republican leader of virtue, dignity, and honor. Sensitive to his public audience, Washington weighed every word, gesture, and decision with painstaking care. His vaunted reputation gave him great political leverage, but he dreaded losing his impeccable aura with any public controversy. He wanted the convention to succeed but feared that if it did collapse he would have to wear its failure. By the spring of 1787, however, his worries shifted: perhaps he would appear selfish and disengaged if he stayed away. On May 13, Madison, who had already reached Philadelphia, felt a thrill of optimism when ringing church bells, roaring cannon, and cheering crowds announced that Washington had arrived.[68]

The delegates slowly assembled, riding in from far-flung states over the muddy roads of spring. Of the union's great leaders, only Adams, Jay, and Jefferson did not attend, kept away by their duties as diplomats. The fifty-five delegates were mature, wealthy, and well-educated gentlemen from prestigious families. Aside from two Catholics, all were Protestants, and 70 percent belonged to the relatively elitist Episcopal Church. None adhered to the more plebeian evangelical churches. At a time when few men (and no women) had access to higher education, twenty-nine of the delegates held college degrees. Professionally, they were a mix of lawyers, merchants, great planters, and landlords. Twenty-five owned slaves. Aside from the wealthy Pennsylvania merchants, the richest delegates came from Virginia and South Carolina, where they possessed vast plantations worked by scores of the enslaved. Most had federal experience as congressmen (forty-two) or Continental officers (thirty). No delegate embodied the perspective of the American majority: the hinterland farmers of modest means. Consequently, almost all rejected populist measures for debtor relief.[69]

Opening their proceedings in late May, the delegates met in the Pennsylvania State House, now known as Independence Hall, which had served as the wartime home for Congress. On their first day, the delegates unanimously chose Washington to preside over their sessions. They also adopted strict rules of secrecy, barring attendance by outsiders or any public discussion by members of the proceedings. To discourage snoopers, delegates kept the hall's windows and doors shut through the heat and humidity of a Philadelphia summer. By excluding public feedback, they sought frank discussions. Madison later insisted, "No Constitution would ever have been adopted by the convention if the debates had been public." Devoted to a secular, legal project, the delegates also rejected proposals to appoint chaplains or hold morning prayers before their sessions.[70]

Never did all fifty-five delegates meet together, as many came and went for weeks at a time to attend to private business in their home states. Just fifteen spoke with any regularity, and only Madison kept a detailed record of their proceedings. In mid-July, during the most critical sessions, only ten states had representation. Following the precedent of Congress under the Articles, each delegation, no matter how large or small the state, could cast but one vote, so Delaware had the same weight as Virginia in the convention.[71]

Despite their similar backgrounds, consensus proved elusive, for the delegates had robust egos fed by long experience as leaders in their home states. A critic described one especially cantankerous delegate, Elbridge Gerry, as a "Grumbletonian" fond of "objecting to everything he did not propose." Despite frequent invocations to pursue the common good, everyone pressed the interest of his own state. Benjamin Franklin sighed that whenever "you assemble a number of men to have the advantage of their joint wisdom, you inevitably assemble with those men all their prejudices, their passions, their errors of opinion, their local interests, and their selfish views. From such an assembly can a perfect production be expected?"[72]

Seizing the initiative, Madison framed the "Virginia Plan," which that state's governor, Edmund Randolph, presented to the convention on May 29. The plan proposed a powerful national government with executive and judicial branches as well as a bicameral legislature. Larger states would have greater weight in both houses based on their population or contributions to federal revenue. The members of both houses would be directly elected, rather than chosen by state legislatures. Indeed, this national government would control state governments through a power to veto any state law. Because this veto would doom debtor relief measures, Randolph concluded that the plan provided "sufficient checks against democracy."[73]

Delegates from smaller states balked at the Virginia Plan as consolidating a powerful nation at their expense. Fearing the big states, William Paterson of New Jersey insisted that his state would never accept the Virginia Plan: "She would be swallowed up. I would rather submit to a monarch, to a despot, than to such a fate." Paterson presented an alternative plan in mid-June. Following the narrow mandate provided by Congress to the convention, the "New Jersey Plan" preserved the diffuse union of the Articles, with additional powers to tax the people and regulate overseas and interstate trade. Congress would remain a single chamber in which each state cast one vote regardless of size, and its resolutions would continue to rely on cooperation from the states rather than operate directly on individual citizens. Under the New Jersey Plan, states would retain their sovereignty except for military, foreign, and Indian affairs. Rejecting the "idea of a national government," Paterson concluded, "We have no power to go beyond the federal scheme, and if we had, the people are not ripe for any other."[74]

The parochialism of the New Jersey Plan provoked Alexander Hamilton into presenting his own plan. On June 18, Hamilton delivered a five-hour harangue, the longest at the convention, to denounce both the Virginia and New Jersey plans as too weak. He began with the premise that "all communities divide themselves . . . into the rich and the well-born" and that "the mass of people . . . seldom judge or determine right." Disgusted by state governments, he longed for an imperial regime modeled on Britain's mixed constitution and adapted ever so slightly to republicanism. "The British government is the best in the world, and I doubt much whether anything short of it will do in America," he asserted. Only the House of Representatives would be popularly elected under Hamilton's plan. Both the president and senators should be indirectly elected by electoral colleges and would serve for life terms as republican equivalents of king and lords. The president could veto laws passed by Congress without any override. Hamilton's imperial government also could appoint the governors of every state and each would have a full veto power over acts by state legislatures. He reasoned, "The general power . . . must swallow up the State powers, otherwise it will be swallowed up by them."[75]

Many delegates admired Hamilton's logical rigor and vivid eloquence, but none thought that his plan had any chance of winning popular support. A Connecticut delegate declared that Hamilton's plan "had been praised by everybody" but "supported by none." The delegates could not afford to embrace a controversial British-style mixed constitution. Citing an ancient precedent, Pierce Butler of South Carolina concluded, "We must follow the example of Solon who gave the Athenians not the best Government he could devise but the best they would receive." Although disgusted by state democracy, the delegates still hoped to preserve republican principles in their national government.[76]

After Hamilton's fiery speech, the delegates resumed debating the New Jersey and Virginia Plans. For nearly a month, the convention deadlocked with both sides threatening to bolt and thereby doom the convention. A Delaware delegate, Gunning Bedford, bluntly assured the big state delegates, "I do not, gentlemen, trust you. If you possess the power, the abuse of it could not be checked." Pouring gunpowder on that fire, Gouverneur Morris threatened the small states with conquest if they balked at constitutional change: "The stronger party will make traytors of the weaker, and the gallows and halter will finish the work of the sword." The delegates came to Philadelphia seeking a peace pact to avert civil wars within the fragile union, but their rancor seemed more likely to hasten that bloody collapse.[77]

To break the deadlock, Franklin and the Connecticut delegates proposed a compromise that would grant an equal vote to every state in the Senate while allowing the big states more seats in the House. Under this compromise, the House would be a national institution while the Senate would reflect a federal logic, rendering Congress a composite of the two. By the narrowest of margins, five states to four, with a tenth delegation (Massachusetts) divided, the convention adopted the compromise on July 16. A day later, Madison suffered a second key defeat, when seven of ten delegations rejected his cherished national veto of state laws. Instead, the convention settled for barring states from issuing paper money or otherwise "impairing the obligation of contracts." Connecticut's Roger Sherman considered the convention as a "favorable crisis for crushing paper money."[78]

Slaves

The heated debates over representation exposed a second, even more dangerous fault line between northern and southern states. Slaves comprised less than 4 percent of the northern population compared to 40 percent in the South. Determined to protect their property rights in humans, southern delegates worried about entering a more powerful union that northerners might control. Pierce Butler explained, "The security the South[er]n States want is that their negroes, may not be taken from them." Southerners wanted a union strong enough to defend their states against slave rebellion and foreign invasion but without the authority to tax or emancipate slaves.[79]

Some northern delegates argued that only free citizens should count in allocating seats in the House of Representatives. Gouverneur Morris denounced the inequity that

> the inhabitant of Georgia and South Carolina who goes to the Coast of Africa, and in defiance of the most sacred laws of humanity, tears away his fellow creatures from their dearest connections and damns them to the most cruel bondage, shall have more votes in a government instituted for the protection of the rights of mankind, than the citizen of Pennsylvania or New Jersey who views with a laudable horror so nefarious a practice.

A Massachusetts delegate satirically reasoned that northern oxen should count on a par with southern slaves in representation. Southerners countered that they needed the political clout of slave numbers to protect their property from federal interference.[80]

Rival regional interests, rather than moral qualms, drove the debate, for the delegates regarded blacks as inferior to whites. Every delegate primarily sought a formula for representation meant to protect his state. The convention compromised by adopting the notorious "three-fifths clause," which stipulated that three-fifths of the enslaved population would count in allocating congressional seats and presidential electors to the states.[81]

In August, another heated debate erupted over continuing the import slave trade. On this issue, southern delegates divided. Seeking to expand their operations, planters in the Lower South demanded continued imports from Africa. The Upper South's leaders, however, believed that they had a surplus and could profit by sales to the Lower South. Banning import competition would enhance those profits, but principle also played a role with some delegates, particularly Madison, who insisted that importing more slaves would "dishonor" the nation.[82]

Although outnumbered, the delegates from Georgia and South Carolina had a trump card to play: they cared less about the union than about protecting the import slave trade, while the other delegations reversed that priority. By threatening to bolt from the convention and forsake the union, Lower South delegates called the bluff of their critics. Georgians and Carolinians also discovered that northern men had a price for their scruples. Reliant on shipping and shipbuilding, New Englanders wanted the Constitution to empower Congress to pass "navigation acts" by a mere majority rather than the two-thirds vote previously insisted upon by southern delegates. Favoring northern vessels, such navigation acts would restrict foreign competition and thereby increase mercantile profits and southern shipping costs.[83]

In return for that lower threshold for trade regulation, northeastern delegates agreed that Congress could place no limit on slave imports for twenty years. Oliver Ellsworth of Connecticut declared that, without this deal, the states would "fly into a variety of shapes and directions," which would lead to "bloodshed." Saving the union and promoting profits ultimately mattered more than any moral principles against bondage for others. Thanks to this compromise, the

Lower South would import another 200,000 Africans as slaves during the next twenty years.[84]

Lower South and Upper South delegates reunited to push for a fugitive-slave clause that would compel free-state magistrates to help masters recover runaways. The delegates rejected the legal principle established by the 1772 *Somerset* case in England that escaped slaves could claim freedom by fleeing to a state that did not sustain slavery by positive law. As a price of union, northern courts, juries, and sheriffs would have to sustain the slave system by forcing interstate runaways back into southern bondage. A South Carolina delegate later boasted to his constituents, "We have obtained a right to recover our slaves in whatever part of America they may take refuge, which is a right we had not before."[85]

In the Constitution, delegates adopted euphemisms to avoid the terms "slave" or "slavery," referring instead to "other persons," "such persons as the several States now existing shall think proper to admit," and "any person bound to service or labor." A Maryland member noted that the delegates "anxiously sought to avoid the admission of expressions which might be odious in the ears of Americans, although they were willing to admit into their system those things which the expressions signified." John Dickinson disdained the moral evasion but only in the privacy of his notebook: "What will be said of this new principle of founding a Right to govern Freemen on a power derived from Slaves[?] . . . The omitting [of] the WORD [slaves] will be regarded as an Endeavour to conceal a principle of which we are ashamed."[86]

By adopting the three-fifths clause, prolonging the import slave trade, and providing a fugitive-slave clause, the constitution defended slavery. The delegates understood that southerners would reject a constitution that did not secure their property in human beings. By their moral compromises, delegates bought a chance to ratify their constitution and strengthen the union. Acting for the short term, they unwittingly imperiled the nation in the long-term, for the United States ultimately would divide in a bloody civil war over the expansion of slavery.[87]

*but expansion
fuelled it!*

Delegates longed to believe that slavery eventually would wither without Americans having to make difficult sacrifices. Oliver Ellsworth reasoned, "Let us not intermeddle. As population increases, poor laborers will be so plenty as to render slaves useless. Slavery in time will not be a speck in our country." When the proposed constitution became public, a Rhode Island clergyman asked, "How does it appear in the sight of Heaven, that *these states*, who have been fighting for liberty . . . cannot agree in any political constitution unless it indulge and authorize them to enslave their fellow-men!" But he reluctantly accepted the Constitution as the only alternative to a "state of anarchy, and probably of civil war" in his own time.[88]

Giving priority to shaping Congress, the delegates were slow to define the executive branch. Reacting against the weakness of state governors, the delegates favored a powerful president as a check on Congress. Acting with advice and consent from the Senate, the president could conclude treaties and appoint executive officials and federal judges. The chief executive also had a veto that could only be overridden by two-thirds votes of both houses. Confidence in Washington as the anticipated first president promoted the creation of such a strong office.[89]

The president and a vice president would hold four-year terms with eligibility for indefinite reelection. Both would be indirectly elected through an electoral college chosen by state legislatures (or by elections arranged by those legislatures) rather than selected by either a direct vote of citizens or by Congress. A state's electoral votes would equal its number of representatives plus its two senators. The delegates expected the electors to be well-informed gentlemen superior to common voters.[90]

The delegates spent less time and thought defining the judicial branch but did specify a supreme court and allowed Congress to create additional inferior courts. The delegates asserted that the nation's laws, treaties, and constitution were superior to, and binding upon, state laws and courts.[91]

On September 17, thirty-nine of the persisting forty-two delegates signed the Constitution. The three holdouts included Edmund Randolph, who had begun the convention as Madison's close ally but ended it with new fears that the constitution would threaten Virginia's interests. George Mason of Virginia also defected, declaring that he would "sooner chop off his right hand than put it to the constitution as it now stands." Deeming the proposed government too strong, he predicted that it "would end either in monarchy or a tyrannical aristocracy." Elbridge Gerry, however, insisted that the constitution did not go far enough to contain "democracy, the worst of all political evils."[92]

The compromises over representation discouraged Madison, who doubted that the final constitution was strong enough to solve the political crisis of the 1780s. He assured Jefferson that it would "neither effectually *answer* its *national object* nor prevent the local *mischiefs* which every where *excite disgusts* ag[ain]st the *state governments*." But Madison was willing to sign and try an administration of the new Federal Constitution. Hamilton had even greater doubts, but he dreaded that the alternative was "anarchy and convulsion." Washington aptly described the Federal Constitution as a mixed bag but "the best that could be obtained at this time."[93]

Ratification

After publishing the constitution, its proponents had to ratify it by securing public support in the states. The delegates' reluctant compromises in convention became their best defense against critics who charged them with seeking national consolidation. Denying that they had subordinated the states, supporters ingeniously argued that the *Federal* Constitution evenly split the powers of sovereignty between nation and states to produce "coequal sovereignties," as Madison put it. They cleverly claimed the popular name of "Federalists," which previously had meant a supporter of strong states and a weak confederation. Better still, the newly minted "Federalists" cast their critics as mere contrarians called "Anti-Federalists," whom they characterized as cunning demagogues bent on cheating their creditors. Winning that propaganda battle, the Federalists created labels that stuck with the press and historians ever since.[94]

The so-called Anti-Federalists were a diverse lot in class, region, and religion. Relatively short on genteel leaders, they relied on broad, but diffuse, support from the farmer majority. Those farmers distrusted the wealthy and well-connected men who pushed for the Federal Constitution with such united zeal. In Massachusetts, Rufus King reported that rural people denounced the constitution as "the production of the Rich and ambitious" who meant to exploit "the poor and illiterate." Indeed, critics saw proof of their fears in the "extraordinary Union in favor of the Constitution in this State of the Wealthy." A common farmer, Amos Singletary, complained of "these lawyers, and men of learning, and moneyed men, that talk so finely, and gloss over matters so smoothly, to make us poor little people swallow down the pill." Once they "get all the power and all the money into their own hands" they would "swallow up all us little folks . . . just as the whale swallowed up *Jonah.*"[95]

Anti-Federalists warned that the proposed constitution would centralize power in the hands of an aloof aristocracy. Critics noted that Congress would have fewer members than any state legislature but would rule over thirteen states and a vast western territory. Anti-Federalists added that the people could directly elect only their congressmen, for state legislatures would choose the senators, and an electoral college would elect the president. With the advice and consent of the Senate, that president would appoint federal judges to life terms, and those judges could review and reject any state laws deemed at odds with the Federal Constitution. The president also held veto and appointive powers greater than those permitted to governors under any state constitution. Contrary to republican principles, which favored annual elections, representatives would serve for two years, the president for four, and senators for six. Plus, they could run indefinitely for reelection, potentially serving for life. The large districts, relatively long terms, powerful executive and Senate, and distant government seemed designed for genteel elitists to tax and exploit common people with impunity.[96]

The debate boiled down to the proper scale of representation. Favoring state legislatures, Anti-Federalists insisted that the people needed many representatives, each with an intimate knowledge of a small district. George Mason explained, "Rep[resentative]s should sympathize with their constituents; sh[oul]d think as they think, & feel as they feel." Federalists countered that a nation's larger districts would elect more prestigious men, who could best defend a republic against petty demagogues. An Anti-Federalist, Patrick Henry, noted that the Constitution "presupposes that the chosen few who go to Congress will have more upright hearts, and more enlightened minds, than those who are members of the individual legislatures."[97]

Anti-Federalists insisted that the constitution threatened liberty. In South Carolina, an Anti-Federalist asked his constituents, "What have you been contending for these ten years past? Liberty! What is liberty? The power of governing yourselves. If you adopt this constitution, have you this power? No: you give it into the hands of a set of men who live one thousand miles distant from you." In rural South Carolina, farmers staged a funeral for a coffin labeled "Liberty." In Virginia, Richard Henry Lee marveled, "'Tis really astonishing that the same people, who have just emerged from a long and cruel war in defence of liberty, should now agree to fix an elective despotism upon themselves and their posterity." Anti-Federalists pointed out that the constitution created a national government with greater power than Britain had ever exercised over the colonists.[98] *propaganda*

To refute charges of elitism, Federalists posed as the truest friends of republicanism. In New York, a cynic reported, "You would be surprised did you not know the Man, what an *amazing Republican* [Alexander] Hamilton wishes to make himself be considered." Federalists created a useful fiction: that a united, homogeneous, and sovereign American people created the constitution. Hence the document begins with "We the People" rather than "We the States." James Wilson shrewdly asked, "How comes it . . . that these State governments dictate to their superiors?—to the majesty of the people?" By claiming to speak for this sovereign people, Federalists cast their critics as petty and selfish contrarians.[99]

not notional identity

In 1787, there was scant evidence that the diverse and squabbling Virginians, New Englanders, Carolinians, New Yorkers, and Pennsylvanians thought and acted as Americans. A Federalist privately conceded, "Instead of feeling as a nation, a state is our country. We look with indifference, often with hatred, fear, and aversion to the other states." The delegates crafted a constitution to manage distrust by their states, lest they fall into bloody civil wars. Hamilton warned, "If we should be disunited, . . . our liberties would be prey to the means of defending ourselves against the ambition and jealousy of each other." Mutual suspicion had forced them together. Federalists asserted an American people as an act of faith, hoping thereby to generate a self-fulfilling prophecy for the future. An American national identity emerged later, slowly, painfully, and partially. It would follow from that constitution rather than lie behind its creation.[100]

In 1787–1788, the creative fiction of a sovereign people helped Federalists to change the rules of ratification. Because state legislators were likely to defend their power by rejecting a national constitution, Federalists called for special ratifying conventions in each state. Federalists expected to win more seats in such conventions than in the usual legislative elections. They argued that conventions represented a fundamental resort to the people that was superior to the ordinary acts of a legislature. Consequently, only popular ratification by conventions could legitimate the Federal Constitution and render it binding on future generations. Madison explained that the Constitution "was nothing more than the draught of a plan, nothing but a dead letter, until life and validity were breathed into it by the voice of the people, speaking through the several state conventions."[101]

The Philadelphia delegates also unilaterally declared that nine states, rather than all thirteen, would suffice to ratify the constitution and form a new union. Under the Articles of Confederation, any change required approval by all thirteen state legislatures: a process that would doom the Federal Constitution. When Anti-Federalists protested the new ratification process as violating the Articles, Madison insisted that special conventions could do as they wished: "The people were, in fact, the fountain of all power, and by resorting to them, all difficulties were got over. They could alter constitutions as they pleased." Wilson added, "The House on fire must be extinguished without a scrupulous regard to ordinary rights." Federalists also denounced their opponents as enemies of the imagined sovereign people. "All power," Federalists chanted, "is in the people, and not in the state governments." Only in Rhode Island did Anti-Federalists have the wit to call the Federalists' bluff by holding a more direct appeal to the people: a referendum, where Rhode Islanders voted against the constitution by ten to one.[102]

While claiming to seek the popular will, Federalists tried to limit the ratifying conventions to either approving or rejecting the constitution as a whole, rather than endorse only parts or make ratification contingent upon amendments. By restricting the choice in this way, Federalists maximized their greatest advantage: that they offered an alternative to the ineffectual and unpopular Articles of Confederation. Rather than defend the Articles, most Anti-Federalists proposed sweeping amendments meant to weaken the Federal Constitution.[103]

The Federalists' greatest political liability was their failure to include a bill of rights in their constitution. The Philadelphia delegates had considered such a bill unnecessary and divisive given their lack of consensus on which rights to include or exclude. A South Carolina Federalist explained that bills of rights customarily began by declaring that all men were created equal, and "we should make that declaration with a very bad grace, when a large part of our property consists in men who are actually born slaves." The oversight gave Anti-Federalists their best opening to cast the constitution as a devious scheme to monopolize power and undermine liberty. In many ratifying conventions, Federalists had to give ground by promising to provide a bill of rights once the new government went into operation.[104]

A nationalizing constitution faced an uphill battle given that most voters were common farmers with limited educations, parochial perspectives, and deep suspicions of external, distant power. An unusually frank Federalist conceded that his side needed "to *pack* a [ratifying] Convention whose sense would be different from that of the people."[105]

But Federalists had powerful countervailing advantages in conducting the union's first national political campaign. They rallied most of the wealthiest Americans who could best afford to finance that campaign. Lawyers, merchants, and speculators welcomed a national government that could protect private property from state legislatures. Public creditors eagerly anticipated a federal government with the tax power sufficient to fund the certificates of debt from the war. The investor class also expected that a more secure political climate for large property would attract new investments from Europe to spur economic growth.[106]

In the national campaign, Federalists enjoyed better networks for sharing information and political strategy. As congressmen, Philadelphia delegates, or Continental officers, many had worked with one another across state lines. A Connecticut Anti-Federalist lamented that the Federalists "have got almost all the best Writers (as well as speakers) on their side." A New York Anti-Federalist noted, "The great easily form associations," but "the poor and middling class form them with difficulty." The Federalists especially counted on Washington's prestige, for his endorsement carried great clout with many otherwise wary voters.[107]

By comparison, most Anti-Federal leaders lacked ties in other states. Consequently, their criticisms had a scattershot quality, varying widely from state to state, which invited mockery everywhere by Federalist writers. Dispersed and disconnected, the Anti-Federalists never coalesced into an organized opposition. Throughout the ratification struggle, the better-organized Federalists kept the initiative.[108]

Although a minority in most states, Federalists proved disproportionately conspicuous, for their supporters clustered in and around the seaports, which hosted most of the ratifying conventions. Aedanus Burke described South Carolina Federalists as "All the rich leading men, along the sea coast, and rice settlements with few exceptions, Lawyers, Physicians, and Divines; the Merchants, mechanics, the Populace and mob of Charleston," while Anti-Federalists were "chiefly from the back country where the strength and numbers of our republick be." Seaport merchants, shopkeepers, and artisans (and the more commercialized farmers of the nearby counties) supported the Federal Constitution. They all hoped that a stronger federal government could boost overseas trade. Federal rallies pressured urban leaders with initial doubts about the constitution. Samuel Adams reluctantly came around to Federalism rather than offend his political base, Boston's artisans.[109]

Cities hosted most of the nation's newspapers, and their editors usually agreed with their advertisers and subscribers, who were overwhelmingly Federalists. Eighty of the nation's ninety-two newspapers tilted toward the Federalists, favoring their essays, particularly the celebrated series, *The Federalist*, written by Hamilton (51 essays), Madison (29), and Jay (5). Because postmasters doubled as merchants or printers, most supported Federalism, so Anti-Federalist letters and pamphlets often got lost or delayed in the mail. Thanks to distortions by press and post, readers could gain the misleading impression that the Federal Constitution was wildly popular elsewhere. Northerners read that Patrick Henry had endorsed the constitution when, in fact, he was leading the opposition in Virginia.[110] *misinformation*

While cities favored political networking by Federalists, rural dispersion worked against coordination by Anti-Federalists. Farmers may have been the American majority, but they were poorly situated for political mobilization. For example, only 13,000 of the 70,000 eligible voters (a mere 18 percent) in Pennsylvania turned out to elect convention delegates, largely because the Federalists staged that election abruptly, before many rural people learned much about the proposed constitution.[111]

For all of their warnings against mob rule, Federalists could resort to violence to intimidate opponents. In late September, Federalists pressed the Pennsylvania legislature immediately to authorize a state ratifying convention without holding a full debate. They counted on their majority in the assembly, but Anti-Federalists exploited the requirement for a quorum by staying away. Federalists then recruited toughs to find and drag back to the assembly hall two kicking and screaming Anti-Federalist representatives. Thrust into their seats, they were counted as present, providing the bare quorum needed to authorize a ratifying convention. Vindictive in victory, a Federalist mob then attacked the boardinghouse that hosted many Anti-Federalist representatives, smashing the windows. A staunch Federalist, George Minot, described the Federalist techniques as "*Bad* measures in a *good* cause." Minot conceded, "Never was there a political system introduced by less worthy means."[112]

Federalists maximized their organizational advantages by pressing for quick decisions by ratifying conventions. By January 9, 1788, they had prevailed in five states: Delaware, Pennsylvania, New Jersey, Georgia, and Connecticut. They were more than halfway to the nine states needed to put their new government into operation. That momentum gave them a further advantage. In the remaining states, the growing probability of ratification pulled many waverers off the political fence, lest they be left outside the union and looking in. The promise of an eventual bill of rights also brought around swing delegates.[113]

On January 9, 1788, the end game began in Boston with the opening of the Massachusetts ratifying convention. That state provided a major political test where Federalists would either consolidate their momentum or suffer a staggering setback. Initially, most delegates opposed the Federal Constitution because so many came from poor towns in the hinterland, where voters resented the violent suppression of the recent regulation commonly known as Shays's Rebellion. To shift the balance, Federalists cultivated the ambition and vanity of Hancock, the state's popular governor and a tepid Anti-Federalist. In return for his switch, Federalists promised to support him for the vice-presidency in the new government. They even held out the delicious prospect that, if Virginia failed to ratify, Hancock could become president rather than Washington. In a dramatic appearance before the convention, Hancock announced his conversion and proposed constitutional amendments as mere recommendations. His example swayed enough moderates to bless Federalists with a majority. On February 6, by a vote of 187 to 168, the Massachusetts convention ratified the constitution.[114]

In the spring, two more states ratified overwhelmingly: Maryland in April and South Carolina in May. In both states, the apparent inevitability of national ratification had deflated opposition. A convention heavily skewed against the backcountry and for coastal counties also favored Federalism in South Carolina. By early June, eight states had ratified, leaving the new union just one state short of the minimum.[115]

On June 21, New Hampshire narrowly provided that ninth state, but it was a minor prize compared to two major holdouts: New York and Virginia. A union without them would be painfully incomplete and likely to falter. Both favored Anti-Federalism, for their voters preferred to live in strong states within a weak union. Both states also had especially able, clever, and committed Anti-Federalist leaders: New York's Governor George Clinton and Virginia's Patrick Henry, whom Jefferson considered "the greatest orator that ever lived." Considering his political clout invincible, Jefferson once observed to Madison, "What we have to do I think is devoutly pray for his death." Clinton feared losing the state's robust revenues from taxing imports, for his popularity derived from minimizing internal taxes. Henry dreaded that northerners would dominate a powerful nation and could threaten southern slavery.[116]

At Virginia's ratifying convention, Madison countered by dwelling on the proslavery features of the Constitution: the three-fifths clause, fugitive-slave clause, and federal military support to suppress any slave revolt. A stronger union would benefit Virginia, he argued, more than any other state. After three weeks of debate, Madison's dogged optimism trumped Henry's gloomy eloquence. The Federalists also induced the popular governor, Edmund Randolph, to change sides by assuring him of a cabinet position in the new government. Finally, the Federalists played their ace card by promising prompt amendments once the new government was launched. On June 25, Virginia's delegates voted 89 to 79 to ratify.[117]

New York, however, still remained in the balance. Thanks to Clinton's political machine, New York's Anti-Federalists could organize voters and wage the newspaper war as well or better than Federalists in that one state. Sweeping the rural, upstate counties, Anti-Federalists won a two-to-one majority at the ratifying convention, but news of Virginia's ratification discouraged New York's Anti-Federalists. The downstate counties, including New York City, chose Federalist delegates, who threatened to secede from the state to join the union. Such a move would deprive New York of most of its revenue, which came from commerce flowing through the port. On July 25, the convention ratified by a vote of 30 to 27. Giddy with victory, a Federalist mob sacked the Anti-Federalist printing office in New York City.[118]

After New York ratified, the Constitution had secured eleven states, leaving Rhode Island and North Carolina on the outside. During the winter, Rhode Islanders had overwhelmingly voted against ratification. In early August, North Carolina's delegates met and rejected ratification, 184 to 84. Lacking a major seaport, the state was dominated by farmers and planters, the people most suspicious of a distant government with the power to tax them. North Carolina's Anti-Federalists clung to the idle hope of a new interstate convention that would adopt sweeping amendments to restore more power to the states at the expense of the nation.[119]

In early September, the lame-duck Congress of the Articles of Confederation certified ratification of the Federal Constitution and invited the states to hold elections for Congress and the Electoral College during early 1789. Disheartened by defeat, most Anti-Federalist leaders and voters sat out the first national elections. Low voter turnout enabled Federalists to capture forty-eight of the fifty-nine seats in the House of Representatives. In one Pennsylvania county, merely eighteen men bothered to vote. The electoral college unanimously chose Washington to preside over the new government. Wearied by economic woes and political struggles, most citizens wanted to give the new system a fair if skeptical trial. John Quincy Adams (the son of John Adams) noted that the Federal Constitution "had been extorted from the grinding necessity of a reluctant nation."[120]

Many Americans today celebrate the Federal Constitution as perfectly designed to promote democracy, prosperity, and power: as setting the United States on the road to greatness. In 1789, few Americans were so sure, for they worried that sectional and partisan divisions would tear apart a union that seemed too vast and diverse to last. On the eve of becoming president, George Washington feared being "shipwrecked in sight of the Port." And the nature of that port remained uncertain and depended on the interpretation that his administration and the first Congress would give to the relatively brief and often ambiguous Federal Constitution.[121]

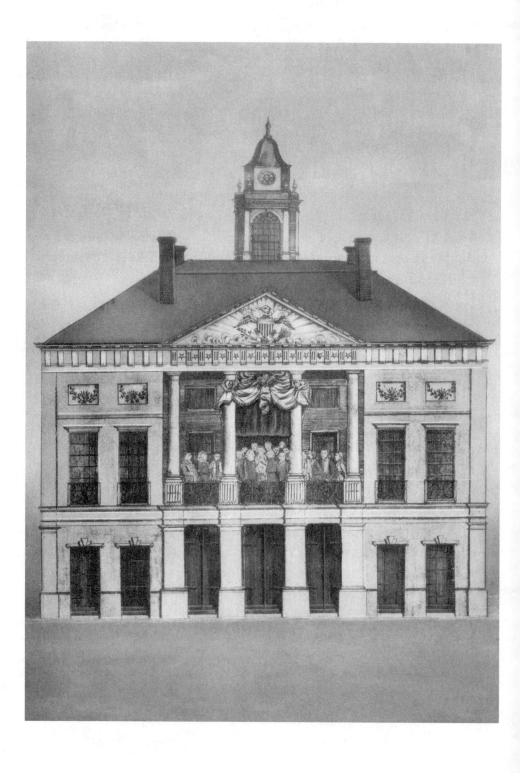

11

PARTISANS

It was for a long time doubtful whether we were to survive
as an independent Republic, or decline from our federal dignity
into insignificant & wretched Fragments of Empire.
—GEORGE WASHINGTON, 1788[1]

The revolution of 1800 . . . was as real a revolution in the
principles of our government as that of [17]76 was in its form.
—THOMAS JEFFERSON, 1819[2]

I mpressed by British precedents, Federalists wanted to create a
nation with the revenue and power to command foreign respect,
attract investment from overseas, and compel citizens to pay taxes
and obey laws. As the new administration's prime mover, Alexander
Hamilton cultivated "a principle of strength and stability in the organization of our government, and vigor in its operations." Washington
agreed, "I do not conceive we can exist long as a nation, without having
lodged somewhere a power which will pervade the whole Union."[3]

But the new nation seemed to teeter between future greatness and
imminent collapse during the 1790s. Although endowed with immense

---

*"Federal Hall, N.Y. 1789—First Capitol of the United States," engraving by Amos
Doolittle, 1790. Doolittle depicts George Washington taking the oath of office as
president on the balcony of Federal Hall. Courtesy of the Library of Congress (LC-
DIG-ds-05278).*

potential for economic and demographic growth, the union remained relatively weak in a dangerous world of more powerful empires. Despite the new constitution, sectional tensions threatened to compound the external danger. At the first Congress, Henry Lee of Virginia declared that he would rather "submit to all the hazards of [civil] war . . . than to live under the rule of a fixed insolent northern majority." The great American nightmare was that foreign powers would exploit the internal divisions of a tenuous union. Moreover, the Federalists were gambling on a radical and risky form of government, a republic, while hoping to prevent its decline, as they saw it, into the anarchy of democracy.[4]

Washington's enormous popularity bought time for Federalists to implement the controversial new constitution. To persuade him to accept the presidency, Hamilton insisted, "It is to little purpose to have *introduced* a system, if the weightiest influence is not given to its firm *establishment* in the outset." Washington dreaded the new office as inevitably contentious and potentially fatal to his cherished reputation. He felt like "a culprit who is going to the place of his execution," as he exchanged "a peaceful abode for an Ocean of difficulties." Washington ensured the Constitution's early survival by administering the new government with careful deliberation, good judgment, and public dignity. John Adams later recalled Washington as "the best actor of Presidency We have ever had." The Spanish ambassador credited the first president for saving "this nation from . . . internal dissentions" but only temporarily, "because it seems impossible that there could be found another man so beloved of all. . . . Disunion will follow."[5]

On April 30, 1789, Washington took his oath of office on the balcony of City Hall, renamed Federal Hall, in New York City, the nation's temporary capital. With a booming overseas trade and 30,000 people, New York was the nation's second-largest city and its fastest-growing. When Washington finished the oath, the listening crowd erupted in shouts and cheers while church bells rang and the master of ceremonies bellowed, "Long Live George Washington, President of the United States." It resembled the announcement of a new king. A friend assured Washington, "You are now a King, under a different name."[6]

Federalists sought to sustain the republic with monarchical pageantry, which they considered essential to build public reverence for the new government. "Neither Dignity nor Authority can be Supported in human Minds, collected into nations . . . without a Splendor and Majesty," John Adams explained. Following his lead, the Senate defined Washington's title as "His Highness the President of the United States of America, and Protector of their Liberties."[7]

Washington's grave dignity perfectly suited his transitional role as a republicanized monarch. In New York City, the city fathers erected a bronze Washington on the pedestal formerly used for a statue of George III. Throughout the nation, tavern keepers had Washington's name and face painted over signs that once honored the king. In the celebrated story "Rip Van Winkle," Washington Irving's title character falls asleep in the colonial era but awakes after the revolution to see his favorite inn with the old "ruby face of King George . . . singularly metamorphosed. The red coat was changed for one of blue and buff, a sword was held in the hand instead of a scepter, the head was decorated with a cocked hat, and underneath was painted in large characters, GENERAL WASHINGTON."[8]

Washington went along with the quasi-regal style, acting with cold formality while wearing a dignified, dark suit accessorized with a ceremonial sword. He rode in a richly decorated coach drawn by six white horses and attended by four servants in orange-and-white livery. During public appearances, officials called him "Your Excellency," and bands sometimes played "God Save the King." Washington made two long tours, in the royal style, through the states to bolster reverence for the new government. Everywhere, people erected triumphal arches, rang bells, fired cannon, and gave welcoming speeches of deference for the new president. When in the capital, he held Tuesday afternoon receptions, known as "levees," where he stood on a stage and bowed stiffly when congressmen and visitors were announced and presented. Washington disliked these awkward performances but considered them essential "to preserve the dignity & respect which was due to the first Magistrate."[9]

Federalists underestimated the backlash that the quasi-regal performances evoked in many Americans, who preferred a plainer style as better suited to preserve their republic. Pennsylvania Senator William Maclay denounced "the fooleries, fopperies, fineries, and pomp of Royal etiquette" as the slippery slope to a complete monarchy. Madison persuaded the House to kill the Senate's monarchical title for the president in favor of the simpler, "President of the United States," which ultimately prevailed. Jefferson denounced the Federalists as "panting after an English constitution of king, lords, and commons, and whose heads are itching for crowns, coronets, and mitres." Meant by Federalists to unify the nation, the regal style instead divided the people.[10]

Rights

Madison became the most active and influential member of the first Congress. He drafted both Washington's inaugural address and the response from the House of Representatives to that speech. Madison feared divisions in the new Congress: "contentions first between federal & antifederal parties, and then between Northern & Southern parties." He added, "Scarcely a day passes without some striking evidence of the delays and perplexities springing merely from the want of precedents." Madison concluded that congressmen were "in a wilderness without a single footstep to guide us."[11]

Madison pushed quickly to amend the Federal Constitution in a carefully targeted fashion. Although he privately derided "the nauseous project of amendments," Madison saw the political imperative of appeasing moderate voters with guarantees for civil liberties. He hoped that his amendments would "kill the opposition every where" and thereby "enable the administration to venture on measures not otherwise safe." While drafting guarantees for freedoms of religion, speech, assembly, and the press, he rejected more substantive amendments proposed by Anti-Federalists to restrict the federal government's powers to levy direct taxes, keep an army in peacetime, or establish a *a legacy of slavery* supreme federal judiciary. Rather than alarm southern leaders, Madison also avoided a philosophical preface on human equality featured in the bills of rights adopted by most states. Consequently, no one called Madison's slate of amendments "the Bill of Rights" until the 1860s.[12]

In October 1789, Congress and the president approved Madison's twelve amendments, but only ten received the necessary approval from three-quarters of the states by the end of 1791. An Anti-Federalist, Aedanus Burke, saw the amendments as more distracting than substantive: as "frothy and full of wind, . . . like a tub thrown out to a whale, to secure the freight of the ship and its peaceable voyage." Another critic complained that the amendments were "calculated merely to amuse, or rather to deceive" because they secured "personal liberty alone, leaving the great points of the Judiciary & direct taxation &c to stand as they are." Anti-Federalists regarded the libertarian amendments as better than nothing.[13]

Madison's amendments did give North Carolinians enough political cover to enter the union in November 1789. Rhode Islanders remained stubbornly independent until Congress put economic screws to the little republic by barring its trade with the United States in May 1790. At the end of that month a special state convention narrowly voted to rejoin the United States, which once again had thirteen states. The union added a fourteenth state with Vermont's admission a year later.[14]

Madison's amendments protected only the free, leaving untouched the slavery suffered by a fifth of the American people. In February 1790, Pennsylvania Quakers and other antislavery activists submitted two petitions to Congress. The petitioners included an aged and dying Benjamin Franklin, who had owned slaves but had developed new scruples. The signers urged Congress to end the overseas slave trade immediately despite the constitutional guarantee for twenty more years of imports. The activists also wanted Congress to adopt a gradual plan to extend liberty "without distinction of colour, to all descriptions of people" and thereby remove "this Inconsistency from the Character of the American People."[15]

Outraged congressmen from Georgia and South Carolina demanded an abrupt rejection of the petitions or they would "blow the trumpet of civil war." A South Carolinian denounced the petitions as "a persecution of the southern inhabitants" by Quakers, whom he derided as traitors during the revolution. As at the Philadelphia convention, northern delegates dared not risk the fragile union by defying congressmen from the Lower South. Madison moved to deflate the controversy, he hoped forever, by resolving "that Congress have no authority to interfere in the emancipation of slaves, or in the treatment of them." Almost every congressman endorsed Madison's gag rule.[16]

Congress and the president also bolstered slavery with positive measures. They guaranteed the system in federal territories south of the Ohio River and admitted Kentucky and Tennessee as slave states in 1792 and 1796. In 1790, Congress rejected black immigrants as potential citizens and, two years later, barred blacks from serving in any state militia. Giving sharp teeth to the Federal Constitution's fugitive-slave clause, Congress adopted the Fugitive Slave Act of 1793 by overwhelming votes (48 to 7 in the House). Overriding state legislatures and courts, the federal law authorized masters or their agents to pursue and seize alleged runaways in another state. Entrusting adjudication to any magistrate, the law denied trial by jury or the protections of habeas corpus to the accused runaways. Tacitly permitting kidnappings, so long as the victims were black, the law empowered southern agents who profited by hunting down and seizing supposed runaways in northern states.[17]

Free blacks sought the law's repeal, but the House refused to receive their petitions. In 1799, congressmen voted 84 to 1 to reject a petition from free blacks claiming equal citizenship. A Georgia congressman bluntly explained, "'We the people' does not mean them." The lone supporter of the petition, George Thacher of Massachusetts, aptly warned that slavery was "a cancer of immense magnitude, that would some time destroy the body politic." During the 1790s, Congress claimed the power to track down escaped slaves in northern states but renounced any authority to hear black protests against reenslavement.[18]

Capital

During the spring and summer of 1789, Congress created executive departments to assist the president: state, war, treasury, and justice. Washington appointed their heads, with the approval of the Senate, and assembled them as a cabinet to consider major issues. In a pivotal development, Washington secured the power to dismiss executive officials without the Senate's approval. Thereby the president obtained control over his administration, averting dependence on majority support in the Senate.[19]

Washington assembled talented but incompatible men in his cabinet, primarily Jefferson as secretary of state and Hamilton as secretary of the treasury. Emulating a British prime minister, Hamilton meant to dominate the administration and build a powerful, centralized nation like Britain. Brash and energetic, he meddled in every department, including foreign affairs, to Jefferson's disgust. Attentive to details and the big picture, Hamilton designed both policy and the bureaucracy to implement it. By deploying patronage, he built support in Congress and the states. A critic grumbled, "Mr. Hamilton is all powerful and fails in nothing which he attempts."[20]

To establish national credit, Hamilton meant to fund, at its full face value, the inflated war debt of the Continental Congress, $51 million, a prodigious sum for the eighteenth century. More boldly still, he proposed to assume the states' war debts as well: another $25 million, increasing the total to $76 million. Rather than pay that debt down to nothing, he meant to finance a permanent national debt, whose annual interest payments of $5 million literally would "interest" public creditors in supporting the nation, for he considered a funded debt a "national blessing." Federal customs duties, excise taxes, and western land sales would generate the revenue to pay that interest and the government's annual operations. To manage those transactions and generate additional capital for investment, Hamilton proposed a national bank modeled on the celebrated and powerful Bank of England. By stabilizing the currency and increasing the stock of capital, he hoped to accelerate and diversify the nation's economic development, promoting a new industrial sector to complement the traditional agricultural base. With this fiscal program, Hamilton enhanced federal power as the great collector of taxes and dispenser of payments. With the money, the administration rebuilt the army and started a navy.[21]

But Hamilton's program faced strong opposition from many southern congressmen, who feared that the new taxes would, at the expense of their region, enrich northern mercantile centers. In June 1790, the House rejected Hamilton's national assumption of state debts. The defeat outraged New Englanders, who had counted on federal relief for the large war debts of their states. Their talk of secession troubled Jefferson, who reported that congressmen "got into the most extreme ill humor with one another," and "this broke out on every question with the most alarming heat" so that "little or nothing could be done from mutual distrust and antipathy."[22]

To defuse tensions, Jefferson hosted a dinner party, where Madison brokered a compromise with Hamilton. In return for moving the capital southward to the banks of the Potomac, Madison and Jefferson would round up southern votes for Hamilton's program. To buy support from Pennsylvania's delegation, the compromise stipulated that Philadelphia would replace New York as the temporary capital during the ten-year construction of a new federal city. The compromise passed Congress but, upon returning home to Virginia, Jefferson and Madison heard from angry constituents who despised Hamilton's program as corrupt. Deeming the compromise his greatest political mistake, Jefferson became Hamilton's relentless foe.[23]

Locating the temporary capital in Philadelphia created a problem for slaveholders, who by state law could keep a slave in Pennsylvania for no more than six months. Washington brought a few household slaves to Philadelphia but shuttled them back to Mount Vernon every few months to keep them from claiming freedom. "I wish to have it accomplished," he explained, "under [some] pretext that may deceive both them and the Public."[24]

Eager to create a grand capital beside his beloved Potomac River,

Washington supported an ambitious plan for a grand city with wide avenues, elaborate circles, and monumental structures. He hoped that a national metropolis would unify the disparate states. Reality, however, lagged far behind his utopian vision. In 1800, the federal government moved to the new federal city named after Washington, but the public buildings remained unfinished and scattered among stumpy cow pastures and piles of construction materials. The muddy, rustic capital struck visitors as an apt metaphor for the weak union with grandiose aspirations. Slaveholders, however, felt relieved by the capital's shift southward to Washington, D.C., where the law sustained slavery and two slave states surrounded the federal district.[25]

West

The Federalists hoped to build a stronger nation through a carefully managed process of western settlement in the Northwest Territory. Distrusting most settlers as ignorant, violent, and indolent, Federalists hoped to improve them through restrictive policies that empowered local elites in the new settlements.

The Federalists' land policy favored speculators over settlers by mandating a minimum price of $2 per acre, a minimum purchase of 640 acres, and full payment down. Unable to meet such terms, common settlers instead had to buy their 160-acre farms on credit from, and at a markup paid to, the speculators. In a further boon to large-scale investors, Congress stipulated that only half of the Northwest Territory could be sold in 640-acre tracts; the rest would be wholesaled in 5,760-acre parcels. Federalists reasoned that a high land price would compel settlers to work harder to raise the money, thereby improving their moral characters. The Federalists also expected some of the speculators to become community leaders who could command deference from their common neighbors. The federal governor of the Northwest Territory, Arthur St. Clair, explained that federal policy would "give the people such a direction as might contribute to make them virtuous and of course happy and a useful part of the United States when they shall be entitled to it." The paternalism of Federalist policies irritated settlers, who welcomed federal power only when deployed against Indians.[26]

Western conditions threatened the fragile new nation premised on expansion. The British and Spanish empires compromised American sovereignty by clinging to forts along the southern shores of the Great Lakes and the lower Mississippi River. From those forts, British and Spanish agents and traders provided guns, ammunition, advice, and encouragement to Indian allies who resisted American expansion. That opposition was especially effective in the Ohio country, where a confederacy united two-dozen native peoples committed to rolling American settlements back to the Ohio River. In a 1791 report, the secretary of war, Henry Knox, conceded that the vast West was more of a menace than an asset: "The United States have come into existence as a nation, embarrassed with a frontier of immense extent." Obliged to defend a long frontier from Georgia to New York, Knox considered the nation "critically circumstanced."[27]

During the fall of 1791, Arthur St. Clair led 1,400 federal soldiers deep into Indian country. Before dawn on November 4, about 1,000 warriors surprised the sleeping troops in their poorly guarded camp. Quickly overwhelmed, they broke and fled, suffering 630 dead in the greatest single victory won by Indians over Americans during their long history of conflict. The victors stuffed the mouths of the enemy dead with soil to mock their fatal lust for Indian land.[28]

Indian victories discredited the national government and halted the sale and settlement of the federal domain in the Ohio country (called the "Northwest Territory" by Americans), depriving the nation of desperately needed revenue. Western settlement also slowed because the Spanish restricted American trade down the Mississippi River to the great port of New Orleans. Prior to 1796, western land sales accounted for only one-tenth of 1 percent of all federal revenues. Indeed, the nation earned three times as much from selling postage. Instead of generating revenue, the territory drained the union's resources as western warfare cost nearly five-sixths of all federal expenditures.[29]

Losing faith in the national experiment, some western leaders flirted with seceding to seek a protective association with the Spanish or the British empire. In 1789, a settlement in Tennessee adopted the name "Miro District," to flatter the Spanish governor of Louisiana and signal alienation from the United States. Federal officials feared that a breakaway West would become a formidable foe, embroiling the continent in bloody new wars.[30]

To impress and control settlers, the federal regime needed to lead and win the war against Indians. Knox insisted, "Government must keep them both in awe by a strong hand, and compel them to be moderate and just." St. Clair agreed that settlers needed to see and feel "that the Government of the Union was not a mere shadow." Then "their progeny would grow up in habits of Obedience and Respect . . . and the Countless multitudes which will be produced in that vast Region would become the Nerves and Sinews of the Union." A federal triumph might convert the West from the nation's greatest threat into its primary asset.[31]

Knox designed the nation's new Indian policy, which combined conciliation with a show of force. A classic Federalist paternalist, he distrusted common settlers as vicious and turbulent, while he nurtured a patronizing sympathy for native peoples. Willing to purchase Indian lands for settlements, he abandoned the confrontational and dangerous theory that natives were conquered peoples who had lost title to their lands. Knox also sought to save money, for he hoped that $16,150 in presents could buy a peace cheaper than the millions needed annually to fight the Indian confederacy. Knox treated chiefs with diplomatic respect and hoped to define a boundary line to separate settlers from natives. Along that line, he meant to interpose federal forts, soldiers, and officials, who then could regulate the pace at which Indians receded and settlement advanced.[32]

Lacking federal lands to sell south of the Ohio River, national leaders balked at the high costs of fighting the Creeks to benefit Georgia's aggressive speculators and settlers. Federal officials instead found a promising negotiating partner in Alexander McGillivray, the Creek spokesman who felt frustrated with his Spanish allies as ineffectual. In 1790, McGillivray visited the federal leaders at New York, seeking their alliance at the expense of Spain and Georgia. The Treaty of New York restored some Creeks lands that Georgia had extorted during the 1780s; provided $1,500 in annual presents to the Creek nation; and secretly put McGillivray on the federal payroll as a general with a $1,200 annual salary.[33]

Although Federalists treated Indians with moderation in the short term, the ultimate goal remained to transfer their lands to settlers. Federal officials simply wanted to assert greater control over that transfer by regulating its pace. Dreading unregulated expansion as anarchic, Federalists tried to compel settlers to live in cohesive and orderly communities led by gentlemen. A slower expansion would oblige settlers to become more deferential to authority and buy time for Indians gradually to adapt to the "civilization" dictated by their American neighbors. To promote a more settled mode of native agriculture, Knox included farm tools and domesticated livestock in the federal presents to Indian chiefs.[34]

Rejecting Knox's offers, the Ohio country Indians remained confederated against the United States, so the Washington administration sent a new invasion force deep into Indian country in August 1794. Commanded by General Anthony Wayne, the invaders defeated confederation warriors at Fallen Timbers and then destroyed their large villages and vast cornfields in the nearby Maumee Valley. Demoralized by the loss of homes and crops, the confederates also resented that British troops had holed up in a fort rather than come to their assistance. Although willing to arm natives, Britons balked at directly confronting the United States. Without a reliable British ally, the confederacy dissolved into acrimony, as the distinct nations made separate deals, conceding the southern two-thirds of Ohio to the United States in the Treaty of Greenville in August 1795. In return, they obtained perpetual annuities totaling $9,500. The United States prevailed by shattering the parallel effort by Indians to build their own union.[35]

The British watched the Indian confederacy dissolve because they had become embroiled in a massive new European war, which eclipsed their interests in North America. Hard-pressed by the French in Europe, the British could ill afford another conflict across the Atlantic. In the Jay Treaty of late 1794, the British reconciled with the United States by agreeing to surrender the border posts along the southern shores of the Great Lakes.[36]

The European war also persuaded the Spanish to back down from their frontier confrontation with the United States. The Spanish overplayed their hand in the Pacific Northwest by trying to drive away British merchant ships trading with natives for sea otter pelts. In May 1789, Captain Esteban José Martínez visited Nootka Sound, beside Vancouver Island, and seized two British ships and their crews. Martínez provoked an international crisis as Britain threatened war and sought armed cooperation from Washington's administration. Spanish officials then learned, to their dismay, that their French allies were too financially strapped to help fight the British. Unprepared for war without an ally, the Spanish made a humiliating peace deal with the British in October 1790, releasing the ships and crews, paying reparations, and accepting that both Britons and Americans could trade with natives in the Northwest. A Spanish official warned that expanding Pacific trade would enrich and empower Americans, who "will become with time for us the most terrible neighbors." Without firing a shot, Americans won a partial claim on the continent's Pacific shores by exploiting the divisions of European empires.[37]

After resolving the Nootka crisis, Spain's rulers joined a British-led coalition against France in the European war. In 1795, French troops invaded Spain, which abruptly deserted the coalition to make a separate peace. Fearing renewed British hostility in North America, the Spanish bought American neutrality with generous terms in the October 1795 Treaty of San Lorenzo. Accepting the American definition of their border as the 31st parallel, the Spanish abandoned their forts and settlements in the Natchez District and forsook their Indian allies east of the Mississippi. The Spanish also opened up the Mississippi River to duty-free American trade. To mollify the Americans, the Spanish sacrificed their vision of a native buffer zone and secession by western settlements.[38]

In a little over a year, three treaties transformed federal prospects in the West. In combination, the Jay Treaty, Treaty of San Lorenzo, and Treaty of Greenville secured American domination in a vast and fertile region that previously had seemed to defy and frustrate national ambitions. Thanks to these diplomatic triumphs, the federal government gained a measure of grudging respect from western settlers.[39]

As the Indian danger receded, western settlement accelerated. In 1805, a traveler noted, "The woods are full of new settlers. Axes were resounding and the trees literally were falling about us as we passed." By 1800, half a million Americans lived west of the Appalachian Mountains, three times as many as in 1790. The newcomers spilled over the western border into Louisiana, where Spanish officials reluctantly welcomed them for want of any way to stop them. New Orleans prospered as the great entrepôt for the farm produce raised by the swelling settler population of the vast Mississippi watershed. While politically still tied to Spain, Louisiana became integrated into the American economy.[40]

Parties

During the mid-1790s, Federalist policies produced peace, prosperity, and popularity. In the West, the Federalists secured favorable treaties with Spain, the western Indians, and the British Empire. Recovering impressively from the depression of the 1780s, the nation's economy boomed after 1792. Hamilton's financial program stabilized the currency and restored investor confidence. The federal assumption of state debts enabled the states to cut their taxes in half. Neutrality in the European war rewarded American shippers with enhanced trade. Merchants paid higher wages, had more ships built, and erected grander homes. Wages for skilled artisans in the seaports doubled between 1790 and 1796. Farmers also reaped higher prices as merchants bought produce for export. The price of flour nearly doubled, to the delight of wheat farmers. In 1795, a Boston newspaper exulted, "The affairs of Europe . . . rain riches upon us; and it is as much as we can do to find dishes to catch the golden shower." Pleased voters rewarded the Federalists, who controlled Congress through the 1790s, unanimously reelected Washington to the presidency in 1792, and more narrowly elected John Adams to succeed him in 1796.[41]

But the Federalist agenda proved divisive, appalling many Americans as a betrayal of the revolution fought against the British model of society and government. Critics regarded Hamilton's fiscal program as a corrupt bid to control congressmen by interesting them in the public funds and a national bank. Benjamin Rush complained, "I sicken every time I contemplate the European Vices that the Secretary's gambling report will necessarily introduce into our infant republic." Jefferson warned Washington "that the ultimate object of all this is to prepare the way for a change, from the present republican form of government, to that of a monarchy, of which the English constitution is to be the model."[42]

In 1791, Madison joined Jefferson in organizing political opposition to Hamilton's program—although Jefferson remained in Washington's cabinet as secretary of state for another three years. The opponents called themselves "Republicans" (not to be confused with today's Republican Party). To build popular support, they founded and subsidized a partisan newspaper, the *National Gazette*, which attacked Hamilton and his centralizing policies. Jefferson and Madison also cultivated political friends in other states, especially New York's Governor George Clinton and Senator Aaron Burr. In the fall of 1792, elections became fiercely contested between Federalists and Republicans.[43]

The organized opposition outraged Washington, who cherished consensus and resented attacks on him for supporting Hamilton's policies. Usually a master of self-control, Washington exploded when accused of betraying the republic. At a cabinet meeting in 1793, Jefferson saw Washington's meltdown: "The President was much inflamed [and] got into one of those passions when he cannot command himself, ran on much on the personal abuse which has been bestowed on him, defied any man on earth to produce one single act of his since he had been in the gov[ernmen]t which was not done on the purest motives" and adding that "he had rather be on his farm than to be made *emperor of the world*, and yet they were charging him with wanting to be a king."[44]

Federalists and Republicans clashed over the degree of democracy needed to sustain republican government. Federalists insisted that stability required government by an elite secure in the public esteem. Common people should deferentially elect men of superior education, wealth, and status, and those elected officials should enjoy immunity from "licentious" criticism. Every stable society, Federalists believed, needed to accept inequality. "There must be," a Federalist preached, "rulers and subjects, masters and servants, rich and poor." By design, Hamilton's policies appealed to wealthy men, "who," he reasoned "are in every society the only firm supporters of government." Congressman Fisher Ames defined his fellow Federalists as "the wise, and good, and rich." Republicans, however, accused the Federalists of betraying the egalitarian legacy of the revolution. By centralizing power and increasing taxes, Federalists allegedly meant to impoverish and subdue common people, thereby subverting the republic in favor of monarchy and aristocracy.[45]

Posing as accessible "Friends of the People," Republicans framed a stark contrast with paternalistic Federalists, who called themselves "Fathers of the People." Although leading Republicans were wealthy Virginia planters and New York lawyers, they deftly appealed to class resentments by common folk against the rich and powerful. In New York City, an election handbill denounced the Federalist mayor as an elitist "who acts as if he thought a poor man had no more rights than a horse." In 1796, Hamilton complained that Republicans "made our election in the view of the common people a question between the Rich & the Poor."[46]

Federalists insisted that the revolution was over and had been a limited struggle for independence, but Republicans countered that the revolution remained incomplete and required the democratic transformation of American society. Attacking the genteel vestiges of colonial hierarchy, Republicans promised to create a liberal society in which an impartial government would secure equal opportunities for common men by refusing any superior privileges for elites. Republicans claimed that equal rights would reward the industrious poor rather than perpetuate the idle rich. Without the allegedly artificial distortions of an elitist government, society would naturally and properly promote equality. Freed from parasitical Federalist rulers, common people could enjoy, as one Jeffersonian put it, "that happy mediocrity of condition" essential for a true republic to endure.[47]

While championing common white voters, most Republicans disdained Indians and African-Americans. Disavowing a class hierarchy, Republicans fostered racial solidarity by insisting that all white men were equal in rights but superior to blacks and natives. Because Federalists emphasized class gradations, they were more open to treating Indians and black people as inferior but worthy objects of elite paternalism. In response, Republicans accused Federalists of undermining white men by coddling Indians and blacks. White supremacy thus sustained and limited the Republican vision of democracy and equality.[48]

Where Federalists wanted national consolidation, Republicans favored a decentralized, consensual union in which most power remained with the states, which they considered more democratic. Offering an Anti-Federalist reading of the Constitution, Republicans insisted that dispersing power would frustrate crypto-aristocrats who would dominate a national government. In turn, Federalists denounced the Republican vision as dangerously naïve and anarchic.[49]

Political enmities bitterly divided communities. A Massachusetts minister noted that the "parties hate each other as much as the French and English hate each [other] in time of war." When a Republican neighbor died, a Federalist declared, "Another God Damned Democrat has gone to Hell, and I wish they were all there." James Fenimore Cooper was the son of a Federalist congressman. In the future novelist's earliest piece of writing, a child's penmanship exercise, Cooper wrote, "If I had a dog that had not more modesty than a Democrat, I would shoote him."[50]

And shoot each other they did in duels over perceived insults, which proliferated as political debates grew nastier and newspapers became partisan, polemical, and scandalmongering. A South Carolinian noted, "Three-fourths of the duels which have been fought in the United States were produced by political disputes." When not dueling, the partisans brawled. Feeling insulted by a Republican publication, a Federalist confronted the author in an Albany street, beating him with a heavy cane. Attracting dozens of partisans from both sides, the fight turned the street into "a tumultuous *sea of heads*, over which clattered a forest of canes; the vast body, now surging this way, now that, as the tide of combat ebbed or flowed."[51]

Political partisans were so edgy and shrill because the stakes seemed so high. The American union and republican government were new, tenuous, and vulnerable, and the nation's potential powers remained open to debate. Federalists and Republicans knew that all previous republics in European history had been unstable, short-lived, and overthrown from within. Edmund Randolph believed that only Washington kept the partisans from launching a civil war: "It is a fact, well known, that the parties in the U.S. are highly inflamed against each other; and that there is but one character, which keeps both in awe. As soon as the sword is drawn, nothing will be able to restrain them."[52]

Paradoxically, a dread of parties drove each group to organize and practice an especially bitter partisanship meant to discredit and destroy the other. Both sides disdained political parties as selfish factions and divisive threats to the common interest of a true republic. In 1789, Jefferson declared, "If I could not go to heaven but with a party, I would not go there at all." Of course, Federalists thought that Jefferson had no chance of going to heaven. Claiming exclusively to speak for the American people, each party cast rivals as insidious conspirators bent on destroying freedom and union. Referring to "the parties of Honest men, and Rogues, into which every country is divided," Jefferson insisted that "the republicans are the *nation*." Federalists agreed with the polarity but reversed it: "Naturally there can but be two parties in a Country; the friends of order and its foes." Both parties believed that the fate of their republic hung in the balance, which gave an edge of desperation to their struggle. Washington's dream of governing by consensus dissolved as the nation polarized between two angry parties, each denying the legitimacy of the other.[53]

Federalists also felt threatened by a revival of the regulator tradition in the backcountry from Pennsylvania south to Georgia as farmers resisted Hamilton's excise tax on alcohol. To denigrate their opponents, Federalists called the resistance "the Whiskey Rebellion," an insult that has stuck in histories. Hamilton's excise tax offended western farmers, who distilled much of their grain into whiskey, which could better bear the cost of overland transportation to markets in the East. Compared to bulky grain, whiskey had a higher value and was more portable and less perishable. Disdaining internal taxes, which they associated with British rule, country people wanted the government exclusively to rely on import duties collected at the seaports. Common farmers resented paying taxes to provide windfall profits to wealthy speculators in the public debt. Regulators sought to give "industrious men of a middle and low class an equal privilege with those of the rich."[54]

Settlers felt as justified in resisting the Federalist excise as they had in opposing Parliament's taxes. Claiming to defend the revolution, they erected liberty poles inscribed with slogans and topped with flags. To nullify the tax in their localities, regulators refused to pay, and ostracized, harassed, intimidated, and tarred-and-feathered any neighbors who broke ranks by helping to collect the tax. In July 1794, five hundred armed regulators marched to the mansion of John Neville, the wealthiest man and leading tax collector in Washington County, Pennsylvania, to demand his resignation. Neville's hired guards opened fire, killing a regulator captain. When the regulators counterattacked, the outnumbered guards surrendered, Neville fled, and the victors burned his mansion, fine furniture, and $4,600 in public debt certificates.[55]

Federalists regarded the regulation as a rebellion that threatened the new constitutional order. They insisted that "busy and restless sons of anarchy" were bringing "us back to those scenes of humiliation and distress from which the new Constitution has so wonderfully extricated us." In August 1794, Washington called 15,000 state militiamen, from New Jersey, Pennsylvania, Maryland, and Virginia, into federal service and sent them into western Pennsylvania. The president deemed this massive force essential because "we had given no testimony to the world of being able or willing to support our government and laws." The Federalists sought to consolidate and end the revolution by discrediting and suppressing the tradition of regulator resistance in backcountry regions.[56]

Standing down, the regulators stayed home rather than confront overwhelming force. Federal troops arrested twenty supposed rebels, whom they hauled back to Philadelphia for trial. They included Herman Husband, an aged religious mystic and a refugee from the bloody suppression of the regulation in North Carolina in 1772. After a year in a frigid jail, Husband was released, but he died of pneumonia on his journey home. Jefferson mocked the expensive expedition as a farce: "An insurrection was announced and proclaimed and armed against, and marched against, but could never be found."[57]

Unamused by Jefferson's wit, Federalists blamed the rural turmoil on local clubs of radicals known as the Democratic-Republican Societies. Federalists denounced such "self-created societies" as a threat to the stability of a republic, for they corroded public respect for elected officials. Addressing Congress, Washington denounced "combinations of men, who, careless of consequences . . . have disseminated, from an ignorance or perversions of fact, suspicions, jealousies, and accusations, of the whole government." If the societies triumphed, he warned, "we may bid adieu to all government in this Country, except mob, or Club government." Unable to compete with Washington's popularity, the Democratic-Republican societies dissolved. With a show of force, Federalists had discredited regulation as an alternative to institutional politics.[58]

Revolutions

American partisan politics also became entangled in a global conflict ignited by the French Revolution. On July 14, 1789, a mob attacked the Bastille, a political prison in Paris. As the American minister to France, Jefferson supported the revolutionaries, and Thomas Paine joined them. The American Revolution had helped to provoke the French Revolution by generating a massive war debt that the crown could not finance and by setting a republican precedent for replacing that monarchy.[59]

Initially, almost all Americans welcomed the revolutionary creation of a sister republic by their wartime allies. Americans hoped that republicanism would become a moral contagion that could liberate the entire world from kings and aristocrats. Americans celebrated French victories, sang their revolutionary songs, waved the tricolored revolutionary flag, wore tricolored cockades on their hats, and even donned red French liberty caps. In Boston, an angry audience rioted and demolished a theater after concluding that a play had mocked a French character.[60]

The French Revolution became more controversial in 1792–1793, when radicals known as "Jacobins," seized power and executed the king, queen, and thousands of other enemies. The radical turn provoked war with other European powers, including Britain. As the French invaded and conquered their Dutch, Swiss, and Italian neighbors, Federalists soured on the new revolution. Already wary of democracy, Federalists came to see in France the anarchic consequences of unchecked popular power. Rejecting the earlier linkage between the two revolutions, Federalists recast the American Revolution as supposedly decorous, orderly, dignified, and solemn—and, therefore, as a complete contrast to the chaotic French version. Federalists began celebrating Britain as the champion of rational liberty, a reassuring bastion of stable government, and the source of profitable commerce.[61]

As the French and British escalated their naval warfare, both powers pressured the United States for assistance. The British counted on America's dependence on British imports and its vulnerability to the superior might of the Royal Navy. The French expected American gratitude for their help in defeating the British during the War of the American Revolution. The Washington administration opted for neutrality because the deeply indebted and politically divided United States could ill afford a new conflict. In April 1793, Washington issued a proclamation of neutrality, barring Americans from assisting the French as privateers or filibusterers.[62]

Despite the violent turn to the new revolution, Republicans still praised France as a sister republic imperiled by the kings of Europe. Jefferson accepted the executions of monarchs and aristocrats as the worthy price of revolution: "The liberty of the whole earth was depending on the issue of the contest, and . . . rather than it should have failed, I would have seen half the earth desolated. Were there but an Adam and an Eve left in every country, and left free, it would be better than as it is now." Jefferson worried that if the French Revolution failed, reactionaries would triumph in America and convert the government "to that kind of Halfway-house, the English constitution."[63]

By continuing to celebrate the French Revolution, Republicans terrified Federalists, who dreaded that their rivals meant to copy the bloody French Jacobins. Cultivating a xenophobic American patriotism, Federalists disdained foreign revolutions as perversions. They cast the Republicans as traitors in league with "foreign disorganizers." Federalists claimed that only the United States could sustain a stable republic—and only so long as they kept European ideas and conspirators away. "Holding the rights of man in one hand, and the seeds of Rebellion in the other, they harangue the mob, preach against the oppression of the laws, [and] rail at all good men," a Federalist warned. A Republican complained that if anyone merely quoted "our declaration of independence, 'that all men are created equal' . . . he is denounced by the modern friends of order as an anarchist Jacobin."[64]

Federalists even cheered the British suppression of republicanism in Ireland. A coalition of Protestant and Catholic radicals had formed "the United Irishmen" to challenge British rule and create an independent Irish republic. In 1798, British troops and Loyalist volunteers brutally suppressed a scattered and uncoordinated rebellion by the United Irishmen. The violence killed at least 20,000, most of them defeated rebels.[65]

British repression accelerated Irish migration to the United States, where most of the newcomers voted for Republicans as the enemies of their enemies, the British. Disgusted Federalists denounced the newcomers as "United Irishmen, Free Masons, and the most God-provoking Democrats on this side of Hell." Adopting a nativist position, Federalists derided most immigrants as too ignorant, poor, violent, and brutish to become citizens. A Federalist journalist declared that "every United Irishman ought to be hunted from the country, as much as a wolf or a tyger." A Federalist congressman insisted, "The time is now come when it will be proper to declare that nothing but birth shall entitle a man to citizenship in this country."[66]

Federalists also blamed the French Revolution for instigating a massive and bloody slave revolt in the Caribbean. The greatest slave revolt in the Americas erupted on the evening of August 22, 1791, later known as the "Night of Fire." On the northern plain of the French West Indian colony of Saint-Domingue, enslaved Africans began to kill overseers and masters and torched the buildings and cane fields of a thousand plantations. The revolt caused an international sensation because Saint-Domingue was the wealthiest colony in the Caribbean, for its 465,000 slaves produced richer crops of coffee and sugarcane than in the entire British West Indies. About the size of Maryland, Saint-Domingue occupied the western third of the island of Hispaniola, with the Spanish holding the eastern two-thirds as their colony of Santo Domingo. Because of brutal work conditions and tropical diseases, slave deaths exceeded births in the colony, so the planters imported thousands to replace the corpses. As a consequence, most of the enslaved in Saint-Domingue were Africans by birth.[67]

The slave revolt exploited the French Revolution, which bitterly

divided the 40,000 white colonists. The revolutionary ideals of liberty, equality, and fraternity were particularly subversive in the highly
unequal, racially divided, and despotic regimes of the Caribbean. An
elite of *grands blancs* owned the largest plantations and dominated the
colony. They tried to exploit the upheaval in France to claim greater
autonomy and free trade for the colony, just as North American planters had done in their revolution. The *grands blancs* faced opposition
from the poorer but more numerous *petits blancs*, primarily recent
immigrants from France who sought greater equality and opportunity.
Hostile to free blacks, known as *gens de couleur*, the common whites
favored a different legacy of the American Revolution: the assertion of
white equality linked to black inequality. Making a fetish of their revolutionary zeal, *petits blancs* proudly wore the tricolored cockade and
abused free blacks who tried to do so. Denied equal rights as citizens,
the colony's 30,000 free blacks felt frustrated and betrayed by a revolution of apparently hollow pretensions. Their alienation weakened
colonial efforts to suppress the spreading slave revolt.[68]

In 1792, France's revolutionary regime sent 6,000 troops to
restore order in the colony. Initially, the regime's commissioners,
Étienne Polverel and Léger-Félicité Sonthonax, hoped to suppress
the slave revolt with help from free blacks, to whom they promised legal equality as French citizens. But that new policy infuriated
many white colonists, who became counterrevolutionaries, taking
up arms to attack the commissioners. In desperation, they promised
freedom to slave rebels who would provide armed assistance. During
the summer of 1793, that appeal turned the tide in the civil war, as the
former rebels captured and burned much of Cap Francois, a haven
for the counterrevolutionaries. Thousands of whites escaped by ship
as refugees bound to Spanish Cuba or the United States.[69]

Faced with an invasion of Saint-Domingue by France's enemies,
Spain and Britain, Sonthonax consolidated black support by issuing
a formal decree, emancipating all of the colony's slaves on August
29, 1793. In early 1794, the revolutionary regime in Paris endorsed
Sonthonax's measures and adopted a sweeping decree emancipating

the slaves throughout the French West Indies without offering any compensation for masters. The revolutionaries also granted equal citizenship to the emancipated and even seated black representatives as members of the national legislature, something that American Patriots never did. The French sought to rally thousands of black men to defend the French West Indies while promoting slave revolts in the British West Indies.[70]

In Saint-Domingue, the preeminent rebel leader was Toussaint Louverture, a literate former slave and pious Catholic. Small, wiry, brilliant, and charismatic, he cultivated an air of command and mystery. Initially suspicious of the French commissioners, he recruited and trained 4,000 men, who comprised the best-disciplined force in the colony. Impressed by the French abolition of slavery, Toussaint turned against the Spanish and British invaders of Saint-Domingue. Defeated by the invaders, Sonthonax fled to France, leaving Toussaint to take command in Saint-Domingue. Harried by his masterful guerrilla warfare, the Spanish and British troops withdrew in defeat. Toussaint took charge of a devastated colony, which had lost a third of its population during a decade of brutal warfare. While governing autonomously, Toussaint continued to profess a token allegiance to France.[71]

Back in France in late 1799, a brilliant and ruthless general, Napoleon Bonaparte, seized power in a military coup. Rejecting the racial radicalism of the French Revolution, Napoleon resolved to restore French control and plantation slavery in Saint-Domingue. In early 1802, 16,000 French troops invaded the colony under the command of Victor-Emmanuel Leclerc, who had married Napoleon's sister. Leclerc defeated and arrested Toussaint, shipping him away to France, where he died in April 1803 of abuse, malnutrition, and cold in a wretched prison.[72]

The French generals ruled Saint-Domingue through terror, butchering thousands of black men, women, and children who had surrendered. By 1804, however, yellow fever and black resistance had killed most of the invaders, including Leclerc. With the resumption of war in Europe, Napoleon could not afford to send more troops to die in the

"Lt. Gnl. Toussaint-L'Ouverture, rettant au Gal anglais," by an unknown engraver. A victorious Toussaint dictates terms of evacuation to British officers, who had invaded Saint-Domingue. Courtesy of the Library of Congress (LC–USZ62-7860).

tropics, so he withdrew his decimated force from Saint-Domingue. Led primarily by Jean-Jacques Dessalines, one of Toussaint's generals, the victorious revolutionaries declared independence. Their new country, named "Haiti," became the second new nation, after the United States, to win sovereignty in the Americas. In a symbolic move, the red and blue Haitian flag eliminated the white of the French tricolor.[73]

Some Americans initially accepted the black revolutionaries as kindred spirits seeking freedom from tyrants. In a set of newspaper essays published in 1791 and 1792, a Connecticut radical, Abraham Bishop, insisted that Caribbean slaves acted with the same motives and equal justice as the American Patriots. Asserting that "freedom is the natural right of all rational beings," Bishop asked, "Is not their cause as just as ours?" But Bishop and other American sympathizers fell silent after 1793, as public opinion hardened against slave rebels.[74]

Before the slave revolt in Saint-Domingue, Americans had celebrated their revolution as a "contagion of liberty" meant to overthrow tyranny everywhere. That contagion seemed more ominous, however, when enslaved blacks claimed freedom by killing white masters. In reporting the violence in Saint-Domingue, American writers dwelled in lurid detail on atrocities committed by blacks while skipping over the greater brutalities committed by their white oppressors. Headlines screamed about the "Horrors of Santo Domingo" and likened slave revolts to the sudden and utter destruction of a volcanic explosion. Deriding black rebels as vicious and ignorant brutes, most writers cast them as "unworthy of liberty."[75]

Although Americans had declared revolution a universal right for the oppressed, they shuddered when the enslaved claimed that right. Shocked by the Saint-Domingue revolt, most Americans retreated from radical and universal claims for their own revolution. In 1794, a South Carolina legislator warned that, if his colleagues continued to declare that "equality is the natural condition of man," they would produce the "ruin of the country, by giving liberty to the slaves, and the desolating [of] the land with fire and sword in the struggles between master and slave."[76]

American slaveholders feared that Saint-Domingue's example would inspire revolts by their slaves. Jefferson declared, "It is high time we should foresee the bloody scenes which our children certainly, and possibly ourselves (South of Patowmac) [will] have to wade through, and try to avert them." In 1797, he added, "But if something is not done and soon done, we shall be the murderers of our own children," for "the revolutionary storm, now sweeping the globe, will be upon us." To fend off that storm, Jefferson favored emancipating and deporting Virginia's slaves over the course of two generations. But his fellow southerners rejected his plan as too expensive and economically debilitating.[77]

In 1800, the southern nightmare nearly became manifest in Jefferson's Virginia. An enslaved blacksmith named Gabriel secretly organized a revolt in and around the state capital, Richmond. "We have as much right to fight for our liberty as any men," declared Jack Ditcher, one of Gabriel's lieutenants. The rebels planned to burn the riverside warehouses as a distraction and then to rush into the heart of town to grab the governor, James Monroe, seize the state arsenal, and plunder the treasury. The rebels hoped then to negotiate for their freedom.[78]

On the appointed night, August 30, a violent thunderstorm lashed Richmond with sheets of rain, washing away many bridges. Blocked by swollen streams and rivers, few rebels could make it to their rendezvous point. The confusion spread alarm among those in on the secret. A few fearful slaves sought to save themselves by revealing the plot to their masters, who alerted militia officers. Called into service, militiamen patrolled the roads and arrested suspects.[79]

The trials commenced on September 11, and executions began the next day. Gabriel died in front of a huge crowd on October 10, when a noose snapped his neck. By December 1, twenty-seven men had paid with their lives for trying but failing at revolution. They met death with a defiant resolve that alarmed a watching master: "The accused have exhibited a spirit, which, if it becomes general, must deluge the Southern country in blood. They manifested a sense of their rights, and contempt of danger, and a thirst for revenge which portend the most unhappy consequences."[80]

Election

In 1800, Gabriel's revolt jolted a nation embroiled in a divisive and crucial election pitting the incumbent Federalist president, John Adams, against his Republican challenger, Thomas Jefferson. To embarrass Jefferson, Federalists linked Gabriel to the revolutions in France and Saint-Domingue, casting all as the malign fruits of egalitarian folly. Federalists ridiculed Republicans who preached the revolutionary rights of man while hanging rebels who claimed those rights as their own. Rather than advocate emancipation, Federalists sought political gain, for they hoped to win conservative votes in proslavery South Carolina.[81]

The Federalists also exploited American diplomatic tensions with France to rally voters against the Republicans. During the 1790s, the neutrality policy of the United States irritated the French as a violation of their 1778 treaty of alliance. In 1797, the French began seizing American merchant ships trading with the British. To even discuss the controversy, French diplomats demanded bribes and tribute from American emissaries dispatched by President Adams. The seizures and indignities outraged popular opinion in America, which the Federalists exploited to prepare for war, enlarging the army and navy and raising taxes. Without declaring formal war, Adams sent warships to attack French vessels in the West Indies in 1798.[82]

Federalists hoped to discredit their domestic critics as treacherous American Jacobins helping the French. Disgusted by the many Irish immigrants who voted Republican, Federalists in Congress adopted new alien laws. One permitted the president summarily to expel any alien deemed "dangerous to the peace and safety of the United States." Another alien law increased the probationary period for naturalization to fourteen years from the previous five. Noah Webster insisted, "The country would be as prosperous and much more happy if no European should set his foot on our shores."[83]

Federalists bristled at criticism by Republican newspapers, especially those edited by immigrants. In 1798, Congress passed a <u>Sedition</u> <u>Act</u> to criminalize public attacks on the national government if a jury deemed the accusations "false, scandalous, and malicious." Those convicted faced up to two years in prison and $2,000 in fines. The ten men convicted under the law included Matthew Lyon, a Republican congressman from Vermont who had accused Adams of being driven by "an unbounded thirst for ridiculous pomp, foolish adulation, or selfish avarice." Lyon served four months in jail and paid a $1,000 fine.[84]

Republicans denounced the Alien and Sedition Acts as further proof that the Federalists were crypto-aristocrats subverting free speech and republicanism. In November 1798, the Kentucky state legislature adopted provocative resolutions written by Jefferson, who insisted that the states had created the union as a diplomatic compact. Therefore, any state legislatures could determine the constitutionality of federal laws and nullify their execution within a state's bounds. Virginia adopted similar (but a bit more tepid) resolutions drafted by Madison. Assailing the Kentucky and Virginia resolutions as "a regular conspiracy to overturn the government," Hamilton advised sending "a clever force" of federal troops southward to "put Virginia to the Test of resistance." By rejecting Hamilton's dangerous advice, Adams averted a civil war.[85]

Both parties instead hoped to crush the other in the national election of 1800. The campaign rhetoric became especially dire and bloody. Depicting Jefferson as a dangerous atheist, a Federalist warned that, under a Republican administration, "murder, robbery, rape, adultery, and incest will be openly taught and practiced, the air will be rent with the cries of distress, the soil will be soaked with blood, the nation black with crimes." A Republican journalist countered by denouncing Adams as "one of the most egregious fools on the continent," who meant to become an American king. Republicans and Federalists brawled in city streets in competitions to sing their songs and display their flags.[86]

Republicans prevailed by highlighting the unpopular federal taxes and Sedition Act prosecutions. In the fall, they captured both houses of Congress and appeared to have elected Jefferson as president and

Aaron Burr as vice president. But Jefferson and Burr had tied in electoral college returns that, per the Federal Constitution, did not then distinguish between votes for the offices of president and vice president. That tie cast the decision into the House of Representatives, which, per the Constitution, would vote by state delegations with each state casting one equal vote, which meant that Jefferson needed to capture at least nine of the sixteen delegations. In early 1801, Federalists of the lame-duck Congress toyed with choosing Burr, a handsome, charming, clever, and indebted opportunist who seemed open to making a deal. For a suspenseful week, the House deadlocked, while Federalists and Republicans muttered about preparing for civil war. Working behind the scenes, Hamilton lobbied for Jefferson as the lesser of two great evils. In mid-February, he persuaded one moderate Federalist to abstain, which broke the deadlock in favor of Jefferson. Another relieved congressman noted that, had the Federalists taken the presidency from Jefferson, "what other result would follow but civil war?" In that event, "his head would not have remained on his shoulders for twenty-four hours afterward."[87]

Sobered by the constitutional crisis over the election, Republicans in Congress crafted the Twelfth Amendment. Ratified by the states, the amendment obliged each member of the electoral college to cast one vote for president and the other for vice president. Thereafter, the president and vice president would almost certainly belong to the same party. Where the founders in 1787 had sought to preclude partisan divisions, the Twelfth Amendment assumed their lamentable inevitability.[88]

Empire of Liberty

In the pivotal election of 1800, most voters decided that their leaders should be friends of the people rather than their fathers. Republicans asserted that they had defended and completed a revolution imperiled by internal enemies. A Republican newspaper exulted, "The Revolution of 1776 is now, and for the *first* time, arrived at its completion," and "the sun of aristocracy [has] set, to rise no more." In Connecticut,

*"President Thomas Jefferson," engraving by Charles Balthazar
Julien Févret de Saint-Mémin, 1805. Courtesy of the
Library of Congress (LC-DIG-ppmsca-31800).*

a Baptist association congratulated Jefferson that republicanism would "prevail through all these States and all the world till Hierarchy and Tyranny be destroyed from the Earth."[89]

Jefferson insisted that the federal government should heed public opinion and tolerate free speech. Congress killed the Sedition Act, while Jefferson pardoned those convicted under that law. To reward their immigrant voters, Republicans reduced the period of naturalization to five years from the punitive fourteen years mandated by the Federalists in 1798. A rueful Noah Webster noted that his fellow Federalists had "attempted to resist the force of public opinion, instead of falling into the current with a view to correct it. In this they have manifested more integrity than address." Democracy had prevailed over deference in the election of 1800.[90]

The victorious Republicans halted the Federalist drive to build a powerful national government. They instead favored a decentralized union that entrusted to the states all responsibilities but foreign affairs, customs collection, a bare-bones military, and the postal service. Jefferson dreaded a peacetime military establishment because its great "expenses and the eternal wars in which it will implicate us, [will] grind us with public burthens, & sink us under them." By cutting the army and navy, Republicans could abolish the unpopular excise and land taxes levied by the Federalists. Jefferson also tried to pay down the national debt that Hamilton had designed for perpetuity. During their twelve years in power, the Federalists had increased that debt from $76 million to $83 million; during his eight years as president, Jefferson reduced it to $57 million.[91]

Glorying in their dispersion of power, Republicans insisted that a minimal and cheap government would inspire a passionate popularity that no monarchy could match. Jefferson claimed that the diffuse United States had the "strongest Government on earth," precisely because its lack of coercive power won popular support. Common militiamen would rush to defend a republic that demanded so little of them. In 1811, the United States spent only $1 per capita, a mere twenty-fifth of the public expenditures in Great Britain. A French traveler reported that Jefferson's administration was "neither seen [n]or felt."[92]

Jefferson shrewdly deployed political symbols and public performance to woo popularity. To show his dependence on common voters, he eliminated the quasi-regal panoply of power favored by the Federalists. *shaping presidency* He sold the presidential coaches with their silver harnesses, and shabby gentility became his fashion statement. A Federalist complained, "Jefferson is the supreme director of measures—he has no levee days—observes no ceremony—often sees company in an undress, sometimes with his slippers on—always accessible to, and very familiar with, the sovereign people." But a British diplomat noted that, when not performing publicly as a democrat, the president indulged in gourmet food, fine wines, and silverware. Jefferson privately lived "upon a more expensive scale than during [the administrations] of either of the former Presidents, but with less of form and ostentation." Thereafter, Americans accepted government by wealthy men so long as they pretended to have common manners.[93]

In his speeches, Jefferson struck a conciliatory tone, declaring in his first inaugural address, "We are all republicans—we are all federalists." But Jefferson preached moderation as the means to ruin the Federalists forever. With soothing rhetoric, he wooed moderate voters to abandon their support for Federalist leaders, whom he privately considered as only "entitled to be protected & taken care of as other insane persons are." He vowed "by the establishment of republican principles," to "sink federalism into an abyss from which there shall be no resurrection for it." He never accepted the legitimacy of opposition to his administration.[94]

Voters rewarded Jefferson's moderate public tone. In 1804, he won reelection in a landslide and Republicans increased their majorities in House and Senate. Never again would Federalists recover the presidency or a majority in either house of Congress. A Republican chortled, "The ejected party is now almost universally considered as having been employed in conjunction with G[reat] B[ritain] in a scheme for the total destruction of the liberties of the people." Burr inadvertently helped the Republicans by turning Federalist, and then in frustration over losing his gubernatorial election in New York, he blamed Hamilton and shot him dead in a duel in July 1804. By winning the duel, Burr lost his popularity and damned his political fortunes forever.[95]

Jefferson was especially indebted to southern voters and legislators, for he won 82 percent of the electoral votes in the South compared to only 27 percent in the North. Southerners also comprised most of the Republican majority in the House of Representatives. Although the Federalists had not challenged slavery, many southerners worried about the future uses of federal power if state sovereignty eroded. The Federalists also offended them by promoting American trade with the black rebels in Saint-Domingue (Haiti).[96]

Attentive to those who had elected him, President Jefferson refused to meddle with slavery, reasoning "that no more good must be attempted than the nation can bear." In 1802, Jefferson's postmaster-general, Gideon Granger, fired the free blacks employed in his department, reasoning that their free movement threatened to promote slave revolts. Jefferson's administration also sought to isolate and ruin Haiti, which he dreaded as a dangerous example to American slaves. Adopting a lurid stereotype, the president denounced the "Cannibals of the terrible republic," denied them diplomatic recognition, and supported a congressional ban on trade with Haiti.[97]

Jefferson slighted the geopolitical benefit that the United States reaped from the black freedom fighters who resisted the French invasion of Saint-Domingue in 1802. Hamilton noted that "the courage and obstinate resistance made by black inhabitants" had destroyed the invaders and induced Napoleon to cut his losses in America by selling Louisiana to the United States at a bargain price in 1803. Three years earlier, Napoleon had extorted that vast colony from the Spanish king. Jefferson's Louisiana Purchase nearly doubled the size of the United States, extending its territorial claims beyond the Mississippi at least as far as the Rocky Mountains. His greatest diplomatic achievement owed much to black rebels whom he dreaded.[98]

Jefferson did support a ban on importing more Africans as slaves, a ban that Congress passed in March 1807 and made effective January 1, 1808: the first year when the Federal Constitution permitted such a prohibition. The overwhelming vote, 113 to 5, in the House of Representatives attested to broad support in the South as well as the North. Most southern leaders reasoned that natural increase by the current slave population sufficed for expanding the plantation economy westward. Noting the example of Saint-Domingue, they also feared that new slaves from Africa were especially prone to revolt. The ban signaled no commitment to abolish slavery or even to meddle with the booming interstate trade in slaves. Indeed, by eliminating foreign competition, Virginians and Marylanders could sell more slaves to the Lower South. The sellers also expected to sleep more securely as the domestic slave trade diffused their surplus slaves to the south and west.[99]

Jefferson also had political debts to pay in the West, where he won overwhelming support from voters, who bristled at Federalist efforts to slow and manage expansion. Where Federalists had treated settlers as "white savages" who needed elite mentors, Republicans celebrated them as industrious farmers who redeemed a wilderness through hard work. Jefferson's administration promoted retail sales of federal land to common settlers by reducing the minimum tract from 640 acres to a more affordable 160 acres, offering a credit of four years, and opening three new land offices in the west.[100]

To get more land for settlers, Jefferson coerced Indians to make massive cessions. He expected territorial officials to "press on the Indians, as steadily and strenuously as they can bear, the extension of our purchases." To reduce Indian resistance, Jefferson encouraged territorial officials to advance goods generously on credit to natives to make them dependent debtors: "When these debts get beyond what the individuals can pay, they become willing to lop th[em off] by a cession of lands." Jefferson hoped that Indians would dissolve their tribal governments and forsake their native identities by accepting acculturation and absorption as Americans. On Jefferson's orders, the territorial governors made thirty cession treaties, procuring 200,000 square miles for a mere penny or two per acre. Governors dealt with older chiefs representing smaller tribes vulnerable to pressure, so the treaties infuriated most of the natives.[101]

Jefferson promoted an "Empire of Liberty," which favored white men at the expense of Indians and blacks. Rather than restrain westward expansion, as the British Empire and Federalists had tried (and failed) to do, Jeffersonians helped settlers dispossess Indians. A democratic but racially defined society would expand relentlessly westward, creating thousands of new farms to sustain relative equality among white men. Jeffersonians recognized that the strength of a diffuse nation lay in helping, rather than hindering, ambitious settlers.[102]

Principles

Jefferson described his election to the presidency as "the revolution of 1800," which he claimed was "as real a revolution in the principles of our government as that of 1776 was in its form." Jefferson's electoral triumph seemed to seal the victory of his political philosophy as the true legacy of the American Revolution. Rejecting Hamilton's vision of a consolidated nation, Jeffersonian Republicans favored a strict construction of the constitution that limited the federal government and favored the states. The Republicans also championed the rights and interests of common white men while accepting their prejudices against blacks and Indians.[103]

The Federalist philosophy, however, endured in a Supreme Court led by John Marshall. In 1801, Jefferson ascended to the presidency shortly after Marshall became chief justice as a last-minute appointment by the outgoing president, John Adams. In March, Marshall administered the presidential oath of office to Jefferson—to the dismay of both men, who despised each other. As a Continental Army captain, Marshall had become a nationalist who disdained the states' rights philosophy of the Republicans. Marshall considered Jefferson "unfit . . . for the chief magistracy" because he would "sap the fundamental principles of the government." Jefferson feared becoming entrapped by Marshall's quick mind and rigorous logic. The new president assured another judge, "So great is his sophistry [that] you must never give him an affirmative answer, or you will be forced to grant his conclusions. Why, if he were to ask me whether it were daylight or not, I'd reply, 'Sir, I don't know, I can't tell.'"[104]

Jefferson held the presidency for eight years, while Marshall served as Chief Justice for thirty-four years thanks to a life tenure provided by the Federal Constitution. Marshall participated in more than a thousand decisions, writing over half of them. Thanks to that prodigious output during a critical generation in the consolidation of the federal union, Marshall had an impact at least comparable to Jefferson's. The

*"Chief Justice John Marshall," engraving by
Charles Balthazar Julien Févret de Saint-Mémin, 1808.
Courtesy of the Library of Congress (LC-USZ62-54940).*

president complained that Federalists had "retired into the Judiciary as a stronghold. There the remains of federalism are to be preserved & fed from the treasury, and from that battery all the works of republicanism are to be beaten down & erased."[105]

Given the Republicans' electoral triumphs, Marshall proceeded carefully and patiently, cultivating a nonpartisan tone and unanimity on the court. To promote solidarity, he arranged for the judges to room and board together during their annual sessions in Washington, D.C. In those close quarters and over many bottles of Madeira, Marshall's amiable manners, keen wit, and sharp mind swayed his colleagues. By 1819, Jefferson and his Republican successor, James Madison, had appointed most of the Supreme Court justices, but the justices had come around to Marshall's Federalist philosophy, to Jefferson's dismay.[106]

Marshall sought to bolster the authority of the Supreme Court as a coequal branch with congress and the presidency. By upholding the Federalist doctrine that the Federal Constitution emanated from a sovereign American people, Marshall refuted the Jeffersonian insistence that it derived from a compact by sovereign states. In *McCulloch v. Maryland* (1819), the Marshall court defended the federal Bank of the United States against a state tax levied to favor state-chartered banks. By broadly interpreting the Federal Constitution's "necessary and proper" clause, Marshall sustained the creation of a national bank. Outraged by the ruling, Jefferson accused Marshall of "working like gravity, without intermission, . . . to press us at last into one consolidated mass."[107]

The Marshall court promoted a national market in which interstate investment and commerce benefited from federal laws that trumped state intervention. Protecting propertied interests against state laws, the Supreme Court insisted that business corporations were private properties that could neither be revoked nor diminished by legislative action. Jefferson raged that this legal doctrine subordinated democratic legislatures to the dictates of a previous generation: "that the earth belongs to the dead, & not the living." But legal protection for corporations reassured investors. Thereafter, corporations proliferated to become the nation's dominant form of business enterprise (supplanting partnerships and sole proprietorships).[108]

Jefferson and Marshall asserted conflicting interpretations of the revolution's legacy. Echoes of their clashing principles have ebbed and flowed in competition ever since, informing the constitutional and political disputes to our own time. In his last years, Marshall lost control over the Supreme Court, which swung toward Jefferson's decentralizing principles. Marshall began to despair of the union and Federal Constitution as doomed by state democracy and sectional rivalry. As if to echo Marshall's despair, Philadelphia's famed Liberty Bell cracked while tolling to mark the news of his death in 1835. But Marshall's principles would revive during the 1860s, when a new and very different Republican Party championed liberty and union as intertwined and inseparable.[109]

Conflicting constitutional principles contributed to the Civil War. Eleven southern states claimed a right to secede from the union as a last, desperate measure to protect slavery. Most northerners, however, fought for the union as perpetual and supreme. Leading that defense of the union, Abraham Lincoln had the good political sense to deploy Marshall's principles in Jeffersonian rhetoric. Lincoln crafted the useful fiction that the founders had favored the freedom of all men, black as well as white. Victory in the Civil War validated Lincoln's combination of Jeffersonian rhetoric with Hamiltonian policies.[110]

But any political victory is temporary. Like a kaleidoscope, we continue in every generation to make new combinations of clashing principles derived from the enduring importance and incompleteness of our revolution. The revolution remains embedded as selective memory in every contemporary debate.

Americans often romanticize the founders of the nation as united and resolute and then present them as a rebuke to our current political divisions. Pundits insist that Americans should return to the ideal vision set by the founders. That begs the question, however, which founders and what vision? Far from being united, they fought over what the revolution meant. Should Americans follow Jefferson's vision of a decentralized country with a weak federal government? Or do we prefer Hamilton's and Marshall's push for a powerful, centralized nation that promotes economic development and global power? Conservatives today embrace Jefferson's stances against taxes and for states' rights, but skip over his opposition to a military establishment, his unease with inequality of wealth, and his push to separate church and state. They like a Hamiltonian military but not Hamiltonian taxes to pay for it. Instead of offering a single, cohesive, and enduring plan, the diverse founders generated contradictions that continue to divide Americans.[111]

12

LEGACIES

There is nothing more common than to confound
the terms of the American Revolution with those of the
late American war. *The American war is over; but this is*
far from being the case with the American Revolution.
—BENJAMIN RUSH, 1787[1]

By promising equal rights in an unequal society, the revolution opened social hierarchies to criticism and potential reform. Some reformers questioned even the unequal family relationships between husbands and wives and parents and children. The challenges troubled gentlemen, who defended their privileged position in traditional class, race, and gender relations. Clinging to the unequal structures of society, John Adams wrote from Congress in 1776: "We have been told that our Struggle has loosened the bands of Government everywhere. That Children and Apprentices were disobedient—that schools and Colledges were grown turbulent—that Indians slighted their Guardians and Negroes grew insolent to their Masters." He feared: "There will be no End of it. New Claims will arise. Women will

---

"Apotheosis of Washington," engraving after John James Barralet, 1802. Father Time and an angel carry Washington to heaven, while Lady Liberty and an American Indian mourn in the foreground. Courtesy of the Library of Congress (LC-USZ62-60993).

demand a Vote. Lads from 12 to 21 will think their Rights not enough attended to, and every Man, who has not a Farthing, will demand an equal Voice with any other in all Acts of State. It tends to confound and destroy all Distinctions, and prostrate all Ranks, to one common Levell." Adams longed for "more Serenity of Temper, a deeper Understanding and more Courage . . . to ride in this Whirlwind."[2]

Postwar migration compounded the social strains introduced by the republican revolution. With more places and more reasons to go, Americans moved farther and more often than ever before, shifting into and out of communities where diverse strangers outnumbered kin and old acquaintances. The rising velocity of movement and the increased competition meant that nothing seemed certain, stable, and predictable. A French visitor marveled, "It is a country in flux; that which is true today as regards its population, its establishments, its prices, its commerce will not be true six months from now." Another traveler added, "Here, all is circulation, motion, and boiling agitation."[3]

Strained by revolution and migration, old hierarchies had to be reinvented in a new republic. Although excluded from formal politics, poorer colonists and women could protest violently as urban mobs and rural regulators. Republicanism discredited the irregular politics of rioters while inviting common white men to participate in electoral politics. Patriots had rejected British claims "virtually" to represent Americans in Parliament, but they defended their own mode of virtual representation: white men with some property alone should govern everyone in the new order.[4]

As their price of admission to regular politics, common white men were supposed to adopt greater self-control. In return for moral discipline, the middle class—a mix of entrepreneurial artisans, small-scale manufacturers, shopkeepers, and commercial farmers—bought political inclusion. Their numbers grew and prosperity increased thanks to the economic boom of the 1790s. Often they measured their characters in dollars and cents. In 1809 an entrepreneurial printer in upstate New York explained himself to John Adams: "[I] began 'the world'

$20 in debt, am now worth Thousands of dollars, gained by my own industry and attention to business. You, sir, have now a sketch of my character."[5]

Once limited to the governing elite, gentility spread to the middle class. Prosperous tradesmen, shopkeepers, and farmers read more, adopted better manners, and wore nicer clothes. Teacups and saucers, carpets, clocks, and looking glasses proliferated in their homes as they entertained more visitors. Watching closely, they measured one another for signs of refinement or vulgarity. A dread of scorn compelled attention to every detail of appearance and performance.[6]

As this self-conscious "vernacular gentility" spread down the social ladder, it also expanded geographically, reaching hundreds of country towns, where prosperous families could obtain urban goods and notions of respectability. Many farmers painted their barns and homes, hired a local artist to depict the family, donned finer clothes on Sunday, and rode to church in new carriages. Numerous in the Northeast and Middle Atlantic, the outposts of middle-class gentility were scarce in the West and scarcest of all in the South, where most rural folk preserved a plain style of life.[7]

While softening the line between the wealthy and middling classes, vernacular gentility drew a harder line between the respectable above and the poor below, derided as coarse and vulgar. Middle-class folk blamed poverty on bad taste and slack morals. In theory, poor people could prosper by improving their manners, reading uplifting books, and acquiring a few genteel goods. But most of the poor struggled just to get by from one day to the next. Urban laborers were often unemployed or underemployed, while many farmers barely eked out a living from hard work on thin, rocky soils. The poor lacked the means or time to acquire the manners and props of respectability.[8]

Vernacular gentility also reinforced a color line as stark and immutable, separating white respectability from ridiculous vulgarity. When free blacks dressed well and held balls, they reaped savage mockery from satirists and brutal attacks from street bullies. A black dentist, Joseph Willson, complained, "The exceedingly illiberal, unjust, and oppressive prejudices of the great mass of the white community" are "enough to crush—effectually crush and keep down—any people."[9]

Culture

Because republics depended on a broad electorate, American leaders felt compelled to reform the morals and manners of citizens. "We have changed our forms of government," Benjamin Rush declared in 1786, "but it remains yet to effect a revolution in our principles, opinions, and manners so as to accommodate them to the forms of government that we have adopted." Seeking a distinctively American and republican culture, reformers worried that the far-flung people of thirteen states remained both too British and too different from one another. In heritage and manners, they shared little that they did not also share with the mother country, and they lacked a unifying American culture.[10]

Improving the people required enhancing their education so that students would become well-informed protectors of republican government. "If the common people are ignorant and vicious," Rush concluded, "a republican nation can never be long free." He sought "to convert men into republican machines" in order to "fit them more easily for uniform and peaceable government." He meant to consolidate the revolution by encouraging "honest mechanics, industrious farmers, peaceable sailors, and . . . good citizens." Putting revolutionary turmoil behind them, citizens needed to become orderly supporters of republican institutions.[11]

Republican reformers wanted to expand schools, which had been few and private (except in New England) before the war. In 1786, Jefferson pitched a secular and public system of education for Virginia. He reasoned that "the tax which will be paid for this purpose is not more that the thousandth part of what will be paid to [the] kings, priests, and nobles who will rise up among us if we leave the people in ignorance." But most citizens preferred to keep their taxes low, so Virginia's legislators rejected Jefferson's plan. Many farmers also wanted to keep their children at work on the farm. Comprehensive, public school systems did not emerge beyond New England until the 1820s and 1830s and only in the other northern states.[12]

Rather than wait on taxpayers, ambitious men and women formed voluntary associations to support schools and libraries, debating clubs and lyceums through subscriptions and tuition. Private cultural institutions proliferated in the populous northeast rather than in the dispersed counties of the South. Serving the middle class, these associations rarely included the poor.[13]

The colonies had supported only nine colleges, which each year collectively graduated fewer than 200 students, most of them from the genteel elite. After the war, reformers sought to expand colleges and recruit more middle-class students. By 1815, the United States sustained thirty-three colleges, but that growth barely kept up with the exploding population. Many rustics still distrusted colleges as training grounds for potential aristocrats. A North Carolinian insisted, "College learned persons give themselves great airs, are proud, and the fewer of them we have amongst us the better." Preferring "the plain, simple, honest matter-of-fact republicanism," he asked, "Who wants Latin and Greek and abstruse mathematics . . . in a country like this?"[14]

The early republic promoted more self-education than public education as many people exploited the greater availability of print. Thanks to rudimentary education at home, about three-quarters of free American adults were literate: one of the highest rates in the world. As printing presses spread beyond the seaports to the commercial villages of the interior, they produced more and cheaper texts. The number of American magazines swelled from just 1 in 1785 to 28 a decade later. The 100 newspapers of 1790 became nearly 400 by 1810. An expanding federal postal system spread letters and publications throughout the nation. The 69 post offices of 1788 mushroomed to 903 in 1800, when the postal system carried nearly 2 million copies of newspapers to far-flung readers, giving the United States the largest and widest circulation in the world. A North Carolina congressman concluded, "If the people hereafter remain uninform'd, it must be their own fault."[15]

Foreign visitors marveled at the number and influence of American newspapers, which became pivotal to republican politics, for shrewd editors could make or break candidates. The French visitor Alexis de Tocqueville noted "Only a newspaper can put the same thought at the same time before a thousand readers." But many moralists worried that newspapers put the wrong thoughts in too many minds, spreading slander rather than insights. In 1807, Jefferson concluded, "Nothing can now be believed which is seen in a newspaper. . . . The man who never looks into a newspaper is better informed than he who reads them." A free press might threaten, rather than bolster, the fragile new republic.[16]

Republican writers and artists hoped to reform a European culture tainted with a traditional reverence for hierarchy. European art and literature relied on aristocratic and royal patrons and celebrated their superiority. Adams warned, "Architecture, Sculpture, Painting, and Poetry have conspir'd against the Rights of Mankind." But the Congregational minister Jeremy Belknap asked, "Why may not a Republic of Letters be realized in America as well as a Republican Government?" Rather than perpetuate the unequal privileges of birth, a republican culture would celebrate equal rights and an open competition that rewarded merit. By enlightening the minds and improving the morals of citizens, reformers hoped to develop a broad public market that could supplant aristocratic patrons in supporting the arts. Such a market supposedly would favor a natural purity of style superior to European artificiality. In 1793, the commissioners for the new national capital sought "a Republican simplicity and that true elegance of proportion, which correspond to a tempered freedom excluding frivolity, the food of little minds."[17]

More than anyone else, Charles Willson Peale shaped the culture of republican uplift. Benefiting from the revolution's boost to social mobility, he rose from an apprentice saddlemaker to prosper as an artist and entrepreneur. In Philadelphia in 1786, Peale created a museum to educate the public and promote "the interests of religion and morality by the arrangement and display of the works of nature and art." In his "Temple of Wisdom," he combined his portraits of leading Patriots with exhibits of natural history: stuffed birds, baboons, squirrels, rattlesnakes, and moose, as well as a fossil mastodon. Emphasizing harmony, order, stability, and coherence, Peale insisted that all knowledge, including politics and the arts, belonged to a unified whole governed by universal principles of nature. By setting a modest admission fee—25 cents—he maximized "its utility; that of giving information generally." By 1815, Peale's Museum annually drew nearly 40,000 visitors.[18]

While professing to reject Old World ways, Americans still longed to impress Europeans. By producing great literature and art, republicans sought to refute intellectuals who insisted that the American environment degraded bodies and minds, rendering them smaller, dimmer, and more feminine. Washington hoped that Americans would prove "not inferior to the rest of the world in the performances of our poets and painters." Jefferson promoted neoclassical public buildings "to improve the taste of my countrymen, to increase their reputation, to reconcile to them the respect of the world, and procure them its praise." By seeking European approval, Americans kept their art derivative and prolonged their cultural dependency.[19]

Republican art and literature rarely impressed Europeans. In 1820, a British critic dismissed American culture as second-rate: "Who reads an American book? Or goes to an American play or looks at an American picture or statue?" Most Americans agreed, preferring British fashions, furniture, art, books, and architecture. Americans wrote only 2 of the 160 plays performed in Philadelphia between 1792 and 1794. Although an Anglophobe in politics, Jefferson could not stop buying British goods: "It is not from a love of the English but a love of myself that I sometimes find myself obliged to buy their manufactures."[20]

Before 1820, American publishers preferred to pirate books and articles from Britain rather than publish American writers. English texts were more fashionable and less expensive for publishers who, by law, had to pay royalties to American authors but not to foreign writers. Susanna Rowson's novel *Charlotte Temple* (1791) sold very well, but she reaped few profits because American printers pirated it from the London edition. Because of that unintended consequence of copy-right law, no American novelist could live by her or his work until the 1820s.[21]

The didactic style of republican art failed commercially, for most Americans preferred entertainment to enlightenment. To make a living, painters had to decorate carriages and tavern signs or paint flattering portraits of paying customers. Grand history paintings and studies of common scenes found few if any buyers. The great portraitist Gilbert Stuart recognized that his art was a commodity. "I expect to make a fortune by Washington alone," he announced before producing multiple copies of his most celebrated portrait. Stuart described each copy as "a hundred dollar bill."[22]

The market rewarded accessibility rather than brilliance. John Marshall's ponderous and expensive multivolume biography of Washington sold few copies. The reading public preferred Mason Locke Weems's brief, cheap, melodramatic, and fanciful version of Washington, which featured his inability to lie about chopping down his neighbor's cherry tree. An exuberant salesman, Weems specialized in "the gay and sprightly kind" of books. A frustrated playwright, William Dunlap, complained that "mercenary managers" preferred to produce "such ribaldry or folly, or worse, as is attractive" to "the uneducated, the idle and profligate" and therefore "productive of profit to themselves."[23]

Churches

Many more Americans attended church and read the Bible than ever attended a play. Consequently, the revolution had the greatest cultural impact in the interplay of religion and republicanism. Before the war, the spread of evangelical Protestantism had promoted individual choice in faith, challenging the tax-supported, government-favored religious establishments of most colonies. In New England, the establishment sustained Congregationalism, while Anglicanism enjoyed official favor in the southern colonies. The religious diversity of the middle colonies had discouraged any official church, save for a weak Anglican establishment in New York. Established churches insisted that well-educated ministers could best prepare and guide common people to cultivate morality and seek salvation.[24]

Evangelicals countered that spiritual truth came spontaneously, emotionally, and directly from God to individuals who sought his grace. Evangelicals argued that common people could find religious truth through free inquiry and should dispense with the inevitable distortions of elite guidance. A Baptist preacher, John Leland, explained, "Every man must give an account of himself to God, and therefore every man ought to be at liberty to serve God in a way that he can best reconcile to his conscience. If government can answer for individuals at the day of judgement, let me be controlled by it in religious matters; otherwise, let men be free."[25]

Evangelicals had an ambivalent relationship to the revolution, which troubled them with its violence, plundering, and swearing soldiers. Devout people sought an eternal salvation deemed superior and at odds with material life and political strife. In 1789, a Methodist preacher described "the true disciple of Christ" as "meek in heart, thirsting after holiness, crucified with Christ, and dead to the world." In 1800, North Carolina Baptists declared it their "duty then to walk as people who are not of the world but chosen of God and bound for the heavenly Canaan." While prioritizing spirituality, evangelicals did not withdraw from the world, for they expected believers to work hard and honestly—and then support church and charity. Methodism's founder, John Wesley, exhorted, "Earn all you can, save all you can, give all you can."[26]

Evangelicals cherished liberty, but they gave the term a distinctive definition as an inspiring liberation from a troubling sense of sin. Unforgiven sin constituted the ultimate slavery, for it consigned sinners to eternity in hell. A Virginian recalled that his painful "conviction for sin became more deep and pungent every hour," until divine grace suddenly gripped his soul and he realized that "my guilt was gone, my conscience at rest, and my soul at liberty." In 1771, Virginia gentry interrupted a Baptist service and whipped the preacher, but he rose up and resumed "singing praises to God . . . and preached with a great deal of liberty."[27]

Despite differing definitions of liberty, a public synergy developed between revolutionary republicanism and evangelical religion. Colonial evangelicals had preached individual choice, or voluntarism, in religion, a concept that helped promote the revolutionary challenge to British rule. Then the triumph of that revolution established individual consent as essential for true religion as well as for popular sovereignty. Evangelicals could draw on the revolution's legacy to challenge church establishments as antirepublican vestiges from the colonial era. The joint assaults of evangelism and republicanism validated a new conception of society as composed of individuals making free choices (save for the enslaved)—just as buyers and sellers allegedly did in a free market.[28]

The First Amendment to the Federal Constitution barred the federal government from creating a church establishment, but that ban did not apply to the states—which became political battlegrounds between religious conservatives and their evangelical critics. Conservatives argued that a republic could not survive without the virtuous and moral citizens promoted by state-mandated financial support for religion. In 1784, Richard Henry Lee defended a religious establishment in Virginia: "The experience of all times shows Religion to be the guardian of morals—and he must be a very inattentive observer in our Country, who does not see that avarice is accomplishing the destruction of religion, for want of a legal obligation to contribute something to its support."[29]

Religious politics made for strange bedfellows as evangelicals allied with secularists to seek disestablishment. Most leading Patriots felt drawn to the anticlerical ideas of the European Enlightenment, but they valued the public morality promoted by churches. Washington esteemed "Religion and morality" as the "great pillars of human happiness, these firmest props of the duties of Men and Citizens." The republic's leaders sought to sustain a broad practice of religion without favoring any one denomination with an establishment. Indeed, they insisted that religion would prosper if all denominations could freely compete for believers.[30]

In Virginia, Jefferson and Madison allied with evangelicals to eliminate public tax support for any church in Virginia. During the pivotal legislative debates, Jefferson was away in Paris as the American minister, leaving the proposed bill to the shrewd management of Madison. Before the war, he had soured on the Anglican alliance with the colonial government because it harassed and jailed Baptist dissidents. In 1774, he wrote, "That diabolical Hell conceived principle of persecution rages among some and to their eternal Infamy the Clergy can furnish their Quota of Imps for such business."[31]

From 1784 to 1786, Madison deftly outmaneuvered the state's governor, Patrick Henry, who wanted a mandatory tithe paid by all taxpayers to support incorporated churches. In the key move, Madison persuaded Presbyterians that they would lose out to Anglicans under Henry's proposal. Madison boasted to Jefferson, "The mutual hatred of these sects has been much inflamed. . . . I am far from being sorry for it." Sectarian rivalry helped Madison make the case for dissolving the church-state alliance.[32]

In 1786, state legislators passed Jefferson and Madison's bill "for establishing Religious Freedom." The legislators reasoned that religious truth, and true freedom, required a completely free market for spiritual ideas: "that the truth is great and will prevail if left to herself, that she is the proper and sufficient antagonist to error, and has nothing to fear from the conflict, unless by human interposition disarmed of her natural weapons, free argument and debate." This doctrine reversed the traditional notion that common people needed spiritual guidance approved by their rulers. Jefferson exulted "to see the standard of reason at length erected, after so many ages during which the human mind has been held in vassalage by kings, priests, and nobles." Less confident in secular rationality, his evangelical allies instead credited the new law to the supervening power of God. Where Jefferson wanted a secular nation, evangelicals wanted a Protestant one but without any one denomination favored by the state.[33]

Virginia's example proved slowly contagious. None of the new states created after the revolution provided for a church establishment, and those of the old states gradually toppled: New York in 1777; Virginia in 1786; South Carolina in 1790; Maryland in 1810; Connecticut in 1818; New Hampshire in 1819; and Massachusetts in 1833.[34]

The turmoil of war weakened established denominations by disrupting churches and the colleges that trained their ministries. After the war, more college students studied law than divinity as lawyers supplanted ministers in social prestige. In 1780 more than a third of New England's Congregational churches lacked a minister because colleges had failed to meet the demand for clergy.[35]

Traditional churches could not keep pace with the growing population expanding westward into hundreds of new settlements. Evangelicals, however, offered many cheaper, less-educated, and more itinerant preachers to fill the vacuum. They lacked social graces, family connections, and formal education. Peter Cartwright confessed that his fellow Methodists "could not, many of us, conjugate a verb or parse a sentence and [we] murdered the king's English almost every lick." Evangelicals insisted that divinely inspired feelings, dreams, and visions provided a better spiritual mandate than any college degree. They promoted an emotional, physical style of worship that often provoked convulsions, known as "the jerks," in listeners absorbed in spiritual ecstasy. This visceral worship appealed to settlers coping with the hardships of frontier life and skeptical of college learning. Evangelical preachers promised personal salvation to thousands of people set in motion by war and its aftermath.[36]

Evangelicals offered individual self-respect and mutual support to common people. Claiming republican values, evangelical preachers exhorted people to reject their traditional, well-educated ministers as clerical aristocrats. In New Hampshire, a beleaguered Congregationalist complained, "Liberty is a great cant word with them. . . . Hence to use their own language, they say, 'Break all these yokes and trammels from off you, and come out of prison; and dare to think, and speak, and act for yourselves.'"[37]

Evangelical churches multiplied, growing faster than the population, as mainstream churches fell behind. From 150 congregations in 1770, Baptists grew to 858 in 1790, becoming America's largest denomination. Methodists expanded from 20 congregations in 1770 to 712 in 1790. By comparison, Anglicans suffered from disestablishment, shrinking from 356 congregations in 1770 to just 170 in 1790. Congregationalists grew, but at a slow pace that lagged behind the swelling population. In addition to their local meetings, Methodists convened massive annual camp meetings that attracted thousands from the hinterland and lasted for up to two weeks.[38]

After the revolution, evangelical worship attracted more prosperous and respectable folk. In 1785 in Virginia, a Methodist preacher reported, "Many of the wealthy people, both men and women, were seen lying in the dust, sweating and rolling on the ground, in their fine broad cloths or silks, crying for mercy." As their respectable support grew, evangelical preachers moderated their identification with the lowly and oppressed as favored by God. Cultivating respectability, the Baptists and Methodists increasingly pushed out black people, who formed their own churches. Rather than mock education and fear wealth, evangelical leaders solicited contributions to found seminaries. During the 1810s and 1820s, the seminaries trained a new generation of moderate evangelical ministers, who distrusted emotionalism and mysticism. While defeating Anglicans and Congregationalists with populist rhetoric, Baptists and Methodists developed their own hierarchical structures of authority, albeit without tax support. Their drift toward the moderate center invited new competition on the left from wilder sects—Disciples of Christ, Shakers, Freewill Baptists, Republican Methodists, and New Israelites. By claiming divine sanction through visions and prophecies, they appealed to those who felt left behind by respectable Methodists and Baptists. American evangelicalism was powerful, diverse, and volatile—ever evolving on both the moderate and radical wings as some preachers pursued respectability and others defied it.[39]

The republican revolution created new circumstances for religious practices, favoring evangelicals at the expense of establishments. At the same time, evangelicalism influenced political culture and practices. Evangelicals opposed religious establishments but supported using the state to enforce public morality and the Sabbath. They also wanted nondenominational Protestant instruction in public schools. In 1812, New York mandated that students learn "the principles of morality" by reading the Bible at the opening and closing of every school day.[40]

Catholic priests adapted to the new America, where they no longer faced persecution but still could not count on a government to suppress Protestants as heretics. To curry favor with France during the revolution, the states had repealed colonial laws barring Catholics from voting and holding office. Catholics made the most of their new legal equality to compete for souls through persuasion. In 1790, John Carroll of Maryland became the first Catholic bishop in America. To enhance Catholicism's appeal to American republicans, Carroll downplayed deference to the pope, and the laity assumed more autonomy to manage their parishes.[41]

After the revolution, the United States developed a unique religious culture in which no denomination commanded either a majority or government support. As evangelicals sought respectability and mainstream churches proselytized for converts, the two partially converged, competing for souls who voluntarily associated in their congregations. Denominational affiliation became less significant as Protestant seekers often cycled through several in their lifelong quests for spiritual truth. A Kentucky preacher declared that at the Last Judgment, the great question "will not be, Were you a Presbyterian—a Seceder—a Covenanter—a Baptist—or a Methodist; but, Did you experience the new birth? Did you accept of Christ and his salvation as set forth in the gospel?"[42]

Protestant theology shifted with the more egalitarian times. During the colonial era, almost all Protestant churches clung to Calvinist doctrines, which emphasized inherent human depravity and utter dependence on divine grace for salvation. The postwar competition for believers led most denominations instead to emphasize individual free will in seeking and gaining salvation. Instead of dwelling on God the all-powerful father, preachers emphasized the mix of the human and divine in Jesus. Under the pressure of competition, most mainstream churches—Presbyterian, Congregationalist, and Lutheran—adopted the new emphasis on outreach, free will, and your own personal Jesus. They founded missionary organizations to compete for believers in the West, where the nation's future emerged through expansion.[43]

American Protestants also adopted a more optimistic reading of the Millennium predicted by the Book of Revelation. Traditional belief held that an apocalyptic conflagration would devastate the earth *before* Christ returned to govern the worthy survivors. During the mid-eighteenth century, the American theologian Jonathan Edwards countered that Christ would return *after* believers established a thousand years of utopian and universal Christianity on earth. To advance the Millennium, Protestants promoted missions throughout the country and around the globe. The violet upheavals and political transformations wrought by the revolution and western expansion seemed so far beyond past experience that Americans readily believed that they lived on the verge of a new heaven on earth.[44]

Visitors from Europe marveled that America's many denominations and lack of a church establishment led to a broader and more intense interest in Christianity. A higher proportion of Americans attended church and adhered to religious values than in any other country of Christendom. Most American households owned a Bible—in stark contrast to Europe. The number of clergymen grew from about 1,800 in 1775 to nearly 40,000 by 1845. That rate of growth exceeded even the impressive increase in population, raising the ratio of minister to people from 1 per 1,500 in 1775 to 1 per 500 in 1845.[45]

After 1800, most Americans regarded republicanism and Protestantism as mutually reinforcing, for both preached individual choice and encouraged voluntary association. In 1833, a Supreme Court justice celebrated Protestant Christianity as "the religion of liberty." Alexis de Tocqueville noted, "The Americans combine the notions of Christianity and of liberty so intimately in their minds that it is impossible to make them conceive of the one without the other." American politicians had to make a show of their religiosity or suffer at the polls. Despite differences and competition, most Protestants believed that the United States had a divine, and perhaps millennial, purpose, advanced by the revolution.[46]

In 1822, the increased blurring of civic life and religion alarmed Jefferson as a betrayal of the separation of church and state that he had championed. He worried, "The atmosphere of our country is unquestionably charged with a threatening cloud of fanaticism." By shattering religious establishments, he had sought the triumph of secular thinking. Instead, disestablishment created space for an increasingly evangelical public culture. Jefferson blamed pious women: "In our Richmond there is much fanaticism, but chiefly among the women: they have their night meetings, and praying-parties, where attended by their priests, and sometimes a hen-pecked husband, they pour forth the effusions of their love to Jesus in terms as amatory and carnal as their modesty would permit them to use to a more earthly lover." Nothing could irritate Jefferson more than the rising combination of female influence with religious fervor.[47]

Mothers

In March 1776, Abigail Adams wrote to urge her husband John and his fellow congressmen to "remember the ladies" by writing new laws to protect them from abusive husbands: "Remember all Men would be Tyrants if they could. Why then, not put it out of the power of the vicious and lawless to use us with cruelty and indignity with impunity[?]" She did not ask for women's political equality but merely sought to modify the law of coverture to protect them from violence. Still, John would not take her request seriously. Responding with a joke, he insisted that men were "In Practice" already "the subjects" of women; "We have only the Name of Masters." Although Abigail and

"Abigail Adams," engraving by Johnson, Wilson & Co. after an original portrait by Gilbert Stuart. Courtesy of the Library of Congress. (LC-USZ62-10016).

John enjoyed a mutually supportive and respectful marriage, he would not consider extending republican equality to women.[48]

During the war, women contributed mightily to the Patriot cause by sustaining farms and shops and families. They also took a new interest in political debates. Some men applauded women for becoming, in the words of Benjamin Rush, "principals in the glorious American con-

wartime empowers women

troversy." But many more men felt uneasy with women claiming even the slightest political relevance.[49]

After the war, as the British danger receded, men sought to restore traditional limits on women as domestic creatures. Jefferson insisted that women should be "too wise to wrinkle their foreheads with politics" and instead should "soothe and calm the minds of their husbands returning ruffled from political debate." Jefferson rejected appointing any woman to political office as "an innovation for which the public is not prepared, nor am I." In New England, a lawyer declared, "A woman in politics is like a monkey in a toy shop. She can do no good, and may do harm." [50]   *separate spheres*

Patriots drew a sharp line between public manhood and female domesticity. Republicanism emphasized the masculinity of the citizen, imagined as willing and able to bear arms in defense of his liberty and the common good. "Effeminate" was the worst insult that a Patriot could hurl at a rival or enemy. This republican formula treated women's active participation in the revolution as valuable but ephemeral—and unnatural in peacetime.[51]

Many women resented a forced retreat into domestic silence on politics. In 1782, Eliza Wilkinson complained, "The men say we have no business with [politics], it is not our sphere! . . . They won't even allow us the liberty of thought, and that is all I want. . . . Surely we may have sense enough to give our opinions to commend or discommend such actions as we may approve or disapprove, without being reminded of our spinning and household affairs as the only matters we are capable of thinking or speaking of with justness and propriety." Abigail Adams agreed: "If a woman does not hold the Reigns of Government, I see no reason for her not judging how they are conducted." After managing and defending family farms during the war, many women rejected traditional beliefs in feminine weakness and incapacity.[52]

Slighting women's contributions to victory, men took all the credit for fighting a war to protect allegedly timid and helpless women. In 1785, a New Jersey widow, Rachel Wells, protested when the state government ignored her petition for financial redress. She reasoned,

"I have Don as much to Carrey on the war as meney that Sett Now at ye healm of government & No Notice [is] taken of me. . . . Now gentlemen is this Liberty?" Another widow, Mary Willing Byrd of Virginia, invoked Patriot principles to demand her political rights as a property owner: "I have paid my taxes and have not been Personally, or Virtually represented."[53]

Patriot leaders balked at treating married women as independent political actors with property rights. This reluctance afflicted wives who remained at home as Patriots while their husbands fled as Loyalists. To punish the men, Patriots ousted wives and confiscated their homes. Despite her bitter protests, Grace Growden Galloway lost her own inherited property, including a mansion, because of her husband Joseph's Loyalism. Citing the law of coverture, the Pennsylvania state government denied that she could own any property. But she preferred to remain poor in Philadelphia rather than join her exiled husband, whom she blamed even more than the Patriot regime.[54]

In only one state, New Jersey, did some women gain the right to vote. In 1776, the state constitution neglected to specify citizenship as male, instead defining voters as "all free inhabitants" who met property and residence requirements—which qualified widows and spinsters (but not married women). Some eligible women exploited that oversight to vote during the 1780s, which led the New Jersey legislature explicitly to accept the practice in a 1790 election law that referred to a voter as "he or she." During the 1790s, most widows preferred Federalist candidates rather than Republicans, who favored expanding rights for common white men while limiting those of women. In 1807, Republicans captured control of the state legislature and rewrote the election law to exclude women while also reducing the property requirement for white men to vote.[55]

Although barred from the formal politics of elections and legislatures, women claimed a larger place in the informal politics of the "civil sphere": the growing realm of conversation, publication, and voluntary societies. Many newspaper and magazine writers sought to improve the status of women. Judith Sargent Murray, the wife of a Massachusetts clergyman, wrote, "I expect to see our young women forming a new era in female history."[56]

Patriots believed that no republic could survive if its citizens lost their virtue: which meant a selfless devotion to the public good. "Virtue, Virtue alone . . . is the basis of a republic," Rush declared. Well-educated mothers and wives would inspire their sons and husbands to cherish and practice virtue. In 1795, a college commencement speaker declared, "Yes, ye fair, the reformation of a world is in your power. . . . Contemplate the rising glory of confederated America. Consider that your exertions can best secure, increase, and perpetuate it. The solidity and stability of the liberties of your country rest with you, since Liberty is never sure, till Virtue reigns triumphant." Women could not govern, but they could shape the men who did. Murray concluded that God had "assigned [to women] the care of making the first impressions on the infant minds of the whole human race, a trust of more importance than the government of provinces, and the marshalling of armies."[57]

Women could and should also serve as moral regulators in a republican society, shunning and disgracing men and women who lacked virtue. As a potential wife, a virtuous young woman could, a young man insisted, "mold the taste, the manners, and the conduct of her admirers, according to her pleasure." He concluded, "By the judicious management of this noble passion, [love,] a passion with which the truly accomplished of the fair sex never fail of inspiring men, what almost miraculous reformations may be brought about?" No longer regarded as the temptress Eve, who corrupted men, the republican woman upheld the moral values needed to sustain the republic. But such "republican mothers" and "republican wives" also reaffirmed the household as their proper place. "To delight, to civilize, and to ameliorate mankind . . . *these are the precious rights of women,*" declared one South Carolinian. In the process, reformers forgot all the pushy women who had helped the revolution as rioters, camp women, and farm managers.[58]

To realize their potential as regulators of values, women needed better education. A traditional education for genteel women had empha-

sized social skills: penmanship, dancing, piano playing, and fine nee-
dlework. Reformers insisted that genteel girls should also learn English
composition, history, geography, mathematics, and some political philosophy. Reformers organized new private schools, beginning in 1787
with the Philadelphia Young Ladies Academy. Similar academies sprang
up throughout the northern states as genteel society came to expect
women to obtain a broader education, which had a trickle-down effect
as many towns began to employ single women as grammar school
teachers.[59]

Reformers refuted critics who insisted that education would
"unsex" women, rendering them manly and repellent. The artist John
Trumbull asserted,

> *And why should girls be learn[e]d or wise,*
> *Books only serve to spoil their eyes.*
> *The studious eye but faintly twinkles*
> *And reading paves the way to wrinkles.*

Reformers replied that young women could display their new learning modestly as another feminine adornment rather than as a challenge to male dominance. In Philadelphia, a male educator insisted
that his female students would "be formed to the habits of obedience,
and a placid, graceful attention to whatever duty they may be concerned in."[60]

The idealized republican woman was an active, equal partner in
marriage but devoted to household affairs. Reform-minded women
imagined their sphere as distinct but equal in value to the more public
world of men. Abigail Adams concluded, "I will never consent to have
our sex considered in an inferiour point of light. Let each planet shine
in their own orbit, God and nature design[e]d it so—if man is Lord,
woman is *Lordess*—that is what I contend for." While claiming greater
respect for women, the concept of the republican mother and wife ultimately reinforced their restriction to domestic roles as helpmeets to
men and bearers of children.[61]

A provocative book by an English radical, Mary Wollstonecraft, went a step too far for most American women. Published in 1792, *A Vindication of the Rights of Women* insisted that women warranted complete equality, including the options to pursue careers and dispense with marriage. Few American readers, however, could get past Wollstonecraft's immoral reputation, for she had twice become pregnant out of wedlock before her early death. A prudish critic denounced her as a "whore whose vices and follies had brought about her providential end." Conservatives regarded Wollstonecraft's downfall as proof that women should cling to the traditional roles of wife and mother. In the postwar generation, the culture reaffirmed that women belonged in the home while giving greater credit to that domestic role as essential to the republic's survival.[62]

Affections

American families felt the impact of a revolution fought for liberty and against tyranny. Republicanism opened all forms of social inequality and domination to criticism in the name of individual rights. More young people had sex before marriage in defiance of their parents. Growing steadily during the eighteenth century, premarital pregnancy peaked during the revolutionary generation at a third of brides. Throwing up their hands, magistrates stopped the traditional prosecutions of young people for fornication. Instead, new mothers sued presumed fathers for support if they had not married yet.[63]

Seeking more "companionate marriages," Americans spoke of "affection" as the proper bond between equals, for people as well as states in the union. Rejecting the overt hierarchy of traditional, patriarchal families, many younger men and women cultivated a greater mutuality within their household relationships. "Mutual esteem, mutual friendship, mutual confidence" and "mutual forbearance" characterized the ideal marriage for Judith Sargent Murray. Most parents allowed daughters to decide on their marital partner: a decision previously shaped by colonial fathers. Through the rhythm method and extended breast-feeding of a current child, many younger couples had

"Barroom Dancing," engraving by John Lewis Krimmel, c. 1820. An African-American fiddler provides the tune for a young couple dancing in a country tavern. Note the picture honoring George Washington over the mantle and the flintlock musket hanging above the door. Courtesy of the Library of Congress (LC-DIG-ppmsca-22808).

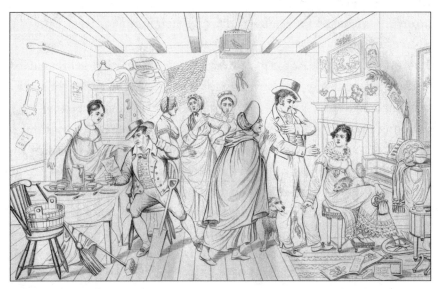

"Return from a Boarding School," engraving by John Lewis Krimmel, from the Analectic Magazine (November 1802). In this satirical engraving, the artist depicts a fashionable and haughty daughter on the far right. She has returned home with the trappings of gentility including a piano and a lap-dog. She spurns her rustic family while her farmer-father (note the shovel) grapples with the bill to pay for it all. Courtesy of the American Antiquarian Society.

fewer pregnancies, reducing the size of their families. Most states also made it easier for women to seek divorces if abandoned or brutalized by their husbands. More couples simply and cheaply "self-divorced" as one bolted from the other to seek happiness outside of marriage. In one of many elopement notices published by jilted men, a Virginian advertised, "Whereas, my wife Annie Dixon has revolted from my bed, and refuses copulation . . . I will not pay any of the debts she contracts."[64]

Cultural republicans substituted consensual marriage for patriarchy as the model for political life. They sought to assure harmony within the family as the foundation of society. Because harmony trumped all, reformers insisted that when a clash did ensue, the wife had to defer to her husband. By law, he still controlled the family's property, but his good standing in society came to depend on treating his wife with some respect, affection, and forbearance. A New England minister insisted that "it was not the design of his great Creator, that he should exercise a tyrannical control, over his female companion; but treat her on the principle of equality, as a joint associate in the common scenes of life." Because deemed radically different in their natures, a man and woman comprised two equal halves of their fulfillment as a united, marital being.[65]

Popular novels featured plots driven by deceptive rakes who seduced and ruined naïve women, who lapsed into prostitution and early deaths in wretched taverns. The novels warned young women to preserve their virginity until they married an upstanding man. Regarded as naturally chaste and virtuous, women were supposed to enforce morality on men. Although overtly moralistic, the novels were so lively and popular that traditionalists detected a dangerous indulgence of the imagination. Novels also enabled individuals to withdraw into private thought, which seemed to subvert the dedication to serving others expected of women. Such conservative denunciations merely increased the popularity of seduction novels with young readers, who cherished the new individualism.[66]

By no means did all families adopt the more egalitarian style. Rural folk often retained traditional families headed by stern patriarchs. In

1788, an elderly New Hampshire man visited New York City and blanched upon meeting fashionable families: "Fathers, mothers, sons & daughters, young & old, all mix together, & talk & joke alike so that you cannot discover any . . . respect shewn to one more than to another. I am not for keeping up a great distance between Parents & Children, but there is a difference between staring & stark mad." Writing to his son in 1799, John Adams blamed America's political turmoil on "a systematical dissolution of the true Family Authority. There can never be any regular Government of a Nation without a marked Subordination of Mothers and Children to the Father." Tellingly, Adams suddenly remembered his forceful wife and urged his son to keep his patriarchal sentiments "a Secret," for their revelation would "infallibly raise a Rebellion against me."[67]

Rather than moving forward in one cultural wave, families became more diverse in their cultural styles in the wake of the revolution. The midwife Martha Moore Ballard grew up in late colonial New England, where she learned to cherish social harmony, deference, and mutual help, so she felt uneasy with the new, more individualistic culture and society promoted by the revolution. She despaired when her aggressive son produced a premarital pregnancy and then took over his mother's house, shunting her to the margins.[68]

In upstate New York, Stephen Arnold taught school and resented his increasingly defiant students. In January 1805, he took out his rage on his six-year-old ward, beating her with a bundle of switches when she failed to produce a word correctly. Four days later, she died of her wounds. Arnold explained "that he wished he was like the old country people, that he could whip her to death; meaning . . . that he wished he possessed a hard heart." But he ran afoul of new ideas of child-rearing, which favored nurturing rather than punishment. His trial for murder attracted great interest because of the new uncertainty about the proper treatment of children by their parents. A jury convicted and the judge sentenced Arnold to death. Initially, the public regarded him as a monster who deserved to die as painfully as possible. But while awaiting execution, Arnold showed such wretched remorse that he attracted growing sympathy. As his pain and suffering became more compelling, his victim's death receded in the public mind. By displaying the sensibility to suffering celebrated by the new culture, he inspired petitions for commuting his execution. At the last minute, with the noose around Arnold's neck, the sheriff produced a commutation from the governor, sending the culprit away to state prison for life. Such long-term incarceration, in lieu of whipping or execution, marked another cultural development of the early republic.[69]

Slaves

In colonial America, slavery was legal, profitable, and accepted throughout British North America, but the enslaved were unevenly distributed, comprising 40 percent of the southern and just 4 percent of the northern population. Aside from Quakers, who rejected slavery as a sin, almost all colonists had regarded human bondage as natural and immutable. In the traditional society of British America, slavery was but the lowest rung in a social hierarchy of dependency, below white indentured servants, tenant farmers, women and children, and wage laborers.[70]

During the 1760s, however, Patriots justified resisting Parliament's taxes by speaking of universal rights and human equality. That libertarian rhetoric exposed Patriot slaveholders to British charges of hypocrisy. Some northern blacks played on that sensitivity in petitions that appropriated Patriot rhetoric to assert their own "Natural and Unalienable Right to that freedom which the Gr[e]at Parent of the Unavers hath Bestowed equally on all menkind." Blacks also exploited the wartime upheaval to run away by the thousands either to join the British or to pass as free in a new state. Hundreds became free, particularly in the north, by serving honorably in the Continental Army.[71]

Many Patriots recognized the gap between their soaring ideals and the sordid practice of slavery. Abigail Adams assured John: "It allways appeared a most iniquitous Scheme to me [to] fight ourselfs for what we

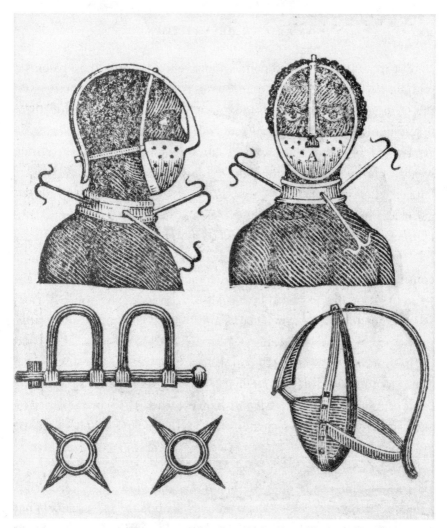

"Iron Mask, Collar, Leg Shackles and Spurs Used to Restrict Slaves," by an unknown engraver, published in Thomas Branagan, The Penitential Tyrant *(New York: Samuel Wood, 1807). This engraving seeks to convey the horrors of plantation slavery to northern readers. Overseers used such devices to punish slaves who had resisted or tried to escape. Courtesy of the Library of Congress (LC-USZ62-31864).*

are daily robbing and plundering from those who have as good right to freedom as we have." A Virginia judge, St. George Tucker, noted that Americans "were imposing upon our fellow men, who differ in complexion from us, a *slavery* ten thousand times more cruel than the utmost extremity of those grievances and oppressions, of which we complained. . . . Should we not have loosed their chains, and broken their fetters?"[72]

But it was far easier to condemn slavery in words than to end it with deeds. Slavery had become woven into the fabric of society and the economy. Slaves comprised so much property that freeing them would bankrupt many masters and ruin their creditors. Political leaders balked at losing the enslaved labor that underwrote their own wealth, high social standing, and the leisure time to read and write. Patrick Henry conceded that slavery was "as repugnant to humanity as it is inconsistent with the bible, and destructive to liberty." But Henry never freed his slaves due to "the general inconvenience of living without them." John Jay headed New York's antislavery society, but he continued to buy slaves and freed them only once he felt fully compensated by years of their hard labor. Although George Mason criticized slavery, he clung to his own slaves and, with consummate insensitivity, named one of them "Liberty."[73]

Patriots liked to believe that slavery was doomed by improving public opinion and declining economic prospects. That self-serving optimism encouraged passive patience rather than prompt action against slavery. In 1774, Benjamin Rush had predicted, "There will be not a Negro slave in North America in 40 years." Two years later he bought his first slave.[74] expansion continues it

As a complex and contradictory movement, the revolution generated proslavery as well as antislavery arguments. Abolitionists insisted on inalienable freedom and natural equality, but conservatives regarded private property rights as essential to liberty. During the mid-1780s, hundreds of Virginians petitioned their legislature against a gradual emancipation proposal as a threat to *their* liberty: "We risked our Lives and Fortunes, and waded through Seas of Blood" to fight a revolution meant to safeguard private property. They denounced abolitionists as covert Loyalists bent on destroying the republic: an equation promoted by the wartime alliance of runaways with British forces.[75]

Crediting white men with courage in defeating British "slavery," Patriots derided their slaves as cowards dishonored for failing to win freedom. Although masters ruthlessly suppressed slave resistance, they depicted the enslaved as too passive to qualify for freedom. By denouncing slavery as degrading, republicanism could deny that the enslaved had the virtue to deserve freedom. During the 1790s, a French visitor noted that "the American people, so excited about their own liberty, don't consider the liberty of others." He concluded that the revolution had increased their contempt for the enslaved: "Doesn't this imply that it would have been better for the people in slavery if liberty had never been mentioned?" Jefferson agreed that southerners were "zealous for their own liberties, but trampling on those of others." Whites especially cherished their own freedom because they denied it to the enslaved.[76] *more grateful for what they have*

Gradualism

Southern strength in the union prevented emancipation at the federal level, obliging reformers to act through state governments. Abolition was possible in northern states, where relatively few voters owned any slaves. But they would support emancipation only if it cost them little or nothing in taxes. In 1777, the independent republic of Vermont had few slaves and adopted a constitution that promised to free females at age eighteen and males at twenty-one. But legal loopholes preserved bondage for some until an 1806 law produced true emancipation.[77]

During the early 1780s, some Massachusetts slaves sued for their freedom, citing the Massachusetts bill of rights, which declared, "All men are born free and equal." In 1781, Elizabeth, a forty-year-old widow of a Continental soldier, ran away from an abusive master, assumed the last name of "Freeman," and persuaded the lawyer Theodore Sedgwick to take her case. Freeman learned of her opportunity "by keeping still and minding things. . . . When she was waiting at table, she heard gentlemen talking over the [state's] Bill of Rights." A county court recognized her freedom and ordered her former master to pay her damages and court costs. Freeman later explained, "Any time while I was a slave, if one minute's freedom had been offered to me, and I had been told I must die at the end of that minute, I would have taken it—just to stand one minute on God's airth a free woman—I would."[78]

In 1783, an enslaved Bostonian, Quok Walker, sued his master for false imprisonment, citing the state's constitution, and the Massachusetts Supreme Judicial Court agreed. The judges ratified a wartime shift in public opinion against slavery. During the war years, the inheritance of slaves and pursuit of runaways had dwindled for want of popular support in Massachusetts. After the ruling, the enslaved in that state could leave masters, for no positive law obliged their return. During the late 1780s, New Hampshire's leaders began to act as if their state constitution also precluded slavery although they lacked any explicit court decision to that effect.[79]

Most northern states gradually emancipated their slaves through laws designed to soften the blow for masters. In 1780, Pennsylvania's legislature declared slavery "disgraceful to any people, and more especially to those who have been contending in the great cause of liberty themselves." But the law freed no slaves then alive, only those born after the law and only once they turned twenty-eight years old. No slave, if properly registered by a master, could become free until 1808. A slave born a day before the act remained enslaved for life. Pennsylvania still had some elderly slaves until 1847, when the state finally and fully abolished the system. Rhode Island (1784), Connecticut (1784), New York (1799), and New Jersey (1804) adopted similar gradual emancipation laws but reduced the age of freedom to twenty-five years for those born after the act became law.[80]

The laws sought primarily (and very gradually) to free northern states of slavery, rather than to ensure freedom for the enslaved. Lawmakers meant to save taxpayers from having to compensate masters for their lost property. Instead, young slaves would pay for their eventual freedom by working without compensation into their mid-twenties. Economic historians calculate that this young labor recouped to masters 95 percent of the slaves' market value. A disappointed Quaker remarked, "If we keep our present slaves in bondage, and only enact laws that their posterity shall be free, we save that part of our tyranny and gain of oppression, which to us [of] the present generation, is of the most value."[81]

Northern legislators acted more from a distaste for slavery than from empathy for the enslaved. Legal loopholes often enabled masters to sell slaves to southern buyers before freedom claimed them. Many blacks also remained trapped in slavery because the laws lacked penalties for violators or resources for enforcement.[82]

Ultimately, the pace of emancipation depended on local opinion. In communities that resented emancipation, masters could, with impunity, keep slaves beyond the legal age limit or sell them away. Where the local majority despised slaveholders, however, masters had to follow the letter of the law or risk ostracism and lawsuits. Emancipation proceeded most rapidly and completely in places, such as Philadelphia, with many Quakers. The laws did give the enslaved a bit of leverage to pressure their masters to negotiate the sale of freedom. John Adams noted that a longing for freedom "filled the Negro[e]s with Discontent, [and] made them lazy, idle, proud, vicious, and at length wholly Useless to their Masters." Weary masters then offered freedom ahead of schedule for a price paid by the slaves from wages made by hiring out. As a Pennsylvania legislator, Charles Willson Peale voted for gradual emancipation, but he refused to free his own slaves until they bought their freedom from him. He sent one woman into the streets to beg for money.[83]

The slow pace of black emancipation stood in marked contrast to the rapid decline of indentured servitude for white people. Common in the colonial era for immigrant laborers, servitude withered during the revolution. By enlisting in Patriot forces, young men could shake off their indentures. The importation of servants lapsed during the war and barely resumed after the peace. In 1784, New York reformers subscribed to liberate newly arrived servants, deeming that status "contrary to . . . the idea of liberty this country has so happily established." With a growing pool of free laborers, thanks to migration from the countryside and Europe, urban employers found wage labor cheaper and less trouble than buying and guarding a servant. Indeed, bosses could discharge redundant workers, without further cost, when business declined in the winter or during a trade recession. While white labor became free, indentured servitude for blacks surged as a halfway status to freedom allowed by masters. After the revolution, citizens rejected servitude as unseemly for fellow whites but clung to it as still appropriate for blacks.[84]

In the northern states, gradual emancipation laws increased the free black population from fewer than 1,000 in 1775 to nearly 50,000 in 1810. But the northern states still had 27,000 slaves that year because the gradual process of emancipation remained incomplete. The freed tended to gravitate from the countryside into the cities, where they found greater comfort and safety in numbers. By 1810, nearly a third of New York State's blacks lived in New York City, and two-fifths of black Pennsylvanians resided in Philadelphia. By providing growing numbers for runaways to hide in, black neighborhoods pressured northern masters to sell early freedom to their remaining slaves. In the greatest boon of freedom, by 1820 most northern black couples could live together and keep their children.[85]

Northern racism intensified as the free black population grew. Tocqueville noted, "The prejudice of race appears to be stronger in the states that have abolished slavery than in those where it still exists." Few blacks could vote or serve on juries, and none held political office. In 1821, New York State abolished the property requirement for white voters but kept it for African Americans, so that only sixteen qualified.[86]

Denied access to education and better-paying jobs, most blacks had to labor as sailors, menial workers, domestic servants, and laundresses. A young black man despaired, "Shall I be a mechanic? No one will employ me; white boys won't work with me. Shall I be a merchant? No one will have me in his office; white clerks won't associate with me. Drudgery and servitude, then, are my prospective portion." Kept at the bottom of society, most free blacks lived from day to day on pittances and without real estate or long-term security. Despite discrimination, a small middle class did develop as some artisans and shopkeepers prospered.[87]

Feeling more uncomfortable with free blacks than with slaves, whites pressured the freed to cluster in the poorest neighborhoods. A traveler reported that, in Philadelphia, any black who ventured into a white neighborhood in winter "is sure to be showered with snowballs by white children." A black preacher ridiculed the increased prejudice against a black man once freed: "He magnifies to a monster of wonderful dimensions, so large that they cannot be made to believe that he is man and a brother." Slaves could join their masters in genteel parlors and public conveyances, but free blacks faced exclusion. Even the antislavery societies of New York and Pennsylvania barred blacks from joining. Prior to 1820, northern magistrates and lawmakers also did little to protect the newly freed from kidnappers who hauled them south for sale.[88]

Claiming exclusive right to the revolution, white toughs drove blacks from public celebrations of the Fourth of July in northern cities. A black activist, Prince Hall, complained that his people had to "bear up under the daily insults we meet on the streets of Boston," and during public holidays "you may truly be said to carry your lives in your hands" when even "helpless old women have their clothes torn off their backs." He noted the irony that southern slaves could gather on Sundays "without molestation."[89]

Black activists created their own urban institutions of mutual support. In Boston, Hall organized a Masonic lodge, which provided members with social security and a sense of community. In Delaware, Richard Allen bought his freedom with wages earned as a sawyer, shoemaker, and wagon driver. A Methodist, he became a spell-binding preacher and moved to Philadelphia, where he also worked as a chimney sweep, founded a black mutual aid association, and published religious tracts. Angered by disrespect from white Methodists, Allen left them to found a thriving black Methodist church.[90]

Black Christians and Masons claimed moral superiority over whites who indulged in the sins of slavery, greed, and hypocrisy. Hall sought to eliminate the "weeds of pride, envy, tyranny, and scorn in this garden of peace, liberty, and equality." Black associations and churches organized petitions and protests against racial discrimination and defended their community against kidnappers. Black churches also provided decent burying grounds for corpses excluded from the cemeteries controlled by whites. <u>Racists resented the pious and respectable blacks, who defied the stereotypes made for them.</u> In Philadelphia a white Methodist complained, "Their aspirings and little vanities have been rapidly growing since they got those separate churches. . . . Thirty to forty years ago, they were much humbler."[91]

Manumissions

Ninety-five percent of American slaves lived in the southern states, where they were essential to profits and property values. Southern whites also clung to slavery because they dreaded living beside thousands of newly freed blacks, people deemed more dangerous than slaves. No southern state legislature adopted gradual emancipation. In 1783, a Virginia legislator proposed such a law, but it failed, to his uncle's delight: "As to your bill for emancipating the slaves, I think it met with a very good fate for we might as well let loose a parcel of Indians or lions, as to let our slaves free without they could be sent from the country." St. George Tucker noted, "Every white man felt himself born to tyrannize, where the blacks were regarded as of no more importance than the brute cattle" and "where every species of degradation towards them was exercised on all occasions."[92]

In 1782, the Virginia legislature did liberalize the legal process of "manumission" by which an individual master could free slaves by a will or deed. The colonial regime had discouraged manumission by requiring legislative approval, which was rarely granted. Patriots, however, insisted that an individual should have the right to dispose of his property freely. But no indebted master could manumit without the consent of creditors, who balked at losing security. Masters with debts and few scruples sold their surplus slaves; only the unusually solvent and principled would manumit them. The manumitters included Washington, who freed his slaves in a last will and testament. Most manumitters, however, were Quakers or evangelicals with religious scruples.[93]

Because most masters clung to slavery, manumitters faced social pressure from their agitated peers, who insisted that freed blacks encouraged slaves to resent and resist continued bondage. An angry neighbor rebuked one manumitter: "It appears to me (witnessing the consequences) that a man has almost as good a right to set fire to his own building, though his neighbor's is to be destroyed by it, as to free his slaves." In 1790, another manumitter, Robert Pleasants, complained that his irritated neighbors had "beat [the freedmen] without cause, and killed & destroyed their Hogs & other property." Then the county court fined Pleasants for allowing "his Negroes to go at large."[94]

Most southern whites insisted that free blacks led depraved lives of vicious larceny and drunken indolence: lounging in their cabins when not preying on the poultry, pigs, orchards, and gardens of their white neighbors. White men also suspected freed blacks of harboring runaways and fencing goods stolen by slaves. Worst of all, free blacks might threaten the slave system by leading a revolt. By dreading the freed as active subversives, Virginians contradicted the stereotype of them as sluggish loungers. But whether seen as lazy, thieving, or scheming, free blacks were cast as proof that emancipation was dangerous to whites.[95]

To reduce their supposed danger, southerners restricted the rights of the freed, who could not vote, serve on juries, or join the militia and could only own a gun with permission from a county court. The freed also had to register with the court and obtain a certificate to display to any suspicious magistrate or slave patroller. No colored person could testify against a white who cheated or struck him or her. When a free black man, Christopher McPherson, founded a school in Richmond, the local authorities drove his teacher from town and confined McPherson in a lunatic asylum. In effect, whites insisted that anyone who set up a school for black children must be crazy. Despite this discrimination, freed people did make important gains: the right to work for wages without corporal punishment or being sold away.[96]

Delaware and Maryland also adopted manumission laws in 1787 and 1790, but the other southern states balked. The postrevolutionary manumissions modestly increased the free black population in Virginia from 2,000 in 1782 (1 percent of all black people) to 20,000 (7 percent) in 1810. Maryland's free black population grew from 4 percent of blacks in 1755 to 20 percent in 1810.[97]

During the mid-1780s, the Virginia legislature rejected a Methodist push for gradual emancipation. Discouraged by this defeat, Methodists and other evangelicals retreated from antislavery activity and allowed church members to keep slaves. In 1798, the Methodist leader Francis Asbury, a former champion of abolition, reported: "I am brought to conclude [that] slavery will exist in Virginia perhaps for ages; there is not a sufficient sense of religion nor of liberty to destroy it." Preferring neighborhood peace and acceptance, southern evangelicals marginalized any radical preachers who continued to agitate for emancipation. Seeking respectability, southern evangelicals reframed their message, urging slaves to obey their masters and wait for freedom and equality in heaven.[98]

To slow growth in the freed population, in 1806 the Virginia legislature discouraged further manumissions. A rare liberal, John Minor, lamented, "In past days these walls have rung with eulogies on liberty. A comparison between those times and the present is degrading to us. We may be equal in intelligence and virtue, but not in the love of liberty." A hard-liner replied, "Tell us not of principles. Those principles have been annihilated by the existence of slavery among us." Under the 1806 revision, masters could still manumit, but the freed had to leave the state within one year or face renewed slavery. Along with a decisive shift in public opinion, the revised law stemmed manumissions in Virginia.[99]

Movement

In Virginia, Patriot reformers promoted greater equality among white men by revising inheritance laws. They doubted that the republic could survive if inequality increased between rich and poor white men. Reformers worried that inherited wealth would consolidate an aristocracy hostile to republican government. Jefferson assured Madison, "I am conscious that an equal division of property is impracticable. But the consequences of this enormous inequality producing so much misery to the bulk of mankind, legislators cannot invent too many devices for subdividing property."[100]

Jefferson and Madison challenged Virginia's colonial laws of "entail and primogeniture," which had enabled a great landowner to bind his heirs never to subdivide or alienate any part of a plantation (including its slaves). Aristocratic in design, entail and primogeniture preserved great estates through the generations at the expense of all the children save the first-born son. Reformers denounced the colonial inheritance laws as the tyranny of a past generation overriding the rights of the living to buy and sell land and slaves as they wished.[101]

The Virginia legislature abolished entails in 1776 and primogeniture in 1785. In 1796, the legislators also eliminated entails on slaves. The reforms empowered entrepreneurial planters to sell surplus lands or borrow against their estates for capital improvements. For example, Jefferson sold his wife's entailed property for the cash needed to rebuild Monticello and expand his wheat fields. While benefiting planters and younger heirs, the reforms afflicted the enslaved. The subdivision of large estates and sales of human chattel by indebted heirs divided enslaved families and ruptured their communities.[102]

By rationalizing their estates, postwar planters sought higher labor productivity and profits, which led them to sell many enslaved children as surplus. That profitable surplus grew as many Virginia and Maryland planters converted their fields to growing wheat, which demanded less labor than tobacco. Planters increasingly valued slave women for their childbearing ability. Jefferson declared, "I consider a woman who brings a child every two years as more valuable than the best man of the farm. What she produces is an addition to the capital, while his labors disappear in mere consumption."[103]

The division of great estates and the growth in sale or rental of slaves increased the number of slaveholders in Virginia. A study of one county found that more than 80 percent of the farmers either owned or hired slaves. More widely distributed, the slaves lived in smaller groups.

About half belonged to farmers who owned ten or fewer. By dispersing and broadening slave ownership, the revolution enhanced popular support for slavery, contributing to the political defeat suffered by Methodist abolitionists during the mid-1780s.[104]

The postrevolutionary era increased the long-distance movement of slaves to frontier districts, where they suffered from harsher conditions. Between 1790 and 1810, about 225,000 whites migrated from the Chesapeake region to points farther south and west. They took along 98,000 slaves, who bore the hardest labor of clearing and cultivating land, usually in summer climes even hotter than they had endured in Virginia. A departing master compelled his slaves to forsake their wives, husbands, parents, and children who belonged to other masters. Francis Fedric remembered "the heart-rending scenes" when his master prepared to move west to Kentucky: "Men and women [were] down on their knees begging to be purchased to go with their wives or husbands . . . children crying and imploring not to have their parents sent away from them; but all their beseeching and tears were of no avail."[105]

Chesapeake masters also sold more slaves to long-distance traders who served the voracious demand for slaves in the Lower South as cotton cultivation expanded. In the colonial era, Virginians sold few slaves beyond their colony. Between 1790 and 1810, however, at least 100,000 slaves moved south and west after sale from Virginia. In 1803, a male field hand sold for about $600 in South Carolina compared to $400 in Virginia: a $200 difference enticing to Virginia sellers and Carolina slave traders.[106]

Inheritance, rentals, interstate movement, and long-distance sales separated children from parents and husbands from wives. A former Virginia slave, William Grimes, recalled, "It is not uncommon to hear mothers say, that they have half a dozen children, but the Lord only knows where they are." He spoke from experience. Grimes was only ten when sold away to a distant master: "It grieved me to see my mother's tears at our separation. I was a heart-broken child . . . but I was compelled to go and leave her." One historian calculates that forced migration and the domestic slave trade "destroyed about one-third of all first slave marriages in the Upper South" prior to 1840.[107]

The revolution enhanced the opportunities for common whites *expansion* to buy or rent slaves and to move west to make new farms. But the enslaved suffered from the more commercial society made by the revolution. As planters sought to retire debts, satisfy multiple heirs, and rationalize their estates, they treated slaves as commodities and disrupted their family ties. By 1800, in Virginia most enslaved husbands and wives lived on different farms, rendering single-parent households the rule rather than the exception. A revolution that benefited white men proved a curse for most southern blacks during the postwar generation.[108]

Cotton

A minor crop during the colonial era, cotton became profitable and widespread in the Lower South after the invention in 1793 of Eli Whitney's cotton gin: a machine to separate valuable fibers from their husks. Planters also benefited from a booming export market as Britain's cotton textile factories multiplied. South Carolina's cotton exports soared from 9,840 pounds in 1790 to 6,425,000 pounds just ten years later. By 1810, exports surged to 50 million pounds, and planters scrambled to buy more slaves from Chesapeake traders.[109]

The most genteel planters cultivated a new, ostensibly paternalistic style of mastery. Adapting to the republican order, masters no longer postured as the monarchs of little kingdoms. Instead, they posed as the fathers of plantation households, with slaves as their permanent children. Masters demanded submission in return for their alleged protection of black people, whom masters deemed incapable of freedom. Born and raised in Pennsylvania, David Ramsay moved to South Carolina, where he married into a great planter family and forsook his former antislavery views during the 1790s. Ramsay assured a northern friend, "Experience proves that they who have been born & grow up in slavery are incapable of the blessings of freedom." If a tad less bloody, the new Christian paternalism sought a more pervasive moral control over the enslaved, in their quarters as well as at work.[110]

At the first hint of resistance, these paternalists expected their overseers to practice the old brutality but less conspicuously. In barns and secluded spots, they whipped backs and inflicted "cat-hauling": dragging a cat by the tail along the bare back of a trussed-up victim. Planters reconciled the old cruelty to the new paternalism by insisting that submissive slaves warranted protection but defiant blacks reaped the brutality deserved by brutes. Christian paternalism served primarily as self-justification to repel attacks of conscience or to deflect criticism by outsiders.[111]

In the Lower South, political leaders and writers renounced the doctrines of universal natural rights and fundamental human equality associated with the revolution. Southerners claimed that they had created a republic solely for white men. In 1806 the Georgia Superior Court insisted that the state's bill of rights "was not made to establish the rights and liberties of slaves or free negroes." In 1804, a rare abolitionist in North Carolina noted: "At present the inhabitants of that state, consider the preservation of their lives, and all they hold dear on earth, as depending on the continuance of slavery; and are even riveting more firmly the fetters of oppression."[112]

Contrary to the wishful thinking of many Patriots, slavery did not wither away after the revolution. Instead, it became more powerfully entrenched in the southern states. From 700,000 in 1790, the number of enslaved doubled to 1.5 million in 1820. As foreign imports faded after 1807, natural increase accounted for most of the population growth. Between 1790 and 1860, slave traders and migrants herded over a million slaves south and west from the Chesapeake to expand southern society to the Mississippi and beyond. Highly profitable, plantation slavery helped drive the capitalist development of the nation. No aberration from the national norm of liberty, the South was an especially vibrant half of the nation, and, in politics, the more powerful half. Masters would never part with so much valuable human property without a fight.[113]

Nature

After 1790, economic growth apparently proved the superiority of America's republican institutions and values, which celebrated individual initiative in markets, elections, and churches. Americans did not invent individualism, which had a long, slow, prior development in Europe. But individualism remained confined to a literate and prosperous minority in eighteenth-century Europe. Most common Europeans remained defined by traditional corporate identities as peasants, laborers, or artisans. Postrevolutionary America was the first society premised on individualism (for and by the free). Only in the United States did most men think of themselves as lone actors making free choices that determined success or failure. And they measured success in dollars made and saved through market transactions. Nowhere else did the culture so insistently judge everyone based on his or her individual choices—in religion, politics, and economics. A successful entrepreneur declared, "Every man stands upon his own merits,—upon his own habits of industry and frugality." This cultural transformation was so sweeping and enduring that readers today have a hard time imagining a past not composed of autonomous individuals preoccupied with their selves. The primary beneficiaries of this emerging society were prosperous white men, who claimed that success proved their superior merit over all others: the poor, women, Indians, and black people.[114]

Slavery had nicely fit the colonial concept of society as a hierarchy with a monarch at the top and gradations of inequality stretching downward through the aristocracy, gentry, and middle class to laborers, servants, and slaves at the bottom. Challenging that concept, Patriots waged a revolution for equal rights and private property rights. They celebrated the "natural" as the antidote to the "artificial" social distinctions of birth that justified monarchy and aristocracy. Republicans vowed to create a society that allowed only a "natural aristocracy," of talented men, who would emerge in each generation, empowered by accomplishments rather than inheritance.[115]

The denigration of privilege opened slavery to criticism as an "artificial" inequality. Proslavery writers responded by insisting that black racial inferiority was natural and immutable. Reserving civic rights for whites, they excluded and exploited blacks as fit only for slavery. Previously underdeveloped, racial screeds became more elaborate and pseudo-scientific after the revolution. In his celebrated *Notes on the State of Virginia*, Jefferson denounced slavery as brutalizing for both master and slave, but he also argued that blacks were innately inferior to whites in their bodies and minds. Opposed to retaining black people if freed in America, Jefferson urged their deportation back to Africa. The great Patriot champion of equality drew racial limits in the name of a supposed science that grew more popular in the nineteenth century. Racism developed to protect inequality from the implications of revolution.[116]

If racial distinctions were, in fact, mandated by nature, they could not and should not be altered by legal and political action. In 1790, Congress adopted the first American naturalization law, which invited white immigrants to become citizens but barred black people. A white skin naturally qualified an immigrant for citizenship, while a dark skin posed a biological barrier. During the early nineteenth century, American citizenship became tightly associated with whiteness and masculinity, weakening the hopes of blacks and women to claim equality. By "naturalizing" the social barriers of race and gender, American leaders sought to cast them as beyond debate.[117]

But abolitionists and feminists persisted in seeking broader liberties as a better legacy for our ever-contested revolution. Later in the nineteenth century, Americans reworked the legacy of the revolution to seek different ends, including abolishing slavery and extending political rights to women and African Americans. More inclusive versions of the revolution's promise lingered in American minds until circumstances allowed them to pursue, in Abraham Lincoln's phrase, "the better angels of our nature." But no generation will ever settle the revolution once and for all. In a constant ebb and flow, we will debate and advance competing and partial versions of our contradictory revolutionary legacy.[118]

Historians debate how revolutionary the revolution was in its consequences. Some find little substantive change and focus on continuities from the colonial era. Other scholars emphasize expanding economic opportunities and increased political participation by common white men as radical consequences of the revolution. Both views convey only part of the story. The revolution intensified trends already underway, including political assertion by common men, territorial expansion at native expense, and the westward spread of slavery. Acceleration and intensification combined continuity with change.[119]

The greatest transformation came in the terms of political debate. Rather than generate clear resolutions, the revolution created powerful new contradictions. Save for Quakers, colonists had accepted slavery as timeless and immutable. The revolution encouraged more people to oppose slavery as unjust and immoral. Obliged to defend slavery, masters, in turn, created new justifications rooted in biological notions of racial inequality. Those masters also demanded clauses in the Federal Constitution, which made the union contingent upon protecting slavery in the South. In sum, the revolution generated clashing contagions, of slavery and liberty, and pitted them against one another.[120]

The revolution also spawned new contradictions over gender relations. To resist British taxes and fight British troops, Patriots needed support from women as well as men. As consumers and producers, women sustained boycotts and armies, helping to win the revolution for the Patriots. Many women became more outspoken in politics and resisted postwar pressure to resume their public silence. That tension generated a new rhetoric that celebrated women as Republican Mothers and Wives, who taught and sustained the civic values of virtuous citizens. While celebrating women, reformers urged them to remain in domestic roles, nurturing children and husbands rather than pursuing public careers. Women received no new civic rights, but they did gain the cultural ground, as Republican Mothers and Wives, to seek those rights in the next generation.[121]

Clashing definitions of who deserved freedom and equal rights became entangled in new debates and contradictions over political sovereignty. The American Revolution began as a constitutional crisis during the 1760s, when colonists discovered that they faced restrictions and taxes from a centralizing empire. After declaring independence, Patriots initially decentralized power among thirteen essentially sovereign states loosely confederated. During the 1780s, social turmoil within states, boundary disputes between them, western uncertainties, and diplomatic futility generated a countermovement by nationalists. They created a Federal Constitution that survived a bruising battle for ratification by the states. Instead of resolving questions of sovereignty, the Federal Constitution gave them a national focus, as the partisans of states' rights battled with nationalists at the new capital. Constitutional crises flared in every generation as one region or another threatened secession until those threats became real and bloody in 1860–1861.

The Civil War erupted over the terms of westward growth. As defined by the Jeffersonians, the revolution established that the federal government needed to facilitate the settler expansion that had helped to unravel the British Empire in North America. But what sort of territorial development should the nation favor: by free laborers from the north or by the mix of slave and free labor favored by southerners? As Americans dispossessed natives and Hispanics, the victors accumulated territories that invited deadly conflict over what sort of nation should triumph through expansion. The revolution validated rapid expansion but failed to settle what sort of society ultimately would take shape in the West.

In "My Kinsman, Major Molineux," Nathaniel Hawthorne recognized that the revolution changed the terms of political and social debates—rather than resolving them. At story's end, an astute gentleman promises a young man named Robin that he can rise in a revolutionary social order with its own inequalities justified in new terms as the fruits of merit and nature. Hawthorne understood the conflicting aspirations and clashing principles of the revolutionary generation. His prophetic gentleman asked Robin, "May not a man have several voices, Robin, as well as two complexions?"[122]

ACKNOWLEDGMENTS

I began this book while on the faculty at the University of California at Davis, where I benefited from support by the dean, Ron Mangun, and my chairs, Susan Mann, Ted Margadant, David Biale, and Kathy Olmsted.

In 2014, I moved to the University of Virginia, where I accumulated many new debts, particularly to the deans, Meredith Woo and Ian Baucom, and to the utterly competent chair of the history department, Paul Halliday. My scholarship has been enriched by participating in UVA's Early American Seminar, which my amigo Peter Onuf founded and which Max Edelson now conducts with great talent, verve, and humor. The Miller Center at UVA has also provided a rewarding scholarly community thanks especially to Brian Balogh, Will Hitchcock, and Mel Leffler. Chuck McCurdy and other devotees of the Wednesday night gathering at Eddie's Tavern slowed my writing but boosted morale. Playing pool with, and losing to, Gary Gallagher has not been so good for morale but has improved my character and knowledge of nineteenth-century history. I am also grateful to Gary and the fabled Aberdeen Barn for providing therapy sessions for Peter Onuf after his troubling lapses with vegetarian ravioli and spinach quiche. I also thank Grace Hale, Claudrena Herold, Ted Lendon, Christian McMillen, Elizabeth Meyer, John and Mary Miller, R. Hoke Perkins, Kristin Onuf, Elizabeth Thompson, and Elizabeth Varon for insightful advice and explanations regarding the mysteries of UVA. Monti-cello's International Center for Jefferson Studies has also provided an intellectual home thanks to the leadership and expertise of Andrew O'Shaughnessy, Christa Dierksheide, Jack Robertson, and Mary Scott-Fleming.

My delivery to Virginia was memorable thanks to the legendary "carmen," Pablo Ortiz and Christopher Reynolds, who devoted a week to driving across the continent, providing musical education, spiritual guidance, relentless bantering, and happy memories that I will always cherish. But I am grateful that I dodged Chris's insistence on going to Denny's for breakfast. Generous moral support for this celebrated trip came from Ana Peluffo, Alessa Johns, and Gabriel Johns-Reynolds. Above all, Emily Albu was relentlessly kind, generous, thoughtful, and selfless. Plus, her penmanship is flawless. Many times, she has warned that I will never amount to anything until I improve mine.

In 2012, I began writing the book at the Huntington Library thanks to a fellowship arranged by Steve Hindle and in honor of my dear friend and mentor, Robert C. Ritchie. One of the greatest honors and pleasures of my career has been to be the Ritchie Distinguished Fellow with Roy as my office neighbor. For assistance at the Huntington, I also thank Molly Gipson, Juan Gomez, Carolyn Powell, and Jaeda Snow. And I'm grateful to Peter Mancall, Lisa Bitel, Bill Deverell, Jason Sharples, Katie Paugh, and Cynthia Nazarian for many acts of friend-ship during my sojourn at the Huntington.

In the past year, I received insightful comments on several chapters from Richard D. Brown, Max Edelson, Katie Lantz, Peter Onuf, and Andrew O'Shaughnessy. Kevin R. Convey carefully reviewed all ref-erences to pirates and masculinity, subjects to which he has devoted his career, indeed his life. Matt Spooner shared access to his promising work, which greatly improved my understanding of the South during the Revolution.

At the Wylie Agency, I benefited from deft representation by Andrew Wylie and his assistants. Shepherding this book to publication depended on my editor at W. W. Norton & Company, Steve Forman, who carefully nurtured and shaped the project with enthusiasm and professionalism. His colleagues, Travis Carr and Scott Sugarman, helped with innumerable details, especially in sorting out the illustrations. For skilled and thorough copyediting, I thank Fred Wiemer. The excellent maps are the work of the talented Jeffrey L. Ward, and the author's photo is the work of the ever-fabulous Lynn Friedman.

I have primarily dedicated the book to Wyatt, who is the very best of dogs although woefully underappreciated by his masters, the Kelmans, who considered roasting him when snowed in and unable to get to a supermarket during the infamous winter of 2014–2015. But it would not look good to exclude them from the dedication after they have been the very best and most generous of friends to me. Despite Ari Kelman's phobias against adverbs and the word "the," he greatly improved this book by his close and careful reading of every chapter. Unfortunately, very few of his keen and funny comments can be repeated in public. Any persisting flaws in the book must therefore be his fault, so please send all complaints and corrections to him.

In the book's introduction, I wanted to invoke a clever observation by the historian Sarah M. S. Pearsall. When apprised of this sequel to *American Colonies*, she suggested that the title should pay homage to Bruce Willis's *Die Hard* and *Die Harder* films to become *American Revolutions: Colonize Harder*. Pearsall's wit is fitting, for *American Revolutions* interprets the revolutionary era as accelerating colonial processes of change. But Ari made me take that out, for as everyone knows, he has no sense of humor.

I have also dedicated the book to the memory of Caroline Cox, who died far too early, depriving us of her kindness, generosity, and scholarly wisdom, which so enriched the Bay Area Early American seminar. She brilliantly studied the experiences of Continental soldiers, who could also attest that the good die too young.

CHRONOLOGY

1651, Oct.: The English Parliament adopts the first set of Navigation Acts to regulate colonial trade.

1688–89: "Glorious Revolution" in England and her colonies: James II replaced as monarch by William and Mary.

1713, Apr.: Treaty of Utrecht transfers French Acadia to British rule as Nova Scotia.

1739–40: English evangelist George Whitefield tours British America, spreading the "Great Awakening."

1747, Nov.: Knowles riot in Boston over the naval impressment of colonial sailors.

1754, May: George Washington leads Virginian attack on French troops near Fort Duquesne in western Pennsylvania, sparking renewed war between Britain and France.

1754, July: Delegates from seven colonies meet at Albany to propose Benjamin Franklin's "Plan of Union" to unite the colonies more closely to Britain.

1755, July: British army of Gen. Edward Braddock routed by French and Indian force near Fort Duquesne in western Pennsylvania.

1755, Oct.: British and colonial troops expel Francophone Acadians from Nova Scotia.

1756, June: French forces capture British naval base at Minorca in the Mediterranean.

1757, June: Williams Pitt becomes prime minister in Britain.

1758, July: British forces capture the French colonial fortress at Louisbourg on Cape Breton Island.

1758, Nov.: British troops drive the French from Fort Duquesne.

1759, Sept.: British forces seize Quebec, the fortified capital of French Canada.

1760, Apr.: "Tackey's Rebellion" by slaves disrupts Jamaica.

1760, Sept.: The French governor of Canada surrenders the province to British troops.

1760, Oct.: George III becomes monarch of Great Britain.

1762, Jan.: Spain enters the war as France's ally against Britain.

1762, Aug.: British forces capture Havana, the capital of Spanish Cuba.

1762, Oct.: British forces seize Manila, Philippines, from the Spanish.

1763, Feb.: Treaty of Paris transfers Florida, Canada, and the eastern half of the Mississippi watershed to British rule and awards the colony of Louisiana to Spain.

1763, May: Natives around the Great Lakes destroy British forts in "Pontiac's Rebellion."

1763, Oct.: Royal Proclamation seeks to mollify natives by barring colonial settlement west of the Appalachian Mountains while encouraging settlement in new, coastal colonies.

1763, Dec.: Frontier vigilantes, known as the "Paxton Boys," massacre peaceful Indians at Conestoga, Pennsylvania.

1764, Feb.: Paxton Boys march on Philadelphia to intimidate the government of Pennsylvania, which agrees to pay bounties for Indian scalps.

1764, Mar.: Parliament passes the Sugar Act to draw new revenue from the colonies.

1765, Mar.: Parliament passes the Stamp Act, levying an internal tax on the colonists.

1765, Mar.: Pennsylvania settler vigilantes, known as "Black Boys," seize and destroy a British pack train on Indian trade goods.

1765, Aug.: Riots against the Stamp Act erupt in Boston.

1765, Oct.: Stamp Act Congress of colonial delegates meets in New York.

1765, Nov.: Rioters hound the governor of New York.

1766, Mar.: Parliament repeals the Stamp Act but issues the Declaratory Act asserting full sovereignty over the colonies.

1766, June: British troops suppress settler regulators on the Wappinger tract along New York's eastern border with Connecticut.

1766, July: Great Lakes Indians restore peace in a treaty council conducted by Sir William Johnson at Oswego, New York.

1767, June: To better fund customs officers and vice-admiralty courts, Parliament passes the Townshend Duties on goods imported into the colonies.

1768:   Spanish soldiers and missionaries from Mexico begin to occupy California with a system of presidios and missions.

1768–79:   Captain James Cook conducts three voyages of the Pacific Ocean on behalf of the British Empire.

1768, Feb.: Frederick Stump massacres ten Indians in Pennsylvania.

1768, June: Bostonians riot to protest the seizure of John Hancock's ship, *Liberty*, by customs officers.

1768, Oct.: British redcoats occupy Boston to suppress riots and defend customs officers.

1768, Oct.: In the treaty of Hard Labor, South Carolina, John Stuart negotiates a new boundary with southern Indian nations.

1768, Oct.: In the Treaty of Fort Stanwix, New York, Sir William Johnson procures a massive land cession in the Ohio Valley from the Haudenosaunee but at the expense of other natives.

1768, Oct.: Rebellion erupts in New Orleans against Spanish rule.

1769, Aug.: Alejandro O'Reilly's troops crush rebels in New Orleans, restoring Spanish rule.

1770, Jan.: To defend a liberty pole erected in New York City, Patriots brawl with British troops.

1770, Mar.: British troops shoot and kill five rioters in the so-called Boston Massacre.

1770, Apr.: Parliament eliminates the Townshend Duties except for on tea imported by the colonists.

1771, May: North Carolina's eastern militia crushes regulators at Alamance.

1772, June: Lord Mansfield issues a judicial ruling in the Somerset Case, limiting slavery in England and outraging masters in the colonies.

1772, Aug.: British Board of Trade approves a massive land grant and a new colony in the Ohio Valley; Lord Hillsborough resigns as Secretary of State.

1773: British colonial officials make peace with the Black Caribs of St. Vincent in the Caribbean.

1773, May: Parliament reduces the tax on tea belonging to the East India Company, which inflames opposition by colonial merchants.

1773, Dec.: Patriots destroy cargoes of East India Company tea by dumping them into Boston Harbor in the "Boston Tea Party."

1774, Jan.: Virginia militiamen seize Fort Pitt after British troops withdraw.

1774, Feb.: British Crown adopts new regulations to increase imperial control over, and revenue from, grants of frontier land in the American colonies.

1774, Mar.: Parliament passes the Boston Port Act to shut down that port until the colonists compensate the East India Company for the destroyed tea.

1774, May: Parliament passes the Massachusetts Government Act, altering the colony's charter to enhance royal control.

1774, May: Parliament passes the Quebec Act to protect Francophones in Canada and extend the colony's bounds south and west to the Ohio River.

1774, Aug.: Rioters shut down the courts in rural Massachusetts.

1774, Sept.: Colonial delegates assemble as a Continental Congress to coordinate resistance against Parliament's taxes and coercive measures.

1774, Oct.: Congress adopts the "Continental Association," a comprehensive boycott of exports to, and imports from, Britain.

1774, Oct.: Lord Dunmore's War leads to the Battle of Point Pleasant, where Virginian militiamen defeated Shawnee warriors.

1775, Mar.: Land speculators led by Richard Henderson procure most of Kentucky in a shady deal with some Cherokees at the Treaty of Sycamore Shoals.

1775, Apr.: Daniel Boone leads a party of settlers to found Boonesborough in Kentucky.

1775, Apr.: British troops march out of Boston to fight Patriot militiamen at Lexington and Concord, Massachusetts, initiating war.

1775, Apr.: Patriots seize control of New York City.

1775, May: The Continental Congress reconvenes in Philadelphia to take charge of the war effort, but balks at declaring independence.

1775, May: Ethan Allen and the Green Mountain Boys seize Fort Ticonderoga beside Lake Champlain.

1775, June: Virginia Patriots drive Lord Dunmore from Williamsburg to take refuge on a British warship in Chesapeake Bay.

1775, June: Congress appoints George Washington to command the Continental Army.

1775, June: In the Battle of Bunker Hill, British troops recapture high ground near Boston but suffer heavy casualties.

1775, July: Washington takes command of the Patriot forces besieging the British garrison of Boston.

1775, Aug.: George III issues a royal proclamation denouncing the colonial rebellion.

1775, Aug.: At Charles Town, South Carolina, Patriots execute Thomas Jeremiah, a free black accused of plotting a slave revolt with British support.

1775, Nov.: Lord George Germain takes charge of the British war effort as Secretary of State.

1775, Nov.: Continental troops capture St. John and Montreal in Canada.

1775, Nov.: Lord Dunmore's proclamation encourages slaves and servants to escape and help suppress the Patriot rebellion in Virginia.

1775, Nov.: Washington bans recruiting blacks for his Continental Army.

1775, Dec.: Dunmore's new black recruits routed by Patriots at Great Bridge, near Norfolk.

1775, Dec.: Patriot attack on Quebec crushed with heavy casualties, including the death of the Patriot commander, General Richard Montgomery.

1776, Jan.: Thomas Paine publishes *Common Sense* to promote independence, union, and republican government.

1776, Feb.: North Carolina Loyalists defeated at Moore's Creek Bridge.

1776, Mar.: South Carolina Patriot rangers suppress black runaways on islands near Charles Town.

1776, Mar.: Continental Navy captures and plunders New Providence in the Bahamas.

1776, Mar.: By posting cannon on Dorchester Heights, Washington compels the British evacuation of Boston.

1776, May: British forces relieve Quebec and begin to drive Patriot forces out of Canada.

1776, June: Defeat of the British naval attack on Fort Sullivan at the entrance to Charles Town Harbor.

1776, June: New Jersey Patriots sack and arrest William Franklin, the last royal governor in the thirteen rebelling colonies.

1776, June: Richard Henry Lee proposes independence in Congress.

1776, July: Congress votes for independence and promulgates a Declaration of Independence.

1776, July: New Jersey adopts a state constitution that permits widows to vote.

1776, July: Lord William Howe's British army occupies Staten Island, New York.

1776, Aug.: Howe nearly destroys Washington's Continental Army in the Battle of Long Island.

1776, Aug.: Dunmore abandons his last base in Virginia.

1776, Sept.: Failed peace conference held on Staten Island between Patriot congressmen and British commissioners.

1776, Sept.: Howe seizes New York City after crushing Patriot resistance at Kip's Bay; fire subsequently destroys much of the city.

1776, Sept.: Southern militiamen ravage Cherokee villages.

1776, Sept.: Pennsylvania adopts a radical republican constitution.

1776, Oct.: British destroy Benedict Arnold's Patriot flotilla at Valcour Bay on Lake Champlain.

1776, Oct.: Howe defeats Washington at White Plains in Westchester County, north of New York City.

1776, Nov.: British and Hessian troops capture Forts Washington and Lee on opposite banks of the Hudson River; Washington's shattered army retreats across New Jersey.

1776, Dec.: British troops capture General Charles Lee, Washington's second-in-command.

1776, Dec.: Washington counterattacks, capturing a Hessian garrison at Trenton, New Jersey.

1777, Jan.: Washington defeats a British detachment at Princeton, New Jersey.

1777, Mar.: Execution in England of "John the Painter," an arsonist who supported the Patriots.

1777 July: Defeated Cherokees cede 5 million acres to the Patriots in the Carolinas and the future Tennessee.

1777, July: British General Burgoyne captures Fort Ticonderoga.

1777, July: Murder of Jane McCrea by Indians supporting Burgoyne's invasion.

1777, Aug.: At Oriskany, New York, Loyalists and Indians defeat Patriot attempt to relieve siege of Fort Schuyler (formerly Fort Stanwix); British commander subsequently retreats to Canada.

1777, Aug.: Patriot General John Stark defeats Hessians and Loyalists at Hoosick, near Bennington, Vermont.

1777, Sept.: Howe defeats Washington's army at Brandywine, Pennsylvania, and the victors occupy Philadelphia.

1777, Sept.: Patriots led by Arnold halt Burgoyne's advance at Freeman's Farm near Saratoga, New York.

1777, Oct.: Burgoyne surrenders his army to General Gates at Saratoga.

1777, Oct.: Washington's promising counterattack at Germantown, a suburb of Philadelphia, ultimately falls apart.

1777, Nov.: Congress adopts the "Articles of Confederation" for a loose union of thirteen states and submits this to the states for ratification.

1777, Nov.: Patriot vigilantes murder Cornstalk, a Shawnee chief.

1777, Dec.: Washington moves his ragged army into winter quarters at Valley Forge, Pennsylvania.

1778, Jan.: Washington accepts black recruits in the Continental Army.

1778, Feb.: French and Patriot diplomats frame treaties of trade and alliance.

1778, Apr.: Congress unanimously ratifies the French treaties.

1778, Apr.: Collapse of a Patriot raid on West Florida led by James Willing.

1778, May: Sir Henry Clinton replaces Howe as British commander in North America.

1778, June: Congress rejects peace and reconciliation overtures from the British Carlisle Commission.

1778, June: Washington attacks retreating British troops at Monmouth, New Jersey, but the latter complete their retreat to New York City.

1778, July: George Rogers Clark seizes the Francophone settlements of the Illinois country.

1778, Aug.: Collapse of the French and Patriot siege of the British garrison at Newport, Rhode Island.

1778, Sept.: Indian attack on Boonesborough, Kentucky, fails.

1778, Sep.: French forces capture Dominica in the West Indies.

1778, Dec.: British forces seize St. Lucia in the French West Indies.

1778, Dec.: British forces capture Savannah, Georgia.

1779, Feb.: Clark captures Vincennes and imprisons the British commander, Henry Hamilton.

1779, Apr.: Spain enters the war as an ally of France but not of the United States.

1779, June: French forces commanded by Comte d'Estaing capture St. Vincent in the West Indies.

1779, July: D'Estaing's forces seize Grenada in the West Indies.

1779, July: Spanish forces commence the siege of the British garrison at Gibraltar.

1779, Sept.: General John Sullivan completes his destructive attacks on Haudenosaunee villages around the Finger Lakes of New York.

1779, Sept.: The Spanish governor of Louisiana, Bernardo de Gálvez, captures British posts on the lower Mississippi River.

1779, Sept.: John Paul Jones of the Continental Navy captures HMS *Serapis*.

1779, Oct.: Collapse of the French and Patriot siege of the British and Loyalist garrison at Savannah.

1779, Oct.: Philadelphia rioters attack conservatives holed up in the "Fort Wilson" mansion of James Wilson.

1780, Jan.: Gálvez captures the British post at Mobile.

1780, Jan.: Sir George Rodney's fleet relieves the British garrison at Gibraltar.

1780, Mar.: Pennsylvania legislature adopts the first state law for gradual emancipation of the enslaved.

1780, May: Spanish forces repel a British and Indian attack on St. Louis in upper Louisiana.

1780, May: Sir Henry Clinton's British force captures Charles Town, South Carolina, after the surrender of Benjamin Lincoln's Patriot garrison.

1780, May: Banastre Tarleton's British cavalry destroys a Virginia regiment at Waxhaw Creek, South Carolina.

1780, May: Attempted mutiny by Connecticut regiments suppressed by Pennsylvania troops.

1780, July: French expeditionary force, commanded by the Comte de Rochambeau, lands at Newport, Rhode Island.

1780, July: Haudenosaunee allies of the British burn the Oneida villages.

1780, Aug.: At Camden, South Carolina, the British army of Lord Cornwallis crushes Continental troops led by General Gates.

1780, Sep.: In India, Haider Ali, the prince of Mysore, destroys the British-led force defending Pollilur.

1780, Sep.: Benedict Arnold defects to the British.

1780, Oct.: Patriots execute John André, a British officer who had helped Arnold defect.

1780, Oct.: Patriots crush Loyalist force at King's Mountain, South Carolina.

1780, Oct.: Massachusetts adopts a relatively conservative state constitution drafted by John Adams.

1780, Dec.: Britain declares war on the Netherlands.

1780, Dec.: Patriot militias devastate Cherokee villages west of the Appalachian Mountains.

1780, Dec.: British invasion of Virginia begins under Generals Arnold and Philips.

1781, Jan.: Mutiny by the Pennsylvania regiments of the Continental Army at Morristown, New Jersey.

1781, Jan.: Arnold's troops capture and plunder Richmond, Virginia.

1781, Jan.: Daniel Morgan's Patriots crush Tarleton's force at Hannah's Cowpens, South Carolina.

1781, Feb.: Rodney seizes and plunders the Dutch West Indian island of St. Eustatius.

1781, Feb.: Spanish forces capture St. Joseph's, a British post on Lake Michigan.

1781, Feb.: Robert Morris becomes Superintendent of Finance for Congress.

1781, Feb.: Maryland's approval completes the ratification of the Articles of Confederation.

1781, Mar.: Cornwallis defeats Nathanael Greene's Patriot force at Guilford Courthouse, North Carolina.

1781, Mar.: Renewed Patriot raids destroy more Cherokee villages.

1781, Apr.: Defeat of Tupac Amaru in the highlands of Peru.

1781, May: Gálvez defeats the British to capture Pensacola, the capital of West Florida.

1781, May: Cornwallis takes command of British forces in Virginia.

1781, June: Despite repelling Greene's attack, British and Loyalist forces withdraw from Ninety-Six, South Carolina.

1781, June: French forces capture Tobago in the West Indies.

1781, July: Quechan Indians destroy the Spanish post at the Yuma crossing of the Colorado River.

1781, Aug.: Elizabeth Freeman wins freedom in a court suit in Berkshire County, Massachusetts.

1781, Aug.: Rodney departs from the Caribbean to return to England to answer lawsuits and a Parliamentary investigation of his plundering at St. Eustatius.

1781, Sep.: In India, British forces defeat Haider Ali.

1781, Sep.: Greene suffers another tactical defeat at Eutaw Springs, South Carolina, but compels a British strategic retreat to Charles Town.

1781, Sep.: At the mouth to Chesapeake Bay, French admiral de Grasse defeats a British attempt to relieve Cornwallis's army at Yorktown, Virginia.

1781, Oct.: Cornwallis surrenders his army at Yorktown to allied forces commanded by Washington and Rochambeau.

1781, Nov.: British forces capture the Dutch entrepôt of Negapatam in India.

1782, Jan.: British forces capture Trincomalee, a Dutch emporium in India.

1782, Jan.: Lord Germain forced to resign as Secretary of State.

1782, Feb.: British garrison surrenders Minorca to French and Spanish forces.

1782, Feb.: French forces led by de Grasse capture St. Kitts, Montserrat, and Nevis in the West Indies.

1782, Mar.: Prowar administration of Lord North loses its majority in Parliament.

1782, Mar.: Pennsylvania vigilantes massacre Christian Indians at Gnadenhutten in the Ohio country.

1782, Apr.: Loyalists execute a Patriot partisan, Joshua Huddy, outraging Washington and irritating the British high command.

1782, Apr.: British negotiators open peace talks with American commissioners in Paris.

1782, Apr.: Rodney defeats and captures de Grasse in the naval battle of the Saintes in the West Indies.

1782, May: Spanish forces capture the Bahamas from the British.

1782, May: Virginia's legislature permits individual masters to manumit slaves.

1782, June: British-allied Indians defeat attacking militiamen led by William Crawford at Sandusky in the Ohio country.

1782, July: British forces evacuate Savannah, Georgia.

1782, Aug.: John Laurens dies in an ambush near Charles Town, South Carolina.

1782, Sep.: At Gibraltar, British troops destroy an attack by French and Spanish floating batteries.

1782, Oct.: A British relief fleet lifts the siege of Gibraltar.

1782, Nov.: In the Treaty of Paris, American commissioners conclude a preliminary peace agreement with the British, securing favorable terms.

1782, Dec.: Death of Haider Ali in India.

1782, Dec.: British forces withdraw from Charles Town, South Carolina.

1783, Mar.: At Newburgh, New York, Continental officers protest their treatment by Congress.

1783, Apr.: Lord Shelburne resigns as prime minister in Britain.

1783, June: Most of the Continental Army discharged without pay; disgruntled soldiers harass Congress, which flees from Philadelphia.

1783, Aug.: Native nations of the Great Lakes and Ohio countries form a confederation to resist American expansion.

1783, Sep.: Treaty of Paris becomes official with the French and Spanish making peace with the British.

1783, Nov.: British forces complete the evacuation of New York City, their last garrison on the coast of the new United States.

1783, Dec.: Washington surrenders his command to Congress at Annapolis, Maryland..

1784, Apr.: Thomas Jefferson proposes to Congress the first ordinance for organizing territories west of the Appalachian Mountains.

1784, June: Execution of Jean Saint Malo, a maroon leader, by Spanish officials at New Orleans.

1785, May: Congress adopts an ordinance to survey and sell lands in the Northwest Territory (Ohio country).

1786, Jan.: Virginia legislature adopts the "Ordinance of Religious Freedom."

1786, Feb.: Juan Bautista de Anza negotiates a peace treaty with the Comanches on the margins of New Mexico.

1786, Aug.: Congress roiled by John Jay's proposal to bargain away navigation rights on the lower Mississippi River.

1786, Sept.: Annapolis Convention by delegates from five states discuss the constitutional crisis in the United States.

1786, Sept.: Regulators (or "Shaysites") shut down courts in rural Massachusetts.

1786, Nov.: Kentuckians destroy Shawnee villages and execute the chief Molunthy.

1787, Jan.: Regulators ("Shaysites") falter in attack on the federal armory at Springfield, Massachusetts.

1787, Feb.: Regulators ("Shaysites") crushed and dispersed at Petersham, Massachusetts.

1787, May: Federal Constitutional Convention opens in Philadelphia; Virginia Plan proposed.

1787, June: The Federal Convention considers constitutional plans proposed by the New Jersey delegation and by Alexander Hamilton.

1787, July: Congress adopts a Northwest Ordinance to regulate territorial government.

1787, Aug.: Key compromises over representation and slavery save the Federal Convention from dissolving.

1787, Sept.: Federal Convention presents proposed new constitution to Congress, which submits it to the states for ratification.

1788, Jan.: British found a penal colony at Botany Bay, in the future Australia.

1788, Feb.: Federal Constitution secures ratification in Massachusetts.

1788, Mar.: Rhode Island voters overwhelmingly reject the Federal Constitution.

1788, June: Ratification by New Hampshire and Virginia secures the Federal Constitution.

1788, July: New York narrowly ratifies the Federal Constitution.

1788, Aug.: North Carolina rejects the Federal Constitution.

1789, Feb.: Washington unanimously chosen as the first president by the electoral college.

1789, Apr.: New federal government begins in New York City.

1789, May: Spanish Capt. Esteban José Martínez provokes the Nootka Crisis by seizing British ships and crews along the Pacific Northwest coast.

1789, July: French Revolution ignited by a mob's attack on the Bastille, a political prison in Paris.

1789, Sept.: Madison proposes twelve constitutional amendments to secure rights to individuals and the states.

1789, Nov.: North Carolina ratifies the constitution and rejoins the union.

1790, Feb.: Congress rejects antislavery petitions.

1790, May: Rhode Island ratifies the Constitution, restoring the union at thirteen states.

1790, July: Jefferson brokers a compromise that passes Alexander Hamilton's fiscal program while locating the future federal capital on the banks of the Potomac River.

1790, Aug.: A Creek delegation and federal leaders conclude the Treaty of New York.

1790, Oct.: Spain resolves the Nootka crisis by making concessions and offering compensation to Great Britain.

1791, Feb.: Washington approves the Bank of the United States proposed by Hamilton, thereby favoring a "loose construction" of the Federal Constitution.

1791, June: Parliament passes the Canada Act, dividing Quebec into Lower and Upper Canada, each with a mixed constitution.

1791, Aug.: "Night of Fire" initiates a massive slave revolt in Saint-Domingue in the French West Indies.

1791, Nov.: Arthur St. Clair's American army crushed by confederated Indians in the Ohio country.

1791, Dec.: Ratification of ten of Madison's amendments completed, later known as the Bill of Rights.

1792, Dec.: Washington unanimously reelected president by the electoral college.

1793, Feb.: Congress and the president approve a Fugitive Slave Act.

1793, Apr.: Washington proclaims American neutrality in the renewed warfare between Britain and France.

1793, Aug.: French commissioners offer freedom to the enslaved of Saint-Domingue.

1794, Feb.: French revolutionary government liberates all the enslaved of the French West Indies.

1794, July: Regulators attack the mansion of John Neville, a tax collector, in western Pennsylvania.

1794, July: Richard Allen founds the first African Methodist Episcopal Church in Philadelphia.

1794, Aug.: To enforce a federal excise tax, Washington orders the suppression of regulators, called "Whiskey Rebels," in western Pennsylvania.

1794, Aug.: Federal force commanded by General Anthony Wayne defeats confederated natives at the Battle of Fallen Timbers in the Ohio country.

1794, Nov.: On behalf of the United States, John Jay negotiates a treaty resolving disputes with the British Empire, thereby alienating the French.

1795, Aug.: Ohio country natives make peace and cede lands to the United States in the Treaty of Greenville.

1795, Oct.: By the Treaty of San Lorenzo, Spain opens the lower Mississippi to American navigation.

1796, Dec.: John Adams narrowly elected president to succeed Washington; the runner-up, Thomas Jefferson, becomes vice president.

1798, Mar.: British launch bloody suppression of the United Irishmen in Ireland.

1798, Apr.: British troops withdraw from Saint-Domingue, conceding power there to Touissaint Louverture.

1798, May: Federalist-dominated Congress prepares the nation for war against France.

1798, June: Congress passes the Alien Acts to slow the naturalization of aliens and speed the deportation for those who criticize the federal government.

1798, July: Congress passes the Sedition Act to criminalize public criticism of federal leaders.

1798, Nov.: Kentucky legislature passes Jefferson-authored resolutions that threaten to nullify the Alien and Sedition Acts as unconstitutional; Virginia follows suit with a Madison-drafted resolution a month later.

1800, Aug.: Failure of Gabriel's plot to liberate the enslaved in and around Richmond, Virginia.

1800, Oct.: Execution of Gabriel in Richmond.

1800, Oct.: Sierra Leone Company suppresses revolt by former American slaves at Freetown.

1801, Jan.: John Adams appoints John Marshall as chief justice of the U.S. Supreme Court.

1801, Feb.: House of Representatives breaks deadlock to elect Jefferson as president over Aaron Burr.

1801, Mar.: Jefferson inaugurated as the third president of the United States.

1801, July: Toussaint promulgates a new constitution for Saint-Domingue.

1802, May: Toussaint arrested by French forces and shipped away to prison in France, where he died in April 1803.

1803, Feb.: In *Marbury v. Madison*, Marshall claims for the Supreme Court the power to review the constitutionality of federal laws.

1803, Oct.: U.S. Senate approves treaty with France to purchase Louisiana.

1804, Jan.: After crushing French invaders, Jean-Jacques Dessalines declares the independence of Saint-Domingue as the new nation of Haiti.

1804, July: Hamilton dies of a wound suffered in a duel with Aaron Burr.

1804, Dec.: Jefferson overwhelmingly reelected as president.

1806, Jan.: Virginia legislature discourages further manumissions by individuals.

1807, Mar.: Congress adopts a ban on the importation of foreign slaves, effective January 1, 1808.

1809, June: Death of Thomas Paine in New Rochelle, New York.

1819, Mar.: In *McCulloch v. Maryland*, John Marshall's Supreme Court bolsters the nationalist interpretation of the Federal Constitution.

NOTES

INTRODUCTION

1. Nathaniel Hawthorne, "My Kinsman, Major Molineux," in Pearson, ed., *Complete Novels and Selected Tales of Nathaniel Hawthorne*, 1209–23.
2. Chopra, *Choosing Sides*; Jasanoff, *Liberty's Exiles*.
3. Benjamin Franklin to William Franklin, Mar. 22, 1775, Founders Online, National Archives (http://founders.archives.gov/documents/Franklin/01-21-02-0306). For a scholarly book that overtly celebrates the Patriot cause, see Middlekauff, *Glorious Cause*.
4. Rather than call the American Revolutionaries "Whigs" (as they often did), I identify them as "Patriots," which evokes their similarities with later republican rebels and revolutionaries who called themselves Patriots (rather than Whigs).
5. G. Wood, *Empire of Liberty*; G. Wood, *Radicalism of the American Revolution*.
6. Dorothea Gamsby quoted in Crary, ed., *Price of Loyalty*, 49. See also Anderson and Cayton, *Dominion of War*; McDonnell, "Class War," 305–44; Silver, *Our Savage Neighbors*; Spooner, "Origins of the Old South." This paragraph is also indebted to Benjamin Carp, "The Fearsome Consequences of the American Revolution," and Robert G. Parkinson, "untitled," conference papers, Society for Historians of the Early American Republic, July 18, 2015.
7. Hendrickson, "The First Union," 35–53; Hendrickson, *Peace Pact*; Onuf, "Expanding Union," 50–80.

8. Colley, *Captives*, 230–36; Countryman, "Indians, the Colonial Order, and the Social Significance of the American Revolution," 342–62; Elliott, *Empires of the Atlantic World*, 339; Gould, *Persistence of Empire*, 184–85; Hinderaker, *Elusive Empires*, 189, 268–70; Marshall, *Making and Unmaking*, 205–6.

9. For a classic work that slights western issues to concentrate on taxation, see E. S. Morgan, *Birth of the Republic*.

10. Thomas Jefferson to Edmund Pendleton, Aug. 13, 1776, in Boyd et al., eds., *Papers of Thomas Jefferson* vol. 1: 491–94; Calloway, *American Revolution in Indian Country*, 31–32; Griffin, *American Leviathan*, 158.

11. For Atlantic history, see Armitage and Braddick, eds., *The British Atlantic World*; Elliott, *Empires of the Atlantic World*; J. C. Miller, ed., *Princeton Companion to Atlantic History*. For continental approaches, see Fenn, *Pox Americana*; Richter, *Facing East from Indian Country*; A. Taylor, *American Colonies*.

12. For exceptions to the rule, see DuVal, *Independence Lost*; Gould and Onuf, eds., *Empire and Nation*; O'Shaughnessy, *Empire Divided*; Resendez, *Changing National Identities*; A. Taylor, *Civil War of 1812*; A. White, *Encountering Revolution*.

13. DuVal, *Independence Lost*; Fenn, *Encounters*; Saunt, *West of the Revolution*; A. Taylor, *Divided Ground*; Weber, *Spanish Frontier*.

14. John Adams to Hezekiah Niles, Feb. 13, 1818, Founders Online, National Archives (http://founders.archives.gov/documents/Adams/99-02-02-6854); A. Taylor, "Continental Crossings," 182–88.

15. Hickey, "America's Response," 361–79; A. White, *Encountering Revolution*. The phrase "a new birth of freedom" comes from Abraham Lincoln's Gettysburg Address, November 19, 1863.

CHAPTER 1: COLONIES

1. Samuel Johnson quoted in Calloway, *Scratch of a Pen*, 10.

2. Bushman, *King and People*, 11–17, Boston proclamation quoted on 15; anonymous Bostonian quoted in Gould, "Fears of War," 24; Olson, *Making the Empire Work*, 1.

3. Beddard, ed., *Revolutions of 1688*; Israel, ed., *Anglo-Dutch Moment*.

4. Bowen, *Elites*, 82–83; Brewer, *Sinews of Power*, 40, 89–91, 126–34; Greene, *Negotiated Authorities*, 26–28; O'Brien, "Inseparable Connections," 53–77; Rodger, "Sea-Power and Empire," 169–83.

5. Middleton, *Bells of Victory*, 19–20, George II quoted on 19 ("Ministers"); Olson, *Making the Empire Work*, 136–38; Steele, "Anointed," 105–27.

6. Dunn, "Glorious Revolution in America," 445–66; Greene, *Negotiated Authorities*, 84–85; Johnson, "Revolution of 1688–9," 215–40.

7. Greene, *Negotiated Authorities*, 86–88; Murrin, "Political Development," 431–32; Steele, "Anointed," 105–27.

8. Bushman, *King and People*, 3–7, 19–24; Greene, *Negotiated Authorities*, 88–89; McConville, *King's Three Faces*, 7–8, 31–39, 49–50, 63–70, 77–79; E. S. Morgan, *Inventing the People*, 94–107, 120–21; Steele, "Anointed," 114–15; G. Wood, *Radicalism*, 7, 15–16, 49–50, 63–70, 77–79, George III quoted on 15 ("The pride").

9. Elliott, *Empires of the Atlantic World*, 3–114; Weber, *Spanish Frontier*, 25–42, 64–69.

10. Altman, "The Spanish Atlantic," 183–200; Elliott, *Empires of the Atlantic World*, 122–27, 170–72, 275; Faber, *Building the Land of Dreams*, 30–31.

11. Elliott, *Empires of the Atlantic World*, 270–75; Frank, "Demographic, Social, and Economic Change," 41–71; Weber, *Spanish Frontier*, 60–121; Wickman, "Spanish Colonial Floridas," 208–12.

12. Elliott, *Empires of the Atlantic World*, 273–75; Weber, *Spanish Frontier*, 122–46; Wickman, "Spanish Colonial Floridas," 212–16; R. H. Jackson, "Formation of Frontier Indigenous Communities," 145–49.

13. Elliott, *Empires of the Atlantic World*, 273–75; Snyder, *Slavery in Indian Country*, 156; Weber, *Spanish Frontier*, 147–72, Alexander McGillivray quoted on 283; Yirush, *Settlers, Liberty, and Empire*, 184–85.

14. Eccles, *French in North America*, 165–94; Marzagalli, "French Atlantic World," 236–37, 244, 250.

15. Eccles, *French in North America*, 32–130; Marzagalli, "French Atlantic World," 238–42.

16. Eccles, "French Imperial Policy," 25–26; R. White, *Middle Ground*, 50–93; Rushforth, *Bonds of Alliance*, 15–72.

17. Marzagalli, "French Atlantic World," 245–48; Usner, *Indians, Settlers, and Slaves*, 13–43, 77–104.

18. Burnard, *Mastery*, 13–22, Charles Leslie quoted on 14 ("Constant Mine"); Elliott, *Empires of the Atlantic World*, 224–26; Hornsby, *British Atlantic*, 43–63; Marshall, *Making and Unmaking*, 18; Mulcahy, *Hubs of Empire*, 9–83; S. Newman, *New World of Labor*, 54–68, 189–215; O'Shaughnessy, *Empire Divided*, 8–9, 40–41.

19. Berlin, *Many Thousands Gone*, 142–76; Edelson, *Plantation Enterprise*; Gallay, *Indian Slave Trade*, 53–61; Greene, *Imperatives*, 87–142, Philipp Georg Friedrich von Reck quoted on 121 ("walk[ed]"); Hornsby, *British Atlantic*, 111–25; visitor quoted in P. Wood, *Black Majority*, 132 ("Carolina"). For the Santee tragedy, see Merrell, *Indians New World*, 49–51.

20. Berlin, *Many Thousands Gone*, 109–41; Hornsby, *British Atlantic*, 88–111.

21. Hornsby, *British Atlantic*, 148–63; Tully, *Forming American Politics*, 4–8.

22. V. Anderson, *New England's Generation*; Cronon, *Changes in the Land*; Hornsby, *British Atlantic*, 73–88, 126–48; McCusker and Menard, *Economy of British America*, 91–111.

23. Anderson, *Crucible of War*, 113; Hornsby, *British Atlantic*, 205–8; Plank, *Unsettled Conquest*, 40–67.

24. Hornsby, *British Atlantic*, 28–43; Engerman and Gallman, eds., *Cambridge Economic History*, vol. 1:244–45; McCusker and Menard, *Economy of British America*, 111–16.

25. Grant-Costa and Mancke, "Anglo-Amerindian Commercial Relations," 399–401; Hornsby, *British Atlantic*, 63–72; Mancke, "Chartered Enterprise," 250–52.

26. Horn and Morgan, "Settlers and Slaves," 20.

27. Berlin, *Many Thousands Gone*; Blackburn, *Making of New World Slavery*; Eltis, "Africa, Slavery, and the Slave Trade," 274–83; Horn and Morgan, "Settlers and Slaves," 23, 42–44; Kulikoff, *Tobacco and Slaves*, 317–51; Mulcahy, *Hubs of Empire*, 112–45.

28. Bailyn, *Voyagers to the West*, 4; Berlin, "Time, Space, and the Evolution," 113–46; Marshall, *Making and Unmaking*, 25–26; McCusker and Menard, *Economy of British America*, 231–35.

29. Burnard, "Slavery and the Causes," 59–64, Edward Trelawney quoted on 59 ("Negroes"); V. Brown, *Reaper's Garden*, 129–56; Kulikoff, *Tobacco and Slaves*, 381–415; P. D. Morgan, *Slave Counterpoint*, 146–203.

30. Berlin, *Many Thousands Gone*, 123–24; Elliott, *Empires of the Atlantic World*, 168–69; E. S. Morgan, *American Slavery*, 329–44; Reverend Morgan Godwyn, *The Negro's and Indian's Advocate* (1680) reprinted in Hughes, *Versions of Blackness*, 344–52 ("These two words").

31. Elliott, *Empires of the Atlantic World*, 284–85; E. S. Morgan, *American Slavery, American Freedom*.

32. DuVal, *Independence Lost*, 273–74; Elliott, *Empires of the Atlantic World*, 169–72; Faber, *Building the Land of Dreams*, 32–42; Kueth, "Military and Society," 72–74.

33. John Dobell to unknown, July 4, 1746, in Allen D. Chandler, ed., *Colonial Records of the State of Georgia* (Atlanta: Charles P. Byrd, 1915), vol. 25:74 ("Liberty and Property"); Greene, *Imperatives*, 113–42; A. Taylor, *American Colonies*, 243.

34. Doerflinger, *Vigorous Spirit of Enterprise*, 86–88; Marshall, *Making and Unmaking*, 15–16; McCusker and Menard, *Economy of British America*, 250–54; G. Wood, *Radicalism*, 58–59.

35. McCusker and Menard, *Economy of British America*, 75–80, 334–37; Engerman and Gallman, eds., *Cambridge Economic History*, vol. 1:245.

36. Bowen, *Elites*, 32–33; Breen, *Marketplace of Revolution*, 76–82; Colley, *Britons*, 59–60; John Oldmixon quoted in Greene, "Empire and Identity," 216 ("considerable"); Marshall, *Making and Unmaking*, 13–16; E. S. Morgan, *Inventing the People*, 144–45.

37. Bowen, *Elites*, 34–35; Chaplin, "British Atlantic," 228–29; Engerman and Gallman, eds., *Cambridge Economic History*, 337–62; McCusker and

Menard, *Economy of British America*, 75–80, 334–37; Marshall, *Making and Unmaking*, 17; Steele, *English Atlantic*, 78–93, 213–28.

38. Breen, *Marketplace of Revolution*, 33–71, 172–82; Bushman, *Refinement of America*, 308–12, 406–9; Carson, ed., *Consuming Interests*; Marshall, *Making and Unmaking*, 42–45.

39. C. Cox, *Proper Sense of Honor*, 25–28; G. Wood, *Radicalism*, 24–33, Richard Steele quoted on 26 ("distinguish themselves"), Landon Carter quoted on 27, and a Virginia gentleman quoted on 30 ("it would derogate").

40. Breen, *Marketplace of Revolution*, 33–35, 152–158; Bushman, *Refinement of America*, 61–99, 181–97; G. Wood, *Radicalism*, 19–20, 28–29, 38–39, 75–77, unnamed traveler quoted on 135 ("one continued Race").

41. Berkin, *Revolutionary Mothers*, 4–11, William Blackstone quoted on 6; Gundersen, *To Be Useful to the World*, 45–54; Kerber, *Women of the Republic*, 119–21; Norton, *Liberty's Daughters*, 40–65, 170; Sievens, *Stray Wives*, 5–6; Zagarri, *Revolutionary Backlash*, 19–22.

42. Lucy Paradise Barziza to Thomas Jefferson, Mar. 3, 1789, in Boyd et al., eds., *Papers of Thomas Jefferson*, vol. 14:611–12 ("For my part"); Norton, *Liberty's Daughters*, 44–46, 123–24, Grace Growden Galloway quoted on 44–45 ("wretched Wife").

43. Berkin, *Revolutionary Mothers*, 7–8, Mary Holyoke quoted on 8; Kerber, "'I Have Don,'" 233–34; Norton, "What an Alarming Crisis,'" 204–7; Shammas, "Female Social Structure," 69–84; G. Wood, *Empire of Liberty*, 315–16.

44. Murrin, "Religion and Politics," 19–43; Balmer, *Perfect Babel of Confusion*.

45. McLoughlin, *New England Dissent*, 335; G. Wood, *Radicalism*, 19–21, Jonathan Edwards quoted on 19 ("appointed office").

46. Crawford, *Seasons of Grace*; O'Brien, "Eighteenth-Century Publishing Networks," 38–57; Lambert, *"Pedlar in Divinity"*; Stout, *Divine Dramatist*.

47. Lambert, *Inventing the "Great Awakening"*; A. Taylor, *American Colonies*, 346–51; G. Wood, *Radicalism*, 144.

48. Lambert, *Inventing the "Great Awakening"*; Nash, *Unknown American Revolution*, 8–10, Anglican minister quoted on 10 ("screw up").

49. Hall, *Contested Boundaries*; Juster, *Disorderly Women*; Nash, *Unknown American Revolution*, 8–12.

50. Bonomi, *Under the Cope of Heaven*, 152–57; T. D. Hall, *Contested Boundaries*; Nash, *Unknown American Revolution*, 8–12; G. Wood, *Radicalism*, 144–45.

51. Draper, *Struggle for Power*, 36–37; Greene, *Negotiated Authorities*, 32–33; Greene, *Peripheries and Center*, 11–17; E. S. Morgan, *Inventing the People*, 122–29; Olson, *Making the Empire Work*, 13–50; Steele, "Anointed," 105–27.

52. Bushman, *King and People*, 26; Chaplin, "British Atlantic," 220–21, 225–26; Cox, "British Caribbean," 276–77; Greene, *Peripheries and Center*, 62–81;

Marshall, *Making and Unmaking*, 6–7; Olson, *Making the Empire Work*, xii, 118–19; Steele, "Anointed," 105–27.

53. Greene, *Negotiated Authorities*, 85–86; Greene, *Peripheries and Center*, 1–24, 44; Marshall, "Thirteen Colonies," 71, 75; Olson, *Making the Empire Work*, 1–12, 134.

54. Bailyn, *Origins of American*, 17–19; Greene, "Empire and Identity," 210–29; Greene, *Negotiated Authorities*, 25–26; James Otis quoted in Hutchinson, *History of the Colony and Province*, vol. 3:73–74; G. Wood, *Creation of the American Republic*, 10–11.

55. Bailyn, *Origins of American Politics*, 19–23; Butterfield et al, eds., *Diary and Autobiography of John Adams*, vol. 1:296–99 ("monarchical"); E. S. Morgan, *Inventing the People*, 22–26, 41–43; Ryerson, "John Adams, Republican Monarchist," 75, 91–92.

56. Bailyn, *Origins of American Politics*, 59–60, William Douglass quoted on 59 ("By the governor"); E. S. Morgan, *Inventing the People*, 134–35; Ryerson, "John Adams, Republican Monarchist," 81; Steele, "Anointed," 111–12.

57. Bailyn, *Origins of American Politics*, 63–65, 82–83, 88–90; Bushman, *King and People*, 123–32, 159–60; Marshall, *Making and Unmaking*, 29–30, 164–65; E. S. Morgan, *Inventing the People*, 135–36; Tully, *Forming American Politics*, 311–12.

58. Bailyn, *Origins of American Politics*, 63, 86–88; Bushman, *King and People*, 81–85; E. S. Morgan, *Inventing the People*, 175–76; Sydnor, *Gentlemen Freeholders*, 28–32; Tully, *Forming American Politics*, 316–17.

59. E. S. Morgan, *Inventing the People*, 135; G. Wood, *Radicalism*, 119–21.

60. Bailyn, *Origins of American Politics*, 66–70; Bushman, *King and People*, 74–78, 129; Tully, *Forming American Politics*, 333–34, 340–41.

61. Bailyn, *Origins of American Politics*, 70–80; E. S. Morgan, *Inventing the People*, 144–45; Murrin, "Political Development," 436–37.

62. Bushman, *King and People*, 26–27; Countryman, *People in Revolution*, 81; Draper, *Struggle for Power*, 37–41; E. S. Morgan, *Inventing the People*, 140–41; Steele, "Anointed," 110–12, 115.

63. Alexander Spotswood quoted in: E. S. Morgan, *Inventing the People*, 138 ("that he is the best"); Murrin, "Political Development," 444; Sydnor, *Gentlemen Freeholders*, 33–34; Tully, *Forming American Politics*, 317–30, George Thomas quoted on 323 ("the people").

64. Bonomi, *Factious People*, 140–66; Bushman, *King and People*, 104, 121; Gerlach, *Philip Schuyler and the American Revolution*, 102–3, Philip Livingston quoted on 106; Murrin, "Political Development," 444; Kross, "'Patronage Most Ardently Sought,'" 205–31; Tully, *Forming American Politics*, 333–35, 340–54.

65. Bushman, *King and People*, 27–32, 88–90; Tully, *Forming American Politics*, 322–24, *New-York Weekly Journal*, quoted on 344 ("a Banner").

66. Greene, *Negotiated Authorities*, 134–35; E. S. Morgan, *Inventing the People*, 197–98; Sydnor, *Gentlemen Freeholders*, 28–29, 36–38; G. Wood, *Radicalism*, 49.

67. E. S. Morgan, *Inventing the People*, 185; Murrin, "Political Development," 442–43; Sydnor, *Gentlemen Freeholders*, 27–28, 59.

68. Bailyn, *Origins of American Politics*, 88; Tully, *Forming American Politics*, 328–30.

69. Cadwallader Colden to Lords of Trade, Sept. 20, 1764, in Colden, *Colden Letter Books*, vol. 1:363–64 ("consists"); Countryman, *People in Revolution*, 74, 80, 83; Nadelhaft, "'Snarls of Invidious Animals,'" 63–66; Tully, *Forming American Politics*, 343, 353–89; G. Wood, *Radicalism*, 45, for the size of assemblies, see 61.

70. McConville, *King's Three Faces*, 1–2, 57–63, 79; Nash, *Unknown American Revolution*, 47; G. Wood, *Radicalism*, 42. For Carnival, see E. S. Morgan, *Inventing the People*, 204–5.

71. Brunsman, *Evil Necessity*, 225–33, William Shirley quoted on 232 ("Persons"); Bushman, *King and People*, 43–66; Maier, "Popular Uprisings," 3–35; Nash, *Unknown American Revolution*, 18–19, including the Shirley quotation ("working artificers").

72. Countryman, "'Out of the Bounds of the Law,'" 56; Kars, *Breaking Loose Together*, 197; McConville, *Daring Disturbers*, 156–70; McConville, *King's Three Faces*, 171–75; A. Taylor, "'Kind of Warr,'" 3–26; Tully, *Forming American Politics*, 382–84.

73. Bailyn, *Voyagers to the West*, 4–5; Chaplin, "British Atlantic," 223–24, 228; Colley, *Britons*, 5–9, 23–29, 367–68; Conway, *War, State, and Society*, 216–19; Cotton Mather quoted in Elliott, *Empires of the Atlantic World*, 223 ("It is no little"); Greene, "Empire and Identity," 213–18; Samuel Davies quoted in Marshall, *Making and Unmaking*, 41 ("the reduction").

74. Brecher, *Losing a Continent*, 20–21.

75. Eccles, *French in North America*, 198–99; Hinderaker, *Elusive Empires*, 87–133; J. Lawson, *New Voyage to Carolina*, 243.

76. Hinderaker, *Elusive Empires*, 14–45; Steele, *Warpaths*, 179–82.

77. Lee, "Subjects, Clients, Allies," 200–201, Haudenosaunees quoted on 200 ("Our Young Warriors"); Silver, *Our Savage Neighbors*, 39–73.

78. Brecher, *Losing a Continent*, 15–16; Dixon, "'We Speak as One People,'" 50–51; Hinderaker, *Elusive Empires*, 39–45; Lee, "Subjects, Clients, Allies," 198–99, 208–9; Edmond Atkin quoted in Jacobs, ed., *Indians of the Southern Colonial Frontier*, 3–4 ("The importance").

79. Brecher, *Losing a Continent*, 23–25; Calloway, *Scratch of a Pen*, 48–51, Pierre Pouchot quoted on 50 ("They are unwilling"); Hinderaker, *Elusive Empires*, 110–19; Lee, "Subjects, Clients, Allies," 201–2; R. White, *Middle Ground*, 186–245.

80. Calloway, *Scratch of a Pen*, 50; Wraxall, *Abridgment of the Indian Affairs*, 219 ("To preserve").

81. Eccles, "French Imperial Policy," 22–25; Hornsby, *British Atlantic*, 204–5; Liss, *Atlantic Empires*, 1–2; Steele, *Warpaths*, 137–74.

82. F. Anderson, *Crucible of War*, 24–32; Brecher, *Losing a Continent*, 6, 12–14, 27–28; Eccles, *French in North America*, 199–201; Harris, "War, Empire, and the 'National Interest,'" 16–23; Hornsby, *British Atlantic*, 205–10; Marshall, *Making and Unmaking*, 82–83.

83. F. Anderson and D. Cayton, *Dominion of War*, 116–27; Brecher, *Losing a Continent*, 48–58; Eccles, "French Imperial Policy," 27–34, Ange Duquesne de Menneville quoted on 34 ("Nothing"); Hinderaker, *Elusive Empires*, 26–29; Lenman, *Britain's Colonial Wars*, 114–16, 122–23; Parmenter, "The Iroquois," 106–8; Skaggs, "Sixty Years' War," 3–4.

84. Conway, *War, State, and Society*, 224–25; T. Robinson and Duke of Newcastle quoted in Marshall, *Making and Unmaking*, 83 ("so linked" and "insults"); Middleton, *Bells of Victory*, 2.

85. Brecher, *Losing a Continent*, 61; Lenman, *Britain's Colonial Wars*, 120, 122–26; Earl of Halifax quoted in Marshall, *Making and Unmaking*, 90 ("the absurd and false").

86. Brecher, *Losing a Continent*, 59–61; Shannon, *Indians and Colonists*, 174–201, 205–20; Benjamin Franklin, "The Interest of Great Britain Considered," Apr. 17, 1760, Founders Online, National Archives (http://founders.archives.gov/documents/Franklin/01-09-02-0029).

87. F. Anderson, *Crucible of War*, 113–14; F. Anderson and D. Cayton, *Dominion of War*, 127–28; Calloway, *Scratch of a Pen*, 162–64; Lenman, *Britain's Colonial Wars*, 127–29, 136; Marshall, *Making and Unmaking*, 91–92; Plank, *Unsettled Conquest*, 140–57.

88. F. Anderson and D. Cayton, *Dominion of War*, 127–28; Lenman, *Britain's Colonial Wars*, 127–29; Marshall, *Making and Unmaking*, 91–92.

89. F. Anderson and D. Cayton, *Dominion of War*, 123–24; Brecher, *Losing a Continent*, 103–6, 120–22; Colonel Bougainville quoted in Eccles, "French Imperial Policy," 36 ("What can they do"); Lenman, *Britain's Colonial Wars*, 136–38, 140–41; Middleton, *Bells of Victory*, 5.

90. F. Anderson, *Crucible of War*, 208–13; F. Anderson and D. Cayton, *Dominion of War*, 122–23; Jasanoff, *Edge of Empire*, 20–21; Marshall, *Making and Unmaking*, 58–59; Lenman, *Britain's Colonial Wars*, 138, 142; Middleton, *Bells of Victory*, 6–8.

91. F. Anderson, *Crucible of War*, 214–15; Marshall, *Making and Unmaking*, 95–98. For the expenditures and their compensation, see Marshall, "Thirteen Colonies in the Seven Years War," 69–70.

92. F. Anderson, *Crucible of War*, 257–58, 267–85; Kelton, "British and Indian War," 763–92; Lenman, *Britain's Colonial Wars*, 149–50.

93. F. Anderson, *Crucible of War*, 340–409; Lenman, *Britain's Colonial Wars*, 144–46, 150–52; Marshall, *Making and Unmaking*, 98–99; Middleton, *Bells of Victory*, 216–17.

94. F. Anderson, *Crucible of War*, 490, 497–502, 515–17; Jasanoff, *Edge of Empire*, 20–21; P. Lawson, *Imperial Challenge*, 16–17; Lenman, *Britain's Colonial Wars*, 166–68, 171–72; Marshall, *Making and Unmaking*, 8, 61.

95. Burnard, *Mastery*, 10, 103–4, 170–74; Craton, *Testing the Chains*, 125–39.

96. F. Anderson, *Crucible of War*, 479, 503–6; Gould, "Fears of War," 22; P. Lawson, *Imperial Challenge*, 6–7; Lenman, *Britain's Colonial Wars*, 152–53, 166–68.

97. F. Anderson, *Crucible of War*, 505–6; Brechey, *Losing a Continent*, 45, 169–75; Calloway, *Scratch of a Pen*, 7–10; Eccles, *Essays on New France*, 143; Eccles, *French in North America*, 235–38; P. Lawson, *Imperial Challenge*, 17–18; Ragatz, *Fall of the Planter Class*, 112.

98. Brechey, *Losing a Continent*, 181; Calloway, *Scratch of a Pen*, 9–10; Lenman, *Britain's Colonial Wars*, 168–70.

99. Dull, *Diplomatic History*, 14–16, 19; Gould, "Fears of War," 25; Jasanoff, *Edge of Empire*, 21–22; Mapp, "Revolutionary War and Europe's Great Powers," 312–13; O'Shaughnessy, *Men Who Lost America*, 19.

100. Altman, "Spanish Atlantic," 186, 192–97; Chavez, *Spain*, 7, 137; Elliott, *Empires of the Atlantic World*, 295–324; Langley, *Americas in the Age of Revolution*, 147–49; Lynch, ed., *Latin American Revolutions*, 6–11; MacLachlan, *Spain's Empire*, 89–93; Phelan, "Bourbon Innovation," 41–47; Weber *Bárbaros*, 8–12, 100–16, 150–53; Weber, *Spanish Frontier*, 215–20.

101. Calloway, *Scratch of a Pen*, 138–42; Faber, *Building the Land of Dreams*, 28–30; Weber, *Spanish Frontier*, 198–202.

102. Calloway, *Scratch of a Pen*, 162–64, Alejandro O'Reilly quoted on 163 ("with people"); DuVal, *Independence Lost*, 65–70; Weber, *Spanish Frontier*, 202–3.

103. Hackel, *Children of Coyote*, 27–64; Sandos, "Between Crucifix and Cross," 196–229; Weber, *Spanish Frontier*, 236–65.

104. Mapp, "Revolutionary War and Europe's Great Powers," 314–15; Weber, *Spanish Frontier*, 266; Withey, *Voyages of Discovery*.

105. Dull, *Diplomatic History*, 29–30, 36; Mapp, "Revolutionary War and Europe's Great Powers," 313–15.

106. F. Anderson and D. Cayton, *Dominion of War*, 135–39; Henry Ellis quoted in Calloway, *Scratch of a Pen*, 168 ("What did Britain").

107. Calloway, *Scratch of a Pen*, 10–11; Conway, *War, State, and Society*, 240–41; James Otis quoted in Hutchinson, *History of the Colony*, vol. 3:73–74 ("We in America"); Otis quoted in Marshall, *Making and Unmaking*, 104 ("We love").

108. Alden, *General Gage*, 104–5; F. Anderson, *Crucible of War*, 614–15; Draper,

Struggle for Power, 5–25, (London) *Morning Chronicle*, July 1, 1775, quoted on 23; Gould, "Fears of War," 20; Hutchinson, *History of the Colony*, vol. 3:73.

109. Alden, *General Gage*, 106; Brewer, *Sinews of Power*, 114; Bushman, *King and People*, 34–35; Lenman, *Britain's Colonial Wars*, 181; Marshall, *Making and Unmaking*, 71–72.

110. Calloway, *Scratch of a Pen*, 12; Gould, "Fears of War," 24.

111. F. Anderson, *Crucible of War*, 167, 286–88, 519–20, General Wolfe quoted on 288 ("the dirtiest"), William Pitt quoted on 520 ("principally"); Conway, *War, State, and Society*, 223; Marshall, "Thirteen Colonies," 73–75, 82–84; Marshall, *Making and Unmaking*, 92–94, 108–10.

112. William Smith quoted in Marshall, *Making and Unmaking*, 288.

113. Calloway, *Scratch of a Pen*, 10; Conway, *War, State and Society*, 236–37, 240–43; Greene, *Negotiated Authorities*, 40–41; Marshall, *Making and Unmaking*, 104–5, 117–18.

114. F. Anderson, *Crucible of War*, 710; Chaplin, "British Atlantic," 231; Elliott, *Empires of the Atlantic World*, 234; G. Wood, *Americanization of Benjamin Franklin*, 113–14.

115. Conway, *War, State, and Society*, 236–38; Lynd and Waldstreicher, "Free Trade, Sovereignty, and Slavery," 601; Benjamin Franklin, "First Reply to Vindex Patriae," Dec. 28, 1765, B. Franklin, "Fragments of a Pamphlet on the Stamp Act," B. Franklin to Lord Kames, Feb. 25, 1767, and B. Franklin, "Subjects of Subjects," in Labaree et al, eds., *Papers of Benjamin Franklin*, vol. 12:413–16 ("mixed rabble"), vol. 13:72–84 ("fit only"), vol. 14:65, vol. 15:36–38 ("subjects"); B. Franklin to William Franklin, Mar. 22, 1775 ("lowest of Mankind"), Founders Online, National Archives (http://founders.archives.gov/documents/Franklin/01-21-02-0306); Greene, "Empire and Identity," 224–25; Marshall, *Making and Unmaking*, 180, 298–99, James Harris quoted on 299 ("a most complete").

116. F. Anderson, *Crucible of War*, 743–45; Bushman, *King and People*, 186; Chaplin, "British Atlantic," 233; Onuf, "Empire of Liberty," 196–203, Thomas Jefferson quoted on 197.

CHAPTER 2: LAND

1. Sir William Johnson to Thomas Gage, Apr. 8, 1768, in Sullivan et al., eds., *Papers of Sir William Johnson*, vol. 6:186.

2. Draper, *Struggle for Power*, 11–13; Benjamin Franklin, "Observations Concerning the Increase of Mankind, 1751," in Labaree et al., eds., *Papers of Benjamin Franklin*, vol. 4:225–34; McCoy, *Elusive Republic*, 49–51.

3. Earl of Hillsborough to Thomas Gage, July 31, 1770, in Davies, ed., *Documents of the American Revolution*, vol. 2:153–56; Hutchinson, *History of the Colony*, vol. 3:62; Sosin, *Whitehall and the Wilderness*, 167.

4. Draper, *Struggle for Power*, 10; Bailyn, *Voyagers to the West*, 40–42, British newspaper writer quoted on 41; Marshall, *Making and Unmaking*, 321–25.

5. Bailyn, *Voyagers to the West*, 24–28, 37–40, 43–49, Irish observer quoted on 37–38 ("if the numbers"); Marshall, *Making and Unmaking*, 324–25.

6. Bailyn, *Voyagers to the West*, 29–32, Earl of Hillsborough quoted on 30; Benjamin Franklin to William Franklin, Sept. 12, 1766, in Labaree et al., eds., *Papers of Benjamin Franklin*, vol. 13:414; Marshall, *Making and Unmaking*, 323; G. Wood, *Americanization of Benjamin Franklin*, 135.

7. Bailyn, *Voyagers to the West*, 49–55; D. Morgan, *Devious Dr. Franklin*, 117.

8. F. Anderson, *Crucible of War*, 469–71; Calloway, *Scratch of a Pen*, 55–56, 66–69, Yahatastonake quoted on 106, and George Galphin on 110 ("People is mad"); Minweweh quoted in Snyder, "Native Nations," 84 ("Although you have").

9. Calloway, *Scratch of a Pen*, 50–52, George Croghan quoted on 50 ("highest notions") and Sir William Johnson on 52 ("greatly disgusted"); M. Ward, *Breaking the Backcountry*, 216–18; R. White, *Middle Ground*, 275–79.

10. Neolin quoted in Calloway, *Scratch of a Pen*, 70 ("Heaven"); Dixon, "'We Speak as One People,'" 58–59; Dowd, *Spirited Resistance*, 33–36; Shoemaker, *Strange Likeness*, 129–40; M. Ward, *Breaking the Backcountry*, 209–10; R. White, *Middle Ground*, 278–85.

11. Calloway, *Scratch of a Pen*, 71–72; R. White, *Middle Ground*, 285–89.

12. Calloway, *Scratch of a Pen*, 72–75, Turtle's Heart quoted on 72 ("This land"); Dixon, "'We Speak as One People,'" 45; Lenman, *Britain's Colonial Wars*, 177–78; R. White, *Middle Ground*, 269–96.

13. Merrell, *Into the American Woods*, 284–91; Merritt, *At the Crossroads*, 283–94.

14. Calloway, *Scratch of a Pen*, 76–81; Benjamin Franklin, "A Narrative of the Late Massacres in Lancaster County," in Labaree et al., eds., *Papers of Benjamin Franklin*, vol. 11:55; Silver, *Our Savage Neighbors*, 177–81.

15. Alden, *General Gage*, 102–3; Dowd, *War Under Heaven*, 198; Hinderaker, *Elusive Empire*, 160–61; Merrell, *Into the American Woods*, 284–88; Richter, *Facing East*, 203–6; Silver, *Our Savage Neighbors*, 185–90.

16. Alden, *General Gage*, 89–90; Sir William Johnson to Board of Trade, Nov. 13, 1763, in E. B. O'Callaghan, ed., *Documents Relative to the Colonial History*, vol. 7:574 ("without considering"); Treaty of Peace with the Delaware Nation, May 8, 1765, and Johnson to Board of Trade, Aug. 20, 1766, in O'Callaghan, ed., *New York Colonial Documents*, vol 7:739, 852; Skaggs, "Sixty Years' War," 6–7; R. White, *Middle Ground*, 297–314.

17. Thomas Gage to Lord Shelburne, June 13, 1767, in Carter, ed., *Correspondence of General Thomas Gage*, vol. 1:143 ("I find"); Sir William Johnson, speech, July 24, 1766, in O'Callaghan, ed., *New York Colonial Documents*, vol. 7:855; Gage to Johnson, May 28, 1764, in Sullivan et al., eds., *Papers of Sir William Johnson*, vol. 4:433; R. White, *Middle Ground*, 305–6, 314–19.

18. Aron, *How the West Was Lost*, 13–15; McCoy, *Elusive Republic*, 122–23; Earl of Hillsborough to Thomas Gage, July 31, 1770, and Earl of Dunmore to Hillsborough, Nov. 12, 1770, in Davies, ed., *Documents of the American Revolution*, vol. 2:154, 255–56; Griffin, *American Leviathan*, 21–22; Ritcheson, *British Politics*, 63–64.

19. Alden, *General Gage*, 137–38; F. Anderson, *Crucible of War*, 565–71; Calloway, *Scratch of a Pen*, 90–98, 110–11; Campbell, *Speculators in Empire*, 73–74; Sir William Johnson to Board of Trade, Nov. 13, 1763, in O'Callaghan, ed., *New York Colonial Documents*, vol. 7:578; Royal Proclamation, Oct. 7, 1763, in Sosin, ed., *Opening of the West*, 79–81.

20. John Stuart to Earl of Hillsborough, Dec. 2, 1770, in Davies, ed., *Documents of the American Revolution*, vol. 2:280–83; Alden, *General Gage*, 92–96, 135–37, 147; Calloway, *Scratch of a Pen*, 110–11; Holton, "Ohio Indians," 463–64; Lenman, *Britain's Colonial Wars*, 182–83; Piecuch, *Three Peoples*, 31–34; Sosin, *Whitehall and the Wilderness*, 193–94.

21. Abernethy, *Western Lands*, 16; Preston, *Texture of Contact*, 71, 86, 92–97, 190–95; A. Taylor, *Divided Ground*, 3–4.

22. F. Anderson, *Crucible of War*, 565–66; Bailyn, *Voyagers to the West*, 55; Marshall, *Making and Unmaking*, 279–80; Starr, *Tories, Dons, and Rebels*, 2–3; J. L. Wright, *Florida in the American Revolution*, 2; Earl of Hillsborough to Thomas Gage, July 31, 1770, in Davies, ed., *Documents of the American Revolution*, vol. 2:153–56.

23. Gipson, *Coming of the Revolution*, 160–61; Niddrie, "Eighteenth-Century Settlement," 67–71, 76; O'Shaughnessy, *Empire Divided*, 41–42; Ragatz, *Fall of the Planter Class*, 111–12, 117.

24. Burnard, "Slavery and the Causes," 58–59; Niddrie, "Eighteenth-Century Settlement," 67–72; Ragatz, *Fall of the Planter Class*, 113–15, 117.

25. Niddrie, "Eighteenth-Century Settlement," 78; O'Shaughnessy, *Empire Divided*, 60; Ragatz, *Fall of the Planter Class*, 116–18, 127, Valentine Morris quoted on 118.

26. Weber, *Spanish Frontier*, 199–200; Wickman, "Spanish Colonial Floridas," 216; J. L. Wright, *Florida in the American Revolution*, 1.

27. Bailyn, *Voyagers to the West*, 430–37; Gipson, *Coming of the Revolution*, 153–54; Starr, *Tories, Dons, and Rebels*, 4–8, J. L. Wright, *Florida in the American Revolution*, 2–4, 8–12.

28. Bailyn, *Voyagers to the West*, 434–40, Lord Adam Gordon quoted on 434; J. L. Wright, *Florida in the American Revolution*, 2–3.

29. Bailyn, *Voyagers to the West*, 445–50, 457; J. L. Wright, *Florida in the American Revolution*, 3–4.

30. Bailyn, *Voyagers to the West*, 451–61; Gipson, *Coming of the Revolution*, 155; J. L. Wright, *Florida in the American Revolution*, 6–7.

31. Alden, *General Gage*, 106; Bailyn, *Voyagers to the West*, 469–72, James

Grant quoted on 472; J. L. Wright, *Florida in the American Revolution*, 13–14.

32. Bailyn, *Voyagers to the West*, 475–94; Starr, *Tories, Dons, and Rebels*, 6–8, 20–23; J. L. Wright, *Florida in the American Revolution*, 4, 8–12.

33. Franklin, "The Interest of Great Britain Considered," in Labaree et al., eds., *Papers of Benjamin Franklin*, vol. 9:73–74; McCoy, *Elusive Republic*, 51; Cadwallader Colden quoted in G. Wood, *Radicalism*, 114 ("The hopes").

34. Bailyn, *Voyagers to the West*, 486–87; Bushman, *King and People*, 199–206; G. Wood, *Radicalism*, 55–56, 125, 128; Shapiro, "Ethan Allen," 248.

35. Bailyn, *Voyagers to the West*, 482–83; Sir Henry Moore to the Lords of Trade, Jan. 12, 1767, in O'Callaghan, ed., *Documents Relative to the Colonial History*, vol. 7:888–89; G. Wood, *Radicalism*, 125–28.

36. Bailyn, *Voyagers to the West*, 8–20; Griffin, *American Leviathan*, 123; Preston, *Texture of Contact*, 216–18; Sosin, *Revolutionary Frontier*, 43–60, 65–71; John Munro to William Tryon, Nov. 6, 1771, in O'Callaghan, ed., *Documentary History of the State of New York*, vol. 4:453 ("They are crowding"); G. Wood, *Radicalism*, 125–27.

37. Aron, *How the West Was Lost*, 13–14; Charles Woodmason quoted in G. Wood, *Radicalism*, 132–33; H. Ward, *Between the Lines*, 235–36.

38. Bonomi, *Factious People*, 188, 204–11; Kim, *Landlord and Tenant*, 134–35; Thomas Gage to Sir William Johnson, Oct. 4, 1767, in Sullivan et al., eds., *Papers of Sir William Johnson*, vol. 12: 368; Thomas Gage to Lord Shelburne, Oct. 10, 1767, in Carter, ed., *Correspondence of General Thomas Gage*, vol. 1:152.

39. P. D. Nelson, *William Tryon*, 101–5; Earl of Hillsborough to William Tryon, Dec. 4, 1771, and Tryon to the Earl of Dartmouth, June 2, 1773, Tryon to Hillsborough, Apr. 11, 1772, and Tryon to the Earl of Dartmouth, Feb. 8, 1773, in O'Callaghan, ed., *New York Colonial Documents*, vol. 8:285–86, 293 ("I conceive"), 350 ("keep his ground"), and 373–74.

40. William Tryon, "Report on the State of the Province of New York, 1774," in O'Callaghan, ed., *Documentary History of the State of New York*, vol. 1:765–66; Bonomi, *Factious People*, 66–67, 219–20; Handlin and Mark, eds, "Chief Nimham," 196–200.

41. Moss Kent quoted in Countryman, "'Out of the Bounds of the Law,'" 49 ("In a course"); Handlin and Mark, eds., "Chief Nimham," 200–1; Kim, *Landlord and Tenant*, 379–80; Nammack, *Fraud, Politics, and the Dispossession of the Indians*, 76; Samuel Monroe to Sir William Johnson, Mar. 9, and May 12, 1765, and Roger Morris to Johnson, Aug. 12, 1765, in Sullivan et al., eds., *Papers of Sir William Johnson*, vol. 11: 630–31, 735, 884–85.

42. Bonomi, *Factious People*, 222–24; Kim, *Landlord and Tenant*, 381–96; Handlin and Mark, eds., "Chief Nimham," 207–9; Sir Henry Moore to Lords

of Trade, Aug. 12, 1766, in O'Callaghan, ed., *New York Colonial Documents*, vol. 7:849.

43. Bonomi, *Factious People*, 221–22; Handlin and Mark, eds., "Chief Nimham," 206–10; Lords of Trade, report, Aug. 30, 1766, in O'Callaghan, ed., *New York Colonial Documents*, vol. 7:868–870 ("unreasonable Severity" on 870); Lord Shelburne to Sir William Johnson, Oct. 11, 1766, in Sullivan et al., eds., *Papers of Sir William Johnson*, vol. 5:394.

44. Captain Jacobs, speech, Feb. 14, 1767, and Sir William Johnson to Guy Johnson, Feb. 24, 1767, in Sullivan et al., eds., *Papers of Sir William Johnson*, vol. 12:269, 270–73; Sir Henry Moore to Lord Shelburne, Dec. 22, 1766, Johnson to Shelburne, Jan. 15, 1767, and Apr. 1, 1767, and Moore to Shelburne, Dec. 22, 1766, and Apr. 3, 1767, in O'Callaghan, ed., *New York Colonial Documents*, vol. 7:886, 892, 913, and 915; Handlin and Mark, eds., "Chief Nimham," 211–13, 239, 243 ("vexatious"); New York Council, proceedings, Mar. 11, 1767, in Sullivan et al., eds., *Papers of Sir William Johnson*, vol. 5:506.

45. John Morin Scott quoted in Handlin and Mark, eds., "Chief Nimham," 239 ("open"); Yirush, *Settlers, Liberty, and Empire*, 113–41.

46. Kars, *Breaking Loose Together*, 27–75; Kay, "North Carolina Regulation," 75–76, 83–85; Nash, *Unknown American Revolution*, 75.

47. Ekirch, ed., "'New Government of Liberty,'" 632–46; Kars, *Breaking Loose Together*, 18, 24–26, 34, Herman Husbands quoted on 25 ("new government"); Husbands quoted in Kay, "North Carolina Regulation," 88 ("unequal").

48. Kars, *Breaking Loose Together*, 138–142, 182–86; Kay, "North Carolina Regulation," 73–74, 85–88, 97–99; Nash, *Unknown American Revolution*, 104–5.

49. Kars, *Breaking Loose Together*, 186–207, 211–12; Kay, "North Carolina Regulation," 99–103; Nash, *Unknown American Revolution*, 105–7.

50. Countryman, "'Out of the Bounds of the Law,'" 42–43; Jellison, *Ethan Allen*, 18–38; Shapiro, "Ethan Allen," 241–42.

51. Countryman, "'Out of the Bounds of the Law,'" 44–46; Nash, *Unknown American Revolution*, 113.

52. Countryman, "'Out of the Bounds of the Law,'" 47; Jellison, *Ethan Allen*, 34–38, Allen quoted on 34 ("great state" and "junto") and 62; Shapiro, "Ethan Allen," 239–43, Allen quoted on 239 ("God Damn"), 240 ("that his name"), and 243 ("sealed and confirmed").

53. Aron, *How the West Was Lost*, 6–12; Griffin, *American Leviathan*, 121–22, includes Little Carpenter quotation ("lose their Authority"); Hinderaker, *Elusive Empires*, 73–77, 188–89, 208; Holton, "Ohio Indians," 461–62; Merritt, "Native Peoples," 236–37; R. White, *Middle Ground*, 41–49, 131, 183–85.

54. Calloway, *American Revolution in Indian Country*, 172–73; R. White, *Middle Ground*, 388–94, Shawnees and Simon Kenton quoted on 393–94.

55. Aron, *How the West Was Lost*, 7–11, 35; Calloway, *American Revolution in Indian Country*, 162–64; Hinderaker, *Elusive Empires*, 67–71, 178–82; Snyder, *Slavery in Indian Country*, 158; R. White, *Middle Ground*, 324–39.

56. F. Anderson, *Crucible of War*, 566–68, 731–32; Calloway, *Scratch of a Pen*, 99–111, General Thomas Gage quoted on 100 ("too Numerous"); Campbell, *Speculators in Empire*, 74–75, 86; Thomas Gage to Sir William Johnson, June 28, 1767, Apr. 5, and Nov. 9, 1767, and Apr. 3, 1769, in Sullivan et al., eds., *Papers of Sir William Johnson*, vol. 5:574, vol.12:296 ("driving"), 376–80, 709–10; *Virginia Gazette*, Jan. 14, 1773, quoted in Holton, "Ohio Indians," 454; Preston, *Texture of Contact*, 253–55; R. White, *Middle Ground*, 315–65.

57. Griffin, *American Leviathan*, 74–78; John Penn to Sir William Johnson, Mar. 21, 1765, and Thomas Gage to Johnson, May 8, 1765, in Sullivan et al., eds., *Papers of Sir William Johnson*, vol. 11:643–44, 718; Gage to Henry Seymour Conway, May 6, 1766, in Carter, ed., *Correspondence of General Thomas Gage*, vol. 1:91 ("This Spring"); Ward, "'Indians Our Real Friends,'" 75–76.

58. Sir William Johnson to Thomas Gage, June 27, 1766, in Sullivan et al., eds., *Papers of Sir William Johnson*, vol. 12:115; Johnson to Lords of Trade, June 28, and Aug. 20, 1766, in O'Callaghan, ed., *New York Colonial Documents*, vol. 7:837, 852; Benjamin Franklin to Johnson, Sept. 12, 1766, in Labaree et al., eds., *Papers of Benjamin Franklin*, vol. 13:416.

59. Griffin, *American Leviathan*, 82–83; Ward, "'Indians Our Real Friends,'" 76–77; R. White, *Middle Ground*, 344–46; Conoghquieson speech, Mar. 8, 1768, in O'Callaghan, ed., *New York Colonial Documents*, vol. 8:47; Johnson to Gage, June 27, 1766, in Sullivan et al., eds., *Papers of Sir William Johnson*, vol. 12:115; Johnson to Lords of Trade, June 28, and Aug. 20, 1766, in O'Callaghan, ed., *New York Colonial Documents*, vol. 7:837, 852 ("meritorious act" and "this seems"). For the murder of the two Indian women see "A Horrid Murder," *Pennsylvania Gazette*, July 10, 1766; "Court of Oyer and Terminer," *Pennsylvania Journal*, Aug. 7, 1766.

60. Thomas Gage to Lord Shelburne, Jan. 22, 1768, in Carter, ed., *Correspondence of General Thomas Gage*, vol. 1:157 ("At present"); John Stuart quoted in Snyder, "Native Nations," 84; Snyder, *Slavery in Indian Country*, 156.

61. F. *Anderson, Crucible of War*, 568–70, 740; Calloway, *Scratch of a Pen*, 98–99; Holton, "Ohio Indians," 454–58; George Washington to William Crawford, Sept. 17, 1767, in Rhodehamel, ed., *George Washington*, 124–26; Thomas Gage to Sir William Johnson, Apr. 3, 1769, in Sullivan et al., eds., *Papers of Sir William Johnson*, vol. 12:710.

62. Alden, *General Gage*, 133–35, 139–43; Sosin, *Whitehall and the Wilderness*,

165–68, 211–13, Earl of Hillsborough quoted on 213 ("enormous expence"); Ward, "'Indians Our Real Friends,'" 69, 74–79.

63. Griffin, *American Leviathan*, 84–85; Hinderaker, *Elusive Empires*, 168–69; Holton, "Ohio Indians," 460; Sosin, *Whitehall and the Wilderness*, 169–72.

64. Alden, *General Gage*, 147–48; Calloway, *Scratch of a Pen*, 62–65, 99–100; Campbell, *Speculators in Empire*, 139–66; Sosin, *Whitehall and the Wilderness*, 172–80, 194–96, 211.

65. Aron, *How the West Was Lost*, 17–18; Griffin, *American Leviathan*, 88–90, Earl of Hillsborough quoted on 93; Holton, "Ohio Indians," 465–67.

66. Thomas Gage to Sir William Johnson, Sept. 10, 1769, in Sullivan et al., eds., *Papers of Sir William Johnson*, vol. 7:160; Earl of Hillsborough to Sir William Johnson, Jan. 4, 1769, and Congress with the Six Nations at German Flats, July 21, 1770, in E. B. O'Callaghan, ed., *New York Colonial Documents*, vol. 8:145, 236; Holton, "Ohio Indians," 468–70.

67. Abernethy, *Western Lands*, 44–46; F. Anderson, *Crucible of War*, 595, 744–45; Griffin, *American Leviathan*, 87–88; D. Morgan, *Devious Dr. Franklin*, 116–17, 172–73; McCoy, *Elusive Republic*, 51–53, 62–63; Sosin, *Whitehall and the Wilderness*, 183–88, and 199–201, including William Strahan quotation on 199 ("better *Connections*"); G. Wood, *Americanization of Benjamin Franklin*, 135–37; Benjamin Franklin to William Franklin, Sept. 12, 1766, and B. Franklin to Thomas Cushing, Jan. 13, 1772, in Labaree, et al., eds., *Papers of Benjamin Franklin*, vol. 13:414–15 and 19:22–23.

68. Benjamin Franklin to William Franklin, Aug. 17, 1772, in Labaree et al., eds., *Papers of Benjamin Franklin*, vol. 19:243–44; D. Morgan, *Devious Dr. Franklin*, 173–74, 194–95; Ritcheson, *British Politics*, 145–46; Sosin, *Whitehall and the Wilderness*, 189–93, 196–206.

69. Alden, *General Gage*, 148–49; Griffin, *American Leviathan*, 102–9; D. Morgan, *Devious Dr. Franklin*, 229–32; Sosin, *Whitehall and the Wilderness*, 206–10.

70. Alden, *General Gage*, 149–50; Alden, *John Stuart*, 288–90; Sosin, *Whitehall and the Wilderness*, 206–10; George Washington to Lord Botetourt, Oct. 5, 1770, Thomas Gage to John Stuart, Oct. 16, 1770, William Nelson to Earl of Hillsborough, Oct. 18, 1770, and Earl of Dunmore to Hillsborough, Nov. 12, 1770, in Davies, ed., *Documents of the American Revolution*, vol. 2:201–3, 203–4, 205–10 ("such convulsions" on 209), and 255–56.

71. Alden, *General Gage*, 143–45; Griffin, *American Leviathan*, 92–94; Hinderaker, *Elusive Empires*, 170–72; Sosin, *Whitehall and the Wilderness*, 220–22, Thomas Gage quoted on 221 ("I wish"); Gage to Viscount Barrington, Mar. 4, 1772, in Carter, ed., *Correspondence of General Thomas Gage*, vol. 2:137 ("Let them feel").

72. Griffin, *American Leviathan*, 97–99, including John Heckewelder quoted

on 97 ("rove"); Holton, "Ohio Indians," 462; Snyder, *Slavery in Indian Country*, 156–57; Hinderaker, *Elusive Empires*, 170–74, 197–98.

73. Alden, *John Stuart*, 285–93; Griffin, *American Leviathan*, 98–99, 104; Hinderaker, *Elusive Empires*, 170–74; Holton, "Ohio Indians," 471–72; Hugh Wallace to Sir William Johnson, June 3, 1770, in Sullivan et al., eds., *Papers of Sir William Johnson*, vol. 7:711 ("a very good natural").

74. Griffin, *American Leviathan*, 103–7; Sosin, *Whitehall and the Wilderness*, 195–96, 222–29; R. White, *Middle Ground*, 356–57; Frederick Haldimand to Earl of Dartmouth, Nov. 3, 1773, in Davies, ed., *Documents of the American Revolution*, vol. 6:237–38 ("the asylum").

75. Devereux Smith to William Smith, June 10, 1774, in Sosin, ed., *Opening of the West*, 11–14; Griffin, *American Leviathan*, 108–110, Arthur Campbell quoted on 109 ("would be easier"); Hinderaker, *Elusive Empires*, 190–92; Holton, "Ohio Indians," 473–74, William Preston quoted on 474 ("The Oppertun[i]ty"); R. White, *Middle Ground*, 354–64.

76. Hinderaker, *Elusive Empires*, 190–92; Preston, *Texture of Contact*, 280–82; R. White, *Middle Ground*, 354–64.

77. Abernethy, *Western Lands*, 110–13; Aron, *How the West Was Lost*, 20–21; Griffin, *American Leviathan*, 98–101, 111–20, Earl of Dunmore quoted on 123 ("undoubtedly"); Hinderaker, *Elusive Empires*, 192–94; Holton, "Ohio Indians," 474.

78. Griffin, *American Leviathan*, 98–101, 120–23; R. White, *Middle Ground*, 362–64.

79. Aron, *How the West Was Lost*, 35–37, 59–62; Griffin, *American Leviathan*, 121–22.

80. Alden, *John Stuart*, 290–93; Aron, *How the West Was Lost*, 37–38, 59–62; Hinderaker, *Elusive Empires*, 195–96; Snyder, *Slavery in Indian Country*, 157; Sosin, *Revolutionary Frontier*, 36–38, Dragging Canoe quoted on 38 ("bloody ground"), 76–77.

81. Richard Henderson quoted in Aron, *How the West Was Lost*, 65 ("set of scoundrels"); Griffin, *American Leviathan*, 121–22, William Preston quoted on 121 ("When they got"); Henderson quoted in Hinderaker, *Elusive Empires*, 197 ("unless"); Sosin, *Revolutionary Frontier*, 77.

82. Aron, *How the West Was Lost*, 20–21, 66–67; Six Nations Congress, Dec. 1, 1774, in E. B. O'Callaghan, ed., *Documents Relative to the Colonial History*, vol. 8:521 ("who are white Men"); Hinderaker, *Elusive Empires*, 194–95, William Doack quoted on 194 ("When without a king").

83. Calloway, *Scratch of a Pen*, 112–22; Eccles, *French in North America*, 240, 243–44; Marshall, "Incorporation of Quebec," 43–44.

84. M. Anderson, *Battle for the Fourteenth Colony*, 17–18; Calloway, *Scratch of a Pen*, 114–18; Conway, *War, State, and Society*, 238–39; P. Lawson, *Imperial Challenge*, 32–41; Marshall, "Incorporation of Quebec," 44–62.

85. M. Anderson, *Battle for the Fourteenth Colony*, 33–34; Calloway, *Scratch of a Pen*, 118–20, James Murray quoted on 118 ("Licentious Fanaticks") and 119 ("faithful & useful"); P. Lawson, *Imperial Challenge*, 48–51, Murray quoted on 48 ("as I cannot be") and 49 ("disbanded soldiers"); Conway, *War, State, and Society*, 238–39.

86. F. Anderson, *Crucible of War*, 730–31; M. Anderson, *Battle for the Fourteenth Colony*, 34–35; Calloway, *Scratch of a Pen*, 120–21, Montreal merchants quoted on 121 ("Vexatious"); P. Lawson, *Imperial Challenge*, 51–59.

87. F. Anderson, *Crucible of War*, 730–31; M. Anderson, *Battle for the Fourteenth Colony*, 36–37; P. Lawson, *Imperial Challenge*, 72–73, 93–95, Viscount Barrington quoted on 94; Marshall, "Incorporation of Quebec," 44–62, Sir Guy Carleton quoted on 59 ("The Province"); Carleton quoted in Tousignant, "Comment," 64 ("severe Climate"); Ritcheson, *British Politics*, 65.

88. M. Anderson, *Battle for the Fourteenth Colony*, 39–41; Calloway, *Scratch of a Pen*, 121–22; P. Lawson, *Imperial Challenge*, 139–45; Marshall, "Incorporation of Quebec," 59–62; Thomas, *Tea Party to Independence*, 91–98.

89. Sosin, *Whitehall and the Wilderness*, 241–8, Alexander Wedderburn quoted on 245 ("This is the border"); Thomas, *Tea Party to Independence*, 99–104; Ward, "'The Indians Our Real Friends,'" 79–80.

90. M. Anderson, *Battle for the Fourteenth Colony*, 43; Lenman, *Britain's Colonial Wars*, 189–90, *New York Journal* quoted on 190 ("The finger of God"); Marshall, "Incorporation of Quebec," 44.

91. M. Anderson, *Battle for the Fourteenth Colony*, 12, 41–44; English visitor quoted in Breen, *American Insurgents*, 103; Jordan, "Familial Politics," 299–301; McConville, *King's Three Faces*, 281–91; Marston, *King and Congress*, 43; Boston writer quoted in P. Smith, *New Age Now Begins*, 406 ("a superstitious").

92. Holton, *Forced Founders*, 35–38; Richard Henry Lee quoted in Holton, "Ohio Indians," 475 ("worst grievance"); Nash, *Unknown American Revolution*, 172; George Mason's resolutions quoted in Rakove, *Revolutionaries*, 166 ("a premeditated").

93. Earl of Dartmouth to American governors, Feb. 5, 1774, in Davies., ed., *Documents of the American Revolution*, vol. 8:42–45; Bailyn, *Voyagers to the West*, 55–56; Sosin, *Whitehall and the Wilderness*, 226–27.

94. Thomas Jefferson, "Draft of Instructions to the Virginia Delegates," in Boyd et al., eds., *Papers of Thomas Jefferson*, vol. 1:121–37 ("no right"); Edmund Pendleton quoted in Holton, "Ohio Indians," 475 ("the Ministry"); Onuf, *Origins of the Federal Republic*, 81–82; Selby, *Revolution in Virginia*, 199.

95. Countryman, "'Out of the Bounds of the Law,'" 48.

96. Kars, *Breaking Loose Together*, 207–8, Josiah Martin quoted on 208; Kay, "North Carolina Regulation," 104; Nash, *Unknown American Revolution*, 108.

97. Kars, *Breaking Loose Together*, 212; Kay, "North Carolina Regulation," 104–5, James Hunter quoted on 105 ("given" and "hate"); Nash, *Unknown American Revolution*, 163–64.

98. Thomas McKee to Sir William Johnson, June 1, 1765, and Johnson to Thomas Gage, June 19, 1765, in Sullivan et al., eds., *Papers of Sir William Johnson*, vol. 11:760–61, 798–99; Gage to Lord Halifax, June 8, 1765, in Carter, ed., *Correspondence of General Thomas Gage*, vol. 1:61–62; Johnson to Lords of Trade, July n.d., 1765, in O'Callaghan, ed., *New York Colonial Documents*, vol. 7:746–47; George Croghan quoted in Griffin, *American Leviathan*, 91.

99. Countryman, "'Out of the Bounds of the Law,'" 49; Griffin, *American Leviathan*, 240–71; Hinderaker, *Elusive Empires*, 185–87; Kars, *Breaking Loose Together*, 209–10; Captain John Montresor quoted in Kim, *Landlord and Tenant*, 388–89 ("Sons of Liberty"); Nash, *Unknown American Revolution*, 72–73, 84; R. White, *Middle Ground*, 364–65, 418.

CHAPTER 3: SLAVES

1. Nathaniel Niles quoted in Lepore, *Whites of Their Eyes*, 93.

2. Anderson, *Crucible of War*, 560–72, 580, 602; Greene, *Peripheries and Center*, 47–53; R. R. Johnson, "Parliamentary Egotisms," 338–62, Charles Garth quoted on 347 ("the power"); Gould, "Fears of War," 20; Marshall, "Thirteen Colonies," 72, 86–87; Marshall, *Making and Unmaking*, 76–81, 85, 105–7, 159–62; Ritcheson, *British Politics*, 24; G. Wood, *Americanization of Benjamin Franklin*, 118–19.

3. Draper, *Struggle for Power*, 36–37; Greene, *Negotiated Authorities*, 34–40; Greene, *Peripheries and Center*, 12, 28–42; Hendrickson, "The First Union," 37; Charles Thomson to Benjamin Franklin, Sept. 24, 1765, in Labaree et al., eds., *Papers of Benjamin Franklin*, vol. 12:278–80; Bushman, *King and People*, 177; Massachusetts House of Representatives, July 31, 1770, in Hutchinson, *History of the Province*, vol. 3:392; R. R. Johnson, "Parliamentary Egotisms,'" 350–53; Marshall, *Making and Unmaking*, 176–78; Ritcheson, *British Politics*, 26, Francis Bernard quoted on 43 ("perfect states").

4. Bailyn, *Origins of American Politics*, 40–48; R. R. Johnson, "'Parliamentary Egotisms,'" 347–53, Earl of Hillsborough quoted on 348 ("It is essential") and Thomas Hutchinson quoted on 358 ("I know"); McConville, *The King's Three Faces*, 249–61; Marshall, *Making and Unmaking*, 165–68, 178, 181; Ritcheson, *British Politics*, 12–13; G. Wood, "Problem of Sovereignty," 573–75.

5. Bailyn, *Origins of American Politics*, 40–48, Thomas Gordon and John Trenchard quoted on 41 ("Power") and 42 ("We have").

6. G. Wood, *Radicalism of the American Revolution*, 101–5.

7. Bailyn, *Origins of American Politics*, 35–38, 52–54.

8. Bailyn, *Origins of American Politics*, 54–58; Bushman, *King and People*, 123–32.

9. R. R. Johnson, "'Parliamentary Egotisms,'" 349, 356; McConville, *King's Three Faces*, 249–50, 261–69; Benjamin Franklin to the Printer of the *Gazeteer*, Jan. 13, 1768, in Labaree et al., eds., *Papers of Benjamin Franklin*, vol. 15:19 ("To be apprehensive"); Lepore, *Whites of their Eyes*, 59–60, Boston Town Meeting quoted on 59; Maier, *From Resistance to Revolution*, 104–5; Tomlins, "Republican Law," 541–42; G. Wood, *Americanization of Benjamin Franklin*, 126–29; Yirush, "Imperial Crisis," 85–99.

10. F. Anderson, *Crucible of War*, 487–88, 561–63; Bushman, *King and People*, 164–65; Gould, "Fears of War," 32–33; Marshall, *Making and Unmaking*, 275–79; "America Triumphant" quoted in E. S. Morgan and H. Morgan, *Stamp Act Crisis*, 338; Ritcheson, *British Politics*, 9–12, 15–16.

11. F. Anderson, *Crucible of War*, 563–64, 575–76; E. S. Morgan and H. Morgan, *Stamp Act Crisis*, 38–40; O'Shaughnessy, *Empire Divided*, 65–66; Ritcheson, *British Politics*, 17–18.

12. F. Anderson, *Crucible of War*, 572–80; Burnard, *Mastery*, 14–17; Burnard, "Slavery and the Causes," 66–67; Bushman, *King and People*, 142–43; Benjamin Franklin to Peter Collinson, Apr. 30, 1764, in Labaree et al., eds., *Papers of Benjamin Franklin*, vol. 11:180–84; Marshall, *Making and Unmaking*, 281–82; E. S. Morgan and H. Morgan, *Stamp Act Crisis*, 39–44; O'Shaughnessy, *Empire Divided*, 10–17, 28, 32, 65–66; Ritcheson, *British Politics*, 18–19.

13. F. Anderson, *Crucible of War*, 581–87; Bushman, *King and People*, 144–49; Marshall, *Making and Unmaking*, 282; E. S. Morgan and H. Morgan, *Stamp Act Crisis*, 47–48.

14. F. Anderson, *Crucible of War*, 604–16, 642–46; Marshall, *Making and Unmaking*, 285–86; E. S. Morgan and H. Morgan, *Stamp Tax Crisis*, 42–43, 75–98; Ritcheson, *British Politics*, 20–29.

15. F. Anderson, *Crucible of War*, 604–16, 642–46, Charles Townshend quoted on 642 ("If America"); R. R. Johnson, "'Parliamentary Egotisms,'" 347; Edmund Burke quoted in Marshall, *Making and Unmaking*, 167, 286–88; G. Wood, *Americanization of Benjamin Franklin*, 206–7.

16. F. Anderson, *Crucible of War*, 645–47; E. S. Morgan and H. Morgan, *Stamp Act Crisis*, 74–98.

17. F. Anderson, *Crucible of War*, 563, 588–93; Conway, *War, State, and Society*, 244; Nash, *Urban Crucible*, 246–53; Marshall, *Making and Unmaking*, 115–16; E. S. Morgan and H. Morgan, *Stamp Act Crisis*, 48–49; Lynd and Waldstreicher, "Free Trade, Sovereignty, and Slavery," 606–7.

18. F. Anderson, *Crucible of War*, 591–92, 668–69; Nash, *Urban Crucible*, 252–62.

19. F. Anderson, *Crucible of War*, 605–7, 669; Bailyn, *Ordeal of Thomas Hutchinson*, 39–54; Nash, *Urban Crucible*, 273–76.

20. F. Anderson, *Crucible of War*, 669; Bailyn, *Ordeal of Thomas Hutchinson*, 44–45, 67–68; Nash, *Urban Crucible*, 273–78.

21. F. Anderson, *Crucible of War*, 607–8; Bailyn, *Ordeal of Thomas Hutchinson*, 17–18, 62–65, Hutchinson quoted on 64 ("The rights"); Joseph Galloway to Benjamin Franklin, Sept. 20, 1765, in Labaree et al., eds., *Papers of Benjamin Franklin*, vol. 12: 269–70.

22. Fowler, *Samuel Adams*, 30–56; Maier, *Old Revolutionaries*, 17–50, Samuel Adams quoted on 18 ("keep"), and 34 ("I glory"); Joseph Galloway quoted in Rakove, *Revolutionaries*, 59 ("by no means").

23. Butterfield et al., eds., *Diary and Autobiography of John Adams*, vol. 1:100 ("I have"), 259–61 ("Is not"); Anderson, *Urban Crucible*, 683–84; Bailyn, *Ordeal of Thomas Hutchinson*, 39–54, James Otis quoted on 52 ("set the whole").

24. F. Anderson, *Crucible of War*, 608–9; Bushman, *King and People*, 179–82; McConville, *King's Three Faces*, 287–88; Marshall, *Making and Unmaking*, 305–6; Nash, *Urban Crucible*, 279–82, E. S. Morgan and H. Morgan, *Stamp Act Crisis*, 172. The Morgans note that the Patriots were "able to turn the hatred of the poor against the British government instead of against the rich."

25. Bushman, *King and People*, 182–83, Daniel Leonard quoted on 183 ("They were"); Maier, *Old Revolutionaries*, 17–19, 28–29; E. S. Morgan and H. Morgan, *Stamp Act Crisis*, 248.

26. Gould, "Fears of War," 26–28; *Newport Mercury*, Oct. 28, 1765, quoted in Maier, *From Resistance to Revolution*, 51; E. S. Morgan and H. Morgan, *Stamp Act Crisis*, 212; O'Shaughnessy, *Empire Divided*, 82.

27. F. Anderson, *Crucible of War*, 604–7, 660–65; Conway, *War, State and Society*, 245–47, Pennsylvania assemblymen quoted on 245 ("entitled"); R. R. Johnson, "Parliamentary Egotisms,'" 352–53; Patrick Henry quoted in Maier, *From Resistance to Revolution*, 52–53; Marshall, *Making and Unmaking*, 291; E. S. Morgan and H. Morgan, *Stamp Tax Crisis*, 52–58; Benjamin Franklin to John Hughes, Aug. 9, 1765, and Charles Thomson to Benjamin Franklin, Sept. 24, 1765, in Labaree et al., eds., *Papers of Benjamin Franklin*, vol. 12:234–35, 278–80.

28. Charles Thomson to Benjamin Franklin, Sept. 24, 1765, in Labaree et al., eds., *Papers of Benjamin Franklin*, vol. 12:279; McConville, *King's Three Faces*, 249–57, New York writer quoted on 250 ("the pretence") and banner quoted on 256 ("King"); Samuel Adams quoted in Maier, *Old Revolutionaries*, 21–22 ("so sensible"); E. S. Morgan and H. Morgan, *Stamp Act Crisis*, 260–61.

29. F. Anderson, *Crucible of War*, 665–71; Bailyn, *Ordeal of Thomas Hutchinson*, 35–36, 65–69; Bushman, *King and People*, 179–80; E. S. Morgan and

H. Morgan, *Stamp Act Crisis*, 160–68; Nash, *Urban Crucible*, 260–62, 273–81, 293, 293–97.

30. David Hall to Benjamin Franklin, Sept. 6, 1765, and John Hughes to Franklin, Sept. 8–17, 1765, in Labaree et al., eds., *Papers of Benjamin Franklin*, vol. 12:255–59, 264–66; Anderson, *Crucible of War*, 672–76, cheer quoted on 674 ("liberty and property"); Maier, *From Resistance to Revolution*, 54–58; E. S. Morgan and H. Morgan, *Stamp Act Crisis*, 187–96, 203–4, 213; Nash, *Urban Crucible*, 305–7.

31. Alden, *General Gage*, 118–22; F. Anderson, *Crucible of War*, 677–79; Maier, *From Resistance to Revolution*, 67–69; Nash, *Urban Crucible*, 300–304.

32. Joseph Galloway to Benjamin Franklin, Oct. 8, 1765, in Labaree et al., eds., *Papers of Benjamin Franklin*, vol. 12:306; F. Anderson, *Crucible of War*, 671; E. S. Morgan and H. Morgan, *Stamp Act Crisis*, 172–86, 205–17; Nash, *Urban Crucible*, 308.

33. Brebner, *Neutral Yankees*, 157–63; Jarvis, *Eye of All Trade*, 383–84; Lawson, *Imperial Challenge*, 91–93; Mancke, *Fault Lines of Empire*, 72; Piecuch, *Three Peoples*, 23–24; Starr, *Tories, Dons, and Rebels*, 36–42; J. L. Wright, *Florida*, 17–18.

34. Marshall, *Making and Unmaking*, 298–99; E. S. Morgan and H. Morgan, *Stamp Act Crisis*, 215–16; O'Shaughnessy, *Empire Divided*, 81–104.

35. Butterfield et al., eds., *Diary and Autobiography of John Adams*, vol. 1:285; Marshall, *Making and Unmaking*, 298–99; E. S. Morgan and H. Morgan, *Stamp Act Crisis*, 138–39, Christopher Gadsden quoted on 146, for the cartoon see 257.

36. F. Anderson, *Crucible of War*, 679–81; Breen, *Marketplace of Revolution*, 219; E. S. Morgan and H. Morgan, *Stamp Act Crisis*, 139–44, Stamp Act Congress quoted on 143.

37. *Boston Gazette* quoted in F. Anderson, *Crucible of War*, 682–83 ("weavers"); Breen, *Marketplace of Revolution*, 223–29; E. S. Morgan and H. Morgan, *Stamp Act Crisis*, 118–19, 331.

38. F. Anderson, *Crucible of War*, 691–99; Marshall, *Making and Unmaking*, 294–96; E. S. Morgan and H. Morgan, *Stamp Act Crisis*, 231, 327–40, 348; Ritcheson, *British Politics*, 35–51.

39. F. Anderson, *Crucible of War*, 703–13, Declaratory Act quoted on 703; Ritcheson, *British Politics*, 60–67; Marshall, *Making and Unmaking*, 296–97; E. S. Morgan and H. Morgan, *Stamp Act Crisis*, 346–52, 354; Wood; *Americanization of Benjamin Franklin*, 120.

40. F. Anderson, *Crucible of War*, 709; Gipson, *Coming of the Revolution*, 172–73, William Samuel Johnson quoted on 172 ("that they are"); Maier, *From Resistance to Revolution*, 61–62, 107–12; North Carolina legislature quoted

in Conway, *War, State, and Society,* 248; G. Wood, *Americanization of Benjamin Franklin,* 120.

41. Breen, *Marketplace of Revolution,* 235–36, 239–40; Calloway, *Scratch of a Pen,* 20; Maier, *From Resistance to Revolution,* 114–15.

42. Butterfield et al., eds., *Diary and Autobiography of John Adams,* vol. 1:263 ("So universal"); E. S. Morgan and H. Morgan, *Stamp Act Crisis,* 239–40, 265–66.

43. F. Anderson, *Crucible of War,* 681; Maier, *From Resistance to Revolution,* 58–71; Marshall, *Making and Unmaking,* 303; E. S. Morgan and H. Morgan, *Stamp Act Crisis,* 141, 245–50; Nash, *Urban Crucible,* 351–56.

44. Countryman, *American Revolution,* 97–104; Lepore, *Whites of their Eyes,* 29–30, 33–34, 38–40; Maier, *From Resistance to Revolution,* 77–91, 240–42; E. S. Morgan and H. Morgan, *Stamp Act Crisis,* 257–59; Nash, *Urban Crucible,* 304–6, 364–72.

45. Bushman, *King and People,* 177–78, 185–86; Butterfield et al., eds., *Diary and Autobiography of John Adams,* vol. 1:263 ("The people"); John Adams to Mercy Otis Warren, July 27, 1807 ("Was not"), Founders Online, National Archives (http://founders.archives.gov/documents/Adams/99–02–02–5196); Maier, *From Resistance to Revolution,* 88–89; Nash, *Urban Crucible,* 340–50.

46. Maier, *From Resistance to Revolution,* 124; John Holt to Deborah Franklin, Feb. 15, 1766, quoted in E. S. Morgan and H. Morgan, *Stamp Act Crisis,* 249–52.

47. Maier, *From Resistance to Revolution,* 89–112, Francis Bernard quoted on 92 ("prisoner at large"), New York Sons of Liberty quoted on 96 ("are not attempting") and 98 ("farther than"), Newport Sons of Liberty quoted on 101 ("strong Sense"); Marshall, *Making and Unmaking,* 291–93, Bernard quoted on 293 ("meer nominal"); E. S. Morgan and H. Morgan, *Stamp Act Crisis,* 255–56.

48. Bushman, *King and People,* 165–66; Marshall, *Making and Unmaking,* 293; E. S. Morgan and H. Morgan, *Stamp Act Crisis,* 19–35, Francis Bernard quoted on 28 ("give strength").

49. Bushman, *King and People,* 167–68; Marshall, *Making and Unmaking,* 307–8; E. S. Morgan and H. Morgan, *Stamp Act Crisis,* 334–46; Ritcheson, *British Politics,* 99–101; G. Wood, *Americanization of Benjamin Franklin,* 117–20, 130.

50. Breen, *Marketplace of Revolution,* 243–44; Bushman, *King and People,* 169–70; Marshall, *Making and Unmaking,* 306–8, 314; Ritcheson, *British Politics,* 99–100.

51. George Washington to George Mason, Apr. 5, 1769, and Mason to Washington, Apr. 5, 1769, in Abbot et al, eds., *Papers of George Washington,* vol.

8:177–81 ("such an alteration"), and 182–84 ("Our All"); Breen, *Marketplace of Revolution*, 244–47; Tyler, *Smugglers and Patriots*, 139–69.

52. Breen, *Marketplace of Revolution*, 248–65; Benjamin Franklin, "The Rise and Present State of Our Misunderstanding," Nov. 6–8, 1770, in Labaree et al., eds., *Papers of Benjamin Franklin*, vol. 17: 268–73 ("enemies").

53. Breen, *Marketplace of Revolution*, 253–63; Carp, *Rebels Rising*, 50; Maier, *From Resistance to Revolution*, 73–74, New Jersey Patriots quoted on 74; McConville, *King's Three Faces*, 287–88.

54. Breen, *Marketplace of Revolution*, 255–75, Thomas Gage quoted on 255.

55. Fowler, *Baron of Beacon Hill*, 113–20, mob quoted on 119 ("Kill"); Maier, *From Resistance to Revolution*, 127, 129; Tyler, *Smugglers and Patriots*, 121–27, 129–38, 158.

56. Alden, *General Gage*, 157–58; Carp, *Rebels Rising*, 45–46; Fowler, *Baron of Beacon Hill*, 84–85; Maier, *From Resistance to Revolution*, 124–25; Middlekauff, *Glorious Cause*, 166–70, Francis Bernard quoted on 170.

57. Alden, *General Gage*, 156–73, Earl of Hillsborough quoted on 157 ("protect"); Carp, *Rebels Rising*, 52–53; Lepore, *Whites of their Eyes*, 56–57; Maier, *From Resistance to Revolution*, 126–28; Middlekauff, *Glorious Cause*, 173–75, 193–98.

58. Alden, *General Gage*, 174–83; Bailyn, *Ordeal of Thomas Hutchinson*, 157–63; Fowler, *Baron of Beacon Hill*, 123–24; Young, *Shoemaker and the Tea Party*, 36–41.

59. Alden, *General Gage*, 180, 184; James Bowdoin et al., quoted in Bailyn, *Ordeal of Thomas Hutchinson*, 163 ("wicked and designing"); Lepore, *Whites of their Eyes*, 63–64, 86.

60. Champagne, *Alexander McDougall*, 23–26; Maier, Old Revolutionaries, 74–76.

61. Berkin, *Revolutionary Mothers*, 13–25, Anna Green Winslow quoted on 17; Breen, *Marketplace of Revolution*, 229–34, 280–82; Gundersen, *To Be Useful to the World*, 173–75; Kerber, *Women of the Republic*, 15–67; Nash, *Unknown American Revolution*, 141–44, Christopher Gadsden quoted on 141; Norton, *Liberty's Daughters*, 155–66.

62. Oliver, *Origins and Progress*, 97–98 ("Ladys"); Ulrich, "Daughters of Liberty," 211–14; A. Young, "Women of Boston," 196–206, conservative quoted on 206 ("A certain" and "mischief making devils"); Zagarri, *Revolutionary Backlash*, 22–23.

63. Gundersen, *To Be Useful to the World*, 176–78; Kerber, *Women of the Republic*, 15–67; Norton, *Liberty's Daughters*, 157–61, 166–69, 177, *South Carolina Gazette*, quoted on 159; Oliver, *Origins and Progress*, 63–64; Ulrich, "'Daughters of Liberty'" 214–18, 225–31; A. Young, "Women of Boston," 211–13, 216–17.

64. Breen, *Marketplace of Revolution*, 229–34, anonymous writer quoted on

233 ("What should induce"); Kerber, *Women of the Republic*, 82–85, Mercy Otis Warren quoted on 84; Norton, *Liberty's Daughters*, 121–23.

65. Gundersen, *To Be Useful to the World*, 176–77; Norton, *Liberty's Daughters*, 169–72, Charity Clarke quoted on 169, Annis Boudinot Stockton quoted on 171, Eliza Wilkinson quoted on 171–172; Young, "Women of Boston," 209–11.

66. Breen, *Marketplace of Revolution*, 289–93; Carp, *Rebels Rising*, 51–52; Marshall, *Making and Unmaking*, 317–18, 326–31; O'Shaughnessy, *Men Who Lost America*, 50–51; Ritcheson, *British Politics*, 127–33, 136–38.

67. Marshall, *Making and Unmaking*, 326, 330–31; O'Shaughnessy, *Men Who Lost America*, 51–52, Lord North quoted on 52; Ritcheson, *British Politics*, 154–56; Tyler, *Smugglers and Patriots*, 186–92.

68. Breen, *Marketplace of Revolution*, 294–302, *Boston Gazette* quoted on 302; Bushman, *King and People*, 175–76, 186; Carp, *Rebels Rising*, 55–56; Lynd and Waldstreicher, "Free Trade, Sovereignty, and Slavery," 608–9; Thomas, *Tea Party to Independence*, 14–15; Tyler, *Smugglers and Patriots*, 192–98.

69. Breen, *Marketplace of Revolution*, 300–302, *Pennsylvania Packet* quoted on 300 ("filled with"); Carp, *Rebels Rising*, 56–57; Marshall, *Making and Unmaking*, 331; Thomas, *Tea Party to Independence*, 14–25; Tyler, *Smugglers and Patriots*, 199–205; Young, *Shoemaker and the Tea Party*, 42–45.

70. O'Shaughnessy, *Men Who Lost America*, 50–53, Charles Van quoted on 53 ("The town"); Richeson, *British Politics*, 157–59; Thomas, *Tea Party to Independence*, 25–31, Thomas Gage quoted on 25, Lord Buckinghamshire quoted on 31.

71. Marshall, *Making and Unmaking*, 331–32; Ritcheson, *British Politics*, 158–62; Thomas, *Tea Party to Independence*, 48–87.

72. Gould, "Fear of War," 32; Lord Dartmouth quoted in Marshall, "Case for Coercing America," 14 ("constitutional authority"); Thomas, *Tea Party to Independence*, 40–41, 81, 86–87.

73. Greene, *Peripheries and Center*, 22–23; Lynd and Waldstreicher, "Free Trade, Sovereignty, and Slavery," 603–4; Maier, *From Resistance to Revolution*, 53–54; Marshall, *Making and Unmaking*, 50; Boston's assemblymen quoted in E. S. Morgan and H. Morgan, *Stamp Act Crisis*, 52 ("If taxes"); Trenchard and Gordon quoted in Rosswurm, *Arms, Country, and Class*, 195 ("Happiness"). For the fullest discussion of slavery as a Patriot trope, see Dorsey, *Common Bondage*.

74. George Washington to Bryan Fairfax, Aug. 24, 1774, in Abbott et al., eds., *Papers of George Washington*, vol. 10:154–56; Burnard, *Mastery*, 18–21; John Adams, "Humphrey Ploughjogger," Oct. 14, 1765, in Butterfield et al., eds., *Papers of John Adams*, vol. 1:146–48; Dorsey, *Common Bondage*, 22–32; Holton, *Forced Founders*, 46–47, 66; Marshall, *Making and Unmaking*, 25, 49.

75. Eltis, "Africa, Slavery," 272; Lepore, *The Whites of their Eyes*, 26, 58; Marshall, *Making and Unmaking*, 25; Nash, *Unknown American Revolution*, 32–33, 37.

76. Holton, *Forced Founders*, xix–xx, 66–73; Nash, *Unknown American Revolution*, 127; Wolf, *Race and Liberty*, 23–24; P. Morgan, *Slave Counterpoint*, 59–62, 81, 90–95.

77. Berlin, *Many Thousands Gone*, 160, protestors quoted; Nash, *Unknown American Revolution*, 60–61; Van Cleve, *Slaveholders' Union*, 38.

78. C. Brown, *Moral Capital*, 118–26, Ambrose Serle quoted on 120 ("Such men"), and 134; Gould, *Among the Powers*, 53–55; Greene, "Empire and Identity," 226–28; Rakove, *Revolutionaries*, 200–201, Samuel Johnson quoted on 201.

79. Lepore, *Whites of their Eyes*, 27, 75–77; Nash, *Unknown American Revolution*, 137–39.

80. Lepore, *Whites of their Eyes*, 63, 75–76; Nash, *Unknown American Revolution*, 124–28, petitioners quoted on 125.

81. Berlin, *Many Thousands Gone*, 220; Nash, *Unknown American Revolution*, 62–64, 114–28, Patrick Henry quoted on 118, and Benjamin Rush quoted on 121.

82. Lepore, *Whites of their Eyes*, 3–75, James Warren quoted on 74; Nash, *Unknown American Revolution*, 115–18, 122–23, Patrick Henry quoted on 118.

83. McConville, *King's Three Faces*, 175–81; Olwell, "'Domestick Enemies,'" 29–34, Alexander Innes quoted on 29 ("entertained"), George Say quoted on 34 ("was about to alter").

84. C. Brown, *Moral Capital*, 96–100; D. B. Davis, *Slavery in the Age of Revolution*, 471–501; Drescher, *Abolition*, 98–105; Gould, *Among the Powers*, 55–56; Meranze, "Hargrave's Nightmare," 221–22, Lord Mansfield quoted on 223 ("so odious"); Van Cleve, *A Slaveholders' Union*, 17, 311–36.

85. Blumrosen, *Slave Nation*, 15, 20, 30–38; Drescher, *Abolition*, 103–5; Gould, *Among the Powers*, 55–58; Meranze, "Hargrave's Nightmare," 222–24; Van Cleve, *Slaveholders' Union*, 31–38; Waldstreicher, *Slavery's Constitution*, 39–42.

86. Schama, *Rough Crossings*, 16–18, *Virginia Gazette* advertisement quoted on 18; P. Morgan, *Slave Counterpoint*, 461.

87. C. Brown, *Moral Capital*, 134–43; Drescher, *Abolition*, 109; Gould, *Among the Powers*, 57; Olwell, "'Domestick Enemies,'" 21–48; Parkinson, "Manifest Signs of Passion," 53–57; Van Cleve, "Founding a Slaveholders' Union," 120–21.

88. Gould, "Fears of War," 25; Fairfax County Association, Sept. 21, 1774, quoted in F. Anderson and D. Cayton, *Dominion of War*, 106.

89. Alden, *General Gage*, 203–8; Breen, *American Insurgents*, 71–75; Marston, *King and Congress*, 69–70; Thomas, *Tea Party to Independence*, 119–21, 132–33.

90. Gross, *Minutemen*, 68–108; Pruitt, "Self-Sufficiency," 339; Raphael, *First American Revolution*, 21–23.

91. Bailyn, *Ordeal of Thomas Hutchinson*, 392; Breen, *American Insurgents*, 79–80; Brown, *Revolutionary Politics*, 178–209; Bushman, *King and People*, 178, 204–7, Boston Committee of Correspondence quoted on 206 ("If the breath"); Raphael, *First American Revolution*, 46–47.

92. Alden, *General Gage*, 213; Breen, *American Insurgents*, 76–84, Jonathan Parsons quoted on 84 ("the spirit"); Nash, *Unknown American Revolution*, 180.

93. Alden, *General Gage*, 211–12; Breen, *American Insurgents*, 85–93, Peter Oliver quoted on 92 ("the consequences"); Nash, *Unknown American Revolution*, 179–80; Raphael, *First American Revolution*, 63–89, 96–97.

94. Alden, *General Gage*, 215; Breen, *American Insurgents*, 93–94; Rakove, *Revolutionaries*, 52–53; conservative quoted in P. Smith, *New Age Now Begins*, 405 ("In truth"); conservative quoted in Nash, *Unknown American Revolution*, 181 ("Everybody").

95. Alden, *General Gage*, 213–14; Breen, *American Insurgents*, 134–46, Mr. McNeil quoted on 140 ("armed Men" and "surpassed"); Brown, *Revolutionary Politics*, 226–27; Marston, *King and Congress*, 82–83; Thomas, *Tea Party to Independence*, 149–50.

96. Alden, *General Gage*, 213–14; Breen, *American Insurgents*, 147–51; Brown, *Revolutionary Politics*, 228; Loyalist quoted in P. Smith, *New Age Now Begins*, 404 ("I really fear").

97. Brown, *Revolutionary Politics*, 229–36; Marston, *King and Congress*, 84–85; Rakove, *Revolutionaries*, 56–57; Thomas Gage quoted in Shy, "Thomas Gage," 24; Raphael, *First American Revolution*, 105–10, 171–73; Thomas, *Tea Party to Independence*, 158–59.

98. Alden, *General Gage*, 219–20; Breen, *American Insurgents*, 86–105, Samuel Adams quoted on 98; Marston, *King and Congress*, 70–75; Thomas Gage quoted in P. Smith, *New Age*, 418; Thomas, *Tea Party to Independence*, 133–35.

99. Breen, *American Insurgents*, 82; Ferling, *First of Men*, 103–4; Jensen, *Founding of a Nation*, 479–82; Marston, *King and Congress*, 67–69, 76–77; Middlekauff, *Glorious Cause*, 234–44; Henry Laurens quoted in Olwell, *Masters, Slaves, and Subjects*, 227; Thomas, *Tea Party to Independence*, 123–25, 131–32, 156, 174.

100. John Adams to Abigail Adams, Sept. 25, 1774, in Butterfield et al., eds, *Adams Family Correspondence*, vol. 1:163 ("Strangers"); John Adams, diary, Oct. 10, 1774, Butterfield et al, eds., *Diary and Autobiography of John Adams*, vol. 2:146–58 ("Deliberations of Congress").

101. Marston, *King and Congress*, 81–82; Rakove, *Revolutionaries*, 53–54; Thomas, *Tea Party to Independence*, 123.

102. Chopra, *Unnatural Rebellion*, 30–31; Jasanoff, *Liberty's Exiles*, 29–30, Joseph Galloway quoted on 30; Marston, *King and Congress*, 91–92; Thomas, *Tea Party to Independence*, 154–55.

103. Chopra, *Unnatural Rebellion*, 31–32; Jasanoff, *Liberty's Exiles*, 30–31; Marston, *King and Congress*, 93; Middlekauff, *Glorious Cause*, 245–46, Patrick Henry quoted on 245.

104. George Washington to Robert McKenzie, Oct. 9, 1774, in Abbot et al., eds., *Papers of George Washington*, vol. 10:171–172; John Adams to William Tudor, Sept. 29, 1774, in Butterfield et al., eds., *Papers of John Adams*, vol. 2:176–78; Marston, *King and Congress*, 87–91; Rakove, *Revolutionaries*, 59–60.

105. Breen, *American Insurgents*, 165–66; Marston, *King and Congress*, 112–16; Rakove, *Revolutionaries*, 58–59.

106. Breen, *American Insurgents*, 166–68, Congress quoted on 168 ("that all such foes"); Marston, *King and Congress*, 116–22; Middlekauff, *Glorious Cause*, 244–49, Continental Congress quoted on 248 ("every county"); Rakove, *Revolutionaries*, 63–65; Thomas, *Tea Party to Independence*, 167–68.

107. Ammerman, *In the Common Cause*, 103–9; Breen, *American Insurgents*, 169–77, 185–95, 200–201, Reverend Isaac Mansfield, Jr., quoted on 173 ("acquired"); Countryman, *People in Revolution*, 139–41; Holton, *Forced Founders*, 102–3; Marston, *King and Congress*, 124–25.

108. Breen, *American Insurgents*, 190–94, 202; Holton, *Forced Founders*, 103–4; Jensen, *Founding of a Nation*, 524; McConville, *King's Three Faces*, 291–92, 300.

109. Breen, *American Insurgents*, 190–94, 202; James Madison to William Bradford, Jan. 20, 1775, in Hutchinson, et al., eds., *Papers of James Madison*, vol. 1:135; Middlekauff, *Glorious Cause*, 257–58.

110. Breen, *American Insurgents*, 199–206, 224–36; Jensen, *Founding of a Nation*, 522–23; Oliver, *Origin and Progress*, 157 ("stripped naked").

111. Breen, *American Insurgents*, 224–36; Irvin, *Clothed in Robes of Sovereignty*, 69–70; Joseph Jacob quoted in Marston, *King and Congress*, 126 ("the temper"); Leamon, *Jacob Bailey*, 106–8; McConville, *King's Three Faces*, 292–95, Philadelphia committee quoted on 294 ("no person").

112. Samuel Seabury quoted in T. Allen, *Tories*, 162; W. Brown, *Good Americans*, 63–64; Chopra, *Unnatural Rebellion*, 34; Jensen, *Founding of a Nation*, 508–12, Maryland conservative quoted on 520 ("What think you"), see also 526–27.

CHAPTER 4: REBELS

1. Mather Byles quoted in W. Brown, *The Good Americans*, 74.

2. Jonathan Sewall and John Adams quoted in Butterfield et al., eds., *Adams Papers, Adams Family Correspondence*, vol. 1:137n5.

3. O'Shaughnessy, *Men Who Lost America*, 54–55, Lord Sandwich quoted on 327; Thomas, *Tea Party to Independence*, 137–42, 160–61, Lord North quoted on 140.

4. Alden, *General Gage*, 233–41; Jensen, *Founding of a Nation*, 537–38, 569–83; Mackesy, *War for America*, 2; O'Shaughnessy, *Men Who Lost America*, 84; Rakove, *Revolutionaries*, 66–67; Thomas, *Tea Party to Independence*, 159–62.

5. Alden, *General Gage*, 241–44; Gross, *Minutemen*, 109–18; Higginbotham, *War of American Independence*, 58–61; Jensen, *Founding of a Nation*, 584–86; Shy, "Thomas Gage," 27–29.

6. Alden, *General Gage*, 244–47; Gross, *Minutemen* 118–30; Higginbotham, *War of American Independence*, 61–65; Jensen, *Founding of a Nation*, 586–87, Shy, "Thomas Gage," 29.

7. Alden, *General Gage*, 251–59; Higginbotham, *War of American Independence*, 65–66; Jensen, *Founding of a Nation*, 587–93; C. Ward, *War of the Revolution*, vol. 1:76–77.

8. Alden, *General Gage*, 260–65; Higginbotham, *War of American Independence*, 68–70; C. Ward, *War of the Revolution*, vol. 1:59–62.

9. Alden, *General Gage*, 260–68; Higginbotham, *War of American Independence*, 70–75, John Burgoyne quoted on 75; O'Shaughnessy, *Men Who Lost America*, 85–86; Shy, "Thomas Gage," 30–31; Stephenson, *Patriot Battles*, 212–18; C. Ward, *War of the Revolution*, vol. 1:73–93.

10. Alden, *General Gage*, 268–69; Higginbotham, *War of American Independence*, 75–77; M. A. Jones, "Sir William Howe," 47; Oliver, *Origin and Progress*, 127; O'Shaughnessy, *Men Who Lost America*, 85–86; Thomas Gage quoted in Shy, "Thomas Gage," 31; Thomas, *Tea Party to Independence*, 254; C. Ward, *War of the Revolution*, vol. 1:93–96.

11. Chopra, *Unnatural Rebellion*, 33–37, William Smith Jr., quoted on 35–36, John Wetherhead quoted on 36 ("insulted"); Countryman, *People in Revolution*, 144; Kammen, *Colonial New York*, 366–67; Kierner, *Traders and Gentlefolk*, 207; Thomas, *Tea Party to Independence*, 243–45, William Franklin quoted on 243.

12. Gouverneur Morris quoted in Chopra, *Unnatural Rebellion*, 36; James Duane quoted in Countryman, *People in Revolution*, 131–60; Evans, *A Topping People*, 177–94; Jensen, *Founding of a Nation*, 530–32, Cadwallader Colden quoted on 531; W. Nelson, *American Tory*, 3–5; Kammen, *Colonial New York*, 343, 364–68.

13. Countryman, *People in Revolution*, 103–4, 115–16; Jasanoff, *Liberty's Exiles*, 8–9, 27–28; W. Nelson, *American Tory*, 85–86; David Ramsay quoted in Page Smith, *New Age*, 658.

14. Jan Lewis, *Pursuit of Happiness*, 48–50; G. Wood, *Radicalism*, 229–43.

15. Hoffman, "The 'Disaffected,'" 304–5; Kulikoff, *Tobacco and Slaves*, 300–11.

16. W. Brown, *Good Americans*, 122–24; Calhoon, *Loyalists*, 258–59, William Clark quoted on 258 ("to such a pitch"); Countryman, *People Numerous and Armed*, 104–8, Isaac Low quoted on 285 ("The height"); Jasanoff, *Liberty's Exiles*, 9; W. Nelson, *American Tory*, 91–92; P. Smith, *Loyalists and Redcoats*, 58; Van Buskirk, *Generous Enemies*, 38–39.

17. Bonomi, "Religious Dissent," 47–48; Charles Inglis quoted in W. Brown, *Good Americans*, 44 ("It is the Cause"); Bushman, *King and People*, 17–26, 56–60, 74–82, 192–93; Chopra, *Choosing Sides*, 2–3; Colley, *Britons*, 11–54; Jasanoff, *Liberty's Exiles*, 27–28; Potter, *Liberty We Seek*, 10–16, 54–55, 107, 153–57, 172–80.

18. Bannister and Riordan, "Loyalism and the British Atlantic," 8; W. Brown, *Good Americans*, 75; Chopra, *Choosing Sides*, 3; W. Nelson, *American Tory*, 5–18, Martin Howard quoted on 12 ("how thin"); Tiedemann et al., eds., *Other Loyalists*, 11.

19. Oliver Parker quoted in Calhoon, *Loyalists*, 292 ("Take"); Chopra, *Unnatural Rebellion*, 2–4; John Connolly quoted in David, *Dunmore's New World*, 97 ("Committees"); Reverend Bullman quoted in J. W. Harris, *Hanging of Thomas Jeremiah*, 140 ("keep his own rank" and "every silly Clown").

20. W. Brown, *Good Americans*, 58–59, William Franklin quoted on 66; Joseph Galloway quoted in Ferling, *Loyalist Mind*, 49; Nobles, *Divisions Throughout the Whole*, 182.

21. Beeman, *Our Lives*, 197–99; Rakove, *Beginnings*, 70–71; Thomas, *Tea Party to Independence*, 245.

22. Countryman, *People in Revolution*, 131–60; Evans, *A Topping People*, 177–94; Jensen, *Founding of a Nation*, 530–32; Lewis, *Pursuit of Happiness*, 1; W. Nelson, *American Tory*, 3–5; Young, *Democratic Republicans of New York*, 10–32.

23. John Dickinson quoted in E. S. Morgan and H. Morgan, *Stamp Act Crisis*, 261. For Dickinson's background, see Rakove, *Revolutionaries*, 5–9, 23, 81–82. For the Olive Branch Petition, see Beeman, *Our Lives*, 250–51; Rakove, *Beginnings*, 67–68.

24. John Adams to Abigail Adams, June 11, 1775, in Butterfield et al., eds., *Adams Papers, Adams Family Correspondence*, vol. 1:215–17; Maier, *American Scripture*, 13–18; Rakove, *Beginnings of National Politics*, 71–78; Thomas, *Tea Party to Independence*, 247–48.

25. Jensen, *Founding of a Nation*, 606–9; Marston, *King and Congress*, 145–

47; Middlekauff, *Glorious Cause*, 280–81; C. Ward, *War of the Revolution*, vol. 1:64–72.

26. John Adams to James Warren, May 21, 1775, in Butterfield, et al., eds., *Adams Papers*, vol. 3:11; Higginbotham, *War of American Independence*, 150–51; Mackesy, *War for America*, 29–30, 35; C. Ward, *War of the Revolution*, vol. 1:209–10.

27. Higginbotham, *War of American Independence*, 83–85; Jensen, *Founding of a Nation*, 609–10; Marston, *King and Congress*, 140–41, 148–49; Middlekauff, *Glorious Cause*, 280–81.

28. F. Anderson and D. Cayton, *Dominion of War*, 157–58; John Adams, "In Congress, June and July 1775," in Butterfield et al., *Diary and Autobiography of John Adams*, vol. 3:321–24 ("a Gentleman"); Adams to Benjamin Rush, Nov. 11, 1807 ("He possessed"), Founders Online, National Archives (http://founders.archives.gov/documents/Adams/99-02-02-5216); Chernow, *Washington*, 182–87, Eliphalet Dyer quoted on 186 ("He seems discreet"); Higginbotham, *War of American Independence*, 84–86; Marston, *King and Congress*, 148–49.

29. Chernow, *Washington*, 191–92, Thomas Jones quoted on 192 ("What a farce"); Chopra, *Unnatural Rebellion*, 42; McConville, *King's Three Faces*, 306–7; Van Buskirk, *Generous Enemies*, 33.

30. John Adams to Abigail Adams, July 7, 1776, in Butterfield et al., *Adams Papers, Adams Family Correspondence*, vol. 2:37–38 ("Our armies"); C. Cox, "Continental Army," 163–66; C. Cox, *Proper Sense of Honor*, 2–3, 21–26; Shy, *People Numerous and Armed*, 147–48.

31. George Washington to Richard Henry Lee, Aug. 29, 1775, in Chase et al., eds., *Papers of George Washington, Revolutionary War Series*, vol. 1:372–76 ("unaccountable"); Higginbotham, *War of American Independence*, 93–94; Marston, *King and Congress*, 150–52; Washington to Richard Henry Lee, July 10, 1775, to John Augustine Washington, July 27, 1775, to Lund Washington, Aug. 20, 1775, and in Rhodehamel, ed., *Washington*, 177–78, 179–80 ("I found"), 184 ("an exceeding"); Royster, *Revolutionary People*, 59–60.

32. F. Anderson and D. Cayton, *Dominion of War*, 160–164; George Washington, General Orders, Jan. 1, 1776, in Chase et al., eds., *Papers of George Washington, Revolutionary Series*, vol. 3:1–5 ("that an Army"); Higginbotham, *War of American Independence*, 98–101; Martin and Lender, *Respectable Army*, 71–72; Royster, *Revolutionary People*, 61–63, 67–68.

33. C. Cox, "Continental Army," 167–68; Higginbotham, *War of American Independence*, 101–2, 104–5; C. Ward, *War of the Revolution*, vol. 1:104–5, visitor quoted on 104 ("The strictest government"), 120–21.

34. Thomas Gage to Lord Dartmouth, Aug. 20, 1775, in Carter, ed., *Correspondence of General Thomas Gage*, vol. 1:412; Mackesy, *The War for Amer-*

ica, 38; O'Shaughnessy, *Men Who Lost America*, 175; Thomas, *Tea Party to Independence*, 260–80, Lord North quoted on 263–64.

35. Dull, *Diplomatic History*, 44–45; Mackesy, *War for America*, 50–56; O'Shaughnessy, *Men Who Lost America*, 55, 59–60, 167–76; Thomas, *Tea Party to Independence*, 286–87.

36. Burnard, "Slavery and the Causes," 54; Chopra, *Choosing Sides*, 16–20; DuVal, *Independence Lost*, 54–56, 62–63; Mancke, "Early Modern Imperial Governance," 3–20; Mancke, *Fault Lines*, 5, 66; Piecuch, *Three Peoples*, 22–26; Weber, *Spanish Frontier*, 267.

37. Armstrong, "Neutrality," 33–34; Chopra, *Choosing Sides*, 19–20; Longley, "Coming of the New England Planters," 14–28; Mancke, *Fault Lines*, 10–11, 34–35, 160–61.

38. Jasanoff, *Liberty's Exiles*, 167–68; MacNutt, *Atlantic Provinces*, 77–81; Mancke, *Fault Lines*, 3–4, 11–12, 17, 26–27, 77.

39. Clarke, *Siege of Fort Cumberland*, 128–204; Jasanoff, *Liberty's Exiles*, 167; MacNutt, *Atlantic Provinces*, 81–85; Mancke, *Fault Lines*, 77–78, 85–94, 101–2.

40. Burnard, *Mastery*, 14–17; Burnard, "Slavery and the Causes," 66; Craton, "Reluctant Creoles," 314–62; Egerton, *Death or Liberty*, 54–55; Knight, "American Revolution and the Caribbean," 253–54; Marshall, *Making and Unmaking*, 38–39; O'Shaughnessy, *Empire Divided*, 3–7, 19–31, 58–63, 72–74.

41. Burnard, *Mastery*, 14–17; Burnard, "Slavery and the Causes," 56, 58, 63; Chopra, *Choosing Sides*, 17–18; Egerton, *Death or Liberty*, 53–54; Knight, "American Revolution and the Caribbean," 252–53; Marshall, *Making and Unmaking*, 38–39; O'Shaughnessy, *Empire Divided*, 27–29, 34–44, 49–50, 81–82, 250n1, Malachy Postlethwayt quoted on 76 ("on Planting").

42. Frey, "Between Slavery and Freedom," 376–77; Dorchester County Committee of Inspection quoted in Gilbert, *Black Patriots and Loyalists*, 11–12; Holton, *Forced Founders*, 137–40, 151; McConville, *King's Three Faces*, 175–82; McDonnell, *Politics of War*, 22–23, 47–49; Henry Muhlenberg quoted in Nash, *Forgotten Fifth*, 30 ("secretly wished"); Olwell, "'Domestick Enemies,'" 33–34; Van Cleve, *Slaveholders' Union*, 43.

43. Anderson and Cayton, *Dominion of War*, 155–56, Lord Dunmore quoted on 156; David, *Dunmore's New World*, 1–2, 94–106; Hoffman, "The 'Disaffected,'" 281–82; Holton, *Forced Founders*, 141–48; James Madison to William Bradford, June 19, 1775, in Hutchinson et al., eds., *Papers of James Madison*, vol. 1:151–54 ("To say the truth"); Jasanoff, *Liberty's Exiles*, 52–53; McDonnell, *Politics of War*, 49–65; Schwarz, *Twice Condemned*, 181–83.

44. David, *Dunmore's New World*, 100–108; Holton, *Forced* Founders, 153–

56; McDonnell, *Politics of War*, 140–44, 152–59; Pybus, *Epic Journeys of Freedom*, 10–11.

45. Thomas Jefferson to John Randolph, Nov. 29, 1775, in Boyd et al., eds., *Papers of Thomas Jefferson*, vol. 1:268–70; Nash, *Forgotten Fifth*, 26–28; *Pennsylvania Gazette*, July 17, 1776, quoted in Schama, *Rough Crossings*, 8, see also 77; Raphael, *Founders*, 219–20.

46. David, *Dunmore's New World*, 108–9; *Virginia Gazette*, Nov. 24, 1775, quoted in Parkinson, "Manifest Signs of Passion," 57; George Washington to Richard Henry Lee, Nov. 27, 1775, Lund Washington to G. Washington, Dec. 3, 1775, G. Washington to Joseph Reed, Dec. 15, 1775, and G. Washington to R. H. Lee, Dec. 26, 1775, in Chase et al., eds., *Papers of George Washington, Revolutionary War Series*, vol. 2:435–37 ("the World"), 477–82 ("There is not"), 551–54 ("Arch Traitor"), and 610–13 ("that Man").

47. Frey, "Between Slavery and Freedom," 394–95; McDonnell, *Politics of War*, 139–40n7; Mullin, *Flight and Rebellion*, 136; Pybus, *Epic Journeys of Freedom*, 11; Pybus, "Jefferson's Faulty Math," 249; Robert Carter quoted in Morton, *Robert Carter*, 55–56.

48. David, *Dunmore's New World*, 110–12, 117; McDonnell, *Politics of War*, 161–62; Pybus, *Epic Journeys*, 11–12.

49. David, *Dunmore's New World*, 117–26; Egerton, *Death or Liberty*, 72–73; Frey, "Between Slavery and Freedom," 376, 396–98; Fenn, *Pox Americana*, 55–62; Patriot militiaman quoted in Gilbert, *Black Patriots and Loyalists*, 25; McDonnell, *Politics of War*, 249.

50. Frey, "Between Slavery and Freedom," 377–78; Gilbert, *Black Patriots and Loyalists*, 17; Holton, *Forced Founders*, 157–89; McDonnell, *Politics of War*, 134–39; Parkinson, "Manifest Signs of Passion," 57; Piecuch, *Three Peoples*, 43–44; Richard Henry Lee and Edward Rutledge quoted in Raphael, *Founders*, 220.

51. Frey, *Water from the Rock*, 57–58, 61–67; Olwell, *Masters, Slaves, and Subjects*, 228–34, Alexander Innes quoted on 228 ("to grant freedom"), Henry Laurens quoted on 228 ("Inhabitants"), slave quoted on 233 ("God would send"); Raphael, *Founders*, 216–17.

52. Frey, *Water from the Rock*, 57–58, Henry Laurens quoted on 57 ("puffed up"); J. W. Harris, *Hanging of Thomas Jeremiah*, 2–4, 92–96; Olwell, *Masters, Slaves, and Subjects*, 234–235.

53. Frey, *Water from the Rock*, 57–58; J. W. Harris, *Hanging of Thomas Jeremiah*, 142–49; Olwell, *Masters, Slaves and Subjects*, 234–37, William Campbell quoted on 235 ("They openly") and 236 ("murdered" and "asserted"), Henry Laurens quoted on 236 ("Justice"); Campbell quoted in Raphael, *Founders*, 218 ("his implacable").

54. Frey, *Water from the Rock*, 64–66, Charles Town city council quoted on

65; Olwell, *Masters, Slaves, and Subjects*, 241–42, Colonel Stephen Bull quoted on 242.

55. M. Anderson, *Battle for the Fourteenth Colony*, 347–48; Higginbotham, *War of American Independence*, 106–8; Neatby, *Quebec*, 142–47; C. Ward, *War of the Revolution*, vol. 1:135–39.

56. M. Anderson, *Battle for the Fourteenth Colony*, 102–38; Mackesy, *War for America*, 79; Neatby, *Quebec*, 148–49; C. Ward, *War of the Revolution*, vol. 1:140–85.

57. M. Anderson, *Battle for the Fourteenth Colony*, 144–51; Beeman, *Our Lives*, 298; Higginbotham, *War of American Independence*, 108–113; Neatby, *Quebec*, 150–51; C. Ward, *War of the Revolution*, vol. 1:140–85, Richard Montgomery quoted on 185.

58. M. Anderson, *Battle for the Fourteenth Colony*, 151–69, 182–99; Higginbotham, *War of American Independence*, 112–14; Neatby, *Quebec*, 151–52, Sir Guy Carleton quoted on 152; C. Ward, *War of the Revolution*, vol. 1:186–195, H. Ward, *American Revolution*, 268.

59. M. Anderson, *Battle for the Fourteenth Colony*, 300–301, 310–29; Mackesy, *War for America*, 94; Middlekauff, *Glorious Cause*, 339–40; Neatby, *Quebec*, 152–53. For the smallpox epidemic, see Fenn, *Pox Americana*, 63–75.

60. M. Anderson, *Battle for the Fourteenth Colony*, 299–300, 305–6, 329–31, Capt. Charles Douglas quoted on 330 ("a resistance"); John Adams to Abigail Adams, July 7, 1776, in Butterfield et al., eds., *Adams Family Correspondence*, vol. 2:37–38 ("disgraced"); Fenn, *Pox Americana*, 76–77, John Lacey quoted on 76 ("Lice and Maggots"); Neatby, *Quebec*, 152–53; C. Ward, *War of the Revolution*, vol. 1:196–201, John Sullivan quoted on 200.

61. Callahan, "Henry Knox," 239–241; Higginbotham, *War of American Independence*, 105–6; C. Ward, *War of the Revolution*, vol. 1:120–33, British officer quoted on 128.

62. Higginbotham, *War of American Independence*, 105–6; Mackesy, *War for America*, 80–81; C. Ward, *War of the Revolution*, vol. 1:132–33.

63. T. Allen, *Tories*, 148–51; O'Shaughnessy, *Men Who Lost America*, 217; Piecuch, *Three Peoples*, 87–88; P. Smith, *Loyalists and Redcoats*, 22–26; C. Ward, *War of the Revolution*, vol. 2:662–64.

64. Higginbotham, *War of American Independence*, 136–37; Olwell, *Masters, Slaves, and Subjects*, 243–44; O'Shaughnessy, *Men Who Lost America*, 217–18; Piecuch, *Three Peoples*, 90–91; C. Ward, *War of the Revolution*, vol. 2:671–78.

65. Beeman, *Our Lives*, 300–304; Hendrickson, "Escaping Insecurity," 217; Benjamin Franklin to Josiah Quincy, Apr. 15, 1776, in Labaree et al., eds., *Papers of Benjamin Franklin*, vol. 22: 400–402; Maier, *American Scripture*, 27–30; Thomas, *From Tea Party to Independence*, 329.

66. Beeman, *Our Lives*, 305–12; E. Foner, *Tom Paine*, 1–73; P. Foner, ed.,

Complete Writings of Thomas Paine, vol. 1:143–44; Keane, *Tom Paine*, 104; Raphael, *Founders*, 236–37.

67. Beeman, *Our Lives*, 319–20; E. Foner, *Tom Paine*, 73–74, 79; Maier, *American Scripture*, 32–34; Raphael, *Founders*, 239.

68. Thomas Jefferson to Francis Eppes, Jan. 19, 1821 ("No writer"), Founders Online, National Archives (http://founders.archives.gov/documents/Jefferson/98-01-02-1778); E. Foner, *Tom Paine*, 83–85.

69. Beeman, *Our Lives*, 312–18; E. Foner, *Tom Paine*, 74–78; Raphael, *Founders*, 237–38.

70. P. Foner, ed., *Complete Writings*, vol. 1:13–16, and 29.

71. P. Foner, ed., *Complete Writings*, vol. 1:3, 30–31, and 45.

72. P. Foner, ed., *Complete Writings*, vol. 1:17.

73. Chopra, *Choosing Sides*, 28; Chopra, *Unnatural Rebellion*, 44; Cresswell, *Journal*, 136; P. Gould, "Loyalists Respond," 105–22; Jasanoff, *Liberty's Exiles*, 34–35, Charles Inglis quoted on 34; James Chalmers quoted in Keane, *Tom Paine*, 125.

74. Beeman, *Our Lives*, 322–24; John Adams to Benjamin Waterhouse, Oct. 29, 1805, Founders Online, National Archives (http://founders.archives.gov/documents/Adams/99-02-02-5107); Elias Boudinot quoted in L. Gerlach, *Prologue to Independence*, 485; Gouverneur Morris quoted in P. Foner, ed., *Complete Writings*, vol. 1:xviii; Rakove, *Revolutionaries*, 95–96.

75. Beeman, *Our Lives*, 321–22; Charles Lee to George Washington, Jan. 24, 1776, and Washington to Joseph Reed, Jan. 31, 1776, in Chase et al., eds., *Papers of George Washington, Revolutionary War Series*, vol. 3:182–84 ("Have you seen"), and 225–29 ("sound Doctrine"); Joseph Hawley quoted in E. Foner, *Tom Paine*, 86; Jordan, "Familial Politics," 29.

76. Beeman, *Our Lives*, 330–31, Prohibitory Bill quoted on 330; John Adams to Horatio Gates, Mar. 23, 1776, in Butterfield et al., eds., *Papers of John Adams*, vol. 4:58–60 ("It throws"); Marston, *King and Congress*, 60–62; Rakove, *Revolutionaries*, 96–97, John Hancock quoted on 97; Thomas, *Tea Party to Independence*, 297–303; Van Buskirk, *Generous Enemies*, 13–14.

77. Beeman, *Our Lives*, 362–63, New Jersey Provincial Congress quoted on 362; Skemp, *William Franklin*, 192–216.

78. Beeman, *Our Lives*, 327–40, 350–57; Dull, *Diplomatic History*, 49–52; Gould, *Among the Powers*, 1–3; Maier, *American Scripture*, 37–43; Marston, *King and Congress*, 284–87; Rakove, *Beginnings*, 92–100, Richard Henry Lee quoted on 98.

79. Beeman, *Our Lives*, 369–82; John Adams to Abigail Adams, July 3, 1776, in Butterfield et al., eds., *Adams Papers, Adams Family Correspondence*, vol. 2:29–33 ("The Hopes"); Maier, *American Scripture*, 44–46; Rakove, *Beginnings*, 99–100.

80. Beeman, *Our Lives*, 387–407, Declaration of Independence quoted on 395 ("We hold"), and 403 ("merciless"); Maier, *American Scripture*, 104–31; Thomas, *Tea Party to Independence*, 328–29.

81. John Adams to Benjamin Rush, June 21, 1811 ("The Declaration"), and Adams to Timothy Pickering, Aug. 6, 1822, Founders Online, National Archives (http://founders.archives.gov./documents/Adams/99-02-02 5649) and (http://founders.archives.gov/documents/Adams/99-02-02 7674); Irvin, *Clothed in Robes*, 132–39; Maier, *American Scripture*, 150–60.

82. T. Allen, *Tories*, 167; Irvin, *Clothed in Robes*, 140–41; Jasanoff, *Liberty's Exiles*, 35–36; Jordan, "Familial Politics," 306–8; Maier, *American Scripture*, 157–58; McConville, *King's Three Faces*, 298–311; Van Buskirk, *Generous Enemies*, 18. For slaves employed to topple the statue, see Kammen, *Colonial New York*, 371.

83. Jasanoff, *Liberty's Exiles*, 35; Joseph Barton quoted in Higginbotham, *War of American Independence*, 119 ("I could").

84. James Allen quoted in W. Brown, *Good Americans*, 76–77; T. Allen, *Tories*, 190; Rev. Jacob Duché to George Washington, Oct. 8, 1777, in Chase et al., eds., *Papers of George Washington, Revolutionary War Series*, vol. 11:430–37; Moore, *Loyalists*, 23–26, 72–74.

85. Moore, *Loyalists*, 116–18; James Allen quoted in P. Smith, *New Age*, 670–71. For other prominent Patriots who dropped out see, W. Brown, *Good Americans*, 77–79; Calhoon, *Loyalists*, 377–81; Chopra, *Choosing Sides*, 4.

86. Dickinson, "Impact of the War," 357–58; Higginbotham, *War of American Independence*, 151–52, 154; Mackesy, *War for America*, 82–86; O'Shaughnessy, *Men Who Lost America*, 92–93; Van Buskirk, *Generous Enemies*, 17–18; C. Ward, *War of the Revolution*, vol. 1:209.

87. Conway, *War of American Independence*, 39–40; Higginbotham, *War of American Independence*, 154–55; O'Shaughnessy, *Men Who Lost America*, 92–93, General James Grant quoted on 92; C. Ward, *War of the Revolution*, vol. 1:207–9; Spring, *With Zeal*, 124–32.

88. John Adams to George Washington, Jan. 6, 1776, in Butterfield et al., eds., *Papers of John Adams*, vol. 3:395–96 ("Nexus"); Higginbotham, *War of American Independence*, 150–52; O'Shaughnessy, *Men Who Lost America*, 93; Thomas, *Tea Party to Independence*, 329.

89. Ewald Gustav Schaukirk quoted in Chopra, *Unnatural Rebellion*, 71 ("On Monday night"); Jasanoff, *Liberty's Exiles*, 34–35; Solomon Drowne quoted in Van Buskirk, *Generous Enemies*, 17 ("Toory rides").

90. Charles Lee to George Washington, Feb. 19, 1776, and Washington to the New York Convention, Aug. 23, 1776, in Chase et al., eds., *Paper of George Washington, Revolutionary War Series*, vol. 3:339–41 ("Whoever") and vol. 6:114–15 ("many worthy"); Chernow, *Washington*, 229–33, William Tudor

quoted on 230 ("Every brutal"), 235; Higginbotham, *War of American Independence*, 150–52; C. Ward, *War of the Revolution*, vol. 1:229–30.

91. Higginbotham, *War of American Independence*, 155–57; Jones, "Sir William Howe," 52–53; Mackesy, *War for America*, 87–88; O'Shaughnessy, *Men Who Lost America*, 93–95; C. Ward, *War of the Revolution*, vol. 1:211–27.

92. Chernow, *George Washington*, 248–51; Higginbotham, *War of American Independence*, 157–58; Jones, "Sir William Howe," 53–54; Mackesy, *War for America*, 88; O'Shaughnessy, *Men Who Lost America*, 95, 98; C. Ward, *War of the Revolution*, vol. 1:231–36.

93. Dull, *Diplomatic History*, 53; Gruber, *Howe Brothers*, 116–20, Ambrose Serle quoted on 119 ("They met"); O'Shaughnessy, *Men Who Lost America*, 99; Rakove, *Revolutionaries*, 105–6.

94. George Washington, General Orders, Aug. 30, 1776, Washington to John Hancock, Sept. 2, 1776, in Chase et al., eds., *Papers of George Washington, Revolutionary War Series*, vol. 6:162–64 ("Seldom"), 199–201 ("Our situation," "with apprehension" and "With the deepest concern"); C. Ward, *War of the Revolution*, vol. 1:236–40.

95. Chernow, *George Washington*, 253–55, Nathanael Greene quoted on 254; Higginbotham, *War of American Independence*, 160; Mackesy, *War for America*, 89–90; C. Ward, *War of the Revolution*, vol. 1:242–45.

96. Chopra, *Unnatural Rebellion*, 52–58, William Howe quoted on 54 ("free enjoyment"); Higginbotham, *War of American Independence*, 160; Jasanoff, *Liberty's Exiles*, 36–37; Ambrose Serle quoted in Van Buskirk, *Generous Enemies*, 21 ("behaved").

97. Chopra, *Unnatural Rebellion*, 71; Gould, *Among the Powers*, 115.

98. O'Shaughnessy, *Men Who Lost America*, 95–96; Higginbotham, *War of American Independence*, 162–63; Mackesy, *War for America*, 90–93; C. Ward, *War of the Revolution*, vol. 1:255–74.

99. George Washington to John Augustine Washington, Mar. 31, 1776, in Chase et al., eds., *Papers of George Washington, Revolutionary War Series*, vol. 3:566–71 ("first Officer"); Higginbotham, *War for American Independence*, 89, 136–37; Marston, *King and Congress*, 151–52; Piecuch, *Three Peoples*, 89–90; Shy, *A People Numerous and Armed*, 135–45.

100. Chernow, *George Washington*, 262–67, Charles Lee quoted on 263; Shy, *People Numerous and Armed*, 146–54, Joseph Reed quoted on 149; C. Ward, *War of the Revolution*, vol. 1:277–81.

101. George Washington to Samuel Washington, Dec. 18, 1776, in Chase et al., eds., *Papers of George Washington, Revolutionary War Series*, vol. 7:369–72; Shy, *People Numerous and Armed*, 153; C. Ward, *War of the Revolution*, vol. 1:288–89.

102. George Washington to Samuel Washington, Dec. 18, 1776, and G. Washington to John Hancock, Dec. 20, 1776, in Chase et al., eds., *Papers of George Washington, Revolutionary War Series*, vol. 7:369–72 ("Our affairs"), 381–89 ("an end"); G. Washington to Lund Washington, Dec. 10, 1776, in Rhodehamel, ed., *Washington, Writings*, 261; Shy, *People Numerous and Armed*, 149–50; C. Ward, *War of the Revolution*, vol. 1:281–86, Joseph Reed quoted on 281.

103. Calhoon, *Loyalists*, 360–64; George Washington to Charles Lee, Nov. 21, 1776, in Chase et al., eds., *Papers of George Washington, Revolutionary War Series*, vol. 7:193–95) ("will cease"); G. Washington to Lund Washington, Dec. 10, 1776, in Rhodehamel, ed., *George Washington: Writings*, 260 ("from disaffection"); O'Shaughnessy, *Men Who Lost America*, 102–3; Shy, *People Numerous and Armed*, 150–51; P. Smith, *Loyalists and Redcoats*, 42–43.

104. Bodle, *Valley Forge*, 16–19; Ferling, *Loyalist Mind*, 37–39; Rakove, *Revolutionaries*, 106–7, Robert Morris quoted on 106; C. Ward, *War of the Revolution*, vol. 1:285–87.

105. Chernow, *George Washington*, 264–65, Lord Rawdon quoted on 264; Mackesy, *War for America*, 97; C. Ward, *War of the Revolution*, vol. 1:281, 288.

106. T. Allen, *Tories*, 171–72, 198; Gould, *Among the Powers*, 116–17; Gruber, *Howe Brothers*, 190; Jones, "Sir William Howe," 49, 51–57; Loyalist ditty quoted in O'Shaughnessy, *Men Who Lost America*, 96–99; Van Buskirk, *Generous Enemies*, 30–31; C. Ward, *War for America*, 59, 321–22. For Loring and the prison hulks, see Burrows, *Forgotten Patriots*, 10–11, 163–93.

107. Chernow, *George Washington*, 264, James Monroe quoted on 264 ("A deportment"); Thomas Paine, "The American Crisis, Number I," in Rhodehamel, ed., *American Revolution*, 241.

108. George Washington to Jonathan Trumbull, Sr., Dec. 14, 1776, Washington to Joseph Reed, Dec. 23, 1776, in Chase et al., eds., *Papers of George Washington, Revolutionary War Series*, vol. 7:340–41 ("raise"), 423–24 ("necessity").

109. Higginbotham, *War of American Independence*, 166–67; C. Ward, *War of the Revolution*, vol. 1:292–95, officer quoted on 295.

110. Higginbotham, *War of American Independence*, 167–68; C. Ward, *War of the Revolution*, vol. 1:295–305.

111. Bodle, *Valley Forge*, 32–33; Higginbotham, *War of American Independence*, 168–70; George Washington to John Hancock, Jan. 5, 1777, in Rhodehamel, ed., *George Washington: Writings*, 266–68; C. Ward, *War of the Revolution*, vol. 1:306–18.

112. Calhoon, *Loyalists*, 367–68; Fowler, "Loyalty is Now Bleeding," 54 ("tory-hunters"); Higginbotham, *War of American Independence*, 164–70, Stephen

Kimble quoted on 164 ("every species"), James Grant quoted on 165 ("lose you friends"), William Harcourt quoted on 170 ("Though").

113. Bodle, *Valley Forge*, 20–21; Cresswell, *Journal*, 179–80; Rakove, *Revolutionaries*, 115–17; Shy, *People Numerous and Armed*, 226.

114. Anderson and Cayton, *Dominion of War*, 166–67; Conway, "British Army," 186–87; Cresswell, *Journal*, 251–52; General Harvey quoted in Mackesy, *War for America*, 407 ("Our army"); George Washington to John Hancock, Sept. 8, 1776, in Rhodehamel, ed., *George Washington: Writings*, 241; Spring, *With Zeal*, 6–9.

CHAPTER 5: ALLIES

1. Ichabod Ward quoted in Bodle, *Valley Forge*, 129.

2. Dull, *Diplomatic History*, 50–56; Gould, *Among the Powers*, 1–13; Mapp, "Revolutionary War and Europe's Great Powers," 315–16; Sadosky, *Revolutionary Negotiations*, 82–83; Stinchcombe, *American Revolution and the French Alliance*, 7.

3. DeConde, "French Alliance," 13; Kaplan, "Treaties," 155–58; Stinchcombe, *American Revolution and the French Alliance*, 10.

4. DeConde, "French Alliance," 4–6, 13; Dull, *Diplomatic History*, 55–56; Gould, *Among the Powers*, 1–4; Hendrickson, "Escaping Insecurity," 218–19; Kelly, "Treaties," 157–59; Sadosky, *Revolutionary Negotiations*, 83–84; Stinchcombe, *American Revolution and the French Alliance*, 7–9.

5. Chavez, *Spain*, 47; DeConde, "French Alliance," 6; Hendrickson, "Escaping Insecurity," 216; Kaplan, "Treaties," 155–60; Mapp, "Revolutionary War and Europe's Great Powers," 311–13.

6. DeConde, "French Alliance," 9–12; Dull, *Diplomatic History*, 38–39, 48–51, 60; Mapp, "Revolutionary War and Europe's Great Powers," 317; Murphy, "View from Versailles," 109–18; Sadosky, *Revolutionary Negotiations*, 100–101.

7. Chavez, *Spain*, 49; Dull, *Diplomatic History*, 57–65, 78; Mapp, "Revolutionary War and Europe's Great Powers," 317–18; Murphy, "View from Versailles," 118–19; Sadosky, *Revolutionary Negotiations*, 93–95; Stinchcombe, *American Revolution and the French Alliance*, 9–10.

8. Mackesy, *War for America*, 94–96, 106–7; O'Shaughnessy, *Men Who Lost America*, 141–43; C. Ward, *War of the Revolution*, vol. 1:387–97.

9. Billias, "John Burgoyne," 142–55; Mackesy, *War for America*, 107–9, Horace Walpole quoted on 108; O'Shaughnessy, *Men Who Lost America*, 123–32, 142–43, John Burgoyne quoted on 143.

10. Billias, "John Burgoyne," 167–72; Higginbotham, *War of American Independence*, 176–81; Mackesy, *War for America*, 111–18, 121–23; O'Shaughnessy,

Men Who Lost America, 143–45; C. Ward, *War of the Revolution*, vol 1:399–401.

11. Billias, "John Burgoyne," 173–76; Higginbotham, *War of American Independence*, 188–90; Mackesy, *War for America*, 130–31; O'Shaughnessy, *Men Who Lost America*, 145–47; C. Ward, *War of the Revolution*, vol. 1:404–11, John Burgoyne quoted on 404.

12. Billias, "Horatio Gates," 89–93; Higginbotham, *War of American Independence*, 189–91; Pell, "Philip Schuyler," 64–69.

13. W. Brown, *Good Americans*, 120; Mackesy, *War for America*, 131–33; Middlekauff, *Glorious Cause*, 374–76; Silver, *Our Savage Neighbors*, 245–46.

14. Higginbotham, *War of American Independence*, 192–93; Mackesy, *War for America*, 133–34; John Burgoyne quoted in Spring, *With Zeal*, 280; C. Ward, *War of the Revolution*, vol. 1:421–23.

15. Philip Schuyler to John Hancock, June 8, 1776, and Schuyler to George Washington, June 11, 1776, in Peter Force, ed., *American Archives*, 4th ser., vol. 6:762–63, and 819; Graymont, *Iroquois in the American Revolution*, 115–46; Kelsay, *Joseph Brant*, 193–208; Martin and Lender, eds., *Citizen-Soldier*, 73–76, 97–99; C. Ward, *War of the Revolution*, vol. 2:481–91.

16. Mackesy, *War for America*, 133–34; O'Shaughnessy, *Men Who Lost America*, 151–54, John Burgoyne quoted on 154; C. Ward, *War of the Revolution*, vol. 1:421–23.

17. Billias, "Horatio Gates," 93–97; Higginbotham, *War of American Independence*, 194–97, Sergeant Roger Lamb quoted on 197 ("swarmed"); Mackesy, *War for America*, 135–44; O'Shaughnessy, *Men Who Lost America*, 155–58.

18. Middlekauff, *Glorious Cause*, 384; O'Shaughnessy, *Men Who Lost America*, 158–60.

19. Mason Bolton quoted in Calloway, *American Revolution in Indian Country*, 133 ("Scalps"); Campbell, *Annals of Tryon County*, 93–94, 100; Daniel Claus, "Remarks on the Management of the Northern Indian Nations," in O'Callaghan, ed., *New York Colonial Documents*, vol. 8:704; Jasanoff, *Liberty's Exiles*, 45–46; Kelsay, *Joseph Brant*, 222–23; Mintz, *Seeds of Empire*, 156–64.

20. Gruber, *Howe Brothers*, 224–38; Higginbotham, *War of American Independence*, 182–84; M. A. Jones, "Sir William Howe," 58–61; Mackesy, *War for America*, 122–26; O'Shaughnessy, *Men Who Lost America*, 106–7; C. Ward, *War of the Revolution*, vol. 1:328–33.

21. George Washington to John Hancock, Aug. 23, 1777, in Chase et al., eds., *Papers of George Washington, Revolutionary War Series*, vol. 11:52–54 ("the minds"); Gruber, *Howe Brothers*, 238–41; Higginbotham, *War of American Independence*, 185–86; Mackesy, *War for America*, 128–29; C. Ward, *War of the Revolution*, vol. 1:334–55.

22. Bodle, *Valley Forge*, 50; Elias Boudinot quoted in A. Boyd, *Elias Boudinot*, 43; W. Brown, *Good Americans*, 74–76; Butterfield et al., eds., *Diary and Autobiography of John Adams*, vol. 2:263–64 ("that Mass"); Jacob Duché to George Washington, Oct. 8, 1777, in Chase et al., eds., *Papers of George Washington, Revolutionary War Series*, vol. 11:430–37; Gruber, *Howe Brothers*, 241–44; O'Shaughnessy, *Men Who Lost America*, 107–10, British officer quoted on 109 ("tho' by all accounts"); C. Ward, *War of the Revolution*, vol. 1:355–61.

23. Gruber, *Howe Brothers*, 248; Higginbotham, *War of American Independence*, 186–88; M. A. Jones, "Sir William Howe," 61–62; Mackesy, *War for America*, 129–30; C. Ward, *War of the Revolution*, vol. 1:362–71.

24. Bodle, *Valley Forge*, 41–42; Nathanael Greene quoted in Royster, *Revolutionary People*, 116; C. Ward, *War of the Revolution*, vol. 1:371.

25. Chernow, *Washington*, 306, 312–14; Ferling, *Leap in the Dark*, 205–6; Higginbotham, *War of American Independence* 216–17; Royster, *Revolutionary People*, 146–48, 178–85.

26. Higginbotham, *War of American Independence*, 216–17; George Washington to Henry Laurens, Jan. 2, 1778, and Washington to Horatio Gates, Jan. 4, 1778, in Rhodehamel, ed., *Washington, Writings*, 286–89; Martin and Lender, *Respectable Army*, 111–13; C. Ward, *War of the Revolution*, vol. 2:560–61.

27. Henry Knox to George Washington, Nov. 26, 1777, in Chase et al., eds., *Papers of George Washington, Revolutionary War Series*, vol. 12:414–17 ("The people"); Cunliffe, "George Washington," 13–17; John Adams to Benjamin Rush, Mar. 19, 1812 ("Northern"), Founders Online, National Archives (http://founders.archives.gov/documents/Adams/99-02-02-5768); Higginbotham, *War of American Independence*, 217–22.

28. Bodle, *Valley Forge*, 124–26, 136–38; Albigence Waldo quote from Waldo, "Valley Forge," 306–7 ("Poor food"); Middlekauff, *Glorious Cause*, 411–16; George Washington to George Clinton, Feb. 16, 1778, in Rhodehamel, ed., *Washington, Writings*, 292–93 ("starving"); Royster, *Revolutionary People*, 186–88; C. Ward, *War of the Revolution*, vol. 2:543–550.

29. Chernow, *Washington*, 328–29; George Washington to Henry Laurens, Dec. 23, 1777, Washington to John Banister, Apr. 21, 1778, and Washington to James Warren, Mar. 31, 1779, in Rhodehamel, ed., *Washington, Writings*, 281–86 ("I can"), 298–305, and 342 ("Is the paltry").

30. A. Sullivan, "In but Not of the Revolution," chapter 3; Nathanael Greene to George Washington, Feb. 15 and Feb. 16, 1778, in Chase et al., eds., *Papers of George Washington, Revolutionary War Series*, vol. 13:546–48 ("The inhabitants cry"), 557–58 ("poverty and distress").

31. Bodle, *Valley Forge*, 131; Chernow, *Washington*, 332–33, Baron von Steuben quoted on 333 ("but to roast"); Higginbotham, *War of American Independence*, 247; C. Ward, *War of the Revolution*, vol. 2:550–52.

32. Bodle, *Valley Forge*, 199–202; Higginbotham, *War of American Independence*, 247; Martin and Lender, *Respectable Army*, 113–15; C. Ward, *War of the Revolution*, vol. 2:551–55.

33. Kaplan, "Treaties," 160–61; Middlekauff, *Glorious Cause*, 403; Sadosky, *Revolutionary Negotiations*, 96–100.

34. Dull, *Diplomatic History*, 64, 75–77, 85–87; Rakove, *Revolutionaries*, 245, 249–50, 257–58; Warner, *John the Painter*, 108–9, 132–34, 231–32.

35. Dull, *Diplomatic History*, 92–96; Kelly, "Two Treaties," 162–63; Mackesy, *War for America*, 160; Mapp, "Revolutionary War and Europe's Great Powers," 319–20; Stinchcombe, *American Revolution and the French Alliance*, 15.

36. Chavez, *Spain*, 47, 52–81, 87–88, 126–36; Dull, *Diplomatic History*, 108–10; Liss, *Atlantic Empires*, 127–28; Mackesy, *War for America*, 262–63; Mapp, "Revolutionary War and Europe's Great Powers," 318–20; Rakove, *Revolutionaries*, 265–66; Weber, *Spanish Frontier*, 265–66.

37. Dull, *Diplomatic History*, 13–25, 43–44, 121–36; Mapp, "Revolutionary War and Europe's Great Powers," 312, 321–22.

38. Dickinson, "Impact of the War," 359; Dull, *Diplomatic History*, 99–100; Gruber, *Howe Brothers*, 271–73, 278–79; Ritcheson, *British Politics*, 272–85, Carlisle commissioners quoted on 274 ("reestablish"); Sadosky, *Revolutionary Negotiations*, 101–8.

39. Mackesy, *War for America*, 153–54, 159, 187–89; O'Shaughnessy, *Men Who Lost America*, 61–64, *Morning Post* (London) quoted on 64 ("terms" and "race"); Ritcheson, *British Politics*, 258–71; Howe's aide quoted in Spring, *With Zeal*, 127–28 ("The common").

40. Chopra, *Unnatural Rebellion*, 101–5; Conway, "To Subdue America," 393–405; Dull, *Diplomatic History*, 100; Gruber, *Howe Brothers*, 289–90; O'Shaughnessy, *Men Who Lost America*, 115, George Washington to John Bannister, Apr. 21, 1778, in Rhodehamel, ed., *Washington, Writings*, 298–305; Banastre Tarleton quoted on 211; Sadosky, *Revolutionary Negotiations*, 90–91, 108–15; Stinchcombe, *American Revolution and the French Alliance*, 21–23.

41. Gouverneur Morris quoted in Sadosky, *Revolutionary Negotiations*, 91. Morris's threat anticipated the 2009 Quentin Tarantino film *Inglourious Basterds*, which featured an American hit squad that killed and scalped Germans during World War II.

42. Warner, *John the Painter*, xi–xii, 1–11, 58–229.

43. Conway, "British Army," 187–88; Dickinson, "Impact of the War," 355–56; Dull, *Diplomatic History*, 110–11; Piecuch, *Three Peoples*, 124–27, Lord George Germain quoted on 127 ("the War").

44. Mackesy, *War for America*, 213–14; O'Shaughnessy, *Men Who Lost America*, 212–20, 238, Sir Henry Clinton quoted on 212 ("the rebels"); Willcox, "Sir Henry Clinton," 73–75, 78–84, Clinton quoted on 82 ("I am hated").

45. Calhoon, *Loyalists*, 393–96; Chernow, *Washington*, 337–38, British official quoted on 338 ("No man"); Chopra, *Unnatural Rebellion*, 99–101; Ferling, *Loyalist Mind*, 40–50, Joseph Galloway quoted on 50; Gruber, *Howe Brothers*, 254–56, 260–61, 273–75, 280–81, 300–303; M. A. Jones, "Sir William Howe," 61–62; Mackesy, *War For America*, 54–59, 212; O'Shaughnessy, *Men Who Lost America*, 111, 119–20, 210–13.

46. Bodle, *Valley Forge Winter*, 245–49; Chernow, *Washington*, 338–44, Charles Scott quoted on 342 ("Never"); Higginbotham, *War of American Independence*, 246–47; Martin, ed., *Ordinary Courage*, 74–80, quote on 75 ("It was"); O'Shaughnessy, *Men Who Lost America*, 221–22; Shy, *People Numerous and Armed*, 155–58; C. Ward, *War of the Revolution*, vol. 2:572–85.

47. Higginbotham, *War of American Independence*, 247; Martin and Lender, *Respectable Army*, 123–24; Shy, *People Numerous and Armed*, 159–62, Charles Lee quoted on 160.

48. George Washington to Henry Laurens, May 1, 1778, in Chase et al., eds., *Papers of George Washington, Revolutionary War Series*, vol. 15:4–5 ("I believe"); Continental soldiers quoted in Chernow, *Washington*, 335 ("Long Live"); Kaplan, "Treaties," 161–62; Elbridge Gerry quoted in Martin and Lender, *Respectable Army*, 118–20; Stinchcombe, "Americans Celebrate," 41–42; Stinchcombe, *American Revolution and the French Alliance*, 14–24, Henry Livingston quoted on 15 ("America").

49. Chopra, *Unnatural Rebellion*, 97–98; Dull, *French Navy*, 122–23; Higginbotham, *War of American Independence*, 248; Mackesy, *War for America*, 216–19; Stinchcombe, *American Revolution and the French Alliance*, 49–50; C. Ward, *War of the Revolution*, vol. 2:588–93.

50. Higginbotham, *War of American Independence*, 248–49; Stinchcombe, *American Revolution and the French Alliance*, 51–60, John Laurens quoted on 60 ("I saw"); French officer quoted in Stinchcombe, "Americans Celebrate," 45 ("dwarfs").

51. Higginbotham, *War of American Independence*, 249–51; Mackesy, *War for America*, 221–22, 225; Stinchcombe, *American Revolution and the French Alliance*, 56, 60–61.

52. Chopra, *Unnatural Rebellion*, 105–7; Martin and Lender, *Respectable Army*, 124–25; C. Ward, *War of the Revolution*, vol. 2:596–610; H. Ward, *American Revolution*, 121–24, Captain Archibald Robertson quoted on 124 ("A very pretty").

53. C. Cox, *Proper Sense of Honor*, xix, 102–6, Henry Laurens quoted on xix, William Tudor quoted on 105 ("temporary"); Gross, *Minutemen*, 135–36, 150; Royster, *Revolutionary People*, 25–53, 64–67.

54. Anderson and Cayton, *Dominion of War*, 164–66; Bodle, *Valley Forge*, 35–36; Butterfield et al., eds., *Diary and Autobiography of John Adams*, vol. 3:386–88 ("men who could" and "the meanest"); C. Cox, *Proper Sense of Honor*, 1–4, 44–45; Martin and Lender, *Respectable Army*, 69–70, 88–89;

Middlekauff, *Glorious Cause*, 511–12; Royster, *Revolutionary People*, 130–32; H. Ward, *American Revolution*, 212–16; Shy, *People Numerous and Armed*, 172–73.

55. C. Cox, *Proper Sense of Honor*, 13–14; Gross, *Minutemen*, 146–52; Higginbotham, *War of American Independence*, 392–94, draft notice quoted on 393; McDonnell, "Class War?" 323–25; Martin, ed., *Ordinary Courage*, 38 ("I thought"); Shy, *People Numerous and Armed*, 172–73; B. C. Smith, *Freedoms We Lost*, 146–48; H. Ward, *American Revolution*, 212–16, French officer quoted on 215 ("were composed").

56. C. Cox, *Proper Sense of Honor*, 3–4, 10–16; Crow, "Liberty Men and Loyalists," 170–71; Gross, *Minutemen*, 151–52; Higginbotham, *War of American Independence*, 393–96; Martin and Lender, *Respectable Army*, 90–93; McDonnell, "Class War?" 321–23; Royster, *Revolutionary People*, 135–36, 373–78; H. Ward, *American Revolution*, 212–16, Col. Francis Johnston quoted on 215 ("only *Food for* Worms"), Alexander Graydon quoted on 215 ("who would do").

57. C. Cox, *Proper Sense of Honor*, 49–50; Gross, *Minutemen*, 152–53; Higginbotham, *War of American Independence*, 398–99; Middlekauff, *Glorious Cause*, 510–16, Ebenezer Huntington quoted on 511–12; H. Ward, *American Revolution*, 217–19.

58. George Washington to John Jay, Apr. 23, 1779, in Chase et al., eds., *Papers of George Washington, Revolutionary War Series*, vol. 20:174–77 ("a waggon load"); E. Foner, *Tom Paine*, 149–50; Gross, *Minutemen*, 140–41; Higginbotham, "War and State Formation," 63; Irvin, *Clothed in Robes of Sovereignty*, 241–42, 249–50, Oliver Wolcott quoted on 250 ("for little Else"); Middlekauff, *Glorious Cause*, 516–19; Royster, *Revolutionary People*, 298.

59. C. Cox, *Proper Sense of Honor*, 22–23, 50–54, Zebulon Vaughan quoted on 53 ("we are yoused" and "Cu[r]se"); Martin, ed., *Ordinary Courage*, 111 ("venting our spleen"); Martin and Lender, *Respectable Army*, 128–30; Royster, *Revolutionary People*, 295–98.

60. Enoch Poor quoted in Bodle, *Valley Forge*, 128–29 ("If any"); Ebenezer Huntington quoted in H. Ward, *American Revolution*, 239 ("Not a Day").

61. George Washington, General Orders, July 25, 1777, in Chase et al., eds., *Papers of George Washington, Revolutionary War Series*, vol. 10: 402–3 ("How disgraceful"); C. Cox, *Proper Sense of Honor*, 70–71, 103–5; Royster, *Revolutionary People*, 73–74, 301–2.

62. Higginbotham, *War of American Independence*, 399–400; Martin and Lender, *Respectable Army*, 130–33; Royster, *Revolutionary People*, 71–72.

63. Higginbotham, *War of America Independence*, 403–4; Martin and Lender, *Respectable Army*, 161–65; Royster, *Revolutionary People*, 140–41, 299–301; H. Ward, *American Revolution*, 222.

64. Higginbotham, *War of American Independence*, 403–5; Martin and Lender, *Respectable Army*, 162–64; Royster, *Revolutionary People*, 302–6; H. Ward, *American Revolution*, 222–24.

65. George Washington to Samuel Huntington, Jan. 23, 1781 ("Unless this") Founders Online, National Archives (http://founders.archives.gov/doc uments/Washington/99-01-02-04623); Martin and Lender, *Respectable Army*, 164–65; H. Ward, *American Revolution*, 224–25, James Thacher quoted on 224 ("wretched victims").

66. Royster, *Revolutionary People*, 295–98, Eliphalet Wright quoted on 296 ("As affairs"), Ann Glover quoted on 297.

67. Bodle, *Valley Forge*, 130–31, Richard Butler quoted on 130 ("the best"); George Washington, "Farewell Address to the Army," Nov. 2, 1783 ("unparalleled" and "through almost"), Founders Online, National Archives (http://founders.archives.gov/documents/Washington/99-01-02-12012); C. Cox, *Proper Sense of Honor*, 69–70, 172–73, 237–38; Martin, ed., *Ordinary Courage*, 162–68; Royster, *Revolutionary People*, 115–16, 373–78; H. Ward, *American Revolution*, 212–16.

68. Berkin, *Revolutionary Mothers*, 30–31, unnamed Philadelphia woman quoted on 30 ("I will tell"); Breen, *American Insurgents*, 140–41; Kerber, "'History Can Do It No Justice,'" 21–22; Mayer, *Belonging to the Army*, 20; Norton, *Liberty's Daughters*, 156–58.

69. Berkin, *Revolutionary Mothers*, 33–35, "his," "ours," and "my farm" quoted on 33–34, see also 42–43; Gundersen, *To Be Useful to the World*, 189; Kerber, *Women of the Republic*, 41–42, 87–89, Rachel Wells quoted on 87; Norton, *Liberty's Daughters*, 215–220; Pearsall, "Women," 276; Ulrich, "'Daughters of Liberty,'" 234; Young, "Women of Boston," 214.

70. Norton, *Liberty's Daughters*, 216–220, unnamed soldier quoted on 216 ("but must Leave"), Timothy Pickering quoted on 222 ("This war"), and Lucy Flucker Knox quoted on 223 ("quite a woman"), and 224 ("I hope").

71. Berkin, *Revolutionary Mothers*, 44–48, Benjamin Rush quoted on 46; Gundersen, *To Be Useful to the World*, 189–91, Anna Rawle Clifford quoted on 191 ("reminded" and "at length"); Kerber, *Women of the Republic*, 99–106; Norton, *Liberty's Daughters*, 178–85; Pearsall, "Women," 281–83.

72. Berkin, *Revolutionary Mothers*, 48–49; Gundersen, *To Be Useful to the World*, 191–92; Norton, *Liberty's Daughters*, 179–88.

73. George Washington, "General Orders," Aug. 4, 1777, in Chase et al., eds., *Papers of George Washington, Revolutionary War Series*, vol. 10: 496–97 ("absolutely necessary"); Gundersen, *To Be Useful to the World*, 194–98; Kerber, "'History Can Do It No Justice,'" 11–14; Martin, ed., *Ordinary Courage*, 117–18; Mayer, *Belonging to the Army*, 5–6, 12–13, 17.

74. Berkin, *Revolutionary Mothers*, 50–56, unnamed gentleman quoted on

56, Benedict Arnold quoted on 59; Kerber, *Women of the Republic*, 55–60; Norton, *Liberty's Daughters*, 212–13.

75. Berkin, *Revolutionary Mothers*, 41–42, 55–56, 58–60; Gundersen, *To be Useful to the World*, 192–93, 197; Kerber, "'History Can Do It No Justice,'" 13–14; Martin, ed., *Ordinary Courage*, 80; Mayer, *Belonging to the Army*, 20–21, 125–28.

76. Berkin, *Revolutionary Mothers*, 60–61; Gundersen, *To Be Useful to the World*, 193–94; Norton, *Liberty's Daughters*, 174; Young, *Masquerade*, 202–24.

77. Berkin, *Revolutionary Mothers*, 136–42; Gundersen, *To Be Useful to the World*, 180–81; Kerber, *Women of the Republic*, 48–49; Norton, *Liberty's Daughters*, 175–76.

78. Berkin, *Revolutionary Mothers*, 26–40; Gundersen, *To Be Useful to the World*, 179–86; Kulikoff, "War in the Countryside," 216–19; Norton, *Liberty's Daughters*, 196–209, Baroness Frederica von Riedesel quoting a Patriot girl on 172; Norton, "'What an Alarming Crisis,'" 215–17; Pearsall, "Women," 273–76; Young, "Women of Boston," 206–7, 216.

79. Bodle, *Valley Forge*, 125–26; John Adams to Abigail Adams, May 22, 1777, in Butterfield et al., eds., *Adams Family Correspondence*, vol. 2:245–46 ("wearied to Death"); C. Cox, *Proper Sense of Honor*, 25–26, 28–32, 40–41, 60–65; Martin and Lender, *Respectable Army*, 103–7; Conrad-Alexandre Gerard quoted in Murphy, "View from Versailles," 134 ("an epidemic"); Royster, *Revolutionary People*, 86–95, 197–201; Waldo, "Valley Forge," 308.

80. C. Cox, *Proper Sense of Honor*, 47–48; Higginbotham, *War of American Independence*, 401–2, Ebenezer Huntington quoted on 401 ("I despise"); Martin and Lender, *Respectable Army*, 107–10, James Lovell quoted on 108 ("forgotten"), 127–28, 150–51; Alexander McDougall quoted in Royster, *Revolutionary People*, 298 ("for Empire").

81. Shy, *People Numerous and Armed*, 187–88, Moore Fauntleroy quoted on 188.

82. Chernow, *Washington*, 378–79; Martin and Lender, *Respectable Army*, 104–5; Royster, *Revolutionary People*, 289; Wallace, "Benedict Arnold," 163–84.

83. Chernow, *Washington*, 379–80; Irvin, *Clothed in Robes*, 253–57; Royster, *Revolutionary People*, 288–89; Wallace, "Benedict Arnold," 184–86; H. Ward, *American Revolution*, 245.

84. Higginbotham, *War of American Independence*, 402–3; Benedict Arnold, "To the Inhabitants of America," and Arnold to Lord Germain, Oct. 7, 1780, in Rhodehamel, ed., *American Revolution*, 592–95, quotation from 594–95 ("the Reunion"), 596–99; Royster, *Revolutionary People*, 283–86, 289–90; H. Ward, *American Revolution*, 245.

85. O'Shaughnessy, *Men Who Lost America*, 234–36, Sir Henry Clinton quoted on 235 ("the Rebellion"); Wallace, "Benedict Arnold," 186–87; H. Ward, *American Revolution*, 246.

86. Alexander Hamilton to John Laurens, Oct. 11, 1780, in Rhodehamel, ed., *American Revolution*, 600–609; George Washington to Benedict Arnold, Aug. 3, 1780, and Washington to Samuel Huntington, Sept. 26, 1780, in Rhodehamel, ed., *Washington, Writings*, 381–82, 387–88; Wallace, "Benedict Arnold," 186–87.

87. Chernow, *Washington*, 382–83, George Washington quoted on 382 ("Arnold has betrayed"); Alexander Hamilton to John Laurens, Oct. 11, 1780, in Rhodehamel, ed., *American Revolution*, 600–609; George Washington to Henry Clinton, Sept. 30, 1780, and Washington to J. Laurens, Oct. 13, 1780, in Rhodehamel, ed., *George Washington: Writings*, 388–89, 392.

88. Irvin, *Clothed in Robes*, 251–53, 258–59; Martin and Lender, *Respectable Army*, 159–60; George Washington to Samuel Huntington, Sept. 26, 1780, in Rhodehamel, ed., *Washington, Writings*, 387–88; Royster, *Revolutionary People*, 290–94, Samuel Shaw quoted on 290 ("I cannot"), Nathanael Greene quoted on 290 ("How black").

89. Irvin, *Clothed in Robes*, 258; Martin and Lender, *Respectable Army*, 159–60; George Washington to Samuel Huntington, Sept. 26, 1780, in Rhodehamel, ed., *Washington, Writings*, 387–88 ("men of great"); Royster, *Revolutionary People*, 346–47.

90. O'Shaughnessy, *Men Who Lost America*, 235–38, Sergeant Roger Lamb quoted on 237.

91. Gross, *Minutemen*, 153–54; Irvin, *Clothed in Robes*, 251; Martin and Lender, *Respectable Army*, 126–34; O'Shaughnessy, *Men Who Lost America*, 199; Royster, *Revolutionary People*, 308; Shy, *People Numerous and Armed*, 243, 254–55.

92. Murphy, "View from Versailles," 133–39, Marquis de Lafayette quoted on 133, Comte de Vergennes quoted on 138.

93. Higginbotham, *War of American Independence*, 379–80; Murphy, "View from Versailles," 143–45, Comte de Rochambeau quoted on 143; H. Ward, *American Revolution*, 124, Sir Henry Clinton quoted on 124.

CHAPTER 6: LOYALTIES

1. Pierce Butler quoted in Weir, "'Violent Spirit,'" 76.

2. Nathanael Greene quoted in C. Ward, *War of the Revolution*, vol. 2:827.

3. Bannister and Riordan, "Loyalism and the British Atlantic," 6–7, 17; W. Brown, *Good Americans*, 72–73; Thomas McKean quoted in Calhoon, *Loyalists*, 399 ("was not a nation"); Elliott, *Empires of the Atlantic World*, 352; Jasanoff, *Liberty's Exiles*, 9–10; Larkin, "Loyalism," 291–94; New York

writer quoted in H. Ward, *American Revolution*, 259. For mythic memories, see Purcell, *Sealed with Blood*, 1–10.

4. Higginbotham, *War of American Independence*, 134–35; Mackesy, *War for America*, 36–37, William Howe quoted on 36; Sadosky, *Revolutionary Negotiations*, 105; Tiedemann, "Revolution Foiled," 421, 443; Shy, *People Armed and Numerous*, 163–179, 218–19.

5. T. Allen, *Tories*, xx–xxii; Calhoon, "Loyalism and Neutrality," 247; John Adams to Benjamin Rush, Mar. 19, 1812 ("We were about"), Founders Online, National Archives (http://founders.archives.gov/documents/Adams/99-02-02-5768); Fowler, "Loyalty Is Now Bleeding," 49; W. Nelson, *American Tory*, 92; Shy, *People Numerous and Armed*, 166, 183.

6. T. Allen, *Tories*, 188–92; Kim, "Limits of Politicization," 871–73; McDonnell, "The Struggle Within," 107–9, 113–14; Nathanael Greene quoted in Moore, *World of Toil and Strife*, 71 ("notwithstanding"); Thomas Paine, "The American Crisis, Number 1," in Rhodehamel, ed., *American Revolution*, 241–42; George Washington to Lund Washington, Dec. 10, 1776, in Rhodehamel, ed., *Washington, Writings*, 26 ("apprehend"); Tiedemann, "Revolution Foiled," 417–44.

7. Crow, "Liberty Men and Loyalists," 127–28, 137–38; Hoffman, "The 'Disaffected,'" 277–90, 303–4; Kim, "Limits of Politicization," 876, 888; Crèvecoeur, *Letters*, 221 ("malevolent"); Crèvecoeur, *Sketches*, 296 ("We have so many"); Van Buskirk, *Generous Enemies*, 40.

8. Crèvecoeur, *Letters*, 152–53; Nelson, *American Tory*, 149–50; Van Buskirk, *Generous Enemies*, 38–39.

9. Allen and Asselineau, *St. John de Crèvecoeur*, 69; Van Buskirk, *Generous Enemies*, 39; Crèvecoeur, *Sketches*, 291–96 ("we should").

10. Countryman, *People in Revolution*, 119–20; Shy, *People Numerous and Armed*, 166–67. For the fistfight, see W. Lee, *Crowds and Soldiers*, 147.

11. W. Brown, *Good Americans*, 45–48; Calhoon, *Loyalists*, 364–66, 432–35; Chopra, *Choosing Sides*, 1–2; Countryman, *People in Revolution*, 103–30; Fowler, "Liberty Is Now Bleeding," 49–54, writer quoted on 50 ("almost every"); Moore, *World of Toil and Strife*, 64–68.

12. Fowler, "Liberty Is Now Bleeding," 49–54, Joseph Cogil quoted on 53–54 ("The Presbyterians"); Loyalist quoted in Hibbert, *Redcoats and Rebels*, 284 ("Presbyterian sermon"); W. Lee, *Crowds and Soldiers*, 208–9; W. Nelson, *American Tory*, 50–53, 85–93; Tiedemann, "Revolution Foiled," 419, 422; Van Buskirk, *Generous Enemies*, 39.

13. Chopra, *Unnatural Rebellion*, 5; Kim, "Limits of Politicization," 868–79; Piecuch, *Three Peoples*, 231; Thomas Paine quoted in O'Shaughnessy, *Men Who Lost America*, 105.

14. W. Brown, *Good Americans*, 58–59, 87–88, Loyalist quoted on 59 ("We are at present"); Robert Weir quoted in Crow, "Liberty Men and Loyalists,"

159; Fowler, "Loyalty Is Now Bleeding," 49–52; Captain Bowater quoted in Hibbert, *Redcoats and Rebels*, 268 ("They swallow"); Shy, *People Numerous and Armed*, 186–88, Earl of Carlisle quoted on 186.

15. Countryman, *People Numerous and Armed*, 130; Piecuch, *Three Peoples*, 230; Shy, *People Numerous and Armed*, 163–80, 186–88; C. Ward, *War of the Revolution*, vol. 2:810, Nathanael Greene quoted on 827.

16. Philadelphia Quakers quoted in Beeman, *Our Lives*, 324; W. Brown, *Good Americans*, 138–39; Calhoon, *Loyalists*, 170–74; W. Nelson, *American Tory*, 87–91, 106–7; Tiedemann, "Revolution Foiled," 419–34, Queens County man quoted on 434 ("I am for peace").

17. Calhoon, "Loyalism and Neutrality," 254–55; Calhoon, *Loyalists*, 385–90; Chopra *Choosing Sides*, 26–27; Ousterhout, *State Divided*, 165–68, 282–83.

18. James Child quoted in Calhoon, "Evangelical Persuasion," 164 ("Shew him"); Fowler, "Loyalty Is Now Bleeding," 53; Hoffman, "The 'Disaffected,'" 285–91, Robert Gassaway quoted on 285; Klein, "Frontier Planters," 49–50.

19. W. Brown, *Good Americans*, 88, 130–31, John Adams quoted on 144; Fowler, "Loyalty Is Now Bleeding," 50–51, Patriots quoted on 50 ("Those who are" and "Join"); Calhoon, *Loyalists*, 399; Abijah Brown quoted in W. Nelson, *American Tory*, 96 ("a set").

20. W. Brown, *Good Americans*, 122–23, 131–32, James Allen quoted on 131 ("I never"); Fowler, "Loyalty Is Now Bleeding," 53–54; Jasanoff, *Liberty's Exiles*, 26–27; W. Nelson, *American Tory*, 93–115;. Moses Kirkland quoted in Piecuch, *Three Peoples*, 52 ("not allowed").

21. W. Brown, *Good Americans*, 136–45; Calhoon, *Loyalists*, 304–5; Gross, *Minutemen*, 137–38; J. W. Harris, *Hanging of Thomas Jeremiah*, 136–39; Jasanoff, *Liberty's Exiles*, 6–8, 26–27; W. Lee, *Crowds and Soldiers*, 146–49; Philip Fithian quoted in McDonnell, *Politics of War*, 80 ("Tar and Feathers"); W. Nelson, *American Tory*, 93–115; Piecuch, *Three Peoples*, 45–46, 56; Potter, *Liberty We Seek*, 147–52; Tiedemann, "Revolution Foiled," 420–21.

22. W. Nelson, *American Tory*, 97–104, Provincial Congress quoted on 103; Piecuch, *Three Peoples*, 48–57; Tiedemann, "A Revolution Foiled," 417–44.

23. W. Brown, *Good Americans*, 141–42; Calhoon, *Loyalists*, 306–11, Ephraim Whitney quoted on 322 ("Your law"), 398; Shy, *People Numerous and Armed*, 176–77.

24. W. Brown, *Good Americans*, 126–28; Calhoon, *Loyalists*, 322, 400–401; Chopra, *Unnatural Rebellion*, 160–61; Countryman, *People in Revolution*, 172–75; Crow, "Liberty Men and Loyalists," 138–40; W. Nelson, *American Tory*, 97, 146–48, Jonathan Sewall quoted on 147–48, Grace Galloway quoted on 148; Ousterhout, *State Divided*, 286–91.

25. Bodle, "'Ghost of Clow,'" 19–44, William Wright quoted on 32 ("two thirds"); Calhoon, *Loyalists*, 404–7; Crow, "Liberty Men and Loyalists,"

154–55; E. Evans, "Trouble in the Backcountry," 183–93; Hoffman, "The 'Disaffected,'" 288–290, Joseph Dashiell quoted on 288–89 ("With a poor"), and William Perry quoted on 289 ("As soon as").

26. Joshua Wingate Weeks quoted in W. Brown, *The Good Americans*, 124 ("The Congress"); Cresswell, *Journal*, 45–46; Fowler, "Loyalty Is Now Bleeding," 50; Kim, "Limits of Politicization," 874–75; Shy, *People Numerous and Armed*, 178–79.

27. Witness quoted in H. Ward, *American Revolution*, 263–64.

28. Bodle. "'Ghost of Clow,'" 28; Calhoon, *Loyalists*, 328–30; Fowler, "Loyalism Is Now Bleeding," 57–63; Shy, *People Numerous and Armed*, 188–89 ("nasty little"); Van Buskirk, *Generous Enemies*, 35–38; H. Ward, *Between the Lines*, xi–xii, 1–3.

29. Bodle, *Valley Forge*, 126–27, Jedediah Huntington quoted on 126 ("Any army); C. Cox, *Proper Sense of Honor*, 103–5; Davies, "Restoration of Civil Government," 128; Frey, *Water from the Rock*, 90–91; Kim, "Limits of Politicization," 868–85, Nathanael Greene quoted on 885; Van Buskirk, *Generous Enemies*, 42.

30. T. Allen, *Tories*, 188–208; Bodle, *Valley Forge*, 21–22, 126–28; Calhoon, *Loyalists*, 328–30, 362–63; Dwight, *Travels*, vol. 3:471–72; Fowler, "Loyalty Is Now Bleeding," 61–63; Kim, "Limits of Politicization," 878–85; H. Ward, *Between the Lines*, 1–32.

31. Bodle, *Valley Forge*, 84–87; Dwight, *Travels*, vol. 3:471–72; Kim, "Limits of Politicization," 878–83; Van Buskirk, *Generous Enemies*, 42.

32. W. Brown, *Good Americans*, 91–95; Conway, *War of American Independence*, 35, 39–40; Spring, *With Zeal*, 134–136, 280, British officer quoted on 134 ("crafty").

33. W. Brown, *Good Americans*, 110–25, James Robertson quoted on 110; Chopra, *Unnatural Rebellion*, 160–97; Skemp, *William Franklin*, 229–30; P. Smith, *Loyalists and Redcoats*, 56.

34. Chopra, *Unnatural Rebellion*, 60–72; Davies, "Restoration of Civil Government," 111–33; Jasanoff, *Liberty's Exiles*, 36–37; Van Buskirk, *Generous Enemies*, 22.

35. W. Brown, *Good Americans*, 116; Calhoon, *Loyalists*, 373–75; Chopra, *Unnatural Rebellion*, 149–53, 174–80, 223–24; Davies, "Restoration of Civil Government," 128–33; Skemp, *William Franklin*, 227–28; Van Buskirk, *Generous Enemies*, 23–30.

36. Loyalist quoted in T. Allen, *Tories*, 180 ("This robbing"); Lord Rawdon quoted in Berkin, *Revolutionary Mothers*, 41; W. Brown, *Good Americans*, 118–19; Chopra, *Unnatural Rebellion*, 52–70, Sir William Howe quoted on 63 ("that it was not").

37. W. Brown, *Good Americans*, 64–82, Sir William Howe quoted on 64; Chopra, *Unnatural Rebellion*, 113–22, Sir Henry Clinton quoted on 119;

Moore, *Loyalists*, 119–23; Skemp, *William Franklin*, 229–30, Ambrose Serle quoted on 229 ("Alas"); P. Smith, *Loyalists and Redcoats*, 33–43, 66–67; Van Buskirk, *Generous Enemies*, 36–37.

38. W. Brown, *Good Americans*, 97–98; Chopra, *Unnatural Rebellion*,, 113–22; Moore, *Loyalists*, 119–23; P. Smith, *Loyalists and Redcoats*, 60–78; Van Buskirk, *Generous Enemies*, 36–37.

39. T. Allen, *Tories*, 192–96, 207, 315–17; W. Brown, *Good Americans*, 98–100; Egerton, *Death or Liberty*, 65–68; Fowler, "Loyalty Is Now Bleeding," 59; H. Ward, *Between the Lines*, 51–84.

40. T. Allen, *Tories*, 205, 208, 317 ("the Hanging Place"); Calhoon, *Loyalists*, 401–2; Chopra, *Unnatural Rebellion*, 195; Piecuch, *Three Peoples*, 201. For lynching, see Selby, *Revolution in Virginia*, 220. For "Liberty Forever," see H. Ward, *American Revolution*, 267.

41. Calhoon, *Loyalists*, 368–69; Fowler, "Loyalty Is Now Bleeding," 55–61, Richard Lippincott quoted on 57; Skemp, *William Franklin*, 242–43.

42. Chopra, *Unnatural Rebellion*, 168–74; Jasanoff, *Liberty's Exiles*, 70–71; Skemp, *William Franklin*, 220–46.

43. T. Allen, *Tories*, 315–20; W. Brown, *Good Americans*, 106–7; Chopra, *Unnatural Rebellion*, 196; Fowler, "Loyalty Is Now Bleeding," 45–48, Richard Lippincott quoted on 48 ("We the Reffugees"); Jasanoff, *Liberty's Exiles*, 71–72; Skemp, *William Franklin*, 256–65.

44. Burnard, "Slavery and the Causes," 57–58; Frey, *Water from the Rock*, 81–82; Gilbert, *Black Patriots and Loyalists*, 28–29; John Stuart quoted in Griffin, *American Leviathan*, 135; McDonnell, "Class War?" 325–26; Piecuch, *Three Peoples*, 43, 124–36, Lord George Germain quoted on 136 ("Assistance"); Shy, *People Numerous and Armed*, 229–30.

45. Frey, *Water from the Rock*, 82–83, 89; Piecuch, *Three Peoples*, 29, 124–27, 154–55, 159–60; H. Ward, *American Revolution*, 127–28.

46. Berlin, *Many Thousands Gone*, 295–98; Frey, *Water from the Rock*, 89–91, 94–96, 119–22; Mackesy, *War for America*, 158–59; Olwell, *Masters, Slaves, and Subjects*, 244–47, 251–53; Piecuch, *Three Peoples*, 8–11, 129, 158–59, 163.

47. Frey, *Water from the Rock*, 119–22, P. Morgan, "Black Society in the Low-country," 121–22, Eliza Lucas Pinckney quoted on 121; Norton, "'What an Alarming Crisis," 215; Boston King quoted in Olwell, *Masters, Slaves, and Subjects*, 265.

48. Berlin, *Many Thousands Gone*, 295–98, Eliza Lucas Pinckney quoted on 301; Egerton, *Death or Liberty*, 85–86; Frey, *Water from the Rock*, 130–32.

49. Berlin, *Many Thousands Gone*, 293–301; Frey, *Water from the Rock*, 87–88, 102, 114–18; Archibald Campbell quoted in P. D. Morgan, "Black Society," 109 ("Negroes who flock"); Nash, *Race and Revolution*, 57–60; Olwell, *Masters, Slaves, and Subjects*, 246–52, 263–65, Banastre Tarleton quoted on 248; Piecuch, *Three Peoples*, 9.

50. Berlin, *Many Thousands Gone*, 295–96; Egerton, *Death or Liberty*, 86–87; Frey, *Water from the Rock*, 113–114; Olwell, *Masters, Slaves, and Subjects*, 246, Thomas Sumter quoted on 259; Piecuch, *Three Peoples*, 9–11, 44; Ramsay, *History*, vol. 1:320–21.

51. Frey, *Water from the Rock*, 114–15; Gilbert, *Black Patriots and Loyalists*, 13; Olwell, *Masters, Slaves, and Subjects*, 259; Thomas Lynch and Henry Laurens quoted in Piecuch, *Three Peoples*, 44.

52. Conway, *War of American Independence*, 108; Frey, *Water from the Rock*, 84–85; Piecuch, *Three Peoples*, 129–34; C. Ward, *War of the Revolution*, vol. 2:679–81; H. Ward, *American Revolution*, 127–29.

53. Conway, *War of American Independence*, 111–12; Frey, *Water from the Rock*, 84–86, 96–98; O'Shaughnessy, *Men Who Lost America*, 223–24, Archibald Campbell quoted on 223 ("ripped one"); Piecuch, *Three Peoples*, 135–38, 145–49, 169–70, Campbell quoted on 135 ("I have got"), Charles Grey quoted on 172; C. Ward, *War of the Revolution*, vol. 2:681–84, 688–94.

54. Chernow, *Washington*, 211–13, Captain Alexander Graydon quoted on 212 ("had a disagreeable"); Egerton, *Death or Liberty*, 74–76; Higginbotham, *War of American Independence*, 394–95, Philip Schuyler quoted on 395; Nash, *Forgotten Fifth*, 7–10; Raphael, *Founders*, 221–24.

55. Chernow, *Washington*, 213, 333–34, Baron von Closen quoted on 334 ("merry" and "the most neatly"), 354–55; C. Cox, *Proper Sense of Honor*, 16–17; Egerton, *Death or Liberty*, 76–77; Higginbotham, *War of American Independence*, 395–96; Nash, *Forgotten Fifth*, 8–12.

56. Berlin, *Many Thousands Gone*, 298; J. W. Harris, *Hanging of Thomas Jeremiah*, 158–59; Rakove, *Revolutionaries*, 199–203, John Laurens quoted on 202 ("I think") and 223 ("the Groans"); Raphael, *Founders*, 334.

57. Egerton, *Death or Liberty*, 81; J. W. Harris, *Hanging of Thomas Jeremiah*, 159–60; Piecuch, *Three Peoples*, 163–64; Rakove, *Revolutionaries*, 218, 221–24, 228–30, John Laurens quoted on 230 ("It will be" and "the glory").

58. Henry Laurens to George Washington, Mar. 16, 1779, in Chase et al., eds., *Papers of George Washington, Revolutionary War Series*, vol. 19:503–5 ("had we Arms"); Piecuch, *Three Peoples*, 163–64; Rakove, *Revolutionaries*, 231–34; George Washington to Henry Laurens, Mar. 20, 1779, in Rhodehamel, ed., *Washington, Writings*, 337–38; Alexander Hamilton to John Jay, Mar. 14, 1779, in Rhodehamel, ed., *American Revolution*, 523–25.

59. Frey, *Water from the Rock*, 86; Piecuch, *Three Peoples*, 164; Rakove, *Revolutionaries*, 231–33.

60. Egerton, *Death or Liberty*, 83–84; Frey, *Water from the Rock*, 136; Christopher Gadsden quoted in J. W. Harris, *Hanging of Thomas Jeremiah*, 160; Piecuch, *Three Peoples*, 164.

61. George Washington to John Laurens, July 10, 1782 ("I must confess"), Founders Online, National Archives (http://founders.archives.gov/doc

uments/Washington/99-01-02-08890); Rakove, *Revolutionaries*, 235–38, Henry Laurens quoted on 235–36; Raphael, *Founders*, 393–94.

62. Egerton, *Death or Liberty*, 78–79; James Madison to Joseph Jones, Nov. 28, 1780, in Hutchinson et al., eds., *Papers of James Madison*, vol. 2:209–11; McDonnell, *Politics of War*, 388–95; Rakove, *Revolutionaries*, 239–40.

63. McDonnell, *Politics of War*, 261–62, 338–39, 417, 486–87; Evans, *Topping People*, 198; D. B. Davis, *Problem of Slavery in the Age of Revolution*, 78–80.

64. Conway, *War of American Independence*, 115–16; Higginbotham, *War of American Independence*, 356–57; O'Shaughnessy, *Men Who Lost America*, 229–31; Shipton, "Benjamin Lincoln," 202–3, British officer quoted on 203 ("Lincoln limp'd out"); C. Ward, *War of the Revolution*, vol. 2:695–703; Willcox, "Sir Henry Clinton," 85–87.

65. Alexander MacDonald quoted in Conway, *War of American Independence*, 116 ("This Country"); Higginbotham, *War of American Independence*, 357; Charles Town address quoted in Nadelhaft, "'Snarls of Invidious Animals,'" 71; Piecuch, *Three Peoples*, 237–42, Edward Giles quoted on 237 ("With a few exceptions"); P. Smith, *Loyalists and Redcoats*, 128–29.

66. Klein, "Frontier Planters," 63–64; Moore, *World of Toil and Strife*, 62–64; Piecuch, *Three Peoples*, 178–87, Robert Gray quoted on 180 ("enjoy a respite"); Shy, *People Numerous and Armed*, 209; P. Smith, *Loyalists and Redcoats*, 129–33.

67. Klein, "Frontier Planters," 44–47, Oliver Hart quoted on 45 ("Col. Fletchall"); Moore, *World of Toil and Strife*, 61–66; Shy, *People Numerous and Armed*, 231–33, Robert Gray quoted on 232 ("a piece").

68. Moore, *World of Toil and Strife*, 63; Piecuch, *Three Peoples*, 178–87, Robert Biddulph quoted on 182 ("There is"); Shy, *People Numerous and Armed*, 208–9.

69. O'Shaughnessy, *Men Who Lost America*, 249–51, 255–56; Rankin, "Charles Lord Cornwallis," 193–94, 201–3; Willcox, "Sir Henry Clinton," 88–89. For the distribution of British troops see Gruber, "Britain's Southern Strategy," 232.

70. Hibbert, *Redcoats and Rebels*, 270–71, 273; W. Lee, *Crowds and Soldiers*, 177, 186; Moore, *World of Toil and Strife*, 60–61; O'Shaughnessy, *Men Who Lost America*, 256–57; C. Ward, *War of the Revolution*, 701–2, 705–6; H. Ward, *American Revolution*, 133–35.

71. Billias, "Horatio Gates," 99–103, Gates quoted on 100; Higginbotham, *War of American Independence*, 357–60; Mackesy, *War for America*, 342–43; O'Shaughnessy, *Men Who Lost America*, 257–58; C. Ward, *War of the Revolution*, vol. 2:712–35.

72. Conway, *War of American Independence*, 118–19; Higginbotham, *War of American Independence*, 364; O'Shaughnessy, *Men Who Lost America*,

263–65; Piecuch, *Three Peoples*, 198–202; C. Ward, *War of the Revolution*, vol. 2:739–45.

73. Hibbert, *Redcoats and Rebels*, 280–87, prisoner quoted on 284 ("Mrs. Mills"); W. Lee, *Crowds and Soldiers*, 186–90; Piecuch, *Three Peoples*, 198–201, Gov. Rutledge quoted on 201, and Lewis Morris quoted on 238 ("The tories"); C. Ward, *War of the Revolution*, vol. 2:739–45; H. Ward, *American Revolution*, 138–40.

74. Conway, *War of American Independence*, 118–19; J. W. Hall, "'My Favorite Officer,'" 149–68; Higginbotham, *War of American Independence*, 362–63; Thayer, "Nathanael Greene," 109–22; C. Ward, *War of the Revolution*, vol. 2:748.

75. Middlekauff, *Glorious Cause*, 464–67, Nathanael Greene quoted on 466 ("dismal"); Greene quoted in Piecuch, *Three Peoples*, 275 ("where most") Thayer, "Nathanael Greene," 126–28; C. Ward, *War of the Revolution*, vol. 2:748–51, Greene quoted on 750 ("so addicted").

76. Conway, *War of American Independence*, 122–23; Higginbotham, "Daniel Morgan," 291–306; Mackesy, *War for America*, 344–45; O'Shaughnessy, *Men Who Lost America*, 262–63; Thayer, "Nathanael Greene," 109–28, Greene quoted on 109 ("There are few generals").

77. Conway, *War of American Independence*, 123; Higginbotham, "Daniel Morgan," 306–9; O'Shaughnessy, *Men Who Lost America*, 266–68; C. Ward, *War of the Revolution*, vol. 2:751–62.

78. Conway, *War of American Independence*, 123–24; Nathanael Greene to Thomas Jefferson, Feb. 15, 1781, in Boyd et al., eds., *Papers of Thomas Jefferson*, vol. 4:615–16 ("The Army"); O'Shaughnessy, *Men Who Lost America*, 269–71; Thayer, "Nathanael Greene," 129–30.

79. Higginbotham, *War for American Independence*, 369–70; O'Shaughnessy, *Men Who Lost America*, 271–72; Cornwallis quoted in Spring, *With Zeal*, 279; C. Ward, *War of the Revolution*, vol. 2:795–97.

80. Hibbert, *Redcoats and Rebels*, 307–8; P. Smith, *Loyalists and Redcoats*, 154–56; C. Ward, *War of the Revolution*, vol. 2:797–98; H. Ward, *American Revolution*, 148–49.

81. McDonnell, *Politics of War*, 398–401, 435–37; Selby, *Revolution in Virginia*, 221–25, John Page quoted on 222, 271–74; C. Ward, *War of the Revolution*, vol. 2:867–73, Marquis de Lafayette quoted on 873 ("whom the militia"); H. Ward, *American Revolution*, 149–53.

82. O'Shaughnessy, *Men Who Lost America*, 274–76; Selby, *Revolution in Virginia*, 277–83; C. Ward, *War of the Revolution*, vol. 2:872–74; H. Ward, *American Revolution*, 154–55.

83. Ewald, *Diary of the American War*, 305 ("Any place"); McDonnell, *Politics of War*, 438–40; Nash, *Forgotten Fifth*, 32–34; Pybus, "Jefferson's Faulty Math," 243–46.

84. McDonnell, *Politics of War*, 404–34, 440–52, Vincent Redman quoted on 450 ("The Rich"), 467–69, Rockbridge County Petition quoted on 468 ("One day's").

85. Evans, "Executive Leadership," 212–13; McDonnell, *Politics of War*, 404–34, 440–52, William Holland quoted on 445 ("swore by God"); George Mason to Thomas Jefferson, May 14, 1781, in Boyd et al., eds., *Papers of Thomas Jefferson*, vol. 5:647–49 ("The same").

86. Evans, "Executive Leadership," 213–14; McDonnell, *Politics of War*, 440–61, unnamed Virginian and William Bernard quoted on 450 ("he never would" and "That was not enough"), Baron von Steuben quoted on 452 ("little dwarfs"), Henry Lee quoted on 453 ("cut off").

87. Conway, *War of American Independence*, 125–26, John Bannister quoted on 126 ("The People"); McDonnell *Politics of War*, 440–61, George Corbin quoted on 458 ("armed with"), tax collectors quoted on 459 ("Anarchy"); Richard Claiborne to Thomas Jefferson, May 20, 1781, in Boyd et al., eds., *Papers of Thomas Jefferson*, vol. 5:669–70 ("The Citizen").

88. Gruber, "Britain's Southern Strategy," 237–38; Mackesy, *War for America*, 407–11; General O'Hara and Sir Henry Clinton quoted in O'Shaughnessy, *Men Who Lost America*, 278; Selby, *Revolution in Virginia*, 286–88; Rankin, "Charles Lord Cornwallis," 214–15.

89. Nathanael Greene quoted in Hibbert, *Redcoats and Rebels*, 298; Mackesy, *War for America*, 408; C. Ward, *War of the Revolution*, vol. 2:797–810; H. Ward, *American Revolution*, 146–47.

90. Hibbert, *Redcoats and Rebels*, 309–11; Major Frederick Mackenzie quoted in Mackesy, *War for America*, 407 ("The more"); Middlekauff, *Glorious Cause*, 490–93; Piecuch, *Three Peoples*, 245–51; C Ward, *War of the Revolution*, vol. 2:810–25.

91. Frey, *Water from the Rock*, 104–5; Hibbert, *Redcoats and Rebels*, 311–13; Piecuch, *Three Peoples*, 246–56, William Moultrie quoted on 247 ("Rawdontown").

92. Hibbert, *Redcoats and Rebels*, 271–73, British officer quoted on 272 ("The violence"); Nathanael Greene quoted in W. Lee, *Crowds and Soldiers*, 138 ("The whole country").

93. Berlin, *Many Thousands Gone*, 291; Crow, "Liberty Men and Loyalists," 144–46, 162–65; Frey, *Water from the Rock*, 99–104, 112–18; Higginbotham, *War of American Independence*, 360–62; Piecuch, *Three Peoples*, 231–33, Daniel Wallace quoted on 232 ("*Not one*").

94. W. Lee, *Crowds and Soldiers*, 180–82; Moore, *World of Toil and Strife*, 68–75; Norton, "'What an Alarming Crisis,'" 215–16; Olwell, *Masters, Slaves, and Subjects*, 266; H. Ward, *Between the Lines*, 227–39, North Carolinian quoted on 237 ("Fear").

95. Calhoon, *Loyalists in Revolutionary America*, 478; Moses Hall quoted in

W. Lee, *Crowds and Soldiers*, 195; Piecuch, *Three Peoples*, 182; H. Ward, *Between the Lines*, 225–27.

96. Crow, "Liberty Men and Loyalists," 142–45, Elias Brock quoted on 158 ("to see the day"), 170–71; Aedanus Burke quoted in Piecuch, *Three Peoples*, 282 ("kept a tally" and "There are not"); Shy, *People Numerous and Armed*, 231–33; Ward, *Between the Lines*, 222–25, Loyalist quoted on 225 ("As his murderers"), Burke quoted on 239 ("man by custom").

97. Hibbert, *Redcoats and Rebels*, 271–73, French officer quoted on 273 ("Thou shalt"); W. Lee, *Crowds and Soldiers*, 178–79, Salisbury district residents quoted on 179 ("Numbers of persons"); Norton, "'What an Alarming Crisis,'" 216–19.

98. Crow, "Liberty Men and Loyalists," 139–42, Moravians quoted on 161; W. Lee, *Crowds and Soldiers*, 203–7; O'Shaughnessy, *Men Who Lost America*, 258–59; Piecuch, *Three Peoples*, 137–46; Weir, "'The Violent Spirit,'" 75–78, and Archibald Simpson quoted on 77.

99. Frey, *Water from the Rock*, 133–34, 207; Moore, *World of Toil and Strife*, 70–74, Banastre Tarleton quoted on 70; H. Ward, *Between the Lines*, 220–30, 239, traveler quoted on 222 ("most of the plantations"); Weir, "'The Violent Spirit,'" 75–78, William Moultrie quoted on 76 ("no living" and "picking the bones").

100. Shy, *People, Numerous and Armed*, 209–11, 231–34; Piecuch, *Three Peoples*, 230–31, Lord Cornwallis quoted on 230.

101. Crow, "Liberty Men and Loyalists," 167; Klein, "Frontier Planters," 54–62; Otho Williams quoted in Piecuch, *Three Peoples*, 265 ("Yesterday"); H. Ward, *Between the Lines*, 233–34.

102. Calloway, *American Revolution in Indian Country*, 50, 203–7, the Raven of Chota quoted on 204 ("dyed"); Klein, "Frontier Planters," 51–54; Piecuch, *Three Peoples*, 207–10, 258–60, Arthur Campbell quoted on 259 ("The Over Hill Country"); Selby, *Revolution in Virginia*, 199–200.

103. Frey, *Water from the Rock*, 106–7, 134–35, 140–42; Klein, "Frontier Planters," 65–69; Olwell, *Masters, Subjects, and Slaves*, 266–67; Piecuch, *Three Peoples*, 270.

104. W. Brown, *Good Americans*, 60–62, 108, William Rankin quoted on 116; Conway, "British Army," 185–86; Fowler, "Loyalty Is Now Bleeding," 52–53; Piecuch, *Three Peoples*, 127–32, Sir Henry Clinton quoted on 131 ("might induce"); Shy, *People Numerous and Armed*, 234–44; Clinton quoted in P. Smith, *Loyalists and Redcoats*, 27 ("only serves").

105. Gruber, "Britain's Southern Strategy," 237–38; Klein, "Frontier Planters," 64–65; Piecuch, *Three Peoples*, 230–31; Thomas Paine, "The American Crisis, Number I," in Rhodehamel, ed., *American Revolution*, 239, 243; Shy, *People Numerous and Armed*, 233–44; Spring, *With Zeal*, 280–81; Francis Kinloch quoted in Weir, "'The Violent Sort,'" 78 ("The lower sort").

CHAPTER 7: WESTS

1. Western Pennsylvania settlers quoted in Griffin, *American Leviathan*, 178.

2. Palatine District Committee to Albany Committee, May 18, 1775 ("the Indians" and "they are"), in Campbell, *Annals of Tryon County*, 21–22; Nobles, *American Frontiers*, 87–88; Richter, *Facing East*, 214–19.

3. Joseph Brant quoted in Calloway, *American Revolution in Indian Country*, 122; Guy Johnson quoted in Campbell, *Annals of Tryon County*, 55 ("Are you"); D. Richter, *Facing East*, 223.

4. Calloway, *American Revolution in Indian Country*, 34, 43, 91–96; Merrell, *Indians' New World*, 215–21; Merritt, "Native Peoples," 239–40; Snyder, "Native Nations," 85–86.

5. Graymont, *Iroquois in the American Revolution*, 72–74; Griffin, *American Leviathan*, 130–32; American commissioners, speech, Aug. 28, 1775 ("This is a family quarrel"), in O'Callaghan, ed., *New York Colonial Documents*, vol. 8:619; Sadosky, *Revolutionary Negotiations*, 73–75.

6. Lender and Martin, eds., *Citizen-Soldier*, 49–50, Colonel Elias Dayton quoted on 50 ("He would burn"); Gerlach, *Proud Patriot*, 183.

7. Calloway, *American Revolution in Indian Country*, 26–30, 35–37, David Taitt quoted on 45 ("to enjoy"), 165–66; Tilghman, ed., *Memoir of Tench Tilghman*, 88 ("It is plain"); Starr, *Tories, Dons, and Rebels*, 75; R. White, *Middle Ground*, 382–83.

8. Braund, *Deerskins and Duffels*, 167; Calloway, *American Revolution in Indian Country*, 191; Griffin, *American Leviathan*, 126–28; Higginbotham, *War of American Independence*, 320–21; Kelsay, *Joseph Brant*, 166–67.

9. Aron, *How the West was Lost*, 37–38, Dragging Canoe quoted on 38 ("die like men"); Calloway, *American Revolution in Indian Country*, 182–97; Griffin, *American Leviathan*, 133; Piecuch, *Three Peoples*, 68–70; Richter, *Facing East*, 219; Selby, *Revolution in Virginia*, 186–87; Snyder, "Native Nations," 85.

10. Piecuch, *Three Peoples*, 71–73, William Henry Drayton quoted on 72 ("cut up" and "that every"); Selby, *Revolution in Virginia*, 187–88; Snyder, "Native Nations," 85.

11. Anderson and Cayton, *Dominion of War*, 170; Lachlan McIntosh quoted in Braund, *Deerskins and Duffels*, 168 ("out of their"); Calloway, *American Revolution in Indian Country*, 49, 197–201; DuVal, *Independence Lost*, 79–81; Selby, *Revolution in Virginia*, 188.

12. Calloway, *American Revolution in Indian Country*, 132–33; DuVal, *Independence Lost*, 76–78; Griffin, *American Leviathan*, 128–34.

13. Braund, *Deerskins and Duffels*, 166–67; Captain Pipe quoted in Calloway, *American Revolution in Indian Country*, 38 ("We are ridiculed"); Graymont, *Iroquois and the American Revolution*, 86–103; Piecuch, *Three Peo-*

ples, 157–58, Choctaw chief quoted on 158; Venables, "'Faithful Allies,'" 138–39; Philip Schuyler to Congress, Jan. 7, 1777, in New-York Historical Society, *Collections for the Year 1879*, 60.

14. Calloway, *American Revolution in Indian Country*, 142–52; Kelsay, *Joseph Brant*, 272–74, 299–300, 328–30; A. Taylor, *Divided Ground*, 103–5; R. White, *Middle Ground*, 404–6.

15. Joseph Brant, speech, Mar. 14, 1776, in O'Callaghan, ed., *New York Colonial Documents*, vol. 8:671; Emistisiguo quoted in DuVal, *Independence Lost*, 78 ("The Virginians"); Choctaw chief quoted in Snyder, "Native Nations," 84–85 ("The Americans").

16. Calloway, *American Revolution in Indian Country*, 31–32, Silver Heels quoted on 56; Fernando de Leyba quoted in Calloway, "Continuing Revolution," 5 ("causing"); Hinderaker, *Elusive Empires*, 188–89; P. J. Marshall, "First Americans," 40–41.

17. Calloway, *American Revolution in Indian Country*, 141–42; Graymont, *Iroquois in the American Revolution*, 230–33, 236–41; Griffin, *American Leviathan*, 128–29.

18. DuVal, *Independence Lost*, 78–79, John Stuart quoted on 78; Johann Hinrichs quoted in Piecuch, *Three Peoples*, 205 ("Hiding" and "cost"); R. White, *Middle Ground*, 367, 406–7.

19. Graymont, *Iroquois in the American Revolution*, 192–99, James Clinton quoted on 196; Tiouganda, speech, Dec. 11, 1782 ("yet these Rebels"), RG 10 (Indian Affairs), vol. 15:78, Library and Archives Canada.

20. Anderson and Cayton, *Dominion of War*, 174–75; Calloway, *American Revolution in Indian Country*, 51–52; George Washington to John Sullivan, May 31, 1779, in Chase et al., eds., *Papers of George Washington, Revolutionary War Series*, vol. 20:716–19; Graymont, *Iroquois in the American Revolution*, 194–218; Mintz, *Seeds of Empire*, 103–14; Cornplanter quoted in Mt. Pleasant, "Independence for Whom?" 124–25 ("We called you"); Pearsall, "Women," 279–81.

21. Abler, ed., *Chainbreaker*, 114; Calloway, *American Revolution in Indian Country*, 137–41, officer quoted on 272 ("The nests"); Graymont, *Iroquois in the American Revolution*, 221–22; Namias, ed., *Narrative of the Life of Mary Jemison*, 105; Guy Johnson to Lord George Germain, Nov. 11, 1779, in O'Callaghan, ed., *New York Colonial Documents*, vol. 8:779–80.

22. Tiro, *People of the Standing Stone*, 39–48; Guy Johnson to George Germain, Jan. 26, 1776, in O'Callaghan, ed., *New York Colonial Documents* vol. 8:657; Schuyler to the Oneidas, May 11, 1778 ("You will then partake"), Papers of the Continental Congress, Reel 189, p. 281, Library of Congress.

23. Chastellux, "Visit to Schenectady, 1780," 293–94; Graymont, *Iroquois in the American Revolution*, 233–35; Philip Schuyler to Samuel Huntington, Oct. 10, 1780 ("I fear"), Papers of the Continental Congress, Reel 173, p.

541, Library of Congress; A. Taylor, *Divided Ground*, 100–101; Tiro, "A Civil War?" 162–63.

24. Graymont, *Iroquois in the American Revolution*, 230–58; George Clinton to George Washington, Oct. 18, 1780, and Clinton to James Duane, Oct. 29, 1780, in Hastings, ed., *Public Papers of George Clinton*, vol. 6:306–7, 345–47; A. Taylor, *Divided Ground*, 101–2.

25. Aron, *How the West Was Lost*, 37, 63–70; Griffin, *American Leviathan*, 134–38; Hinderaker, *Elusive Empires*, 195–203; C. Ward, *War of the Revolution*, vol. 2:852–53.

26. Griffin, *American Leviathan*, 141–46; Selby, *Revolution in Virginia*, 189–93; C. Ward, *War of the Revolution*, vol. 2:853–56; R. White, *Middle Ground*, 369–71.

27. Griffin, *American Leviathan*, 143–46; Higginbotham, *War of American Independence*, 323–24; Selby, *Revolution in Virginia*, 194–96; C. Ward, *War of the Revolution*, vol. 2:856–60; R. White, *Middle Ground*, 372–78, Henry Hamilton quoted on 378.

28. Calloway, *American Revolution in Indian Country*, 48–49; Selby, *Revolution in Virginia*, 188–89, 196–98, George Rogers Clark quoted on 196; Snyder, "Native Nations," 85.

29. Aron, *How the West Was Lost*, 80–81; Haselby, *Origins*, 169–70; Hinderaker, *Elusive Empires*, 204–6, 224; Onuf, *Origins of the Federal Republic*, 83–84.

30. Aron, *How the West Was Lost*, 64–65, 70–81; Kentucky Setters' petition quoted in Cayton, *Frontier Republic*, 4 ("Slaves to those Engrossers"); Griffin, *American Leviathan*, 146–49, John Dodge quoted on 149 ("officers of the State" and "a Damn'd Set"), John May quoted on 151 ("With what a Jealous Eye"); Selby, *Revolution in Virginia*, 202–3.

31. Griffin, *American Leviathan*, 146–49, Richard Winston quoted on 147 ("set of ignorant asses"), Walter Daniel quoted on 160 ("are now"); Selby, *Revolution in Virginia*, 200–201; R. White, *Middle Ground*, 396–97.

32. Aron, *How the West Was Lost*, 38–41, 47–49; Griffin, *American Leviathan*, 138–41, 158–60, John Butler quoted on 160 ("reduced"), William Irvine quoted on 160 ("It is truly disturbing"); Hinderaker, *Elusive Empires*, 207–10; R. White, *Middle Ground*, 399–404.

33. Aron, *How the West Was Lost*, 30–32, 73; Griffin, *American Leviathan*, 160–63, 174–75; Hinderaker, *Elusive Empires*, 214–15.

34. Aron, *How the West Was Lost*, 48–49; General Armstrong quoted in Calloway, *American Revolution in Indian Country*, 47–48 ("but their huts"); Griffin, *American Leviathan*, 165–66, 178–79; Hinderaker, *Elusive Empires*, 215–16.

35. Calloway, *American Revolution in Indian Country*, 39, 46–48, 167–68, George Rogers Clark quoted on 48 ("to excel them"); Selby, *Revolution in*

Virginia, 189, Clark quoted on 199 ("The same world"); R. White, *Middle Ground*, 368–78, 383–96, Clark quoted on 368 ("he would never spare"), Captain Leonard Helm quoted on 386 ("If there is not").

36. Aron, *How the West Was Lost*, 41–47, 53–54; Griffin, *American Leviathan*, 162–63; R. White, *Middle Ground*, 391–92.

37. Calloway, *American Revolution in Indian Country*, 39, 46–47, 165; Hinderaker, *Elusive Empires*, 213; R. White, *Middle Ground*, 380–402.

38. Griffin, *American Leviathan*, 152–55, 168–75, William Irvine quoted on 175; R. White, *Middle Ground*, 388–89.

39. Lachlan McIntosh quoted in Calloway, *American Revolution in Indian Country*, 38; Griffin, *American Leviathan*, 164–65, William Irvine quoted on 165.

40. Griffin, *American Leviathan*, 167–68, William Irvine quoted on 167; D. Richter, *Facing East*, 222–23, Buckongahelas quoted on 223; R. White, *Middle Ground*, 387–90.

41. Griffin, *American Leviathan*, 168–75, William Irvine quoted on 175; D. Richter, *Facing East*, 222–23; Snyder, "Native Nations," 86; R. White, *Middle Ground*, 390–91.

42. Calloway, "Continuing Revolution," 30–31; Griffin, *American Leviathan*, 168–70; C. Ward, *War of the Revolution*, vol. 2:863–64; R. White, *Middle Ground*, 394–95.

43. Aron, *American Confluence*, 72–73; Elliott, *Atlantic Empires*, 353–55; Mapp, "Revolutionary War and Europe's Great Powers," 318–19; Weber, *Spanish Frontier*, 265–68.

44. DuVal, "Independence for Whom?" 99, 107–8; Faber, *Building the Land of Dreams*, 30–32; Foley, *Genesis of Missouri*, 98–107; Furstenberg, "Significance," 656–57; Kastor, *Nation's Crucible*, 26–34; Weber, *Spanish Frontier*, 223, 227–30.

45. Chavez, *Spain and the Independence*, 107–12; DuVal, *Independence Lost*, 35–42, 116–24; Starr, *Tories, Dons, and Rebels*, 72–73; Weber, *Spanish Frontier*, 267.

46. DuVal, *Independence Lost*, 92–95, 122–23, 128–29; Piecuch, *Three Peoples*, 106–7; Starr, *Tories, Dons, and Rebels*, 81–83, William Dunbar quoted on 82 ("frequently indulged").

47. Chavez, *Spain and the Independence*, 104–5; DuVal, *Independence Lost*, 105–6; Piecuch, *Three Peoples*, 106–8; Starr, *Tories, Dons, and Rebels*, 87–98, Joseph Nunn quoted on 98 ("the bare walls").

48. Chavez, *Spain and the Independence*, 106–7; Piecuch, *Three Peoples*, 106–8; Starr, *Tories, Dons, and Rebels*, 116–21.

49. Chavez, *Spain and the Independence*, 166–72; DuVal, *Independence Lost*, 126–27, 146–52; Piecuch, *Three Peoples*, 149, 157; Starr, *Tories, Dons, and Rebels*, 72–73; Weber, *Spanish Frontier*, 267–68.

50. Chavez, *Spain and the Independence*, 172–97; Dull, *French Navy*, 233–34; DuVal, *Independence Lost*, 152–217; Piecuch, *Three Peoples*, 256–57, 262–65; Starr, *Tories, Dons, and Rebels*, 1, 196–215; Usner, *Indians, Settlers, and Slaves*, 143; Weber, *Spanish Frontier*, 268–69.

51. DuVal, *Independence Lost*, 275–76; Usner, *Indians, Settlers, and Slaves*, 140–41.

52. Aron, *American Confluence*, 73–74; Calloway, *American Revolution in Indian Country*, 42–43; Piecuch, *Three Peoples*, 157–58, 308; Saunt, *West of the Revolution*, 188–208, Manuel de Montiano quoted on 199 ("More than anything").

53. Chavez, *Spain and the Independence*, 204–5; Elliott, *Empires of the Atlantic World*, 355–56; Godoy, "Bourbon Taxes," 80–87; Liss, *Atlantic Empires*, 145–46; Lynch, ed., *Latin American Revolutions*, 21–23; Phelan, "Bourbon Innovation," 42–44; Walker, *Tupac Amaru Rebellion*, 1–6.

54. Chavez, *Spain and the Independence*, 204; Elliott, *Empires of the Atlantic World*, 356–60; MacLachlan, *Spain's Empire*, 101–2; Walker, *Smoldering Ashes*, 19–27; Walker, *Tupac Amaru Rebellion*, 7–17.

55. Burkholder and Chandler, "Creole Participation," 53–54; Elliott, *Empire of the Atlantic World*, 361–68; Liss, *Atlantic Empires*, 136–37, Manuel Antonio Florez quoted on 136 ("News"); Phelan, "Bourbon Innovation," 46–49.

56. Bobb, *Viceregency*, 162–66; Costell and Hornbeck, "Alta California," 303–32; Sandos, "Between Crucifix and Lance," 196–229; Saunt, *West of the Revolution*, 72–82, Francisco Palau quoted on 81 ("The only ones"); Weber, *Spanish Frontier*, 242–46.

57. Weber, *Spanish Frontier*, 256–60.

58. MacLachlan, *Spain's Empire*, 107–9; Saunt, *West of the Revolution*, 91–94, Antonio Maria Bucareli quoted on 91–92; Weber, *Spanish Frontier*, 204–212.

59. Lynch, ed., *Latin American Revolutions*, 15; Saunt, *West of the Revolution*, 58; Weber, *Spanish Frontier*, 204–212, Marques de Rubi quoted on 212, José de Gálvez quoted on 248.

60. Lynch, ed., *Latin American Revolutions*, 19–20; MacLachlan, *Spain's Empire*, 114–18; Phelan, "Bourbon Innovation," 41–49.

61. Burkholder and Chandler, "Creole Participation," 51–52; Liss, *Atlantic Empires*, 134–35; Lynch, ed., *Latin American Revolutions*, 16–17; Phelan, "Bourbon Innovation," 41–42; Rivadeneira, "America for the Americans," 58–70.

62. Langley, *Americas in the Age of Revolution*, 152–58, Venezuelan aristocrats quoted on 157 ("a system"); Liss, *Atlantic Empires*, 159 ("*limpieza*"); Rivadeneira, "America for the Americans," 67 ("positively ugly").

63. Liss, *Atlantic Empires*, 142–45, 166–68, 191, Miranda quoted on 142 ("the infallible preliminary") and 143 ("Good God"); Lynch, ed., *Latin American Revolutions*, 29, 32, 36.

64. Langley, *Americas in the Age of Revolution*, 158–65; Liss, *Atlantic Empires*, 130–31, 136, 167; Lynch, ed., *Latin American Revolutions*, 5–6, 11–17, 19–21; MacLachlan, *Spain's Empire*, 132–35; Walker, *Tupac Amaru Rebellion*, 267–78; Weber, *Spanish Frontier*, 274–75.

65. Lynch, ed., *Latin American Revolutions*, 18–24, 29–34, 37–38.

66. Carlson, *Plains Indians*; L. Fowler, "Great Plains," 1–55; E. West, *Way to the West*, 3–12.

67. Fenn, *Encounters*, 8–34; Fowler, "Great Plains," 1–55; E. West, *Way to the West*, 13–50.

68. E. West, *Way to the West*, 51–84.

69. Hämäläinen, *Comanche Empire*, 18–67; Saunt, *West of the Revolution*, 124–68; Weber, *Spanish Frontier*, 214; R. White, "Winning of the West," 319–43.

70. Saunt, *West of the Revolution*, 91–115; Weber, *Spanish Frontier*, 220–26, Pedro Fermin de Mendinueta quoted on 221–22 ("to the most deplorable").

71. Weber, *Spanish Frontier*, 230–35.

72. Saunt, *West of the Revolution*, 148–68.

73. Saunt, *West of the Revolution*, 148–68; White, "Winning of the West," 319–43.

74. Fenn, *Encounters*, 154–59; Fenn, *Pox Americana*, 3–79.

75. Fenn, *Encounters*, 155–62, William Warren quoted on 162 ("the lodges").

76. Fenn, *Encounters*, 165–72; Saunt, *West of the Revolution*, 148–68, Jean Baptiste Truteau, quoted on 155 ("Their very name"); White, "Winning of the West," 319–43.

77. Aron, *American Confluence*, 22–26, 36–38, 88–91; DuVal, *Native Ground*, 103–27; Saunt, *West of the Revolution*, 169–86, Athanase de Mézières quoted on 181 ("no lack").

78. Thomas Jefferson to Robert Smith, July 13, 1804, Founders Online, National Archives (http://founders.archives.gov/documents/Jefferson/99-01-02-0067).

79. Anderson and Cayton, *Dominion of War*, 169–70; Thomas Jefferson to Edmund Pendleton, Aug. 13, 1776, and Jefferson to Samuel Huntington, Feb. 9, 1780, in Boyd et al., *Papers of Thomas Jefferson*, vol. 1:491–94 ("will settle"), vol. 3:286–89 ("endeavours" and "necessary"); Griffin, *American Leviathan*, 134–35; Hinderaker, *Elusive Empires*, 185–87, 227–28; Onuf, "Empire of Liberty," 209–10; Richter, *Facing East*, 216–18.

CHAPTER 8: OCEANS

1. Alexander Hamilton to John Laurens, June 30, 1780, in Syrett, ed., *Papers of Alexander Hamilton*, vol. 2:347–48.

2. Miller, *World of Jack Aubrey*, 8–12; O'Shaughnessy, *Men Who Lost America*, 314.

3. Miller, *World of Jack Aubrey*, 13–25.

4. Mackesy, *War for America*, 170–74; O'Shaughnessy, *Men Who Lost America*, 327–29, Earl of Sandwich quoted on 329.

5. O'Shaughnessy, *Empire Divided*, 155–57; O'Shaughnessy, *Men Who Lost America*, 294, 330–32, James Gambier quoted on 331 ("choice of difficulties"); H. Ward, *American Revolution*, 184–85.

6. Jasanoff, *Liberty's Exiles*, 229–30; Middlekauff, *Glorious Cause*, 525–28; O'Shaughnessy, *Men Who Lost America*, 332; H. Ward, *American Revolution*, 184.

7. Middlekauff, *Glorious Cause*, 529–34; H. Ward, *American Revolution*, 184–86.

8. Mackesy, *War for America*, 166–68, 175–79; O'Shaughnessy, *Men Who Lost America*, 329–30.

9. Conway, *War of American Independence*, 157; Dull, *French Navy*, 107–8; Mackesy, *War for America*, 190–96; O'Shaughnessy, *Men Who Lost America*, 332–35, George Germain quoted on 334; H. Ward, *American Revolution*, 186–87.

10. Conway, *War of American Independence*, 141–42; Dull, *French Navy*, 107–24; Mackesy, *War for America*, 190–96, 225; O'Shaughnessy, *Men Who Lost America*, 334–36.

11. Conway, *War of American Independence*, 133–34; Mackesy, *War for America*, 182–86, 225–26; O'Shaughnessy, *Men Who Lost America*, 294–95.

12. Mackesy, *War for America*, 182–83, 227–28; O'Shaughnessy, *Empire Divided*, 199.

13. Knight, "American Revolution and the Caribbean," 246–48; Mackesy, *War for America*, 228–29; O'Shaughnessy, *Empire Divided*, 171.

14. Mackesy, *War for America*, 182–84, 229–31; Marshall, *Making and Unmaking*, 363–64, George III quoted on 363; O'Shaughnessy, *Empire Divided*, 169, 171, 206–8; O'Shaughnessy, *Men Who Lost America*, 294–95, 342–43.

15. Mackesy, *War for America*, 181–86, unnamed official quoted on 183 ("The war"); O'Shaughnessy, *Empire Divided*, 169, 208–10; Sir Henry Clinton quoted in O'Shaughnessy, *Men Who Lost America*, 342.

16. Dull, *French Navy*, 123–24; Mackesy, *War for America*, 231–32, 275–78; O'Shaughnessy, *Empire Divided*, 208–9; O'Shaughnessy, *Men Who Lost America*, 295, 340–41; H. Ward, *American Revolution*, 188.

17. Chavez, *Spain and the Independence*, 138–39; Conway, *War of American Independence*, 142–44; Dull, *French Navy*, 136–58; Mackesy, *War for America*, 250, 263, 279–97, 324–25, the Earl of Sandwich quoted on 250, George III quoted on 263; O'Shaughnessy, *Men Who Lost America*, 340.

18. Conway, *War of American Independence*, 135–37; Dull, *French Navy*, 159–62, 187; Mackesy, *War for America*, 275–78; O'Shaughnessy, *Empire*

Divided, 169–70, 209–10; O'Shaughnessy, *Men Who Lost America*, 340–41; H. Ward, *American Revolution*, 188.

19. O'Shaughnessy, *Empire Divided*, 161–63; O'Shaughnessy, *Men Who Lost America*, 294.

20. O'Shaughnessy, *Empire Divided*, 173–74, 179–80.

21. O'Shaughnessy, *Empire Divided*, 162–67.

22. Conway, *War of American Independence*, 138; Mackesy, *War for America*, 334; O'Shaughnessy, *Empire Divided*, 169, 174–75.

23. O'Shaughnessy, *Empire Divided*, 175–81, Stephen Fuller quoted on 181 ("a policy").

24. DuVal, "Independence for Whom?" 100–109; Elliott, *Empires of the Atlantic*, 107–8; O'Shaughnessy, *Empire Divided*, 181.

25. O'Shaughnessy, *Empire Divided*, 185–205, legislature of Barbados quoted on 201 ("the delusion").

26. Mackesy, *War for America*, 307–9, 323–24, 329–30, George III quoted on 308.

27. Mackesy, *War for America*, 319–321; O'Shaughnessy, *Empire Divided*, 221; O'Shaughnessy, *Men Who Lost America*, 292–93, 304.

28. Mackesy, *War for America*, 321–322; O'Shaughnessy, *Men Who Lost America*, 293–96.

29. Conway, *War of American Independence*, 138; Dull, *French Navy*, 188–90; Mackesy, *War for America*, 323–34, 415; O'Shaughnessy, *Men Who Lost America*, 293.

30. Conway, *War of American Independence*, 138–39, Dull, *French Navy*, 174–76, 207–9; Mackesy, *War for America*, 377–79, 416; O'Shaughnessy, *Empire Divided*, 214–17; O'Shaughnessy, *Men Who Lost America*, 289–99, Sir George Rodney quoted on 299.

31. Conway, *War of American Independence*, 139; Mackesy, *War for America*, 416–17; O'Shaughnessy, *Empire Divided*, 217–24, Sir Samuel Hood quoted on 221 ("wickedly rapacious"), Sir George Rodney quoted on 223 ("best harpsichord"); O'Shaughnessy, *Men Who Lost America*, 299–306.

32. Conway, *War of American Independence*, 139; Dull, *French Navy*, 238; Mackesy, *War for America*, 417–20; O'Shaughnessy, *Men Who Lost America*, 308–9.

33. Mackesy, *War for America*, 417–20; O'Shaughnessy, *Empire Divided*, 225–26, 231; O'Shaughnessy, *Men Who Lost America*, 306–8.

34. Dull, *French Navy*, 239–45, Chevalier de la Luzerne quoted on 243; O'Shaughnessy, *Empire Divided*, 230–31; O'Shaughnessy, *Men Who Lost America*, 308–9.

35. Chavez, *Spain and the Independence*, 200–203, Francisco de Saavedra quoted on 201; Dull, *French Navy*, 243–44, 247; Mackesy, *War for America*, 419; O'Shaughnessy, *Men Who Lost America*, 311; C. Ward, *War of the Revolution*, vol. 2:884–85.

36. Dull, *French Navy*, 245–46; Mackesy, *War for America*, 423–25; O'Shaughnessy, *Men Who Lost America*, 311–13; C. Ward, *War of the Revolution*, vol. 2:884–85.

37. Conway, *War of America Independence*, 127; Mackesy, *War for America*, 428–29; Selby, *Revolution in Virginia*, 294–301; Stinchcombe, *American Revolution and the French Alliance*, 147–48; C. Ward, *War of the Revolution*, vol. 2:880–86.

38. Mackesy, *War for America*, 425–27; Middlekauff, *Glorious Cause*, 560–62; O'Shaughnessy, *Men Who Lost America*, 278–82; Rankin, "Charles Lord Cornwallis," 214–18; Selby, *Revolution in Virginia*, 287–303; C. Ward, *War of the Revolution*, vol. 2:885–87, 895.

39. George Washington to Thomas Lee, Oct. 12, 1781 ("passive"), Founders Online, National Archives (http://founders.archives.gov/documents/Washington/99-01-02-07141); Middlekauff, *Glorious Cause*, 564–70, Johann Conrad Doehla quoted on 569 ("whose heads"); O'Shaughnessy, *Men Who Lost America*, 279–80; Selby, *Revolution in Virginia*, 303–8, anonymous soldier quoted on 307 ("fled"); C. Ward, *War of the Revolution*, vol. 2:887–94.

40. Feltman, *Journal*, 6 ("numbers"); St. George Tucker quoted in Coleman, *St. George Tucker*, 74 ("An immense"); McDonell, *Politics of War*, 440–43, 476–89; Parkinson, "Manifest Signs of Passion," 60; Pybus, "Jefferson's Faulty Math," 256–57.

41. Mackesy, *War for America*, 427–28, Sir Henry Clinton quoted on 427; O'Shaughnessy, *Men Who Lost America*, 280–81; Rankin, "Charles Lord Cornwallis," 219–20; Selby, *Revolution in Virginia*, 308–9; C. Ward, *War of the Revolution*, vol. 2:894–95.

42. Chopra, *Unnatural Rebellion*, 193–96; Jasanoff, *Liberty's Exiles*, 56–57.

43. Alexander Hamilton to John Laurens, June 30, 1780, in Syrett, ed., *Papers of Alexander Hamilton*, vol. 2:347–48 ("If we"); Dull, *Diplomatic History*, 119–20, 139–40; Mackesy, *War for America*, 433; Rakove, *Beginnings of National Politics*, 268–69, 273–74; Stinchcombe, *American Revolution and the French Alliance*, 133–34, 151–53, Daniel Jenifer quoted on 153 ("Our affairs" and "Congress is"); C. Ward, *War of the Revolution*, vol. 2:879–80.

44. Dickinson, "Impact of the War," 360–62, Lord North quoted on 360 ("The torrent"); Dull, *Diplomatic History*, 137–38, 143; Jasanoff, *Liberty's Exiles*, 63–64; Mackesy, *War for America*, 434–35; O'Shaughnessy, *Men Who Lost America*, 41–42, 76–78; Nathaniel Wraxall quoted in C. Ward, *War of the Revolution*, vol. 2:895 ("as he would" and "Oh God"); E. Wright, "British Objectives," 8–10.

45. O'Shaughnessy, *Men Who Lost America*, 41–42, 77–78; Perkins, "Peace of Paris," 197–98; E. Wright, "British Objectives," 12–13, 22.

46. Dull, *Diplomatic History*, 138–39; Mackesy, *War for America*, 436–37, Vergennes quoted on 436; O'Shaughnessy, *Men Who Lost America*, 313.

47. Chavez, *Spain and the Independence*, 145–47; Conway, *War of American Independence*, 146–48; Dull, *French Navy*, 232–36, 267–68; Mackesy, *War for America*, 436–38, 454–56; O'Shaughnessy, *Men Who Lost America*, 313–14, Lord John Cavendish quoted on 313.

48. Mackesy, *War for America*, 439–40, 444–45, 457; O'Shaughnessy, *Men Who Lost America*, 313–14.

49. Conway, *War of American Independence*, 140; Dull, *French Navy*, 283–84; Mackesy, *War for America*, 458–59; O'Shaughnessy, *Men Who Lost America*, 314–15; H. Ward, *American Revolution*, 188–90.

50. O'Shaughnessy, *Men Who Lost America*, 315–16, Nathaniel Wraxall quoted on 316 ("The country").

51. O'Shaughnessy, *Empire Divided*, 237; O'Shaughnessy, *Men Who Lost America*, 316–17.

52. Chavez, *Spain and the Independence*, 147–49; Conway, *War of American Independence*, 144–45, 148; Dull, *French Navy*, 279–81, 307–9; Mackesy, *War for America*, 482–84; H. Ward, *American Revolution*, 187.

53. Conway, *War of American Independence*, 150–53; Dull, *French Navy*, 123; Jasanoff, *Edge of Empire*, 20–31, 40, 47–50; Marshall, *Making and Unmaking of Empires*, 196–97, 207–28.

54. Conway, *War of American Independence*, 150–53, Thomas Munro quoted on 152 ("the severest"); Dull, *French Navy*, 229; Jasanoff, *Edge of Empire*, 152–59, Haidar Ali quoted on 159; Mackesy, *War for America*, 380; Marshall, *Making and Unmaking of Empires*, 196–97, 230–32, 366–67; H. Ward, *American Revolution*, 190–91.

55. Conway, *War of American Independence*, 154–57; Dull, *French Navy*, 313–14; Jasanoff, *Edge of Empire*, 159–60; Mackesy, *War for America*, 390, 494–500; Marshall, *Making and Unmaking of Empires*, 367–70; H. Ward, *American Revolution*, 186–87.

56. Dull, *Diplomatic History*, 118–19; Morris, *Peacemakers*, 209–17; Rakove, *Revolutionaries*, 266–67, Congress quoted on 267; Stinchcombe, *American Revolution and the French Alliance*, 153–69.

57. Hinderaker, *Elusive Empires*, 222–27; Perkins, "Peace of Paris," 194–95.

58. Lint, "Preparing for Peace," 39–42; Comte de Vergennes quoted in Morris, *Peacemakers*, 326 ("foolishness" and "But you will agree"); Stinchcombe, *American Revolution and the French Alliance*, 156–57.

59. Chavez, *Spain and the Independence*, 211–12, Conde de Aranda quoted on 212; Dull, "Diplomacy of Trust," 112–13; Dull, *Diplomatic History*, 142–43, 146–48; DuVal, *Independence Lost*, 231–32; E. Wright, "British Objectives," 6–7.

60. Chopra, *Unnatural Rebellion*, 203–4; Morris, *Peacemakers*, 285–86; Lord

Shelburne quoted in Perkins, "Peace of Paris," 198; E. Wright, "British Objectives," 10–12.

61. O'Connell, *Irish Politics*, 16–20; Wickwire, *Cornwallis*, 209–13; Watson, *Reign of George III*, 387–88.

62. W. Brown, *Good Americans*, 157; Frey, *British Soldier in America*, 4: McDowell, *Ireland in the Age of Imperialism and Revolution*, 240–46; Morley, *Irish Opinion and the American Revolution*, 137–43, 168–69; O'Connell, *Irish Politics*, 25–30; Watson, *Reign of George III*, 221–25.

63. O'Connell, *Irish Politics*, 22–23; Morley, *Irish Opinion*, 332; Wickwire, *Cornwallis*, 214–15; Watson, *Reign of George III*, 242–46, 388–90.

64. Elliott, *Empires of the Atlantic World*, 367; Franklin to Samuel Cooper, June 28, 1782, Labaree et al., eds., *Papers of Benjamin Franklin*, vol. 37:563 ("We have no safety"); McDowell, "Ireland in 1800," 695–96.

65. Dull, *Diplomatic History*, 139, 144–50; Jasanoff, *Liberty's Exiles*, 84–85; Marshall, *Making and Unmaking*, 364–65; Perkins, "Peace of Paris," 197–99, Lord Shelburne quoted on 198; Rakove, *Revolutionaries*, 273–74; Ritcheson, "Britain's Peacemakers," 70–75; E. Wright, "British Objectives," 14–18.

66. John Adams to Arthur Lee, Oct. 10, 1782, and Adams to Jonathan Jackson, Nov. 8, 1782, in Butterfield et al., eds., *Papers of John Adams*, vol. 13:523–26 ("Those Chains"), and vol. 14:43–47 ("to keep us down"); Benjamin Franklin to Robert R. Livingston, July 22, 1783, in Butterfield et al., eds., *Adams Family Correspondence*, vol. 5:251–52 ("always"); Chavez, *Spain and the Independence*, 209–10; Dull, *Diplomatic History*, 148–50.

67. John Adams, Diary, Nov. 30, 1782, in Butterfield et al., eds., *Diary and Autobiography of John Adams*, vol. 3:82–85; Hutson, "American Negotiators," 52–69; Lint, "Preparing for Peace," 50–51; Morris, *Peacemakers*, 308–10; Rakove, *Revolutionaries*, 275–80.

68. W. Brown and Senior, *Victorious in Defeat*, 24–27; Chopra, *Unnatural Rebellion*, 207–8; Dull, *Diplomatic History*, 148–50; Jasanoff, *Liberty's Exiles*, 86–87; Morris, *Peacemakers*, 351–85; Rakove, *Revolutionaries*, 281–85; Pybus, *Epic Journeys*, 60–61; Watson, *Reign of George III*, 242–43; E. Wright, "British Objectives," 23.

69. Dull, *Diplomatic History*, 145; DuVal, *Independence Lost*, 232–34; Marshall, *Making and Unmaking*, 358–61; Morris, *Peacemakers*, 263–70, 301–3; Neatby, *Quebec*, 208–9; Ritcheson, *Aftermath of Revolution*, 4–5; C. Stuart, "Lord Shelburne," 245–46, Shelburne quoted on 245 ("If we"); R. Stuart, *United States Expansionism*, 22–24; Watson, *Reign of George III*, 249.

70. Morris, *Peacemakers*, 382–85, Comte de Vergennes quoted on 383; Perkins, "Peace of Paris," 215–16; Sadosky, *Revolutionary Negotiations*, 116–17.

71. Black, *George III*, 248; Jasanoff, *Liberty's Exiles*, 124; George III quoted in

Marshall, *Making and Unmaking*, 358 ("knavery"); O'Shaughnessy, *Men Who Lost America*, 42–43, George III quoted on 42 ("scrupulous attachment").

72. Black, *George III*, 252–53; Dull, *Diplomatic History*, 159–60; Jasanoff, *Liberty's Exiles*, 122–25; Mackesy, *War for America*, 509–10; Marshall, *Making and Unmaking*, 360–62; Ritcheson, *Aftermath of Revolution*, 5–6, 12, 18–20, 31–45, 50–56, 63–69; O'Shaughnessy, *Men Who Lost America*, 78–79; Watson, *Reign of George III*, 253–56.

73. John Adams to Robert R. Livingston, July 17, 1783, in Giunta, ed., *Emerging Nation*, vol. 2:195; Graham, *British Policy and Canada*, 56–59, 65, 71; McCusker, "British Mercantilist Policies," 337–62; Milobar, "Conservative Ideology," 57–58; Ritcheson, *Aftermath of Revolution*, 6; Watson, *Reign of George III*, 253–56; E. Wright, "British Objectives," 24–25.

74. Chavez, *Spain and the Independence*, 208, 210–11; Dull, *Diplomatic History*, 151–55, Vergennes quoted on 153; DuVal, *Independence Lost*, 235–37; Lint, "Preparing for Peace," 46–47; Rakove, *Revolutionaries*, 287–88.

75. Chavez, *Spain and the Independence*, 210–11; Dull, *Diplomatic History*, 155–60; Mackesy, *War for America*, 506–9; Marshall, *Making and Unmaking*, 364–65.

76. Dull, *Diplomatic History*, 161–62; Lint, "Preparing for Peace," 42–43; Rakove, *Revolutionaries*, 287–88; Sadosky, *Revolutionary Negotiations*, 126–27.

77. Dull, *Diplomatic History*, 160–61; Marshall, *Making and Unmaking*, 361–62, 378–79, Lord Macartney quoted on 362; O'Shaughnessy, *Men Who Lost America*, 4–5, 360–61.

78. Colley, *Captives*, 236–38; Drescher, "Emperors of the World," 133–35; Gould, *Persistence of Empire*, 210–13; Jasanoff, *Liberty's Exiles*, 122.

79. Jasanoff, *Liberty's Exiles*, 97; Marshall, *Making and Unmaking*, 375–79; Richardson, *Moral Imperium*, 99–100, 103–26.

80. Burnard, "Freedom, Migration, and the American Revolution," 295–314; D. B. Davis, "American Slavery and the American Revolution," 263–64; Jasanoff, *Liberty's Exiles*, 147; Knight, "American Revolution and the Caribbean," 248–49, 254–55; O'Shaughnessy, *Empire Divided*, 238–45, Thomas Clarkson quoted on 245 ("As long as"); Ritcheson, *Aftermath of Revolution*, 8–13.

81. Burnard, "Freedom, Migration, and the American Revolution," 295–314; D. B. Davis, "American Slavery and the American Revolution," 272–80; O'Shaughnessy, *Empire Divided*, 246–48.

CHAPTER 9: SHOCKS

1. J. Mullryne Tattnall quoted in Jasanoff, *Liberty's Exiles*, 106.

2. W. Brown, *Good Americans*, 198–200; Chopra, *Unnatural Rebellion*, 197–

98; Jasanoff, *Liberty's Exiles*, 65–70; E. Jones, "British Withdrawal," 259–64; Moore, *Loyalists*, 134–35.

3. George Washington to William Gordon, Mar. 8, 1785, in Abbot et al., eds., *Papers of George Washington, Confederation Series*, vol. 2:411–14; Egerton, *Death or Liberty*, 91; Hargrove, "Southern Patriot," 199–200; Jasanoff, *Liberty's Exiles*, 69–73; E. Jones, "The British Withdrawal," 263–64, 270–71, 277–78; Piecuch, *Three Peoples*, 282–83, 323–24.

4. W. Brown, *Good Americans*, 215–16; Chopra, *Unnatural Rebellion*, 199; Jasanoff, *Liberty's Exiles*, 75–84, 103–16, Elizabeth Johnston quoted on 105; E. Jones, "The British Withdrawal," 259–285.

5. Crow, "Liberty Men and Loyalists," 169–170, Thomas Wade quoted on 170 ("We had to kill"); Frey, *Water from the Rock*, 132–34; Moore, *World of Toil and Strife*, 74; Piecuch, *Three Peoples*, 246–56, 273–75, William Lee quoted on 256 ("Many of them").

6. Egerton, *Death or Liberty*, 152; Frey, *Water from the Rock*, 226–28, trial record of Lewis quoted on 227 ("King of England's Soldiers") and James Jackson quoted on 227 ("Their leaders"); Holton, *Unruly Americans*, 220–21; R. Klein, *Unification of a Slave State*, 114–20; Moore, *Loyalists*, 145–46; Olwell, *Masters, Slaves, and Subjects*, 274–81; Piecuch, *Three Peoples*, 289–98.

7. Berlin, *Many Thousands Gone*, 263–64; Frey, *Water from the Rock*, 218; Kulikoff, "Uprooted Peoples," 144–45; McDonnell, *Politics of War*, 490–91; P. Morgan, *Slave Counterpoint*, 384; unnamed merchant quoted in Norton, *Liberty's Daughters*, 275.

8. Blakeley and Grant, eds., *Eleven Exiles*, 270–71; W. Brown, *Good Americans*, 199–201, 215–16; Jasanoff, *Liberty's Exiles*, 5–6, 92–102; E. Jones, "British Withdrawal," 260–61; Moore, *Loyalists*, 134–35, 145–46, 150–52; P. Smith, "Sir Guy Carleton," 130–32.

9. Beeman, *Plain Honest Men*, 10–12; Bouton, *Taming Democracy*, 70–72; Jensen, *New Nation*, 56–57; Middlekauff, *Glorious Cause*, 593–98; Rakove, *Revolutionaries*, 84–86, 409–10.

10. Jensen, *New Nation*, 60–67, Stephen Higginson quoted on 82 ("Their professed"); Holton, *Unruly Americans*, 66–68; Kohn, "Inside History," 187–96; Larson, *Return of George Washington*, 9–10; J. Martin and Lender, *Respectable Army*, 188–89; Rakove, *Beginnings of National Politics*, 298–312.

11. Beeman, *Plain, Honest Men*, 12–13; Bouton, *Taming Democracy*, 69–70; Hendrickson, *Peace Pact*, 203–4; Kohn, "Inside History," 196–97, 201; Rakove, *Beginnings of National Politics*, 310–12, Gouverneur Morris quoted on 310; Rakove, *Revolutionaries*, 409–10.

12. Jensen, *New Nation*, 69–71; Kohn, "Inside History," 197–207; J. Martin and Lender, *Respectable Army*, 186–91, Alexander Hamilton quoted on 189; R. Morris, *Forging of the Union*, 44–47, Gouverneur Morris quoted on

46; Rakove, *Beginnings of National Politics*, 317–18; John Armstrong, "The Newburgh Address," March 1783, and George Washington to Joseph Jones, Mar. 12, 1783, in Rhodehamel, ed., *American Revolution*, 774–77 ("country that tramples"), and 778–80.

13. Beeman, *Plain, Honest Men*, 3–6; Jensen, *New Nation*, 71–72; Kohn, "Inside History," 202, 207–15; Larson, *Return of George Washington*, 12–18; J. Martin and Lender, *Respectable Army*, 189–93; Rakove, *Revolutionaries*, 410–11; Samuel Shaw to the Rev. Eliot, April 1783, in Rhodehamel, ed., *American Revolution*, 786–89; George Washington, "Speech to the Officers of the Army," March 15, 1783, in Rhodehamel, ed. *George Washington: Writings*, 496–500 ("open"); Alexander Hamilton to George Washington, Mar. 25, 1783, in Syrett, ed., *Papers of Alexander Hamilton*, vol. 3:305–7 ("I confess").

14. Jensen, *New Nation*, 80–82; J. Martin and Lender, *Respectable Army*, 194–96; R. Morris, *Forging of the Union*, 52–53; George Washington to Alexander Hamilton, Apr. 22, 1783, in Syrett, ed., *Papers of Alexander Hamilton*, vol. 3:334–37.

15. Larson, *Return of Washington*, 16–23; J. P. Martin, ed., *Ordinary Courage*, 161–62 (all quotations); J. Martin and Lender, *Respectable Army*, 194–96; R. Morris, *Forging of the Union*, 53–54.

16. Rakove, *Beginnings of National Politics*, 334–36; Rosswurm, *Arms, Country, and Class*, 246–47, Philadelphia militiamen quoted on 247; P. Smith, *New Age Now Begins*, vol. 2:1774–80, North Carolina delegate quoted on 1778 ("hated"), Benjamin Rush quoted on 1779.

17. George Washington, "Proclamation for the Cessation of Hostilities" Apr. 18, 1783, and John Adams to Benjamin Rush, June 21, 1811, Founders Online, National Archives (http://founders.archives.gov/documents/Washington/99-01-02-11104) and (http://founders.archives.gov/documents/Adams/99-02-02-5649); Beeman, *Plain, Honest Men*, 13–14; Larson, *Return of Washington*, 3–8, 23, 26–30; Middlekauff, *Glorious Cause*, 582–84; P. Smith, *New Age Now Begins*, vol. 2:1780–81.

18. Beeman, *Plain, Honest Men*, 6–7; Thomas Jefferson to George Washington, Apr. 16, 1784, in Boyd et al., eds., *Papers of Thomas Jefferson*, vol. 7:105–10 ("prevented"); Larson, *Return of Washington*, 3–8, 23, George III quoted on 6.

19. George Washington to James Madison, Dec. 16, 1786, in Abbot et al., eds., *Papers of George Washington, Confederation Series*, vol. 4:457–59; Chernow, *Washington*, 497–500; C. Cox, *Proper Sense of Honor*, 241–42; Holton, *Unruly Americans*, 69–71; Main, *Anti-Federalists*, 106–9, Farmington town records quoted on 108–9 ("to dissolve"); G. Wood, *Creation of the American Republic*, 399–400.

20. Blakeley and Grant, eds., *Eleven Exiles*, 265–66, 272–73, Boston King

quoted on 266; Chopra, *Choosing Sides*, 47–48, 168–71, Sir Guy Carleton quoted on 170–71; Egerton, *Death or Liberty*, 202–6; Jasanoff, *Liberty's Exiles*, 80–81, 94–95.

21. Gilbert, *Black Patriots and Loyalists*, 177–78, 188–96; James Madison to Thomas Jefferson, May 13, 1783, in Hutchinson et al., eds., *Papers of James Madison*, vol. 7:39–42 ("a palpable"); Jasanoff, *Liberty's Exiles*, 95–96; McColley, *Slavery and Jeffersonian Virginia*, 85–87; Moore, *Loyalists*, 137, 151–52; Olwell, *Masters, Slaves, and Subjects*, 268–70; Pybus, *Epic Journeys*, 61–72.

22. Blakeley and Grant, eds., *Eleven Exiles*, 273–86, Boston King quoted on 279; Chopra, *Choosing Sides*, 49–50; Egerton, *Death or Liberty*, 206–9, David George quoted on 209 ("The old Negro"); Gilbert, *Black Patriots and Loyalists*, 208–15; Jasanoff, *Liberty's Exiles*, 181–85, 293–95, David George quoted on 182 ("almost naked"); Moore, *The Loyalists*, 207–10, 213–14; Pybus, *Epic Journeys*, 144–48.

23. Blakeley and Grant, eds., *Eleven Exiles*, 284–86, John Clarkson quoted on 284 ("No distinction"); Holton, *Unruly Americans*, 27; Jasanoff, *Liberty's Exiles*, 295–302, Thomas Peters quoted on 301.

24. Egerton, *Death or Liberty*, 214–16, unnamed woman quoted on 216 ("that she might"); Gilbert, *Black Patriots and Loyalists*, 219–22, 229–31; Jasanoff, *Liberty's Exiles*, 301–4.

25. Gilbert, *Black Patriots and Loyalists*, 219–22, 229–31, Thomas Perronet Thompson quoted on 231 ("While"); Jasanoff, *Liberty's Exiles*, 304–9; Moore, *The Loyalists*, 219–21; Nash, "Thomas Peters," 76–84.

26. Granville Sharp quoted in Burnard, "Freedom, Migration, and the American Revolution," 307; Egerton, *Death or Liberty*, 216–19; Gilbert, *Black Patriots and Loyalists*, 229–42; Jasanoff, *Liberty's Exiles*, 312–16, Daddy Moses quoted on 316 ("Free Town" and "Town of Slavery").

27. Egerton, *Death or Liberty*, 219–21; Gilbert, *Black Patriots and Loyalists*, 241–43 ("Their government"), Thomas Perronet Thompson quoted on 243; Jasanoff, *Liberty's Exiles*, 318–22.

28. John Adams, Diary, Nov. 10, 1782, in Butterfield et al., eds., *Diary and Autobiography of John Adams*, vol. 3:48–49; Chopra, *Choosing Sides*, 44–45, *Royal American Gazette*, Dec. 26, 1782, quoted on 45 ("licks"); Chopra, *Unnatural Rebellion*, 198, 206; Jasanoff, *Liberty's Exiles*, 63–64, 85–86; Moore, *The Loyalists*, 142–43; Ritcheson, "Britain's Peacemakers," 96–100.

29. Albany resolutions, May 19, 1783 ("never to be"), MG 21, vol. 21, 763:121, reel A-681, Library and Archives Canada (Ottawa) (hereafter LAC); Brown and Senior, *Victorious in Defeat*, 25–29, George Clinton quoted on 25; W. Brown, *Good Americans*, 174–77, Nathanael Greene quoted on 177; Calloway, *Crown and Calumet*, 7–8; Chopra, *Unnatural Rebellion*, 210–13; Crow, "Liberty Men and Loyalists," 175; Jasanoff, *Liberty's Exiles*, 98;

Aedanus Burke quoted in R. Klein, *Unification of a Slave State*, 118; Main, *Political Parties*, 46–47; Moore, *Loyalists*, 148–49; Piecuch, *Three Peoples*, 288; Weir, "Violent Spirit," 91; Zeichner, "Loyalist Problem," 289–95.

30. W. Brown, *Good Americans*, 180–88; Jasanoff, *Liberty's Exiles*, 6, 126–29, 137–40; Moore, *Loyalists*, 150. Some estimates of the Loyalist diaspora run as high as 100,000 people.

31. W. Brown, *Good Americans*, 180–88; Jasanoff, *Liberty's Exiles*, 137–50, Alexander Wallace quoted on 142–43.

32. Brown, *Good Americans*, 150–60, 192, Thomas Hutchinson quoted on 160; Jasanoff, *Liberty's Exiles*, 6, 9, 119–52, Louisa Wells quoted on 119 ("The Isle"); Moore, *The Loyalists*, 143–44.

33. Jasanoff, *Liberty's Exiles*, 229–31, 240–41; Troxler, "Uses of the Bahamas," 185–92.

34. Brown and Senior, *Victorious in Defeat*, 21–52; Chopra, *Choosing Sides*, 46–47; Chopra, *Unnatural Rebellion*, 212; Cruikshank, ed., "Records of Niagara, 1784–7," 80–81, 95; Jasanoff, *Liberty's Exiles*, 10–11, 93–94, 159–61; Moore, *Loyalists*, 152–54, 161–70; Moore, "Disposition to Settle," 53–79.

35. W. Brown, *Good Americans*, 203–9, Polly Dibblee quoted on 206–7, Sarah Frost quoted on 208 ("sat down"); Gilbert, *Black Patriots and Loyalists*, 213–14; Jasanoff, *Liberty's Exiles*, 165–74; Moore, *Loyalists*, 183–223, Sarah Frost quoted on 154 ("roughest land").

36. W. Brown, *Good Americans*, 210–11; Gates, *Land Policies of Upper Canada*, 15; Hansen and Brebner, *Mingling of the Canadian and American Peoples*, 60–62; Hunter, *Quebec to Carolina*, 70 ("It does"); Moore, "Disposition to Settle," 68–71.

37. Lord Sydney to Henry Hope, Aug. 22, 1785 ("Sufferers"), MG 11, vol. 48:36, LAC; Cometti, ed., *American Journals*, 146; G. Craig, *Upper Canada*, 35–38; John Stuart quoted in Jasanoff, *Liberty's Exiles*, 218 ("great Influx" and "compared"). For population growth, see McCalla, *Planting the Province*, 249. For increased American taxes, see Holton, "'From the Labour of Others,'" 275–76.

38. Cometti, ed., *American Journals*, 298–301; Lord Dorchester to Lord Sydney, Oct. 14, 1788 ("should on all occasions"), MG 11, vol. 51:203, LAC.; Jasanoff, *Liberty's Exiles*, 188; Edward Winslow quoted in Moore, *The Loyalists*, 187.

39. Burt, *Old Province*, vol. 1:378–81; A. Taylor, "Hungry Year," 145–81; Pauley, "Fighting the Hessian Fly," 485–507; Lord Grenville to Lord Dorchester, Oct. 20, 1789 ("the minds"), in Shortt and Doughty, eds., *Documents*, 970; Prince Edward quoted in Guillet, *Early Life*, 213 ("My Father").

40. Neatby, *Quebec*, 87–141, 172, and 181–92; Lanctot, *Canada and the American Revolution*, 17–18.

41. Upton, *Loyal Whig*, 150, 167; Greenwood, *Legacies of Fear*, 8–9; Colley,

Britons, 11–54; Milobar, "Conservative Ideology," 52; Harlow, *Founding*, vol. 2:725–26.

42. Greenwood, *Legacies of Fear*, 10–11; William Smith, Jr., to Lord Dorchester, Feb. 5, 1790, in Shortt and Doughty, eds., *Documents*, 1018–19; Harlow, *Founding*, vol. 2:731–32, 747–48; Jasanoff, *Liberty's Exiles*, 89–92; McConville, *King's Three Faces*, 227, 229n18; Upton, *Loyal Whig*, 104–33, 154–88, 199, and 204.

43. Upton, *Loyal Whig*, 136–142, Smith quoted on 141; Upton, ed., *Diary*, vol. 1:276.

44. Hugh Finlay to Evan Nepean, Apr. 4, and July 30, 1788, MG 11, vol. 61, LAC; Henry Hope to Lord Dorchester, May 1, 1787, MG 11, vol. 40:374, LAC.

45. G. Craig, *Upper Canada*, 15–19; Greenwood, *Legacies of Fear*, 35–38; Harlow, *Founding*, vol. 2:751–52; Milobar, "Conservative Ideology," 45, 61–63; Upton, *Loyal Whig*, 161–66, 177, 189–92, 202; Lord Grenville, "Discussion of Petitions and Counter Petitions Re Change of Government in Canada," and Grenville to Lord Dorchester, Oct. 20, 1789, in Shortt and Doughty, eds., *Documents*, 976, and 987–88.

46. Harlow, *Founding*, vol. 2:760–62; Mason, "American Loyalist Diaspora," 244; Lord Grenville, "Discussion of Petitions and Counter Petitions Re Change of Government in Canada [1789]," in Shortt and Doughty, eds., *Documents*, 983–86 (982: "the constitution" and 983: "no care"); Lord Thurlow to Grenville, Sept. 10, 1789, in Cruikshank, ed., *Correspondence of Simcoe*, vol. 1:4–5.

47. Lord Dorchester to William W. Grenville, Feb. 8, 1790, in Shortt and Doughty, eds., *Documents*, 1004.

48. Young, *Democratic Republicans*, 237.

49. McCalla, *Planting the Province*, 17–19, 352n27; Potter, *Liberty We Seek*, 172.

50. Lord Grenville, "Discussion of Petitions and Counter Petitions Re Change of Government in Canada [1789]," in Shortt and Doughty, eds., *Documents*, 985–86; "An Act for Laying and Collecting of Assessments and Rates," *Upper Canada Gazette*, July 25, 1793; John Graves Simcoe to Henry Dundas, Aug. 2, 1794, and the Upper Canada Civil Establishments for 1794 and 1795 in Cruikshank, ed., *Correspondence of Simcoe*, vol. 3:1–2, 250, and vol. 4:167; Craig, *Upper Canada*, 29; McCalla, *Planting the Province*, 17–19, 352n27, and 352n28. American emigrant quoted in Maude, *Visit to the Falls*, 60. For New York's tax rate, see Young, *Democratic Republicans*, 27, 61.

51. Bushman, *King and People*, 85–86; Morgan, *Inventing the People*, 239–62; Greenwood and Wright, "Parliamentary Privilege," 412–15; Lord Grenville, "Discussion of Petitions and Counter Petitions Re Change of Government in Canada [1789]," in Shortt and Doughty, eds., *Documents*, 984–86 ("would afford").

52. Burt, *Old Province*, vol. 2:116–58; Upton, *Loyal Whig*, 150–51, and 167; G. Craig, *Upper Canada*, 17–19; Lord Grenville to Lord Dorchester, Oct. 20, 1789, in Shortt and Doughty, eds., *Documents*, 987–89; Greenwood, *Legacies of Fear*, 43–44.

53. Greenwood, *Legacies of Fear*, 45; G. Craig, *Upper Canada*, 17–19; "Discussion of Petitions and Counter Petitions Re Change of Government in Canada [1789]," in Shortt and Doughty, eds., *Documents*, 977.

54. Garner, *Franchise and Politics*, 82–90; "List of the Poll and Candidates for the County of Leeds," June 21, 1804, MG 24, B 7 (Charles Jones Papers), vol. 1:275, LAC.

55. Lord Thurlow to W. W. Grenville, Sept. 10, 1789, in Cruikshank, ed., *Correspondence of Simcoe*, vol. 1:4–5 ("have given"); Jasanoff, *Liberty's Exiles*, 13–14; Milobar, "Conservative Ideology," 64.

56. Bonomi, *Factious People*, 34–39, and 114–15; Countryman, *People in Revolution*, 76–79, 166–69; Varga, "Election Procedures and Practices," 249–77; G. Wood, *Radicalism*, 287–305; Young, *Democratic Republicans*, 17–22. For the reactionary nature of the postwar empire, see Bayly, *Imperial Meridian*, 1–15; E. Gould, "American Independence," 107–41.

57. Jasanoff, *Liberty's Exiles*, 193–97.

58. David, *Dunmore's New World*, 143–72; Jasanoff, *Liberty's Exiles*, 227–44, John Maxwell quoted on 232; ("It will be"), and Lord Sydney quoted on 236–37; Troxler, "Uses of the Bahamas," 192–96.

59. Graymont, *Iroquois in the American Revolution*, 259–62; Calloway, *Crown and Calumet*, 7–8; Frederick Haldimand to Baron von Riedesel, Apr. 26, 1783 ("My soul"), in Stone, ed., *Memoirs, and Letters and Journals*, vol. 2:168–69.

60. Allan MacLean to Frederick Haldimand, May 18, 1783 ("that the Indians") MG 21 (Haldimand Papers), #21763, p. 118, LAC; Calloway, *American Revolution in Indian Country*, 273–77; Calloway, *Crown and Calumet*, 8–9; DuVal, *Independence Lost*, 236–38, unnamed Creek chief quoted on 238; Jasanoff, *Liberty's Exiles*, 106–7.

61. Allen, *His Majesty's Indian Allies*, 56–57; François de Barbé-Marbois to Comte de Vergennes, Sept. 30, and Oct. 30, 1784, in Giunta, ed., *Emerging Nation*, vol. 2:451, 482–83; Ritcheson, *Aftermath of Revolution*, 4–6, 33–37, 59–69; Wright, *Britain and the American Frontier*, 2, 16, 20–26, 36, 42–43, 80–86.

62. Samuel Kirkland, diary, July 7, 1788 ("that Congress"), Lothrop Family Papers, Dartmouth College; Allen, *His Majesty's Indian Allies*, 56–57; Calloway, *Crown and Calumet*, 14; DuVal, *Independence Lost*, 253–55, 294–98; Furstenberg, "Significance," 663; White, *Middle Ground*, 413–17, 433–43, 447–48; Wright, *Britain and the American Frontier*, 69–72.

63. John Adams to Hezekiah Niles, Feb. 13, 1818, Founders Online, National

Archives (http://founders.archives.gov/documents/Adams/99-02-02-6854); Edling, "More Perfect Union," 390–91; Higginbotham, "War and State Formation," 94; G. Wood, *Creation of the American Republic*, 354–59.

64. James Madison quoted in Edling, "Consolidating a Revolutionary Republic," 169; Hendrickson, "First Union," 40–42; Onuf, "Empire of Liberty," 198–99; Rakove, *Beginnings of National Politics*, 142–43, 156–64, 178–79; Sadosky, *Revolutionary Negotiations*, 84–85.

65. Hendrickson, "First Union," 37–39, 45; Higginbotham, "War and State Formation," 60–61, 64; Irvin, *Clothed in Robes of Sovereignty*, 274–76; Rakove, *Beginnings of National Politics*, 148–76, John Witherspoon quoted on 158 ("the smaller"); G. Wood, *Creation of the American Republic*, 357.

66. Edling, "Consolidating a Revolutionary Republic," 170–71; Gould, *Among the Powers*, 10–11; Hendrickson, "First Union," 36–37; Rakove, *Origins of National Politics*, 158–59; G. Wood, *Creation of the American Republic*, 356–57.

67. Edling, "Consolidating a Revolutionary Republic," 170–71; John Adams to Thomas Jefferson, Mar. 1, 1787 ("diplomatic assembly"), Founders Online, National Archives (http://founders.archives.gov/documents/Adams/99-02-02-0072); Hendrickson, "First Union," 37–42; Rakove, *Origins of National Politics*, 163–92, Thomas Burke quoted on 167; G. Wood, *Creation of the American Republic*, 355–56.

68. Onuf, *Origins of the Federal Republic*, 76–79, 86–90; Rakove, *Origins of National Politics*, 159–60, 163–91.

69. Jensen, *New Nation*, 26–27; Onuf, *Origins of the Federal Republic*, 75–76, 87–101, 103–18, Joseph Jones quoted on 92 ("common fund"); Rakove, *Origins of National Politics*, 285–88, 352.

70. Edling, "Consolidating a Revolutionary Republic," 176; Edling, "More Perfect Union," 391–92; Gould, *Among the Powers*, 127; Rakove, *Origins of National Politics*, 163–92; Chevalier de La Luzerne quoted in Sadosky, *Revolutionary Negotiations*, 118 ("an incomplete").

71. Cayton, *Frontier Republic*, 2–3; Onuf, *Origins of the Federal Republic*, 154–60, Benjamin Rush quoted on 160; Sadosky, *Revolutionary Negotiations*, 129–30.

72. Griffin, *America's Revolution*, 251; Onuf, *Origins of the Federal Republic*, 154–60.

73. Beeman, *Plain, Honest Men*, 215–16; Hinderaker, *Elusive Empires*, 228–31; Jensen, *New Nation*, 352–54; Onuf, *Origins of the Federal Republic*, 42–46; Onuf, *Statehood and Union*, 46–49.

74. Griffin, *America's Revolution*, 251–52; Hinderaker, *Elusive Empires*, 242; Holton, *Unruly Americans*, 141–42; Jensen, *New Nation*, 355–57; Onuf, *Statehood and Union*, 53–55.

75. Cayton, *Frontier Republic*, 13–32; Jensen, *New Nation*, 355–57; Onuf, *Statehood and Union*, 42–43.

76. Cayton, *Frontier Republic*, 24–25, Richard Henry Lee quoted on 25; Hendrickson, *Peace Pact*, 228–29; Onuf, *Origins of the Federal Republic*, 170–71; Onuf, *Statehood and Union*, 58–66; Rakove, *Beginnings of National Politics*, 352–53.

77. Beeman, *Plain, Honest Men*, 216–18; Hendrickson, *Peace Pact*, 228–30; Onuf, *Statehood and Union*, 110–13; Van Cleve, *Slaveholders' Union*, 153–67.

78. Calloway, *American Revolution in Indian Country*, 280–81; Cayton, *Frontier Republic*, 2–9, James Tilton quoted on 2 ("slip out"); squatter notice quoted in Jensen, *New Nation*, 357; R. Morris, *Forging the Union*, 223–27.

79. John Jay to Thomas Jefferson, Dec. 14, 1786, in Boyd et al., eds., *Papers of Thomas Jefferson*, vol. 10:596–99; Cayton, *Frontier Republic*, 6–11; Griffin, *America's Revolution*, 250–51; Hinderaker, *Elusive Empires*, 227–31, 238–40, unnamed surveyor quoted on 239 ("lawless set").

80. Calloway, *American Revolution in Indian Country*, 278–83, Philip Schuyler quoted on 278; DuVal, *Independence Lost*, 236–37; Arthur Lee, speech, Oct. 20, 1784 ("You are"), in N. Craig, ed., *Olden Time*, 424–25; Lee quoted in Potts, *Arthur Lee*, 270 ("Animals"); Richter, "Onas," 141–43; Sadosky, *Revolutionary Negotiations*, 135–38.

81. Calloway, *American Revolution in Indian Country*, 282–83; Griffin, *America's Revolution*, 220–21; Hinderaker, *Elusive Empires*, 232–36; Sadosky, *Revolutionary Negotiations*, 128–30, 138–39; R. White, *Middle Ground*, 416–17; Richard Butler, "Fort Stanwix Proceedings," in N. Craig, ed., *Olden Time*, vol. 2:413, 425.

82. Hinderaker, *Elusive Empires*, 240–41; Nichols, *Red Gentlemen*, 65–68; R. White, *Middle Ground*, 438–40.

83. Cayton, *Frontier Republic*, 23–24; DuVal, *Native Ground*, 174–75; Furstenberg, "Significance," 659–65; Louis Guillaume Otto to Comte de Montmorin, Mar. 5, 1787, in Giunta, ed., *Emerging Nation*, vol. 2:210–11; Hilton, "Loyalty and Patriotism," 15; Jensen, *New Nation*, 170–73, Rufus King quoted on 171–72 ("every emigrant"); Lewis, *American Union*, 14–22; Onuf, *Statehood and Union*, 54–57; George Washington to Benjamin Harrison, Oct. 10, 1784, in Rhodehamel, ed., *George Washington: Writings*, 559–67, quotation from 563; Weber, *Spanish Frontier*, 281–82.

84. Thomas Jefferson to Richard Henry Lee, July 12, 1785, in Boyd et al., eds., *Papers of Thomas Jefferson*, vol. 8:286–88 ("our states"); DuVal, *Independence Lost*, 314–20, David Campbell quoted on 332 ("I think").

85. Aron, *American Confluence*, 71–73; DuVal, "Choosing Enemies," 234; Francisco Rendón to Don José de Gálvez, Feb. 12, 1785, in Giunta, ed.,

Emerging Nation, vol. 2:197; Barthelemi Tardiveau to Count de Aranda, July 17, 1792, Baron Carondelet to Aranda, c. 1793 ("unmeasured ambition"), and Josef Vidal to Marquis de Casa-Calvo, Sept. 27, 1800, in Houck, ed., *Spanish Regime*, vol. 1:360, vol. 2:13, 289–90; Nasatir, *Borderland in Retreat*, 35–36; Weber, *Spanish Frontier*, 272–80, Vicente Manuel de Zéspedes quoted on 272 ("distinguished").

86. Foley, *Genesis of Missouri*, 98–107; Kastor, *Nation's Crucible*, 26–34; McCalla, *Planting the Province*, 15–17, 249; Weber, *Spanish Frontier*, 276–78.

87. Patrick Murray to John Graves Simcoe, Dec. 23, 1791 ("We are"), MG 23 H I 1, 3rd ser. (Simcoe Transcripts), vol. 1:367, LAC; Calloway, *American Revolution in Indian Country*, 277–78; DuVal, "Choosing Enemies," 235–36; DuVal, *Independence Lost*, 239–40, 246–52, 256–58, 310–12, Alexander McGillivray quoted on 248 ("the protection"), Bernardo de Gálvez quoted on 266; Nasatir, *Borderland in Retreat*, 41–42; Weber, *Spanish Frontier*, 278–79, 282–84, McGillivray quoted on 282 ("Crown of Spain").

88. Aron, *American Confluence*, 78; Din, "Immigration Policy of Miró," 161; DuVal, *Independence Lost*, 318–20; Faber, *Building the Land of Dreams*, 37–38, Esteban Rodriguez Miró quoted on 38 ("written"); Liss, *Atlantic Empires*, 148; Weber, *Spanish Frontier*, 279.

89. Aron, *American Confluence*, 78, 82; Foley, *Genesis of Missouri*, 67–68; Weber, *Spanish Frontier*, 280–85.

90. DuVal, *Independence Lost*, 320–22; Esteban Rodríguez Miró quoted in Hilton, "Being and Becoming Spanish," 10; Vicente Manuel de Zéspedes quoted in Weber, *Spanish Frontier*, 280 ("The best").

91. John Gordon quoted in Hilton, "Being and Becoming Spanish," 18 ("May God"); Weber, *Spanish Frontier*, 278–81.

92. Thomas Jefferson to George Washington, Apr. 2, 1791, in Boyd et al., eds., *Papers of Thomas Jefferson*, vol. 20:95–98 ("the means"); Alexander McGillivray quoted in DuVal, *Independence Lost*, 323.

93. Lord Grenville to Lord Dorchester, Oct. 20, 1789 ("It appears"), MG 11, vol. 59:234, LAC; Graham, *British Policy and Canada*, 118–28, and 131–32; Harlow, *Founding*, vol. 2:596–603; Lord Sheffield quoted in Onuf, "Expanding Union," 58; Upton, *Loyal Whig*, 173; Wright, *Britain and the American Frontier*, 44.

94. Henry Hamilton to Lord Sydney, July 8, 1785, MG 11, vol. 48:45, reel B-39, LAC; Allen, *His Majesty's Indian Allies*, 67–68; Calloway, *Crown and Calumet*, 17; Alexander McGillivray quoted in DuVal, *Independence Lost*, 253; John Adams to John Jay, Oct. 15, and Dec. 3, 1785 ("they rely"), in Giunta, ed., *Emerging Nation*, vol. 2:864–65 and 940–41; James Monroe to Thomas Jefferson, Nov. 1, 1784, in Hamilton, ed., *Writings of Monroe*, vol. 1:43–44; R. White, *Middle Ground*, 416–17.

95. DuVal, *Independence Lost*, 288–89; Holton, *Unruly Americans*, 28; Klein, *Unification of a Slave State*, 164–65; McCusker and Menard, *Economy of British America*, 367–75; Schoen, "Positive Goods and Necessary Evils," 163–64.

96. Berkin, *Brilliant Solution*, 21; John Jay to Thomas Jefferson, Dec. 14, 1786, in Boyd et al., eds., *Papers of Thomas Jefferson*, vol. 10:596–99; Alexander McGillivray quoted in DuVal, *Independence Lost*, 253; Ritcheson, *Aftermath of Revolution*, 45.

97. Beeman, *Plain, Honest Men*, 14–15; Berkin, *Brilliant Solution*, 21–23; DuVal, *Independence Lost*, 333–34, Diego de Gardoqui quoted on 334 ("almost without"); Edling, *Revolution in Favor of Government*, 86–87; John Jay to John Adams, Oct. 14, 1785 ("Our federal"), and Adams to Jay, Oct. 15, and Dec. 3, 1785, in Giunta, ed., *Emerging Nation*, vol. 2:863, 864–65, 940–41; Holton, *Unruly Americans*, 137–38, 143–44.

98. Thomas Jefferson to James Madison, Sept. 1, 1785, in Boyd et al., eds., *Papers of Thomas Jefferson*, vol. 8:360–63 ("supposed"); Edling, *Revolution*, 85–88, Lord Sheffield quoted on 87; E. Gould, *Among the Powers*, 113–21, 125–27; Hendrickson, "Escaping Insecurity," 218–19, Josiah Tucker quoted on 219 ("Their Fate"); Opal, "Republic in the World," 596; George Washington to Benjamin Harrison, Jan. 18, 1784, and Washington to Henry Lee, Oct. 31, 1786, in Rhodehamel, ed., *George Washington: Writings*, 551–53 ("worst consequences" on 552), 609 ("be more exposed"); Ritcheson, *Aftermath of Revolution*, 15–17.

99. James Monroe to Thomas Jefferson, Nov. 1, 1784, in S. M. Hamilton, ed., *Writings of Monroe*, vol. 1:43–44; McCoy, "James Madison and Visions of American Nationality," 244–45; Timothy Bloodworth quoted in R. Morris, *Forging the Union*, 243 ("that the Confederated compact"), see also 93–95; Onuf, *Origins of the Federal Republic*, 149–50; Polishook, *Rhode Island*, 53–80; George Washington to Benjamin Harrison, Jan. 18, 1784, in Rhodehamel, ed., *George Washington: Writings*, 551–53; Alexander Hamilton to John Jay, July 25, 1783, in Syrett, ed., *Papers of Alexander Hamilton*, vol. 3:416–17.

100. Thomas Jefferson to James Madison, Jan. 30, 1787, in Boyd et al., eds., *Papers of Thomas Jefferson*, vol. 11:92–97; Hendrickson, *Peace Pact*, 205–6; McCoy, "James Madison and Visions of American Nationality," 227–45; Onuf, *Origins of the Federal Republic*, 168–69; Rakove, *Beginnings of National Politics*, 349–51; Van Cleve, *Slaveholders' Union*, 111–12, 159–61, Patrick Henry quoted on 159.

101. William Gordon to John Adams, Sept. 7, 1782, in Butterfield et al., eds., *Papers of John Adams*, vol. 13:447–53 ("If America"); Hendrickson, *Peace Pact*, 205–6; Jensen, "Sovereign States," 228–29, 234–37; McCoy, "James Madison and Visions of American Nationality," 227–45, William Grayson

quoted on 244 ("great national contest" and "whether"); Onuf, *Origins of the Federal Republic*, 168–69; Rothman, *Slave Country*, 14–15.

102. Benjamin Franklin quoted in Berkin, *Brilliant Solution*, 164; Greene, *Imperatives*, 332–33; Hendrickson, "Escaping Insecurity," 219–20; Lepore, *A Is for American*, 19–20, Alexander Hamilton quoted on 19; David Ramsay quoted in R. Morris, *Forging of the Union*, 93 ("That once"); Onuf, "Epilogue," 288–90; Onuf, "Expanding Union," 59–60.

103. DuVal, *Independence Lost*, 319–20, John Jay quoted on 320; Gould, *Among the Powers of the Earth*, 130–34; James Lewis, *American Union*, 6. Hendrickson, *Peace Pact*, 203–7, 216–18.

104. DuVal, *Independence Lost*, 268–69; A. Taylor, *Divided Ground*, 113–19.

CHAPTER 10: REPUBLICS

1. Samuel Ellsworth quoted in Szatmary, *Shays' Rebellion*, 56.

2. George Washington to James Madison, Dec. 16, 1786, in Abbot et al., eds., *Papers of George Washington, Confederation Series*, vol. 4:457–59.

3. Kierner, *Traders and Gentle Folk*, 201–4, Robert R. Livingston, Jr., quoted on 240–41; Main, "American States," 23–27; E. S. Morgan, *Inventing the People*, 249–50; G. Wood, *Empire of Liberty*, 29–30.

4. Bouton, "Trials of the Confederation," 383–84, Robert Morris quoted on 384; G. Wood, *Creation of the American Republic*, 495–97, Louis Otto quoted on 495 ("Although"). For the sources of Morris's wealth, see G. Wood, "Interests and Disinterestedness," 96–99.

5. Kulikoff, *Tobacco and Slaves*, 300–11; Lewis, *Pursuit of Happiness*, 48–50; Main, *Political Parties*, 16–17; E. S. Morgan, *Inventing the People*, 247–48; Nadelhaft, "'Snarls of Invidious Animals,'" 67–68; B. C. Smith, *Freedoms We Lost*, 181–82.

6. Kulikoff, *Tobacco and Slaves*, 300–11; Jan Lewis, *Pursuit of Happiness*, 48–50.

7. Bouton, *Taming Democracy*, 31–58; Holton, *Unruly Americans*, 3–17, 165–68; Kulikoff, "War in the Countryside," 228–29; McDonnell, "Class War," 305–44; Nadelhaft, "'The Snarls of Invidious Animals,'" 62–94; Charles Carroll quoted in Rakove, *Revolutionaries*, 188–89; Rosswurm, *Arms, Country, and Class*, 76–108.

8. Bouton, *Taming Democracy*, 64–65; E. S. Morgan, *Inventing the People*, 247–48; Main, *Political Parties*, 125–26; Rakove, *Revolutionaries*, 353–54.

9. Countryman, *People in Revolution*, 196–202, 287–88; Kierner, *Traders and Gentlefolk*, 209, 212, 234–35; Maier, *Ratification*, 320–24, Philip Schuyler quoted on 322; Main, *Political Parties*, 126–27; Young, *Democratic Republicans of New York*, 34–39.

10. Edward Carrington to Thomas Jefferson, June 9, 1787, in Boyd et al., eds.,

Jefferson Papers, vol. 11:408–9 ("Demagogues"); Connecticut writer quoted in Holton, *Unruly Americans*, 165 ("be content"); G. Wood, *Creation of the American Republic*, 475–83, James Otis quoted on 476 ("When the pot boils") and 494–95, Federalist quoted on 494 ("horse-jockey").

11. Chernow, *Alexander Hamilton*, 7–186; Elkins and McKitrick, *Age of Federalism*, 93–102; E. S. Morgan, *Inventing the People*, 249–50; Rakove, *Revolutionaries*, 401–5; G. Wood, *Creation of the American Republic*, 475–83; G. Wood, *Empire of Liberty*, 89–90.

12. Middlekauff, *Glorious Cause*, 604–5; Morgan, *Birth of the Republic*, 88–90; Rakove, *Revolutionaries*, 171–72; G. Wood, *Creation of the American Republic*, 127–32.

13. John Adams, "Thoughts on Government, April 1776," in Butterfield et al., eds., *Papers of John Adams*, vol. 4:86–93 ("How few"); E. S. Morgan, *Birth of the Republic*, 89–90; Rakove, *Revolutionaries*, 169–71; G. Wood, *Creation of the American Republic*, 127–34.

14. Bouton, *Training Democracy*, 54; Middlekauff, *Glorious Cause*, 606–8; E. S. Morgan, *Birth of the Republic*, 90–91, Virginia's constitution quoted on 91; Rakove, *Revolutionaries*, 172–75.

15. Beeman, *Old Dominion*, 28, 53; Evans, *Topping People*, 192; Thomas Mann Randolph quoted in D. Jordan, *Political Leadership*, 14 ("no more than"); E. S. Morgan, *Birth of the Republic*, 91–92; Nadelhaft, "'Snarls of Invidious Animals,'" 69–70; Rakove, *Revolutionaries*, 173–77; G. Wood, *Creation of the American Republic*, 135–50, Delaware Patriot quoted on 135 ("executive power"); McDonnell, *Politics of War*, 519, 524–26; Wolf, *Race and Liberty*, 126–27.

16. John Adams, "Thoughts on Government, April 1776," in Butterfield et al., eds., *Papers of John Adams*, vol. 4:86–93 ("should be"); Holton, *Unruly Americans*, 168–71, 200; E. S. Morgan, *Inventing the People*, 244–45; Nadelhaft, "'Snarls of Invidious Animals,'" 68; Rakove, *Revolutionaries*, 176; G. Wood, *Creation of the American Republic*, 162–72, Patriots quoted on 166 ("Where annual").

17. Bouton, *Taming Democracy*, 53; John Adams to James Sullivan, May 26, 1776, in Butterfield et al., eds., *Papers of John Adams*, vol. 4:208–13 ("Such is the Frailty"); Holton, *Unruly Americans*, 170; E. S. Morgan, *Birth of the Republic*, 93–94; Rakove, *Revolutionaries*, 174–80, 189; G. Wood, *Creation of the American Republic*, 168–69.

18. Bouton, "Trials of the Confederation," 379; Countryman, "Some Problems of Power," 160, 169–71; Holton, *Unruly Americans*, 12–17; E. S. Morgan, *Inventing the People*, 248–51; G. Wood, *Creation of the American Republic*, 150–61, 489–90.

19. Bouton, *Taming Democracy*, 51–58, militia captain quoted on 68; Brunhouse, *Counter-Revolution in Pennsylvania*, 12–15; Joseph Shippen quoted

in Main, *Political Parties*, 178 ("violent"); Rakove, *Revolutionaries*, 181–83; Rosswurm, *Arms, Country, and Class*, 100–8; Ryerson, "Republican Theory and Partisan Reality," 99–115; G. Wood, *Creation of the American Republic*, 88–89.

20. Bouton, *Taming Democracy*, 51–58; Brunhouse, *Counter-Revolution in Pennsylvania*, 12–15; Rakove, *Revolutionaries*, 180–84; Ryerson, "Republican Theory and Partisan Reality," 103–9; G. Wood, *Creation of the American Republic*, 137–38, 226–32, Philadelphia newspaper quoted on 229 ("the more simple") and 230 ("Two or more").

21. Bouton, *Taming Democracy*, 56; Brunhouse, *Counter-Revolution in Pennsylvania*, 16–19; Main, *Political Parties*, 177–78; Rosswurm, *Arms, Country, and Class*, 101–2; Rakove, *Revolutionaries*, 185; Ryerson, "Republican Theory and Partisan Reality," 108, 116–18.

22. Bouton, *Taming Democracy*, 62–64; Brunhouse, *Counter-Revolution in Pennsylvania*, 15–17; Main, *Political Parties*, 178–79; Rosswurm, *Arms, Country, and Class*, 103–7, 123–24, 138–39, 158–62, William Hooper quoted on 106 ("Taverns"); Ryerson, "Republican Theory and Partisan Reality," 110–13, 118–19; G. Wood, *Creation of the American Republic*, 232–37, Benjamin Rush quoted on 233, and Hooper quoted on 233 ("an execrable").

23. John Adams, "Thoughts on Government, April 1776," in Butterfield et al., eds., *Papers of John Adams*, vol. 4:86–93; Ryerson, "Republican Theory and Partisan Reality," 111–12; G. Wood, *Creation of the American Republic*, 442–63.

24. E. S. Morgan, *Birth of the Republic*, 91–93; Rakove, *Revolutionaries*, 185; G. Wood, *Creation of the American Republic*, 569–80, John Adams quoted on 575 ("the most stupendous"), and 578 ("as unjust").

25. E. S. Morgan, *Inventing the People*, 258–59; Patterson, "Roots of Massachusetts Federalism," 39–41; Rakove, *Revolutionaries*, 192–95; G. Wood, *Creation of the American Republic*, 340–41, 574–80, Adams quoted on 575 ("but three"), and 578 ("that the people's rights").

26. E. S. Morgan, *Inventing the People*, 255–56; Ryerson, "Republican Theory and Partisan Reality," 111–12; G. Wood, *Creation of the American Republic*, 442–63, *New Hampshire Gazette* quoted on 449 ("become centinels").

27. Kulikoff, "War in the Countryside," 217–24; Lindert and Williamson, "American Incomes," 725–65, quotations from 741 ("America's greatest"), 752 ("economic disaster"); McCusker and Menard, *Economy of British America*, 361–74. For mortality, see C. Cox, "Continental Army," 162.

28. Bouton, "Trials of the Confederation," 372–74; Edling, *Revolution in Favor of Government*, 84–85.

29. Bouton, "Trials of the Confederation," 372, 382–83; St. George Tucker quoted in Evans, *Topping People*, 196; William Allison quoted in P. Hamilton, *Making and Unmaking*, 74–75 ("We have"); Jensen, *New Nation*, 177–

93, 314–15; R. Klein, *Unification of a Slave State*, 125–29; Main, *Political Parties*, 61–62; McCusker and Menard, *Economy of British America*, 369–70; R. Morris, *Forging of the Union*, 130–37.

30. Foner, *Tom Paine*, 149–50; Main, "American States," 9–12; Rakove, *Revolutionaries*, 189–90; B. C. Smith, *Freedom We Lost*, 140–42.

31. Countryman, *American Revolution*, 143–44; B. C. Smith, *Freedoms We Lost*, 140–51, *Boston Gazette* quoted on 151 ("greedy Muckworms").

32. Alexander, "Fort Wilson Incident," 593–600; Bouton, *Taming Democracy*, 66–68; Abigail Adams to John Adams, July 31, 1777, in Butterfield et al., eds., *Book of Abigail and John*, 184–85; Countryman, "Some Problems of Power," 174–77; Foner, *Tom Paine*, 150–53; Kerber, *Women of the Republic*, 43–44; Main, *Political Parties*, 48–49, 127; B. C. Smith, *Freedoms We Lost*, 143–68.

33. Alexander, "Fort Wilson Incident," 593–12; Bouton, *Taming Democracy*, 66–69; Brunhouse, *Counter-Revolution in Pennsylvania*, 68–76; Countryman, *American Revolution*, 154–56; Foner, *Tom Paine*, 174–78; Rosswurm, *Arms, Country, and Class*, 177–227, broadside quoted on 178; B. C. Smith, *Freedoms We Lost*, 179–80.

34. Bouton, *Taming Democracy*, 70–75; Countryman, *American Revolution*, 147–50; Countryman, "Some Problems of Power," 175–76; Foner, *Tom Paine*, 152–58, 178–82; Rosswurm, *Arms, Country, and Class*, 194–99; B. C. Smith, *Freedoms We Lost*, 140–43, 155–58; G. Wood, *Creation of the American Republic*, 413–20, Robert Morris quoted on 419 ("It is inconsistent").

35. Bouton, "Trials of the Confederation," 375–75; Buel, "Public Creditor Interest," 47–56; Countryman, *American Revolution*, 156–57; Foner, *Tom Paine*, 171–73; Holton, *Unruly Americans*, 30–31, 59–60; Jensen, *New Nation*, 309; Main, *Political Parties*, 86–87; Patterson, "Federalist Reaction," 102–3.

36. Bouton, *Taming Democracy*, 80–83; Holton, *Unruly Americans*, 29–32, Greenwich, Massachusetts inhabitants quoted on 29 ("Our Grievances").

37. Bouton, *Taming Democracy*, 136; Bouton, "Trials of the Confederation," 374–77; Holton, *Unruly Americans*, 27–45; *Massachusetts Centinel* writer quoted on 32 ("great possessors" and "abominable system"); Jensen, *New Nation*, 304–6; Main, *Political Parties*, 51–52; Richards, *Shays's Rebellion*, 80–81, Rhode Island workman quoted on 84 ("Soldiers blood").

38. Bouton, "Trials of the Confederation," 373–75; Holton, *Unruly Americans*, 32–38, 43–44, 90, Connecticut writer quoted on 103 ("a country"); Jensen, *New Nation*, 309; R. Morris, *Forging the Union*, 35–36; Richards, *Shays's Rebellion*, 79–80.

39. Bouton, "Trials of the Confederation," 374–78, Massachusetts farmers quoted on 376 ("it cost them"), New York writer quoted on 378 ("The secu-

rity"); John Reed quoted in Holton, *Unruly Americans*, 131 ("Has not"); Main, *Political Parties*, 127.

40. Bouton, "Trials of the Confederation," 374–79, Delaware farmers quoted on 376; Holton, *Unruly Americans*, 55–58, 77–81; Jensen, *New Nation*, 306–7, 311–12; Main, *Political Parties*, 51–52.

41. Breen, *George Washington's Journey*, 91–92; Polishook, *Rhode Island*, 131–61; Richards, *Shays's Rebellion*, 74–76, 83–85, *United States Chronicle* quoted on 84 ("Fool's Island"); Szatmary, *Shays' Rebellion*, 50–51, 57–58; Van Cleve, "Anti-Federalists' Toughest Challenge," 544–45, Noah Webster quoted on 554 ("the little detestable corner").

42. Abigail Adams to Isaac Smith, Sr., Mar. 12, 1787, in Butterfield et al., eds., *Adams Family Correspondence*, vol. 8:8–10; Holton, *Unruly Americans*, 46–54; Main, *Political Parties*, 65–66.

43. Bouton, "Trials of the Confederation," 376–77; Holton, *Unruly Americans*, 133–34; Jensen, *New Nation*, 307–8, 310–11; R. Morris, *Forging of the Union*, 258–59; Szatmary, *Shays' Rebellion*, 44–50.

44. Bouton, "Trials of the Confederation," 376–77; Holton, *Unruly Americans*, 108–9; Patterson, "Federalist Reaction," 113–14; Szatmary, *Shays' Rebellion*, 37–44, 56–67.

45. Buel, "Public Creditor Interest," 52–54; Holton, *Unruly Americans*, 74–75; Jensen, *New Nation*, 309–11; Nobles, "Satan, Smith, Shattuck and Shays," 223–24; Patterson, "Roots of Massachusetts Federalism," 49–51; Richards, *Shays's Rebellion*, 8–9; Szatmary, *Shays' Rebellion*, 37–47, *Worcester Magazine* quoted on 47 ("When we"); Fisher Ames quoted in G. Wood, *Creation of the American Republic*, 397 ("The people").

46. Bouton, "Trials of the Confederation," 380–81; R. D. Brown, "Shays's Rebellion," 115; Nobles, "Satan, Smith, Shattuck and Shays," 219–24; Nobles, "Shays's Neighbors," 199–202; Richards, *Shays's Rebellion*, 9–12, 63–64; Szatmary, *Shays' Rebellion*, 58–69.

47. John Jay to Thomas Jefferson, Dec. 14, 1786, in Boyd et al., eds., *Papers of Thomas Jefferson*, vol. 10:596–99; Nobles, "Satan, Smith, Shattuck and Shays," 215–24, conservative catechism quoted on 216; Nobles, "Shays's Neighbors," 197–99; Richards, *Shays's Rebellion*, 16–22, 26–27, 113–14; Szatmary, *Shays' Rebellion*, 70–77.

48. R. D. Brown, "Shays's Rebellion," 115–17; Nobles, "Satan, Smith, Shattuck, and Shays," 225–28; Patterson, "Federalist Reaction," 115–16; Richards, *Shays's Rebellion*, 23–42, 77–79; Szatmary, *Shays' Rebellion*, 83–118.

49. Henry Knox quoted in George Washington to James Madison, Nov. 5, 1786, in Abbot et al., eds., *Papers of George Washington, Confederation Series*, vol. 4:331–32; John Jay to Thomas Jefferson, Dec. 14, 1786, in Boyd et al., eds., *Papers of Thomas Jefferson*, vol. 10:596–99; Richards, *Shays's Rebellion*, 1–3, 109–11, 129–32; Henry Lee to George Washington, Nov. 11, 1786,

and Edward Carrington to Edmund Randolph, Dec. 8, 1786, in P. Smith, ed., *Letters of Delegates*, vol. 24:26, and 43–45; G. Wood, *Creation of the American Republic*, 412.

50. Beeman, *Plain, Honest Men*, 16–17; Flexner, *George Washington*, 98–100; Holton, *Unruly Americans*, 10–12, 145–53; Szatmary, *Shays' Rebellion*, 78–79, 120–30, James Wilson quoted on 130.

51. R. D. Brown, "Shays's Rebellion," 119–21; Buel, "Public Creditor Interest," 55–56; Holton, *Unruly Americans*, 76–77; R. Morris, *Forging of the Union*, 264–65; Nobles, "Satan, Smith, Shattuck, and Shays," 228–29; Richards, *Shays's Rebellion*, 38–39, 118–19.

52. Bouton, *Taming Democracy*, 159; Bouton, "Trials of the Confederation," 379–80; David Ramsay to Thomas Jefferson, Apr. 7, 1787, in Boyd, et al., eds., *Papers of Thomas Jefferson*, vol. 11:279; Holton, *Unruly Americans*, 110–15; Jensen, *New Nation*, 178, 311–12, Edmund Randolph quoted on 312; R. Klein, *Unification of a Slave State*, 127–28; R. Morris, *Forging of the Union*, 156–57; Van Cleve, "Anti-Federalists' Toughest Challenge," 529–30.

53. Bouton, *Taming Democracy*, 70–71; Holton, *Unruly Americans*, 12–13, 86–88, 157–59; 165; E. S. Morgan, *Inventing the People*, 253–54; Rakove, *Revolutionaries*, 175, 361–62; George Washington to Henry Lee, Oct. 31, 1786, in Rhodehamel, ed., *George Washington: Writings*, 608–10, quotation on 608; G. Wood, *Creation of the American Republic*, 393–403, 415–25, David Ramsay quoted on 403, John Jay quoted on 424–25.

54. Benjamin Rush quoted in Breen, *George Washington's Journey*, 89; James Madison, "Federalist Number 48," in Hutchinson et al., eds., *Papers of James Madison*, vol. 10:456–60; Rakove, *Revolutionaries*, 362–63; G. Wood, *Creation of the American Republic*, 403–8, 431–32.

55. George Washington to James Madison, Mar. 31, 1787, in Abbot et al., eds., *Papers of George Washington, Confederation Series*, vol. 5:114–17; J. Boyd, *Number 7*, 6–10; Flexner, *George Washington*, 96n, 105; Holton, *Unruly Americans*, 21–22, 179; Noah Webster quoted in Jensen, *New Nation*, 107–8; Reuter, "'Petty Spy' or Effective Diplomat," 477–79; Syrett, ed., *Papers of Hamilton*, vol. 26:198n4, and 324n3; Szatmary, *Shays' Rebellion*, 81–82, Nathaniel Gorham quoted on 82 ("on the failure"); G. Wood, *Empire of Liberty*, 31.

56. Bouton, *Taming Democracy*, 70–75, Robert Morris quoted on 73 ("establishing the Power" and "The Possession of Money"); Holton, *Unruly Americans*, 99–100; James Madison, "The Federalist Number 10," in Hutchinson et al., eds., *Papers of James Madison*, vol. 10:263–70 ("republican remedy"); G. Wood, *Creation of the American Republic*, Benjamin Lincoln quoted on 220.

57. Bouton, *Taming Democracy*, 172–77; Richards, *Shays's Rebellion*, 125–28; Alexander Hamilton, "Conjectures About the New Constitution," Sept.

17–30, 1787, in Syrett, ed., *Papers of Alexander Hamilton*, vol. 4:275–77 ("most men"); G. Wood, *Creation of the American Republic*, 463–67; A. Young, *Liberty Tree*, 193–95.

58. Beeman, *Plain, Honest Men*, 25–27; Elkins and McKitrick, *Age of Federalism*, 79–82; Rakove, *Original Meanings*, 36–38; Rakove, *Revolutionaries*, 341–53; G. Wood, *Empire of Liberty*, 61.

59. Beeman, *Plain, Honest Men*, 27–28; James Madison to Thomas Jefferson, Oct. 17, 1788, in Hutchinson et al., eds., *Paper of James Madison*, vol. 11:295–300 ("it is much more"); James Madison, "Term of the Senate," June 26, 1787, in Hutchinson et al., *Papers of James Madison*, vol. 10:76–78 ("protect the minority"); Hendrickson, *Peace Pact*, 212–18; Holton, *Unruly Americans*, 6–7; Kornblith and Murrin, "Making and Unmaking," 55; Rakove, *Original Meanings*, 39–45.

60. Holton, *Unruly Americans*, 8–9; Nadelhaft, "'Snarls of Invidious Animals,'" 88–89; Rakove, *Original Meanings*, 46–51; G. Wood, *Creation of the American Republic*, 471–75; A. Young, *Liberty Tree*, 193–94.

61. Beeman, *Plain, Honest Men*, 28–29; James Madison, "Vices of the Political System," in Hutchinson et al., eds., *Papers of James Madison*, vol. 9:345–58; E. S. Morgan, *Inventing the People*, 268–70; G. Wood, *Creation of the American Republic*, 499–504.

62. Beeman, *Plain, Honest Men*, 28–29; James Madison, "Vices of the Political System," Madison, "Term of the Senate," June 26, 1787, and Madison to Thomas Jefferson, Oct. 24, 1787, in Hutchinson et al., eds., *Papers of James Madison*, vol. 9:345–58 ("a rage"), vol. 10:76–78, and 205–20 ("No common interest"); Rakove, *Original Meanings*, 50–52; G. Wood, *Creation of the American Republic*, 504–5.

63. Beeman, *Plain, Honest Men*, 28–29; James Madison, "Vices of the Political System," and Madison, "Term of the Senate," June 26, 1787, in Hutchinson et al., eds., *Papers of James Madison*, vol. 9:356–57 ("extract"), vol. 10:76–78, and 263–70 ("who possess"); Kornblith and Murrin, "Making and Unmaking," 55–56; G. Wood, *Creation of the American Republic*, 505–18.

64. Beeman, *Plain, Honest Men*, 18–21, Congress quoted on 20; Berkin, *Brilliant Solution*, 24–25; James Madison to Thomas Jefferson, Oct. 24, 1787, in Hutchinson et al., eds., *Papers of James Madison*, vol. 10:212 (all Madison quotations); G. Wood, *Creation of the American Republic*, 327, 473.

65. Berkin, *Brilliant Solution*, 177; Bouton, *Taming Democracy*, 172; Holton, *Unruly Americans*, 14–15, 162–63; David Ramsay quoted in R. Klein, *Unification of a Slave State*, 165; Kornblith and Murrin, "Making and Unmaking," 54–56; Elbridge Gerry and Roger Sherman quoted in R. Morris, *Forging of the Union*, 278–79; Nadelhaft, "'Snarls of Invidious Animals,'" 88–89; Charles Carroll quoted in Rakove, *Revolutionaries*, 188; Richards, *Shays's Rebellion*, 133–34.

66. David Ramsay to Thomas Jefferson, Apr. 7, 1787, in Boyd et al., eds., *Papers of Thomas Jefferson*, vol. 11:280; Madison, "Term of the Senate," June 26, 1787, in Hutchinson et al., eds., *Papers of James Madison*, vol. 10:76–78.

67. Beemen, *Plain, Honest Men*, 44–52, 65, 91–92, Patrick Henry quoted on 92; Berkin, *Brilliant Solution*, 118–19; Bouton, *Taming Democracy*, 176–77; R. Morris, *Forging of the Union*, 257, 269–75; Polishook, *Rhode Island*, 184–85.

68. Beemen, *Plain, Honest Men*, 29–33; Berkin, *Brilliant Solution*, 32–35; Breen, *George Washington's Journey*, 86–88; Flexner, *George Washington*, 86–95, 102–11; Longmore, *Invention of George Washington*, 179–83; Maier, *Ratification*, 1–7, 17–26.

69. Beeman, *Plain, Honest Men*, 58–60, 64–68, 180–81; Kornblith and Murrin, "Making and Unmaking," 54; R. Morris, *Forging of the Union*, 268–75; Noll, *America's God*, 164–65.

70. Beeman, *Plain, Honest Men*, 68–69, 82–84, 177–80, 360, James Madison quoted on 83; R. Morris, *Forging of the Union*, 276–77; Rakove, *Revolutionaries*, 367–68; Van Dorn, *Grand Rehearsal*, 23–29; Waldstreicher, *Slavery's Constitution*, 71–72.

71. Beeman, *Plain, Honest Men*, 55–57, 60–63; R. Morris, *Forging of the Union*, 257; Rakove, *Revolutionaries*, 367–68.

72. Benjamin Franklin quoted in Beeman, *Plain, Honest Men*, 360; William Lewis quoted in Rossiter, *Grand Convention*, 233 ("Grumbletonian").

73. Beeman, *Plain, Honest Men*, 42–43, 52–53, 86–91, Edmund Randolph quoted on 89; E. S. Morgan, *Inventing the People*, 270–71; Rakove, *Original Meanings*, 59–61; Rakove, *Revolutionaries*, 360–61, 366–67; Waldstreicher, *Slavery's Constitution*, 72–74; G. Wood, *Creation of the American Republic*, 467, 524–26.

74. Beeman, *Plain, Honest Men*, 148–49, William Paterson quoted on 148 ("idea" and "We have no power") and 149 ("She would be swallowed up"), 160–62; Hendrickson, *Peace Pact*, 221–23; Rakove, *Revolutionaries*, 368–75.

75. Beeman, *Plain, Honest Men*, 164–70; R. Elkins and McKitrick, *Age of Federalism*, 104–5; Raphael, *Mr. President*, 68–72; James Madison, "Version of Hamilton's Speech," June 18, 1787, and Robert Yates, "Version of Alexander Hamilton's Speech," June 18, 1787, in Syrett, ed., *Papers of Alexander Hamilton*, vol. 4:187–95 ("The British Government" and "the mass"), 195–202 ("all communities divide" and "The general power").

76. Beeman, *Plain, Honest Men*, 169–70, William Samuel Johnson quoted on 170 ("had been praised"); Holton, *Unruly Americans*, 191–93; Raphael, *Mr. President*, 72–76; Rossiter, *Grand Convention*, 178; A. Young, *Liberty Tree*, 183–85, 198, Pierce Butler quoted on 199.

77. Beeman, *Plain, Honest Men*, 170–89, 200–204, Gunning Bedford quoted on

184, Gouverneur Morris quoted on 204; Berkin, *Brilliant Solution*, 102–12; Hendrickson, *Peace Pact*, 223–25, 240; Rakove, *Original Meanings*, 67–69; Rakove, *Revolutionaries*, 368–77.

78. Beeman, *Plain, Honest Men*, 218–25; Berkin, *Brilliant Solution*, 112–13; Bouton, *Taming Democracy*, 177–78; Holton, *Unruly Americans*, 8–9, 182–84; R. Morris, *Forging of the Union*, 281–83; Rakove, *Original Meanings*, 69–70; Van Cleve, "Anti-Federalists' Toughest Challenge," 545–47, Roger Sherman quoted on 546.

79. Beeman, *Plain, Honest Men*, 153–55; Greene, *Imperatives*, 328–30, 335–39; Hendrickson, *Peace Pact*, 225–26; Van Cleve, *Slaveholders' Union*, 103–5, 113–14; Pierce Butler quoted in Waldstreicher, *Slavery's Constitution*, 86.

80. Beeman, *Plain, Honest Men*, 206–15, 310–17, Gouverneur Morris quoted on 316–17; Hendrickson, *Peace Pact*, 232–34; Waldstreicher, *Slavery's Constitution*, 77–78.

81. Hendrickson, *Peace Pact*, 226–31; R. Morris, *Forging of the Union*, 283–84; Rakove, *Revolutionaries*, 371–74; Van Cleve, *Slaveholders' Union*, 115–17; Waldstreicher, *Slavery's Constitution*, 79–87.

82. Beeman, *Plain, Honest Men*, 319–27, James Madison quoted on 327; Hendrickson, *Peace Pact*, 234–35; R. Morris, *Forging of the Union*, 285–86; Waldstreicher, *Slavery's Constitution*, 93–98.

83. Beeman, *Plain, Honest Men*, 325–29; Finkelman, "Making a Covenant with Death," 217–21; Hendrickson, *Peace Pact*, 235–37; Jensen, "Sovereign States," 241–47; Waldstreicher, *Slavery's Constitution*, 97–100; Wiecek, "Witch at the Christening," 180–81.

84. Beeman, *Plain, Honest Men*, 326–34; Berkin, *Brilliant Solution*, 113–14; Hendrickson, *Peace Pact*, 237–39; Oliver Ellsworth quoted in Rossiter, *Grand Convention*, 217.

85. Beeman, *Plain, Honest Men*, 329–30; Davis, *Problem of Slavery*, 125–26; Charles Cotesworth Pinckney quoted in Finkelman, "Making a Covenant with Death," 224 ("We have obtained"); Meranze, "Hargrave's Nightmare," 219–38; Rakove, *Original Meanings*, 70–73; Van Cleve, "Founding a Slaveholders' Union," 122, 129–31; Waldstreicher, *Slavery's Constitution*, 3–19, 141–45. For the greater relative weight of the South in the union than in the empire, see Van Cleve, *Slaveholders' Union*, 41.

86. Beeman, *Plain, Honest Men*, 212–15, 327–35, John Dickinson quoted on 215, Luther Martin quoted on 327 ("anxiously sought"); Rossiter, *Grand Convention*, 266–69; Waldstreicher, *Slavery's Constitution*, 85–86, 99–100.

87. Beeman, *Plain, Honest Men*, 330–36; Finkelman, "Making a Covenant with Death," 190–93; R. Morris, *Forging of the Union*, 286–87; Rossiter, *Grand Convention*, 266–69; Van Cleve, *Slaveholders' Union*, 19; Waldstreicher, *Slavery's Constitution*, 101–5; Wiecek, "Witch at the Christening," 181–84.

88. Beeman, *Plain, Honest Men*, 323–29, Oliver Ellsworth quoted on 325;

Samuel Hopkins quoted in D. B. Davis, *Problem of Slavery*, 299 ("state of anarchy"); Hendrickson, "Escaping Insecurity," 223–24; Hopkins quoted in Zilversmit, *First Emancipation*, 156 ("How does it").

89. Beeman, *Plain, Honest Men*, 240–55, 299–307; Berkin, *Brilliant Solution*, 116–48, 178; R. Klein, *Unification of a Slave State*, 166; Rakove, *Revolutionaries*, 379–80; G. Wood, *Empire of Liberty*, 72–73.

90. Beeman, *Plain, Honest Men*, 253; Berkin, *Brilliant Solution*, 116–48; R. Morris, *Forging of the Union*, 287–91, George Mason quoted on 288; Rakove, *Revolutionaries*, 379–80; Rossiter, *Grand Convention*, 218–24.

91. Beeman, *Plain, Honest Men*, 236–39, 349–52; R. Morris, *Forging of the Union*, 291–92.

92. Beeman, *Plain, Honest Men*, 355–68, George Mason quoted on 355–56 ("would end"), Elbridge Gerry quoted on 364; Berkin, *Brilliant Solution*, 160–68; Maier, *Ratification*, 39–49, Mason quoted on 43 ("sooner chop"); R. Morris, *Forging of the Union*, 275, 296–97; Rossiter, *Grand Convention*, 232–37; Waldstreicher, *Slavery's Constitution*, 99–101.

93. George Washington to Benjamin Harrison, Sept. 24, 1787, in Abbot et al., eds., *Papers of George Washington, Confederation Series*, vol. 5:339–40 ("the best"); Beeman, *Plain, Honest Men*, 355–68; James Madison to Thomas Jefferson, Sept. 6, 1787, in Hutchinson, et al., eds., *Papers of James Madison*, vol. 10:163–65; Maier, *Ratification*, 36–39; Rakove, *Revolutionaries*, 381–84, 414–15; Alexander Hamilton, "Remarks on Signing the Constitution," Sept. 17, 1787, in Syrett, ed., *Papers of Alexander Hamilton*, vol. 4:253.

94. Beeman, *Plain, Honest Men*, 375, 380–81, 407–8; Berkin, *Brilliant Solution*, 175–77; Cornell, *Other Founders*, 162; Hendrickson, "Escaping Insecurity," 221–23; Holton, *Unruly Americans*, 250–51; Maier, *Ratification*, 157; Van Cleve, "Anti-Federalists' Toughest Challenge," 554–55; G. Wood, *Creation of the American Republic*, 527–30, 543–47, James Madison quoted on 529; A. Young, *Liberty Tree*, 208.

95. Beeman, *Plain, Honest Men*, 377–78, 387; Bouton, *Taming Democracy*, 187–88, 191–94; Cornell, *Other Founders*, 22–34, 40–42, 48–49; Holton, *Unruly Americans*, 236–37; Amos Singletary quoted in Maier, *Ratification*, 185–86; Main, *Anti-Federalists*, 253–54; Rufus King quoted in Richards, *Shays's Rebellion*, 143; A. Young, *Liberty Tree*, 203–4.

96. Beeman, *Plain, Honest Men*, 408–10; Berkin, *Brilliant Solution*, 176–77; Holton, *Unruly Americans*, 9–10, 235–36; R. Klein, *Unification of a Slave State*, 168–69; Kornblith & Murrin, "Making and Unmaking," 55–56; Nadelhaft, "'Snarls of Invidious Animals,'" 89–90. In 1913, an amendment to the Constitution allowed for the popular election of United States senators.

97. Bouton, *Taming Democracy*, 178–79; George Mason quoted in Holton, *Unruly Americans*, 167; E. S. Morgan, *Inventing the People*, 272–79; Patrick Henry quoted in G. Wood, *Creation of the American Republic*, 507.

98. Beeman, *Plain, Honest Men*, 372–73, 382; Cornell, *Other Founders*, 30–31; James Lincoln quoted in R. Klein, *Unification of a Slave State*, 168 ("What"); Maier, *Ratification*, 413; G. Wood, *Creation of the American Republic*, 519–23, Richard Henry Lee quoted on 469.

99. Lepore, *A Is for American*, 27; Charles Tillinghast quoted in Main, *Anti-Federalists*, 238 ("You would be"); E. S. Morgan, *Inventing the People*, 267–68; G. Wood, *Creation of the American Republic*, 523–31, 562–64, James Wilson quoted on 531 ("How comes it").

100. Beeman, *Plain, Honest Men*, 380–81; Bouton, *Taming Democracy*, 182; Haselby, *Origins*, 1; Jensen, "Sovereign States," 226–28, Fisher Ames quoted on 228 ("Instead of feeling"); Lepore, *A Is for American*, 27–31; Murrin, "Roof Without Walls," 341–48; Alexander Hamilton, "Federalist No. 8," Nov. 20, 1787, in Syrett, ed, *Papers of Alexander Hamilton*, vol. 4:326–32 ("If we should be disunited").

101. James Madison, "Jay's Treaty, [Apr. 6] 1796," in Hutchinson et al., eds., *Papers of James Madison*, vol. 16:290–301 ("was nothing more"); Rakove, *Original Meanings*, 339–65.

102. Beeman, *Plain, Honest Men*, 293–95, 391–92; Holton, *Unruly Americans*, 180–81, James Wilson quoted on 180; James Madison, "Method of Ratifying the Constitution," in Hutchinson et al., eds., *Papers of James Madison*, vol. 10:160 ("The people"); Maier, *Ratification*, 223–24; Main, *Anti-Federalists*, 212–13, 249; E. S. Morgan, *Inventing the People*, 280–82; Rakove, *Original Meanings*, 99–112, 128–9; G. Wood, *Creation of the American Republic*, 532–36, unnamed Federalists quoted on 534 ("All power").

103. Beeman, *Plain, Honest Men*, 370–71, 374–75; Maier, *Ratification*, 55–56, 430–31; Main, *Anti-Federalists*, 255–56; Rakove, *Original Meanings*, 114–16.

104. Cornell, *Other Founders*, 58–59; Holton, *Unruly Americans*, 252–53, 256–58; Maier, *Ratification*, 56–57, Charles Cotesworth Pinckney quoted on 249 ("we should make"); Main, *Anti-Federalists*, 158–61; E. S. Morgan, *Inventing the People*, 282–83; G. Wood, *Creation of the American Republic*, 536–43.

105. Beeman, *Plain, Honest Men*, 394; Holton, *Unruly Americans*, 249–50; Main, *Anti-Federalists*, 252–54, George Minot quoted on 202 ("to *pack*").

106. Bouton, *Taming Democracy*, 172–73, 179–81; Holton, *Unruly Americans*, 227–32, 239–40; Main, *Anti-Federalists*, 191–92; Van Cleve, "Anti-Federalists' Toughest Challenge," 533.

107. Beeman, *Plain, Honest Men*, 370–74, Hugh Ledlie quoted on 384 ("have got"); Berkin, *Brilliant Solution*, 174–76; Melancton Smith quoted in Holton, *Unruly Americans*, 237 ("The great"); Main, Anti-Federalists 252–54; G. Wood, *Creation of the American Republic*, 485–87.

108. Beeman, *Plain, Honest Men*, 410–11; Main, *Anti-Federalists*, 192–93, 204, 252–54; G. Wood, *Creation of the American Republic*, 485–87.

109. Beeman, *Plain, Honest Men*, 378–79; Aedanus Burke quoted in R. Klein, *Unification of a Slave State*, 170–71; Maier, *Ratification*, 163–65; Main, *Anti-Federalists*, 190, 205, 256–57; Richards, *Shays's Rebellion*, 143; A. Young, *Liberty Tree*, 61–66, 206–8.

110. Beeman, *Plain, Honest Men*, 406–8; Berkin, *Brilliant Solution*, 172–74; Bouton, *Taming Democracy*, 181; Holton, *Unruly Americans*, 249–52; Main, *Anti-Federalists*, 249–52; Rakove, *Revolutionaries*, 387–90, 415–17.

111. Bouton, *Taming Democracy*, 182–83; Holton, *Unruly Americans*, 237–38.

112. Beeman, *Plain, Honest Men*, 375–77, 379; Bouton, *Taming Democracy*, 180–81; George Minot quoted in Holton, *Unruly Americans*, 252 ("Never"); Main, *Anti-Federalists*, 187–88, Minot quoted on 202 ("*Bad* measures").

113. Beeman, *Plain, Honest Men*, 382–85; Maier, *Ratification*, 413; Main, Anti-Federalist, 187–220, 252–55.

114. Beeman, *Plain, Honest Men*, 386–91; Maier, *Ratification*, 155–213; Main, *Anti-Federalists*, 200–209; Richards, *Shays's Rebellion*, 143–50; Szatmary, Shays' *Rebellion*, 133.

115. Beeman, *Plain, Honest Men*, 392–97, 401; R. Klein, *Unification of a Slave State*, 167–70; Maier, *Ratification*, 214–17.

116. Beeman, *Old Dominion*, 7–8; Einhorn, "Patrick Henry's Case," 549–73; Thomas Jefferson to James Madison, Dec. 8, 1784, in Hutchinson et al., eds., *Papers of James Madison*, vol. 8:177–80 ("devoutly pray"); Jefferson to William Wirt, Aug. 4, 1805 ("greatest orator"), Founders Online, National Archives (http://founders.archives.gov/documents/Jefferson/99-01-02-2187); Maier, *Ratification*, 225–37, 241–53, 314–16, 320–26; Main, *Anti-Federalists*, 213–42; Waldstreicher, *Slavery's Constitution*, 144.

117. Beeman, *Plain, Honest Men*, 395–400; Beeman, *Old Dominion*, 3–13; D. B. Davis, *Problem of Slavery*, 125–26; McCoy, "James Madison and Visions," 226–32, 244–47; Maier, *Ratification*, 255–314; Shalhope, *John Taylor*, 50–57; Van Cleve, "Founding a Slaveholders' Union," 129–31; Waldstreicher, *Slavery's Constitution*, 3–19, 141–45.

118. Beeman, *Plain, Honest Men*, 400–403; Maier, *Ratification*, 327–400; Main, *Anti-Federalists*, 233–41; Morris, *Forging of the Union*, 312–13; Van Cleve, "Anti-Federalists" Toughest Challenge," 555–56.

119. Beeman, *Plain, Honest Men*, 403–5; Maier, *Ratification*, 403–23; Main, *Anti-Federalists*, 242–48; Morris, *Forging of the Union*, 315–16.

120. Bouton, *Taming Democracy*, 192–93; Maier, *Ratification*, 429–38; Morris, *Forging of the Union*, 316–17, John Quincy Adams quoted on 317.

121. George Washington to James Madison, Sept. 23, 1788, in Hutchinson et al., eds., *Papers of James Madison*, vol. 11:261–62. For the modern cult of the perfect Federal Constitution, see Kammen, *Machine That Would Go of Itself*, 3–39; Lepore, *Whites of their Eyes*, 112–13, 118–25.

CHAPTER 11: PARTISANS

1. George Washington to Henry Lee, Sept. 22, 1788, in Abbott, et al., eds., *Papers of George Washington, Confederation Series*, vol. 6:529.
2. Thomas Jefferson to Spencer Roane, Sept. 6, 1819, Founders Online, National Archives (http:/founders.archives.gov/documents/Jeffer son/98-01-02-0734).
3. George Washington to John Jay, Aug. 15, 1786, in Abbott et al., eds., *Papers of George Washington, Confederation Series*, vol. 4:212–13 ("I do not"); Hendrickson, "Escaping Insecurity," 221; Alexander Hamilton, "New York Ratifying Convention Remarks," June 24, 1788, in Syrett, ed., *Papers of Alexander Hamilton*, vol. 5:67–74 ("a principle").
4. Hendrickson, "Escaping Insecurity," 221–25; Opal, "Republic in the World," 598–600; Henry Lee to James Madison, Mar. 13, 1790, and Apr. 13, 1790, in Hutchinson et al., eds., *Papers of James Madison*, vol. 13:102–3, 136–37 ("submit").
5. John Adams to Benjamin Rush, June 21, 1811 ("best actor"), Founders Online, National Archives (http://founders.archives.gov/documents/ Adams/99-02-02-5649); Beeman, *Plain, Honest Men*, 412–17; Breen, *George Washington's Journey*, 1–5; Diego de Gardoqui quoted in DuVal, *Independence Lost*, 339 ("this nation"); Ferling, *Leap in the Dark*, 310–12; Longmore, *Invention of George Washington*, 181–82; Alexander Hamilton to George Washington, Aug. 13, 1788, in Syrett, ed., *Papers of Alexander Hamilton*, vol. 5:201–2 ("It is to little purpose"); George Washington to Henry Knox, Apr. 1, 1789, in Rhodehamel, ed., *Washington, Writings*, 726 ("a culprit"); G. Wood, *Empire of Liberty*, 78, 85–86.
6. Chernow, *Washington*, 559–71; Elkins and McKitrick, *Age of Federalism*, 43–46; Ferling, *Leap in the Dark*, 308–13; James McHenry to George Washington, Mar. 29, 1789, in Abbott et al., eds., *Papers of George Washington, Presidential Series*, vol. 1:461 ("You are now"); G. Wood, *Empire of Liberty*, 55–56, 64–65, Robert Livingston quoted on 64–65 ("Long Live"), 74–75.
7. John Adams to George Washington, May 17, 1789, Abbott et al., eds., *Papers of George Washington, Presidential Series*, vol. 2:314 ("Neither Dignity"); Thomas Jefferson to James Madison, July 29, 1789, in Boyd et al., eds., *Papers of Thomas Jefferson*, vol. 15:315–16; G. Wood, *Empire of Liberty*, 72–76.
8. Longmore, *Invention of George Washington*, 208–10, Washington Irving quoted on 209–10; G. Wood, *Empire of Liberty*, 1–2; Zagarri, "American Revolution," 485–86.
9. George Washington to David Stuart, July 26, 1789, in Abbott et al., eds., *Papers of George Washington, Presidential Series*, vol. 3:322 ("to preserve");

Chernow, *Washington*, 576–79; Freeman, *Affairs of Honor*, 45–46, 52–53, 74–75; Waldstreicher, *In the Midst of Perpetual Fetes*, 118–22; G. Wood, *Empire of Liberty*, 76–85. For Washington's national tours, see Breen, *George Washington's Journey*.

10. Thomas Jefferson to Thomas Paine, June 19, 1792, in Boyd et al., eds., *Papers of Thomas Jefferson*, vol. 20:312–13 ("panting after"); Ferling, *Leap in the Dark*, 332–35, 340–41; Freeman, *Affairs of Honor*, 14–15, 74–76; G. Wood, *Empire of Liberty*, 84–85, William Maclay quoted on 84.

11. James Madison to Edmund Randolph, Mar. 1, 1789, and May 31, 1789, and Madison to Thomas Jefferson, June 30, 1789, in Hutchinson et al., eds., *Papers of James Madison*, vol. 11: 453–54 ("contentions"), vol. 12:190 ("Scarcely"), 267–72 ("in a wilderness"); Rakove, "Structure of Politics," 286–87; G. Wood, *Empire of Liberty*, 55–62.

12. James Madison to Richard Peters, Aug. 19, 1789, in Hutchinson et al., eds., *Papers of James Madison*, vol. 12:346–47 ("nauseous project," "kill," and "enable"); Ketcham, *James Madison*, 289–92; Rakove, *Revolutionaries*, 393–95; G. Wood, *Empire of Liberty*, 71–72.

13. Cornell, *Other Founders*, 158–63, Aedanus Burke quoted on 162; R. Ellis, "Persistence of Antifederalism," 297–99; Holton, *Unruly Americans*, 256–58; Maier, *Ratification*, 446–56, 459–64; Morris, *Forging of the Union*, 317–20; William Grayson quoted in G. Wood, *Empire of Liberty*, 71 ("calculated" and "personal liberty").

14. Maier, *Ratification*, 457–59; Morris, *Forging of the Union*, 315–16, Polishook, *Rhode Island*, 207–30.

15. Chernow, *Washington*, 622–23, George Washington quoted on 624; Egerton, *Death or Slavery*, 253–54; Ketcham, *James Madison*, 315; Nash, *Race and Revolution*, 38–40, antislavery petition quoted on 40 ("without distinction"); Parkinson, "Manifest Signs of Passion,'" 49–50, petition quoted on 50 ("this Inconsistency").

16. Chernow, *Washington*, 623–24; Egerton, *Death or Slavery*, 254–55; Madison quoted in Ketcham, *James Madison*, 315–16; Nash, *Race and Revolution*, 38–42, James Jackson quoted on 39 ("blow the trumpet"); Parkinson, "'Manifest Signs of Passion,'"49–68, William Loughton Smith quoted on 50 ("persecution"); R. Smith, *Civic Ideals*, 142–43.

17. Richards, *Slave Power*, 71–72; Robinson, *Slavery in the Structure*, 285–90; R. Smith, *Civic Ideals*, 143–44; Van Cleve, "Founding a Slaveholders' Union," 130–32.

18. Litwack, *North of Slavery*, 33–34, George Thacher quoted on 34; Nash, *Race and Revolution*, 77–79; Newman, *Freedom's Prophet*, 146–48, Georgia congressman quoted on 148.

19. Chernow, *Washington*, 595–605; Elkins and McKitrick, *Age of Federalism*, 50–58; Ferling, *Leap in the Dark*, 309–13; G. Wood, *Empire of Liberty*, 86–88.

20. Chernow, *Alexander Hamilton*, 288–92; Elkins and McKitrick, *Age of Federalism*, 95, 114–16; Ferling, *Leap in the Dark*, 315–18; Freeman, *Affairs of Honor*, 55–56, 160–61; G. Wood, *Empire of Liberty*, 89–94, William Maclay quoted on 92 ("Mr. Hamilton"), 108–9.

21. Ferling, *Leap in the Dark*, 316, 318–21; Elkins and McKitrick, *Age of Federalism*, 114–23, 297–304; Alexander Hamilton, "Fact No. 1," Sept. 11, 1792, in Syrett, ed., *Papers of Alexander Hamilton*, vol. 12:361–65 ("national blessing"); G. Wood, *Empire of Liberty*, 92–109; Zagarri, "American Revolution," 486–87.

22. Thomas Jefferson, "Account of the Bargain on the Assumption and Residence Bills," in Boyd et al., eds., *Papers of Thomas Jefferson*, vol. 17:205–7 (contains quotations); Elkins and McKittrick, *Age of Federalism*, 154–61; Ferling, *Leap in the Dark*, 323–28.

23. Chernow, *Washington*, 630–33; G. Wood, *Empire of Liberty*, 139–44; Zagarri, "American Revolution," 487.

24. Chernow, *Washington*, 636–39; Fehrenbacher, *Slaveholding Republic*, 59; Nash and Soderlund, *Freedom by Degrees*, 123; George Washington to Tobias Lear, Apr. 12, 1791, in Abbott et al., eds., *George Washington Papers, Presidential Series*, vol. 8:85 ("I wish").

25. Chernow, *Washington*, 662–63, 794–95; R. B. Davis, ed., *Jeffersonian America*, 49; Elkins and McKitrick, *Age of Federalism*, 171–82; McNamara, "Republican Art and Architecture," 514; G. Wood, *Empire of Liberty*, 79–80, 288–91; Yokota, *Unbecoming British*, 227.

26. Cayton, *Frontier Republic*, 12–32; Hinderaker, *Elusive Empires*, 253–54; Merrell, "Declarations of Independence," 210; Nichols, *Red Gentlemen and White Savages*, 180–85, Arthur St. Clair quoted on 185; Onuf, "Settlers, Settlements, and New States," 173–80, 185–87, 190–91; Rohrbough, *Land Office Business*, 15–19.

27. Henry Knox, report, Jan. 22, 1791, *American State Papers, Indian Affairs*, vol. 1:112; Cayton, "'Radicals in the Western World,'" 80–82; Nichols, *Red Gentlemen and White Savages*, 98–127; Onuf, "Settlers, Settlements, and New States," 171–72.

28. Henry Knox report, Dec. 26, 1791, in Abbott et al., eds., *Papers of George Washington, Presidential Series*, vol. 9:318; Nichols, *Red Gentlemen and White Savages*, 125–26, 139–40; R. White, *Middle Ground* 454.

29. Cayton, *Frontier Republic*, 12–32; Ferguson, *Power of the Purse*, 289–343; D. Jones, *License for Empire*, 163; M. Rohrbough, *Land Office Business*, 15.

30. DuVal, *Independence Lost*, 335–36, for "Miro District" see 335; Onuf, "Expanding Union," 59–60; Onuf, "Settlers, Settlements, and New States," 183.

31. Henry Knox, report, June 15, 1789, *American State Papers, Indian Affairs*, vol. 1:113; Arthur St. Clair to George Washington, Aug. 1789, in C. Carter,

ed., *Territorial Papers*, vol. 2:212; Cayton, *Frontier Republic*, 12–50; Onuf, "Liberty, Development, and Union," 179–213.

32. Henry Knox, reports, June 15, 1789, July 7, 1789, and Jan. 4, 1790, *American State Papers, Indian Affairs*, vol. 1:12–14, 53–54, 60; Cayton, *Frontier Republic*, 18, 43; Cayton, "Radicals in the 'Western World,'" 77–96; Hendrickson, "Escaping Insecurity," 225–27; D. Jones, *License for Empire*, 157–79; Horsman, "Indian Policy," 39–44, 47; Nichols, *Red Gentlemen and White Savages*, 81–84, 106–8, 113–14.

33. DuVal, *Independence Lost*, 295–309; Nicholas, *Red Gentlemen and White Savages*, 118–27; Ritcheson, *Aftermath of Revolution*, 174–76.

34. Henry Knox, reports, June 15, 1789, and July 7, 1789, *American State Papers, Indian Affairs*, vol. 1:12–14, 53–54; Horsman, "Indian Policy," 44–47; Prucha, *Great Father, 60.*

35. R. White, *Middle Ground*, 467–68; J. L. Wright, *Britain and the American Frontier*, 95–97; Zeisberger, *Diary*, vol. 2:378.

36. Timothy Pickering to Anthony Wayne, Apr. 15, 1795, in Knopf, ed., *Anthony Wayne*, 407; Nugent, *Habits of Empire*, 47, 53; R. White, *Middle Ground*, 474–75; G. Wood, *Empire of Liberty*, 130–31.

37. Cook, *Flood Tide of Empire*, 132, 169–75; Gould, *Among the Powers*, 124, 165; Servando Teresa de Mier quoted in Liss, *Atlantic Empires*, 190 ("will become"); Weber, *Spanish Frontier*, 285–88.

38. Din, "Spain's Immigration Policy," 266–67; Faber, *Building the Land of Dreams*, 39–40; Foley, *Genesis of Missouri*, 76–78; Liss, *Atlantic Empires*, 147–48; Weber, *Spanish Frontier*, 274–75, 289–90.

39. Nichols, *Red Gentlemen and White Savages*, 171–76; J. L. Wright, *Britain and the American Frontier*, 92–98.

40. Faber, *Building the Land of Dreams*, 40–42; Foley, *Genesis of Missouri*, 77, 80–92; Zenon Trudeau to Manuel Gayoso de Lemos, Jan. 15, 1798, in Houck, ed., *Spanish Regime in Missouri*, vol. 2:247–56; Nasatir, *Borderland in Retreat*, 38; A. Taylor, "'Great Change Begins,'" 265–90; G. Wood, *Empire of Liberty*, 316–17, traveler quoted on 316 ("The woods").

41. Edling and Kaplanoff, "Alexander Hamilton's Fiscal Reforms," 713–44; Elkins and McKitrick, *Age of Federalism*, 439–41, 443, 842–43, *Columbian Centinel* quoted on 441; G. Wood, *Empire of Liberty*, 200–202.

42. Thomas Jefferson to George Washington, May 23, 1792, and Sept. 9, 1792, in Boyd et al., eds., *Papers of Thomas Jefferson*, vol. 23:535–40 (quotation on 539: "That the ultimate object"), and vol. 24:351–59; Elkins and McKitrick, *Age of Federalism*, 265–70; Benjamin Rush to James Madison, Mar. 10, 1790, in Hutchinson et al., eds., *Papers of James Madison*, vol. 13:97–99 ("I sicken"); G. Wood, *Empire of Liberty*, 140–41.

43. Elkins and McKitrick, *Age of Federalism*, 282–92; Ferling, *Leap in the Dark*, 334–40.

44. Thomas Jefferson, "Notes of Cabinet Meeting," Aug. 2, 1793, in Boyd et al,

eds., *Papers of Thomas Jefferson*, vol. 26:601–3; Elkins and McKitrick, *Age of Federalism*, 443; Ferling, *Leap in the Dark*, 345–46; Macleod, "Thomas Paine," 215–17; G. Wood, *Empire of Liberty*, 155–58, 198–201.

45. Appleby, *Inheriting the Revolution*, 26–27, Fisher Ames quoted on 32; Jedediah Morse quoted in Banner, *To the Hartford Convention*, 57 ("There must be"); Bouton, "William Findley," 239–41; Elkins and McKitrick, *Age of Federalism*, 19–29, 750–52; Fischer, *Revolution*, 1–17, 250–51; Rakove, "Structure of Politics," 279–84; A. Taylor, "From Fathers to Friends of the People," 465–91; Alexander Hamilton to George Washington, Sept. 9, 1792, in Abbott et al., eds., *Papers of George Washington, Presidential Series*, vol. 11:91–94 ("who"); G. Wood, *Empire of Liberty*, 105–10, 162–64, 203.

46. Alexander Hamilton to Rufus King, May 4, 1796, in Syrett, ed., *Papers of Alexander Hamilton*, vol. 20:158–59 ("made our election"); A. Taylor, "From Fathers to Friends," 465–91; New York handbill quoted in G. Wood, *Empire of Liberty*, 336 ("who acts").

47. Appleby, *Capitalism*, 51–53, 70–78, 90–94; Fischer, *Revolution*, 197–99; Shankman, *Crucible of American Democracy*, 3–8, *Philadelphia Aurora* quoted on 3 ("that happy"); Zagarri, "American Revolution," 492–94.

48. Ben-Atar and Oberg, "Introduction," 9–11; Cotlar, *Tom Paine's America*, 65–67; Egerton, "Empire of Liberty," 309–30; Sidbury, "Thomas Jefferson," 199–201; Zagarri, "American Revolution," 495–96.

49. Onuf, *Jefferson's Empire*, 53–56, 83, 95.

50. Appleby, *Inheriting the Revolution*, 27–28, 35; James Fenimore Cooper quoted in A. Taylor, *William Cooper's Town*, 297; William Bentley and an unnamed Federalist, quoted in G. Wood, *Empire of Liberty*, 333 ("parties," and "Another God Damned").

51. Appleby, *Inheriting the Revolution*, 30–31, 41–45; Freeman, *Affairs of Honor*, 167–80; Gorham Worth quoted in A. Taylor, *William Cooper's Town*, 367–68 ("a tumultuous sea"); Warren, *Jacobin and Junto*, 183–214; G. Wood, *Empire of Liberty*, 333–34, South Carolinian quoted on 333 ("Three-fourths").

52. "Marcellus," *Albany Centinel*, Apr. 1, 1800; Buel, *Securing the Revolution*, ix–xii, 91–92; Elkins and McKitrick, *Age of Federalism*, 263–64; Freeman, *Affairs of Honor*, 1–10; Howe, "Republican Thought," 147–51; Edmund Randolph to George Washington, July 30, 1794, in Abbott et al., eds., *Papers of George Washington, Presidential Series*, vol. 16:523–30 ("It is a fact"); G. Wood, *Empire of Liberty*, 162–63.

53. *Massachusetts Mercury* quoted in Appleby, *Inheriting the Revolution*, 28 ("Naturally"); Thomas Jefferson to Francis Hopkinson, Mar. 13, 1789, Jefferson to William B. Giles, Dec. 31, 1795, in Boyd et al., eds., *Papers of Thomas Jefferson*, vol. 14:650 ("If I could not go"), vol. 28:565–67 ("the parties of"), and Jefferson to William Duane, Mar. 28, 1811, in Looney et al., eds., *Papers of Thomas Jefferson, Retirement Series*, vol. 3:506–9 ("the

republicans"); Buel, *Securing the Revolution*, 91–92; Howe, "Republican Thought," 147–65; Lepore, *A Is for American*, 25–26; G. Wood, *Empire of Liberty*, 160–61.

54. Bouton, *Taming Democracy*, 236–37, Regulators quoted on 236 ("industrious men"); Bouton, "William Findley," 233–40; Elkins and McKitrick, *Age of Federalism*, 461–62; Slaughter, *Whiskey Rebellion*, 127–35; G. Wood, *Empire of Liberty*, 134–35.

55. Bouton, *Taming Democracy*, 224–26, 230–38; Bouton, "William Findley," 241–47; Elkins and McKitrick, *Age of Federalism*, 462–63; Slaughter, *Whiskey Rebellion*, 164–69, 177–89; G. Wood, *Empire of Liberty*, 135–36.

56. Bouton, "William Findley," 239–40; Elkins and McKitrick, *Age of Federalism*, 463–65; 476–82; George Washington, address to Congress, Nov. 19, 1794, in Rhodehamel, ed., *George Washington, Writings*, 887–95; Slaughter, *Whiskey Rebellion*, 133–35, *Gazette of the United States* quoted on 133–34 ("busy and restless" and "us back"); G. Wood, *Empire of Liberty*, 111, 136–38.

57. Bouton, *Taming Democracy*, 241–42; Elkins and McKitrick, *Age of Federalism*, 482–84; Slaughter, *Whiskey Rebellion*, 203–4, 206–20; G. Wood, *Empire of Liberty*, 138–39, Thomas Jefferson to James Monroe, May 26, 1795, in Boyd et al., eds., *Papers of Thomas Jefferson*, vol. 28:359 ("An insurrection").

58. Bouton, *Taming Democracy*, 241–42; Elkins and McKitrick, *Age of Federalism*, 466, 484–88; George Washington to Daniel Morgan, Oct. 8, 1794, in Abbott et al., eds., *Papers of George Washington, Presidential Series*, vol. 17:40 ("we may bid adieu"); Washington, annual message to Congress, Nov. 19, 1794, in Rhodehamel, ed., *George Washington: Writings*, 887–95, quotation on 893 ("combinations"); G. Wood, *Empire of Liberty*, 196–97, 203–4.

59. Blackburn, *Overthrow of Colonial Slavery*, 164–65; Gordon-Reed, *Hemingses of Monticello*, 468–69; Messer, "Feel the Terror," 23–25; G. Wood, *Empire of Liberty*, 174–75, 179–80.

60. Lepore, *A Is for American*, 42; J. Miller, *Crisis in Freedom*, 4–7; Popkin, "Liberty," 162–63; Waldstreicher, *In the Midst of Perpetual Fetes*, 126–28; G. Wood, *Empire of Liberty*, 175–79, 185–86; Zagarri, "American Revolution," 489–90.

61. Cotlar, *Thomas Paine's America*, 99; Elkins and McKitrick, *Age of Federalism*, 303–30; Perkins, *First Rapprochement*, 12–14; Popkin, "Liberty," 163–65; G. Wood, *Empire of Liberty*, 176–78; Zagarri, "American Revolution," 488–90.

62. Cotlar, *Tom Paine's America*, 86–88; Elkins and McKitrick, *Age of Federalism*, 336–54; Ferling, *Leap in the Dark*, 359–61; A. White, *Encountering Revolution*, 106–7; G. Wood, *Empire of Liberty*, 182–85.

63. Thomas Jefferson to William Carmichael, Dec. 15, 1787, Jefferson to George

Mason, Feb. 4, 1791, Jefferson to William Short, Jan. 3, 1793, Jefferson to Joseph Fay, Mar. 18, 1793, and Jefferson to Tench Coxe, May 1, 1794, in Boyd et al., eds., *Papers of Thomas Jefferson*, vol. 12:424, vol. 19:241 ("to that kind"), vol. 25:14 ("The liberty"), 402, and vol. 28:67; Bradburn, *Citizenship Revolution*, 16–17; Waldstreicher, *In the Midst of Perpetual Fetes*, 115–17; G. Wood, *Empire of Liberty*, 179–84; Zagarri, "American Revolution," 490.

64. Cotlar, *Tom Paine's America*, 82–114, David Osgood quoted on 93 ("foreign disorganizers"), Timothy Dwight quoted on 103 ("Holding"), Abraham Bishop quoted on 105 ("our declaration"); Lepore, *A Is for American*, 53–55; S. Newman, "Paine, Jefferson, and Revolutionary Radicalism," 79–81; G. Wood, *Empire of Liberty*, 177–79.

65. Curtin, *United Irishmen*, 2–4, 21–22, 25–31, 261–81; Durey, *Transatlantic Radicals*, 93–102, 116, 130–32; McDowell, "Age of the United Irishmen," 291–301, 349–63; Watson, *Reign of George III*, 302, 356–59, 397–99; Wickwire and Wickwire, *Cornwallis*, 221–29.

66. Bradburn, *Citizenship Revolution*, 148–67, 224–27, 233–34; Bric, "Irish Immigrant," 163–68; Carter, "Wild Irishman," 332–45; Whelan, "Green Atlantic," 225–28; D. Wilson, *United Irishmen*, Uriah Tracy quoted on 1 ("United Irishmen"), William Cobbett quoted on 45 ("every United Irishman"); Robert Goodloe Harper speech, June 19, 1798, *Annals of Congress*, 5th Congress, 2nd Session, 1991–92 ("The time").

67. Blackburn, *Overthrow*, 163–64; Dubois, "Unworthy of Liberty," 47–49; Dubois and Scott, "African Revolutionary," 148–51; Geggus, *Haitian Revolutionary Studies*, 5–6; A. White, *Encountering Revolution*, 10–11, 14–15.

68. Blackburn, "Achievement," 118–23; Blackburn, *Overthrow of Colonial Slavery*, 168–69, 175–76, 183–90; D. B. Davis, *Slavery in the Age of Revolution*, 140–44; Dubois, *Colony of Citizens*, 112–13; Geggus, *Haitian Revolutionary Studies*, 6–12; Popkin, "Liberty," 166–67; A. White, *Encountering Revolution*, 3–4, 15–16, 20.

69. Blackburn, *Overthrow of Colonial Slavery*, 195–200, 215–16; D. B. Davis, *Slavery in the Age of Revolution*, 144–45; Dubois, *Colony of Citizens*, 112–14, 155–56; Geggus, *Haitian Revolutionary Studies*, 7–8, 11–14; W. Jordan, *White over Black*, 376–77; Langley, *Americas in the Age of Revolution*, 106–14, 118; A. White, *Encountering Revolution*, 16–17.

70. Blackburn, *Overthrow of Colonial Slavery*, 224–26, 235–36; D. B. Davis, *Slavery in the Age of Revolution*, 145–47; Drescher, *Abolition*, 147–49, 160–62; Dubois, *Colony of Citizens*, 156–57, 166–67, 204–5; Dubois and Scott, "African Revolutionary," 142–43; Geggus, *Haitian Revolutionary Studies*, 15–16; 22; Popkin, "Liberty," 170–73; A. White, *Encountering Revolution*, 104.

71. Blackburn, "Achievement," 127–30; Blackburn, *Overthrow of Colonial Slavery*, 204–5, 218–22, 242–44; Dubois, *Colony of Citizens*, 295, 306–7;

Egerton, *Death or Liberty*, 269–70; Geggus, *Haitian Revolutionary Studies*, 15–25; Langley, *Americas in the Age of Revolution*, 118–23, A. White, *Encountering Revolution*, 162–63.

72. Blackburn, *Overthrow of Colonial* Slavery, 245–53; D. B. Davis, *Slavery in the Age of Revolution*, 150–51; Dubois, *Colony of Citizens*, 344–45, 366–73; Geggus, *Haitian Revolutionary Studies*, 25–26.

73. Blackburn, *Overthrow of Colonial* Slavery, 253–55; D. B. Davis, *Slavery in the Age of Revolution*, 151; Dubois, "Unworthy of Liberty," 46–47, 56–61; Geggus, *Haitian Revolutionary Studies*, 26–27; A. White, *Encountering Revolution*, 4.

74. W. Jordan, *White over Black*, 377–78; A. White, *Encountering Revolution*, 134–38, Abraham Bishop quoted on 135.

75. V. Brown, "Vapor of Dread," 195–96, Bryan Edwards quoted on 195 ("Horrors"); Dubois, "Unworthy of Liberty?" 45–46, 50–51, quote on 46 ("unworthy"); Hickey, "America's Response to the Slave Revolt," 361–79; W. Jordan, *White over Black*, 379–80, 394; Sidbury, "Saint Domingue in Virginia," 531–52; A. White, *Encountering Revolution*, 2–5, 206–7.

76. Dubois, *Avengers of the New World*, 305–6; Egerton, *Death or Liberty*, 263–64; Henry William DeSaussure quoted on 264 ("equality" and "ruin"); W. Jordan, *White over Black*, 386–91; Riley, "Slavery and the Problem of Democracy," 230–31; Rugemer, "Caribbean Slave Revolts," 95–97; A. White, *Encountering Revolution*, 2–3, 204–9.

77. Thomas Jefferson to James Monroe, July 14, 1793, in Boyd et al., eds., *Papers of Thomas Jefferson*, vol. 26:503 ("It is high time"); Thomas Jefferson to St. George Tucker, Aug. 28, 1797, in Lipscomb and Bergh, eds., *Writings of Thomas Jefferson*, vol. 9:417–19 ("But if something"); Hickey, "America's Response," 362–64; Sidbury, "Saint Domingue in Virginia," 531–52; D. Jordan, *Political Leadership*, 122.

78. John Randolph to Joseph H. Nicholson, Sept. 26, 1800, in Bruce, ed., *John Randolph*, vol. 2:250; Egerton, *Gabriel's Rebellion*, 20–53, 64–65, Jack Ditcher quoted on 40 ("We have as much right"); Schwarz, "Gabriel's Challenge," 287–94; Mullin, *Flight and Rebellion*, 141, 156–57; Nicholls, *Whispers of Rebellion*, 25–29; Sidbury, *Ploughshares into Swords*, 6–7.

79. Egerton, *Gabriel's Rebellion*, 69–79; L. K. Ford, *Deliver Us from Evil*, 52; Mullin, *Flight and Rebellion*, 151; Nicholls, *Whispers of Rebellion*, 57–70.

80. Egerton, *Gabriel's Rebellion*, 83–112; Nicholls, *Whispers of Rebellion*, 72–92; John Randolph to Joseph H. Nicholson, Sept. 26, 1800, in Bruce, ed., *John Randolph*, vol. 2:250 ("The accused"); L. K. Ford, *Deliver Us from Evil*, 53; Sidbury, *Ploughshares into Swords*, 7.

81. Ferling, *Leap in the Dark*, 458–68; Freeman, "Corruption and Compromise," 87–120; Pasley, "1800 as a Revolution," 121–52.

82. Cotlar, *Tom Paine's America*, 97–98; DeConde, *Quasi-War*, 117–21; Per-

kins, *First Rapprochement*, 92–98, 101–13; Ritcheson, *Aftermath*, 331–52; R. Stuart, *United States Expansionism*, 39–40; G. Wood, *Empire of Liberty*, 197–98.

83. Bradburn, *Citizenship Revolution*, 148–67; Kettner, *Development of American Citizenship*, 244–45; Noah Webster quoted in J. Lepore, *A Is for American*, 55; J. Miller, *Crisis in Freedom*, 47–48, 67–70, 163–65, 189; J. M. Smith, *Freedom's Fetters*, 22–34, 51–56, 61–62, 66–67, 90–91, 163–65; A. Taylor, "Alien and Sedition Acts," 63–76.

84. Elkins and McKitrick, *Age of Federalism*, 709–11, Matthew Lyon quoted on 710; J. Miller, *Crisis in Freedom*, 67–70, 75–76, 81–85; Pasley, *"Tyranny of Printers,"* 118–25, 176–78; J. M. Smith, *Freedom's Fetters*, 94–95, 278–79, 419–21; A. Taylor, "Alien and Sedition Acts," 66–68; Whelan, "Green Atlantic," 226.

85. Read, *Power versus Liberty*, 144–47; Simon, *What Kind of Nation*, 52–53, 57–62; Alexander Hamilton to Theodore Sedgwick, Feb. 2, 1799, in Syrett, ed., *Papers of Alexander Hamilton*, vol. 22:452–54 ("regular conspiracy," "clever," and "put Virginia"); Tomlins, "Republican Law," 552–54.

86. Ferling, *Leap in the Dark*, 458–68, James T. Callender quoted on 459 ("one of the most egregious fools"); G. Wood, *Empire of Liberty*, 268–71, Theodore Dwight quoted on 586 ("murder").

87. Ackerman, *Failure of the Founding Fathers*, 97–99, 203–6, Samuel Smith quoted on 204 ("what other" and "his head"); Jonas Platt to James Kent, Feb. 11, 1801, James Kent Papers, reel 2, Library of Congress; Elkins and McKitrick, *Age of Federalism*, 741–750; Ferling, *Leap in the Dark*, 468–75; Freeman, "Corruption and Compromise," 91; James Lewis, "'What Is to Become,'" 8–11, 14–21; Onuf, *Jefferson's Empire*, 82, 100–102; Pasley, "1800 as a Revolution," 122–23; Alexander Hamilton to James A. Bayard, Jan. 16, 1801, in Syrett, ed., *Papers of Alexander Hamilton*, vol. 25:319–24.

88. Ackerman, *Failure of the Founding Fathers*, 203–6; Simon, *What Kind of Nation*, 207–8.

89. Ackerman, *Failure of the Founding Fathers*, 100–108, *Philadelphia Aurora* quoted on 107 ("The Revolution"); Haseby, *Origins*, 29–30, Danbury Baptist Association quoted on 29.

90. Appleby, *Inheriting the Revolution*, 32–33; Noah Webster quoted in Fischer, *Revolution of American Conservatism*, 151–52; Grabbe, "European Immigration," 197–202; Simon, *What Kind of Nation*, 134–35.

91. Ackerman, *Failure of the Founding Fathers*, 149–50; Bradburn, *Citizenship Revolution*, 281–82; Thomas Jefferson to Elbridge Gerry, Jan. 26, 1799, in Boyd et al., eds., *Papers of Thomas Jefferson*, vol. 30:645–53 ("expenses"); Kettner, *Development of American Citizenship*, 245–46; James Lewis, "'What Is to Become,'" 3; Onuf, *Jefferson's Empire*, 80–81, 85, 93; Pasley, "1800 as a Revolution," 122–25; Simon, *What Kind of Nation*, 135–37, 150–51.

92. Thomas Jefferson, "First Inaugural Address," Mar. 4, 1801, in Boyd et al., *Papers of Thomas Jefferson*, vol. 33:148–52 ("strongest"); Bradburn, *Citizenship Revolution*, 1; Hendrickson, *Peace Pact*, 258–59; French traveler quoted in Hunt, ed., *First Forty Years*, 362; Onuf, "Expanding Union," 64–67; Onuf, *Jefferson's Empire*, 107–8, 117–21.

93. Meacham, *Thomas Jefferson*, 353–54, 363–68, Edward Thornton quoted on 364 ("more expensive scale"), Robert Troup quoted on 366 ("Jefferson is"); Simon, *What Kind of Nation*, 140–41.

94. Thomas Jefferson to William Hylton, June 15, 1801, and Jefferson to Levi Lincoln, Oct. 25, 1802, in Boyd et al., eds., *Papers of Thomas Jefferson*, vol. 34:262 ("entitled"), vol. 38:565–66 ("revolution"); Elkins and McKitrick, *Age of Federalism*, 753–54; Meacham, *Thomas Jefferson*, 349–51; Simon, *What Kind of Nation*, 141–46; Zagarri, "American Revolution," 496.

95. Ackerman, *Failure of the Founding Fathers*, 207–9; William Branch Giles to Thomas Jefferson, June 1, 1801, in Boyd et al., *Papers of Thomas Jefferson*, vol. 34:228 ("The ejected party"); Elkins and McKitrick, *Age of Federalism*, 753–54; Simon, *What Kind of Nation*, 208.

96. Beeman, *The Old Dominion*, xii–xiii; Hickey, "America's Response," 365–68; Riley, "Slavery and the Problem of Democracy," 230–31.

97. Thomas Jefferson to Aaron Burr, Feb. 11, 1799, and Jefferson to Walter Jones, Mar. 31, 1801, in Boyd et al., eds., *Papers of Thomas Jefferson*, vol. 31:22–23 ("Cannibals") and vol. 33:506 ("no more good"); V. Brown, "Vapor of Dread," 195–96; D. B. Davis, *Slavery in the Age of Revolution*, 152; W. Jordan, *White over Black*, 385–86; John, *Spreading the News*, 140–41; Onuf, *Mind of Thomas Jefferson*, 252–55; P. Riley, "Slavery and the Problem of Democracy," 230–31; Rothman, *Slave Country*, 34; A. White, *Encountering Revolution*, 163–65.

98. Dubois, *Avengers of the New World*, 304; Egerton, *Death or Liberty*, 269–70; Faber, *Building the Land of Dreams*, 43–46; Alexander Hamilton, "Purchase of Louisiana," in Syrett, ed., *Papers of Alexander Hamilton*, vol. 26:130 ("the courage"); A. White, *Encountering Revolution*, 162–64.

99. Blackburn, *Overthrow of Colonial Slavery*, 286; Deyle, *Carry Me Back*, 24; Drescher, *Abolition*, 137; Fehrenbacher and McAfee, *Slaveholding Republic*, 136–47; Mason, "Necessary but Not Sufficient," 18.

100. Cayton, "Radicals in the 'Western World,'" 83–89; Hinderaker, *Elusive Empires*, 255–57; Nichols, *Red Gentlemen and White Savages*, 193–97, 201; Rohrbough, *Land Office Business*, 23–41.

101. Thomas Jefferson to William Henry Harrison, Feb. 27, 1803, and Jefferson to William C. C. Claiborne, May 24, 1803, in Boyd et al., eds., *Papers of Thomas Jefferson*, vol. 39:589–92, quotation on 590 ("When these debts"), vol. 40:422–23 ("press on the Indians"); Horsman, *Expansion*, 104–14, 142–

57; Nichols, *Red Gentlemen and White Savages*, 193–97; R. White, *Middle Ground*, 473–74, 496–500.

102. For the first use of the phrase "Empire of Liberty," see Thomas Jefferson to George Rogers Clark, Dec. 25, 1780, in Boyd et al., eds, *Papers of Thomas Jefferson*, vol. 4:237; Calloway, "Continuing Revolution," 31–32; DuVal, *Independence Lost*, 343–45; Hinderaker, *Elusive Empires*, 267–70; Onuf, "Imperialism and Nationalism," 21–40.

103. Jefferson to Spencer Roane, Sept. 6, 1819 ("revolution of 1800"), Founders Online, National Archives (http://founders.archives.gov/documents/Jefferson/98-01-02-0734); Baptist, *Half Has Never Been Told*, 7–16; Hinderaker, *Elusive Empires*, 268–70; Pasley, "1800 as a Revolution," 121–47; Sidbury, "Thomas Jefferson," 199–14; White, *Middle Ground*, 515–17.

104. John Marshall to Alexander Hamilton, Jan. 1, 1801, in Hobson et al., eds., *Papers of John Marshall*, vol. 6:46–47 ("unfit" and "sap"); Newmyer, *John Marshall*, 80–81; G. Wood, *Empire of Liberty*, 434–36, Thomas Jefferson quoted on 434 ("So great").

105. Ackerman, *Failure of the Founding Fathers*, 149–51; Thomas Jefferson to John Dickinson, Dec. 19, 1801, in Boyd et al., eds, *Papers of Thomas Jefferson*, vol. 36:165–66 ("retired"); Simon, *What Kind of Nation*, 148–49, 192–93.

106. Newmyer, *John Marshall*, 148–52; Simon, *What Kind of Nation*, 152, 161.

107. Thomas Jefferson to Spencer Roane, Sept. 6, 1819, and Jefferson to Archibald Thweatt, Jan. 19, 1821 ("working like gravity"), Founders Online, National Archives (http://founders.archieves.gov/documents/Jefferson/98-01-02-0734 and 98-01-02-1782); Newmyer, *Supreme Court Justice*, 125–27; Simon, *What Kind of Nation*, 272–75; G. E. White, *Marshall Court*, 541–52; G. Wood, *Empire of Liberty*, 455–56.

108. Thomas Jefferson to William Plumer, July 21, 1816, in Looney et al., eds., *Papers of Thomas Jefferson, Retirement Series*, vol. 10:260–61 ("that the earth"), Newmyer, *John Marshall*, 271–72; Newmyer, *Supreme Court Justice*, 129–36; G. Wood, *Empire of Liberty*, 458–66.

109. Newmyer, *John Marshall*, 464–67; Newmyer, *Supreme Court Justice*, 196–205; Simon, *What Kind of Nation*, 294–301.

110. Haselby, *Origins*, 21–22; Maier, *American Scripture*, 201–8; Newmyer, *Supreme Court Justice*, 378–83; Onuf, "Imperialism and Nationalism," 23–24, 40.

111. For the celebration of founders as offering the antidote for modern politics, see Lepore, *Whites of Their Eyes*. For a revisionist view, see Waldstreicher, *Runaway America*.

CHAPTER 12: LEGACIES

1. Benjamin Rush quoted in Kerber, "'History Can Do It No Justice,'" 17n26.

2. John Adams to Abigail Smith Adams, Apr. 14, and Apr. 28, 1776, in Butterfield et al., eds., *Book of Abigail and John*, 122–23 ("We have been told"), 126 ("more Serenity"); John Adams to James Sullivan, May 26, 1776, in Butterfield et al., eds., *Papers of John Adams*, vol. 4:208–13 ("There will be"); Kerber, "'History Can Do It No Justice,'" 10–12, 38–42; Kerber, *Women of the Republic*, 189, 269; Jan Lewis, "Republican Wife," 693–94; Lyons, "Discipline," 567–68; Main, "American States," 24–29; Young, "Women of Boston," 215–16.

3. Appleby, *Inheriting the Revolution*, 6–7, Duc de La Rochefoucauld quoted on 6 ("It is a country"), Michel Chevalier quoted on 7 ("Here"); Faber, *Building the Land of Dreams*, 3–4; R. Gross, "Confidence Man," 303–9; A. Taylor, "Unhappy Stephen Arnold," 118–19; G. Wood, "Significance of the Early Republic," 1–20.

4. R. D. Brown, *Strength of a People*, 86–87; John Adams to James Sullivan, May 26, 1776, in Butterfield et al., eds., *Papers of John Adams*, vol. 4:208–13; Onuf, "Epilogue," 298–99; Tomlins, "Republican Law," 540–41; Yokota, *Unbecoming British*, 11.

5. Bushman, *Refinement of America*, 208–22; Elihu Phinney quoted in A. Taylor, "Unhappy Stephen Arnold," 108; G. Wood, *Empire of Liberty*, 27–31.

6. Bushman, *Refinement of America*, 208–22, 404–5; Jaffee, *New Nation of Goods*, ix–xv; A. Taylor, "Unhappy Stephen Arnold," 118; G. Wood, *Empire of Liberty*, 355–56; Yokota, *Unbecoming British*, 92–95.

7. Bushman, *Refinement of America*, 208 ("vernacular gentility"), 222–27, 353–54, 381–82, 390–98; Jaffee, *New Nation of Goods*, 47–101; McNamara, "Republican Art and Architecture," 509–10.

8. Bushman, *Refinement of America*, 420–25, 446–47; Rockman, *Scraping By*, 158–93.

9. Bushman, *Refinement of America*, 420–25, 434–40, 446–47, Joseph Willson quoted on 440; Rockman, *Scraping By*, 194–230; Sweet, *Bodies Politic*, 378–92.

10. R. D. Brown, *Strength of a People*, 85–88; Lepore, *A Is for American*, 17–18; Onuf, "Epilogue," 297–98; G. Wood, *Empire of Liberty*, 469–75, Benjamin Rush quoted on 474–75.

11. R. D. Brown, *Strength of a People*, 85–86, 93–99, Benjamin Rush quoted on 99 ("If the common people" and "honest mechanics"); G. Wood, *Empire of Liberty*, 469–71, Benjamin Rush quoted on 473 ("to convert").

12. Thomas Jefferson to George Wythe, Aug. 13, 1786, in Boyd et al., eds., *Papers of Thomas Jefferson*, vol. 10:245 ("the tax"); R. D. Brown, *Strength*

of a People, 91–101, 146–47; Haselby, *Origins*, 45–46, 48; G. Wood, *Empire of Liberty*, 471–74.

13. Appleby, *Inheriting the Revolution*, 195–96; R. D. Brown, *Strength of a People*, 92–114; Ferling, *Leap in the Dark*, 481–82; Opal, *Beyond the Farm*, 97–109.

14. Brown, *Strength of a People*, 146–47, North Carolinian quoted on 147; G. Wood, *Empire of Liberty*, 472.

15. John Steele quoted in R. D. Brown, *Strength of a People*, 91 ("If the people"), see also 111–12; J. Ellis, *After the Revolution*, 162–63; Hatch, *Democratization of American Christianity*, 25–26; John, *Spreading the News*, 17–18, 50–54; O'Donnell, "Print Culture," 519–22; Pasley, *Tyranny of Printers*, 8–9; G. Wood, *Empire of Liberty*, 476–79.

16. Appleby, *Inheriting the Revolution*, 102–3; R. D. Brown, *Strength of a People*, 86–89; Thomas Jefferson to John Norvell, June 11, 1807, Founders Online, National Archives (http://founders.archives.gov/documents/Jefferson/99-01-02-5737); Pasley, *Tyranny of Printers*, 2–16, Alexis de Tocqueville quoted on 4; O'Donnell, "Print Culture," 523–24; Waldstreicher, *In the Midst of Perpetual Fetes*, 95–97, 101–5, 109–13, 226–31.

17. J. Ellis, *After the Revolution*, 8–12, 19–21, 24–30, 43, 53–54, 61–63; John Adams to John Trumbull, Jan. 1, 1817, Founders Online, National Archives (http://founders.archives.gov/documents/Adams/99-02-02-6684); McNamara, "Republican Art and Architecture," 499–500; Jan Lewis, "Republican Wife," 690–92; G. Wood, *Empire of Liberty*, 543–55, 560–61, Washington, D.C., commissioners quoted on 543, Jeremy Belknap quoted on 544.

18. J. Ellis, *After the Revolution*, 41–71, Charles Willson Peale quoted on 69 ("Temple"); McNamara, "Republican Art and Architecture," 510–11; G. Wood, *Empire of Liberty*, 555–56, Peale quoted on 556 ("the interests" and "its utility").

19. R. D. Brown, *Knowledge Is Power*, 198–99; J. Ellis, *After the Revolution*, 57–58; McNamara, "Republican Art and Architecture," 511–13; George Washington to Marquis de Lafayette, May 28, 1788, in Rhodehamel, ed., *George Washington: Writings*, 680–81 ("not inferior"); Thomas Jefferson to James Madison, Sept. 20, 1785, in Boyd et al., eds., *Papers of Thomas Jefferson*, vol. 8:534–35 ("to improve").

20. Jefferson to Marquis de Lafayette, Nov. 3, 1786, in Boyd et al., eds., *Papers of Thomas Jefferson*, vol. 10:505–6 ("It is not"); A. White, *Encountering Revolution*, 14; G. Wood, *Empire of Liberty*, 543–55, Sydney Smith quoted on 543 ("Who reads"); Yokota, *Unbecoming British*, 8–18.

21. Davidson, *Revolution and the Word*, 15–37; Gilmore, "Literature of the Revolutionary and Early National Periods," 625–26, 644, 676; O'Donnell, "Print Culture," 524–25; G. Wood, *Empire of Liberty*, 559–60; Yokota, *Unbecoming British*, 10–11.

22. Appleby, *Inheriting the Revolution*, 115–17; McNamara, "Republican Art and Architecture," 506–9, Gilbert Stuart quoted on 507; G. Wood, *Empire of Liberty*, 563–71.

23. J. Ellis, *After the Revolution*, 70–71, 154–56, William Dunlap quoted on 155; J. Green, *Mathew Carey*, 10–17; O'Donnell, "Print Culture," 524–25, Mason Locke Weems quoted on 525; G. Wood, *Empire of Liberty*, 563–71.

24. Bonomi, *Under the Cope of Heaven*, 152–57; Butler, "Coercion, Miracle, Reason," 3–9; Murrin, "Religion and Politics," 19–43.

25. Nash, *Unknown American Revolution*, 8–12; Noll, *America's God*, 173–74; John Leland quoted in Ragosta, *Religious Freedom*, 86.

26. Calhoon, "Evangelical Persuasion," 156–66, Kehukee Baptist Association quoted on 171 ("duty"); John Wesley quoted in Haselby, *Origins*, 122; Marini, "Religion, Politics, Ratification," 201–3, James O'Kelly quoted on 202 ("true disciple" and "meek").

27. Calhoon, "Evangelical Persuasion," 156–66, Edward Baptist quoted on 157 ("conviction" and "my guilt"), John Williams quoted on 159 ("singing praises").

28. Appleby, *Inheriting the Revolution*, 250–51; R. D. Brown, *Strength of a People*, 146; Noll, *America's God*, 165, 187–90; G. Wood, *Empire of Liberty*, 576–77.

29. Appleby, *Inheriting the Revolution*, 32; Gaustad, "Religious Tests," 222–23, 226–29; Haselby, *Origins*, 33–34; Richard Henry Lee to James Madison, Nov. 26, 1784, in Hutchinson et al., eds., *Papers of James Madison*, vol. 8:149; Ragosta, *Religious Freedom*, 76–78; G. Wood, *Empire of Liberty*, 583–84.

30. George Washington, Farewell Address, Sept. 19, 1796 ("Religion"), Founders Online, National Archives (http://founders.archives.gov/documents/Washington/99-01-02-00963); Marini, "Religion, Politics, Ratification," 195–96; Noll, *America's God*, 203–4; G. Wood, *Empire of Liberty*, 576–78, 585–86.

31. Haselby, *Origins*, 26–33; James Madison to William Bradford, Jan. 24, 1774, in Hutchinson et al., eds., *Papers of James Madison*, vol. 1:104–8.

32. Haselby, *Origins*, 33–38; James Madison to Thomas Jefferson, Aug. 20, 1785, in Hutchinson et al., eds., *Papers of James Madison*, vol. 8:344–47.

33. Ahlstrom, *Religious History*, 380; Thomas Jefferson to James Madison, Dec. 16, 1786, in Boyd et al., eds., *Papers of Thomas Jefferson*, vol. 10:604; R. D. Brown, *Strength of a People*, 92–93, Virginia statute quoted on 92; Butler, "Coercion, Miracle, Reason," 20–24; Haselby, *Origins*, 28–30; Noll, *America's God*, 163–64; Ragosta, *Religious Freedom*, 7–39, 74–100.

34. Ahlstrom, *Religious History*, 380; Gaustad, "Religious Tests," 218–20; Gilje, *Making of the American Republic*, 202; Noll, *America's God*, 167; G. Wood, *Empire of Liberty*, 591.

35. Ahlstrom, *Religious History*, 368–69, 374–75; Appleby, *Inheriting the Rev-*

olution, 109–10; Hatch, *Democratization of American Christianity*, 4–5, 19–22; Marini, "Religion, Politics, Ratification," 194–95.

36. Appleby, *Inheriting the Revolution*, 183–84, 197–98; Haselby, *Origins*, 117–19, 128–29, 133–36; Noll, *America's God*, 169–70, 179–80, 187–88; G. Wood, *Empire of Liberty*, 595–96, Peter Cartwright quoted on 596.

37. Appleby, *Inheriting the Revolution*, 198–99; Calhoon, "Evangelical Persuasion," 159–62; Gilje, *Making of the American Republic*, 204–5; Hatch, *Democratization of American Christianity*, 4–16, 26–27, 44–45; G. Wood, *Empire of Liberty*, 615–16, unnamed Congregationalist quoted on 615 ("Liberty").

38. D. Andrews, *Methodists*, 76; Haselby, *Origins*, 120–21; Hatch, *Democratization of American Christianity*, 3–4; Marini, "Religion, Politics, Ratification," 193–95, 197–99; Noll, *America's God*, 165–70, 180–82, 196–97; G. Wood, *Empire of Liberty*, 578–81.

39. Ahlstrom, *Religious History*, 433–35; Butler, "Coercion, Miracle, Reason," 26–28; Frey, *Water from the Rock*, 251–56, Jesse Lee quoted on 251 ("Many"); Haselby, *Origins*, 121–22; Hatch, *Democratization of American Christianity*, 15–16; Marini, "Religion, Politics, Ratification," 198–203; Noll, *America's God*, 254–55; G. Wood, *Empire of Liberty*, 595–96, 608–16.

40. R. D. Brown, *Strength of a People*, 98–99, 106–7, 146, New York state law quoted on 104; Butler, "Coercion, Miracle, Reason," 26–27; A. Taylor, "The Plough-Jogger," 385–86.

41. Ahlstrom, *Religious History*, 379–80, 529–39; G. Wood, *Empire of Liberty*, 591–92.

42. Ahlstrom, *Religious History*, 383–84; Appleby, *Inheriting the Revolution*, 203–4; Noll, *America's God*, 206–7; G. Wood, *Empire of Liberty*, 582–83, 589–91, 611–12, James McGready quoted on 611 ("will not be").

43. Appleby, *Inheriting the Revolution*, 187–88, 192, 201–4; Haselby, *Origins*, 1–4, 19–21; Noll, *America's God*, 256–63; G. Wood, *Empire of Liberty*, 608–10.

44. Hatch, *Democratization of American Christianity*, 6–7; Noll, *America's God*, 256–63; G. Wood, *Empire of Liberty*, 616–18.

45. Hatch, *Democratization of American Christianity*, 3–5; Noll, *America's God*, 204–6.

46. R. D. Brown, *Strength of a People*, 98–99; Haselby, *Origins*, 18–20; Noll, *America's God*, 204–6, Joseph Story quoted on 204 ("the religion"); G. Wood, *Empire of Liberty*, 613–14, Alexis de Tocqueville quoted on 614.

47. Thomas Jefferson to Benjamin Waterhouse, June 26, 1822, and Jefferson to Thomas Cooper, Nov. 2, 1822 ("The atmosphere" and "In our Richmond"), Founders Online, National Archives (http://founders.archives.gov/documents/Jefferson/98-01-02-2905 and 98-01-02-3137); Appleby, *Inheriting the Revolution*, 183–84; Haselby, *Origins*, 46–48.

48. Abigail Adams to John Adams, Mar. 31, 1776, J. Adams to A. Adams, Apr. 14, 1776, and A. Adams to J. Adams, May 7, 1776, in Butterfield et al., eds., *Book of Abigail and John*, 120–21 (all A. Adams quotations), 122–23 (all J. Adams quotations), and 126–27; Berkin, *Revolutionary Mothers*, 157–58; Norton, *Liberty's Daughters*, 50–51, 163–64; Young, "Women of Boston," 181–83, 213–15.

49. Benjamin Rush quoted in Berkin, *First Generations*, 180; Gundersen, *To Be Useful to the World*, 176–78; Kerber, *Women of the Republic*, 46–47.

50. Thomas Jefferson to Anne Willing Bingham, May 11, 1788, in Boyd et al., eds., *Papers of Thomas Jefferson*, vol. 13:151–52 ("too wise" and "soothe"); Thomas Jefferson to Albert Gallatin, Jan. 13, 1807 ("an innovation"), Founders Online, National Archives (http://founders.archives.gov/doc uments/Jefferson/99-01-02-4862); Norton, *Liberty's Daughters*, 161–63, 190–91; Norton, "'What an Alarming Crisis,'" 224–25; Jeremiah Mason quoted in Wood, *Empire of Liberty*, 507 ("woman in politics"); Zagarri, *Revolutionary Backlash*, 6–7.

51. Appleby, *Inheriting the Revolution*, 30; Kerber, "'History Can Do It No Justice,'" 29–33; Kerber, "'I Have Don,'" 227–33, 250–51.

52. Abigail Adams to Elizabeth Smith Shaw Peabody, July 19, 1799 ("If a woman"), in Founders Online, National Archives (http://founders.archives. gov/documents/Adams/99-03-02-0428); Norton, *Liberty's Daughters*, 188–91, 228–29, Eliza Wilkinson quoted on 188–89; Norton, "'What an Alarming Crisis,'" 220–22; Zagarri, *Revolutionary Backlash*, 5–6.

53. Gundersen, *To Be Useful to the World*, 177–78; Kerber, "'I Have Don,'" 227–28; Norton, *Liberty's Daughters*, 225–27, Rachel Wells quoted on 225 and Mary Willing Byrd quoted on 226; G. Wood, *Empire of Liberty*, 507.

54. Berkin, *Revolutionary Mothers*, 93–96; Gundersen, *To Be Useful to the World*, 188–89; Kerber, *Women of the Republic*, 51–52; Norton, *Liberty's Daughters*, 44–45, 217–18; Norton, "'What an Alarming Crisis,'" 220–21.

55. Berkin, *Revolutionary Mothers*, 159–60; Gundersen, *To Be Useful to the World*, 178–79; Norton, *Liberty's Daughters*, 191–93, New Jersey election law quoted on 191.

56. Berkin, *Revolutionary Mothers*, 150–52, 154–55; Kerber, "'I Have Don,'" 234–36, 239–41, Judith Sargent Murray quoted on 241; Norton, *Liberty's Daughters*, 238–55; Skemp, "America's Mary Wollstonecraft," 289–303; Young, "Women of Boston," 217–18.

57. Abigail Adams to John Adams, Aug. 14, 1776, in Butterfield et al., eds., *Book of Abigail and John*, 153; Gunderson, *To Be Useful to the World*, 100–101; Kerber, "'History Can Do It No Justice,'" 36–39, Columbia commencement speaker quoted on 37–38 ("Yes, ye fair"); Norton, *Liberty's Daughters*, 242–49, Benjamin Rush quoted on 242 ("Virtue"), Judith Sargent Murray quoted on 249 ("assigned"); Skemp, "America's Mary Wollstonecraft," 293.

58. Kerber, "'History Can Do It No Justice,'" 39–40; Kerber, *Women of the Republic*, v–vi, 11–12; Columbia College commencement speaker quoted in Jan Lewis, "Republican Wife," 701 ("mold the taste" and "By the judicious"); Norton, *Liberty's Daughters*, 243–44; William Loughton Smith quoted in Zagarri, *Revolutionary Backlash*, 177 ("To delight").

59. Appleby, *Inheriting the Revolution*, 105–7; Berkin, *Revolutionary Mothers*, 152–53; Gunderson, *To Be Useful to the World*, 99–102; Kerber, *Women of the Republic*, 199–201; Jan Lewis, "Republican Wife," 702–3; Norton, *Liberty's Daughters*, 252–55, 272–76.

60. Berkin, *Revolutionary Mothers*, 156–57; Gunderson, *To Be Useful to the World*, 100–102; Kerber, *Women of the Republic*, 185; 198–99, John Trumbull quoted on 185; Norton, *Liberty's Daughters*, 265–68, Samuel Magaw quoted on 268 ("be formed").

61. Abigail Adams to Elizabeth Smith Shaw Peabody, July 19, 1799 ("I will never consent"), in Founders Online, National Archives (http://founders.archives.gov/documents/Adams/99-03-02-0428); Gunderson, *To Be Useful to the World*, 100–102; Kerber, *Women of the Republic*, 210–14; Norton, *Liberty's Daughters*, 247–50.

62. Kerber, "'I Have Don,'" 236–39; Kerber, *Women of the Republic*, 222–31, 282–83; Norton, *Liberty's Daughters*, 250–52, 289–94; Skemp, "America's Mary Wollstonecraft," 300–302, an unidentified critic quoted on 300 ("whore"); Zagarri, "Rights of Man and Woman," 203–30.

63. Gross, *Minutemen and Their World*, 181–85; Gunderson, *To Be Useful to the World*, 138–40; Lyons, "Discipline," 562–63; Ulrich, *Midwife's Tale*, 147–60.

64. Jan Lewis, "Republican Wife," 689–90; Lyons, "Discipline," 560–70, Henry Dixon quoted on 565 ("Whereas"); Norton, *Liberty's Daughters*, 229–42, Judith Sargent Murray quoted on 234–35; Sievens, *Stray Wives*, 4–9; G. Wood, *Empire of Liberty*, 341–42, 495–500.

65. Appleby, *Inheriting the Revolution*, 192–93; Jan Lewis, "Republican Wife," 693–713; Sievens, *Stray Wives*, 12–13, Reverend Martin Tullar quoted on 12; G. Wood, *Empire of Liberty*, 498.

66. Davidson, *Revolution and the Word*, 55–79; Isaac, "Stories," 229–35; Jan Lewis, "The Republican Wife," 696–701, 718–20; Lyons, "Discipline," 570–71; Ulrich, *Midwife's Tale*, 158–60.

67. John Adams to Thomas Boylston Adams, Oct. 17, 1799, Founders Online, National Archives (http://founders.archives.gov/documents/Adams/99-03-02-0482); Lyons, "Discipline," 566–68; Norton, *Liberty's Daughters*, 235–38, Paine Wingate quoted on 236 ("Fathers"); A. Taylor, "Unhappy Stephen Arnold," 103–4; G. Wood, *Empire of Liberty*, 340–41, 500.

68. D. Cohen, "Homicidal Compulsion," 725–64; Ulrich, *Midwife's Tale*, 291–308.

69. Halttunen, "Humanitarianism," 303–34; A. Taylor, "Unhappy Stephen Arnold," 96–121, Arnold quoted on 104 ("that he wished").

70. Berlin, *Many Thousands Gone*, 237–38; Blackburn, *Overthrow of Colonial Slavery*, 120; Nash, *Race and Revolution*, 8–10; Van Cleve, *Slaveholders' Union*, 20–31; S. White, *Somewhat More Independent*, 16–18; Wood, *Empire of Liberty*, 517–18; Zilversmit, *First Emancipation*, 55–84, 162.

71. Boston petition of the enslaved quoted in Berlin, *Many Thousands Gone*, 229–32; Kaplan and Kaplan, *Black Presence*, 11–16, 44–68, 203–4; Nash, *Race and Revolution*, 58–59; G. Wood, *Empire of Liberty*, 517–20; Zilversmit, *First Emancipation*, 85–112. For blacks in the Continental Army, see Egerton, *Death or Liberty*, 95.

72. Abigail Adams to John Adams, Sept. 22, 1774, in Butterfield et al., eds., *Adams Family Correspondence*, vol. 1:161–62; Litwack, *North of Slavery*, 6–9; Nash, *Race and Revolution*, 10; S. G. Tucker, *Dissertation on Slavery*, 1–2; Van Cleve, *Slaveholders' Union*, 93–94.

73. Patrick Henry quoted in Deyle, *Carry Me Back*, 26 ("general inconvenience"); Henry quoted in L. K. Ford, *Deliver Us from Evil*, 23 ("repugnant"); Nash, *Race and Revolution*, 11–12, 44–45; Rakove, *Revolutionaries*, 163–64 (refers to George Mason's slave named "Liberty"). For Jay, see Zilversmit, *First Emancipation*, 166–67.

74. D. B. Davis, *Problem of Slavery*, 316–17; Frey, *Water from the Rock*, 246; Nash, *Race and Revolution*, 11–12, 15–17; Van Cleve, *Slaveholders' Union*, 93–94; Benjamin Rush quoted in G. Wood, *Empire of Liberty*, 519.

75. Mullin, *Flight and Rebellion*, 134; Pittsylvania County, Virginia, Petition, quoted in Schmidt and Wilhelm, "Early Proslavery Petitions," 139; Zilversmit, *First Emancipation*, 142–46, 166–67.

76. Thomas Jefferson to Marquis de Chastellux, Sept. 2, 1785, in Boyd et al., eds., *Papers of Thomas Jefferson*, vol. 8:467–70 ("zealous"); D. B. Davis, *Problem of Slavery*, 257; Furstenberg, "Beyond Freedom and Slavery," 1295–1330; Parkinson, "Manifest Signs of Passion," 59–65; Roberts and Roberts, eds., *Moreau de St. Méry's American Journey*, 310 ("the American people"); Rothman, *Slave Country*, 8–9; Van Cleve, *Slaveholders' Union*, 42–45; Zilversmit, *First Emancipation*, 144, 200.

77. Egerton, *Death or Liberty*, 96–97; Van Cleve, *Slaveholders' Union*, 49; Whitfield, *Problem of Slavery*, 3–41; Zilversmit, *First Emancipation*, 110–11, 131–32, 142–46.

78. Egerton, *Death or Liberty*, 104–5, 169–71, Elizabeth Freeman quoted on 171 ("Any time"); Kaplan and Kaplan, *Black Presence*, 244–48, Harriet Martineau quoted on 244–45 ("by keeping"); Littwack, *North of Slavery*, 10–11.

79. Blackburn, *Overthrow of Colonial Slavery*, 117–20; Egerton, *Death or Liberty*, 93–95, 104–9; Van Cleve, *Slaveholders' Union*, 59–62, 66–68; G. Wood, *Empire of Liberty*, 519–20; Zilversmit, *First Emancipation*, 113–17. For the role of public opinion regarding emancipation in Massachusetts, see

Gloria McCahon Whiting, "The Negroes have left: African Americans and the Politics of Emancipation in Revolutionary Massachusetts," Massachusetts Historical Society conference on the American Revolution, April 2015.

80. Blackburn, *Overthrow of Colonial Slavery*, 117–18, 272–74; Egerton, *Death or Liberty*, 97–100; Nash and Soderlund, *Freedom by Degrees*, 103–6; Sweet, *Bodies Politic*, 249–51; Waldstreicher, *Slavery's Constitution*, 50, 60–61; S. White, *Somewhat More Independent*, 38; Zilversmit, *First Emancipation*, 119–37, 192–200.

81. Egerton, *Death or Liberty*, 100–101; Nash, *Race and Revolution*, 34–35, David Cooper quoted on 35 ("If we keep"); Nash and Soderlund, *Freedom by Degrees*, 103–4, 167–68; Van Cleve, *Slaveholders' Union*, 60–62, 74–75, 89–90; G. Wood, *Empire of Liberty*, 520.

82. Berlin, *Many Thousands Gone*, 228, 232–33; Zilversmit, *First Emancipation*, 115–16, 208–9, 216–17.

83. John Adams to Jeremy Belknap, Mar. 21, 1795 ("filled the Negros"), Founders Online, National Archives (http://founders.archives.gov/documents/Adams/99-02-02-1659); Berlin, *Many Thousands Gone*, 235–36; Nash and Soderlund, *Freedom by Degrees*, 108, 156–57; Sweet, *Bodies Politic*, 253–60.

84. Nash and Soderlund, *Freedom by Degrees*, 35–36, 75–76, 167–76; Rockman, *Scraping By*, 49–70; Rosswurm, *Arms, Country, and Class*, 16; Salinger, "Artisans," 64–69; G. Wood, *Empire of Liberty*, 345–47, New York reformers quoted on 345.

85. Berlin, *Many Thousands Gone*, 228–29, 233–44; Berlin, "Revolution in Black Life," 363–64; Nash, "Forging Freedom," 6–8, 20–40; Nash and Soderlund, *Freedom by Degrees*, 170–72; Van Cleve, *Slaveholders' Union*, 64–68, 74–75, 79–80, 89–90; S. White, *Somewhat More Independent*, 24–38, 147–49.

86. Appleby, *Inheriting the Revolution*, 28; Litwack, *North of Slavery*, 64–77, 94–96, Alexis de Tocqueville quoted on 65 ("The prejudice"); Melish, *Disowning Slavery*, 84–162; Nash, "Forging Freedom," 9–11, 15–17.

87. Berlin, *Many Thousands Gone*, 239–48; W. Jordan, *White over Black*, 410–14; Litwack, *North of Slavery*, 153–59, young black man quoted on 154 ("Shall I be"); Nash and Soderlund, *Freedom by Degrees*, 167–80, 187–93; Newman, *Freedom's Prophet*, 58; Van Cleve, *Slaveholders' Union*, 79–88.

88. W. Jordan, *White over Black*, 416–22, Moreau de St. Méry quoted on 416 ("snowballs"); Nash, "Forging Freedom," 40–43; R. Newman, *Transformation*, 88–89; Sweet, *Bodies Politic*, 252–53, 353–92, Hosea Easton quoted on 392 ("He magnifies"); Van Cleve, *Slaveholders' Union*, 99–100.

89. Prince Hall quoted in Kaplan and Kaplan, *Black Presence*, 212–14; Litwack, *North of Slavery*, 15–18; Nash, *Race and Revolution*, 49–50; Newman, *Freedom's Prophet*, 146–47.

90. W. Jordan, *White over Black*, 422–26; Kaplan and Kaplan, *Black Presence*,

96–99; Nash, "Forging Freedom," 43–48; Newman, *Freedom's Prophet*, 1–19, 54–77.

91. Berlin, *Many Thousands Gone*, 254; Kaplan and Kaplan, *Black Presence*, 202–14, Prince Hall quoted on 212; Nash, "Forging Freedom," 48; Nash, *Race and Revolution*, 65–79, John F. Watson quoted on 73 ("Their aspirings"); Newman, *Transformation*, 86–95; S. White, *Somewhat More Independent*, 144–45, 194–206.

92. St. George Tucker to Jeremy Belknap, June 29, 1795, in Belknap, ed., "Queries," 405–7; Berlin, *Many Thousands Gone*, 263–64; D. B. Davis, *Problem of Slavery*, 256–57; Frey, *Water from the Rock*, 217–18; Rothman, *Slave Country*, 2–3; Van Cleve, *Slaveholders' Union*, 93–96, Peter Minor quoted on 96 ("As to your bill").

93. Berlin, *Many Thousands Gone*, 279–80; Nash, *Race and Revolution*, 17–18; Van Cleve, *Slaveholders' Union*, 94–96; Wolf, *Race and Liberty*, xi–xii, 6.

94. Dunn, "Black Society," 74; Morton, *Robert Carter*, 251, 260–65, anonymous neighbor quoted on 266–67 ("It appears"); McColley, *Slavery and Jeffersonian Virginia*, 156; Robert Pleasants, "Memorial to the Governor and Council of State," c. 1790, Pleasants Family Papers, Brock Collection, box 13, folder 18, Huntington Library.

95. St. George Tucker to Jeremy Belknap, June 29, 1795, in Belknap, "Queries," 407; Ely, *Israel on the Appomattox*, 9; James Madison to Edward Coles, Sept. 3, 1819, in Hunt, ed., *Writings of James Madison*, vol. 8:455; W. Jordan, *White over Black*, 580–81; Kulikoff, *Tobacco and Slaves*, 432.

96. Berlin, "Revolution in Black Life," 375–76; Ely, *Israel on the Appomattox*, 8–11; L. K. Ford, *Deliver Us from Evil*, 68; Nicholls, "Passing Through This Troublesome World," 59–68; S. G. Tucker, *Dissertation on Slavery*, 9.

97. Blackburn, *Overthrow of Colonial Slavery*, 275–76; Dunn, "Black Society," 61–63; Ely, *Israel on the Appomattox*, 71; Wolf, *Race and Liberty*, 143; Morgan, *Slave Counterpoint*, 489–90; Nash, *Race and Revolution*, 18–19; Nicholls, "Passing Through This Troublesome World," 65–68.

98. D. B. Davis, *Problem of Slavery*, 200–209, 303–4; Dunn, "Black Society," 80–81; Frey, *Water from the Rock*, 246–48, 275–76; Haselby, *Origins*, 148–49; Jan Lewis, "Problem of Slavery," 285–86; McColley, *Slavery and Jeffersonian Virginia*, 142; Schmidt and Wilhelm, eds., "Early Proslavery Petitions," 133–43; Sobel, *The World They Made Together*, 207–9; Wolf, *Race and Liberty*, 93–95, Francis Asbury quoted on 129. For a radical Baptist who felt marginalized and obliged to leave Virginia see C. Allen, ed., "David Barrow's *Circular Letter*," 440–51.

99. L. K. Ford, *Deliver Us from Evil*, 65; W. Jordan, *White over Black*, 575–76, John Minor quoted on 575; Wolf, *Race and Liberty*, 121–26, Thomas Robertson quoted on 124 ("Tell us not").

100. Thomas Jefferson to James Madison, Oct. 28, 1785, in Boyd et al., eds.,

Papers of Thomas Jefferson, vol. 8:681–83 ("I am conscious"); H. Brewer, "Entailing Aristocracy," 307; Grossberg, "Citizens and Families," 14.

101. H. Brewer, "Entailing Aristocracy," 307–46; Grossberg, "Citizens and Families," 3–27; McGarvie, "Transforming Society," 1393–1425.

102. St. George Tucker to Jeremy Belknap, Nov. 27, 1795, in Belknap, ed., "Queries Relating to Slavery," 421; H. Brewer, "Entailing Aristocracy," 339–40; Deyle, *Carry Me Back*, 35–36; Dunn, "Black Society in the Chesapeake," 67; Jefferson, *Notes on the State of Virginia*, 125–27; "McColley, *Slavery and Jeffersonian Virginia*, 27–30; Stanton and Bear, eds., *Jefferson's Memorandum Book*, vol. 1:354n90.

103. Bailor, "John Taylor of Caroline," 300; Deyle, *Carry Me Back*, 28; Dunn, "Tale of Two Plantations," 43–51; Thomas Jefferson to John Wayles Eppes, June 30, 1820 ("I consider"), Founders Online, National Archives (http://founders.archives.gov/documents/Jefferson/98-01-02-1352); Frey, *Water from the Rock*, 219–20; Jan Lewis, *Pursuit of Happiness*, 142–43; Stanton, "'Those Who Labor for My Happiness,'" 150; Walsh, "Rural African Americans," 329–31.

104. Deyle, *Carry Me Back*, 31–33; Dunn, "After Tobacco," 346; Dunn, "Black Society in the Chesapeake," 67; Walsh, "Rural African Americans," 327, 339.

105. Dunn, "Black Society in the Chesapeake," 59; Fedric, *Slave Life in Virginia and Kentucky*, ix; Kulikoff, "Uprooted Peoples," 149; Kulikoff, *Tobacco and Slaves*, 429–30; J. B. Lee, *Price of Nationhood*, 258–61; Sidbury, *Ploughshares into Swords*, 29, 31.

106. Deyle, "Abominable New Trade," 833–34; Deyle, *Carry Me Back*, 16–21, 38; W. Jordan, *White over Black*, 321; Kulikoff, "Uprooted Peoples," 149–51.

107. Deyle, *Carry Me Back*, 34–35; Grimes, *Life of William Grimes*, 33 ("grieved me"), and 43 ("Lord only knows"); Gudmestad, *Troublesome Commerce*, 8 ("destroyed"); Sidbury, "Saint Domingue in Virginia," 539.

108. Berlin, *Many Thousands Gone*, 265–66; P. Morgan, *Slave Counterpoint*, 503–8; Sobel, *World They Made Together*, 108.

109. Berlin, *Many Thousands Gone*, 307–10; Egerton, *Death or Liberty*, 248–53; Faber, *Building the Land of Dreams*, 41–42; Frey, *Water from the Rock*, 214–22.

110. Calhoon, "Evangelical Persuasion," 167–68, David Ramsay quoted on 168; Frey, *Water from the Rock*, 232–34; Olwell, *Masters, Slaves, and Subjects*, 282–83.

111. Frey, *Water from the Rock*, 235–44.

112. Berlin, "Revolution in Black Life," 360–61; unnamed North Carolinian quoted in D. B. Davis, *Problem of Slavery*, 199 ("At present"); Egerton, *Death or Slavery*, 158–60; Frey, *Water from the Rock*, 240–42, Georgia Superior Court quoted on 241.

113. Baptist, *Half Has Never Been Told*, 1–3, 20–27, 35–37; Berlin, "Revolution in Black Life," 351–52; Rothman, *Slave Country*, x–xi, 1–35.

114. Appleby, *Inheriting the Revolution*, 4–11, 250–56, Frederic W. Lincoln quoted on 253.

115. Appleby, "Thomas Jefferson," 167; G. Wood, *Empire of Liberty*, 551–52.

116. Appleby, *Inheriting the Revolution*, 261–62; D. B. Davis, *Problem of Slavery*, 299–306; Egerton, *Death or Slavery*, 222–47; Frey, *Water from the Rock*, 240–41; Haselby, *Origins*, 39–40; Jefferson, *Notes*, 128–33, 150–51; W. Jordan, *White over Black*, 429–569; Nash, *Race and Revolution*, 16–17, 177–81; Olwell, *Masters, Slaves, and Subjects*, 282–83.

117. Appleby, *Inheriting the Revolution*, 159–60; Edwards, *People and Their Peace*, 8–10; Hinderaker, *Elusive Empires*, 260–62; W. Jordan, *White over Black*, 533–38; Skemp, "America's Mary Wollstonecraft," 300; Yokota, *Unbecoming British*, 216–22; Zagarri, "American Revolution," 495–97.

118. Abraham Lincoln, "First Inaugural Address," Mar. 4, 1861, Abraham Lincoln Online, (http:/www.abrahamlincolnonline.org/Lincoln/speeches/linaug.htm).

119. Greene, "Colonial History and National History," 235–50; G. Wood, *Radicalism of the American Revolution*; Gray and Kamensky, eds., *Oxford Handbook*, 1–9.

120. For the contagion of liberty, see Bailyn, *Ideological Origins*; G. Wood, *Empire of Liberty*. For the early republic as a retreat for women's rights, see Zagarri, *Revolutionary Backlash*. For the contagion of slavery, see Greene, "Colonial History and National History," 235–50; Tomlins, *Freedom Bound*; and Brooke, "Trouble with Paradox," 549–57.

121. Gundersen, *Useful to the World*; Kerber, *Women of the Republic*; Norton, *Liberty's Daughters*; Zagarri, *Revolutionary Backlash*.

122. Nathaniel Hawthorne, "My Kinsman, Major Molineux," in Pearson, ed., *Complete Novels and Selected Tales of Nathaniel Hawthorne*, 1209–23.

BIBLIOGRAPHY

Abbott, William W., "Lowcountry, Backcountry: A View of Georgia in the American Revolution," in Ronald Hoffman, Thad W. Tate, and Peter J. Alfbert, eds., *An Uncivil War: The Southern Backcountry During the American Revolution* (Charlottesville: University Press of Virginia, 1985): 321–32.

Abbott, William W., et al., eds., *The Papers of George Washington, Confederation Series*, 6 vols. (Charlottesville: University Press of Virginia, 1992–97).

Abbott, William W., et al., eds., *The Papers of George Washington, Presidential Series*, 10 vols. to date (Charlottesville: University Press of Virginia, 1987–).

Abernethy, Thomas Perkins, *Western Lands and the American Revolution* (New York: D. Appleton-Century Co., 1937).

Abler, Thomas S., ed., *Chainbreaker: The Revolutionary War Memoirs of Governor Blacksnake* (Lincoln: University of Nebraska Press, 1989).

Ackerman, Bruce, *The Failure of the Founding Fathers: Jefferson, Marshall, and the Rise of Presidential Democracy* (Cambridge: Harvard University Press, 2005).

Adair, Douglass, and John A Schiutz, eds., *Peter Oliver's Origin & Progress of the American Rebellion* (Stanford, Calif.: Stanford University Press, 1967).

Adams, Charles F., ed., *The Works of John Adams, Second President of the United States, with a Life of the Author*, 10 vols. (Boston: Little, Brown, 1850–56).

Ahlstrom, Sydney E., *A Religious History of the American People* (New Haven: Yale University Press, 1972).

Alden, John Richard, *General Gage in America, Being Principally a History of His Role in the American Revolution* (Baton Rouge: Louisiana State University Press, 1948).

Alden, John Richard, *John Stuart and the Southern Colonial Frontier* (Ann Arbor: University of Michigan Press, 1944).

Alexander, John K., "The Fort Wilson Incident of 1779: A Case Study of the Revolutionary Crowd," *William and Mary Quarterly*, 3rd ser., vol. 31 (Oct. 1974): 589–612.

Allen, Carlos R., Jr., ed., "David Barrow's *Circular Letter* of 1798," *William and Mary Quarterly*, 3rd ser., vol. 20 (July 1963): 440–51.

Allen, Gay Wilson, and Roger Asselineau, *St. John de Crèvecoeur: The Life of an American Farmer* (New York: Viking, 1987).

Allen, Robert S. *His Majesty's Indian Allies: British Indian Policy in the Defence of Canada, 1774–1815* (Toronto: Dundurn Press, 1992).

Allen, Thomas B., *Tories: Fighting for the King in America's First Civil War* (New York: HarperCollins, 2010).

Altman, Ida, "The Spanish Atlantic, 1650–1780," in Nicholas Canny and Philip Morgan, eds., *The Atlantic World, c. 1450–c.1850* (New York: Oxford University Press, 2011): 183–200.

Ammerman, David, *In the Common Cause: American Response to the Coercive Acts of 1774* (Charlottesville: University Press of Virginia, 1974).

Anderson, Fred, *Crucible of War: The Seven Years' War and the Fate of Empire in British North America, 1754–1766* (New York: Knopf, 2000).

Anderson, Fred, *A People's Army: Massachusetts Soldiers and Society in the Seven Years War* (Chapel Hill: University of North Carolina Press, 1984).

Anderson, Fred, and Andrew, Cayton, *The Dominion of War: Empire and Liberty in North America, 1500–2000* (New York: Penguin, 2005).

Anderson, Mark R., *The Battle for the Fourteenth Colony: America's War of Liberation in Canada, 1774–1776* (Hanover N.H.: University Press of New England, 2013).

Anderson, Virginia DeJohn, *New England's Generation: The Great Migration and the Formation of Society and Culture in the Seventeenth Century* (New York: Cambridge University Press, 1991).

Andrews, Dee E., *The Methodists and Revolutionary America, 1760–1800: The Shaping of an Evangelical Culture* (Princeton: Princeton University Press, 2000).

[Anonymous], "Canadian Letters: Description of a Tour thro' the Provinces of Lower and Upper Canada in the Course of the Years 1792 and '93," *Canadian Antiquarian and Numismatic Journal*, 3rd ser., vol. 9 (1912): 85–168.

Appleby, Joyce, *Capitalism and a New Social Order: The Republican Vision of the 1790s* (New York: NYU Press, 1984).

Appleby, Joyce, *Inheriting the Revolution: The First Generation of Americans* (Cambridge: Harvard University Press, 2000).

Appleby, Joyce, "Thomas Jefferson and the Psychology of Democracy," in James Horn, Jan Ellen Lewis, and Peter S. Onuf, eds., *The Revolution of 1800: Democracy, Race, and the New Republic* (Charlottesville: University of Virginia Press, 2002): 155–72.

Aptheker, Herbert, *American Negro Slave Revolts* (New York: Columbia University Press, 1943).

Armitage, David, and Michael J. Braddick, eds., *The British Atlantic World, 1500–1800* (New York: Palgrave Macmillan, 2002).

Armstrong, Maurice W., "Neutrality and Religion in Revolutionary Nova Scotia," in G. A. Rawlyk, ed. *Historical Essays on the Atlantic Provinces* (Toronto: McClelland & Stewart, 1967): 33–43.

Aron, Stephen, *American Confluence: The Missouri Frontier from Borderland to Border State* (Bloomington: Indiana University Press, 2006).

Aron, Stephen, *How the West Was Lost: The Transformation of Kentucky from Daniel Boone to Henry Clay* (Baltimore: Johns Hopkins University Press, 1996).

Bailor, Keith M., "John Taylor of Caroline: Continuity, Change, and Discontinuity in Virginia's Sentiments toward Slavery, 1790–1820," *Virginia Magazine of History and Biography*, vol. 75 (July 1967): 290–304.

Bailyn, Bernard, *The Ideological Origins of the American Revolution* (Cambridge: Harvard University Press, 1967).

Bailyn, Bernard, *Origins of American Politics* (New York: Knopf, 1968).

Bailyn, Bernard, *Voyagers to the West: A Passage in the Peopling of America on the Eve of the Revolution* (New York: Knopf, 1986).

Bailyn, Bernard, and Philip D. Morgan, eds., *Strangers Within the Realm: Cultural Margins of the First British Empire* (Chapel Hill: University of North Carolina Press, 1991).

Banner, James M., Jr., *To the Hartford Convention: The Federalists and the Origins of Party Politics in Massachusetts, 1789–1815* (New York: Knopf, 1970).

Bannister, Jerry, and Liam Riordan, "Loyalism and the British Atlantic, 1660–1840," in Bannister and Riordan, eds., *The Loyal Atlantic: Remaking the British Atlantic in the Revolutionary Era* (Toronto: University of Toronto Press, 2012): 3–36.

Baptist, Edward E., *The Half Has Never Been Told: Slavery and the Making of American Capitalism* (New York: Basic Books, 2014).

Bayly, C. A., *Imperial Meridian: The British Empire and the World, 1780–1830* (London: Addison Wesley Longman, 1989).

Beddard, Robert, ed., *The Revolutions of 1688* (Oxford: Clarendon Press, 1991).

Beeman, Richard R., *The Old Dominion and the New Nation, 1788–1801* (Lexington: University Press of Kentucky, 1972).

Beeman, Richard R., *Plain, Honest Men: The Making of the American Constitution* (New York: Random House, 2009).

Beeman, Richard R., "The Political Response to Social Conflict in the Southern Backcountry: A Comparative View of Virginia and the Carolinas During the Revolution," in Ronald Hoffman, Thad W. Tate, and Peter J. Albert, eds., *An Uncivil War: The Southern Backcountry During the American Revolution* (Charlottesville: University Press of Virginia, 1985): 213–39.

Beeman, Richard R., *The Varieties of Political Experience in Eighteenth-Century America* (Philadelphia: University of Pennsylvania Press, 2004).

Belknap, Jeremy, ed., "Queries Relating to Slavery in Massachusetts," Massachusetts Historical Society, *Collections*, 5th ser., vol. 3 (1877): 378–431.

Bellisles, Michael A., *Revolutionary Outlaws: Ethan Allen and the Struggle for Independence on the Early American Frontier* (Charlottesville: University Press of Virginia, 1993).

Ben-Atar, Doron, and Barbara B. Oberg, "Introduction: The Paradoxical Legacy of the Federalists," in Ben-Atar and Oberg, eds., *Federalists Reconsidered* (Charlottesville: University of Virginia Press, 1998): 1–16.

Berkin, Carol, *A Brilliant Solution: Inventing the American Constitution* (New York: Harcourt, 2002).

Berkin, Carol, *First Generations: Women in Colonial America* (New York: Hill & Wang, 1996).

Berkin, Carol, *Revolutionary Mothers: Women in the Struggle for America's Independence* (New York: Knopf, 2005).

Berlin, Ira, *Many Thousands Gone: The First Two Centuries of Slavery in North America* (Cambridge: Harvard University Press, 1998).

Berlin, Ira, "The Revolution in Black Life," in Alfred F. Young, ed., *The American Revolution: Explorations in the History of American Radicalism* (DeKalb: Northern Illinois University Press, 1976): 349–82.

Berlin, Ira, "Time, Space, and the Evolution of Afro-American Society on British Mainland North America," in Philip D. Morgan, ed., *Diversity and Unity in Early North America* (New York: Routledge, 1993): 113–46.

Billias, George Athan, "Horatio Gates," in Billias, ed., *George Washington's Generals and Opponents: Their Exploits and Leadership* (New York: Da Capo Press, 1994), vol. 1:79–108.

Billias, George Athan, "John Burgoyne: Ambitious General," in Billias, ed., *George Washington's Generals and Opponents: Their Exploits and Leadership* (New York: Da Capo Press, 1994), vol. 2:142–92.

Black, Jeremy, *George III: America's Last King* (New Haven: Yale University Press, 2006).

Blackburn, Robin, "The Achievement of the Haitian Revolution, 1791–1804," in Thomas Bender, Lauren Dubois, and Richard Rabinowitz, eds., *Revolution!: The Atlantic World Reborn* (New York: New-York Historical Society, 2011): 115–38.

Blackburn, Robin, *The Making of New World Slavery: From the Baroque to the Modern, 1492–1800* (New York: Verso, 1997).

Blackburn, Robin, *The Overthrow of Colonial Slavery, 1776–1848* (New York: Verso, 1988).

Blakeley, Phyllis R., and John N. Grant, eds., *Eleven Exiles: Accounts of Loyalists of the American Revolution* (Toronto: Dundurn Press, 1982).

Blumrosen, Alfred W., and Ruth G., *Slave Nation: How Slavery United the Colonies and Sparked the American Revolution* (Naperville, Ill.: Sourcebooks, 2005).

Bobb, Bernard E., *The Viceregency of Antonio Maria Bucareli in New Spain, 1771–1779* (Austin: University of Texas Press, 1962).

Bodle, Wayne, "'The Ghost of Clow': Loyalist Insurgency in the Delmarva Peninsula," in Joseph S. Tiedemann, Eugene R. Fingerhut, and Robert W. Venables, eds., *The Other Loyalists: Ordinary People, Royalism, and the Revolution in the Middle Colonies, 1763–1787* (Albany: State University of New York Press, 2009): 19–44.

Bodle, Wayne, *The Valley Forge Winter: Civilians and Soldiers in War* (University Park: Pennsylvania State University Press, 2002).

Bonomi, Patricia U., *A Factious People: Politics and Society in Colonial New York* (New York: Columbia University Press, 1971).

Bonomi, Patricia U., "Religious Dissent and the Case for American Exceptionalism," in Ronald Hoffman and Peter J. Albert, eds., *Religion in a Revolutionary Age* (Charlottesville: University Press of Virginia, 1994): 31–51.

Bonomi, Patricia U., *Under the Cope of Heaven: Religion, Society, and Politics in Colonial America* (New York: Oxford University Press, 1986).

Bouton, Terry, *Taming Democracy: "The People," the Founders, and the Troubled Ending of the American Revolution* (New York: Oxford University Press, 2007).

Bouton, Terry, "The Trials of the Confederation," in Edward G. Gray and Jane Kamensky, eds., *The Oxford Handbook of the American Revolution* (New York: Oxford University Press, 2013): 370–87.

Bouton, Terry, "William Findley, David Bradford, and the Pennsylvania Regulation of 1794," in Alfred F. Young, Gary Nash, and Ray Raphael, eds., *Revolutionary Founders: Rebels, Radicals, and Reformers in the Making of the Nation* (New York: Knopf, 2012): 233–51.

Bowen, H. V., *Elites, Enterprise, and the Making of the British Overseas Empire, 1688–1775* (New York: St. Martin's Press, 1996).

Boyd, Adams, *Elias Boudinot: Patriot and Statesman, 1740–1821* (Princeton: Princeton University Press, 1952).

Boyd, Julian P., *Number 7: Alexander Hamilton's Secret Attempts to Control American Foreign Policy, with Supporting Documents* (Princeton: Princeton University Press, 1964).

Bradburn, Douglas, *The Citizenship Revolution: Politics and the Creation of the American Union, 1774–1804* (Charlottesville: University of Virginia Press, 2009).

Braund, Kathryn E. Holland, *Deerskins & Duffels: The Creek Indian Trade with Anglo-America, 1685–1815* (Lincoln: University of Nebraska Press, 1993).

Brebner, John Bartlett, *The Neutral Yankees of Nova Scotia: A Marginal Colony*

During the Revolutionary Years (New York: Columbia University Press, 1937).

Brecher, Frank W., *Losing a Continent: France's North American Policy, 1753–1763* (Westport, Conn.: Greenwood Press, 1998).

Breen, T. H., *American Insurgents, American Patriots: The Revolution of the People* (New York: Hill & Wang, 2011).

Breen, T. H., *George Washington's Journey: The President Forges a New Nation* (New York: Simon & Schuster, 2015).

Breen, T. H., *The Marketplace of Revolution: How Consumer Politics Shaped American Independence* (New York: Oxford University Press, 2004).

Brewer, Holly, "Entailing Aristocracy in Colonial Virginia: 'Ancient Feudal Restraints' and Revolutionary Reform," *William and Mary Quarterly*, vol. 54 (Apr. 1997): 307–46.

Brewer, John, *The Sinews of Power: War, Money, and the English State, 1688–1783* (New York: Knopf, 1989).

Bric, Maurice J., "The Irish Immigrant and the Broadening of the Polity in Philadelphia, 1790–1800," in Eliga H. Gould and Peter S. Onuf, eds., *Empire and Nation: The American Revolution in the Atlantic World* (Baltimore: Johns Hopkins University Press, 2005): 159–77.

Brooke, John L., "Trouble with Paradox," *William and Mary Quarterly*, vol. 67 (July 2010): 549–57.

Brown, Christopher Leslie, *Moral Capital: Foundations of British Abolitionism* (Chapel Hill: University of North Carolina Press, 2006).

Brown, Richard D., *Knowledge Is Power: The Diffusion of Information in Early America, 1700–1865* (New York: Oxford University Press, 1989).

Brown, Richard D., *Revolutionary Politics in Massachusetts: The Boston Committee of Correspondence and the Towns, 1772–1774* (Cambridge: Harvard University Press, 1970).

Brown, Richard D., "Shays's Rebellion and the Ratification of the Federal Constitution in Massachusetts," in Richard Beeman, Stephen Botein, and Edward C. Carter II, eds., *Beyond Confederation: Origins of the Constitution and American National Identity* (Chapel Hill: University of North Carolina Press, 1987): 113–27.

Brown, Richard D., *The Strength of a People: The Idea of an Informed Citizenry in America, 1650–1870* (Chapel Hill: University of North Carolina Press, 1996).

Brown, Richard Maxwell, "Back Country Rebellions and the Homestead Ethic in America, 1740–1799," in Brown and Don E. Fehrenbacher, eds., *Tradition, Conflict, and Modernization: Perspectives on the American Revolution* (New York: Academic Press, 1977), 76–85.

Brown, Roger H., *Redeeming the Republic: Federalists, Taxation, and the Origins of the Constitution* (Baltimore: Johns Hopkins University Press, 1993).

Brown, Vincent, *The Reaper's Garden: Death and Power in the World of Atlantic Slavery* (Cambridge: Harvard University Press, 2008).

Brown, Vincent, "A Vapor of Dread: Observations on Racial Terror and Vengeance in the Age of Revolution," in Thomas Bender, Lauren Dubois, and Richard Rabinowitz, eds., *Revolution!: The Atlantic World Reborn* (New York: New-York Historical Society, 2011): 177–98.

Brown, Wallace, and Hereward Senior, *Victorious in Defeat: The Loyalists of the American Revolution in Exile* (New York: Facts on File, 1984).

Bruce, William Cabell, *John Randolph of Roanoke, 1773–1833*, 2 vols. (New York: Putnam, 1922).

Brunhouse, Robert L., *The Counter-Revolution in Pennsylvania* (New York: Octagon Books, 1971).

Brunsman, Denver, *The Evil Necessity: British Naval Impressment in the Eighteenth-Century Atlantic World* (Charlottesville: University of Virginia Press, 2013).

Buel, Richard, Jr., "The Public Creditor Interest in Massachusetts Politics, 1780–86," in Robert A. Gross, ed., *In Debt to Shays: The Bicentennial of an Agrarian Rebellion* (Charlottesville: University Press of Virginia, 1993): 47–56.

Buel, Richard, Jr., *Securing the Revolution: Ideology in American Politics, 1789–1815* (Ithaca: Cornell University Press, 1972).

Burkholder, Mark A., and D. S. Chandler, "Creole Participation, Spanish Reaction," in John Lynch, ed., *Latin American Revolutions, 1808–1826: Old and New World Origins* (Norman: University of Oklahoma Press, 1994): 50–57.

Burnard, Trevor, "Freedom, Migration, and the American Revolution," in Eliga H. Gould and Peter S. Onuf, eds., *Empire and Nation: The American Revolution in the Atlantic World* (Baltimore: Johns Hopkins University Press, 2005): 295–314.

Burnard, Trevor, *Mastery, Tyranny, and Desire: Thomas Thistlewood and His Slaves in the Anglo-Jamaican World* (Chapel Hill: University of North Carolina Press, 2004).

Burnard, Trevor, "'Prodigious Riches': The Wealth of Jamaica Before the American Revolution," *Economic History Review*, 2nd ser., vol. 64 (Aug. 2001): 506–24.

Burnard, Trevor, "Slavery and the Causes of the American Revolution in Plantation British America," in Andrew Shankman, ed., *The World of the Revolutionary American Republic: Land, Labor, and the Conflict for a Continent* (New York: Routledge, 2014): 54–76.

Burrows, Edwin G., *Forgotten Patriots: The Untold Story of American Prisoners During the Revolutionary War* (New York: Basic Books, 2008).

Burt, Alfred Leroy, *The Old Province of Quebec*, 2 vols. (Toronto: McClelland & Stewart, 1968).

Bushman, Richard L., *King and People in Provincial Massachusetts* (Chapel Hill: University of North Carolina Press, 1985).

Bushman, Richard, *The Refinement of America: Persons, Houses, Cities* (New York: Knopf, 1992).

Butler, Jon, "Coercion, Miracle, Reason: Rethinking the American Religious Experience in the Revolutionary Age," in Ronald Hoffman and Peter J. Albert, eds., *Religion in a Revolutionary Age* (Charlottesville: University Press of Virginia, 1994): 1–30.

Butterfield, Lyman H., et al., eds., *The Adams Papers, Adams Family Correspondence,* 11 vols. to date (Cambridge: Harvard University Press, 1963–)

Butterfield, Lyman H., et al., eds., *The Book of Abigail and John: Selected Letters of the Adams Family, 1762–1784* (Cambridge: Harvard University Press, 1975).

Butterfield, Lyman H., et al., eds., *Diary and Autobiography of John Adams,* 4 vols. (Cambridge: Harvard University Press, 1961–62).

Calhoon, Robert M., "The Evangelical Persuasion," in Ronald Hoffman and Peter J. Albert, eds., *Religion in a Revolutionary Age* (Charlottesville: University Press of Virginia, 1994): 156–183.

Calhoon, Robert M., "Loyalism and Neutrality," in Jack P. Greene and J. R. Pole, eds., *Blackwell Encyclopedia of the American Revolution* (Cambridge, Mass.: Basil Blackwell, 1991): 247–59.

Calhoon, Robert M., *The Loyalists in Revolutionary America, 1760–1781* (New York: Harcourt Brace Jovanovich, 1973).

Callahan, North, "Henry Knox: American Artillerist," in George Athan Billias, ed., *George Washington's Generals and Opponents: Their Exploits and Leadership* (New York: Da Capo Press, 1994), vol. 1:239–59.

Calloway, Colin G., *The American Revolution in Indian Country: Crisis and Diversity in Native American Communities* (New York: Cambridge University Press, 1995).

Calloway, Colin G., "The Continuing Revolution in Indian Country," in Frederick E. Hoxie, Ronald Hoffman, and Peter J. Albert, eds., *Native Americans and the Early Republic* (Charlottesville: University Press of Virginia, 1999): 3–33.

Calloway, Colin G., *Crown and Calumet: British-Indian Relations, 1783–1815* (Norman: University of Oklahoma Press, 1987).

Calloway, Colin G., *The Scratch of a Pen: 1763 and the Transformation of North America* (New York: Oxford University Press, 2006).

Campbell, William J., *Speculators in Empire: Iroquoia and the 1768 Treaty of Fort Stanwix* (Norman: University of Oklahoma Press, 2012).

Campbell, William W., *Annals of Tryon County; or, the Border Warfare of New York During the Revolution* (New York: Dodd, Mead, 1924).

Canny, Nicholas, ed., *Europeans on the Move: Studies on European Migration, 1500–1800* (New York: Oxford University Press, 1994).

Cappon, Lester J., ed., *The Adams-Jefferson Letters: The Complete Correspondence Between Thomas Jefferson and Abigail and John Adams*, 2 vols.(Chapel Hill: University of North Carolina Press, 1959).

Carlson, Paul H., *The Plains Indians* (College Station: Texas A&M University Press, 1998).

Carp, Benjamin L., *Rebels Rising: Cities and the American Revolution* (New York: Oxford University Press, 2007).

Carson, Cary, et al., eds., *Of Consuming Interests: The Style of Life in the Eighteenth Century* (Charlottesville: University Press of Virginia, 1994).

Carter, Clarence Edward, ed., *The Correspondence of General Thomas Gage with the Secretaries of State, 1763–1775*, 2 vols. (New Haven: Yale University Press, 1931–33).

Carter, Clarence Edward, ed., *The Territorial Papers of the United States*, 28 vols. (Washington, D.C.: Government Printing Office, 1934–75).

Carter, Edward C., Jr., ed., *The Virginia Journals of Benjamin Henry Latrobe, 1795–1798*, 2 vols. (New Haven: Yale University Press, 1977).

Carter, Edward C., Jr., "'A Wild Irishman' Under Every Federalist's Bed: Naturalization in Philadelphia, 1789–1806," *Pennsylvania Magazine of History and Biography*, vol. 94 (July 1970): 331–46.

Cashin, Edward J., "'But Brothers, It Is Our Land We Are Talking About': Winners and Losers in the Georgia Backcountry," in Ronald Hoffman, Thad W. Tate, and Peter J. Albert, eds., *An Uncivil War: The Southern Backcountry During the American Revolution* (Charlottesville: University Press of Virginia, 1985): 240–75.

Cayton, Andrew R. L., *The Frontier Republic: Ideology and Politics in the Ohio Country, 1780–1825* (Kent, Ohio: Kent State University Press, 1986).

Cayton, Andrew R. L., "Radicals in the 'Western World': The Federalist Conquest of Trans-Appalachian North America," in Doron Ben-Atar and Barbara Oberg, eds., *Federalists Reconsidered* (Charlottesville: University of Virginia Press, 1998): 77–96.

Champagne, Roger J., *Alexander McDougall and the American Revolution in New York* (Schenectady, N.Y.: Union College Press, 1975).

Chaplin, Joyce, *An Anxious Pursuit: Agricultural Innovation and Modernity in the Lower South, 1730–1815* (Chapel Hill: University of North Carolina Press, 1993).

Chaplin, Joyce E., "The British Atlantic," in Nicholas Canny and Philip Morgan, eds., *The Atlantic World, c. 1450–c. 1850* (New York: Oxford University Press, 2011): 219–34.

Chase, Philander D., et al., eds., *The Papers of George Washington, Revolutionary War Series*, 22 vols. to date (Charlottesville: University of Virginia Press, 1985–).

Chastellux, Marquis de, "Visit to Schenectady, 1780," in Dean R. Snow, Charles

T. Gehring, and William A. Starna, eds., *In Mohawk Country: Early Narratives About a Native People* (Syracuse, N.Y.: Syracuse University Press, 1996): 292–94.

Chavez, Thomas E., *Spain and the Independence of the United States: An Intrinsic Gift* (Albuquerque: University of New Mexico Press, 2002).

Chernow, Ron, *Alexander Hamilton* (New York: Penguin Books, 2004).

Chernow, Ron, *Washington: A Life* (New York: Penguin Press, 2010).

Chopra, Ruma, *Choosing Sides: Loyalists in Revolutionary America* (New York: Rowman & Littlefield, 2013).

Chopra, Ruma, *Unnatural Rebellion: Loyalists in New York City During the Revolution* (Charlottesville: University of Virginia Press, 2011).

Clarke, Ernest A., *The Siege of Fort Cumberland, 1776: An Episode in the American Revolution* (Kingston: McGill-Queen's University Press, 1995).

Cogliano, Francis D., *Emperor of Liberty: Thomas Jefferson's Foreign Policy* (New Haven: Yale University Press, 2014).

Cohen, Daniel A., "Homicidal Compulsion and the Conditions of Freedom: The Social and Psychological Origins of Familicide in America's Early Republic," *Journal of Social History*, vol. 28 (Summer 1995): 725–64.

Colden, Cadwallader, *The Cadwallader Colden Letter Books*, 2 vols. (New York: New-York Historical Society, 1876–1877).

Coleman, Mary H., *St. George Tucker, Citizen of No Mean City* (Richmond: Dietz Press, 1938).

Colley, Linda, *Britons: Forging the Nation, 1707–1837* (New Haven: Yale University Press, 1992).

Colley, Linda, *Captives: Britain, Empire, and the World, 1600–1850* (London: Jonathan Cape, 2002).

Cometti, Elizabeth, ed., *The American Journals of Lt. John Enys* (Syracuse, N. Y. : Syracuse University Press, 1976).

Conway, Stephen, "The British Army and the War of Independence," in Edward G. Gray and Jane Kamensky, eds., *The Oxford Handbook of the American Revolution* (New York: Oxford University Press, 2013): 177–93.

Conway, Stephen, "To Subdue America: British Army Officers and the Conduct of the Revolutionary War," *William and Mary Quarterly*, 3rd ser., vol. 48 (July 1986): 381–407.

Conway, Stephen, *The War of American Independence, 1775–1783* (New York: St. Martin's, 1995).

Conway, Stephen, *War, State, and Society in Mid-Eighteenth-Century Britain and Ireland* (New York: Oxford University Press, 2006).

Cook, Warren L., *Flood Tide of Empire: Spain and the Pacific Northwest, 1543–1819* (New Haven: Yale University Press, 1973).

Cornell, Saul, *The Other Founders: Anti-Federalism & the Dissenting Tradition in America, 1788–1828* (Chapel Hill: University of North Carolina Press, 1999).

Costell, Julia G., and David Hornbeck, "Alta California: An Overview," in David

Hurst Thomas, ed., *Columbian Consequences: Archaeological and Historical Perspectives on the Spanish Borderland West* (Washington, D.C.: Smithsonian Institution Press, 1989): 303–32.

Cotlar, Seth, *Tom Paine's America: The Rise and Fall of Transatlantic Radicalism in the Early Republic* (Charlottesville: University of Virginia Press, 2011).

Countryman, Edward, *The American Revolution* (New York: Hill & Wang, 1985).

Countryman, Edward, "Indians, the Colonial Order, and the Social Significance of the American Revolution," *William and Mary Quarterly*, 3rd ser., vol. 53 (Apr. 1996): 342–62.

Countryman, Edward, *A People in Revolution: The American Revolution and Political Society in New York, 1760–1790* (Baltimore: Johns Hopkins University Press, 1981).

Countryman, Edward, "'Out of the Bounds of the Law': Northern Land Rioters in the Eighteenth Century," in Alfred F. Young, ed., *The American Revolution: Explorations in the History of American Radicalism* (DeKalb: Northern Illinois University Press, 1976): 37–69.

Countryman, Edward, "Some Problems of Power in New York, 1777–1782," in Ronald Hoffman and Peter J. Albert, eds., *Sovereign States in an Age of Uncertainty* (Charlottesville: University Press of Virginia, 1981): 157–84.

Cox, Caroline, "The Continental Army," in Edward G. Gray and Jane Kamensky, eds., *The Oxford Handbook of the American Revolution* (New York: Oxford University Press, 2013): 161–76.

Cox, Caroline, *A Proper Sense of Honor: Service and Sacrifice in George Washington's Army* (Chapel Hill: University of North Carolina Press, 2004).

Cox, Edward L., "The British Caribbean in the Age of Revolution," in Eliga H. Gould and Peter S. Onuf, eds., *Empire and Nation: The American Revolution in the Atlantic World* (Baltimore: Johns Hopkins University Press, 2005): 275–94.

Craig, Gerald M., *Upper Canada: The Formative Years, 1784–1841* (Toronto: McClelland & Stewart, 1963).

Craig, Neville B., ed., *The Olden Time*, 2 vols. (Pittsburgh: Wright & Charlton, 1848).

Crary, Catherine S., ed., *The Price of Loyalty: Tory Writings from the Revolutionary Era* (New York: McGraw-Hill, 1973).

Craton, Michael, "Reluctant Creoles: The Planters' World in the British West Indies," in Bernard Bailyn and Philip Morgan, eds., *Strangers Within the Realm: Cultural Margins of the First British Empire* (Chapel Hill: University of North Carolina Press, 1991): 314–62.

Craton, Michael, *Testing the Chains: Resistance to Slavery in the British West Indies* (Ithaca: Cornell University Press, 1982).

Cresswell, Nicholas, *The Journal of Nicholas Cresswell, 1774–1777* (New York: Dial Press, 1924).

Crèvecoeur, J. Hector St. John de, *Letters from an American Farmer and Other*

Essays, edited by Dennis D. Moore (Cambridge: Harvard University Press, 2013).

Crèvecoeur, J. Hector St. John de, *Sketches of Eighteenth-Century America*, edited by Henri L. Bourdin, Ralph Gabriel, and Stanley T. Williams (New Haven: Yale University Press, 1925).

Cronon, William, *Changes in the Land: Indians, Colonists, and the Ecology of New England* (New York: Hill & Wang, 1983).

Crow, Jeffrey J., "Liberty Men and Loyalists: Disorder and Disaffection in the North Carolina Backcountry," in Ronald Hoffman, Thad W. Tate, and Peter J. Albert, eds., *An Uncivil War: The Southern Backcountry During the American Revolution* (Charlottesville: University Press of Virginia, 1985): 125–78.

Cruikshank, E. A., ed., *The Correspondence of Lieut. Governor John Graves Simcoe, with Allied Documents Relating to His Administration of the Government of Upper Canada*, 5 vols. (Toronto: Ontario Historical Society, 1923–31).

Cruikshank, E. A., "The King's Royal Regiment of New York," Ontario Historical Society, *Papers and Records*, vol. 27 (1931): 193–323.

Cruikshank, E. A., ed., *The Political Adventures of John Henry: The Record of an International Imbroglio* (Toronto: Macmillan, 1936).

Cunliffe, Marcus, "George Washington: George Washington's Generalship," in George Athan Billias, ed., *George Washington's Generals and Opponents: Their Exploits and Leadership* (New York: Da Capo Press, 1994), vol. 1:3–21.

Curtin, Nancy J., *The United Irishmen: Popular Politics in Ulster and Dublin, 1791–1798* (Oxford: Clarendon Press, 1994).

David, James Corbett, *Dunmore's New World: The Extraordinary Life of a Royal Governor in Revolutionary America* (Charlottesville: University of Virginia Press, 2013).

Davidson, Cathy N., *Revolution and the Word: The Rise of the Novel in America* (New York: Oxford University Press, 1987).

Davies, K. G., ed., *Documents of the American Revolution, 1770–1783*, 21 vols. (Shannon: Irish University Press, 1972–1985).

Davies, K. G., "The Restoration of Civil Government by the British in the War of Independence," in Esmond Wright, ed., *Red, White and True Blue: The Loyalists in the Revolution* (New York: AMS Press, 1976): 111–33.

Davis, David Brion, "American Slavery and the American Revolution," in Ira Berlin and Ronald Hoffman, eds., *Slavery and Freedom in the Age of the American Revolution* (Charlottesville: University Press of Virginia, 1983): 262–80.

Davis, David Brion, *The Problem of Slavery in the Age of Revolution, 1770–1823* (Ithaca: Cornell University Press, 1975).

Davis, John, *Travels of Four Years and a Half in the United States of America During 1798, 1799, 1800, 1801, and 1802*, 2 vols. (New York: Henry Holt 1909, reprint of London, 1803).

DeConde, Alexander, "The French Alliance in Historical Speculation," in Ronald

Hoffman and Peter J. Albert, eds., *Diplomacy and Revolution: The Franco-American Alliance of 1778* (Charlottesville: University Press of Virginia, 1981): 1–37.

DeConde, Alexander, *The Quasi-War: The Politics and Diplomacy of the Undeclared War with France, 1797–1801* (New York: Scribner, 1966).

Dexter, Franklin B., ed., *Diary of David McClure, Doctor of Divinity, 1748–1820* (New York: Knickerbocker Press, 1899).

Deyle, Steven, "An 'Abominable' New Trade: The Closing of the African Slave Trade and the Changing Patterns of U.S. Political Power, 1808–1860," *William and Mary Quarterly*, 3rd ser., vol. 66 (Oct. 2009): 833–50.

Deyle, Steven, *Carry Me Back: The Domestic Slave Trade in American Life* (New York: Oxford University Press, 2005).

Dickinson, Harry T., "The Impact of the War on British Politics," in Edward G. Gray and Jane Kamensky, eds., *The Oxford Handbook of the American Revolution* (New York: Oxford University Press, 2013): 355–69.

Din, Gilbert C., "The Immigration Policy of Governor Esteban Miró in Spanish Louisiana," *Southwestern Historical Quarterly*, vol. 73 (Oct. 1969): 155–75.

Din, Gilbert C., "Spain's Immigration Policy in Louisiana and the American Penetration, 1792–1803," *Southwestern Historical Quarterly*, vol. 76 (Jan. 1973): 255–76.

Dippel, Horst, *Germany and the American Revolution, 1770–1800* (Chapel Hill: University of North Carolina Press, 1977).

Dixon, David, "We Speak as One People': Native Unity and the Pontiac Indian Uprising," in Daniel P. Barr, ed., *The Boundaries Between Us: Natives and Newcomers Along the Frontiers of the Old Northwest Territory, 1750–1850* (Kent, Ohio: Kent State University Press, 2006): 44–65.

Doerflinger, Thomas M., *A Vigorous Spirit of Enterprise: Merchants and Economic Development in Revolutionary Philadelphia* (Chapel Hill: University of North Carolina Press, 1986).

Dorsey, Peter A. *Common Bondage: Slavery as Metaphor in Revolutionary America* (Knoxville: University of Tennessee Press, 2009).

Dowd, Gregory Evans, *A Spirited Resistance: The North American Indian Struggle for Unity, 1745–1815* (Baltimore: Johns Hopkins University Press, 1992).

Dowd, Gregory Evans, *War Under Heaven: Pontiac, the Indian Nations, and the British Empire* (Baltimore: Johns Hopkins University Press, 2002).

Draper, Theodore, *A Struggle for Power: The American Revolution* (New York: Random House, 1996).

Drayton, Richard, "Knowledge and Power," in P.J. Marshall, ed., *The Oxford History of the British Empire, II: The Eighteenth Century* (New York: Oxford University Press, 1998): 231–52.

Drescher, Seymour, *Abolition: A History of Slavery and Antislavery* (New York: Cambridge University Press, 2009).

Drescher, Seymour, "Emperors of the World: British Abolitionism and Imperialism," in Derek R. Peterson, ed., *Abolitionism and Imperialism in Britain, Africa, and the Atlantic* (Athens: Ohio University Press, 2010): 129–49.

Dubois, Laurent, *Avengers of the New World: The Story of the Haitian Revolution* (Cambridge: Harvard University Press, 2004).

Dubois, Laurent, *A Colony of Citizens: Revolution & Slave Emancipation in the French Caribbean, 1787–1804* (Chapel Hill: University of North Carolina Press, 2004).

Dubois, Laurent, "Unworthy of Liberty?: Slavery, Terror, and Revolution in Haiti," in Isaac Land, ed., *Enemies of Humanity: The Nineteenth-Century War on Terrorism* (New York: Palgrave Macmillan, 2008): 45–62.

Dubois, Laurent, and Julius S. Scott, "An African Revolutionary in the Atlantic World," in Thomas Bender, Laurent Dubois, and Richard Rabinowitz, eds., *Revolution!: The Atlantic World Reborn* (New York: New-York Historical Society, 2011): 139–57.

Dull, Jonathan R., *A Diplomatic History of the American Revolution* (New Haven: Yale University Press, 1985).

Dull, Jonathan R., *The French Navy and American Independence: A Study of Arms and Diplomacy, 1774–1787* (Princeton: Princeton University Press, 1975).

Dull, Jonathan R., "Vergennes, Rayneval, and the Diplomacy of Trust," in Ronald Hoffman and Peter J. Albert, eds., *Peace and the Peacemakers: The Treaty of 1783* (Charlottesville: University Press of Virginia, 1986): 101–31.

Dun, James Alexander, "Atlantic Antislavery, American Ambition: The Problem of Slavery in the United States in an Age of Disruption, 1770–1808," in Andrew Shankman, ed., *The World of the Revolutionary American Republic: Land, Labor, and the Conflict for a Continent* (New York: Routledge, 2014): 218–45.

Dunn, Richard S., "After Tobacco: The Slave Labour Pattern on a Large Chesapeake Grain-and-Livestock Plantation in the Early Nineteenth Century," in John J. McCusker and Kenneth Morgan, eds., *The Early Modern Atlantic Economy* (New York: Cambridge University Press, 2000), 344–63.

Dunn, Richard S., "Black Society in the Chesapeake, 1776–1810," in Ira Berlin and Ronald Hoffman, eds., *Slavery and Freedom in the Age of the American Revolution* (Urbana: University of Illinois Press, 1983): 49–82.

Dunn, Richard S., "The Glorious Revolution in America," in Nicholas Canny and Alaine Low, eds., *The Origins of Empire: British Overseas Enterprise to the Close of the Seventeenth Century* (New York: Oxford University Press, 1998): 445–66.

Dunn, Richard S., *Sugar and Slaves: The Rise of the Planter Class in the English West Indies, 1624–1733* (Chapel Hill: University of North Carolina Press, 1972).

Dunn, Richard S., "A Tale of Two Plantations: Slave Life at Mesopotamia in Jamaica and Mounty Airy in Virginia, 1799 to 1828," *William and Mary Quarterly* 3rd ser., vol. 34 (Jan. 1977): 32–65.

DuVal, Kathleen, "Choosing Enemies: The Prospects for an Anti-American

Alliance in the Louisiana Territory," *Arkansas Historical Quarterly*, vol. 62 (Autumn 2003): 233–52.

DuVal, Kathleen, "Independence for Whom?: Expansion and Conflict in the South and Southwest," in Andrew Shankman, ed., *The World of the Revolutionary American Republic: Land, Labor, and the Conflict for a Continent* (New York: Routledge, 2014): 97–115.

DuVal, Kathleen, *Independence Lost: Lives on the Edge of the American Revolution* (New York: Random House, 2015).

DuVal, Kathleen, *On Native Ground: Indians and Colonists in the Heart of the Continent* (Philadelphia: University of Pennsylvania Press, 2006).

Dwight, Timothy, *Travels in New-England and New-York*, 4 vols. (London, 1823).

Eccles, W. J., *Essays on New France* (Toronto: Oxford University Press, 1987).

Eccles, W. J., *The French in North America, 1500–1783* (East Lansing: Michigan State University Press, 1998).

Eccles, W. J., "French Imperial Policy for the Great Lakes Basin," in David Curtis Skaggs and Larry L. Nelson, eds., *The Sixty Years' War for the Great Lakes, 1754–1814* (East Lansing: Michigan State University Press, 2001): 21–42.

Edelson, S. Max, *Plantation Enterprise in Colonial South Carolina* (Cambridge: Harvard University Press, 2006).

Edling, Max M., "A More Perfect Union: The Framing and Ratification of the Constitution," in Edward G. Gray and Jane Kamensky, eds., *The Oxford Handbook of the American Revolution* (New York: Oxford University Press, 2013): 388–406.

Edling, Max M., *A Revolution in Favor of Government: Origins of the U.S. Constitution and the Making of the American State* (New York: Oxford University Press, 2003).

Edling, Max M., and Mark D. Kaplanoff, "Alexander Hamilton's Fiscal Reforms: Transforming the Structure of Taxation in the Early Republic," *William and Mary Quarterly*, 3rd ser., vol. 61 (Oct. 2004): 713–44.

Edwards, Laura F., *The People and Their Peace: Legal Culture and the Transformation of Inequality in the Post-Revolutionary South* (Chapel Hill: University of North Carolina Press, 2009).

Egerton, Douglas R., *Death or Liberty: African Americans and Revolutionary America* (New York: Oxford University Press, 2009).

Egerton, Douglas R., "The Empire of Liberty Reconsidered," in James Horn, Jan Ellen Lewis, and Peter S. Onuf, eds., *The Revolution of 1800: Democracy, Race, and the New Republic* (Charlottesville: University of Virginia Press, 2002): 309–30.

Egerton, Douglas R., *Gabriel's Rebellion: The Virginia Slave Conspiracies of 1800 and 1802* (Chapel Hill: University of North Carolina Press, 1993).

Einhorn, Robin L., "Patrick Henry's Case Against the Constitution: The Structural Problem with Slavery," *Journal of the Early Republic*, vol. 22 (Winter 2002): 549–73.

Ekirch, A. Roger, *Bound for America: The Transportation of British Convicts to the Colonies, 1718–1775* (New York: Oxford University Press, 1987).

Ekirch, A. Roger, ed., "'A New Government of Liberty': Hermon Husband's Vision of Backcountry North Carolina, 1755," *William and Mary Quarterly*, 3rd ser., vol. 34 (1977): 632–46.

Ekirch, A. Roger, "*Poor Carolina*': Politics and Society in Colonial North Carolina, 1729–1776 (Chapel Hill: University of North Carolina Press, 1981).

Elkins, Stanley, and Eric McKitrick, *The Age of Federalism* (New York: Oxford University Press, 1993).

Elliott, J. H., *Empires of the Atlantic World: Britain and Spain in America, 1492–1830* (New Haven: Yale University Press, 2006).

Ellis, Joseph J., *After the Revolution: Profiles of Early American Culture* (New York: W. W. Norton, 1979).

Ellis, Richard E., "The Persistence of Antifederalism after 1789," in Richard Beeman, Stephen Botein, and Edward C. Carter II, eds., *Beyond Confederation: Origins of the Constitution and American National Identity* (Chapel Hill: University of North Carolina Press, 1987): 295–314.

Ells, Margaret, "Loyalist Attitudes," in G. A. Rawlyk, ed. *Historical Essays on the Atlantic Provinces* (Toronto: McClelland & Stewart, 1967): 44–60.

Eltis, David, "Africa, Slavery, and the Slave Trade, Mid-Seventeenth to Mid-Eighteenth Centuries," in Nicholas Canny and Philip Morgan, eds., *The Atlantic World, c. 1450–c. 1850* (New York: Oxford University Press, 2011): 271–86.

Ely, Melvin Patrick, *Israel on the Appomattox: A Southern Experiment in Black Freedom from the 1790s Through the Civil War* (New York: Knopf, 2004).

Engerman, Stanley L., and Robert E. Gallman, eds., *The Cambridge Economic History of the United States: Volume I, the Colonial Era* (New York: Cambridge University Press, 1996).

Engstrand, Iris H. W., "Seekers of the 'Northern Mystery': European Exploration of California and the Pacific," in Ramón A. Gutiérrez and Richard J. Orsi, eds., *Contested Eden: California Before the Gold Rush* (Berkeley: University of California Press, 1998): 78–110.

Evans, Emory G., "Executive Leadership in Virginia, 1776–1781: Henry, Jefferson, and Nelson," in Ronald Hoffman and Peter J. Albert, eds., *Sovereign States in an Age of Uncertainty* (Charlottesville: University Press of Virginia, 1981): 185–225.

Evans, Emory G., *A "Topping People": The Rise and Decline of Virginia's Old Political Elite, 1680–1790* (Charlottesville: University of Virginia Press, 2009).

Evans, Emory G., "Trouble in the Backcountry: Disaffection in Southwest Virginia During the American Revolution," in Ronald Hoffman, Thad W. Tate, and Peter J. Albert, eds., *An Uncivil War: The Southern Backcountry*

During the American Revolution (Charlottesville: University Press of Virginia, 1985): 179–212.

Ewald, Johann von, *Diary of the American War: A Hessian Journal*, translated and edited by Joseph P. Tustin (New Haven: Yale University Press, 1979).

Faber, Eberhard L., *Building the Land of Dreams: New Orleans and the Transformation of Early America* (Princeton: Princeton University Press, 2016).

Farrand, Max, ed., *The Records of the Federal Convention of 1787*, 3 vols. (New Haven: Yale University Press, 1966).

Fedric, Francis, *Slave Life in Virginia and Kentucky: A Narrative by Francis Fedric, Escaped Slave* (Baton Rouge: Louisiana State University Press, 2010).

Fehrenbacher, Don E., and Ward M. McAfee, *The Slaveholding Republic: An Account of the United States Government's Relations to Slavery* (New York: Oxford University Press, 2001).

Feltman, William, *The Journal of Lieut. William Feltman of the First Pennsylvania Regiment, 1781–1782* (Philadelphia: Historical Society of Pennsylvania, 1853).

Fenn, Elizabeth A. *Encounters at the Heart of the World: A History of the Mandan People* (New York: Hill & Wang, 2014).

Fenn, Elizabeth A., *Pox Americana: The Great Smallpox Epidemic of 1775–82* (New York: Hill & Wang, 2001).

Ferling, John E., *The First of Men: A Life of George Washington* (Knoxville: University of Tennessee Press, 1988).

Ferling, John E., *A Leap in the Dark: The Struggle to Create the American Republic* (New York: Oxford University Press, 2003).

Ferling, John E., *The Loyalist Mind: Joseph Galloway and the American Revolution* (University Park: Pennsylvania State University Press, 1977).

Ferling, John E., *Setting the World Ablaze: Washington, Adams, Jefferson, and the American Revolution* (New York: Oxford University Press, 2000).

Finkelman, Paul, "Slavery and the Constitutional Convention: Making a Covenant with Death," in Richard Beeman, Stephen Botein, and Edward C. Carter II, eds., *Beyond Confederation: Origins of the Constitution and American National Identity* (Chapel Hill: University of North Carolina Press, 1987): 188–225.

Fischer, David Hackett, *The Revolution of American Conservatism: The Federalist Party in the Era of Jeffersonian Democracy* (New York: Harper & Row, 1965).

Fitzpatrick, John C., ed., *The Writings of George Washington*, 39 vols. (Washington, D.C: U.S. Government Printing Office, 1931–1944).

Flexner, James Thomas, *George Washington and the New Nation (1783–1793)* (Boston: Little, Brown, 1969).

Fogleman, Aaron Spencer, *Hopeful Journeys: German Immigration, Settlement, and Political Culture in Colonial America, 1717–1775* (Philadelphia: University of Pennsylvania Press, 1996).

Foley, William E., *The Genesis of Missouri: From Wilderness Outpost to State-hood* (Columbia: University of Missouri Press, 1989).

Foner, Eric, *Tom Paine and Revolutionary America* (New York: Hill & Wang, 1976),

Foner, Philip, ed., *The Complete Writings of Thomas Paine,* 2 vols. (New York: Citadel Press, 1945).

Force, Peter, ed., *American Archives,* 9 vols. (Washington, D.C.: U.S. Congress, 1837–53).

Ford, Lacy K., *Deliver Us from Evil: The Slavery Question in the Old South* (New York: Oxford University Press, 2009).

Ford, Worthington C., ed., *Journals of the Continental Congress, 1774–1789,* 34 vols. (Washington, D.C.: Government Printing Office, 1904–37).

Fowler, David J., "'Loyalty Is Now Bleeding in New Jersey': Motivations and Mentalities of the Disaffected,'" in Joseph S. Tiedemann, Eugene R. Finger-hut, and Robert W. Venables, eds., *The Other Loyalists: Ordinary People, Royalism, and the Revolution in the Middle Colonies, 1763–1787* (Albany: State University of New York Press, 2009): 45–80.

Fowler, Loretta, "The Great Plains from the Arrival of the Horse to 1885," in Bruce G. Trigger and Wilcomb E. Washburn, eds., *The Cambridge History of the Native Peoples of the Americas,* 2 vols. (New York: Cambridge University Press, 1996), vol. 1, part 2: 1–55.

Fowler, William M., Jr., *The Baron of Beacon Hill: A Biography of John Hancock* (Boston: Houghton Mifflin, 1980).

Fowler, William M., Jr., *Samuel Adams: Radical Puritan* (New York: Longman, 1997).

Frank, Ross, "Demographic, Social, and Economic Change in New Mexico," in Robert H. Jackson, ed., *New Views of Borderlands History* (Albuquerque: University of New Mexico Press, 1998): 41–71.

Freeman, Joanne B., *Affairs of Honor: National Politics in the New Republic* (New Haven: Yale University Press, 2001).

Freeman, Joanne B., "Corruption and Compromise in the Election of 1800: The Process of Politics on the National Stage," in James Horn, Jan Ellen Lewis, and Peter S. Onuf, eds., *The Revolution of 1800: Democracy, Race, and the New Republic* (Charlottesville: University of Virginia Press, 2002): 87–120.

Frey, Sylvia R., "Between Slavery and Freedom: Virginia Blacks in the American Revolution," *Journal of Southern History,* vol. 49 (Aug. 1983): 375–98.

Frey, Sylvia R., *The British Soldier in America: A Social History of Military Life in the Revolutionary Period* (Austin: University of Texas Press, 1981).

Frey, Sylvia R., *Water from the Rock: Black Resistance in a Revolutionary Age* (Princeton: Princeton University Press, 1991).

Fryer, Mary Beacock, and Christopher Dracott, *John Graves Simcoe, 1752–1806: A Biography* (Toronto: Dundurn Press, 1998).

Furstenberg, François, "Beyond Freedom and Slavery: Autonomy, Virtue, and

Resistance in Early American Political Discourse," *Journal of American History*, 89 (Mar. 2003): 1295–1330.

Furstenberg, François, *In the Name of the Father: Washington's Legacy, Slavery, and the Making of a Nation* (New York: Penguin Books, 2006).

Furstenberg, François, "The Significance of the Trans-Appalachian Frontier," *American Historical Review*, vol. 113 (June 2008): 647–77.

Gallay, Alan, *The Indian Slave Trade: The Rise of the English Empire in the American South, 1670–1717* (New Haven: Yale University Press, 2002).

Garner, John, *The Franchise and Politics in British North America* (Toronto: University of Toronto Press, 1969).

Gates, Lillian F., *Land Policies of Upper Canada* (Toronto: University of Toronto Press, 1968).

Gates, Lillian F., "Roads, Rivals, and Rebellion: The Unknown Story of Asa Danforth, Jr.," *Ontario History*, vol. 76 (Sept. 1984): 233–54.

Gaustad, Edwin S., "Religious Tests, Constitutions, and 'Christian Nation,'" in Ronald Hoffman and Peter J. Albert, eds., *Religion in a Revolutionary Age* (Charlottesville: University Press of Virginia, 1994): 218–35.

Geggus, David Patrick, *Haitian Revolutionary Studies* (Bloomington: Indiana University Press, 2002).

Gerlach, Don R., *Philip Schuyler and the American Revolution in New York, 1733–1777* (Lincoln: University of Nebraska Press, 1964).

Gerlach, Don R., *Proud Patriot: Philip Schuyler and the War of Independence, 1775–1783* (Syracuse: Syracuse University Press, 1987),

Gerlach, Larry, *Prologue to Independence: New Jersey in the Coming of the Revolution* (New Brunswick: Rutgers University Press, 1976).

Gilbert, Alan, *Black Patriots and Loyalists: Fighting for Emancipation in the War for Independence* (Chicago: University of Chicago Press, 2012).

Gilje, Paul A., *The Making of the American Republic, 1763–1815* (Upper Saddle River, N. J.: Pearson, 2006).

Gilmore, Michael T., "The Literature of the Revolutionary and Early National Periods," in Sacvan Bercovitch, ed., *The Cambridge History of American Literature, 1590–1820* (New York: Cambridge University Press, 1994): 539–694.

Gipson, Lawrence Henry, *The Coming of the Revolution, 1763–1775* (New York: Harper & Row, 1962).

Giunta, Mary A. ed., *The Emerging Nation: The Foreign Relations, A Documentary History of the United States Under the Article of Confederation*, 2 vols. (Washington, D.C.: United States Government Printing Office, 1996–1998).

Godoy, Scarlett O'Phelan, "Bourbon Taxes, Indian Resistance," in John Lynch, ed., *Latin American Revolutions, 1808–1826: Old and New World Origins* (Norman: University of Oklahoma Press, 1994): 80–87.

Gordon-Reed, Annette, *The Hemingses of Monticello: An American Family* (New York: W. W. Norton, 2008).

Gould, Eliga H., "American Independence and Britain's Counter-Revolution," *Past and Present*, no. 154 (Feb. 1997): 107–141.

Gould, Eliga H., *Among the Powers of the Earth: The American Revolution and the Making of a New World Empire* (Cambridge: Harvard University Press, 2012).

Gould, Eliga H., "The Empire that Britain Kept," in Edward G. Gray and Jane Kamensky, eds., *The Oxford Handbook of the American Revolution* (New York: Oxford University Press, 2013): 465–80.

Gould, Eliga H., "Fears of War, Fantasies of Peace: British Politics and the Coming of the American Revolution," in Gould and Peter S. Onuf, eds., *Empire and Nation: The American Revolution in the Atlantic World* (Baltimore: Johns Hopkins University Press, 2005): 19–34.

Gould, Eliga H., "The Making of an Atlantic State System: Britain and the United States, 1795–1825," in Julie Flavell and Stephen Conway, eds., *Britain and America Go to War: The Impact of War and Warface in Anglo-America, 1754–1815* (Gainesville: University Press of Florida, 2004): 241–65.

Gould, Eliga H., *The Persistence of Empire: British Political Culture in the Age of the American Revolution* (Chapel Hill: University of North Carolina Press, 2000).

Gould, Eliga H., and Peter S. Onuf, eds., *Empire and Nation: The American Revolution in the Atlantic World* (Baltimore: Johns Hopkins University Press, 2005).

Gould, Philip, "Loyalists Respond to *Common Sense*: The Politics of Authorship in Revolutionary America," in Jerry Bannister and Liam Riordan, eds., *The Loyal Atlantic: Remaking the British Atlantic in the Revolutionary Era* (Toronto: University of Toronto Press, 2012): 105–27.

Grabbe, Hans-Jurgen, "European Immigration to the United States in the Early National Period, 1783–1820," *American Philosophical Society, Proceedings*, vol. 133 (June 1989): 190–214.

Graham, Gerald S., *British Policy and Canada, 1774–1791: A Study in Eighteenth-Century Trade Policy* (Westport, Conn.: Greenwood Press, 1974).

Grant-Costa, Paul, and Elizabeth Mancke, "Anglo-Amerindian Commercial Relations," in H. V. Bowen, Elizabeth Mancke, and John G. Reid, eds., *Britain's Oceanic Empire: Atlantic and Indian Ocean Worlds, c. 1550–1850* (New York: Cambridge University Press, 2012): 370–406.

Gray, Edward G., and Jane Kamensky, eds., *The Oxford Handbook of the American Revolution* (New York: Oxford University Press, 2013).

Graymont, Barbara, *The Iroquois in the American Revolution* (Syracuse, N.Y.: Syracuse University Press, 1972).

Green, James N., *Mathew Carey: Publisher and Patriot* (Philadelphia: Library Company of Philadelphia, 1985).

Greene, Jack P., "Colonial History and National History: Reflections on a Continuing Problem," *William and Mary Quarterly*, 3rd ser., vol. 64 (Apr. 2007): 235–50.

Greene, Jack P., "Empire and Identity from the Glorious Revolution to the American Revolution," in Peter J. Marshall, ed., *The Oxford History of the British Empire, II: The Eighteenth Century* (New York: Oxford University Press, 1998): 208–30.

Greene, Jack P., *Imperatives, Behaviors, and Identities: Essays in Early American Cultural History* (Charlottesville: University Press of Virginia, 1992).

Greene, Jack P., *Negotiated Authorities: Essays in Colonial Political and Constitutional History* (Charlottesville: University Press of Virginia, 1994).

Greene, Jack P., *Peripheries and Center: Constitutional Development in the Extended Polities of the British Empire and the United States, 1607–1788* (Athens: University of Georgia Press, 1986).

Greenwood, F. Murray, *Legacies of Fear: Law and Politics in Quebec in the Era of the French Revolution* (Toronto: University of Toronto Press, 1993).

Greenwood, F. Murray, and Barry Wright, "Parliamentary Privilege and the Repression of Dissent in the Canadas," in Greenwood and Wright, eds., *Canadian State Trials*, 2 vols. (Toronto: University of Toronto Press, 1996): 409–49.

Griffin, Patrick, *American Leviathan: Empire, Nation, and Revolutionary Frontier* (New York: Hill & Wang, 2007).

Griffin, Patrick, *America's Revolution* (New York: Oxford University Press, 2013).

Gross, Robert A., "The Confidence Man and the Preacher: The Cultural Politics of Shays's Rebellion," in Gross, ed., *In Debt to Shays: The Bicentennial of an Agrarian Rebellion* (Charlottesville: University Press of Virginia, 1993): 297–320.

Gross, Robert A., *The Minutemen and Their World* (New York: Hill & Wang, 1976).

Grossberg, Michael, "Citizens and Families: A Jeffersonian Vision of Domestic Relations and Generational Change," in James Gilreath, ed., *Thomas Jefferson and the Education of a Citizen* (Hanover: University Press of New England, 1999): 3–27.

Gruber, Ira D., "Britain's Southern Strategy," in W. Robert Higgins, ed., *The Revolutionary War in the South: Power, Conflict, and Leadership* (Durham, N.C.: Duke University Press, 1979): 205–38.

Gruber, Ira D., *The Howe Brothers and the American Revolution* (New York: Antheneum, 1972).

Gudmestad, Robert H., *A Troublesome Commerce: The Transformation of the Interstate Slave Trade* (Baton Rouge: Louisiana State University Press, 2003).

Guillet, Edwin C., *Early Life in Upper Canada* (Toronto: Ontario Publishing Co., 1933).

Gundersen, Joan R., *To Be Useful to the World: Women in Revolutionary America, 1740–1790* (Chapel Hill: University of North Carolina Press, 2006).

Guzzardo, John C., "Democracy Along the Mohawk: An Election Return, 1773," *New York History*, vol. 57 (Jan. 1976): 37–52.

Guzzardo, John C., "Sir William Johnson's Official Family: Patron and Clients in an Anglo-American Empire, 1742–1777," (Ph.D. diss.: Syracuse University, 1975).

Hackel, Steven W., ed. *Alta California: Peoples in Motion, Identities in Formation 1769–1850* (Berkeley: University of California Press, 2010).

Hackel, Steven W., *Children of Coyote, Missionaries of Saint Francis: Indian-Spanish Relations in Colonial California, 1769–1850* (Chapel Hill: University of North Carolina Press, 2005).

Hall, John W., "'My Favorite Officer': George Washington's Apprentice, Nathanael Greene," in Robert M. S. McDonald, ed., *Sons of the Father: George Washington and His Protégés* (Charlottesville: University of Virginia Press, 2013): 149–68.

Hall, Timothy D., *Contested Boundaries: Itineracy and the Reshaping of the Colonial American Religious World* (Durham, N.C.: Duke University Press, 1994).

Hämäläinen, Pekka, *The Comanche Empire* (New Haven: Yale University Press, 2009).

Halttunen, Karen, "Humanitarianism and the Pornography of Pain in Anglo-American Culture," *American Historical Review*, vol. 100 (Apr. 1995): 303–34.

Hamilton, Philip, *The Making and Unmaking of a Revolutionary Family: The Tuckers of Virginia, 1752–1830* (Charlottesville: University of Virginia Press, 2003).

Hamilton, Phillip, "Revolutionary Principles and Family Loyalties: Slavery's Transformation in the St. George Tucker Household of Early National Virginia," *William and Mary Quarterly*, 3rd ser., vol. 55 (Oct. 1998): 531–56.

Hammond, John Craig, "'Uncontrollable Necessity': The Local Politics, Geopolitics, and Sectional Politics of Slavery Expansion," in Hammond, John Craig, and Matthew Mason, eds., *Contesting Slavery: The Politics of Bondage and Freedom in the New American Nation* (Charlottesville: University of Virginia Press, 2011): 138–60.

Hancock, David, "Atlantic Trade and Commodities, 1402–1815," in Nicholas Canny and Philip Morgan, eds., *The Atlantic World, c. 1450–c.1850* (New York: Oxford University Press, 2011): 324–40.

Handlin, Oscar, and Irving Mark, eds., "Chief Nimham v. Roger Morris, Beverly Robinson, and Philip Philipse—An Indian Land Case in Colonial New York," *Ethnohistory*, vol. 11 (Summer 1964): 193–246.

Hanson, J. Howard, and Samuel Ludlow Frey, eds., *The Minute Book of the Committee of Safety of Tyron County, the Old New York Frontier* (New York: Dodd, Mead 1905).

Hargrove, Richard J., "Southern Patriot: John Laurens," in W. Robert Higgins, ed., *The Revolutionary War in the South: Power, Conflict, and Leadership* (Durham, N.C.: Duke University Press, 1979): 182–202.

Harlow, Vincent T., *The Founding of the Second British Empire, 1763–1793*, 2 vols. (London: Longmans, Green, 1964).

Harris, Bob, "War, Empire, and the 'National Interest' in Mid-Eighteenth-Century Britain," in Julie Flavell and Stephen Conway, eds., *Britain and America Go to War: The Impact of War and Warfare in Anglo-America, 1754–1815* (Gainesville: University Press of Florida, 2004): 13–40.

Harris, J. William, *The Hanging of Thomas Jeremiah: A Free Black Man's Encounter with Liberty* (New Haven: Yale University Press, 2009).

Haselby, Sam, *The Origins of American Religious Nationalism* (New York: Oxford University Press, 2015).

Hastings, Hugh, ed., *Public Papers of George Clinton, First Governor of New York, 1777–1795, 1801–1804*, 10 vols. (Albany: New York State Printers, 1899–1914).

Hatch, Nathan O., *The Democratization of American Christianity* (New Haven: Yale University Press, 1989).

Hatley, M. Thomas, "The Three Lives of Keowee: Loss and Recovery in Eighteenth-Century Cherokee Villages," in Peter H. Wood, Gregory A. Waselkov, and Hatley, eds., *Powhatan's Mantle: Indians in the Colonial Southeast* (Lincoln: University of Nebraska Press, 1989): 223–48.

Hawthorne, Nathaniel, "My Kinsman, Major Molineux," in Norman Holmes Pearson, ed., *The Complete Novels and Selected Tales of Nathaniel Hawthorne* (New York: Random House, 1937), 1209–23.

Haycox, Stephen, et al., eds., *Enlightenment and Exploration in the North Pacific, 1741–1805* (Seattle: University of Washington Press, 1997).

Haynes, Sam W., *Unfinished Revolution: The Early American Republic in a British World* (Charlottesville: University of Virginia Press, 2010).

Hendrickson, David C., "Escaping Insecurity: The American Founding and the Control of Violence," in Patrick Griffin, et al., eds., *Between Sovereignty and Anarchy: The Politics of Violence in the American Revolutionary Era* (Charlottesville: University of Virginia Press, 2015): 216–42.

Hendrickson, David C., "The First Union: Nationalism versus Internationalism in the American Revolution," in Eliga H. Gould and Peter S. Onuf, eds., *Empire and Nation: The American Revolution in the Atlantic World* (Baltimore: Johns Hopkins University Press, 2005): 35–53.

Hendrickson, David C., *Peace Pact: The Lost World of the American Founding* (Lawrence: University Press of Kansas, 2003).

Hibbert, Christopher, *Redcoats and Rebels: The American Revolution Through British Eyes* (New York: W. W. Norton, 2002).

Hickey, Donald R., "America's Response to the Slave Revolt in Haiti, 1791–1806," *Journal of the Early Republic*, vol. 2 (1982): 361–79.

Higginbotham, Don, "Daniel Morgan: Guerrilla Fighter," in George Athan Billias, *George Washington's Generals and Opponents: Their Exploits and Leadership* (New York: Da Capo Press, 1994), vol. 1:291–16.

Higginbotham, Don, "War and State Formation in Revolutionary America," in Eliga H. Gould and Peter S. Onuf, eds., *Empire and Nation: The American Revolution in the Atlantic World* (Baltimore: Johns Hopkins University Press, 2005): 54–71.

Higginbotham, Don, *The War of American Independence: Military Attitudes, Policies, and Practice, 1763–1789* (Boston: Northeastern University Press, 1983).

Hilton, Sylvia L., "Loyalty and Patriotism on North American Frontiers: Being and Becoming Spanish in the Mississippi Valley, 1776–1803," in Hilton and Gene Allen Smith, eds., *Nexus of Empire: Negotiating Loyalty and Identity in the Revolutionary Borderlands, 1760s–1820s* (Gainesville: University Press of Florida, 2010): 8–38.

Hinderaker, Eric, *Elusive Empires: Constructing Colonialism in the Ohio Valley, 1673–1800* (New York: Cambridge University Press, 1997).

Hobson, Charles F., et al., eds., *The Papers of John Marshall*, 12 vols. (Chapel Hill: University of North Carolina Press, 1974–2006).

Hochschild, Adam, *Bury the Chains: Prophets and Rebels in the Fight to Free an Empire's Slaves* (Boston: Houghton Mifflin, 2005).

Hodges, Graham R. G. "The Laboring Republic," in Edward G. Gray and Jane Kamensky, eds., *The Oxford Handbook of the American Revolution* (New York: Oxford University Press, 2013): 578–94.

Hodges, Graham R. G., *Slavery and Freedom in the Rural North: African Americans in Monmouth County, New Jersey, 1665–1865* (Madison Wis.: Madison House, 1997).

Hoffer, Peter Charles, *The Treason Trials of Aaron Burr* (Lawrence: University Press of Kansas, 2008).

Hoffman, Ronald, "The 'Disaffected' in the Revolutionary South," in Alfred F. Young, ed., *The American Revolution: Explorations in the History of American Radicalism* (DeKalb: Northern Illinois University Press 1976): 273–316.

Holton, Woody, *Forced Founders: Indians, Debtors, Slaves, and the Making of the American Revolution in Virginia* (Chapel Hill: University of North Carolina Press, 1999).

Holton, Woody, "'From the Labour of Others': The War Bonds Controversy and the Origins of the Constitution in New England," *William and Mary Quarterly* 3rd ser., vol. 61 (Apr. 2004): 271–316.

Holton, Woody, "Ohio Indians and the Coming of the American Revolution in Virginia," *Journal of Southern History*, vol. 60 (Aug. 1994): 453–78.

Holton, Woody, *Unruly Americans and the Origins of the Constitution* (New York: Hill & Wang, 2007).

Horn, James, and Philip D. Morgan, "Settlers and Slaves: European and African Migrations to Early Modern British America," in Elizabeth Mancke and

Carole Shammas, eds., *The Creation of the British Atlantic World* (Baltimore: Johns Hopkins University Press, 2005): 19–44.

Hornsby, Stephen J., *British Atlantic, American Frontier: Spaces of Power in Early Modern British America* (Hanover, N.H.: University Press of New England, 2005).

Horsman, Reginald, *Expansion and American Indian Policy, 1783–1812* (East Lansing: Michigan State University Press, 1967).

Horsman, Reginald, "The Indian Policy of an 'Empire for Liberty,'" in Frederick E. Hoxie, Ronald Hoffman, and Peter J. Albert, eds., *Native Americans and the Early Republic* (Charlottesville: University Press of Virginia, 1999): 37–61.

Houck, Louis, ed., *The Spanish Regime in Missouri*, 2 vols. (Chicago: R. R. Donnelley & Sons, 1909).

Hough, Franklin B. ed., *Proceedings of the Commissioners of Indian Affairs, Appointed by Law for the Extinguishment of Indian Titles in the State of New York*, 2 vols. (Albany, N.Y.: Joel Munsell, 1861).

Howe, John R., Jr., "Republican Thought and the Political Violence of the 1790s," *American Quarterly*, vol. 19 (Summer 1967): 147–65.

Hughes, Derek, ed., *Versions of Blackness: Key Texts on Slavery from the Seventeenth Century* (Cambridge: Cambridge University Press, 2007).

Hughes, Sarah S., "Slaves for Hire: The Allocations of Black Labor in Elizabeth City County, Virginia, 1782–1810," *William and Mary Quarterly*, 3rd ser., vol. 35 (Apr. 1978): 260–86.

Hunt, Gaillard, ed., *The First Forty Years of Washington Society: Portrayed by the Family Letters of Mrs. Samuel Harrison Smith (Margaret Bayard)* (New York: Scribner, 1906).

Hunt, Gaillard, ed., *The Writings of James Madison*, 9 vols. (New York: Scribner, 1900–1910).

Hutchinson, Thomas, *The History of the Colony and Province of Massachusetts Bay*, Lawrence Shaw Mayo, ed., 3 vols. (Cambridge: Harvard University Press, 1936).

Hutchinson, William T., et al., eds, *The Papers of James Madison, Congressional Series*, 17 vols. to date (Chicago and Charlottesville: University of Chicago Press and University of Virginia Press, 1962–)

Hutson, James H., "The American Negotiators: The Diplomacy of Jealousy," in Ronald Hoffman and Peter J. Albert, eds., *Peace and the Peacemakers: The Treaty of 1783* (Charlottesville: University Press of Virginia, 1986): 52–69.

Innes, Stephen, *Creating the Commonwealth: The Economic Culture of Puritan New England* (New York: W. W. Norton, 1995).

Irvin, Benjamin H., *Clothed in Robes of Sovereignty: The Continental Congress and the People Out of Doors* (New York: Oxford University Press, 2011).

Isaac, Rhys, "Stories and Constructions of Identity: Folk Tellings and Diary Inscriptions in Revolutionary Virginia," in Ronald Hoffman, Mechel Sobel, and Fredrika J. Teute, eds., *Through a Glass Darkly: Reflections on Personal Identity in Early America* (Chapel Hill: University of North Carolina Press, 1997): 206–37.

Isenberg, Nancy, *Fallen Founder: The Life of Aaron Burr* (New York: Viking, 2007).

Israel, Jonathan, ed., *The Anglo-Dutch Moment: Essays on the Glorious Revolution and Its World Impact* (New York: Cambridge University Press, 1991).

Jackson, Robert H., "The Formation of Frontier Indigenous Communities: Missions in California and Texas," in Jackson, ed., *New Views of Borderlands History* (Albuquerque: University of New Mexico Press, 1998): 131–56.

Jacobs, Wilbur R., ed., *Indians of the Southern Colonial Frontier: The Edmond Atkin Report and Plan of 1755* (Columbia: University of South Carolina Press, 1954).

Jaffee, David, *A New Nation of Goods: The Material Culture of Early America* (Philadelphia: University of Pennsylvania Press, 2010).

Jarvis, Michael J., *In the Eye of All Trade: Bermuda, Bermudians, and the Maritime Atlantic World, 1680–1783* (Chapel Hill: University of North Carolina Press, 2010).

Jasanoff, Maya, *Edge of Empire: Lives, Culture, and Conquest in the East, 1750–1850* (New York: Knopf, 2005).

Jasanoff, Maya, *Liberty's Exiles: American Loyalists in the Revolutionary World* (New York: Knopf, 2011).

Jefferson, Thomas, *Notes on the State of Virginia*, with an introduction by Peter S. Onuf (New York: Barnes & Noble, 2010 reprint of 1785 original).

Jellison, Charles A., *Ethan Allen: Frontier Rebel* (Syracuse, N.Y.: Syracuse University Press, 1969).

Jensen, Merrill, *The Founding of a Nation: A History of the American Revolution, 1763–1776* (Indianapolis: Hackett Publishing, 1968).

Jensen, Merrill, *The New Nation: A History of the United States During the Confederation, 1781–1789* (New York: Knopf, 1950).

Jensen, Merrill, "The Sovereign States: Their Antagonisms and Rivalries and Some Consequences," in Ronald Hoffman and Peter J. Albert, eds., *Sovereign States in an Age of Uncertainty* (Charlottesville: University Press of Virginia, 1981): 226–50.

John, Richard R., *Spreading the News: The American Postal System from Franklin to Morse* (Cambridge: Harvard University Press, 1995).

Johnson, Richard R., "'Parliamentary Egotisms': The Clash of Legislatures in the Making of the American Revolution," *Journal of American History*, vol. 74 (Sept. 1987): 338–62.

Johnson, Richard R., "The Revolution of 1688–9 in the American Colonies," in Jonathan I. Israel, ed., *The Anglo-Dutch Moment: Essays on the Glorious Revolution and Its World Impact* (New York: Cambridge University Press, 1991): 215–40.

Johnson, Ronald Angelo, *Diplomacy in Black and White: John Adams, Toussaint Louverture, and Their Atlantic World Alliance* (Athens: University of Georgia Press, 2014).

Jones, Dorothy V., *License for Empire: Colonialism by Treaty in Early America* (Chicago: University of Chicago Press, 1982).

Jones, Eldon, "The British Withdrawal from the South, 1781–1785," in W. Robert Higgins, ed., *The Revolutionary War in the South: Power, Conflict, and Leadership* (Durham, N.C.: Duke University Press, 1979): 259–85.

Jones, Maldwyn A., "Sir William Howe: Conventional Strategist," in George Athan Billias, ed., *George Washington's Generals and Opponents: Their Exploits and Leadership* (New York: Da Capo Press, 1994), vol. 2:39–72.

Jordan, Daniel P., *Political Leadership in Jefferson's Virginia* (Charlottesville: University Press of Virginia, 1983).

Jordan, Winthrop D., "Familial Politics: Thomas Paine and the Killing of the King, 1776," *Journal of American History*, vol. 60 (Sept. 1973): 294–308.

Jordan, Winthrop D, *White over Black: American Attitudes Toward the Negro, 1550–1812* (Chapel Hill: University of North Carolina Press, 1968).

Juster, Susan, *Disorderly Women: Sexual Politics and Evangelicalism in Revolutionary New England* (Ithaca: Cornell University Press, 1994).

Kammen, Michael, *Colonial New York: A History* (New York: Oxford University Press, 1975).

Kammen, Michael, *A Machine that Would Go of Itself: The Constitution in American Culture* (New York: Vintage Books, 1986).

Kaplan, Lawrence S., "The Treaties of Paris and Washington, 1778 and 1949: Reflections on Entangling Alliances," in Ronald Hoffman and Peter J. Albert, eds., *Diplomacy and Revolution: The Franco-American Alliance of 1778* (Charlottesville: University Press of Virginia, 1981): 151–94.

Kaplan, Sidney, and Emma Nogrady Kaplan, *The Black Presence in the Era of the American Revolution* (Amherst: University of Massachusetts Press, 1989).

Karras, Alan L., *Sojourners in the Sun: Scottish Migrants in Jamaica and the Chesapeake, 1740–1800* (Ithaca: Cornell University Press, 1993).

Kars, Marjoleine, *Breaking Loose Together: The Regulator Rebellion in Pre-Revolutionary North Carolina* (Chapel Hill: University of North Carolina Press, 2002).

Kastor, Peter J., *The Nation's Crucible: The Louisiana Purchase and the Creation of America* (New Haven: Yale University Press, 2004).

Kay, Marvin L. Michael, "The North Carolina Regulation, 1766–1776," in Alfred F. Young, ed., *The American Revolution: Explorations in the History of American Radicalism* (DeKalb: Northern Illinois University Press, 1976): 71–123.

Keane, John, *Tom Paine: a Political Life* (Boston: Little Brown, 1995).

Kelsay, Isabel *Joseph Brant, 1743–1807: Man of Two Worlds* (Syracuse, N.Y.: Syracuse University Press, 1984).

Kelton, Paul, "The British and Indian War: Cherokee Power and the Fate of

Empire in North America," *William and Mary Quarterly*, 3rd ser., vol. 69 (Oct. 2012): 763–92.

Kerber, Linda K., "'History Can Do It No Justice': Women and the Reinterpretation of the American Revolution," in Ronald Hoffman and Peter J. Albert, eds., *Women in the Age of the American Revolution* (Charlottesville: University Press of Virginia, 1989): 3–42.

Kerber, Linda K., "'I Have Don . . . much to Carrey on the Warr': Women and the Shaping of Republican Ideology After the American Revolution," in Harriet B. Applewhite and Darline G. Levy, eds., *Women and Politics in the Age of Democratic Revolution* (Ann Arbor: University of Michigan Press, 1990): 227–57.

Kerber, Linda K., *Women of the Republic: Intellect and Ideology in Revolutionary America* (Chapel Hill: University of North Carolina Press, 1980).

Ketcham, Ralph, *James Madison: A Biography* (Charlottesville: University Press of Virginia, 1990).

Kettner, James H., *The Development of American Citizenship, 1608–1870* (Chapel Hill: University of North Carolina Press, 1978).

Kierner, Cynthia A., *Traders and Gentlefolk: The Livingstons of New York, 1675–1690* (Ithaca: Cornell University Press, 1992).

Kim, Sung Bok, *Landlord and Tenant in Colonial New York: Manorial Society, 1664–1775* (Chapel Hill: University of North Carolina Press, 1978).

Kim, Sung Bok, "The Limits of Politicization in the American Revolution: The Experience of Westchester County, New York," *Journal of American History*, vol. 80 (Dec. 1993): 868–89.

Kirk, Russell, *John Randolph of Roanoke* (Indianapolis: Liberty Press, 1978).

Klein, Milton M. *The American Whig: William Livingston of New York* (New York: Garland Publishing, 1990).

Klein, Rachel N., "Frontier Planters and the American Revolution: The South Carolina Backcountry, 1775–1782," in Ronald Hoffman, Thad W. Tate, and Peter J. Albert, eds., *An Uncivil War: The Southern Backcountry During the American Revolution* (Charlottesville: University Press of Virginia, 1985): 37–69.

Klein, Rachel N., *Unification of a Slave State: The Rise of the Planter Class in the South Carolina Backcountry, 1760–1808* (Chapel Hill: University of North Carolina Press, 1990).

Knight, Franklin W., "The American Revolution and the Caribbean," in Ira Berlin and Ronald Hoffman, eds., *Slavery and Freedom in the Age of the American Revolution* (Charlottesville: University Press of Virginia, 1983): 237–61.

Knopf, Richard C., ed., *Anthony Wayne: A Name in Arms: The Wayne-Knox-Pickering-McHenry Correspondence* (Pittsburgh: University of Pittsburgh Press, 1960).

Kohn, Richard H., "The Inside History of the Newburgh Conspiracy: America and the Coup d'Etat," *William and Mary Quarterly*, 3rd ser., vol. 27 (Apr. 1970): 187–220.

Kornblith, Gary J., and John M. Murrin, "The Making and Unmaking of an American Ruling Class," in Alfred F. Young, ed., *Beyond the American Revolution: Explorations in the History of American Radicalism* (DeKalb: Northern Illinois University Press, 1993): 27–79.

Kramnick, Isaac, *Republicanism and Bourgeois Radicalism: Political Ideology in Late Eighteenth-Century England and America* (Ithaca: Cornell University Press, 1990).

Kross, Jessica, "Patronage Most Ardently Sought': The New York Council, 1665–1775," in Bruce C. Daniels, ed., *Power and Status: Officeholding in Colonial America* (Middletown, Conn.: Wesleyan University Press, 1986): 205–31.

Kuethe, Allan J., "Military and Society," in John Lynch, ed., *Latin American Revolutions, 1808–1826: Old and New World Origins* (Norman: University of Oklahoma Press, 1994): 71–79.

Kulikoff, Allan, *Tobacco and Slaves: The Development of Southern Cultures in the Chesapeake, 1660–1800* (Chapel Hill: University of North Carolina Press, 1986).

Kulikoff, Allan, "Uprooted Peoples: Black Migrants in the Age of the American Revolution," in Ira Berlin and Ronald Hoffman, eds., *Slavery and Freedom in the Age of the American Revolution* (Urbana: University of Illinois Press, 1983): 143–71.

Kulikoff, Allan, "The War in the Countryside," in Edward G. Gray and Jane Kamensky, eds., *The Oxford Handbook of The American Revolution* (New York: Oxford University Press, 2013): 216–33.

Labaree, Leonard W., ed., *The Papers of Benjamin Franklin*, 40 vols. to date (New Haven: Yale University Press, 1959–).

Lambert, Frank, *Inventing the "Great Awakening"* (Princeton: Princeton University Press, 1999).

Lambert, Frank, *"Pedlar in Divinity": George Whitefield and the Transatlantic Revivals, 1737–1770* (Princeton: Princeton University Press, 1994).

Lanctot, Gustave, *Canada and the American Revolution, 1774–1783* (Cambridge: Harvard University Press, 1967).

Landers, Jane, *Black Society in Spanish Florida* (Urbana: University of Illinois Press, 1999).

Langley, Lester D., *The Americas in the Age of Revolution, 1750–1850* (New Haven: Yale University Press, 1996).

Larkin, Edward, "Loyalism," in Edward G. Gray and Jane Kamensky, eds., *The Oxford Handbook of the American Revolution* (New York: Oxford University Press, 2013): 291–310.

Larson, Edward J., *The Return of George Washington, 1783–1789* (New York: HarperCollins, 2014).

Lawson, John, *A New Voyage to Carolina*, ed. Hugh Talmage Lefler (Chapel Hill: University of North Carolina Press, 1967).

Lawson, Philip, *The Imperial Challenge: Quebec and Britain in the Age of the American Revolution* (Montreal: McGill-Queen's University Press, 1989).

Leamon, James S., *The Reverend Jacob Bailey, Maine Loyalist: For God, King, Country, and for Self* (Amherst: University of Massachusetts Press, 2012).

Leichtle, Kurt E., and Bruce G. Carveth, *Crusade Against Slavery: Edward Coles, Pioneer of Freedom* (Carbondale: Southern Illinois University Press, 2011).

Lee, Jean Butenhoff, *The Price of Nationhood: The American Revolution in Charles County* (New York: W. W. Norton, 1994).

Lee, Richard Henry, *Life of Arthur Lee, LL.D.* (Boston: Wells & Lily, 1829).

Lee, Wayne E., *Crowds and Soldiers in Revolutionary North Carolina: The Culture of Violence in Riot and War* (Gainesville: University Press of Florida, 2001).

Lee, Wayne E., "Subjects, Clients, Allies, or Mercenaries?: The British Use of Irish and Amerindian Military Power, 1500–1800," in H. V. Bowen, Elizabeth Mancke, and John G. Reid, eds., *Britain's Oceanic Empire: Atlantic and Indian Ocean Worlds, c. 1550–1850* (New York: Cambridge University Press, 2012): 179–217.

Lenman, Bruce P., *Britain's Colonial Wars, 1688–1783* (New York: Routledge, 2001).

Lepore, Jill, *A Is for American: Letters and Other Characters in the Newly United States* (New York: Knopf, 2002).

Lepore, Jill, *The Whites of Their Eyes: The Tea Party's Revolution and the Battle over American History* (Princeton: Princeton University Press, 2010).

Lewis, James E., Jr., *The American Union and the Problem of Neighborhood: The United States and the Collapse of the Spanish Empire, 1783–1829* (Chapel Hill: University of North Carolina Press, 1998).

Lewis, James E., Jr., "'What Is to Become of Our Government?': The Revolutionary Potential of the Election of 1800," in James Horn, Jan Ellen Lewis, and Peter S. Onuf, eds., *The Revolution of 1800: Democracy, Race, and the New Republic* (Charlottesville: University of Virginia Press, 2002): 3–29.

Lewis, Jan E., "The Problem of Slavery in Southern Political Discourse," in David Thomas Konig, ed., *Devising Liberty: Preserving and Creating Freedom in the New American Republic* (Stanford, Calif.: Stanford University Press, 1995): 265–97.

Lewis, Jan E., *The Pursuit of Happiness: Family and Values in Jefferson's Virginia* (New York: Cambridge University Press, 1983).

Lewis, Jan E., "The Republican Wife: Virtue and Seduction in the Early Republic," *William and Mary Quarterly*, 3rd ser., vol. 44 (Oct. 1987): 689–721.

Lindert, Peter H., and Jeffrey G. Williamson, "American Incomes Before and After the Revolution," *Journal of Economic History*, vol. 73 (Sept. 2013): 725–65.

Lint, Gregory, "Preparing for Peace: The Objectives of the United States, France, and Spain in the War of the American Revolution," in Ronald Hoffman and Peter J. Albert, eds., *Peace and the Peacemakers: The Treaty of 1783* (Charlottesville: University Press of Virginia, 1986): 30–51.

Lipscomb, Andrew A., and Albert Ellery Bergh, eds., *The Writings of Thomas Jefferson*, 20 vols. (Washington, D.C.: Thomas Jefferson Memorial Association, 1903–4).

Liss, Peggy K., *Atlantic Empires: The Network of Trade and Revolution, 1713–1826* (Baltimore: Johns Hopkins University Press, 1983).

Litwack, Leon F., *North of Slavery: The Negro in the Free States, 1790–1860* (Chicago: University of Chicago Press, 1961).

Longley, R. S., "The Coming of the New England Planters to the Annapolis Valley," in Margaret Conrad, ed., *They Planted Well: New England Planters in Maritime Canada* (Fredericton, New Brunswick: Acadiensis Press, 1988): 14–28.

Longmore, Paul K., *The Invention of George Washington* (Charlottesville: University Press of Virginia, 1999).

Looney, J. Jefferson, et al., eds., *The Papers of Thomas Jefferson, Retirement Series*, 11 vols. to date (Princeton: Princeton University Press, 2004–).

Lynch, John, ed., *Latin American Revolutions, 1808–1826: Old and New World Origins* (Norman: University of Oklahoma Press, 1994).

Lynd, Staughton, and David Waldstreicher, "Free Trade, Sovereignty, and Slavery: Toward an Economic Interpretation of American Independence," *William and Mary Quarterly*, 3rd ser., vol. 68 (Oct. 2011): 597–630.

Lyons, Clare A., "Discipline, Sex, and the Republican Self," in Edward G. Gray and Jane Kamensky, eds., *The Oxford Handbook of the American Revolution* (New York: Oxford University Press, 2013): 560–77.

Mackesy, Piers, *The War for America, 1775–1783* (Lincoln: University of Nebraska Press, 1993).

MacLachlan, Colin M., *Spain's Empire in the New World: The Role of Ideas in Institutional and Social Change* (Berkeley: University of California Press, 1988).

Macleod, Emma, "Thomas Paine and Jeffersonian America," in Simon P. Newman and Peter S. Onuf, eds., *Paine and Jefferson in the Age of Revolutions* (Charlottesville: University of Virginia Press, 2013: 209–28.

MacNutt, W. S., *The Atlantic Provinces: The Emergence of Colonial Society, 1712–1857* (Toronto: McClelland & Steward, 1965).

Maier, Pauline, *American Scripture: Making the Declaration of Independence* (New York: Knopf 1997).

Maier, Pauline, *From Resistance to Revolution: Colonial Radicals and the Development of American Opposition to Britain, 1765–1776* (New York: Knopf, 1973).

Maier, Pauline, *The Old Revolutionaries: Political Lives in the Age of Samuel Adams* (New York: W. W. Norton, 1990).

Maier, Pauline, "Popular Uprisings and Civil Authority in Eighteenth Century America," *William and Mary Quarterly*, 3rd ser., vol. 27 (Jan. 1970): 3–35.

Maier, Pauline, *Ratification: The People Debate the Constitution, 1787–1788* (New York: Simon & Schuster, 2010).

Main, Jackson Turner, "The American States in the Revolutionary Era," in Ronald Hoffman and Peter J. Albert, eds., *Sovereign States in an Age of Uncertainty* (Charlottesville: University Press of Virginia, 1981): 1–30.

Main, Jackson Turner, *The Antifederalists: Critics of the Constitution, 1781–1788* (New York: W. W. Norton, 1961).

Main, Jackson Turner, "Government by the People: The American Revolution and the Democratization of the Legislatures," *William and Mary Quarterly*, 3rd ser., vol. 23 (July 1966): 391–407.

Main, Jackson Turner, *Political Parties Before the Constitution* (Chapel Hill: University of North Carolina Press, 1973).

Malone, Dumas, *Jefferson and the Ordeal of Liberty* (Boston: Little, Brown, 1962).

Mancke, Elizabeth, "Chartered Enterprises and the Evolution of the British Atlantic World," in Mancke and Carole Shammas, eds., *The Creation of the British Atlantic World* (Baltimore: Johns Hopkins University Press, 2005): 237–62.

Mancke, Elizabeth, "Early Modern Imperial Governance and the Origins of Canadian Political Culture," *Canadian Journal of Political Science*, vol. 32 (Mar. 1999): 3–20.

Mancke, Elizabeth, *The Fault Lines of Empire: Political Differentiation in Massachusetts and Nova Scotia, Ca. 1760–1830* (New York: Routledge, 2005).

Manning, William R., ed., *Diplomatic Correspondence of the United States: Canadian Relations, 1784–1860*, 3 vols. (Washington, D.C.: Carnegie Endowment for International Peace, 1940).

Mapp, Paul W., "The Revolutionary War and Europe's Great Powers," in Edward G. Gray and Jane Kamensky, eds., *The Oxford Handbook of the American Revolution* (New York: Oxford University Press, 2013): 311–26.

Marini, Stephen A., "Religion, Politics, and Ratification," in Ronald Hoffman and Peter J. Albert, eds., *Religion in a Revolutionary Age* (Charlottesville: University Press of Virginia, 1994): 184–217.

Marshall, Peter J., "The Case for Coercing America," in Marshall, ed., *"A Free Though Conquering People": Eighteenth-Century Britain and its Empire* (Burlington, Vt.: Ashgate Publishing, 2003): sec. VII: 9–22.

Marshall, Peter J., "First Americans and Last Loyalists: An Indian Dilemma in War and Peace," in Esmond Wright, ed., *Red, White, and True Blue: The Loyalists in the Revolution* (New York: AMS Press, 1976): 33–53.

Marshall, Peter J., "The Incorporation of Quebec in the British Empire, 1763–1774," in Virginia Bever Platt and David Curtis Skaggs, eds., *Of Mother Country and Plantations: Proceedings of the Twenty-Seventh Conference in*

Early American History (Bowling Green, Ohio: Bowling Green State University Press, 1971): 42–61.

Marshall, Peter J., *The Making and Unmaking of Empires: Britain, India, and America, c. 1750–1783* (Oxford: Oxford University Press, 2005).

Marshall, Peter J., "The Thirteen Colonies in the Seven Years' War: The View from London," in Julie, Flavell and Stephen Conway, eds., *Britain and America Go to War: The Impact of War and Warfare in Anglo-America, 1754–1815* (Gainesville: University Press of Florida, 2004): 69–92.

Marston, Jerrilyn Greene, *King and Congress: The Transfer of Political Legitimacy, 1774–1776* (Princeton: Princeton University Press, 1987).

Martin, James Kirby, ed., *Ordinary Courage: The Revolutionary War Adventures of Joseph Plumb Martin* (St. James, N.Y.: Brandywine Press, 1993).

Martin, James Kirby, and Mark E. Lender, eds., *Citizen-Soldier: The Revolutionary War Journal of Joseph Bloomfield* (Newark: New Jersey Historical Society, 1982).

Martin, James Kirby, and Mark E. Lender, eds., *A Respectable Army: The Military Origins of the Republic, 1763–1789* (Arlington Heights, Ill.: Harlan Davidson, 1982).

Marzagalli, Silvia, "The French Atlantic World in the Seventeenth and Eighteenth Centuries," in Nicholas Canny and Philip Morgan, eds., *The Atlantic World, c. 1450–c. 1850* (New York: Oxford University Press, 2011): 235–51.

Mason, Keith, "The American Loyalist Diaspora and the Reconfiguration of the British Atlantic World," in Eliga H. Gould and Peter S. Onuf, *Empire and Nation: The American Revolution in the Atlantic World* (Baltimore: Johns Hopkins University Press, 2005): 239–59.

Mason, Mathew, "Necessary but Not Sufficient: Revolutionary Ideology and Antislavery Action in the Early Republic," in John Craig Hammond and Matthew Mason, eds., *Contesting Slavery: The Politics of Bondage and Freedom in the New American Nation* (Charlottesville: University of Virginia Press, 2011): 11–31.

Maude, John, *Visit to the Falls of Niagara in 1800* (London: Longman, Rees, 1826).

Mayer, Holly, *Belonging to the Army: Camp Followers and Community During the American Revolution* (Columbia: University of South Carolina Press, 1996).

McCalla, Douglas, *Planting the Province: The Economic History of Upper Canada 1784–1870* (Toronto: University of Toronto Press, 1992).

McColley, Robert, *Slavery and Jeffersonian Virginia* (Urbana: University of Illinois Press, 1964).

McConville, Brendan, *The King's Three Faces: The Rise and Fall of Royal America, 1688–1776* (Chapel Hill: University of North Carolina Press, 2006).

McConville, Brendan, *These Daring Disturbers of the Public Peace: The Strug-*

gle for Property and Power in Early New Jersey (Ithaca: Cornell University Press, 1999).

McCoy, Drew R., The Elusive Republic: Political Economy in Jeffersonian America (Chapel Hill: University of North Carolina Press, 1980).

McCoy, Drew R., "James Madison and Visions of American Nationality in the Confederation Period: A Regional Perspective," in Richard Beeman, Stephen Botein, and Edward C. Carter II, eds., Beyond Confederation: Origins of the Constitution and American National Identity (Chapel Hill: University of North Carolina Press, 1987): 226–58.

McCusker, John., and Russell R. Menard, The Economy of British America, 1670–1789 (Chapel Hill: University of North Carolina Press, 1985).

McDonnell, Michael A., "Class War: Class Struggles During the American Revolution in Virginia," William and Mary Quarterly, 3rd ser., vol. 63 (Apr. 2006): 305–44.

McDonnell, Michael A., The Politics of War: Race, Class, and Conflict in Revolutionary Virginia (Chapel Hill: University of North Carolina Press, 2007).

McDonnell, Michael A., "The Struggle Within: Colonial Politics on the Eve of Independence," in Edward G. Gray and Jane Kamensky, eds., The Oxford Handbook of the American Revolution (New York: Oxford University Press, 2013): 103–20.

McDowell, R. B., "The Age of the United Irishmen: Revolution and the Union, 1794–1800," in T. W. Moody and W. E. Vaughan, eds., A New History of Ireland, IV: Eighteenth-Century Ireland, 1691–1800 (Oxford: Clarendon Press, 1986): 339–73.

McDowell, R. B., "Ireland in 1800," in T. W. Moody and W. E. Vaughan, eds., A New History of Ireland, IV: Eighteenth-Century Ireland, 1691–1800 (Oxford: Clarendon Press, 1986): 657–712.

McDowell, R. B., Ireland in the Age of Imperialism and Revolution, 1760–1801 (Oxford: Clarendon Press, 1979).

McGarvie, Mark Douglas, "Transforming Society Through Law: St. George Tucker, Women's Property Rights, and an Active Republican Judiciary," William and Mary Law Review, 47 (Feb. 2006): 1393–1425.

McLoughlin, William G., New England Dissent, 1630–1833 (Cambridge: Harvard University Press, 1971).

McNamara, Martha J., "Republican Art and Architecture," in Edward G. Gray and Jane Kamensky, eds., The Oxford Handbook of the American Revolution (New York: Oxford University Press, 2013): 499–518.

Meacham, Jon, Thomas Jefferson: The Art of Power (New York: Random House, 2012).

Melish, Joanne Pope, Disowning Slavery: Gradual Emancipation and "Race" in New England, 1780–1860 (Ithaca: Cornell University Press, 1998).

Meranze, Michael, "Hargrave's Nightmare and Taney's Dream," UC Irvine Law Review, vol. 4:219–38.

Merrell, James H., "Declarations of Independence: Indian-White Relations in the New Nation," in Jack P. Greene, ed., *The American Revolution: Its Character and Limits* (New York: New York University Press, 1987): 197–223.

Merrell, James H., *The Indians' New World: Catawbas and their Neighbors from European Contact through the Era of Removal* (Chapel Hill: University of North Carolina Press, 1989).

Merrell, James H., *Into the American Woods: Negotiators on the Pennsylvania Frontier* (New York: W. W. Norton, 1999).

Merritt, Jane T., *At the Crossroads: Indians and Empires on a Mid-Atlantic Frontier, 1700–1763* (Chapel Hill: University of North Carolina Press, 2003).

Merritt, Jane T., "Native Peoples in the Revolutionary War," in Edward G. Gray and Jane Kamensky, eds., *The Oxford Handbook of the American Revolution* (New York: Oxford University Press, 2013): 234–49.

Messer, Peter C., "Feel the Terror: Edmund Burke's *Reflections on the Revolution in France*," in Isaac Land, ed., *Enemies of Humanity: The Nineteenth-Century War on Terrorism* (New York: Palgrave Macmillan, 2008): 23–44.

Middlekauff, Robert, *Benjamin Franklin and his Enemies* (Berkeley: University of California Press, 1996).

Middlekauff, Robert, *The Glorious Cause: The American Revolution, 1763–1789* (New York: Oxford University Press, 1982).

Middleton, Richard, *The Bells of Victory: The Pitt-Newcastle Ministry and the Conduct of the Seven Years' War, 1757–1762* (New York: Cambridge University Press, 1985).

Miller, David, *The World of Jack Aubrey: Twelve-Pounders, Frigates, Cutlasses, and Insignia of His Majesty's Royal Navy* (Philadelphia: Courage Books, 2003).

Miller, John C., *Crisis in Freedom: The Alien and Sedition Acts* (Boston: Little, Brown, 1951).

Miller, Joseph C., ed., *The Princeton Companion to Atlantic History* (Princeton: Princeton University Press, 2015).

Milobar, David, "Conservative Ideology, Metropolitan Government, and the Reform of Quebec, 1782–1791," *International History Review*, vol. 12 (Feb. 1990): 45–64.

Mintz, Max M., *Seeds of Empire: The American Revolutionary Conquest of the Iroquois* (New York: New York University Press, 1999).

Moore, Christopher, *The Loyalists: Revolution, Exile, Settlement* (Toronto: McClelland & Stewart, 1994).

Moore, Peter N., *World of Toil and Strife: Community Transformation in Backcountry South Carolina, 1750–1805* (Columbia: University of South Carolina Press, 2007).

Morgan, David T., *The Devious Dr. Franklin, Colonial Agent: Benjamin Franklin's Years in London* (Macon, Ga.: Mercer University Press, 1996).

Morgan, Edmund S., *American Slavery, American Freedom: The Ordeal of Colonial Virginia* (New York: W. W. Norton, 1975).

Morgan, Edmund S., *Birth of the Republic, 1763–89* (Chicago: University of Chicago Press, 2013).

Morgan, Edmund S., *Inventing the People: The Rise of Popular Sovereignty in England and America* (New York: W. W. Norton, 1988).

Morgan, Edmund S., ed., *Prologue to Revolution: Sources and Documents on the Stamp Act Crisis, 1764–1766* (Chapel Hill: University of North Carolina Press, 1959).

Morgan, Edmund S., and Helen M. Morgan, *The Stamp Act Crisis: Prologue to Revolution* (New York: Collier Books, 1962).

Morgan, Philip D., "Black Society in the Lowcountry 1760–1810," in Ira Berlin and Ronald Hoffman, eds., *Slavery and Freedom in the Age of the American Revolution* (Charlottesville: University Press of Virginia, 1983): 83–141.

Morgan, Philip D., *Slave Counterpoint: Black Culture in the Eighteenth-Century Chesapeake and Lowcountry* (Chapel Hill: University of North Carolina Press, 1998).

Morley, Vincent, *Irish Opinion and the American Revolution, 1760–1783* (New York: Cambridge University Press, 2002).

Morris, Richard B., *The Forging of the Union: 1781–1789* (New York: Harper & Row, 1987).

Morris, Richard B., *The Peacemakers: The Great Powers and American Independence* (New York: Harper & Row, 1965).

Morton, Louis, *Robert Carter of Nomini Hall: A Virginia Tobacco Planter of the Eighteenth Century* (Charlottesville: University Press of Virginia, 1964).

Mt. Pleasant, Alyssa, "Independence for Whom?: Expansion and Conflict in the Northeast and Northwest," in Andrew Shankman, ed., *The World of the Revolutionary American Republic: Land, Labor, and the Conflict for a Continent* (New York: Routledge, 2014): 116–33.

Mulcahy, Matthew, *Hubs of Empire: The Southeastern Lowcountry and British Caribbean* (Baltimore: Johns Hopkins University Press, 2014).

Mullin, Gerald W., *Flight and Rebellion: Slave Resistance in Eighteenth-Century Virginia* (New York: Oxford University Press, 1972).

Murphy, Orville T., "The View from Versailles: Charles Gravier Comte de Vergennes's Perceptions of the American Revolution," in Ronald Hoffman and Peter J. Albert, eds., *Diplomacy and Revolution: The Franco-American Alliance of 1778* (Charlottesville: University Press of Virginia, 1981): 107–49.

Murrin, John M., "The Jeffersonian Triumph and American Exceptionalism" *Journal of the Early Republic*, vol. 20 (Spring 2000): 1–25.

Murrin, John M. "Political Development," in Jack P. Greene and J. R. Pole, eds., *Colonial British America: Essays in the New History of the Early Modern Era* (Baltimore: Johns Hopkins University, 1984): 408–456.

Murrin, John M., "Religion and Politics in America from the First Settlements to the Civil War," in Mark A. Noll, ed., *Religion and American Politics:*

From the Colonial Period to the 1980s (New York: Oxford University Press, 1990): 19–43.

Murrin, John M., "A Roof Without Walls: The Dilemma of American National Identity," in Richard Beeman, Stephen Botein, and Edward C. Carter II, eds., *Beyond Confederation: Origins of the Constitution and American National Identity* (Chapel Hill: University of North Carolina Press, 1987): 333–48.

Nadelhaft, Jerome J., "'The Snarls of Invidious Animals': The Democratization of Revolutionary South Carolina," in Ronald Hoffman and Peter J. Albert, eds., *Sovereign States in an Age of Uncertainty* (Charlottesville: University Press of Virginia, 1981): 62–94.

Namias, June, ed., *Narrative of the Life of Mary Jemison by James Seaver* (Norman: University of Oklahoma Press, 1992).

Nammack, Georgiana C., *Fraud, Politics, and the Dispossession of the Indians: The Iroquois Land Frontier in the Colonial Period* (Norman: University of Oklahoma Press, 1969).

Nasatir, Abraham P., *Borderland in Retreat: From Spanish Louisiana to the Far Southwest* (Albuquerque: University of New Mexico Press, 1976).

Nash, Gary B., "Forging Freedom: The Emancipation Experience in the Northern Seaport Cities, 1775–1820," in Ira Berlin and Ronald Hoffman, eds., *Slavery and Freedom in the Age of the American Revolution* (Charlottesville: University Press of Virginia, 1983): 3–48.

Nash, Gary B., *The Forgotten Fifth: African Americans in the Age of Revolution* (Cambridge: Harvard University Press, 2006).

Nash, Gary B., *Race and Revolution* (Madison, Wis.: Madison House, 1990).

Nash, Gary B., *Red, White, and Black: The Peoples of Early America* (Englewood Cliffs, N. J.: Prentice Hall, 1992).

Nash, Gary B., "Thomas Peters: Millwright and Deliverer," in Nash and David G. Sweet, eds., *Struggle and Survival in Colonial America* (Berkeley: University of California Press, 1981): 69–85.

Nash, Gary B., *The Unknown American Revolution: The Unruly Birth of Democracy and the Struggle to Create America* (New York: Penguin Books, 2006).

Nash, Gary B., *The Urban Crucible: Social Change, Political Consciousness, and the Origins of the American Revolution* (Cambridge: Harvard University Press, 1979).

Nash, Gary B., and Jean R. Soderlund, *Freedom by Degrees: Emancipation in Pennsylvania and Its Aftermath* (New York: Oxford University Press, 1991).

Neatby, Hilda, *Quebec: the Revolutionary Age, 1760–1791* (Toronto: McClelland & Stewart, 1966).

Nelson, Paul David, *William Tryon and the Course of Empire: A Life in British Imperial Service* (Chapel Hill: University of North Carolina Press, 1990).

Nelson, William H., *The American Tory* (Oxford: Clarendon Press, 1964).

Newman, Richard S., *Freedom's Prophet: Bishop Richard Allen, the AME Church, and the Black Founding Fathers* (New York: New York University Press, 2008).

Newman, Richard S., *The Transformation of American Abolitionism: Fighting Slavery in the Early Republic* (Chapel Hill: University of North Carolina Press, 2002).

Newman, Simon P., *A New World of Labor: The Development of Plantation Slavery in the British Atlantic* (Philadelphia: University of Pennsylvania Press, 2013).

Newman, Simon P., "Paine, Jefferson, and Revolutionary Radicalism in Early National America," in Newman and Peter S. Onuf, eds., *Paine and Jefferson in the Age of Revolutions* (Charlottesville: University of Virginia Press, 2013): 71–94.

Newmyer, R. Kent, *John Marshall and the Heroic Age of the Supreme Court* (Baton Rouge: Louisiana State University Press, 2001).

Newmyer, R. Kent, *Supreme Court Justice Joseph Story: Statesman of the Old Republic* (Chapel Hill: University of North Carolina Press, 1985).

Nichols, David Andrew, *Red Gentlemen & White Savages: Indians, Federalists, and the Search for Order on the American Frontier* (Charlottesville: University of Virginia Press, 2008).

Nicholls, Michael L, "Passing Through This Troublesome World: Free Blacks in the Early Southside," *Virginia Magazine of History and Biography*, vol. 92 (Jan. 1984): 50–70.

Nicholls, Michael L., *Whispers of Rebellion: Narrating Gabriel's Conspiracy* (Charlottesville: University of Virginia Press, 2012).

Niddrie, D. L., "Eighteenth-Century Settlement in the British Caribbean," *Transactions of the Institute of British Geographers*, no. 40 (Dec. 1966): 67–80.

Nobles, Gregory H., *American Frontiers: Cultural Encounters and Continental Conquest* (New York: Hill & Wang, 1997).

Nobles, Gregory H., *Divisions Throughout the Whole: Politics and Society in Hampshire County, Massachusetts, 1740–1775* (New York: Cambridge University Press, 1983).

Nobles, Gregory H., "'Satan, Smith, Shattuck, and Shays': The People's Leaders in the Massachusetts Regulation of 1786," in Alfred F. Young, Gary Nash, and Ray Raphael, eds., *Revolutionary Founders: Rebels, Radicals, and Reformers in the Making of the Nation* (New York: Knopf, 2012): 215–31.

Nobles, Gregory H., "Shays's Neighbors: The Context of Rebellion in Pelham, Massachusetts," in Robert A. Gross, ed., *In Debt to Shays: The Bicentennial of an Agrarian Rebellion* (Charlottesville: University Press of Virginia, 1993): 185–203.

Noll, Mark, *America's God: From Jonathan Edwards to Abraham Lincoln* (New York: Oxford University Press, 2002).

Norton, Mary Beth, *Liberty's Daughters: The Revolutionary Experience of American Women, 1750–1800* (Boston: Little, Brown, 1980).

Norton, Mary Beth, "'What an Alarming Crisis Is This': Southern Women and the American Revolution," in Jeffrey J. Crow and Larry E. Tise, eds., *The Southern Experience in the American Revolution* (Chapel Hill: University of North Carolina Press, 1978): 203–34.

Norton, Mary Beth, Herbert G. Gutman, and Ira Berlin, "The Afro-American Family in the Age of Revolution," in Berlin and Hoffman, eds., *Slavery and Freedom in the Age of the American Revolution* (Charlottesville: University of Virginia Press, 1983): 175–91.

Nugent, Walter, *Habits of Empire: A History of American Expansion* (New York: Vintage Books, 2009).

O'Brien, Brendan, *Speedy Justice: The Tragic Last Voyage of His Majesty's Vessel Speedy* (Toronto: University of Toronto Press, 1992).

O'Brien, Patrick K., "Inseparable Connections: Trade, Economy, Fiscal State, and the Expansion of Empire, 1688–1815," in P.J. Marshall, ed., *The Oxford History of the British Empire, II: The Eighteenth Century* (New York: Oxford University Press, 1998): 53–77.

O'Brien, Susan, "Eighteenth-Century Publishing Networks in the First Years of Transatlantic Evangelicalism," in Mark A. Noll et al., eds., *Evangelicalism: Comparative Studies of Popular Protestantism in North America, the British Isles, and Beyond, 1700–1990* (New York: Oxford University Press, 1994): 38–57.

O'Callaghan, Edmund Bailey, ed., *The Documentary History of the State of New York*, 4 vols. (Albany: Weed, Parsons, & Co., 1849–51).

O'Callaghan, Edmund Bailey, ed., *Documents Relative to the Colonial History of the State of New York*, 15 vols. (Albany: Weed, Parsons & Co., 1853–1887).

O'Connell, Maurice R., *Irish Politics and Social Conflict in the Age of the American Revolution* (Philadelphia: University of Pennsylvania Press, 1965).

O'Donnell, Catherine, "Print Culture After the Revolution," in Edward G. Gray and Jane Kamensky, eds., *The Oxford Handbook of the American Revolution* (New York: Oxford University Press, 2013): 519–39.

Olson, Alison Gilbert, *Making the Empire Work: London and American Interest Groups, 1690–1790* (Cambridge: Harvard University Press, 1992).

Olwell, Robert, "'Domestick Enemies': Slavery and Political Independence in South Carolina, May 1775–March 1776," *Journal of Southern History*, vol. 55 (Feb. 1989): 21–48.

Olwell, Robert, *Masters, Slaves, and Subjects: The Culture of Power in the South Carolina Low Country, 1740–1790* (Ithaca: Cornell University Press, 1998).

Olwell, Robert, "Seeds of Empire: Florida, Kew, and the British Imperial Meridian in the 1760s," in Elizabeth Mancke and Carole Shammas, eds., *The Creation of the British Atlantic World* (Baltimore: Johns Hopkins University Press, 2005): 263–82.

Onuf, Peter S., "The Empire of Liberty: Land of the Free and Home of the Slave," in Andrew Shankman, ed., *The World of the Revolutionary American Republic: Land, Labor, and the Conflict for a Continent* (New York: Routledge, 2014): 195–217.

Onuf, Peter S., "Epilogue," in Patrick Griffin et al., eds., *Between Sovereignty and Anarchy: The Politics of Violence in the American Revolutionary Era* (Charlottesville: University of Virginia Press, 2015): 285–301.

Onuf, Peter S., "The Expanding Union," in David T. Konig, ed., *Devising Liberty: Preserving and Creating Freedom in the New American Republic* (Stanford, Calif.: Stanford University Press, 1995): 50–80.

Onuf, Peter S., "Imperialism and Nationalism," in Ian Tyrrell and Jay Sexton, eds., *Empire's Twin: U.S. Anti-Imperialism from the Founding Era to the Age of Terrorism* (Ithaca: Cornell University Press, 2015): 21–40.

Onuf, Peter S., *Jefferson's Empire: The Language of American Nationhood* (Charlottesville: University of Virginia Press, 2000).

Onuf, Peter S., *The Mind of Thomas Jefferson* (Charlottesville: University of Virginia Press, 2007).

Onuf, Peter S., *The Origins of the Federal Republic: Jurisdictional Controversies in the United States, 1775–1787* (Philadelphia: University of Pennsylvania Press, 1983).

Onuf, Peter S., "Settlers, Settlements, and New States," in Jack P. Greene, ed., *The American Revolution: Its Character and Limits* (New York: New York University Press, 1987): 179–213.

Onuf, Peter S., *Statehood and Union: A History of the Northwest Ordinance* (Bloomington: Indiana University Press, 1987).

Opal, Jason M., *Beyond the Farm: National Ambitions in Rural New England* (Philadelphia: University of Pennsylvania Press, 2008).

Opal, Jason M., "The Republic in the World, 1783–1803," in Edward G. Gray and Jane Kamensky, eds., *The Oxford Handbook of the American Revolution* (New York: Oxford University Press, 2013): 595–611.

O'Shaughnessy, Andrew Jackson, *An Empire Divided: The American Revolution and the British Caribbean* (Philadelphia: University of Pennsylvania Press, 2000).

O'Shaughnessy, Andrew Jackson, *The Men Who Lost America: British Leadership, the American Revolution, and the Fate of the Empire* (New Haven: Yale University Press, 2013).

Ousterhout, Anne, *A State Divided: Opposition in Pennsylvania to the American Revolution* (New York: Greenwood Press, 1987).

Parker, D. W., ed., "Secret Reports of John Howe, 1808," *American Historical Review*, vol. 17 (Oct. 1911): 70–102 and vol. 17 (Jan. 1912): 332–54.

Parkinson, Robert G., "'Manifest Signs of Passion': The First Federal Congress, Antislavery, and Legacies of the Revolutionary War," in John Craig Hammond and Matthew Mason, eds., *Contesting Slavery: The Politics of Bond-*

age and Freedom in the New American Nation (Charlottesville: University of Virginia Press, 2011): 49–68.

Parmenter, Jon W., "The Iroquois and the Native American Struggle for the Ohio Valley, 1754–1794," in David Curtis Skaggs and Larry L. Nelson, eds., *The Sixty Years' War for the Great Lakes, 1754–1814* (East Lansing: Michigan State University Press, 2001): 105–24.

Pasley, Jeffrey L., "1800 as a Revolution in Political Culture: Newspapers, Celebrations, Voting, and Democratization in the Early Republic," in James Horn, Jan Ellen Lewis, and Peter S. Onuf, eds., *The Revolution of 1800: Democracy, Race, and the New Republic* (Charlottesville: University of Virginia Press, 2002): 121–52.

Pasley, Jeffrey L., *"The Tyranny of Printers": Newspaper Politics in the Early American Republic* (Charlottesville: University of Virginia Press, 2001).

Patterson, Stephen E., "The Federalist Reaction to Shays's Rebellion," in Robert A. Gross, ed., *In Debt to Shays: The Bicentennial of an Agrarian Rebellion* (Charlottesville: University Press of Virginia, 1993): 101–18.

Patterson, Stephen E., "The Roots of Massachusetts Federalism: Conservative Politics and Political Culture Before 1787," in Ronald Hoffman and Peter J. Albert, eds., *Sovereign States in an Age of Uncertainty* (Charlottesville: University Press of Virginia, 1981): 31–61.

Pauley, Philip J., "Fighting the Hessian Fly: American and British Responses to Insect Invasion" *Environmental History*, vol. 7, no. 3 (2002): 485–507.

Pearsall, Sarah M. S., "Women in the American Revolutionary War," in Edward G. Gray and Jane Kamensky, eds., *The Oxford Handbook of the American Revolution* (New York: Oxford University Press, 2013): 273–290.

Pell, John H. G., "Philip Schuyler: The General as Aristocrat," in George Athan Billias, ed., *George Washington's Generals and Opponents: Their Exploits and Leadership* (New York: Da Capo Press, 1994), vol. 1:54–78.

Perkins, Bradford, *The First Rapprochement: England and the United States, 1795–1805* (Philadelphia: University of Pennsylvania Press, 1955).

Perkins, Bradford, "The Peace of Paris: Patterns and Legacies," in Ronald Hoffman and Peter J. Albert., eds., *Peace and the Peacemakers: The Treaty of 1783* (Charlottesville: University Press of Virginia, 1986): 190–229.

Perkins, Bradford, *Prologue to War: England and the United States, 1805–1812* (Berkeley: University of California Press, 1963).

Peterson, Mark A, "The War in the Cities," in Edward G. Gray and Jane Kamensky, eds., *The Oxford Handbook of the American Revolution* (New York: Oxford University Press, 2013): 194–215.

Peterson, Merrill D., *Thomas Jefferson and the New Nation: A Biography* (New York: Oxford University Press, 1970).

Phelan, John Leddy, "Bourbon Innovation, American Responses," in John Lynch, ed., *Latin American Revolutions, 1808–1826: Old and New World Origins* (Norman: University of Oklahoma Press, 1994): 41–49.

Phillips, Kim Tousley, *William Duane, Radical Journalist in the Age of Jefferson* (New York: Garland Publishing, 1989).

Piecuch, Jim, *Three Peoples, One King: Loyalists, Indians, and Slaves in the Revolutionary South, 1775–1782* (Columbia: University of South Carolina Press, 2008).

Plank, Geoffrey, *An Unsettled Conquest: The British Campaign Against the Peoples of Acadia* (Philadelphia: University of Pennsylvania Press, 2001).

Plumb, J. H., *The Growth of Political Stability in England, 1675–1725* (Boston: Houghton Mifflin, 1967).

Polishook, Irwin H., *Rhode Island and the Union, 1774–1795* (Evanston, Ill.: Northwestern University Press, 1969).

Popkin, Jeremy D., "Liberty in Black, White, and Color: A Trans-Atlantic Debate," in Thomas Bender, Lauren Dubois, and Richard Rabinowitz, eds., *Revolution!: The Atlantic World Reborn* (New York: New-York Historical Society, 2011): 159–76.

Potter, Janice, *The Liberty We Seek: Loyalist Ideology in Colonial New York and Massachusetts* (Cambridge: Harvard University Press, 1983).

Potts, Louis, *Arthur Lee: A Virtuous Revolutionary* (Baton Rouge: Louisiana State University Press, 1981).

Preston, David L., *The Texture of Contact: European and Indian Settler Communities on the Frontiers of Iroquoia, 1667–1783* (Lincoln: University of Nebraska Press, 2009).

Prucha, Francis Paul, *American Indian Policy in the Formative Years: The Indian Trade and Intercourse Acts, 1790–1834* (Cambridge: Harvard University Press, 1962).

Prucha, Francis Paul, *The Great Father: The United States Government and the American Indians* (Lincoln: University of Nebraska Press, 1984).

Pruitt, Betty Hobbs, "Self-Sufficiency and the Agricultural Economy of Eighteenth-Century Massachusetts," *William and Mary Quarterly*, 3rd ser., vol. 41 (July 1984): 333–64.

Purcell, Sarah J., *Sealed with Blood: War, Sacrifice, and Memory in Revolutionary America* (Philadelphia: University of Pennsylvania Press, 2002).

Purvis, Thomas L., "Patterns of Ethnic Settlement in Late Eighteenth-Century Pennsylvania," *Western Pennsylvania Historical Magazine*, vol. 70 (Apr. 1987): 107–22.

Pybus, Cassandra, *Epic Journeys of Freedom: Runaway Slaves of the American Revolution and their Global Quest for Liberty* (Boston: Beacon Press, 2006).

Pybus, Cassandra, "Jefferson's Faulty Math: The Question of Slave Defections in the American Revolution," *William and Mary Quarterly*, 3rd ser., vol. 62 (Apr. 2005): 243–64.

Quaife, Milo M., ed., *The John Askin Papers*, 2 vols. (Detroit: Library Commission, 1928–31).

Ragatz, Lowell Joseph, *The Fall of the Planter Class in the British Caribbean, 1763–1833* (New York: Century Co., 1928).

Ragosta, John, *Religious Freedom: Jefferson's Legacy, America's Creed* (Charlottesville: University of Virginia Press, 2013).

Rakove, Jack N., *The Beginnings of National Politics: An Interpretive History of the Continental Congress* (Baltimore: Johns Hopkins University Press, 1979).

Rakove, Jack N. *Original Meanings: Politics and Ideas in the Making of the Constitution* (New York: Random House, 1996).

Rakove, Jack N., *Revolutionaries: A New History of the Invention of America* (Boston: Houghton, Mifflin, Harcourt, 2010).

Rakove, Jack N., "The Structure of Politics at the Accession of George Washington," in Richard Beeman, Stephen Botein, and Edward C. Carter II, eds., *Beyond Confederation: Origins of the Constitution and American National Identity* (Chapel Hill: University of North Carolina Press, 1987): 261–94.

Ramsay, David, *The History of the American Revolution*, 2 vols. (New York: Gale, 2010)

Randolph, Thomas Jefferson, *The Speech of Thomas J. Randolph in the House of Delegates of Virginia on the Abolition of Slavery* (Richmond: Samuel Shepherd & Co., 1832).

Rankin, Hugh F., "Charles Lord Cornwallis: Study in Frustration," in George Athan Billias, ed., *George Washington's Generals and Opponents: Their Exploits and Leadership* (New York: Da Capo Press, 1994), vol. 2:193–232.

Raphael, Ray, *The First American Revolution: Before Lexington and Concord* (New York: New Press, 2002).

Raphael, Ray, *Founders: The People Who Brought You a Nation* (New York: New Press, 2009).

Raphael, Ray, *Mr. President: How and Why the Founders Created a Chief Executive* (New York: Random House, 2013).

Read, James H., *Power versus Liberty: Madison, Hamilton, Wilson, and Jefferson* (Charlottesville: University of Virginia Press, 2000).

Resendez, Andres, *Changing National Identities at the Frontier: Texas and New Mexico, 1800–1850* (New York: Cambridge University Press, 2004).

Reuter, Frank T., "'Petty Spy' or Effective Diplomat: The Role of George Beckwith," *Journal of the Early Republic*, vol. 10 (Winter 1990): 471–92.

Rhodehamel, John, ed., *The American Revolution* (New York: Library of America, 2001).

Rhodehamel, John, ed., *George Washington: Writings* (New York: Library of America, 1997).

Richards, Leonard L., *Shays's Rebellion: The American Revolution's Final Battle* (Philadelphia: University of Pennsylvania Press, 2002).

Richards, Leonard L., *The Slave Power: The Free North and Southern Domination, 1780–1860* (Baton Rouge: Louisiana State University Press, 2000).

Richardson, Ronald Kent, *Moral Imperium: Afro-Caribbeans and the Transformation of British Rule, 1776–1838* (New York: Greenwood Press, 1987).

Richter, Daniel, *Facing East from Indian Country: A Native History of Early America* (Cambridge: Harvard University Press, 2003).

Richter, Daniel, "Onas, the Long Knife: Pennsylvanians and Indians, 1783–1794," in Frederick E. Hoxie, Ronald Hoffman, and Peter J. Albert, eds., *Native Americans and the Early Republic* (Charlottesville: University of Virginia Press, 1999): 125–61.

Riddell, William Renwick, ed., *La Rochefoucault-Liancourt's Travels in Canada, 1795* (Toronto: Ontario Bureau of Archives, 1917).

Riley, Padraig, "Slavery and the Problem of Democracy in Jeffersonian America," in John Craig Hammond and Matthew Mason, eds., *Contesting Slavery: The Politics of Bondage and Freedom in the New American Nation* (Charlottesville: University of Virginia Press, 2011): 227–46.

Ritcheson, Charles R., *Aftermath of Revolution: British Policy Toward the United States, 1783–1795* (Dallas: Southern Methodist University Press, 1969).

Ritcheson, Charles R., "Britain's Peacemakers, 1782–1783: 'To an Astonishing Degree Unfit for the Task'?" in Ronald Hoffman and Peter J. Albert, eds., *Peace and the Peacemakers: The Treaty of 1783* (Charlottesville: University Press of Virginia, 1986): 70–100.

Ritcheson, Charles R., *British Politics and the American Revolution* (Norman: University of Oklahoma Press, 1954).

Rivandeneira, Antonio Joaquin de, "America for the Americans," in John Lynch, ed., *Latin American Revolutions, 1808–1826: Old and New World Origins* (Norman: University of Oklahoma Press, 1994): 58–70.

Rives, George Lockhart, ed., *Selections from the Correspondence of Thomas Barclay, Formerly British Consul-General at New York* (New York: Harper & Brothers, 1894).

Roberts, Kenneth, and Anna M. Roberts, eds., *Moreau de St. Méry's American Journey, 1793–1798* (New York: Doubleday, 1947).

Robinson, Donald, *Slavery in the Structure of American Politics, 1765–1820* (New York: W. W. Norton, 1979).

Rockman, Seth, *Scraping By: Wage Labor, Slavery, and Survival in Early Baltimore* (Baltimore: Johns Hopkins University Press, 2008).

Rodger, N. A. M., "Sea-Power and Empire, 1688–1793," in P. J. Marshall, ed., *The Oxford History of the British Empire, II: The Eighteenth Century* (New York: Oxford University Press, 1998): 169–83.

Rossiter, Clinton, *1787: The Grand Convention* (New York: Macmillan, 1966).

Rosswurm, Steven, *Arms, Country, and Class: The Philadelphia Militia and "Lower Sort" During the American Revolution, 1775–1783* (New Brunswick: Rutgers University Press, 1987).

Rothman, Adam, *Slave Country: American Expansion and the Origins of the Deep South* (Cambridge: Harvard University Press, 2005).

Royster, Charles, *A Revolutionary People at War: The Continental Army and American Character, 1775–1783* (Chapel Hill: University of North Carolina Press, 1979).

Rugemer, Edward B., "Caribbean Slave Revolts and the Origins of the Gag Rule: A Contest Between Abolitionism and Democracy, 1797–1835," in John Craig Hammond and Matthew Mason, eds., *Contesting Slavery: The Politics of Bondage and Freedom in the New American Nation* (Charlottesville: University of Virginia Press, 2011): 94–113.

Rushforth, Brett, *Bonds of Alliance: Indigenous and Atlantic Slaveries in New France* (Chapel Hill: University of North Carolina Press, 2012).

Ryerson, Richard Alan, "John Adams, Republican Monarchist: An Inquiry into the Origins of His Constitutional Thought," in Eliga H. Gould and Peter S. Onuf, eds., *Empire and Nation: The American Revolution in the Atlantic World* (Baltimore: Johns Hopkins University Press, 2005): 72–92.

Ryerson, Richard Alan, "Republican Theory and Partisan Reality in Revolutionary Pennsylvania: Toward a New View of the Constitutionalist Party," in Ronald Hoffman and Peter J. Albert, eds., *Sovereign States in an Age of Uncertainty* (Charlottesville: University Press of Virginia, 1981): 95–133.

Sadosky, Leonard J., *Revolutionary Negotiations: Indians, Empires, and Diplomats in the Founding of America* (Charlottesville: University of Virginia Press, 2009).

Salinger, Sharon V., "Artisans, Journeymen, and the Transformation of Labor in Late Eighteenth-Century Philadelphia," *William and Mary Quarterly*, 3rd ser., vol. 40 (Jan. 1983): 62–84.

Sandos, James A., "Between Crucifix and Lance: Indian-White Relations in California, 1769–1848," in Ramón A. Gutiérrez and Richard J. Orsi, eds., *Contested Eden: California Before the Gold Rush* (Berkeley: University of California Press, 1998): 196–229.

Saunt, Claudio, *West of the Revolution: An Uncommon History of 1776* (New York: W. W. Norton, 2014).

Schama, Simon, *Rough Crossings: Britain, the Slaves, and the American Revolution* (New York: HarperCollins, 2006).

Schmidt, Fredrika Teute, and Barbara Ripel Wilhelm, "Early Proslavery Petitions in Virginia," *William and Mary Quarterly*, 3rd ser., vol. 30 (Jan. 1973): 133–46.

Schoen, Brian, "Positive Goods and Necessary Evils: Commerce, Security, and Slavery in the Lower South, 1787–1837," in John Craig Hammond and Matthew Mason, eds., *Contesting Slavery: The Politics of Bondage and Freedom in the New American Nation* (Charlottesville: University of Virginia Press, 2011): 161–82.

Schwarz, Philip J., "Gabriel's Challenge: Slaves and Crime in Late Eighteenth-

Century Virginia," *Virginia Magazine of History and Biography*, vol. 90 (July 1982): 283–309.

Schwarz, Philip J., *Twice Condemned: Slaves and the Criminal Law of Virginia, 1705–1865* (Baton Rouge: Louisiana State University Press, 1988).

Selby, John E., *The Revolution in Virginia, 1775–1783* (Williamsburg, Va.: Colonial Williamsburg Foundation, 1988).

Sexton, Jay, *The Monroe Doctrine: Empire and Nation in Nineteenth-Century America* (New York: Hill & Wang, 2011).

Shalhope, Robert E., *John Taylor of Caroline: Pastoral Republican* (Columbia: University of South Carolina Press, 1980).

Shankman, Andrew, *Crucible of American Democracy: The Struggle to Fuse Egalitarianism and Capitalism in Jeffersonian Pennsylvania* (Lawrence: University Press of Kansas, 2004).

Shannon, Timothy J., *Indians and Colonists at the Crossroads of Empire: The Albany Congress of 1754* (Ithaca: Cornell University Press, 2000).

Shapiro, Darline, "Ethan Allen: Philosopher-Theologian to a Generation of American Revolutionaries," *William and Mary Quarterly*, 3rd ser., vol. 21 (Apr. 1964):236–55.

Sharp, James Roger, *American Politics in the Early Republic: The New Nation in Crisis* (New Haven: Yale University Press, 1993).

Sheehan, Bernard W., *Seeds of Extinction: Jeffersonian Philanthropy and the American Indian* (Chapel Hill: University of North Carolina Press, 1973).

Shipton, Clifford K., "Benjamin Lincoln: Old Reliable," in George Athan Billias, ed., *George Washington's Generals and Opponents: Their Exploits and Leadership* (New York: Da Capo Press, 1994), vol. 1:193–211.

Shoemaker, Nancy, *A Strange Likeness: Becoming Red and White in Eighteenth-Century North America* (New York: Oxford University Press, 2004).

Shortt, Adam, and Arthur G. Doughty, eds., *Documents Relating to the Constitutional History of Canada, 1759–1791: Part Two, 1774–1791* (Ottawa: J. de L. Tache, 1918).

Shy, John, *A People Numerous and Armed: Reflections on the Military Struggle for American Independence* (Ann Arbor: University of Michigan Press, 1990).

Shy, John, "Thomas Gage," in George Athan Billias, ed., *George Washington's Generals and Opponents: Their Exploits and Leadership* (New York: Da Capo Press, 1994), vol. 2:3–38.

Sidbury, James, *Ploughshares into Swords: Race, Rebellion, and Identity in Gabriel's Virginia, 1730–1810* (New York: Cambridge University Press, 1997).

Sidbury, James, "Saint Domingue in Virginia: Ideology, Local Meanings, and Resistance to Slavery, 1790–1800," *Journal of Southern History*, vol. 63 (1997): 531–52.

Sidbury, James, "Thomas Jefferson in Gabriel's Virginia," in James Horn, Jan Ellen Lewis, and Peter S. Onuf, eds., *The Revolution of 1800: Democracy,*

Race, and the New Republic (Charlottesville: University of Virginia Press, 2002): 199–219.

Sievens, Mary Beth, *Stray Wives: Marital Conflict in Early National New England* (New York: New York University Press, 2005).

Silver, Peter, *Our Savage Neighbors: How Indian War Transformed Early America* (New York: W. W. Norton, 2008).

Simon, James F., *What Kind of Nation: Thomas Jefferson, John Marshall, and the Epic Struggle to Create a United States* (New York: Simon & Schuster, 2002).

Skaggs, David Curtis, "The Sixty Years' War for the Great Lakes, 1754–1814: An Overview," in Skaggs and Larry L. Nelson, eds., *The Sixty Years' War for the Great Lakes, 1754–1814* (East Lansing: Michigan State University Press, 2001): 1–20.

Skemp, Sheila L., "America's Mary Wollstonecraft: Judith Sargent Murray's Case for the Equal Rights of Women," in Alfred F. Young, Gary Nash, and Ray Raphael, eds., *Revolutionary Founders: Rebels, Radicals, and Reformers in the Making of the Nation* (New York: Knopf, 2012): 289–303.

Skemp, Sheila L., *William Franklin: Son of a Patriot, Servant of a King* (New York: Oxford University Press, 1990).

Slaughter, Thomas P., *The Whiskey Rebellion: Frontier Epilogue to the American Revolution* (New York: Oxford University Press, 1986).

Smith, Barbara Clark, *The Freedoms We Lost: Consent and Resistance in Revolutionary America* (New York: New Press, 2010).

Smith, James Morton, *Freedom's Fetters: The Alien and Sedition Laws and American Civil Liberties* (Ithaca: Cornell University Press, 1966).

Smith, Michael, *A Geographical View of the Province of Upper Canada; and Promiscuous Remarks on the Government* (Philadelphia: Thomas and Robert Desilver, 1813).

Smith, Paul H., ed., *Letters of Delegates to Congress, 1774–1789*, 25 vols. (Washington, D.C.: Library of Congress, 1976–1998).

Smith, Paul H., *Loyalists and Redcoats: A Study in British Revolutionary Policy* (Chapel Hill: University of North Carolina Press, 1964).

Smith, Paul H., "Sir Guy Carleton: Soldier-Statesman," in George Athan Billias, ed., *George Washington's Generals and Opponents: Their Exploits and Leadership* (New York: Da Capo Press, 1994), vol. 2:103–41.

Smith, Rogers M., *Civic Ideals: Conflicting Visions of Citizenship in U.S. History* (New Haven: Yale University Press, 1997).

Snyder, Christina, "Native Nations in the Age of Revolution," in Andrew Shankman, ed., *The World of the Revolutionary American Republic: Land, Labor, and the Conflict for a Continent* (New York: Routledge, 2014): 77–94.

Snyder, Christina, *Slavery in Indian Country: The Changing Face of Captivity in Early America* (Cambridge: Harvard University Press, 2010).

Sobel, Mechal, *The World They Made Together: Black and White Values in Eighteenth-Century Virginia* (Princeton: Princeton University Press, 1987).

Sosin, Jack M., ed., *The Opening of the American West* (Columbia: University of South Carolina Press, 1969).

Sosin, Jack M., *The Revolutionary Frontier, 1763–1783* (New York: Holt, Rinehart & Winston, 1967).

Sosin, Jack M., *Whitehall and the Wilderness: The Middle West in British Colonial Policy, 1760–1775* (Lincoln: University of Nebraska Press, 1961).

Spooner, Matthew, "Origins of the Old South: The Reconstruction of Southern Slavery, 1776–1808," (Ph.d. diss.: Columbia University, 2014).

Spring, Mathew H., *With Zeal and with Bayonets Only: The British Army on Campaign in North America, 1775–1783* (Norman: University of Oklahoma Press, 2008).

Stanton, Lucia C., "'Those Who Labor for My Happiness': Thomas Jefferson and His Slaves," in Peter S. Onuf, ed., *Jeffersonian Legacies* (Charlottesville: University Press of Virginia, 1993), 147–80.

Stanton, Lucia C., and James A. Bear, Jr., eds., *Jefferson's Memorandum Books: Accounts, with Legal Records and Miscellany, 1767–1826*, vol. 1 (Princeton: Princeton University Press, 1997).

Starr, J. Barton, *Tories, Dons, and Rebels: The American Revolution in British West Florida* (Gainesville: University Press of Florida, 1976).

Steele, Ian K., "The Anointed, the Appointed, and the Elected," in P. J. Marshall, ed., *The Oxford History of the British Empire, II: The Eighteenth Century* (New York: Oxford University Press, 1998): 105–27

Steele, Ian K., *The English Atlantic, 1675–1740: An Exploration of Communication and Community* (New York: Oxford University Press, 1986).

Steele, Ian K., *Warpaths: Invasions of North America* (New York: Oxford University Press, 1994).

Stephenson, Michael, *Patriot Battles: How the War of Independence Was Fought* (New York: HarperCollins, 2007).

Stinchcombe, William C., *The American Revolution and the French Alliance* (Syracuse, N.Y.: Syracuse University Press, 1969).

Stinchcombe, William C., "Americans Celebrate the Birth of the Dauphin," in Ronald Hoffman and Peter J. Albert, eds., *Diplomacy and Revolution: The Franco-American Alliance of 1778* (Charlottesville: University Press of Virginia, 1981): 39–71.

Stone, William L., trans., *Memoirs, Letters, and Journals of Major General Riedesel, During His Residence in America*, 2 vols. (New York: New York Times, 1969).

Stout, Harry S., *The Divine Dramatist: George Whitefield and the Rise of Modern Evangelicalism* (Grand Rapids, Mich.: Eerdmans, 1991).

Stuart, Charles, "Lord Shelburne," in Hugh Lloyd-Jones, Valerie Pearl, and Blair Worden, eds., *History and Imagination: Essays in Honour of H. R. Trevor-Roper* (London: Gerald Duckworth & Co., 1981): 243–53.

Stuart, Reginald C., *United States Expansionism and British North America, 1775–1871* (Chapel Hill: University of North Carolina Press, 1988).

Sullivan, Aaron, "In but Not of the Revolution: Loyalty, Liberty, and the British Occupation of Philadelphia" (Ph.d. diss.: Temple University, 2014).

Sullivan, James, et al., eds., *The Papers of Sir William Johnson*, 14 vols. (Albany: University of the State of New York, Division of Archives and History, 1921–1962).

Sweet, John Wood, *Bodies Politic: Negotiating Race in the American North, 1730–1830* (Baltimore: Johns Hopkins University Press, 2003).

Sydnor, Charles S., *Gentlemen Freeholders: Political Practices in Washington's Virginia* (Chapel Hill: University of North Carolina Press, 1952).

Syrett, Harold C., ed., *The Papers of Alexander Hamilton*, 27 vols. (New York: Columbia University Press, 1961–87).

Szatmary, David P., *Shays' Rebellion: The Making of an Agrarian Insurrection* (Amherst: University of Massachusetts Press, 1980).

Taylor, Alan, "The Alien and Sedition Acts," in Julian E. Zelizer, ed., *The American Congress: The Building of Democracy* (Boston: Houghton Mifflin, 2004): 63–76.

Taylor, Alan, *American Colonies* (New York: Penguin, 2001).

Taylor, Alan, "'The Art of Hook and Snivey': Political Culture in Rural New York During the 1790s," *Journal of American History*, vol. 79 (March 1993): 1371–96.

Taylor, Alan, *The Civil War of 1812: American Citizens, British Subjects, Irish Rebels and Indian Allies* (New York: Knopf, 2011).

Taylor, Alan, "Continental Crossings," *Journal of the Early Republic*, vol. 24 (Summer 2004): 182–88.

Taylor, Alan, *The Divided Ground: Indians, Settlers, and the Northern Borderland of the American Revolution* (New York: Knopf, 2006).

Taylor, Alan, "From Fathers to Friends of the People: Political Personas in the Early Republic," *Journal of the Early Republic*, vol. 11 (Winter 1991): 465–91.

Taylor, Alan, "'The Great Change Begins': Settling the Forest of Central New York," *New York History*, vol. 76 (July 1995): 265–90.

Taylor, Alan, "'The Hungry Year': 1789 on the Northern Border of Revolutionary America," in Alessa Johns, ed., *Dreadful Visitations: Confronting Natural Catastrophe in the Age of Enlightenment* (New York: Routledge, 1999): 145–81.

Taylor, Alan, "'A Kind of Warr': The Contest for Land on the Northeastern Frontier, 1750–1820," *William and Mary Quarterly*, 3rd ser., vol. 46 (Jan. 1989): 3–26.

Taylor, Alan, "Land and Liberty on the Post-Revolutionary Frontier," in David T. Konig, ed., *Devising Liberty: Preserving and Creating Freedom in the New American Republic* (Stanford: Stanford University Press, 1995): 81–108.

Taylor, Alan, "A Northern Revolution of 1800?: Upper Canada and Thomas Jefferson," in James Horn, Jan Ellen Lewis, and Peter S. Onuf, eds., *The Revolution of 1800: Democracy, Race, and the New Republic* (Charlottesville: University of Virginia Press, 2002): 383–409.

Taylor, Alan, "The Plough-Jogger: Jedediah Peck and the Democratic Revolution," in Alfred F. Young, Gary Nash, and Ray Raphael, eds., *Revolutionary Founders: Rebels, Radicals, and Reformers in the Making of the Nation* (New York: Knopf, 2012): 375–87.

Taylor, Alan, "The Unhappy Stephen Arnold': An Episode of Murder and Penitence in the Early Republic," in Ronald Hoffman, Mechal Sobel, and Fredrika J. Teute, eds., *Through a Glass Darkly: Reflections on Personal Identity in Early America* (Chapel Hill: University of North Carolina Press, 1997): 96–121.

Taylor, John, *Arator, Being a Series of Agricultural Essays, Practical and Political* (Georgetown: J. M. and J. B. Carter, 1813).

Taylor, Robert J., *Western Massachusetts in the Revolution* (Providence, R.I.: Brown University Press, 1954).

Thayer, Theodore, "Nathanael Greene: Revolutionary War Strategist," in George Athan Billias, *George Washington's Generals and Opponents: Their Exploits and Leadership* (New York: Da Capo Press, 1994), vol. 1:109–36.

Thomas, Peter D. G., *Tea Party to Independence: The Third Phase of the American Revolution, 1773–1776* (Oxford: Clarendon Press, 1991).

Tiedemann, Joseph S., "A Revolution Foiled: Queens County, New York, 1775–1776," *Journal of American History*, vol. 75 (Sept. 1988): 417–44.

Tiedemann, Joseph S., Eugene R. Fingerhut, and Robert W. Venables, eds., *The Other Loyalists: Ordinary People, Royalism, and the Revolution in the Middle Colonies, 1763–1787* (Albany: State University of New York Press, 2009).

Tilghman, Oswald, ed., *Memoir of Lieut. Col. Tench Tilghman, Secretary and Aid to Washington* (Albany: J. Munsell, 1876).

Tiro, Karim M., "A Civil War?: Rethinking Iroquois Participation in the American Revolution," *Explorations in Early American Culture*, vol. 4 (2000): 148–65.

Tiro, Karim M., *The People of the Standing Stone: The Oneida Nation from the Revolution through the Era of Removal* (Amherst: University of Massachusetts Press, 2011).

Tomlins, Christopher, *Freedom Bound: Law, Labor, and Civic Identity in Colonizing English America, 1580–1865* (New York: Cambridge University Press, 2010).

Tomlins, Christopher, "Republican Law," in Edward G. Gray and Jane Kamensky, eds., *The Oxford Handbook of the American Revolution* (New York: Oxford University Press, 2013): 540–59.

Tousignant, Pierre, "Comment on Professor Marshall's Paper," in Virginia Bever Platt and David Curtis Skaggs, eds., *Of Mother Country and Plantations:*

Proceedings of the Twenty-Seventh Conference in Early American History (Bowling Green Ohio: Bowling Green State University Press, 1971): 63–66.

Troxler, Carole Watterson, "Uses of the Bahamas by Southern Loyalist Exiles," in Jerry Mannister and Liam Riordan, eds., *The Loyal Atlantic: Remarking the British Atlantic in the Revolutionary Era* (Toronto: University of Toronto Press, 2012): 185–207.

Tucker, Robert W., and David C. Hendrickson, *Empire of Liberty: The Statecraft of Thomas Jefferson* (New York: Oxford University Press, 1992).

Tucker, St. George, *A Dissertation on Slavery: With a Proposal for the Gradual Abolition of It in the State of Virginia* (Philadelphia: Mathew Carey, 1796).

Tully, Alan, *Forming American Politics: Ideals, Interests and Institutions in Colonial New York and Pennsylvania* (Baltimore: John Hopkins University Press, 1994).

Tyler, John W., *Smugglers & Patriots: Boston Merchants and the Advent of the American Revolution* (Boston: Northeastern University Press, 1986).

Ulrich, Laurel, "Daughters of Liberty': Religious Women in Revolutionary New England," in Ronald Hoffman and Peter J. Albert, eds., *Women in the Age of the American Revolution* (Charlottesville: University Press of Virginia 1989): 211–43.

Ulrich, Laurel Thatcher. *A Midwife's Tale: The Life of Martha Ballard Based on Her Diary, 1785–1812* (New York: Alfred A. Knopf, 1990).

Upton, Leslie F. S., ed., *The Diary and Selected Papers of Chief Justice William Smith, 1784–1793*, 2 vols.(Toronto: Champlain Society, 1963).

Upton, Leslie F. S., *The Loyal Whig: William Smith of New York and Quebec* (Toronto: University of Toronto Press, 1969).

Usner, Daniel H., Jr., *Indians, Settlers, and Slaves in a Frontier Exchange Economy: The Lower Mississippi Valley Before 1783* (Chapel Hill: University of North Carolina Press, 1992).

Van Buskirk, Judith L., *Generous Enemies: Patriots and Loyalists in Revolutionary New York* (Philadelphia: University of Pennsylvania Press, 2002).

Van Cleve, George William, "The Anti-Federalists' Toughest Challenge: Paper Money, Debt Relief, and the Ratification of the Constitution," *Journal of the Early Republic*, vol. 34 (Winter 2014): 529–60.

Van Cleve, George William, "Founding a Slaveholders' Union, 1770–1797," in John Craig Hammond and Matthew Mason, eds., *Contesting Slavery: The Politics of Bondage and Freedom in the New American Nation* (Charlottesville: University of Virginia Press, 2011): 117–37.

Van Cleve, George William, *A Slaveholders' Union: Slavery, Politics, and the Constitution in the Early Republic* (Chicago: University of Chicago Press, 2010).

Van Dorn, Carl, *The Great Rehearsal: The Story of the Making and Ratifying of the Constitution of the United States* (New York: Penguin Books, 1986).

Varga, Nicholas, "Election Procedures and Practices in Colonial New York," *New York History*, vol. 41 (1960): 249–77.

Venables, Robert W., "'Faithful Allies of the King': The Crown's Haudenosaunee Allies in the Revolutionary Struggle for New York," in Joseph S. Tiedemann, Eugene R. Fingerhut, and Robert W. Venables, eds., *The Other Loyalists: Ordinary People, Royalism, and the Revolution in the Middle Colonies, 1763–1787* (Alb,any: State University of New York Press, 2009): 131–57.

Vinson, Ben, III, *Bearing Arms for His Majesty: The Free Colored Militia in Colonial Mexico* (Stanford, Calif.: Stanford University Press, 2001).

Waldo, Albigence, "Valley Forge, 1777–1778: Diary of Surgeon Albigence Waldo, of the Connecticut Line," *Pennsylvania Magazine of History and Biography*, vol. 21 (1897): 299–323.

Waldstreicher, David, *In the Midst of Perpetual Fetes: The Making of American Nationalism, 1776–1820* (Chapel Hill: University of North Carolina Press, 1997).

Waldstreicher, David, *Runaway America: Benjamin Franklin, Slavery, and the American Revolution* (New York: Hill & Wang, 2005).

Waldstreicher, David, *Slavery's Constitution: From Revolution to Ratification* (New York: Hill & Wang, 2009).

Walker, Charles F., *Smoldering Ashes: Cuzco and the Creation of Republican Peru, 1780–1840* (Durham, N.C.: Duke University Press, 1999).

Walker, Charles F., *The Tupac Amaru Rebellion* (Cambridge: Harvard University Press, 2014).

Wallace, Anthony F. C., *The Death and Rebirth of the Seneca* (New York: Knopf, 1970).

Wallace, Willard M., "Benedict Arnold: Traitorous Patriot," in George Athan Billias, ed., *George Washington's Generals and Opponents: Their Exploits and Leadership* (New York: Da Capo Press, 1994), vol. 1:163–92.

Walsh, Lorena S., "Rural African Americans in the Constitutional Era in Maryland, 1776–1810," *Maryland Historical Magazine* 84 (Winter 1989): 327–41.

Ward, Christopher, *The War of the Revolution*, 2 vols. (New York: Macmillan, 1952).

Ward, David C., *Charles Willson Peale: Art and Selfhood in the Early Republic* (Berkeley: University of California Press, 2004).

Ward, Harry M., *The American Revolution: Nationhood Achieved, 1763–1783* (New York: St. Martin's Press, 1995).

Ward, Harry M., *Between the Lines: Banditti of the American Revolution* (Westport, Conn.: Praeger, 2002).

Ward, Matthew C., *Breaking the Backcountry: The Seven Years' War in Virginia and Pennsylvania, 1754–1765*(Pittsburgh: University of Pittsburgh Press, 2003).

Ward, Matthew C., "'The Indians Our Real Friends': The British Army and the Ohio Indians, 1758–1772," in Daniel P. Barr, ed., *The Boundaries Between*

Us: Natives and Newcomers Along the Frontiers of the Old Northwest Territory, 1750–1850 (Kent, Ohio: Kent State University Press, 2006): 66–86.

Warner, Jessica, *John The Painter: Terrorist of the American Revolution* (New York: Thunder's Mouth Press, 2004).

Warren, Charles, *Jacobin and Junto, or Early American Politics as Viewed in the Diary of Dr. Nathaniel Ames, 1758–1822* (New York: Benjamin Blom, 1968).

Waters, John J., Jr., *The Otis Family in Provincial and Revolutionary Massachusetts* (Chapel Hill: University of North Carolina Press, 1968).

Watson, J. Steven, *The Reign of George III, 1760–1815* (Oxford: Clarendon Press, 1960).

Weber, David J., *Bárbaros: Spaniards and Their Savages in the Age of Enlightenment* (New Haven: Yale University Press, 2005).

Weber, David J., *The Spanish Frontier in North America* (New Haven: Yale University Press, 1992).

Weir, Robert M., "'The Violent Spirit': The Reestablishment of Order and the Continuity of Leadership in Post-Revolutionary South Carolina," in Ronald Hoffman, Thad W. Tate, and Peter J. Albert, eds., *An Uncivil War: The Southern Backcountry During the American Revolution* (Charlottesville: University Press of Virginia, 1985): 70–98.

West, Elliott, *The Way to the West: Essays on the Central Plains* (Albuquerque: University of New Mexico Press, 1995).

Whelan, Kevin, "The Green Atlantic: Radical Reciprocities Between Ireland and America in the Long Eighteenth Century," in Kathleen Wilson, ed., *A New Imperial History: Culture, Identity, and Modernity in Britain and the Empire, 1660–1840* (New York: Cambridge University Press, 2004): 216–38.

White, Ashli, *Encountering Revolution: Haiti and the Making of the Early Republic* (Baltimore: Johns Hopkins University Press, 2010).

White, G. Edward, *The Marshall Court and Cultural Change, 1815–35* (New York: Macmillan, 1988).

White, Richard, *The Middle Ground: Indians, Empires, and Republics in the Great Lakes Region, 1650–1815* (New York: Cambridge University Press, 1991).

White, Richard, "The Winning of the West: The Expansion of the Western Sioux in the Eighteenth and Nineteenth Centuries," *Journal of American History*, vol. 65 (Sept. 1978): 319–43.

White, Shane, *Somewhat More Independent: The End of Slavery in New York City, 1770–1810* (Athens: University of Georgia Press, 1991).

Whitfield, Harvey Amani, *The Problem of Slavery in Early Vermont, 1777–1810* (Barre: Vermont Historical Society, 2014).

Whittemore, Charles P., "John Sullivan: Luckless Irishman," in George Athan Billias, ed., *George Washington's Generals and Opponents: Their Exploits and Leadership* (New York: Da Capo Press, 1994), vol. 1:137–62.

Wickman, Patricia R., "The Spanish Colonial Floridas," in Robert H. Jackson, ed., *New Views of Borderlands History* (Albuquerque: University of New Mexico Press, 1998): 193–225.

Wickwire, Franklin and Mary Wickwire, *Cornwallis: The Imperial Years* (Chapel Hill: University of North Carolina Press, 1980).

Wiecek, William M., "The Witch at the Christening: Slavery and the Constitution's Origins," in Leonard W. Levy and Dennis J. Mahoney, eds., *The Framing and Ratification of the Constitution* (New York: Macmillan, 1987): 167–84.

Willcox, William B., "Sir Henry Clinton: Paralysis of Command," in George Athan Billias, ed., *George Washington's Generals and Opponents: Their Exploits and Leadership* (New York: Da Capo Press, 1994), vol. 2:73–102.

Williams, Glyndwr, "The Pacific: Exploration and Exploitation," in P.J. Marshall, ed., *The Oxford History of the British Empire, vol. 2: The Eighteenth Century* (New York: Oxford University Press, 1998): 552–75.

Wilson, David. A., *United Irishmen, United States: Immigrant Radicals in the Early Republic* (Ithaca: Cornell University Press, 1998).

Withey, Lynne, *Voyages of Discovery: Captain Cook and the Exploration of the Pacific* (New York: Morrow, 1987).

Wokeck, Marianne S., *Trade in Strangers: The Beginnings of Mass Migration to North America* (University Park: Pennsylvania State University Press, 1999).

Wolf, Eva Sheppard, *Race and Liberty in the New Nation: Emancipation in Virginia from the Revolution to Nat Turner's Rebellion* (Baton Rouge: Louisiana State University Press, 2006).

Wood, Gordon S., *The Americanization of Benjamin Franklin* (New York: Penguin Press, 2004).

Wood, Gordon S. *The Creation of the American Republic, 1776–1787* (Chapel Hill: University of North Carolina Press, 1969).

Wood, Gordon S., *Empire of Liberty: A History of the Early Republic, 1789–1815* (New York: Oxford University Press, 2009).

Wood, Gordon S., "Interests and Disinterestedness in the Making of the Constitution," in Richard Beeman, Stephen Botein, and Edward C. Carter II, eds., *Beyond Confederation: Origins of the Constitution and American National Identity* (Chapel Hill: University of North Carolina Press, 1987): 69–109.

Wood, Gordon S., ed., *John Adams: Revolutionary Writings, 1755–1775* (New York: Library of America, 2011).

Wood, Gordon S., "The Problem of Sovereignty," *William and Mary Quarterly*, 3rd ser., vol. 68 (Oct. 2011): 573–77.

Wood, Gordon S., *The Radicalism of the American Revolution* (New York: Knopf, 1992).

Wood, Gordon S., "The Significance of the Early Republic," *Journal of the Early Republic*, vol. 8 (Spring, 1988): 1–20.

Wood, Peter H., *Black Majority: Negroes in Colonial South Carolina from 1670 Through the Stono Rebellion* (New York: Knopf, 1974).

Wraxall, Peter, *An Abridgment of the Indian Affairs Contained in Four Folio Volumes, Transacted in the Colony of New York, from the Year 1678 to the Year 1751*, edited by Charles Howard McIlwain (Cambridge: Harvard University Press, 1915).

Wright, Esmond, "The British Objectives, 1780–1783: 'If Not Dominion Then Trade,'" in Ronald Hoffman and Peter J. Albert, eds., *Peace and the Peacemakers: The Treaty of 1783* (Charlottesville: University Press of Virginia, 1986): 3–29.

Wright, J. Leitch, Jr., *Britain and the American Frontier, 1783–1815* (Athens: University of Georgia Press, 1975).

Wright, J. Leitch, Jr., *Florida in the American Revolution* (Gainesville: University Press of Florida, 1975).

Yirush, Craig B., "The Imperial Crisis," in Edward G. Gray and Jane Kamensky, eds., *The Oxford Handbook of The American Revolution* (New York: Oxford University Press, 2013): 85–102.

Yirush, Craig B., *Settlers, Liberty, and Empire: The Roots of Early American Political Theory, 1675–1775* (New York: Cambridge University Press, 2011).

Yokota, Kariann Akemi, *Unbecoming British: How Revolutionary America became a Postcolonial Nation* (New York: Oxford University Press, 2014).

Young, Alfred F., *The Democratic Republicans of New York: The Origins, 1763–1797* (Chapel Hill: University of North Carolina Press, 1967).

Young, Alfred F., *Liberty Tree: Ordinary People and the American Revolution* (New York: New York University Press, 2006).

Young, Alfred F., *Masquerade: The Life and Times of Deborah Sampson, Continental Soldier* (New York: Knopf, 2004).

Young, Alfred F., *The Shoemaker and the Tea Party: Memory and the American Revolution* (Boston: Beacon Press, 1999).

Young, Alfred F., "The Women of Boston: 'Persons of Consequence' in the Making of the American Revolution," in Harriet B. Applewhite and Darline G. Levy, eds., *Women and Politics in the Age of Democratic Revolution* (Ann Arbor: University of Michigan Press, 1990): 181–226.

Zagarri, Rosemarie, "The American Revolution and a New National Politics," in Edward G. Gray and Jane Kamensky, eds., *The Oxford Handbook of the American Revolution* (New York: Oxford University Press, 2013): 483–98.

Zagarri, Rosemarie, *Revolutionary Backlash: Women and Politics in the Early American Republic* (Philadelphia: University of Pennsylvania Press, 2007).

Zagarri, Rosemarie, "The Rights of Man and Woman in Post-Revolutionary America," *William and Mary Quarterly*, 3rd ser., vol. 55 (Apr. 1998): 203–30.

Zeisberger, David, *Diary of David Zeisberger: A Moravian Missionary Among the Indians of Ohio*, 2 vols., edited by Eugene F. Bliss (Cincinnati: Historical and Philosophical Society of Ohio, 1885).

Zilversmit, Arthur, *The First Emancipation: The Abolition of Slavery in the North* (Chicago: University of Chicago Press, 1967).

INDEX